SCREEN INPUT/OUTPUT TECHNIQUES USING TURBO PASCAL

Andy Stuart

COPYRIGHT

Copyright © 1987 Andy Stuart

Published by Management Information Source, Inc.
1107 N.W. 14th Avenue
Portland, Oregon 97209
(503) 222-2399

First Printing

ISBN 0-943518-28-8

Library of Congress Catalog Card Number: 87-7892

All rights reserved. Reproduction or use, without express permission, of editorial or pictorial content, in any manner is prohibited. No patent liability is assumed with respect to the use of the information contained herein. While every precaution has been taken in the preparation of this book, neither the publisher nor the author assume responsibility for errors or omissions. Neither is any liability assumed for damages resulting from the use of the information contained herein.

IBM PC is a trademark of IBM Corporation.

MS-DOS is a trademark of Microsoft Corporation.

Turbo Pascal is a trademark of Borland International.

ACKNOWLEDGMENTS

Among the people I know, I would like to especially thank my mother, Helen Stuart, whose supportive wisdom and continued interest helped me to keep going when the going was tough, and my wife Diane for her role as official listening post and sounding board during the creative development and evolution of this book.

Other very important people in this project were Vern Little, who first saw my programs run; Gary Little, my agent, who opened the right doors; Chris Williams of MIS, Inc., who saw the market potential; and, last but not least, Kim Thomas, the senior editor. She and her support staff performed the metamorphosis from manuscript to finished product.

Among those whom I do not know, I want to thank Mr. Philippe Kahn of Borland International. Turbo Pascal has provided me with a solid and reliable programming environment for the development of the topics in this book. Indeed, this book would have been impossible for me to produce without it.

TABLE OF CONTENTS

PREFACE vii
    Target Groups vii
    Book Development viii
    Chapter Overviews viii

PART I: TECHNIQUES 1

    CHAPTER 1: GETTING STARTED 3
        Typing Conventions 4
        Diagrams 7
        Modular Programming: The Concept 8
        Theoretical Background: Definitions 9

    CHAPTER 2: THE MEMORY/SCREEN MEMORY CONNECTION 23
        Module: CHRINOUT.INC
        (character in, character out include file) 24
        CHRINOUT: Notes 26
        Module: CH2DEM1.DRV
        (chapter 2 demo1 driver) 29
        CH2DEM1.DRV: Notes 29
        Module: CH2DEM2.DRV
        (chapter 2 demo2 driver) 31
        CH2DEM2.DRV: Notes 32
        Module: CH2DEM3.DRV
        (chapter 2 demo3 driver) 33
        CH2DEM3.DRV: Notes 35

    CHAPTER 3: CREATING SCREEN WINDOWS 39
        Module: WINDOWS.INC
        (windows include file) 40
        WINDOWS.INC: Notes 42
        Module: WINDOW.DRV
        (windows driver routine) 45
        WINDOW.DRV: Notes 46

CHAPTER 4: SCREEN SAVE AND REDISPLAY 51
    Module: SCR_S_D.INC
    (screen save and redisplay include file) 53
    SCR_S_D.INC: Notes 55
    Module: SSD.DRV
    (screen save and redisplay driver file) 62
    SSD.DRV: Notes 65
    Module: SCRTOPR.DRV
    (screen to printer driver routine) 69
    SCRTOPR.DRV: Notes 71

CHAPTER 5: HORIZONTAL SCROLLING — METHOD 1 75
    Module: H_S1.INC
    (horizontal scrolling method 1 include file) 76
    H_S1.INC: Notes 84
    Module: H_S1.DRV
    (horizontal scrolling method 1 driver file) 94
    H_S1.DRV: Notes 96

CHAPTER 6: HORIZONTAL SCROLLING — METHOD 2 99
    Module: H_S2.INC
    (horizontal scrolling method 2 include file) 101
    H_S2.INC: Notes 103
    Module: H_S2.DRV
    (horizontal scrolling method 2 driver file) 112
    H_S2.DRV: Notes 114

CHAPTER 7: VERTICAL SCROLLING — METHOD 1 119
    Module: V_S1.INC
    (vertical scrolling method 1 include file) 120
    V_S1.INC: Notes 126
    Module: V_S1.DRV
    (vertical scrolling method 1 driver file) 132
    V_S1.DRV: Notes 135

CHAPTER 8: VERTICAL SCROLLING—METHOD 2.................**137**
    Module: V_S2.INC
      (vertical scrolling method 2 include file)......................138
    V_S2.INC: Notes 141
    Module: V_S2.DRV
      (vertical scrolling method 2 driver file).........................149
    V_S2.DRV: Notes 152

CHAPTER 9: VERTICAL SCROLLING—METHOD 3.................**157**
    Module: V_S3.INC
      (vertical scrolling method 3 include file)......................158
    V_S3.INC: Notes 161
    Module: V_S3.DRV
      (vertical scrolling method 3 driver file).........................164
    V_S3.DRV: Notes 166
    Conclusion 167

PART II: APPLICATIONS...**169**

CHAPTER 10: DATA INPUT AND REVISION...........................**171**
    Module: EI_ER.INC
      (enter integer, enter real include file).............................176
    EI_ER.INC: Notes 177
    Module: DOLLARS.INC
      (dollars include file) 181
    DOLLARS.INC: Notes 183
    Module: DATES.INC
      (dates include file) 186
    DATES.INC: Notes 189
    Module: DATA_IR.DRV
      (data input, revise driver routine).................................195
    DATA_IR.DRV: Notes 203

CHAPTER 11: VERTICAL AND HORIZONTAL SCROLLING WINDOWS **213**
    Module: VH_S2.INC
      (vertical and horizontal scroll method 2)....................214
    Module: VHSCROLL.DRV
      (vertical and horizontal scrolling driver)....................223
    VHSCROLL.DRV: Notes...228
    Limitations 235

CHAPTER 12: SCROLLING GRAPH AND NUMBER TABLE 237
    Program: H_GRAPH.DRV
      (horizontal graphics driver applications program).......................238
    H_GRAPH.DRV: Notes...254
    Limitations 264

CHAPTER 13: SCREEN I/O AND THE DISK 269
    Module: FILENAME.INC
      (file name include file)..274
    FILENAME.INC: Notes..276
    Module: TEXTWRIT.INC
      (text writer include file) 280
    TEXTWRIT.INC: Notes 283
    Module: FILMAN.DRV
      (file manager driver file)..288
    FILMAN.DRV: Notes..304
    Limitations 313

CHAPTER 14: GENERAL PRINCIPLES.. 317
    Module: TYPEDEF.INC
      (type definitions include file)...318
    TYPEDEF.INC: Notes...321
    Module: REWRITSC.INC
      (rewrite screen include file) 331
    REWRITSC.INC: Notes...333
    Module: S_D_SC.INC
      (save and redisplay screen include file) 336
    S_D_SC.INC: Notes...339
    Module: MULT_SCR.DRV
      (multiple screen driver routine) 341
    MULT_SCR.DRV: Notes...348

CHAPTER 15: MORE GENERAL PRINCIPLES 355
    Installation Of Horizontal Scrolling...356
    Overall Organization 361
    TYPDEF15.INC
      (TYPEDEF.INC from Chapter 14)..357
    REWRSC15.INC
      (REWRITSC.INC from Chapter 14)...358
    MULTSC15.DRV
      (MULT_SCR.DRV from Chapter 14)..359

CHAPTER 16: REVIEW AND EXTENSIONS 367
    Module: TYPDEF16.INC
    (type definition chapter 16 include file) 369
    TYPEDEF16.INC: Notes..376
    Module: REWRSC16.INC
    (rewrite screen chapter 16 include file) 381
    REWRSC16.INC: Notes..386
    Module: S_D_SC16.INC
    (save redisplay screen chapter 16 include file) 400
    Module: TXTWR16.INC
    (text write chapter 16 include file)...403
    TXTWR16.INC: Notes 407
    Module: MULTSC16.DRV
    (multiple screen chapter 16 driver)...409
    MULTSC16.DRV: Notes 429

APPENDIX A: SCREEN LAYOUT FORM 439

INDEX 441

DISKETTE ORDER FORM 459

PREFACE

Have you ever wondered how professional applications programs are able to scroll data up, down, and sideways on the computer screen? Or how display windows loaded with information can pop up over something else, scroll around for awhile, and then disappear at the touch of a key, leaving that something else completely unchanged? Have you ever wondered why these programs don't crash when you feed them bad input? Or how these programs can possibly allow you to make 100 input data entries in a vertical line and then permit you to scroll them for review and revision?

To me, screen input/output (screen I/O) has always seemed like magic, and it seems equally magical that I have never succeeded in finding any comprehensive information about screen I/O in one place. Sure, there are odd bits and pieces in magazines and journals (lines of Basic DATA Statements followed by line after line of those mindless numbers), or a tantalizingly empty paragraph here and there in the odd computer book, but nothing that actually says "here's how to do it." Like magic and every bit as elusive.

This book deals in depth and exclusively with screen I/O techniques — what they are, how they work, and how to write them yourself — and is the product of my earlier frustration and later curiosity.

Target Groups

The programs in this book are written in Borland International's Turbo Pascal language and are designed to run on an IBM PC or true compatible with at least 128K of RAM memory. If you have an internal RAM disk drive, all the better. This book best addresses the needs of the following two groups of users:

Students: having completed a first course in the Pascal Language, students are probably ready to see the language actually "do something" that would be useful for later project work but refreshingly different right now. Incidental to the main goal of the book is the opportunity for students to review many Turbo Pascal concepts and see them in action. I have gone out of my way to dust these concepts off and bring them to life in a relevant context. Included are lots of practical programming tricks and tips.

Professionals: as researchers, engineers, educators, or business people with a grounding in the Pascal language, most professionals are more than likely familiar with the relevant off-the-shelf or "canned" software available for their professions. They are probably also aware that particular needs can be frustratingly special and that prewritten software doesn't always address those specific needs. So if, as a professional, you need to write your own customized applications programs, an investment in this book will save you hours of programming time and will lend visual appeal, flexibility, and professionalism to your programming efforts. You supply the intellegence; let me teach you how to frame your programs to enhance their communication potential.

Book Development

This book is a comprehensive study of screen I/O techniques. To best develop this theme, I have divided the book into two main parts. In Part One, I have developed a set of short demonstration programs to illustrate specific screen I/O concepts. The explanatory text and diagrams that accompany the programs are intended to clarify difficult or unfamiliar sections of the code. These demonstration programs are relatively short and can be typed into the computer so that the reader can immediately see the particular technique in action. In Part Two, I have developed several "pseudo applications" programs. The purpose of each of these programs is to illustrate the different ways that the basic tools of Part One can be coordinated into fully integrated applications programs. I have used the label "pseudo applications" for these programs because the data that has been created for use inside them has no basis in "real world" activity. Exactly what information is included and how that information is generated is in the sole domain of the reader. As in Part One, the accompanying text and diagrams are designed to bring the specific and often complex details of the program code to life and to show clearly and dramatically their dynamic workings.

Chapter Overviews

Part One consists of ten chapters. Chapter 1 introduces several basic but essential screen I/O concepts and outlines the typing conventions used throughout the rest of the book.

In Chapter 2, you will learn a speedy technique for screen display and how to take text stored in ordinary memory, display that text directly to the screen, and assign it to the video memory array. This technique is an alternative to the familiar "write" statement and is much faster.

Chapter 3 covers how to program customized screen display windows. This chapter offers you the opportunity to put the material from the previous chapter to practical use. As with the previous chapter and the chapters to follow, the module created can be reused in future programs (with minor modifications), thereby minimizing the total amount of required typing.

In Chapter 4, the converse of the screen output operation of Chapter 2 is introduced. Here, you will learn how to "pick off" images displayed on the video screen and save them directly into character arrays in memory for later redisplay to both screen and printer.

The next two chapters cover the topic of horizontal scrolling. Chapter 5 teaches this technique using the screen saving and redisplay methods learned earlier. Chapter 6 covers horizontal scrolling from a different viewpoint: how to systematically address appropriate sections of the one-dimensional video memory array.

Vertical scrolling techniques are discussed in the next three chapters. Chapter 7 uses the "screen save/redisplay" method first seen in Chapter 5. Chapter 8 uses the "index address method" of Chapter 6. Chapter 9 introduces a quick and dirty method using Turbo Pascal's INSLINE and DELLINE functions. As far as I have seen, there is no horizontal scrolling analogue for this method.

Chapter 10 is the last chapter of Part One. Here, I address two key topics in the area of data input. The first is **validation** or the technique that assures that the input data you feed into the computer is in the correct format and that it is within some legally pre-specified range. The second is **input data revision**. Here, you will learn programming techniques that allow you to enter data and then change your mind and reenter the data at some later time without interrupting the flow of the program. Validation ensures that input data is correct, and revision provides freedom to choose between legal alternatives. This chapter is comprehensive and fully self-contained. The demonstration program is long and serves double duty as a pseudo application since it covers a wide range of input types.

Chapter 11 is the first chapter of Part Two. Here, you will learn how to combine scrolling techniques to build a 20×20 bidirectional scrolling multiplication table, complete with moving row and column index labels.

In Chapter 12, you will combine vertical and horizontal scrolling with screen save/redisplay into the same program. After you have filled a vertically scrollable number table with typed input data, the program takes over and converts the data into a horizontally scrollable bar chart. At this point, the program returns control to you and allows you to scroll the bar chart horizontally. Then, when you want to view the entered numbers, the program will overlay part of the chart with the scrollable number table, using the screen save/redisplay technique of Chapter 4.

In Chapter 13, you will explore the connection between screen I/O tools and disk storage; that is, you will learn how to connect scrollable display tables with information from the disk as well as from the keyboard. More specifically, you will develop a program that uses data previously saved to disk as a source of input for your scrolling routines. In addition, you will build some simple techniques that allow you to revise the data onscreen, scroll that altered data, and save it back to disk—all at your option.

In the last three chapters of this book, you will learn about **type definition files**. The creation of one of these simple data structures will enable you to create multiple windows on your video screen. In Chapter 14, you will begin by learning how type definition files are defined and created. Their operation will then be illustrated by creating three on-screen, overlapping, vertically scrollable pop-up windows. Chapter 15 illustrates how to install horizontal scrolling capability into one of the previous chapter's windows. Finally, the book concludes with Chapter 16. The program developed here is more than a pseudo applications program, as it can be used in future screen I/O work. Briefly, it calculates the video memory offset value equivalent to each and every row/column combination on the 25×80 monochrome screen. The result is a scrollable, two-dimensional data table with 25 rows and 80 columns, each row/column cell containing a unique integer (video memory array offset index or "j table value") whose range lies between 0 and 3999. In Chapter 16, three screens are provided, each screen containing the same data; however, each screen is limited to a different section of the overall 25×80 array. Chapter 16 also develops the generalized technique of adding scrollable row and column index labels to all your display screens. In the interest of completeness and practical utility, a scrollable pop-up text file is installed which can be called on to overlay the on-screen system of scrollable display windows. This type of file will usually contain useful notes pertaining to the screens you are scrolling or could hold "help me" information.

This book communicates to the reader a solid understanding of the concepts and techniques that lie behind the magic of screen input/output programming. I hope that I have provided you with a comprehensive set of tools that will be useful in all future applications programs that you write.

Andy Stuart
White Rock, B.C.

PART I

TECHNIQUES

Note to programmers: The program listings in this book have been printed directly from the original program disks to ensure that no errors were introduced through rekeyboarding.

The letter "l" and the number "1" are represented in the program code by the same character. If, in the code, you see a character pattern that appears to be three letter "l"'s in a row, assume it to be two letter "l"'s and a single number "1." For example,

```
v_scroll1
```

would be read as "v scroll one."

You will also see character patterns that appear to be two letter "l"'s in a row. From the context, you should be able to quickly determine whether or not each pattern is the letter "l" followed by the number "1" or just two letter "l"'s.

Finally, if you see what appears to be the letter "l" at the end of a variable name and the spelling seems wrong, then assume that the letter "l" is in fact the number "1."

This should eliminate any confusion.

CHAPTER 1

GETTING STARTED

1 Getting Started

Have you ever read a piece of what you know to be clear, concisely written, logical Pascal code and come away without the foggiest notion of what it is trying to accomplish?

This chapter introduces two ways used in this book to overcome the above problem. The first is the adoption of standardized typing conventions that will be used in all the programs throughout the book. The second is the liberal use of diagrams, which can illustrate relationships that would otherwise require tedious explanation.

This chapter then continues with a discussion of the concept of **modularity**—what it means and how you can put the concept to use in your programs. Finally, this chapter concludes by defining and illustrating definitions central to screen input/output programming and used repeatedly throughout the rest of the book.

TYPING CONVENTIONS

Understanding a new and unfamiliar piece of computer code requires mental concentration and two steps. The first step is associated with the process of sorting out what the procedures and the parameters are and remembering what the variable types mean. You must hold all these "housekeeping" details inside your head at the same time you attempt the second step of understanding how all these "actors" work together to achieve their common programming goal. Often, however, the two steps will overlap. You may feel off balance in a situation where you're trying to figure out how everything works together while at the same time not really knowing what each part is. It's no fun watching a play and not knowing who the players are. The group of typing conventions described below are designed to minimize such difficulties. It is hoped that the way in which the computer code is presented will allow you the maximum amount of energy to understand how the code pulls together as a unit to achieve its purpose.

1) Line numbers have been added to make reference easier in the explanatory text that accompanies the computer code. When typing the programs, *do not* type these line numbers.

2) Wherever possible in the programs, all block indents have been spaced in even multiples of 5: e.g., 1, 5, 10, 15, etc.

3)   Procedures and subprocedures will be formatted as follows:

```
{=========================================================================}
0005    procedure     OUTER(variable1    : integer;
0010                        var variable2 : an_array);
0015
0020
0025
0030   {-------------------------------------------------------------------}
0035
0040       procedure     INNER(variable43   : char;
0045                           q_tot       : real;
0050                           var piU int : integer);
0055
0060
0065       Begin     {sub procedure inner}
0070          .
0075          .
0080       End;      {sub procedure inner}
0085   {-------------------------------------------------------------------}
0090
0095    Begin     {procedure outer}
0100       .
0105       .
0110       .
0115    End;      {procedure outer}
{=========================================================================}
```

4)   The names of all user-defined functions and procedures will be in uppercase letters. The variables in the parameter lists, procedures, functions, and main routines will all be in lowercase letters. To clarify understanding in the procedure and function parameter lists, the parameters are placed underneath one another. For example,

```
        USER_FUNCTION(first_variable    : integer;
                     second_variable    : integer;
                     third_variable     : real)    : real;

        USER_PROCEDURE(variable1        : integer;
                      variable2         : real;
                      variable3         : char;
                      var variable4     : boolean);
```

1 Getting Started

5) Certain Turbo Pascal built-in functions and procedures are designated by uppercase letters. For example,

```
x_coord := WHEREX;
select := count MOD 5;      {...a built-in function}
INSLINE;                    {..a built-in procedure}
DELLINE;
BUFLEN := 4;
d_str := CONCAT('$',COPY(d_str_temp,1,3));
```

However, the most commonly used procedures and functions, such as "Clreol," "window," "gotoxy," "write," "delay," etc., are not in uppercase because doing so would not increase clarity of the code.

6) Note that fairly extensive use is made of bracketed comments ({*....*}) throughout the programs in this book. Brackets hold statements such as "delay(1000)" or "write(bell)" that will aid you in tracing the program's execution and in typing in programs, e.g., "write('   ');" {10 blanks}. They will also be used as side comments to help you understand the logical flow in a typical section of code. These, like the line numbers above, do not have to be typed in.

7) In the explanatory text that accompanies the programs, you will come across notations such as the following:

        < qRET > or < q >< RET >

which means that you must type the small letter "q" and then press the carriage return key.

Notations such as

        < Ctrl/K >

are referred to as simultaneous keystrokes, and are executed by pressing and holding down the Control key and simultaneously pressing the "K" key.

Getting Started 1

8) In situations where a line to be typed is too long for a line in the text, the same stacked format is adopted as for procedures. Note in this example the way the brackets are placed:

```
d_str := CONCAT('$',COPY(d_str_temp,1,3),','
                    ,COPY(d_str_temp,4,3),','
                    ,COPY(d_str_temp,7,6));
```

9) **Note to programmers:** The program listings in this book have been printed directly from the original program disks to ensure that no errors were introduced through rekeyboarding.

   The letter "l" and the number "1" are represented in the program code by the same character. If, in the code, you see a character pattern that appears to be three letter "l"'s in a row, assume it to be two letter "l"'s and a single number "1." For example,

   ```
   v_scroll1
   ```

   would be read as "v scroll one." This should eliminate any confusion (also see p.1).

DIAGRAMS

The diagrams used in this book are of two types. The first is a "Screen Layout," which shows you exactly how the screen will look at certain stages during the execution of a typical program, almost like a snapshot of the computer screen; however, it is also an important planning tool and has been used (along with my trusty dividers and a ruler) in developing the screen layouts for every program in this book. If you are ever unsure about how to begin to code a program, start by planning your output screens on these layout sheets (see Appendix A). The coding will be much easier once a goal is in sight.

The second type of diagram used in this book is a "conceptual layout." These figures (schematic diagrams) are presented to illustrate concepts more clearly. Indeed, one well-drawn picture is worth a thousand typewritten words.

1 Getting Started

MODULAR PROGRAMMING: THE CONCEPT

One powerful method of problem solving that is particularly well-suited for computers is the method of "divide and conquer" (more properly, "divide and understand"). It rests on the assumption that large complex problems may be best solved by

- dividing the problem into smaller, more easily handled sub-problems (tasks)

- solving (programming) each subproblem on its own in isolation

- recombining solutions to individual subproblems to arrive at the solution for the original problem

The idea behind **modular programming** is systematic simplification. That is, by isolating the complex details of specialty activities inside a procedure, you can obtain a main program whose overall problem-solving strategy is clear, easy to follow, and uncomplicated by operational details.

In this book, for example, the aim is to create a set of screen utility modules whose job is to handle specialized screen input/output programming tasks such as

- creating screen window borders

- scrolling screen data horizontally and vertically

- saving screen areas into computer memory variables

- redisplaying saved screen areas from memory and back onto the screen

- validating input data (checking for errors)

- revising input data

Getting Started 1

Once written and debugged, each utility or module can then be saved to disk as part of a screen utility library and reused in any future applications programs that you write.

All the utility modules you create in this book will be given the file name extention ".inc" (include). Once the utility is written and saved to disk, you will have created a specialty tool that you may use in your future programs by simply typing

```
{$i filename.inc}
```

where "filename" represents any legal file name. In this book, all screen I/O utility (library) modules are "included" just after the program's declaration section and just before the start of the program's internal procedures. When declaring a utility module in a program, note that each module must have its own separate brackets and format, as shown above, and that you may use as many or as few modules as you need. In several places, the phrase "external procedure" has replaced "utility" to distinguish between those procedures created and saved to disk separately and those procedures (internal procedures) created and saved along with the program. Use of the phrase "external procedure" is in no way connected with Turbo Pascal's use of the phrase as a reserved word designating a procedure or function written in assembler code.

THEORETICAL BACKGROUND: IMPORTANT DEFINITIONS

To help explanations flow smoothly in the following chapters, some essential background definitions will be covered.

Segment: Offset

In this book you will often come across the code "MEM[bwseg : bwofs + j]." Definitions of the words **segment** and **offset** provide the key to understanding the above code.

1 Getting Started

Generally, a segment is a continuous block or section of computer memory that is dedicated by the programmer or manufacturer to perform a particular task. The most common tasks are storing program instructions or storing data.

More particularly, the video segment is a specially reserved block of RAM memory whose task is to store video data (ASCII codes together with their attributes) for display on the video screen. In memory, the video segment for the Monochrome monitor is preset to start at hex address $B000:$0000 or absolute address $B0000 (720,896 decimal) in the million-byte address space. You might ask how it is that the segment address ("bwseg") and the offset address ("bwofs") are combined to form the starting point of the video memory segment. The answer to that question is beyond the scope of this book. Any text on IBM Assembler Language will provide a detailed explanation. The point to remember is that the phrase "bwseg : bwofs" is equivalent to "$b000 : $0000" (or $b800 : $0000 if you have a graphics monitor) in this book, and together they designate the memory address of the very first character (more correctly, the character's numeric ASCII code) in video memory. Remember, the numeric ASCII codes are first transformed by the the special video circuitry to create the characters you see on the screen. Each character you see on the screen is stored in video memory as its numeric ASCII counterpart. The length of the video segment is 4000 bytes and can be visualized as a one-dimensional array 4000 rows deep by 1 column wide (see Figure 1.1).

An offset is defined as the number of bytes from the beginning of the video memory segment (address $b000 : $0000). The range of the offset values for the 4000-byte video segment is integers 0 to 3999 *inclusive*. The offset provides addressing access to any of those 4000 video data bytes located within the video segment. In the above code, then, the variable "j" represents the offset value (screen pointer value) in the video memory array MEM. The offset will be discussed further in the next section.

In summary, the code "MEM[bwseg : bwofs + j]" refers to the one-dimensional video memory array (MEM) whose starting point is "bwseg : bwofs" and whose offset into the array from that designated starting point is "j." The overall phrase (depending on the value of "j") represents a single address within the 4000-byte video segment used to drive the Monochrome screen (see Figure 1.2).

Getting Started **1**

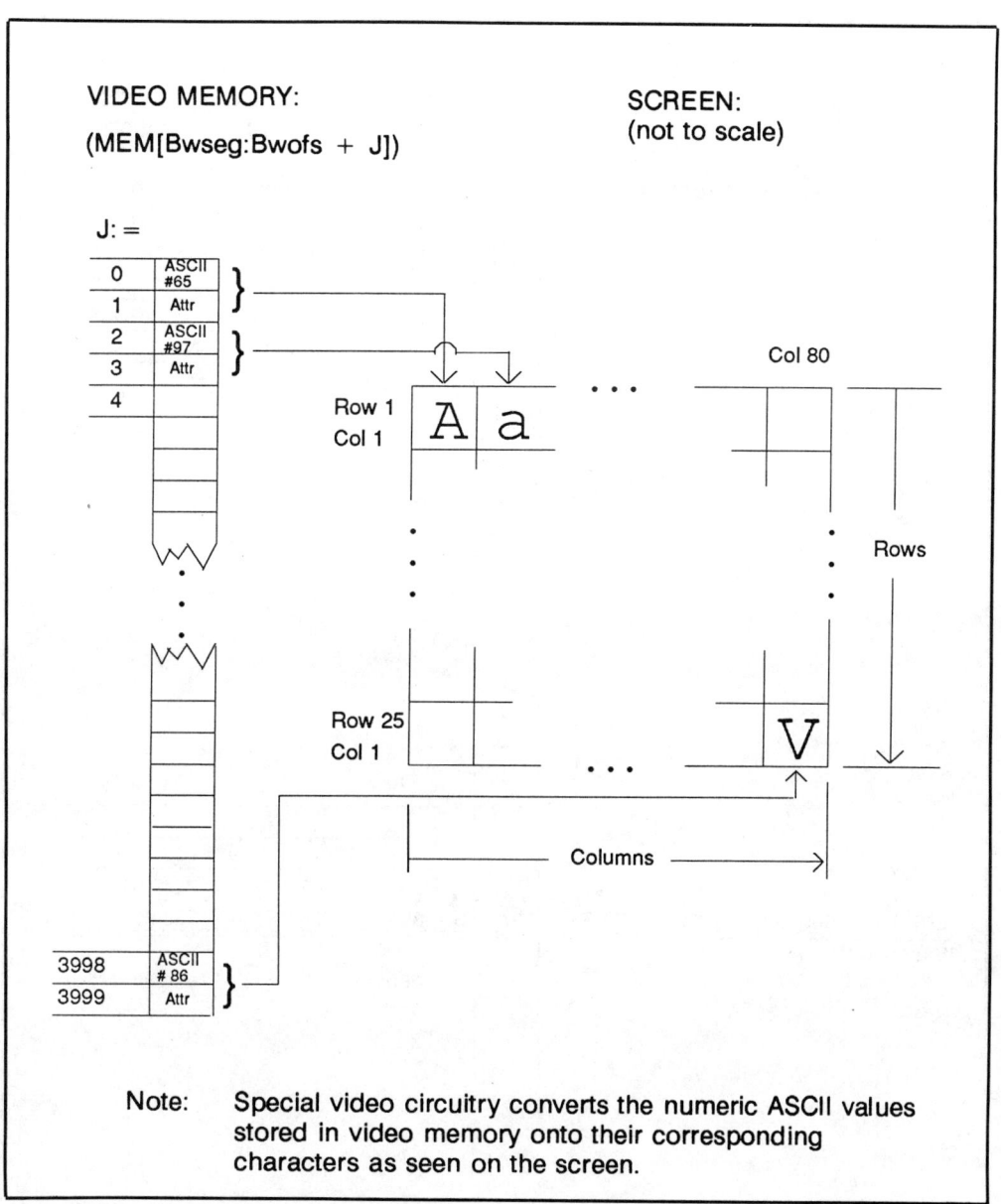

Figure 1.1 Relationship Between Video Memory and Screen Locations

1 Getting Started

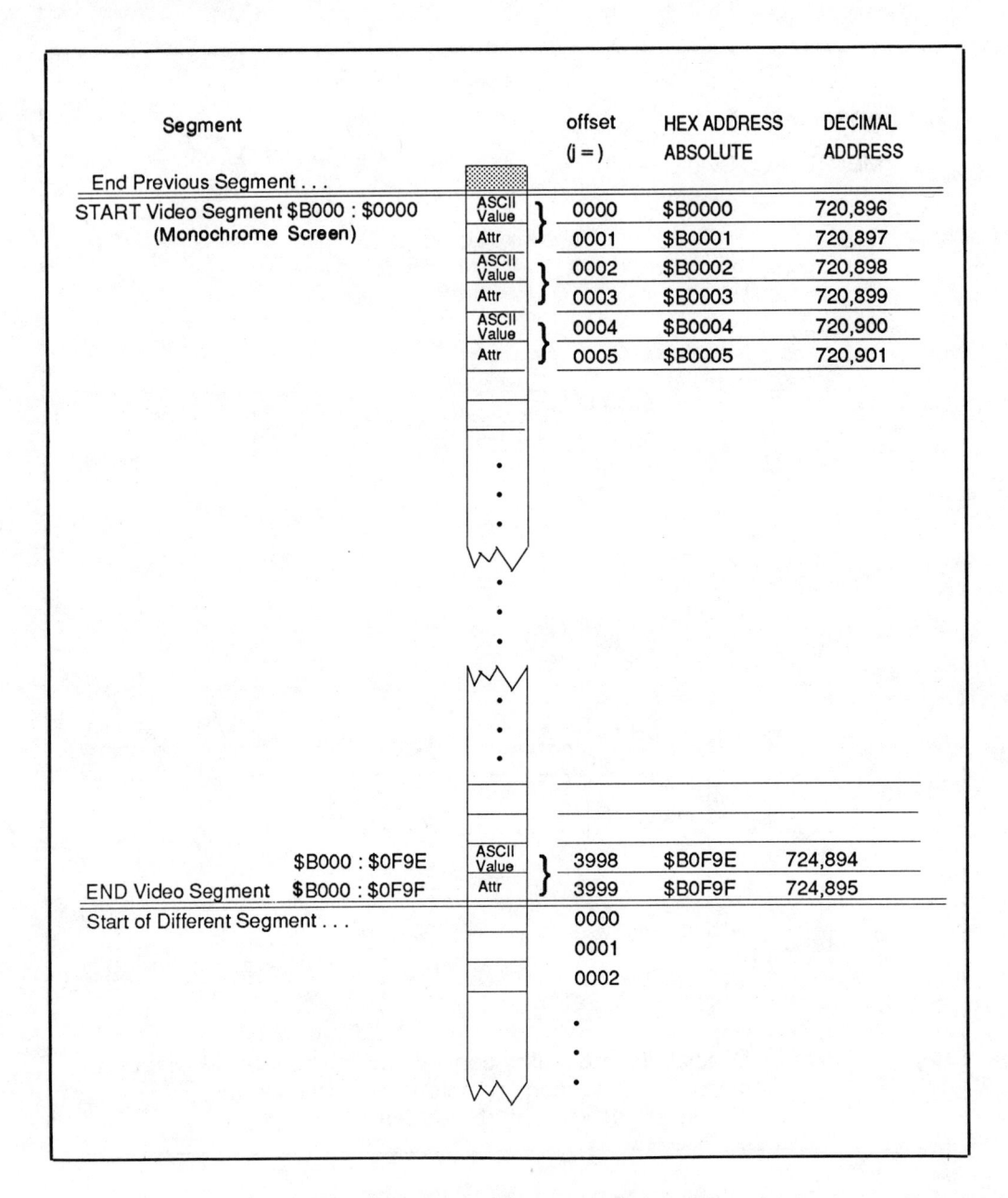

Segment	offset (j =)	HEX ADDRESS ABSOLUTE	DECIMAL ADDRESS
End Previous Segment . . .			
START Video Segment $B000 : $0000 (Monochrome Screen)	ASCII Value 0000	$B0000	720,896
	Attr 0001	$B0001	720,897
	ASCII Value 0002	$B0002	720,898
	Attr 0003	$B0003	720,899
	ASCII Value 0004	$B0004	720,900
	Attr 0005	$B0005	720,901
$B000 : $0F9E	ASCII Value 3998	$B0F9E	724,894
END Video Segment $B000 : $0F9F	Attr 3999	$B0F9F	724,895
Start of Different Segment . . .	0000		
	0001		
	0002		

Figure 1.2 Video Memory Addresses

12

Getting Started 1

Video Memory and Video Screen

An important connection exists between the contents of that special area of the computer's memory called the **video memory** and the familiar row/column coordinate locations on the video screen. If the video memory is designated by the programmer as the standard output device, special video circuits inside the computer will be activated to continually scan the 4000 video memory locations starting at $B000 : $0000 ($B0000 absolute) and put out directly to the screen video signals that depend on the video data that is stored in each of the 4000 locations of the video memory. It is worth repeating that the screen characters themselves are *not* stored in the even-numbered video memory location; only their corresponding ASCII code numbers are. The actual translation of the ASCII code number into the character you see on the screen is accomplished by special video scanning circuitry wired into the video memory segment.

How then does the special video circuitry map or assign a given row/column screen coordinate to that particular screen coordinate's corresponding offset location (address) inside video memory?

The video circuitry uses the following formula for this mapping process (a 25-row by 80-column monochrome display screen is assumed).

   j := ((row - 1) * 160) + ((col - 1) * 2)

The formula first tells you it will take two different input parameters — the row and the column coordinates of a video screen location — and combine them to produce the corresponding video memory offset address j. Note that when using row 25 and column 80, the "j" offset address is only 3998.

The expressions "(row - 1)" and "(col - 1)" are special adjustments that allow the first offset address j to have a value of 0 when row 1 and column 1 on the screen are addressed. This convention allows the first screen location at row 1, column 1 to have a 0 offset value.

The number 160 says that in any given screen row, there are 160 bytes. How can there be 160 bytes in a screen row if each screen row is defined to have only 80 characters? The answer is that each character is fully described by two bytes, not one byte. The first byte (always located in an even-numbered address offset in video memory: 0, 2, 4, 6... 3998) always holds the ASCII value of the screen display. The second

13

1 Getting Started

or successor byte (always located at an odd-numbered video memory offset—1, 3, 5, 7... 3999) represents the attributes of the previous byte, that is, its background and foreground color, whether the character is blinking or not, and whether it is in high intensity or not. So the first character at row 1, column 1 is represented by the bytes located at offset 0 and offset 1 in screen memory, and the last screen character at row 25, column 80 is represented in screen memory by offset bytes 3998 and 3999 in screen memory. There are exactly 4000 screen memory locations accounted for in screen memory (0-3999 *inclusive* equals 4000).

The number constant "160" also says that for any character in a given screen column, the character directly below it (same column) is exactly 160 bytes higher in video memory. Use the formula and prove this for yourself.

The number constant "2" says that for a character located in any given screen row, the character to the right of and adjacent to it (in the same row) is exactly two bytes higher in video memory. Remember, the character's attribute byte follows the character in video memory.

Parameter

The word **parameter** has been mentioned only casually so far. A parameter is a variable constant. This paradox is not enlightening, however, because a parameter exhibits the characteristics of both a variable and a constant. This dual role can only be exhibited in the context of a procedure or a function. When either a procedure or a function is called with a parameter, that particular parameter will act like a variable because it can take any of a number of different values; however, once the value of the parameter has been assigned, the procedure (or function) will treat that value as a constant in its current computations. When the procedure or function is finished, the parameter again takes on the characteristics of a variable, waiting to be assigned another and probably different value on the next call.

Windows

Have you noticed that the parameters in the built-in "window" procedure are listed with the screen column first and then the screen row? At first, this may seem strange because you may be more comfortable with the ordering of parameters by row first, then column.

Getting Started **1**

If, however, you visualize the xy axis in the upper left-hand corner of the computer screen with the x axis cutting horizontally to the right across the columns and the y axis dropping down vertically through the screen rows, the rationale for the column first, row next ordering in the window procedure will be clear (see Figure 1.3).

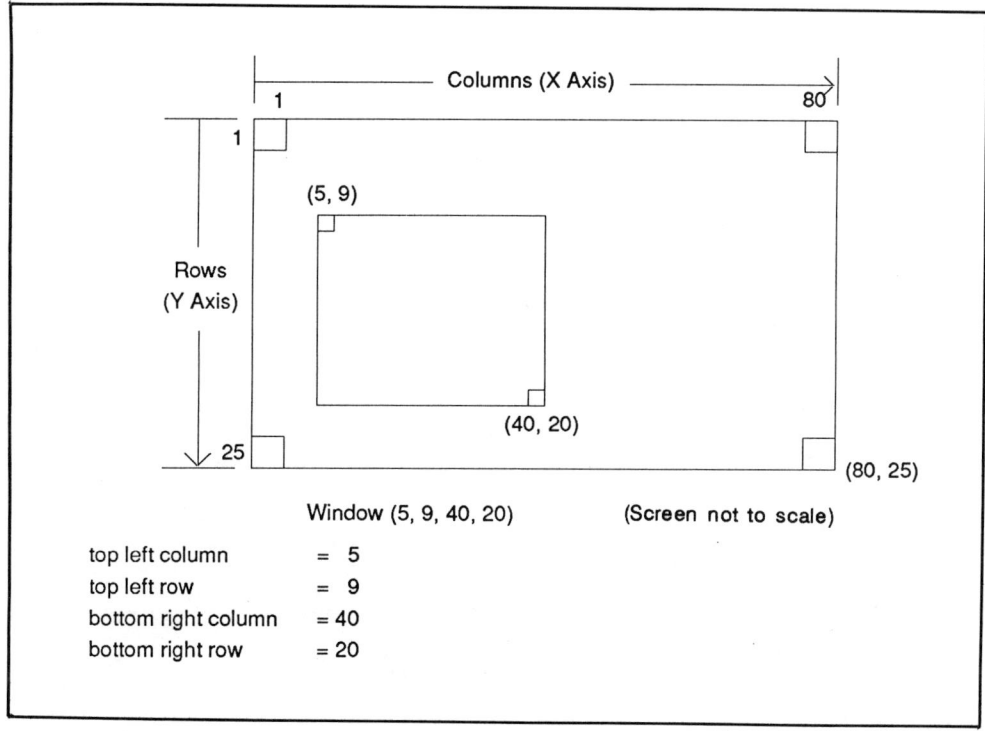

Figure 1.3 WINDOW STATEMENT

1 Getting Started

Note that the familiar x axis, y axis reading order is preserved; however, the orientation of the xy axis on the screen results in the screen column being the first coordinate and the row being the second coordinate of any screen location.

For the sake of completeness, the exact meaning of the following built-in procedure and functions should now be clear:

"GOTOXY" The letter "X" means the x screen coordinate (across the columns). The letter "Y" means the y screen coordinate (down the rows). Thus, the cursor is positioned on the screen by first moving it to the desired column and then down from there to the desired row (see Figure 1.4).

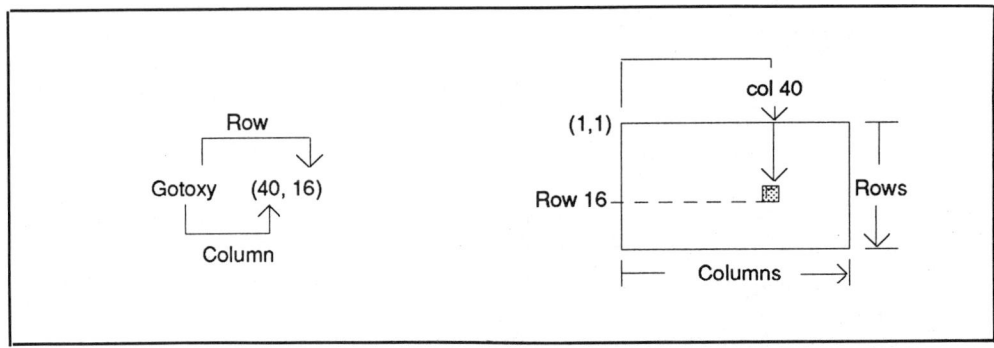

Figure 1.4 GOTOXY STATEMENT

"WHEREX" This function reads the cursor's current column position on the screen into a variable. "X" indicates column.

"WHEREY" This function reads the cursor's current row position on the screen into another variable. "Y" indicates row. If the cursor is placed on the screen at some location (perhaps as a result of a "write" operation or a "gotoxy" procedure), the column and row coordinates of the given location can be determined using these two functions together. Formatting text to be written to the screen is one use of these operations (see Figure 1.5).

Getting Started 1

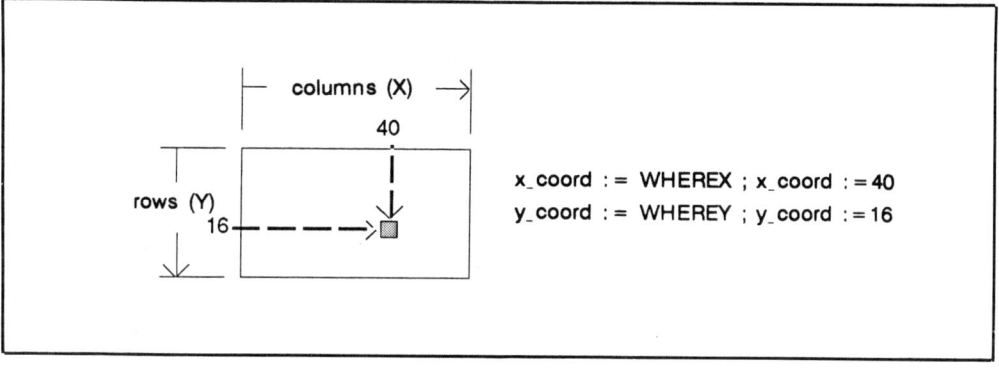

Figure 1.5 WHEREX, WHEREY STATEMENTS

INSTALLATION NOTES

Now turn briefly to the practical problem of getting the programs to run correctly with various system combinations of DOS version number, Turbo Pascal version number, and video monitor (screen) type.

To begin, make sure that the DOS disk v.xx is in Drive A. In the following table, find the combination that matches your own configuration and perform the DOS command in the right-most column. Continue from that point to either instruction A or B to adjust your disk programs.

1 Getting Started

B: For Graphics Screens

- Make sure your versions of "Turbo.com" and "Turbo.msg" are on the same disk as the program. The disk with the programs plus the Turbo programs is called the Program Disk.

- Insert the Program Disk in Drive B. At the B prompt, type

    turbo

    to activate the Turbo Pascal program

- At the Turbo prompt (>), type

    w

    for "work file" and type in the program name

    chrinout.inc

    and press the Return key. From the Turbo prompt, type

    e

    for "edit." The "chrinout.inc" file will appear on the screen, ready for editing.

- Since you need to activate the GRAPHICS screen video memory addresses, you must remove the brackets ({ and }) that appear under the "const" headers that surround "$b800" and "$0000." Removing these brackets will activate these addresses. Be sure that you activate these addresses under *both* procedures CHR_IN and CHR_OUT. Also be sure that both address pairs, "$b000" and "$0000," for the MONOCHROME screen in CHR_IN and CHR_OUT are deactivated (bracketed).

- After these changes are made, save the file to disk by pressing <Ctrl/K>, then <Ctrl/D>, and then, from the Turbo prompt, press <s> (for save).

- If you want to run the program "ssd.drv," follow the above instructions as per "chrinout.inc" *except* use the file name "ssd.drv," and perform the same editing process on the single memory location pair located under the "const" heading in that program.

- After making your changes to "chrinout.inc" and "ssd.drv," at the DOS Drive B prompt, enter the command

    erase *.bak

    to remove "chrinout.bak" and "ssd.bak" (backup files) from the Program Disk. You should remove these files to avoid running out of space on your Program Disk.

Final Note: since the program files and the Turbo Pascal files nearly fill the entire disk, it is suggested that you recopy the Turbo programs and any ".drv" and associated ".inc" and ".txt" files that you want to run onto a separate diskette. This is particularly important for the program "filman.drv" in Chapter 13, where you will create and save a number of new disk files. Also, be sure that Turbo's TINST (Turbo screen installation file) has set "Turbo.com" to *either* the "default display mode" *or* to the screen mode corresponding to the argument in the DOS MODE command (i.e., "monochrome display," "b/w display 80×25," or "color display 80×25").

CHAPTER 2

THE MEMORY/SCREEN MEMORY CONNECTION

2 The Memory/Screen Memory Connection

In this chapter, you will begin to apply material you learned in the previous chapter. More specifically, this chapter introduces the two procedures that lie at the heart of speedy I/O screen routines: the procedure CHR_IN (character from screen into memory) and CHR_OUT (character from memory out to screen). These procedures, because they are so short, come packaged together in an ".inc" file called "chrinout" (character in and out). Three short demonstration programs will illustrate the use of CHR_OUT here; the demonstration of CHR_IN will be covered in Chapter 4 where it will be used to save text directly off the screen and store that text into memory variables for later redisplay.

MODULE: CHRINOUT.INC

The first module to create and save is "chrinout.inc." Boot up the Turbo program and respond to the Turbo ">" prompt by typing the letter "w" (for workfile). *Do not* type the quotation marks. On the screen directly below the ">" prompt, you will see the following: **Work file name:__**. Respond to this prompt by typing (upper or lowercase) the file name **chrinout.inc**. You will then see the message:

```
Loading A:CHRINOUT.INC
New File
>
```

Respond to the ">" prompt by typing the letter "e" (for edit). At this point, the screen will blank out, and the Turbo text editor line will appear across the top of the first line of the screen. You are now ready to type in the first file. Remember, *do not* type the line numbers. They are for reference only.

```
{=====================================================================}
0005  {chrinout.inc}
0010
0015  {This ".inc" file contains the memory-to-screen and the
0020   screen-to-memory character write routines.
0025   On disk as "chrinout.inc"
0030  }
0035  {---------------------------------------------------------------}
0040
0045  procedure      CHR_IN(    j   : integer;
0050                        var ch  : char);
0055
0060      const
0065          {* FOR MONOCHROME SCREENS ONLY *}
0070          {
0075          bwseg = $b000;
```

continued...

...from previous page

```
0080                    bwofs = $0000;
0085                    }
0090
0095                    {* FOR GRAPHICS SCREENS ONLY *}
0100                    {
0105                    bwseg = $b800;
0110                    bwofs = $0000;
0115                    }
0120
0125        Begin
0130             ch := chr(MEM[bwseg : bwofs + j]);
0135        End;
0140   {------------------------------------------------------------------}
0145
0150   procedure      CHR_OUT(j,ch : integer);
0155
0160        const
0165                    {* FOR MONOCHROME SCREENS ONLY *}
0170                    {
0175                    bwseg = $b000;
0180                    bwofs = $0000;
0185                    }
0190
0195                    {* FOR GRAPHICS SCREENS ONLY *}
0200                    {
0205                    bwseg = $b800;
0210                    bwofs = $0000;
0215                    }
0220
0225        Begin
0230             MEM[bwseg : bwofs + j] := ch;
0235        End;
{==================================================================}
```

After you have correctly typed the above code into the computer, save it to disk with the following keystrokes:

- press <Ctrl/K>, then <Ctrl/D>

- at the ">" prompt, type the letter "s" (for save)

On the second line below the prompt, the computer will respond with **SAVING B:CHRINOUT.INC** and then will display the ">" prompt on the following line. *Do not* attempt to compile this module at this time.

2 The Memory/Screen Memory Connection

CHRINOUT: NOTES

The above "include" file is called "chrinout.inc," which means "character in, character out." Notice in the code that for each procedure, there are two different sets of video base addresses given, and both are bracketed. If you have a monochrome screen attached to your system, use the two sets marked FOR MONOCHROME SCREENS ONLY. If you have a graphics screen, use the two sets marked FOR GRAPHICS SCREENS ONLY. Be careful that you activate the correct addresses for *both* the screen character read procedure CHR_IN and the screen character display procedure CHR_OUT.

CHR_IN

The procedure CHR_IN takes a single character that has been displayed on the video screen and saves it into a memory variable (probably an array of characters). Label 1 in Figure 2.1 refers to line 0045. Here, the screen location of the character to be saved is held in the integer variable "j." Label 2 refers to line 0130 and says that the content of the screen memory location MEM[bwseg : bwofs + j] (an integer ASCII value) is converted into its corresponding character. Remember, the screen memory array MEM[bwseg : bwofs + j] holds only ASCII integer values, not characters; the character you see on the screen at a given "j" location is the result of electronic conversion of the number into the corresponding character by special video circuitry inside the computer. Label 3 refers to the "var"'d variable "ch" at line 0050, again in the parameter list. The character variable created at line 0130 is passed from this procedure into the memory variable where it is stored for later use. You will see a good example of this procedure in Chapter 4, where you will save text already on the screen into a memory variable, and then later display the contents of that memory variable back onto the screen.

CHR_OUT

The procedure CHR_OUT is the converse of CHR_IN. It takes a single character (probably from an array of characters in the computer's memory) and displays that character directly onto the video screen. Follow the code in the procedure below. Label 1 in Figure 2.2 refers to line 0150. Here, "j" is a screen memory offset value calculated in the routine that is calling CHR_OUT. "Ch" is derived from the memory

The Memory/Screen Memory Connection 2

CHR_IN — A character already written on the computer screen is "picked off" the screen and saved into a memory variable (probably an array of characters or an array of Boolean).

SCREEN:

SCREEN MEMORY:

MEMORY VARIABLE:

j := ((row-1)*160) +)col-1)*2

① Line 0045: J offset value calculated in main routine is taken in by "CHR_IN"

② Line 0130: the contents of the screen (video) memory location, MEM[Bwseg:Bwofs+J] (an integer ASCII value), is converted into its corresponding screen character

③ Line 0050: the character created at line 0130 is passed out to the main routine from the procedure into an indexed memory array variable

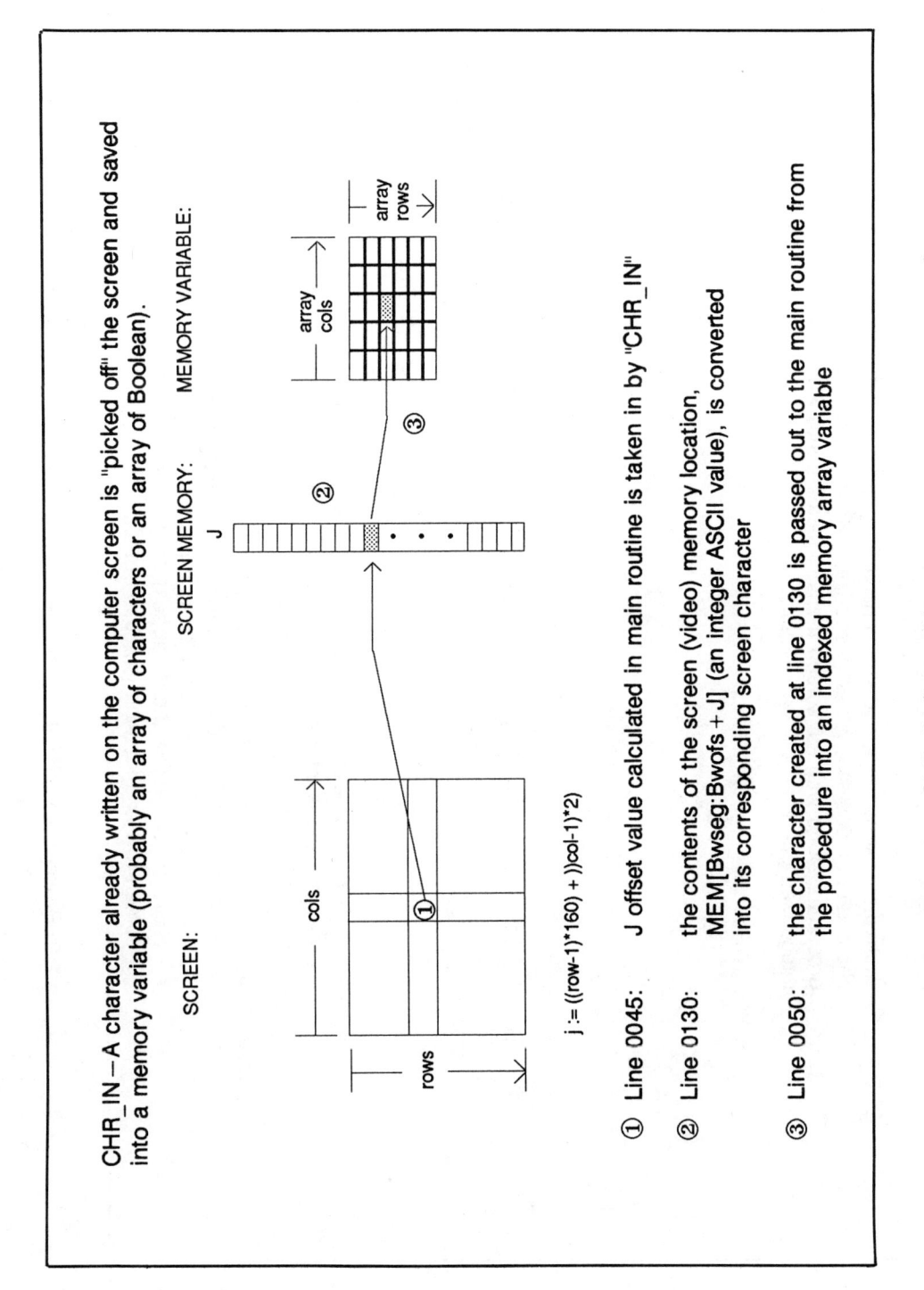

Figure 2.1 Procedure CHR_IN (from video memory or screen to memory)

2 The Memory/Screen Memory Connection

CHR_OUT — A character stored in a memory variable (probably an array of characters or Boolean) is first integerized and then passed into the procedure along with the screen memory location into which the integerized character will be assigned.

MEMORY VARIABLE: SCREEN MEMORY: SCREEN:

$j := ((row-1)*160) + ((col-1)*2)$

① Line 0150   "J" is calculated from the main routine. "Ch" is taken from the memory variable and is integerized as a result of the ORD function in a CHR_OUT procedure call in the main routine.

② Line 0230   The character (in its integerized form) to be displayed from the memory variable and onto the screen is assigned its screen (video) memory location according to the value of "J." Once this is done, the character will automatically appear on the screen in the corresponding screen row and location (see the formula).

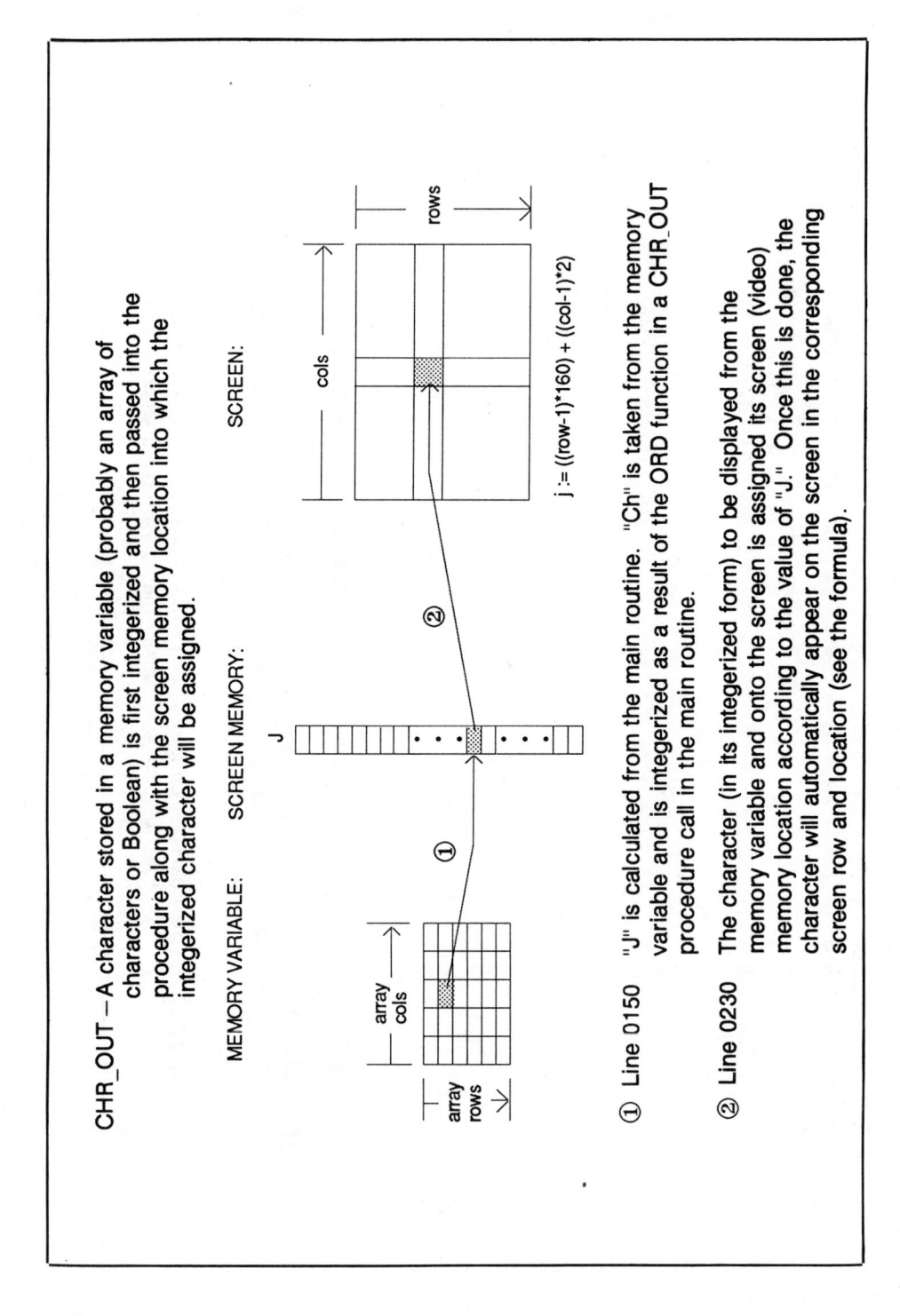

Figure 2.2 Procedure CHR_OUT (from memory to video memory or screen)

variable (a character) and is "integerized" by the ORD function inside the CHR_OUT procedure call located in the main routine. Label 2 refers to line 0230, where the target character (in its integerized form) is assigned its screen (video) memory location as previously given by "j." Once this assignment is made, the character corresponding to its ASCII integer value will appear on the screen in its proper ("j") location. Remember, the specialized video circuitry of the screen memory will electronically convert stored ASCII numbers located in the video memory array (MEM[bwseg : bwofs + j]) into their corresponding characters prior to their display on the screen.

MODULE: CH2DEM1.DRV (CHAPTER 2, DEMONSTRATION 1)

```
{=========================================================================}
0005 program   ch2dem1(input,output);
0010 {
0015   On disk as "ch2dem1.drv"
0020 }
0025 var
0030        i,j : integer;
0035        exit : boolean;
0040
0045 {=========================================================================}
0050 {$i chrinout.inc}
0055 {=========================================================================}
0060
0065 Begin     {main}
0070      window(1,1,80,25);clrscr;
0075      i := 1;
0080      WHILE (i<3123) DO {choose your own number...}
0085      Begin
0090         REPEAT
0095            exit := true;
0100            j := RANDOM(4000); {an integer 0 - 3999 inclusive}
0105            IF ODD(j) THEN
0110               exit := false;
0115         UNTIL (exit = true);{stay in loop until even j  chosen}
0120         CHR_OUT(j , ORD('*'));{CHR_OUT needs integer parameters}
0125         i := i + 1;
0130      End;
0135 End.     {main}
{=========================================================================}
```

CH2DEM1.DRV: NOTES

When run, this program will display 3122 "*" characters directly to the video screen from the screen memory. The idea behind this display is to show that once the "j" value is obtained, you can use that value in the CHR_OUT procedure of "chrinout.inc" to display directly to the screen (line 0120). Examine the REPEAT..UNTIL loop (line 0090). Note that, in this case, the "j" value has not been calculated, but (for illustration purposes) it has been obtained directly using the built-in

2 The Memory/Screen Memory Connection

RANDOM procedure. Line 0105 emphasizes that each character in screen memory has two parts; the character itself (an ASCII number representing the character itself at each even-numbered "j" address) and the character's attribute (at the following odd-numbered "j" address; see Figure 2.3).

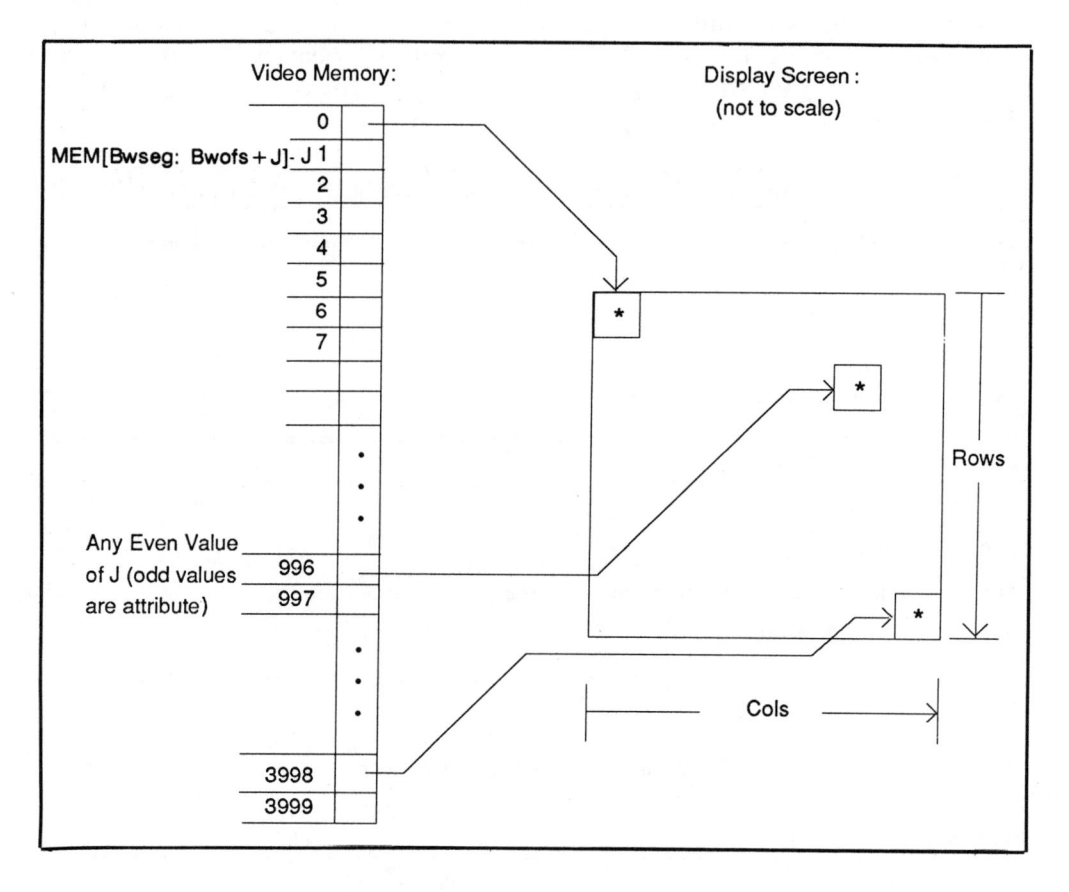

Figure 2.3 CH2DEM1.DRV

MODULE: CH2DEM2.DRV (CHAPTER 2, DEMONSTRATION 2)

```
{================================================================}
0005 program   ch2dem2(input,output);
0010 {
0015    Demonstrates the relationship between the screen
0020    rows and columns and the video screen memory location, j
0025    On disk as "ch2dem2.drv"
0030 }
0035
0040 var
0045       row,col,
0050       j            : integer;
0055       ch           : char;
0060       i            : integer;
0065
0070 {================================================================}
0075 {$i chrinout.inc}
0080 {================================================================}
0085
0090 function    RANDOM_COLUMN : integer;
0095
0100       Begin
0105            random_column := 1 + RANDOM(80);
0110            {1 + (0 - 79 inclusive)}
0115       End;
0120 {----------------------------------------------------------------}
0125
0130 function    RANDOM_ROW : integer;
0135
0140       Begin
0145                random_row := 1 + RANDOM(25);
0150                {1 + (0 - 24 inclusive)}
0155       End;
0160 {----------------------------------------------------------------}
0165
0170 function    CALCULATE_J(c , r : integer) : integer;
0175
0180       Begin
0185            calculate_j := ((r - 1) * 160) + ((c - 1) * 2);
0190       End;
0195 {----------------------------------------------------------------}
0200
0205 Begin {main}
0210       window(1,1,80,25);clrscr;
0215       FOR i := 1 to 2000 DO      {choose your own....}
0220       Begin
0225            col := RANDOM_COLUMN;
0230            row := RANDOM_ROW;
0235            j   := CALCULATE_J(col,row);
0240            CHR_OUT(j , ORD('*');
0245            {CHR_OUT needs integer (ORD) parameter}
0250            {* delay(1000); *}
0255       End;
0260 End.   {main}
{================================================================}
```

2 The Memory/Screen Memory Connection

CH2DEM2.DRV: NOTES

This program, at least from screen appearances, does exactly the same thing as CH2DEM1.DRV above; however, there is a difference. In the above program, the value of "j" was obtained directly using a RANDOM procedure. In this program, "j"'s value is calculated from given row and column values on the screen. To obtain the needed row and column input values, the RANDOM function is again used in the two procedures RANDOM_COLUMN and RANDOM_ROW (lines 0090 & 0130). These column and row values are then combined inside the procedure CALCULATE_J. The result is a single, unique video screen memory location into which CHR_OUT will place the "*" character for display on the screen (see Figure 2.4).

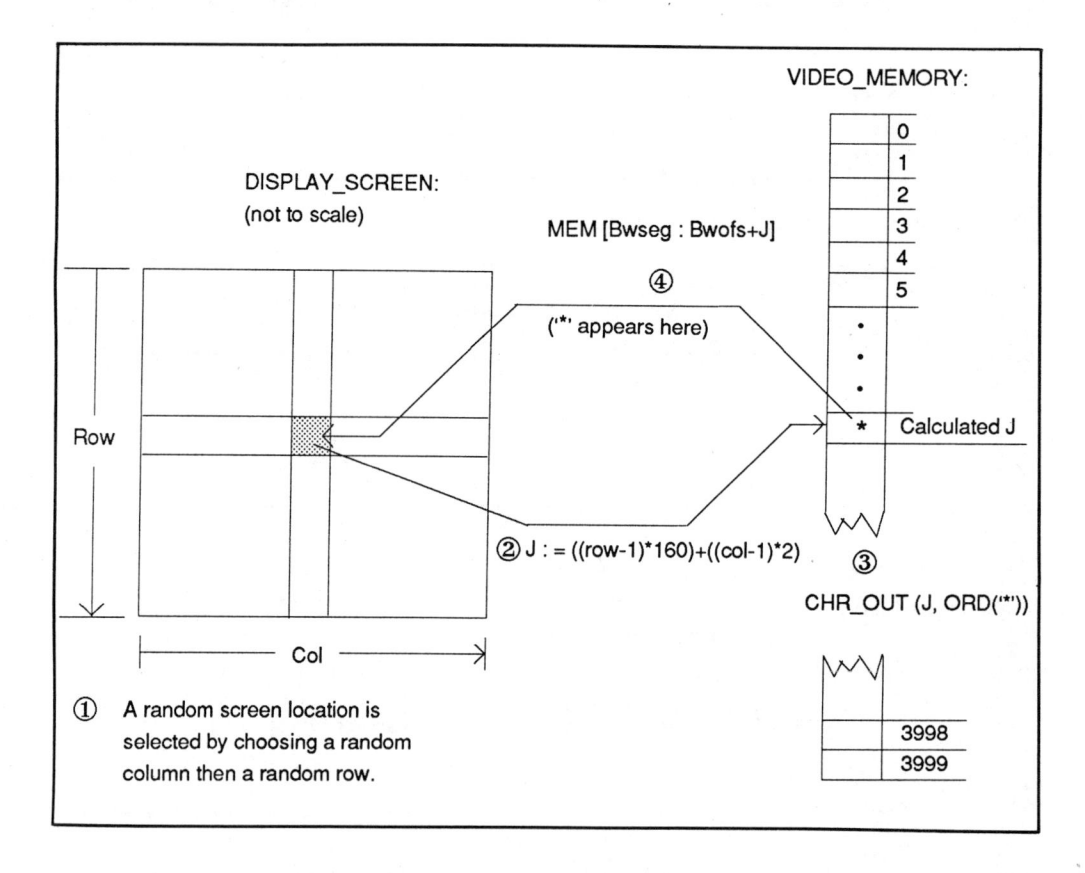

Figure 2.4 CH2DEM2.DRV

The Memory/Screen Memory Connection **2**

MODULE: CH2DEM3.DRV (CHAPTER 2, DEMONSTRATION 3)

```
{==========================================================================}
0005 program   ch2dem3(input,output);
0010 {
0015   This program is a simplified version of J.H. Conway's famous
0020   game called "LIFE". On disk as "ch2dem3.drv"
0025 }
0030
0035 const
0040        bell = #$07;
0045
0050 type
0055        screen    = array[1..25,1..80] of boolean;
0060
0065 var
0070        row,col         : integer;
0075        old_screen,
0080        new_screen      : screen;
0085
0090 {==========================================================================}
0095 {$i chrinout.inc}
0100 {==========================================================================}
0105
0110 procedure      DISPLAY_NEW_SCREEN(var new_screen : screen);
0115
0120 var
0125        row,col         : integer;
0130        j               : integer;
0135
0140 Begin     {procedure display_new_screen}
0145      FOR row := 1 to 25 DO
0150      Begin
0155           FOR col := 1 to 80 DO
0160           Begin
0165                j := ((row - 1) * 160) + ((col - 1) * 2);
0170                IF (new_screen[row,col] = true) THEN
0175                    CHR_OUT(j,ORD('*'));
0180
0185                IF (new_screen[row,col] = false) THEN
0190                    CHR_OUT(j,ORD(' '));   {1 blank}
0195           End;
0200      End;
0205 End;      {procedure display_new_screen}
0210 {--------------------------------------------------------------------------}
0215
0220 procedure      INITIALIZE(var new_screen : screen);
0225
0230 var
0235        row,col,
0240        i,j,
0245        random_row,
0250        random_col      : integer;
0255
0260 Begin     {procedure initialize}
0265      window(1,1,80,25);
0270      FOR row := 1 to 25 DO
0275      Begin
0280           FOR col := 1 to 80 DO
0285           Begin
0290                new_screen[row,col] := false;
```

continued...

33

2   The Memory/Screen Memory Connection

...from previous page

```
0295              End;
0300          End;
0305
0310          FOR i := 1 to 200 DO      {could be any number you wish....}
0315          Begin
0320              random_row := 1 + RANDOM(25);
0325              random_col := 1 + RANDOM(80);
0330              new_screen[random_row,random_col] := true;
0335          End;
0340 End;         {procedure initialize}
0345 {---------------------------------------------------------------}
0350
0355 procedure      VISIT_NEIGHBOUR (r , c              : integer
0360                                 var old_screen    : screen;
0365                                 var new_screen    : screen);
0370
0375 var
0380       n_count   : integer;
0385
0390 Begin     {procedure visit_neighbour}
0395       n_count := 0;
0400       IF (old_screen[r - 1 , c] = true) THEN
0405            n_count := n_count + 1;
0410       IF (old_screen[r - 1 , c - 1] = true) THEN
0415            n_count := n_count + 1;
0420       IF (old_screen[r , c - 1] = true) THEN
0425            n_count := n_count + 1;
0430       IF (old_screen[r + 1 , c - 1] = true) THEN
0435            n_count := n_count + 1;
0440       IF (old_screen[r + 1 , c] = true) THEN
0445            n_count := n_count + 1;
0450       IF (old_screen[r + 1 , c + 1] = true) THEN
0455            n_count := n_count + 1;
0460       IF (old_screen[r , c + 1] = true) THEN
0465            n_count := n_count + 1;
0470       IF (old_screen[r - 1 , c + 1] = true) THEN
0475            n_count := n_count + 1;
0480
0485       IF (old_screen[r,c] = false) THEN   {old screen loc. is "off"}
0490       Begin
0495            IF (n_count = 3) THEN
0500                 new_screen[r,c] := true
0505                 {turn new screen loc. "on"}
0510            ELSE
0515                 new_screen[r,c] := false;
0520                 {turn new screen loc. "off"}
0525       End
0530       ELSE                                {old screen loc. is "on"}
0535       Begin
0540            IF (n_count = 2) OR (n_count = 3) THEN
0545                 new_screen[r,c] := true
0550                 {turn new screen loc. "on"}
0555            ELSE
0560                 new_screen[r,c] := false;
0565                 {turn new screen loc. "off"}
```

continued...

The Memory/Screen Memory Connection   2

...from previous page

```
0570        End;
0575 End;        {procedure visit_neighbour}
0580 {-----------------------------------------------------------------}
0585
0590 Begin    {ch2dem3.drv}
0595     window(1,1,80,25);clrscr;
0600     INITIALIZE(new_screen);
0605     DISPLAY_NEW_SCREEN(new_screen);
0610     REPEAT
0615         FOR row := 1 to 25 DO
0620         Begin
0625             FOR col := 1 to 80 DO
0630             Begin
0635                 old_screen[row,col] := new_screen[row,col];
0640             End;
0645         End;
0650
0655         FOR row := 2 to 24 DO
0660         Begin
0665             FOR col := 2 to 78 DO
0670             Begin
0675                 VISIT_NEIGHBOUR(row,col,
0680                                 old_screen,
0685                                 new_screen);
0690             End;
0695         End;
0700         DISPLAY_NEW_SCREEN(new_screen);
0705     UNTIL (KEYPRESSED = true);
0710 End.        {program ch2dem3.drv}
{=========================================================================}
```

CH2DEM3.DRV: NOTES

This demonstration program is a simplified version of the game of LIFE invented by the English mathematician J.H. Conway. In addition to being fun to run, this program offers a good opportunity to use the CHR_OUT procedure along with some array data structures so you can understand how to translate memory variables into screen display output. Following are the procedures involved.

Initialize

This procedure starts the program by populating the whole Boolean array "new_screen" with the value "false" (line 0290). It then randomly populates 200 of the 4000 possible array locations with the Boolean value "true" (lines 0310-0335). Note that the size of the Boolean variable (25×80) exactly matches the size of the video screen.

2 The Memory/Screen Memory Connection

Display_New_Screen

Once "new_screen" is populated, each row and column of the display screen is scanned (loops at lines 0145 and 0155). If the value of the Boolean "new_screen" at the corresponding row and column value on the screen is "true," then CHR_OUT will "turn on" that screen location by displaying an asterisk (*) there. Conversely, if the value is "false," then CHR_OUT will "turn off" that screen location by displaying a blank (' ') there (see line 0190).

Visit_Neighbour

After "new_screen" is displayed on the video screen, it is immediately assigned to the Boolean array variable "old_screen" at line 0635. The assignment is made so that the procedure VISIT_NEIGHBOUR can convert "old_screen" into a different "new_screen" according to some specialized rules. These rules are as follows (lines 0400-0485):

- If a given cell (screen location) has the value "false" ("off") and VISIT_NEIGHBOUR indicates that three neighbouring cells are "on," then the given cell will also be turned "on." But, if 0, 1, 2, 4, 5, 6, 7, or 8 neighbours are "true" ("on"), then this cell will be turned "off."

- If a given cell is "true" ("on") and VISIT_NEIGHBOUR indicates either two or three neighbouring cells are "true" ("on"), then this cell will stay "on." But if 0, 1, 4, 5, 6, 7, or 8 neighbours are "on" ("true"), then this cell will be turned "off" ("false").

Note that the array variables are "var"'d; that is, even though they are global variables, they are subject to change by a procedure of more limited scope. To supplement understanding of lines 0400-0485, refer to Figure 2.5.

The Memory/Screen Memory Connection 2

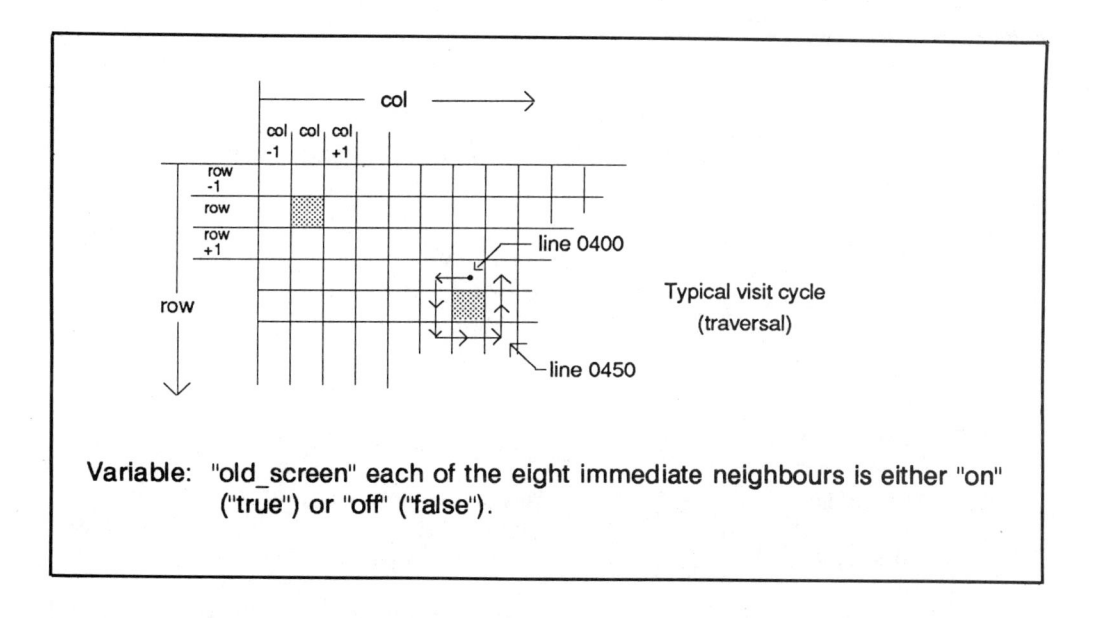

Variable: "old_screen" each of the eight immediate neighbours is either "on" ("true") or "off" ("false").

Figure 2.5 Procedure VISIT_NEIGHBOUR

Main Routine

Before reading further, examine Figure 2.6. The numbered labels you see relate to the REPEAT..UNTIL loop between lines 0610 and 0705. At label 1, "new_screen" is moved into "old_screen." At label 2, "new screen" is created from "old_ screen" using the conversion rules of VISIT_NEIGHBOUR. Note that only rows 2-24 and columns 2-78 inclusive are traversed (visited) in the FOR..DO loops that surround VISIT_NEIGHBOUR. As stated above, this is a simplified version that allows VISIT_NEIGHBOUR to check all eight neighbours around each and every cell included in the row and column boundaries (Figure 2.5). At label 3, the procedure DISPLAY_SCREEN is called to display the newly created array "new_screen." It is displayed onto the screen one character at a time — either an asterisk (*) or a blank (' ') — using CHR OUT from the "chrinout.inc" external procedure package.

2   The Memory/Screen Memory Connection

INSIDE MEMORY: VIDEO SCREEN:

new screen

③ Line 0700
Display "new_screen"
to video screen
then goto step ①

② Line 0675
Create
"new_screen"
from
"old_screen"
using
the
procedure
"VISIT_NEIGHBOUR"

① Lines 0610 - 0635

Assign "new_screen" into
"old_screen"

old screen

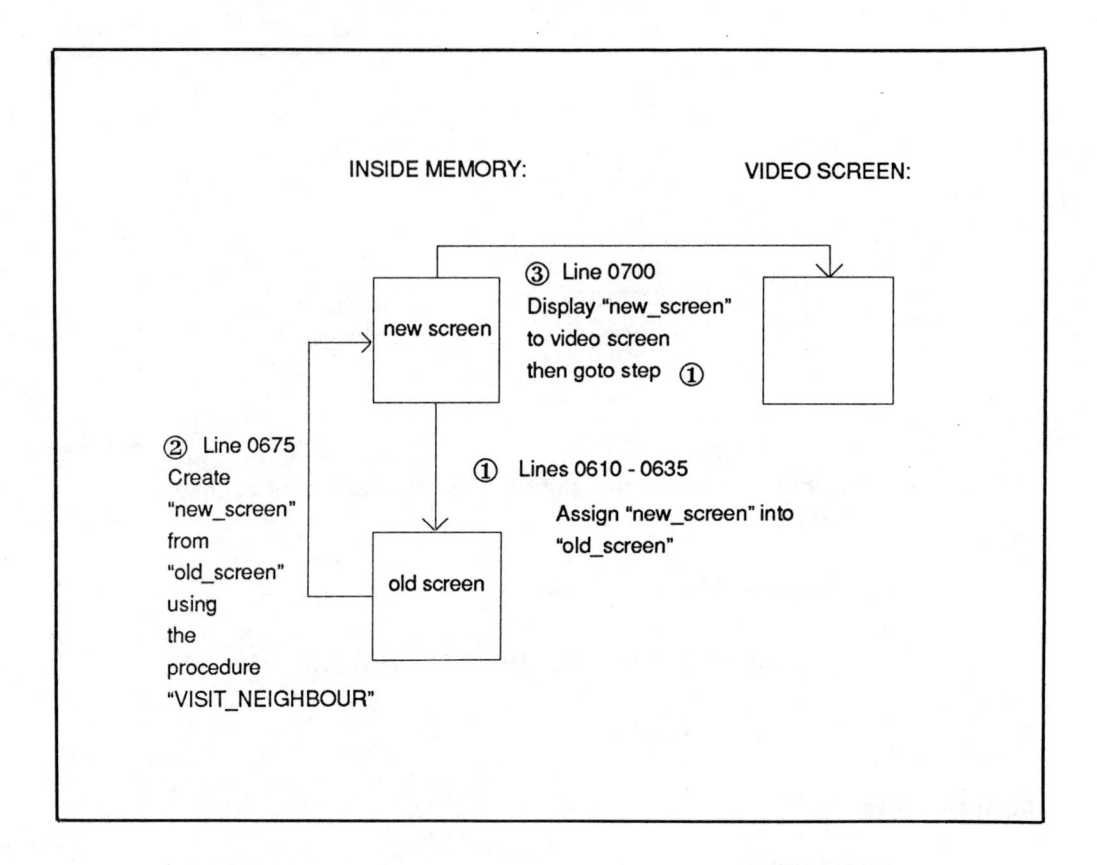

Figure 2.6 Inside REPEAT..UNTIL Loop of Main Routine

CHAPTER 3

CREATING SCREEN WINDOWS

3   Creating Screen Windows

Window bordering or **framing** is the process of enclosing or isolating a defined screen area inside a box of line and corner characters. This chapter presents Pascal code which will enable you to "frame" text that has been written to the computer screen. The chief purpose of this exercise is to enhance screen readability by organizing its contents into portions that are easy for the eye to follow.

Typical applications for this technique are help menus, data input screens, data output screens, input or output data scrolling, and command windows.

Below, a working program is presented that will illustrate window bordering by creating four text borders on the computer's screen. As you will see, coding for this windowing task is separated into three different parts: two separate modules to be typed and saved as ".inc" or "include files" and a small ".drv" or "driver" program file that creates a suitable environment in which to activate the include files to perform their predesignated tasks.

MODULE: WINDOWS.INC

The first module to create and save to disk is WINDOWS.INC. Follow the same file creation and saving steps that you used for the CHRINOUT.INC module above. Remember, *do not* attempt to compile this module on its own. Just save it to disk for now.

```
{==========================================================================}
0005  {windows.inc}
0010  {This ".inc" file contains the window border routine
0015   for the demo program Part 1. It must be used in
0020   conjunction with "chrinout.inc" above.
0025  }
0030  {--------------------------------------------------------------------}
0035
0040  procedure WINDOW_BORDER(tlc,tlr,brc,brr,bord_st : integer);
0045
0050  var
0055        hll,vll                         : integer;
0060        tl_corn , t_h_lin , tr_corn,
0065        l_v_lin , r_v_lin,
0070        bl_corn , b_h_lin , br_corn : integer;
0075
0080  {--------------------------------------------------------------------}
0085
0090        procedure BORDER_STYLE_TABLE(var top_left__corner,
0095                                     var top_horizontal_line,
0100                                     var top_right_corner,
```

continued...

...from previous page

```
0105                                    var left_vertical_line,
0110                                    var right_vertical_line,
0115                                    var bottom_left_corner,
0120                                    var bottom_horizontal_line,
0125                                    var bottom_right_corner : integer);
0130
0135        Begin    {sub-procedure border_style_table}
0140            CASE (bord_st) OF
0145
0150            1 : Begin
0155                    top_left_corner          := 201;
0160                    top_horizontal_line      := 205;
0165                    top_right_corner         := 187;
0170                    left_vertical_line       := 186;
0175                    right_vertical_line      := 186;
0180                    bottom_left_corner       := 200;
0185                    bottom_horizontal_line   := 205;
0190                    bottom_right_corner      := 188;
0195                End;
0200
0205            2 : Begin
0210                    top_left_corner          := 218;
0215                    top_horizontal_line      := 196;
0220                    top_right_corner         := 191;
0225                    left_vertical_line       := 179;
0230                    right_vertical_line      := 179;
0235                    bottom_left_corner       := 192;
0240                    bottom_horizontal_line   := 196;
0245                    bottom_right_corner      := 217;
0250                End;
0255
0260            3 : Begin
0265                    top_left_corner          := 213;
0270                    top_horizontal_line      := 205;
0275                    top_right_corner         := 184;
0280                    left_vertical_line       := 179;
0285                    right_vertical_line      := 179;
0290                    bottom_left_corner       := 212;
0295                    bottom_horizontal_line   := 205;
0300                    bottom_right_corner      := 190;
0305                End;
0310
0315            4 : Begin
0320                    top_left_corner          := 214;
0325                    top_horizontal_line      := 196;
0330                    top_right_corner         := 183;
0335                    left_vertical_line       := 186;
0340                    right_vertical_line      := 186;
0345                    bottom_left_corner       := 211;
0350                    bottom_horizontal_line   := 196;
0355                    bottom_right_corner      := 189;
0360                End;
0365            END; {case}
0370        End;
0375  {----------------------------------------------------------------}
0380
0385        procedure    WINDOW_LINE(r,c,n,ch,d : integer);
0390
0395        var
0400            i,j      : integer;
0405
```

continued...

3 Creating Screen Windows

...from previous page

```
0410        Begin      {sub procedure window_line}
0415              j := ((r - 1) * 160) + ((c - 1) * 2);  {j = f(row & col)}
0420              FOR i := 1 to n DO
0425              Begin
0430                    CHR_OUT(j,ch); {ch passed to procedure "x" as k. }
0435                    IF d = 0 THEN {direction is down...}
0440                          j := j + 160
0445                    ELSE           {direction is across.}
0450                          j := j + 2;
0455              End;
0460        End;        {sub-procedure window_line}
0465 {-------------------------------------------------------------------}
0470
0475 Begin      {procedure window_border}
0480        {NOTE: use of ABSOLUTE screen coordinates not relative ones}
0485
0490        window(1,1,80,25);{all window borders in absolute coords.}
0495        hll := brc - tlc + 1;   {includes both end points}
0500        vll := brr - tlr + 1;   {includes both end points}
0505        BORDER_STYLE_TABLE(tl_corn , t_h_lin , tr_corn, {top}
0510                           l_v_lin , r_v_lin ,         {sides}
0515                           bl_corn , b_h_lin , br_corn; {bottom}
0520
0525        gotoxy(tlc , tlr);write(chr(tl_corn)); {top left corner}
0530        WINDOW_LINE(tlr , tlc+1 , hll-1 , t_h_lin , 1 ); {across top}
0535        gotoxy(brc , tlr);write(chr(tr_corn)); {top right corner}
0540        gotoxy(tlc , tlr+1);    {reposition cursor}
0545        WINDOW_LINE(tlr+1 , tlc , vll-1 , l_v_lin , 0 ); {down lhs}
0550        gotoxy(brc , tlr+1);    {reposition cursor}
0555        WINDOW_LINE(tlr+1 , brc , vll-1 , r_v_lin , 0 ); {down rhs}
0560        gotoxy(tlc , brr);write(chr(bl_corn)); {bottom left corner}
0565        WINDOW_LINE(brr , tlc+1 ,hll-1 , b_h_lin , 1 ); {across bot}
0570        gotoxy(brc , brr);write(chr(br_corn)); {bottom right corner}
0575 End;       {procedure window_border}
{=====================================================================}
```

WINDOWS.INC: NOTES

WINDOWS.INC will be the next include file described. This ".inc" file has two procedures. The first is WINDOW_BORDER. It is called from the driver routine with six parameters that provide information about the row and column screen coordinates, the upper left and lower right corners of the window frame, and the length of the horizontal and vertical window lines. The purpose of this procedure is to lay out the individual steps that will create the screen border.

Border_Style_Table

The purpose of this subprocedure is to supply its calling procedure, WINDOW_BORDER, with the border style characters for the window to be created (lines 0150-0355). As a subprocedure, BORDER_STYLE_TABLE has access to the parameter list of WINDOW_BORDER and will use the variable "bord_st" (border style number) there (line 0040). This subprocedure is thus activated by a supplied "bord_st" value inside the CASE..END structure, starting at line 0140. For example, if the value of "bord_st" is "4," the set of assignment statements starting at line 0320 will be activated. These assignment statements put the ASCII equivalent integer values of the required border characters into the corresponding positions in the parameter list. Note that all the variables in the parameter list are prefixed with the reserved word "var." This means that these variables can be exported from BORDER STYLE_TABLE for use in WINDOW_BORDER. In this case, the variable values are created inside this subprocedure and then passed out into the parameter list of the procedure call at line 0505 by way of the parameter list at lines 0090-0125. Once the values of the BORDER STYLE_TABLE parameter list are filled with the correct values, they are used at lines 0525-0570 in the body of the main calling procedure, WINDOW_BORDER.

Window_Line

The subprocedure WINDOW_LINE is called from within WINDOW BORDER and actually draws the border lines on the screen. The first two parameters of WINDOW_LINE determine the starting screen row and column coordinates. The third parameter, "n," tells the procedure the number of times to repeat drawing a border character on the screen. The parameter "ch," which corresponds to the number passed in from WINDOW_BORDER, is the ASCII representation of the actual line character to be drawn on the screen. And "d," the last parameter, is the direction in which the line will be drawn. A "0" represents the vertical direction (top to bottom), and a "1" represents the horizontal direction (left to right).

The first two parameters — "r" and "c" — are combined by the formula at line 0415 to calculate the integer-valued offset into the video memory segment (called the "j" value or screen pointer). The row and column values are each reduced by one to show that row 1 and column 1, from the human point of view, are actually the 0 offset or first row and column from the computer's point of view.

3 Creating Screen Windows

The expression (r - 1) is multiplied by 160 (80 * 2) to show that the same columns in adjacent rows are actually 160 bytes apart in screen adaptor memory. Each screen character consists of two bytes: one byte (256 unique combinations of 8 bits) defines the unique character itself, and the second byte defines the attributes of that character (underlined, blinking, intensity, foreground color, and background color). The expression (c-1) is multiplied by 2 to show that adjacent characters in the same screen row are only two bytes apart in the screen adaptor memory. Again, each screen display character consists of a character byte followed immediately by its attribute byte inside the screen adaptor memory. On the screen, both character and attribute appear merged into one character.

The integer value "j," then, is the calculated offset value of the screen character inside screen adaptor memory. It is a single number derived from the row and column screen coordinates passed in from the procedure WINDOW_BORDER. The "j" value is passed through to CHR OUT.

The third parameter, "n," is found in the loop at line 0420 and tells WINDOW_LINE how many times to repeat the single-screen character-writing procedure CHR_OUT. Parameter "n" corresponds to the length of the horizontal or vertical line to be drawn.

The fourth parameter, "ch," is passed into WINDOW_LINE from each of lines 0530-0565 in the body of the main procedure WINDOW_BORDER. Exactly which window border character is passed into WINDOW BORDER depends on which part of the window border is being drawn. For example, the invocation of WINDOW_LINE at line 0545 (moving down the left-hand side) will require the ASCII value of the variable "l v_lin" (left vertical line). If you were displaying border style #4, the value used would be ASCII value 186 (now resident in "l_v_lin" of BORDER_STYLE_TABLE at line 0335). The integer value of the ASCII character is then passed into CHR_OUT where it is converted into a character and displayed to the screen as a character.

The last parameter, "d," tells the WINDOW_LINE procedure whether to draw the line horizontally across the screen or vertically down the screen. At this point, note that "j," the screen adaptor memory starting offset value, is calculated only once at line 0415, and that calculation was prior to entry into the FOR..DO loop on the next line. If "d"=0, the direction is down from the starting screen location as defined by "r" and "c" at line 0415. Remember, a vertical drop of one screen line corresponds to a forward jump of 160 bytes in screen adaptor memory, as referenced by "j" in line 0440. If d=1, the direction is defined to be across or to the right of the original row and column coordinates of the video screen. In terms of the "j" offset value in the screen adaptor memory, it means that the offset value will be increased by two bytes each time a character is written to the screen adaptor memory while it only appears as one character (character and its attribute) on the video screen.

The procedure WINDOW_LINE, then, derives its speed from writing the window border characters directly into the screen adaptor memory locations one at a time. This procedure is much quicker than using a series of "write(....)" statements.

In later programs, you will see how characters already on the computer screen can be "picked off" the screen and saved into computer memory for future redisplay. The procedure CHR_IN will find its use there.

MODULE: WINDOW.DRV

The last module to type and save is the module WINDOW.DRV. This module is the one that activates previous modules.

```
{============================================================}
0005 program window(input,output);
0010         { This ".drv" file illustrates the creation of
0015           window borders.  It uses the ".inc" files
0020           "chrinout.inc" and "windows.inc"
0025           together to achieve its task.
0030           On disk as "windo.drv".
0035         }
0040
0045 const
0050       bell = #$07;
0055
0060 var
0065       tl_col,tl_row,
0070       br_col,br_row,
0075       bord_st          : integer
0080
0085
0090 {============================================================}
0095
0100 {$i chrinout.inc} {"chrinout.inc" is invoked by "windows.inc" }
0105 {$i windows.inc}  {module and MUST be prior to it............}
0110
0115 {============================================================}
0120
0125 Begin     {driver}
```

continued...

3 Creating Screen Windows

...from previous page

```
0130        window(1,1,80,25);clrscr;
0135        TEXTCOLOR(0);TEXTBACKGROUND(15)
0140        gotoxy(26,2)
0145        write(' BORDER STYLE DEMO CHAPTER 3 ');
0150        TEXTCOLOR(15);TEXTBACKGROUND(0);
0155        tl_col := 30 ; tl_row := 12;
0160        br_col := 50 ; br_row := 17;
0165        border_style := 1; {the last parameter in list....}
0170        WINDOW_BORDER(tl_col,tl_row,
0175                      br_col,br_row,
0180                      border_style);
0185        gotoxy(34,23);write('Border Style #1');
0190        {* delay(2000); *}
0195
0200        {a shorter alternative way to create a window border....}
0205        WINDOW_BORDER(11,4,70,21,2); {border style #2}
0210        gotoxy(34,20);write('Border Style #2');
0215        {* delay(2000) *}
0220
0225        WINDOW_BORDER(21,7,59,18,3); {border style #3}
0230        gotoxy(34,17);write('Border Style #3');
0235        {* delay(2000) *}
0240
0245        WINDOW_BORDER(31,10,50,15,4); {border style #4}
0250        gotoxy(34,14);write('Border Style #4');
0255        {* delay(2000) *}
0260 End.           {driver}
{================================================================}
```

WINDOW.DRV: NOTES

A **driver routine** (in the most widely used sense) refers to a software routine written to control the input and output or exchange of character data between the computer's microprocessor and the attached peripherals (plotters, floppy disks, RAM disks, hard disks, printers, keyboards, modems, etc.). DOS and BIOS routines contain all the factory-supplied driver routines for the IBM computer and its standard peripherals.

Here, WINDOW.DRV will be called a driver routine because its job is to supply parameters to user-written modules, thus enabling or activating them to perform the tasks for which they were designed. In this chapter and in each chapter of Part One, a small driver routine is included that will activate the module being demonstrated. All these modules will be suffixed with the ".drv" extention.

In the driver routine, the parameters used in the procedure calls that activate the corresponding procedures in the "include" files are named in the "var" section of the declaration block. Numeric values are assigned in two different ways in this routine. The first way (lines 0155-0160) is easier to understand but takes more time to code. Later, you will probably want to directly invoke the "window border" driver as shown at line 0205. Note that assignment of these values could have also been done from the keyboard or disk peripherals using the READ statement in the program code of the driver routine. A final point about driver routines: to avoid confusion, it is best to ensure that the parameter names used in the driver routines are distinguishable from their counterparts inside the ".inc" modules. Attaining this distinction often boils down to creative spelling (e.g., "tl_col" in "window.drv" corresponds to "tlc" in WINDOW_ BORDER and "top_ left_ corner" in BORDER STYLE_ TABLE). Again, the object of developing ".inc" routines is library-building, that is, writing specialized utility routines (like the window drawing routine) only once and then making them globally available for use by other programs by way of the Turbo Pascal "$i" (read as "dollars include") compiler directive.

Lines 0100 and 0105 contain the " $i " ("dollars include") compiler directive of the Turbo compiler. This directive means "Interrupt compiling of the main program; find the routine CHRINOUT.INC and include it in the overall compilation; then, find the routine WINDOWS.INC and include it in the overall compilation also." Once these routines are "include compiled," the compiler continues to compile the rest of the driver routine. As the driver program is being compiled, the screen looks like this:

```
    >
    COMPILING (successive flashing line numbers)
```

You can tell when an "include" file is being compiled because the screen will display a flashing capital letter " I ":

```
    >
I   COMPILING (successive flashing line numbers)
```

Once the driver routine and its ".inc" utility files have been compiled, the Turbo prompt (>) will appear. Respond by pressing <r> (for run). The screen will appear as seen in Figure 3.1

3 Creating Screen Windows

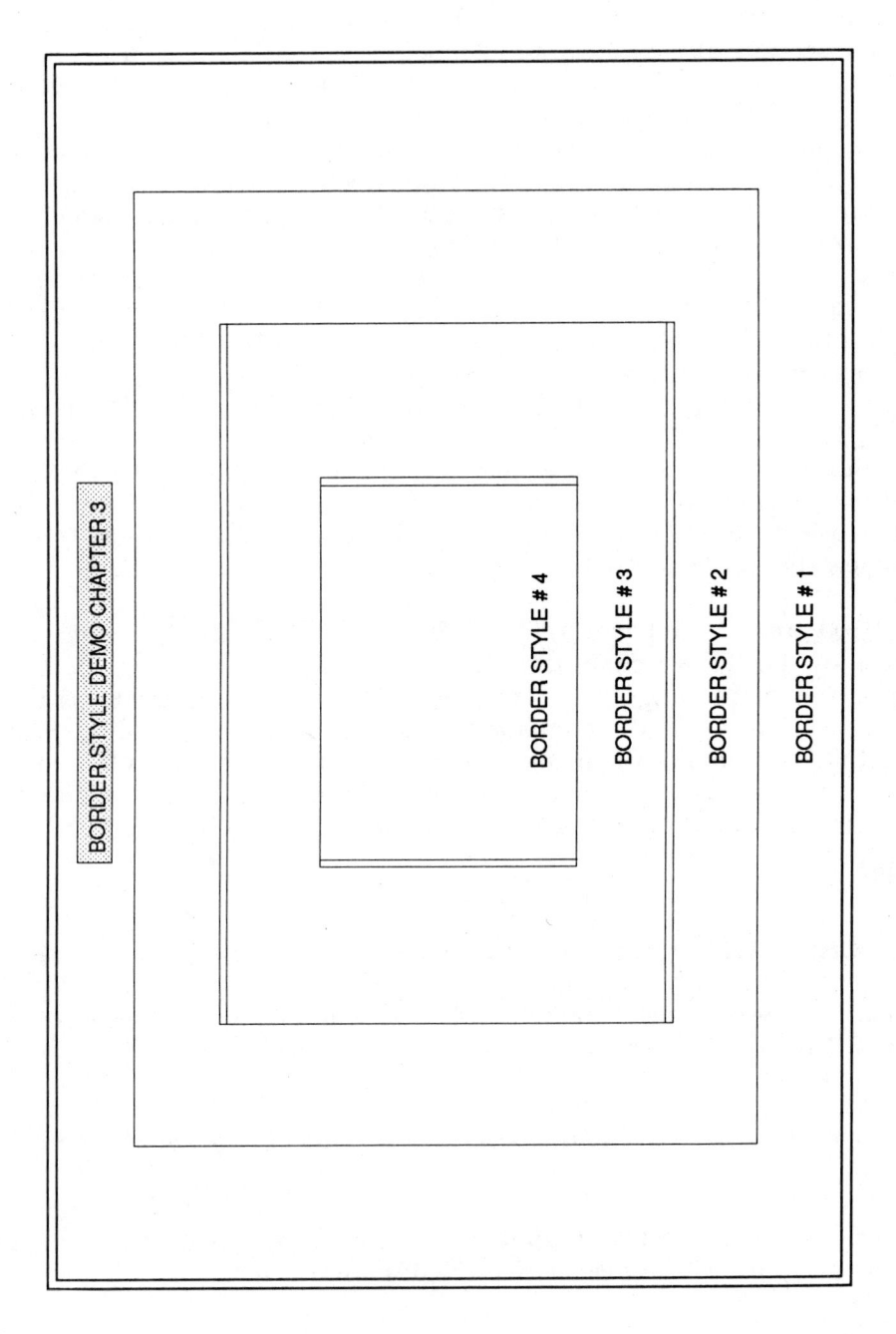

Figure 3.1 Some Window Border Styles

Creating Screen Windows 3

Before the conclusion of this chapter, look at Figures 3.2 and 3.3. The first provides four border style alternatives in addition to those shown in the procedure BORDER_STYLE_TABLE. Figure 3.3 summarizes the various routines introduced thus far along with their variable names and corresponding English translations. Since these will be used consistently throughout the rest of the book, they have been grouped here for reference.

Different window border line styles can be created using these ASCII values in vertical combination:

Top Left Corner	chr(178)	chr(249)	chr(219)	chr(219)
Across Top	chr(178)	chr(249)	chr(205)	chr(223)
Top Right Corner	chr(178)	chr(249)	chr(219)	chr(219)
Down Left Side	chr(178)	chr(249)	chr(186)	chr(219)
Down Right Side	chr(178)	chr(249)	chr(186)	chr(219)
Bottom Left Corner	chr(178)	chr(249)	chr(219)	chr(219)
Across Bottom	chr(178)	chr(249)	chr(205)	chr(220)
Bottom Right Corner	chr(178)	chr(249)	chr(219)	chr(219)

Figure 3.2 Variations

3 Creating Screen Windows

ROUTINE:	VARIABLES:	READ AS:
WINDOW.DRV	tl_col	top left column
	tl_row	top left row
	br_col	bottom right column
	br_row	bottom right row
	h_line_len	horizontal line length
	v_line_len	vertical line length

{--}

WINDOWS.INC

procedure:		
WINDOW_BORDER	tlc	top left column
	tlr	top left row
	brc	bottom right column
	brr	bottom right row
	hll	horizontal line length
	vll	vertical line length
procedure:		
WINDOW_LINE	r	row
(called from	c	column
"window_border")	n	number
	ch	character
	d	direction

{--}

CHRINOUT.INC

procedure:		
CHR_IN	bwseg	black and white segment (monochrome and graphics)
&		
CHR_OUT	bwofs	black and white offset (monochrome and graphics)
	j	a screen character's variable offset value inside the screen memory segment. Also called a screen pointer.
	ch	a screen character (represented as 8-bit ASCII value in any given screen memory offset location)

The procedure CHR_OUT is called from inside the procedure WINDOW_LINE but has been separated because it is called by several other procedures in later chapters.

Figure 3.3 Variable Names Chapters 1-3

CHAPTER 4

SCREEN SAVE AND REDISPLAY

4 Screen Save and Redisplay

This chapter discusses two important screen I/O techniques. The first is a screen saving technique in which text already displayed on the video screen is saved directly from the screen into an array variable in memory. The second is a screen redisplay technique in which previously saved screen images (stored in an array) can be moved from the array and back onto the screen under program control.

These techniques are useful in the following situations:

- where programmers want to separate screen input and output data screens to avoid overcrowding on the video display. After all the input data is entered on the screen, the whole input screen can be saved to make way for the output results. Whenever programmers need to recall the input screen, they only need to press a predefined key.

- in program debugging where users may want to set up a screen of intermediate variable results, which will help trace the evolution of certain variables. These intermediate variables are created by setting up "write" statements inside the algorithm and then saving the text generated by these "write" statements to a separate screen for later redisplay and examination.

- where programmers are interested in fast, previously created, reuseable templates that can be displayed directly from memory to the screen rather than "painted on" by the much slower "write" statements. Typical examples would be pop-up menus, command lines, and data table templates. Only assembler language routines are faster.

The second part of this chapter will show you how to develop a program that will transfer an image on the video screen into hard copy from the printer. It too uses CHR_IN to transfer the character contents directly from the video screen into a memory array variable. Note that this program has not been developed into an ".inc" module as it is not completely inside the realm of pure screen I/O; however, it is included here because of its tremendous potential for use in future work. You can customize the program to fit your own future needs.

Screen Save and Redisplay 4

MODULE: SCR_S_D.INC

The mnemonic "scr_s_d.inc" reads as "screen save and re-display" and is another of the "include" or library files. This module provides two services. The first is to save (copy) the character contents as displayed on the computer screen (and in screen memory) into regular computer memory. The second is to redisplay the previously saved screen image onto the video screen as discussed in Chapter 2. The computer coding for this module follows. Type it in and then save it to disk as "scr_s d.inc".

```
{=========================================================================}
0005 {scr_s_d.inc}          {"SCReen Save and Display"}
0010
0015 { This ".inc" module provides services to save a part (or whole)
0020   of screen TO memory and re-display a part (or whole) of the
0023   screen FROM memory back onto the screen
0025   On disk as "scr_s_d.inc"
0030 }
0035
0040 {-----------------------------------------------------------------}
0045
0050 procedure      SAVE_PART_SCREEN(tlc,tlr,brc,brr : integer;
0055                         var copy_of_part_scr : screen_copy);
0060
0065 var
0070      i,j,k    : integer;
0075      hll,vll  : integer;
0080
0085 Begin     {procedure save_part_screen}
0090      window(1,1,80,25);
0095      hll := brc - tlc + 1;
0100      vll := brr - tlr + 1;
0105      gotoxy(tlc,tlr);
0110      FOR i := 1 to vll DO         {down thru rows}
0115      Begin
0120           j := ((tlr - 1) * 160) + ((tlc - 1) * 2);
0125           FOR k := 1 to hll DO    {across thru columns}
0130           Begin
0135                CHR_IN(j,copy_of_part_scr[i,k]);
0140                { source(j) , destination(copy_of...) }
0145                j := j + 2;
0150           End;
0155           tlc := tlc;             {same column.........}
0160           tlr := tlr + 1;         {drop down to next row}
0165      End;
0170 End;      {procedure save_part_screen}
0175 {-----------------------------------------------------------------}
0180
```

continued...

4 Screen Save and Redisplay

...from previous page

```
0185  procedure RE_DISPLAY_PART_SCREEN(tlc,tlr,brc,brr,
0190                            var copy_of_part_scr : screen_copy);
0195
0200  type
0205       screen_copy_buf     = ARRAY[1..384] OF char;
0210
0215  var
0220       i,j,k,
0225       hll,vll,
0230       count,
0235       count_of_chars_per_line : integer;
0240
0245       part_scr_disp_buf    : screen_copy_buf;
0250
0255  Begin     {procedure re_display_part_screen}
0260       window(1,1,80,25);
0265       hll := brc - tlc + 1;
0270       vll := brr - tlr + 1;
0275       count_of_chars_per_line := 1;
0280       count := 0;
0285       FOR i := 1 to vll DO    {down thru rows.....}
0290       Begin
0295            FOR k := 1 to hll DO {across thru columns}
0300            Begin
0305                 count := count + 1;
0310                 part_scr_disp_buf[count] := copy_of_part_scr[i,k];
0315            End;
0320       End;
0325
0330       j := ((tlr - 1) * 160) + ((tlc - 1) * 2);
0335       {give CHR_OUT it's initial value}
0340       FOR count := 1 to 384 DO     {12 * 32}
0345       Begin
0350            CHR_OUT(j,ORD(part_scr_disp_buf[count]));
0355            { destination(j) , source(ORD(.......) }
0360            count_of_chars_per_line := count_of_chars_per_line + 1;
0365            IF (count_of_chars_per_line > hll) THEN
0370            Begin
0375                 tlr := tlr + 1;
0380                 j := ((tlr - 1) * 160) + ((tlc - 1) * 2);
0385                 count_of_chars_per_line := 1;
0390            End
0395            ELSE
0400                 j := j + 2;   {every second, EVEN numbered screen }
0405                               {memory loc. is the character part}
0410       End;
0415  End;     {procedure re_display_part_screen}
{=====================================================================}
```

SCR_S_D.INC: NOTES

SAVE_PART_SCREEN

The first procedure in this module is called SAVE_PART_SCREEN. This procedure, however, can be used to save a part or full screen of character text to regular memory from the special screen memory. The size of the screen to be saved (up to the maximum of 25×80) will depend on the array type specified in the parameter list (line 0055). In this example, the type "screen_copy" is defined in the declaration section of the main routine to be "ARRAY[1..12,1..32] of char."

The first four parameters that must be supplied by any driver routine are the "tlc" (top left column), "tlr" (top left row), "brc" (bottom right column), and "brr" (bottom right row). "Tlc" and "tlr" together delineate the upper left corner of the rectangular screen area to be saved, and the next two delineate the lower right corner of the screen area to be saved.

The last parameter passed into the procedure from the driver routine is called "copy_of_part_scr" (read as "copy of part screen"). Note several points concerning this parameter. First, it is prefixed by the reserved word "var," which means that the ADDRESS of this variable (not its actual numeric contents) is placed onto the stack. Passing a reference address to the stack saves space on the stack (4 bytes for the address vs. 384 bytes for a copy of this 12 by 32 array of characters) and also allows the procedure to communicate its results directly back to the globally defined variable "copy_of_part_screen" in the driver routine. Second, this parameter's type, "screen_copy," is a programmer-defined type, in this case a 12-row by 32-column array representing the dimensions of the screen image portion to be saved into regular memory. Third, the type "screen_copy" has already been defined inside the driver routine at line 0090 and is global to the ".inc" procedure; however, if the "$ include" procedures had been declared directly beneath the "program" label, as implied by all the Turbo Pascal manuals, the compilation would have aborted. Failure to compile would occur because the type "screen_copy" in the parameter list of the "include" procedures would not have been defined at the time it was needed. For this reason, all "include" procedures in this book will be placed just after the "var" section in the driver routines.

4 Screen Save and Redisplay

Before you examine the operation of this procedure, first look at its local variables. "I" is a row counter and indexes the number of screen rows to be saved from the screen. "K" is a column counter and indexes the number of screen columns to be saved from the screen. "Vll" (vertical line length) is the upper index value of the row counter. It represents the maximum number of screen rows that will be saved by this procedure and is defined as the difference between "brr" (bottom right row) and "tlr" (top left row) plus 1. This formulation (line 0100) includes both row end points. "Hll" (horizontal line length) is the upper index of the column counter. It represents the maximum number of screen columns that will be saved and is defined as the difference between "brc" (bottom right column) and "tlc" (top left column) plus 1. This formulation (line 0095) again must include both column end points. "J" is the numeric offset value in the video memory array MEM[bwseg : bwofs] and is derived from the screen row and column values in the formula at line 0120.

To visualize the operation of the body of the SAVE_PART_SCR procedure, refer to Figure 4.1. In that figure, the procedure saves to screen memory the area on the screen whose upper left corner is at column 25, row 8 and whose lower right corner is column 56, row 19. The dimensions of the screen area to save are 12 rows (19 - 8 + 1....both end points included) and 32 columns (56 - 25 + 1....both end points included). The row index is "i," and "vll" is 12. The column index is "k," and the "hll" is 32.

The procedure saves the defined screen area one row at a time (line 0110). It starts with row 8, col 25, saves the character at that location (line 0135), and then moves on (line 0145) to save each individual screen character in all 32 columns of row 8 (via loop at line 0125). When all 32 columns of row 8 are saved, the procedure then jumps to row 9, col 25 (lines 0155 and 0160) and saves all 32 columns in that row to screen memory. This procedure continues up to and including row 19, columns 25 through 56 inclusive.

The objective of the procedure SAVE_PART_SCREEN is to map the contents of a series of screen memory offset values ("j") into a programmer-created array variable called "copy_of_part_screen." The mapping of the row component of the index "[i,k]" is controlled by the "i" variable in the outer loop at line 0110. The mapping of the column component of the index "[i,k]" (given the i'th row) is controlled by the "k" variable at line 0125. Before the contents of screen memory offset location "j" can be mapped into the "[i,k]" of the variable, "j" must first be

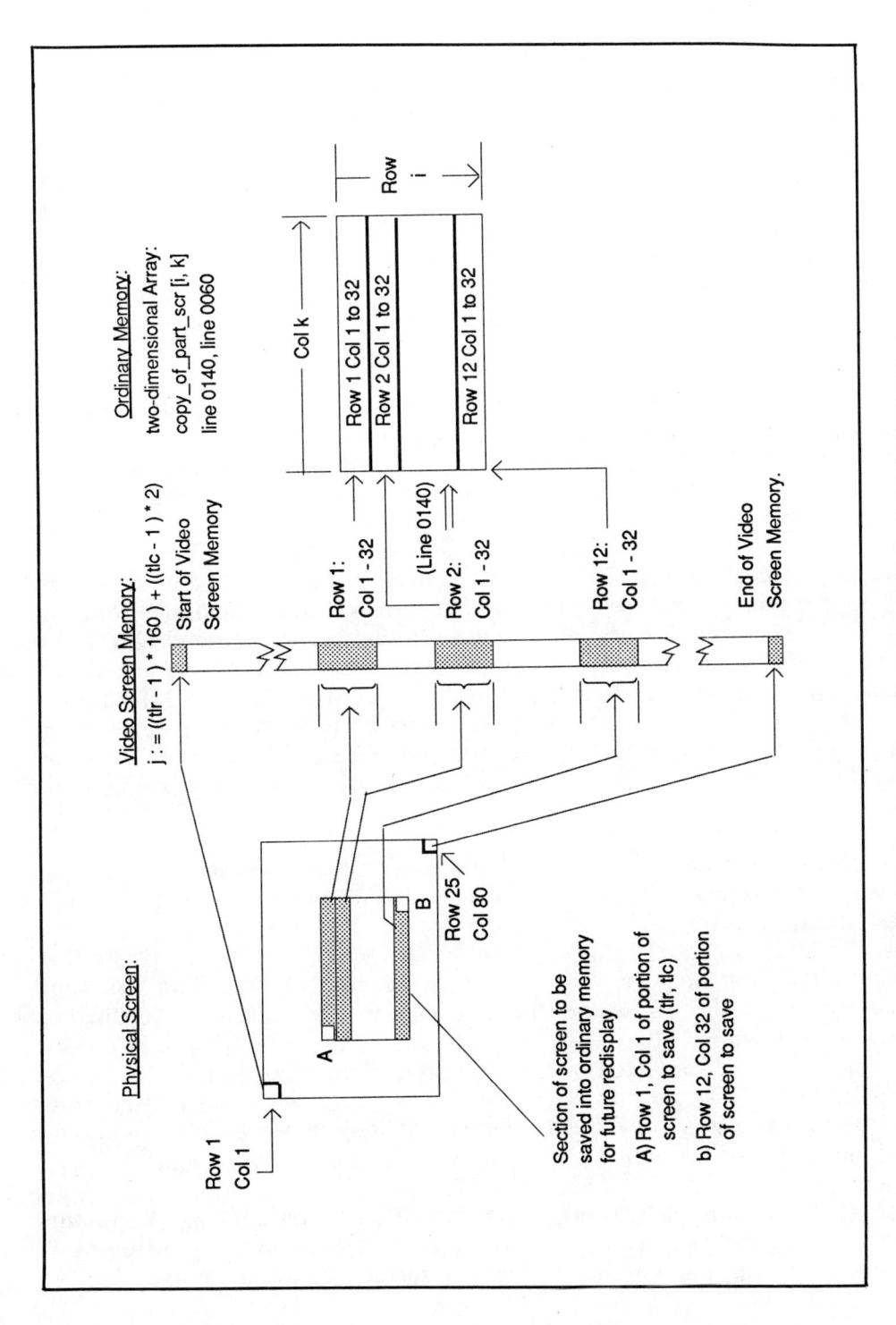

Figure 4.1 Schematic of Procedure SAVE_PART_SCREEN

4 Screen Save and Redisplay

calculated using the desired screen row ("tlr") and column ("tlc"). This calculation is done at line 0120 just after the row is assigned. The initial values for "tlc" and "tlr" are supplied by the values in the parameter list and after that from lines 0155 and 0160. With "j" as the start of a calculated row, successive values of "j" along the given row are then calculated at line 0145 inside the inner loop at line 0145 for use back up at line 0120 in the next iteration. Line 0135 is the core of the procedure. Here, the procedure CHR_IN (from "chrinout.inc") reads the character contents of the screen memory at offset value "j" and copies them into the screen saver array variable "copy_of_part_scr" at index [i,k].

At this point, one character from the screen has been transferred into a location inside the array variable. As mentioned above, line 0145 then increments "j" by 2. If "hll" is less than or equal to 32, then "k" is incremented by 1, and line 0135 performs its screen character-to-array mapping task once again at the next "j" location. If "hll" is greater than 32, then screen row index "i" must be increased by 1 in preparation for the calculation of a new row starting value, "j," at line 0120. If "i" is less than or equal to 12 ("vll" for rows), then the inner loop at line 0125 is entered into, and line 0135 performs another 32 ("hll") times its screen memory-to-character array mapping with a changed "i" index. If "i" is greater than 12, then each of the 384 (12×32) characters at the various locations in the screen memory will have been mapped (transferred) into the memory array "copy_of_part_scr," and the operation of saving a block of screen text into an array variable is finished.

The above explanation is a detailed one. Now, examine the same screen-saving operation from a more general point of view and consider a few questions.

How is the first step of this procedure accomplished? That is, how does the procedure translate the actual row and column coordinates into screen memory offset ("j") values? Since you are saving only a portion of each row, you need a starting point. This starting point is calculated at line 0120. At the start of the procedure, its value comes from the parameter list at line 0050. Once initiated, however, the values of "tlc" and "tlr" are supplied from lines 0155 and 0160.

Also, since you are saving only a portion of each row and you know the starting point for each row, you only need to increase the "j" value by 2 to find the adjacent character position inside screen memory. "J" in screen memory will increase by 2 for each increase of 1 in the column index at line 0145. "J" increases by 2 because each col, row coordinate on the computer's screen is the equivalent of two screen memory locations — one for the actual character and the second for its attribute.

Next, how is the second step of this procedure accomplished? That is, how are the screen memory contents of each j-valued screen memory offset location assigned into the array variable "copy_of_part_scr[i,k]"? The answer lies at line 0135 and the procedure CHR_IN, part of which has been reproduced below for reference. This specialized screen-mapping procedure takes the contents of a given screen memory location (indexed by j), converts the ASCII value there into its corresponding character (CHR function), and then assigns that character into a variable ("ch"), which is then passed out of the procedure and into the indexed array variable "copy_of_part_scr[i,k]." Note that each component of the array "copy_of_part_scr" is of the type "char" (character) as well so that assignment from the procedure into the array is legal:

```
procedure CHR_IN(j : integer : var ch : char);
        .
        etc.
        .
Begin
     ch := CHR(MEM[bwseg : bwofs + j]);
End;
```

In the procedure, line 0135 will be repeated for each of the 384 screen characters (12 rows × 32 col/row). Refer to Figure 4.2 for a visual representation of this procedure.

RE_DISPLAY_PART_SCREEN

The second procedure in this module is called RE_DISPLAY_PART_SCREEN. This procedure takes a previously saved screen from ordinary memory and displays it back onto the video screen at a location of the programmer's choice. This overall operation takes place in two steps. Lines 0285-0320 handle the first step, and lines 0340-0410 handle the second step.

4   Screen Save and Redisplay

The parameters supplied to this procedure by the driver routine will determine where on the screen the previously saved screen image will be redisplayed. The location is set by the upper left corner ("tlc" and "tlr") and the lower right corner ("brc" and "brc").

In the local variable or "var" section of this procedure, there are three new variables introduced. In the first part, "count" and "part_scr_disp buf" (read as "part screen display buffer") are used. "Part_scr_disp_buf" is a local array variable set up when the procedure is called. It is a one-dimensional array and holds the individual characters currently being held in the two-dimensional array variable "copy_of_part_scr." "Count" is the index for this one-dimensional array. "Count_of_char_per_line" (read as "count of characters per line") is a variable that controls the maximum number of allowable characters per row to be redisplayed on the computer screen from the one-dimensional array "part_screen_disp buf."

To visualize the operation of this procedure, refer to Figure 4.2. The starting point for this procedure is the previously saved screen image stored in the two-dimensional array of characters in the parameter list at line 0190.

The first part of the procedure converts the two-dimensional array "copy_of_part_scr" into a one-dimensional array, "part_scr_disp_buf." This conversion is necessary because the screen memory array (MEM[bwseg : bwofs + j]) used in the CHR_OUT procedure at line 0350 is a one-dimensional array. In the first part, each character of "part_scr_disp_buf[count]" is built up from the corresponding character in the two-dimensional array "copy_of_part_scr[i,k]" using the FOR..DO loops between lines 0285 and 0320. Line 0310 is where the actual assignment or conversion occurs.

The second part of this procedure is where all the characters saved in the "part_scr_disp_buf" are actually redisplayed onto the computer screen. Line 0330 calculates the starting screen memory "j" value. This value corresponds to the upper left corner of the rectangular screen section to be redisplayed. This value is dependent on the "tlc" and "tlr" values passed to the procedure in the parameter list. You then enter a loop indexed by the variable "count," whose range is between 1 and the number of characters in the buffer (384 at line 0340). The actual map-

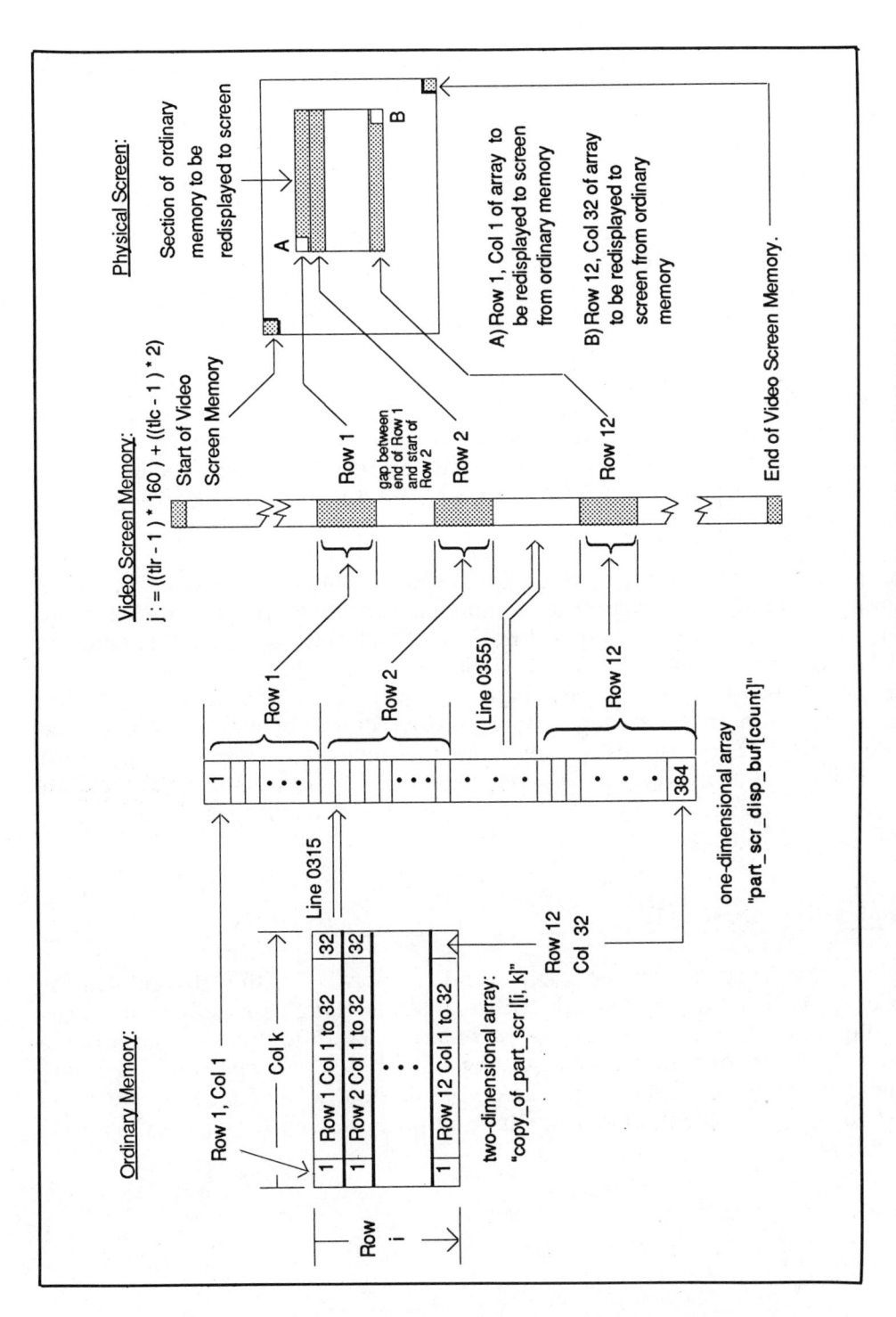

Figure 4.2 Schematic of Procedure RE_DISPLAY_PART_SCREEN

4 Screen Save and Redisplay

ping of each character from "part_scr_disp_buf" to the video screen memory is done by the procedure CHR_OUT at line 0350. The effect of the assignment statement

```
MEM[bwseg : bwofs + j] := ch;
```

in CHR_OUT is to "poke" the ASCII integer equivalent of a character ("ch") into a video screen memory location indexed by "j." Note that the conversion from a character into the ASCII integer equivalent is accomplished by the transfer function ORD at line 0350.

The magic of conversion is that when the ASCII value represented here by the integer "ch" is assigned or mapped into the video screen memory, the specialized scanning circuitry wired into these "j" locations will convert that ASCII value into its corresponding character representation and present it onto the screen at a location in accordance with its "j" offset value.

Once one character is displayed onto the screen, the variable "count_of_chars_per_line" is increased by 1 and compared to the maximum number of characters allowed per line, "hll." If this count is less than or equal to "hll," then you stay on the same line but move to the next character location in screen memory at j + 2 and display another character from that location. If, however, "count_of_chars_per_line" exceeds "hll," then you drop down to the next screen row (line 0375), recalculate a new row starting position for "j" in screen memory (line 0380), and reset the "count_of_chars_per_line" back to 1. The procedure ends when the "count" index exceeds 384.

MODULE: SSD.DRV

SSD.DRV (read as "screen save and display") is the driver routine used to activate the previously written "scr_s_d.inc" procedure package. It illustrates the use of the above service module by first creating a block of text on the screen, saving this block of text into ordinary memory using an array of characters, and, finally, redisplaying the exact text in three different places on the computer screen. The code appears as follows:

Screen Save and Redisplay 4

```
       {=====================================================================}
0005   program   ssd(input,output);   {"screen save and display"}
0010                                  { on disk as "ssd.drv"    }
0015
0020   const
0025         {* FOR MONOCHROME SCREENS ONLY *}
0030         {
0035          bwseg = $b000;
0040          bwofs = $0000;
0045         }
0050
0055         {* FOR GRAPHICS SCREENS ONLY *}
0060         {
0065          bwseg = $b800;
0070          bwofs = $0000;
0075         }
0080
0085   type
0090         screen_copy    = ARRAY[1..12,1..32] of char;
0095
0100   var
0105         t1_col,t1_row,
0110         br_col,br_row, : integer;
0115
0120         copy_of_part_scr    : screen_copy;
0125         command_choice      : char;
0130         exit_flag           : boolean;    {required by "scr_s_d.inc"}
0135
0140   {=====================================================================}
0145
0150   {$i chrinout.inc}{MUST BE FIRST. All other ".inc" files use it}
0155   {$i windows.inc} {includes procedure "window_border"}
0160   {$i scr_s_d.inc} {make sure that all ".inc" files on same disk}
0165
0170   {=====================================================================}
0175
0180   procedure      CREATE_RESIDENCE_RECORD;
0185
0190   type
0195         str16     = string[16];
0200
0205   var
0210         first_name,last_name,
0215         address,city,state,
0220         zip,telephone           : str16;
0225
0230   Begin     {procedure create_residence_record}
0235         window(1,1,80,25);clrscr;
0240         gotoxy(33,9);write('RESIDENCE RECORD');
0245         gotoxy(27,11);write('First Name:');
0250         gotoxy(27,12);write('Last Name.:');
0255         gotoxy(27,13);write('Address...:');
0260         gotoxy(27,14);write('City......:');
0265         gotoxy(27,15);write('State.....:');
0270         gotoxy(27,16);write('Zip.......:');
0275         gotoxy(27,17);write('Telephone.:');
0280         {Now fill in the information by typing from the keyboard....}
0285         gotoxy(39,11);read(first_name);
0290         gotoxy(39,12);read(last_name);
0295         gotoxy(39,13);read(address);
0300         gotoxy(39,14);read(city);
0305         gotoxy(39,15);read(state);
```

continued...

4 Screen Save and Redisplay

...from previous page

```
0310          gotoxy(39,16);read(zip);
0315          gotoxy(39,17);read(telephone);
0320   End;
0325   {------------------------------------------------------------------}
0330
0335   procedure      CREATE_COMMAND_LINES;
0340
0345   Begin
0350          window(1,1,80,25);
0355          TEXTCOLOR(0);TEXTBACKGROUND(15);    {"0" = no color,or black}
0360          gotoxy(24,21);
0365          write(' > SAVE/RE-DISPLAY SCREEN DEMO < ');
0370          gotoxy(8,22);
0375          write('Record to Appear at: Location 1="1"   Location 2="2" ',
0380                'Location 3="3" ');
0385          gotoxy(8,23);
0390          write('                               ');          {31 blanks}
0395          gotoxy(57,23);
0400          write('To Quit: Press "q" ');
0405          TEXTCOLOR(15);TEXTBACKGROUND(0);  {"15" = all colors, or white}
0410   End;
0415   {------------------------------------------------------------------}
0420
0425   Begin     {main program}
0430          window(1,1,80,25);clrscr;
0435          WINDOW_BORDER(1,1,80,24,3);  {border style #3}
0440          tl_col := 25 ; tl_row := 8;
0445          br_col := 56 ; br_row := 19;
0450          WINDOW_BORDER(tl_col,tl_row,br_col,br_row,3);
0455          {or....WINDOW BORDER(25 , 8 , 56 , 19 , 3)
0460          CREATE_RESIDENCE_RECORD;
0465          SAVE_PART_SCREEN(25,8,56,19,copy_of_part_scr);
0470          CREATE_COMMAND_LINES;
0475          exit_flag := false;
0480          window(1,1,80,20);
0485          FILLCHAR(MEM[bwseg : bwofs],3200,'.');
0490          {3200 = 1600 * 2 = (80 * 20) * 2}
0495
0500          REPEAT
0505             gotoxy(40,23);
0510             read(KBD,command_choice);
0515             CASE (command_choice) OF
0520
0525               '1': Begin
0530                      RE_DISPLAY_PART_SCREEN(46,2,77,13,
0535                                             copy_of_part_scr);
0540                      read(KBD,command_choice);
0545                      window(1,1,80,20);
0550                      FILLCHAR(MEM[bwseg : bwofs],3200,'.');
0555                    End;
0560
0565               '2': Begin
0570                      RE_DISPLAY_PART_SCREEN(3,8,34,19,
0575                                             copy_of_part_scr);
0580                      read(KBD,command_choice);
0585                      window(1,1,80,20);
0590                      FILLCHAR(MEM[bwseg : bwofs],3200,'.');
0595                    End;
0600
```

continued...

Screen Save and Redisplay 4

...from previous page

```
0605               '3': Begin
0610                       RE_DISPLAY_PART_SCREEN(25,8,56,19,
0615                                         copy_of_part_scr);
0620                       read(KBD,command_choice);
0625                       window(1,1,80,20);
0630                       FILLCHAR(MEM[bwseg : bwofs],3200,'.');
0635                   End;
0640
0645               'q': Begin
0650                       exit_flag := true;
0655                   End
0660
0665               ELSE
0670                   {entered into when NONE of above characters entered}
0675               END;      {case}
0680         UNTIL (exit_flag = true);
0685 End.        {main program}
{=================================================================}
```

SSD.DRV: NOTES

The declaration section of the driver program contains (and *must* contain) all the variables and their types needed by the ".inc" modules. At line 0120, note that the variable "copy_of_part_screen" has the type "screen_copy" and that "screen_copy," in turn, is defined as the type "ARRAY[1..12,1..32] of char" above at line 0090. You may wonder if it wouldn't be simpler to just write the declaration

```
copy_of_part_scr : ARRAY[1..12,1..32] of char;
```

at line 0120.

It would be correct only if you did *not* need to pass the array variable into procedures. In this case, you *do* need to pass the array into procedures, and, therefore, you must declare the array variable as shown at lines 0090 and 0120. In any event, it is better to develop the habit of defining your array variables under a type declaration; then, define the variable to be of the pre-defined type. If you don't use this method of array declaration, you will not be able to pass array variables into procedures for modification.

Another point about the array variable: the name used in the calling statement parameter lists is the same as the name used in the procedure parameter lists. The names don't have to be the same; it is done here only to avoid confusion at this point. You can give the parameters any names you want. But remember, their type *must* be the same.

4 Screen Save and Redisplay

All the external procedures used by this program are included, starting at line 0150. The concept of **modularity** can be illustrated here. Assume that for some reason you do not want windowing. To omit the windowing feature from this program, you would simply exclude the "windows.inc" module at line 0155 as well as all procedure calls in the driver routine that invoke the border drawing package.

You may wonder why these external routines are not placed underneath the "program" label near the beginning of the program. Modules that do not have array-type variables in their parameter list could most certainly be placed there; however, procedures that have an array variable in their parameter list cannot be placed there because during compilation, the compiler will come across the type "screen_copy" in the parameter list of the module procedures *before* the particular variable has been defined (declared). The compiler will then stop. So, as a general and safe rule, all external procedures modules (".inc" modules) will be declared *after* the "var" section and before the internal procedures of any program or driver routine.

The rest of this driver routine is quite straightforward. At line 0180, the internal procedure CREATE_RESIDENCE_RECORD writes the text to be saved onto the screen and then asks you to fill in some data of your own (see Figure 4.3). The external procedure SAVE_PART SCREEN from the "scr_s_d.inc" module is then invoked at line 0465 with the proper parameters to save the screen image into the array "copy_of_part_scr."

Take a moment to examine the parameter list. The first four parameters define the upper left and lower right boundaries of the screen area you want to save. The fifth parameter is the memory array variable "copy_of_part_scr" into which you will save the screen's text contents for later redisplay back onto the screen.

At line 0485, you fill with 3200 dots the video screen memory whose starting segment:offset location is $b000:$0000 (or $b0000 absolute).

At line 0480, you create a window on the screen, starting at col 1, row1 and ending in the lower right corner at col 80, row 20. This window is the equivalent of 80×20 (or 1600) screen locations or 1600×2 (or 3200) video screen memory locations. Remember, each screen location has both a character byte and an attribute byte. At line 0485, you use the FILLCHAR procedure with the parameter MEM[bwseg:bwofs], which

Screen Save and Redisplay **4**

you will recognize as the very first location in the computer's video screen memory. The FILLCHAR procedure then fills 3200 video screen memory locations with dots starting at $b000:$0000 ($b0000 absolute). This procedure creates a background against which the saved section of screen can be redisplayed.

The programmer-controlled redisplay of the previously saved screen text is coded within a REPEAT...UNTIL control loop between lines 0500 and 0680. The important point is that the location on the screen where the screen image is to reappear is controlled by the first four parameters in the parameter lists at lines 0530, 0565, and 0610.

Once the screen is redisplayed at a chosen location (1, 2, or 3), it will stay there until you press any key, at which time the 80 by 20 screen will be filled with dots and then will wait until you again type the number corresponding to your new choice of location or press "q" to quit the demonstration.

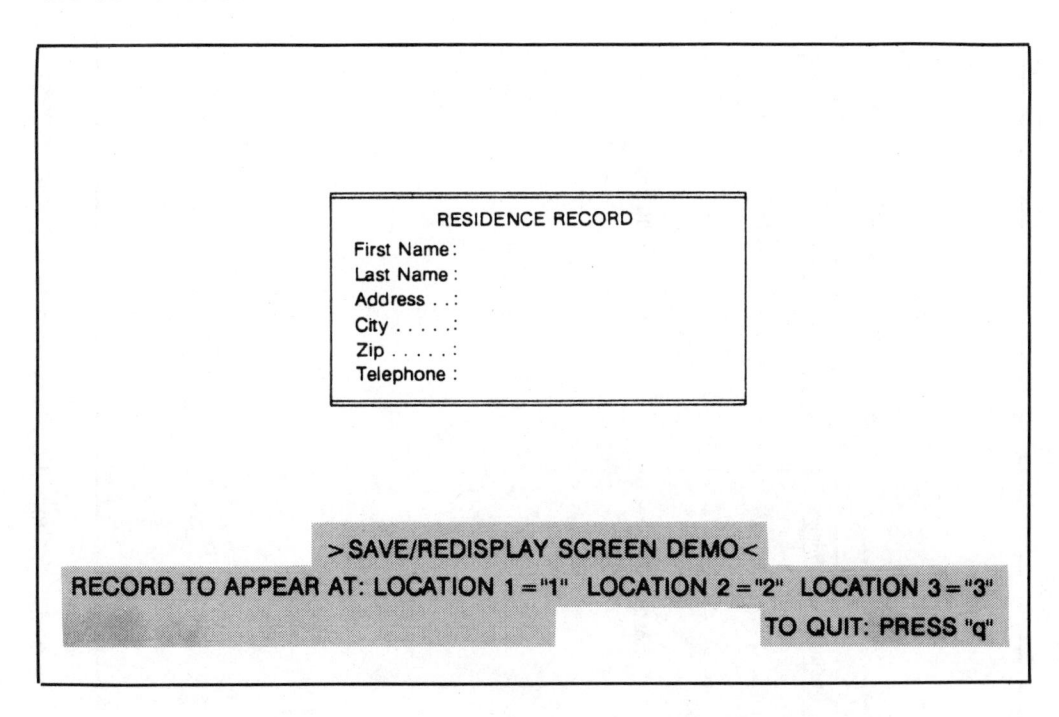

Figure 4.3 Initialized Screen for Program SSD.DRV

67

4 Screen Save and Redisplay

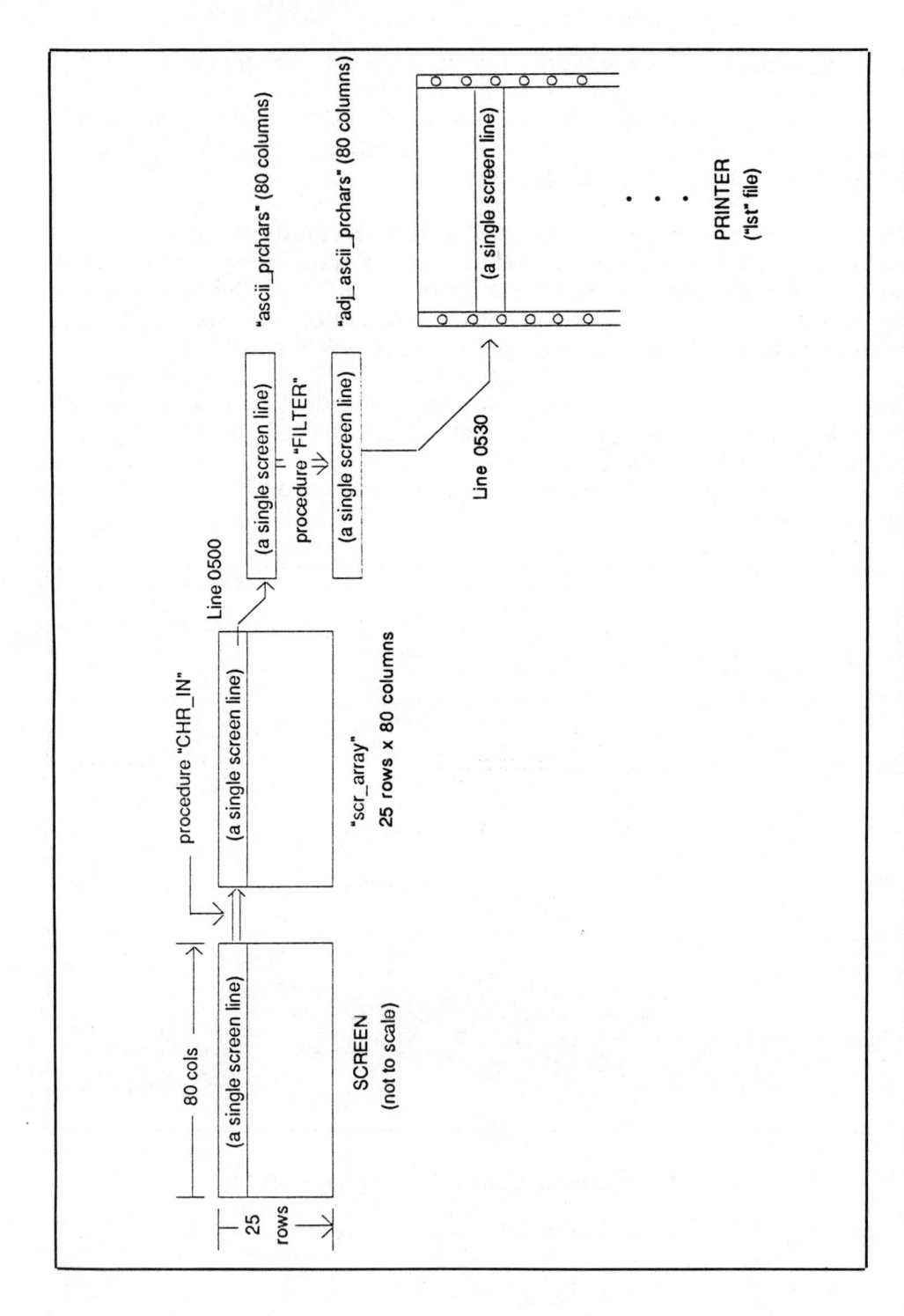

Figure 4.4 Schematic Showing how DISPLAY_SCREEN_CONTENTS is translated to Printed Copy

Screen Save and Redisplay 4

MODULE: SCRTOPR.DRV (SCREEN TO PRINTER)

This section briefly explores the connection between the video screen and the printer and answers the following question: how can you transfer an image on the video screen directly into hardcopy from the printer? If you look at Figure 4.4, the answer should become more obvious. The first crucial step is to "pick off" the video screen image and save it into an array of characters stored in memory. As you can see, this is the role of the external procedure CHR_IN. Once the whole screen image is saved into the array, the overall strategy is to convert each original 80-character screen line of text in the array into an 80-character line of text that can be displayed sensibly by the printer. This is the role of the procedure FILTER. This procedure actually filters out screen characters that cannot be correctly displayed by the printer and converts them into characters that can. Once this task is finished, the converted line of video screen text is sent to the printer. The code follows, after which the screen-to-printer conversion process will be explained in greater depth.

```
{==========================================================================}
0005 program    scrtopr(input,output);
0010
0015 {"Screen to printer". On Disk as "scrtopr.drv" }
0020
0025 const
0030       bell = #$07;
0035
0040 type
0045       border_chars        = 179..218; {ascii char codes}
0050       border_set          = SET OF border_chars;
0055       {the universal set defined....}
0060       arr80               = ARRAY[1..80] of char;
0065       scr_arr             = ARRAY[1..25,1..80] of char;
0070
0075 var
0080       hor_lines,          {each set variable can be a full set}
0085       vert_lines,         {or a sub-set of the universal set}
0090       tl_corners,
0095       bl_corners,
0100       tr_corners,
0105       br_corners          : border_set;
0110
0115       row,col,j           : integer;
0120       scr_array           : scr_arr;
0125       ascii_prchars,
0130       adj_ascii_prchars   : arr80;
0135
0140 {==========================================================================}
```

continued...

4   Screen Save and Redisplay

...from previous page

```
0145  {$i chrinout.inc}
0150  {$i windows.inc}
0155  {===================================================================}
0160
0165  procedure      SET_UP;
0170
0175  Begin      {procedure set_up}
0180       gotoxy(30,2);write('SCREEN TO PRINTER DEMO');
0185       WINDOW_BORDER(1,1,80,24,2);
0190       gotoxy(3,23);write('style #2');
0195       WINDOW_BORDER(4,4,20,20,4);
0200       gotoxy(6,19);write('STYLE #4');
0205       WINDOW_BORDER(10,6,70,15,3);
0210       gotoxy(12,14);write('style number 3');
0215       WINDOW_BORDER(60,17,77,20,1);
0220       gotoxy(62,19);write('Style Number 1');
0225       gotoxy(30,23);write('This is Line 23 of the Screen!?#$');
0230  End;       {procedure set_up}
0235  {-------------------------------------------------------------------}
0240
0245  procedure      FILTER(var a_pc      : arr80;    {in....}
0250                         var a_a_pc   : arr80);   {out...}
0255
0260  var
0265       k    : integer;
0270
0275  Begin     {procedure filter}
0280       FOR k := 1 to 80 DO
0285       Begin
0290            IF (ORD(a_pc[k]) IN hor_lines) THEN          { = }
0295                 a_a_pc[k] := chr(61);
0300
0305            ELSE IF (ORD(a_pc[k]) IN vert_lines) THEN    { | }
0310                 a_a_pc[k] := chr(124);
0315
0320            ELSE IF (ORD(a_pc[k]) IN tl_corners) THEN    { = }
0325                 a_a_pc[k] := chr(61);
0330
0335            ELSE IF (ORD(a_pc[k]) IN bl_corners) THEN    { = }
0340                 a_a_pc[k] := chr(61);
0345
0350            ELSE IF (ORD(a_pc[k]) IN tr_corners) THEN    { = }
0355                 a_a_pc[k] := chr(61);
0360
0365            ELSE IF (ORD(a_pc[k]) IN br_corners) THEN    { = }
0370                 a_a_pc[k] := chr(61);
0375
0380       ELSE
0385                 a_a_pc[k] := a_pc[k];
0390       End;
0395  End; {procedure filter}
0400  {-------------------------------------------------------------------}
0405
0410  Begin     {scrtopr.drv}
0415       { start with the set variable assignments }
0420       hor_lines      := [196 , 205];
0425       vert_lines     := [179 , 186];
0430       tl_corners     := [201 , 213 , 214 , 218];
0435       bl_corners     := [192 , 200 , 211 , 212];
0440       tr_corners     := [183 , 184 , 187 , 191];
```

continued...

...from previous page

```
0445         br_corners      := [188 , 189 , 190 , 217];
0450
0455         SET_UP;   {windows and text to screen}
0460         gotoxy(1,1);
0465         FOR row := 1 to 25 DO
0470         Begin
0475             FOR col := 1 to 80 DO
0480             Begin
0485                 j := ((row - 1) * 160) + ((col - 1) * 2);
0490                 CHR_IN(j , scr_array[row,col]);
0495                 {goes in , comes out of procedure}
0500                 ascii_prchars[col] := scr_array[row,col];
0505             End;
0510             FILTER(ascii_prchars , adj_ascii_prchars);
0515             {          into proc... , out of proc...}
0520
0525             FOR col := 1 to 80 DO
0530                 write(lst , adj_ascii_prchars[col]);
0535                 {writes whole screen line to printer file,"lst"}
0540             IF row < 25 THEN {stop screen from scrolling up at end}
0545                 writeln;
0550         End;
0555         gotoxy(3,20);
0560 End. {scrtopr.drv}
{=====================================================================}
```

SCRTOPR.DRV: NOTES

First, look at the Declaration Section. Under the "type" heading, notice "border_ chars" (border characters) at line 0045. The integers "179..218" are a subrange type and represent the ASCII character code numbers for all of the window-bordering characters. Notice that they all lie above the value of 128, the maximum value allowed for the standard character set for non-graphics printers. If you tried to display one of these characters on the printer, you would fail. For example, if you attempt to display the screen character corresponding to ASCII code #205 (a horizontal double bar), the printer would come back with the letter "M" because

205 - 128 = 77

which is the ASCII code for the uppercase letter "M." A non-graphics printer adjusts to ASCII code values that are greater than 128 by subtracting 128 from the given value and printing that character whose corresponding ASCII code value is their numeric difference.

Under the "var" heading, notice lines 0080-0105. These are the set variable declarations. Each of them has the potential to contain all 40 characters as symbolized by their ASCII code numbers (line 0045). The

4 Screen Save and Redisplay

actual codes they contain (subsets) are shown at lines 0420-0445 in the main routine. Notice that "tl_..." stands for "top left," "bl_..." stands for "bottom left," and so on. The variable "scr_array" (screen array) is exactly the same size as the 80×25 video screen since you are saving one whole screen of characters into memory. "Ascii_prchars" (ASCII print characters) represents one line of "scr_array" and can contain ASCII codes greater than 128 as well as less than 128. "Adj_ascii_prchars" (adjusted ASCII print characters) is derived from "ascii_prchars" (via FILTER) and contains only ASCII character codes that can be accurately displayed by the printer.

SET_UP

This procedure is straightforward. It produces on the video screen an image that will later be reproduced on paper by the printer. As you can see from Figure 4.5, the reproduction on a non-graphics printer is not exact. For example, each of the two different horizontal line types of the border characters (ASCII code #196 and #205) is replaced by the ASCII code #61—a code number less than 128. Similarly, each ASCII code number greater than 128 and used in the window borders on the video screen is replaced by an "equivalent" ASCII code whose value is less than 128 for "reproduction" on the printer.

FILTER

This procedure takes two parameters. "A_pc" corresponds to "ascii prchars" from the main routine, and "a_a_pc" corresponds to "adj_ascii prchars." Each line of video screen text sent is converted by this procedure from "a_pc" into "a_a_pc" and sent back out to the main routine where it is printed on paper. The FOR..DO loop starting at line 0280 looks at each 80-character screen line passed in. Each screen character of a given line is checked for membership in one of the window border character sets defined at the start of the main routine. If membership in one of these sets is determined (lines 0290, 0305, 0320, 0335, 0350, 0365), then the appropriate assignment to the set of accurately printable characters (those whose ASCII codes are less than 128) is made. If membership cannot be determined, then the assignment at line 0380 is made, and the character to be printed will be the same as the character sent in *but only* if the ASCII code is less than 128.

There are two points to note. First, since "a_pc[k]" is a single character, you must use the ORD function to convert it into an integer before you test for membership in any given set. Remember, the set of win-

Screen Save and Redisplay 4

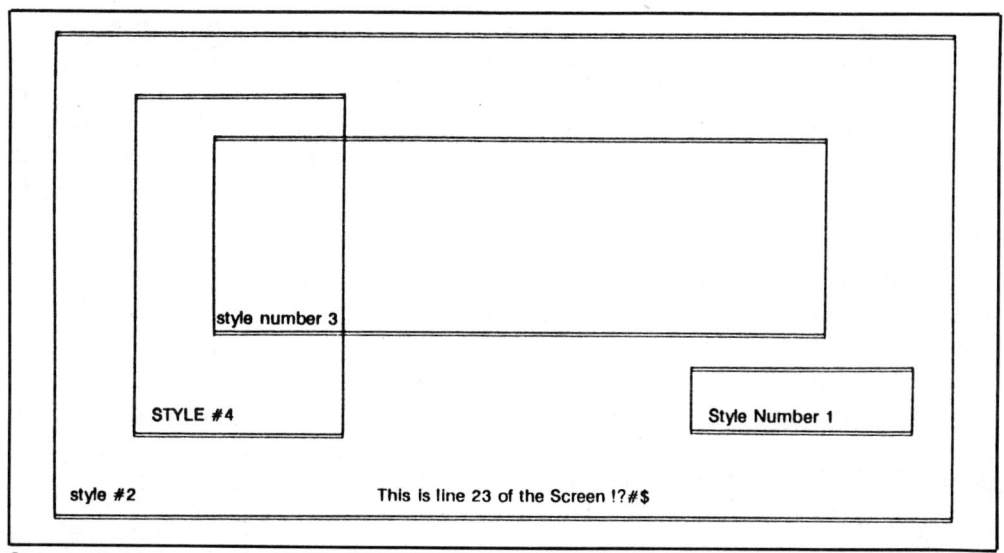

Screen Image:

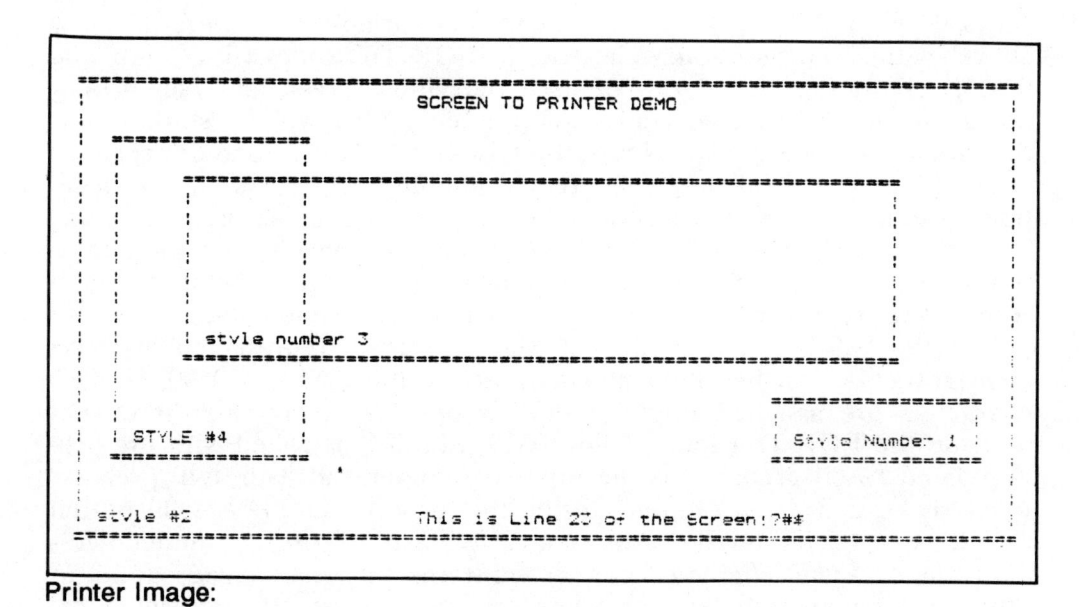

Printer Image:

Figure 4.5 Screen to Printer Demonstration Output

73

4 Screen Save and Redisplay

dow border ASCII codes is a subrange of integers as you see in the "type" definitions above. Second, the series of IF..THEN and ELSE IF..THEN statements (filters) only checks for window border characters (ASCII codes 179..218) and nothing else. This means that any character code above 128 and not within the given range will only be picked up by line 0380 and assigned the equivalent sub-128 ASCII code value used by non-graphics printers. For example, the summation symbol (ASCII code #228) would be "made printable" by first subtracting 128 and then displaying the character corresponding to the number 100 (228 - 128), the ASCII code value for the letter "d." This conversion process can produce some strange-looking printouts if you try to print ASCII codes that are greater than 128 and (in this program) not within the defined subrange, 179..218. For purposes here, this routine is satisfactory since the screen I/O programs and modules use only character code values below 128 or between 179 and 218.

Main Routine

Lines 0420-0445 define the values of the set variables that were declared above in the "var" section. The pair of FOR..DO loops (lines 0465 and 0475) delimit the boundaries of both the video screen and "scr_array," the array into which each character on the screen will be stored using the procedure CHR_IN. Notice that in CHR_IN the one-dimensional video memory offset location "j" (corresponding to the row/column location formula at line 0490) is sent into the procedure as input and that the character "picked off" the screen from the given row/column location is exported as output from the procedure for storage in the corresponding row/column location of "scr_array" (line 0490). At this point, the ASCII code value of the character represented by "scr array[row,col]" can be either above or below 128. At line 0500, 80 such characters are assigned into the one-dimensional array "ascii_prchars." Outside the FOR..DO loop at line 0510, FILTER is called with the just-populated "ascii_prchars" as the input parameter and "adj_ascii_prchars" to hold the converted output. Inside this procedure, any special border characters encountered are converted into their "under 128 equivalents"; any characters under 128 are left unchanged, and any others (that you probably won't be using anyway) would be printed out in surprising but understandable ways as you saw above. After exit from FILTER, you have the printer-printable one-dimensional array "adj_ascii_prchars" (adjusted ASCII print characters), which represents one line of the video screen that can now be "accurately" printed out on paper (lines 0525 & 0530). For one full-screen image, this procedure will be repeated 25 times, once for each screen row. See Figure 4.5 again for a visual representation.

CHAPTER 5

HORIZONTAL SCROLLING: METHOD 1

5 Horizontal Scrolling: Method 1

In many, perhaps most, practical applications, the quantity of data either as input to the screen or output on the screen exceeds the physical 80 column × 25 row limits.

For example, say you have created an array in ordinary memory that is 4 columns wide and 100 rows deep. How can you display this array on the regular 80 by 25 screen? The width of the screen is adequate, but the 25-row depth will cause previously displayed data to scroll off the top line of the screen and be lost from the display.

You could try to "freeze" the scrolling by pressing the <Ctrl/Num Lock> keys simultaneously and "unfreeze" the screen by pressing the <Return> key. This method of scrolling control is clumsy and inelegant on the one hand and one directional on the other.

Or suppose you have created an array in memory that is only 4 rows deep and 100 columns wide. How can you display this "oversized" array on your screen?

Screen scrolling is a method of presenting input and/or output data onto the screen in just those situations where the data is either deeper or wider than the 25-row or 80-column (or both) limits of the computer screen display. It makes oversized rows and/or columns of data in the computer's memory "fit" into the screen limits.

In this chapter and in Chapter 6, you will learn two very different techniques of screen scrolling in the horizontal direction. This chapter deals with horizontal scrolling using the screen saving and redisplay techniques developed in Chapter 4. In the next chapter, you will learn to perform the horizontal scrolling function using a radically different method.

MODULE: H_S1.INC

Below, the module H_S1.INC (read as "Horizontal Scroll One.Inc") is presented. Familiarize yourself with the overall layout of the module as illustrated in Figure 5.1. The main procedure here is H_SCROLL1. This procedure, in turn, incorporates five additional subprocedures also shown in Figure 5.1. Note that the procedures work in teams: MOVE PARTSCR_LEFT with DISP_NEW_RIGHT_COL and MOVE PARTSCR_RIGHT with DISP_NEW_LEFT_COL. To accomplish the scrolling effect, assume that the screen already holds 5 six-character-wide display columns of scrollable data as shown in Figure 5.2.

Horizontal Scrolling: Method 1 **5**

Main Procedure: H_Scroll1

Subprocedures: Save_Part_Scr

                       Re_Disp_Part_Scr

                       Move_Partscr_Left
                          (a) Save_Part_Scr
                          (b) Re_Disp_Part_Scr

                       Disp_New_Right_Col

                       Move_Partscr_Right
                          (a) Save_Part_Scr
                          (b) Re_Disp_Part_Scr

                       Disp_New_Left_Col

Note: Move_Partscr_Left   Read as: Move Partscreen TO the Left
            Move_Partscr_Right   Read as: Move Partscreen TO the Right

---

Figure 5.1 Procedures and Subprocedures of Module "h_s1.inc"

5 Horizontal Scrolling: Method 1

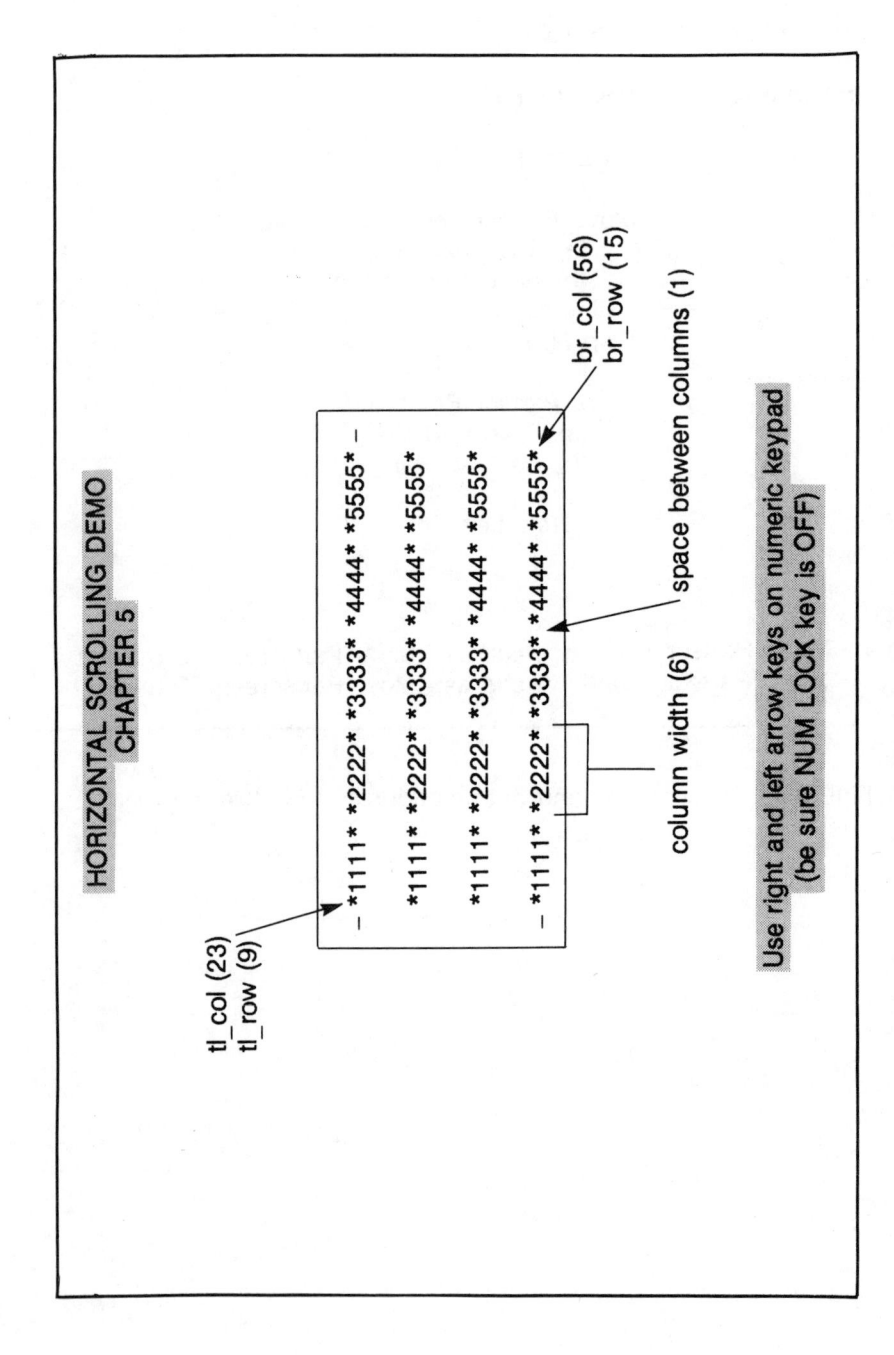

Figure 5.2 Initialized Screen for Horizontal Scrolling — Screen Save/Redisplay Method

Horizontal Scrolling: Method 1

To achieve a "scrolling right" effect (towards the right or larger integers), the already displayed right-hand four columns starting at column 30 are first saved into memory using the array variable "copy_of_part_scr." This saved portion of the screen is then immediately redisplayed from memory back onto the screen but starting at the first column (col. 23). Once this four-column section of screen has been moved left, the next larger column of the data array, "array_contents," is written to the screen with "write" statements in the loop starting at line 0740 of the subprocedure DISP_NEW_RIGHT_COL.

To achieve a "scroll left" effect (movement towards the left or smaller numbers), the already displayed four left-hand columns (starting at col. 23) are first saved into memory using the array variable "copy_of_part_scr." This saved portion of the screen is then immediately redisplayed from the variable back to the screen but now starting at column 30. Once this move is done, the next smaller column of the data array "array_contents" is written to the screen with the write statement in the loop at line 0955 in the subprocedure DISP_NEW_LEFT_COL.

Following is the code for the module H_S1.INC:

```
{============================================================================}
0005  {h_s1.inc}
0010  { This ".inc" file contains all the file saving and scrolling
0015    routines that are OVERHEAD REQUIREMENTS of the program
0020    "h_s1.drv".
0025    On disk as "h_s1.inc".
0030  }
0035
0040  {----------------------------------------------------------------------}
0045
0050  procedure       H_SCROLL1(tlc,tlr,brc,brr,
0055                            col_width,
0060                            sp_betw_cols           : integer;
0065                            var array_contents     : a);
0070
0075  label
0080        rep_read;
0085
0090  const
0095        bell              = #$07;
0100        scroll_left       = #$4b;
0105        scroll_right      = #$4d;
0110        carriage_ret      = #$0d;
0115
0120  var
0125        hll,vll           : integer; {derived from tlc,tlr etc....}
0130        adj_tl_col,
```

continued...

5 Horizontal Scrolling: Method 1

...from previous page

```
0135        adj_br_col      : integer;
0140        scroll_choice   : char;
0145        exit_scroll     : boolean;
0150        i,j             : integer;      {counter variables....}
0155
0160        i_tot , k_tot : integer;
0165        x_coord,y_coord: integer;
0170  {------------------------------------------------------------------}
0175
0180        procedure SAVE_PART_SCR(tlc,tlr,brc,brr       : integer;
0185                            var copy_of_part_scr      : screen_copy);
0190
0195        var
0200            i,k,
0205            hll,vll : integer;
0210
0215        Begin    {sub-procedure save_part_scr}
0220            window(1,1,80,25);
0225            hll := brc - tlc + 1;
0230            vll := brr - tlr + 1;
0235            gotoxy(tlc,tlr);
0240            FOR i := 1 to vll DO     {down thru rows}
0245            Begin
0250                j := ((tlr - 1) * 160) + ((tlc - 1) * 2);
0255                FOR k := 1 to hll DO   {across thru columns}
0260                Begin
0265                    CHR_IN(j,copy_of_part_scr[i,k]);
0270                    { source(j) , destination(copy......) }
0275                    j := j + 2;
0280                End;
0285                tlc := tlc;        {same column..........}
0290                tlr := tlr + 1;    {drop down to next row}
0295            End;
0300        End;      {sub-procedure save_part_scr}
0305  {------------------------------------------------------------------}
0310
0315        procedure    RE_DISP_PART_SCR(tlc,tlr,brc,brr  : integer;
0320                            var copy_of_part_scr       : screen_copy);
0325
0330        var
0335            i,j,k,
0340            hll,vll,
0345            count,
0350            count_of_chars_per_line : integer;
0355
0360        Begin     {sub-procedure re_disp_part_scr}
0365            window(1,1,80,25);
0370            hll := brc - tlc + 1;
0375            vll := brr - tlr + 1;
0380            count_of_chars_per_line := 1;
0385            count := 0;
0390            FOR i := 1 to vll DO     {DOWN thru rows.....}
0395            Begin
0400                FOR k := 1 to hll DO {ACROSS thru columns}
0405                Begin
0410                    count := count + 1;
0415                    screen_copy_buffer[count] :=
0420                        copy_of_part_scr[i,k];
0425                End;
0430            End;
```

continued...

Horizontal Scrolling: Method 1

...from previous page

```
0435
0440                j := ((tlr - 1) * 160) + ((tlc - 1) * 2);
0445                {supply CHR_OUT with it's initial value....}
0450                FOR count := 1 to 189 DO       {7 * 27}
0455                Begin
0460                   CHR_OUT(j,ORD(screen_copy_buffer[count]));
0465                   { destination(j) , source(ORD(.......) }
0470                   count_of_chars_per_line :=
0475                      count_of_chars_per_line + 1;
0480                   IF (count_of_chars_per_line > hll) THEN
0485                   Begin
0490                      tlr := tlr + 1;
0495                      j := ((tlr - 1) * 160) + ((tlc - 1) * 2);
0500                      count_of_chars_per_line := 1;
0505                   End
0510                   ELSE
0515                      j := j + 2;
0520                   {every second, even numbered screen}
0525                   {memory loc. is the character part}
0530                End;
0535          End;    {sub-procedure re_disp_part_scr}
0540  {-----------------------------------------------------------------}
0545
0550          procedure MOVE_PARTSCR_LEFT(tlc,atlc,tlr,
0555                                      brc,abrc,brr : integer);
0560                     {make room on the right hand side    }
0565                     {assoc. with "display_new_right_col"}
0570
0575          Begin     {sub-procedure move_partscr_left}
0580             { atlc := 30 ; tlr := 9;    }
0585             {  brc := 56 ; brr := 15;   }
0590             { contains info to be moved TO lhs}
0595             SAVE_PART_SCR(atlc,tlr,brc,brr,
0600                           copy_of_part_scr);
0605
0610             window(tlc,tlr,abrc,brr);  {(23,9,49,15);}
0615             clrscr;
0620             {  tlc := 23 ; tlr := 9;    }
0625             {  abrc := 49 ; brr := 15; }
0630             { info saved FROM rhs is moved TO lhs}
0635             RE_DISP_PART_SCR(tlc,tlr,abrc,brr,
0640                              copy_of_part_scr);
0645          End;      {sub-procedure move_partscr_left}
0650  {-----------------------------------------------------------------}
0655
0660          procedure DISP_NEW_RIGHT_COL(k_tot,i_tot : integer);
0665                     {associated with "move_partscr_left"}
0670          var
0675             i,k,
0680             start_of_rightmost_col : integer;
0685
0690          Begin      {sub-procedure disp_new_right_col}
0695             window(1,1,80,25);
0700             k := k_tot;
0705             start_of_rightmost_col := brc - (col_width - 1);
0710                                    {   56 - (  6 - 1);    }
0715             gotoxy(start_of_rightmost_col,tlr);  {(51,9);}
0720             x_coord := WHEREX ; y_coord := WHEREY;
0725             FOR i := 1 to 4 DO
```

continued...

5 Horizontal Scrolling: Method 1

...from previous page

```
0730              Begin
0735                  gotoxy(x_coord,y_coord);
0740                  write(array_contents[k + 4 , i]);
0745                  {* delay(2000); *}
0750                  x_coord := x_coord ; y_coord := y_coord + 2;
0755              End;
0760         End;      {sub-procedure disp_new_right_col}
0765     {----------------------------------------------------------------}
0770
0775         procedure       MOVE_PARTSCR_RIGHT(tlc,atlc,tlr,
0780                                            brc,abrc,brr : integer);
0785                     {make room on the left hand side          }
0790                     {associated with "disp_new_left_col"      }
0795
0800         Begin    {sub-procedure move_partscr_right}
0805             {   tlc := 23 ; tlr := 9;   }
0810             {   abrc := 49 ; brr := 15; }
0815             {   contains info to be moved TO rhs}
0820             SAVE_PART_SCR(tlc,tlr,abrc,brr,
0825                             copy_of_part_scr);
0830
0835             window(atlc,tlr,brc,brr);   { window(30,9,56,15); }
0840             clrscr;{*delay(2000);*}
0845             {   atlc := 30 ; tlr := 9;  }
0850             {   brc := 56 ; brr := 15;  }
0855             {   info saved FROM lhs is moved TO rhs}
0860             RE_DISP_PART_SCR(atlc,tlr,brc,brr,
0865                             copy_of_part_scr);
0870         End;      {sub-procedure move_partscr_right}
0875     {----------------------------------------------------------------}
0880
0885         procedure DISP_NEW_LEFT_COL(k_tot,i_tot : integer);
0890              {associated with "move_partscr_right"}
0895
0900         var
0905             i,k    : integer;
0910
0915         Begin    {sub-procedure disp_new_left_col}
0920             window(1,1,80,25);
0925             k := k_tot;
0930             gotoxy(tlc,tlr);   { (23,9);}
0935             x_coord := WHEREX ; y_coord := WHEREY;
0940             FOR i := 1 to 4 DO
0945             Begin
0950                  gotoxy(x_coord,y_coord); {*delay(1000);*}
0955                  write(array_contents[k,i]); {** NOT k - 4 !! **}
0960                  x_coord := x_coord ; y_coord := y_coord + 2;
0965             End;
0970         End;      {sub-procedure disp_new_left_col}
0975     {----------------------------------------------------------------}
0980
0985  Begin    {procedure h_scroll1}
0990       window(tlc,tlr,brc,brr);
0995       exit_scroll := false; {initialize exit condition}
1000       adj_tl_col := tlc + (col_width + sp_betw_cols);
1005            {      23 + (     6      +      1     ) = 30  }
1010       adj_br_col := brc - (col_width + sp_betw_cols);
1015            {      56 - (     6      +      1     ) = 49  }
1020       i_tot := 1;
1025       k_tot := 1;
1030
```

continued...

82

Horizontal Scrolling: Method 1

...from previous page

```
1035        REPEAT
1040            rep_read:      {a label followed by a colon}
1045            read(KBD,scroll_choice); {hit left or right arrow key...}
1050            CASE(scroll_choice) OF
1055
1060            scroll_left : Begin     {Left Arrow Key pressed}
1065                              i_tot := i_tot + 0;
1070                              k_tot := k_tot - 1;
1075                              IF(k_tot < 1) THEN
1080                              Begin
1085                                  k_tot := 1;
1090                                  goto rep_read;
1095                              End;
1100                              MOVE_PARTSCR_RIGHT(tlc,
1105                                      adj_tl_col,tlr,
1110                                      brc,adj_br_col,brr);
1115                              DISP_NEW_LEFT_COL(k_tot,i_tot);
1120                          End; {scroll_left}
1125
1130            scroll_right : Begin    {Right Arrow Key  pressed}
1135                              i_tot := i_tot + 0;
1140                              k_tot := k_tot + 1;
1145                              IF (k_tot > 5) THEN
1150                              Begin
1155                                  k_tot := 5;
1160                                  goto rep_read;
1165                              End;
1170                              MOVE_PARTSCR_LEFT(tlc,adj_tl_col,tlr,
1175                                          brc,adj_br_col,brr);
1180                              DISP_NEW_RIGHT_COL(k_tot,i_tot);
1185                          End;   {scroll_right}
1190
1195            carriage_ret : Begin
1200                              exit_scroll := true;
1205                              write(bell);
1210                          End;
1215
1220            ELSE
1225                {if none of above choices is selected...}
1230                {nothing--go back and press correct key.}
1235            END; {case statement}
1240        UNTIL exit_scroll = true;
1245 End;      {procedure h_scroll1}
{================= END OF "h_sl.inc" overhead   file==================}
```

5 Horizontal Scrolling: Method 1

H_S1.INC: NOTES

H_SCROLL1

The procedure H_SCROLL1 orchestrates the activities of the five sub-procedures in this module. The parameters listed, starting at line 0050, are

- the overall dimensions of the display window: top left column ("tlc"), top left row ("tlr"), bottom right column ("brr"), and bottom right row ("brr").

- the column width ("col_width"), which for this example is six characters wide and holds the contents of the string data to be displayed. Remember that in all the scrolling routines you do, the contents of the scrolling arrays will always be strings of characters. If a program of yours is to scroll a table of calculated numbers (of real or integer type), then *before* they can be scrolled on the screen, they must first be converted to string variables and stored in memory as an array of strings.

- the space between columns ("sp_betw_cols"), which is another required formatting variable used to separate the columns on the screen display. In this example, only one space has been placed between adjacent columns.

- the array variable used to hold the actual data to be scrolled on the screen. This variable is called "array_contents." Refer to Figure 5.3.

In the "const" section of the declaration, the scan code of the Right Arrow key is represented as a constant at line 0105. Likewise, the scan codes of the Left Arrow and Return keys are shown at lines 0100 and 0110.

Horizontal Scrolling: Method 1

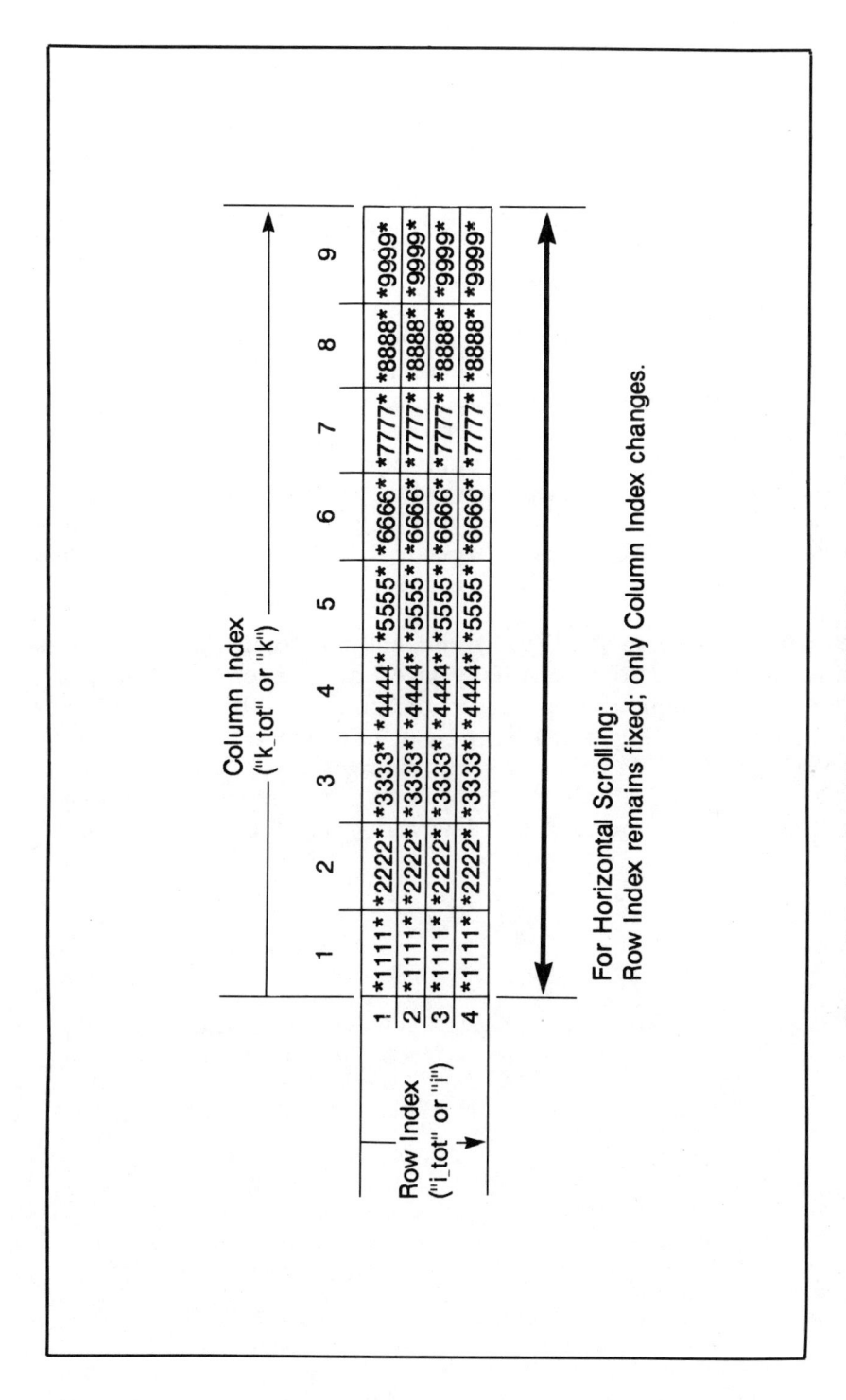

	1	2	3	4	5	6	7	8	9
1	*1111*	*2222*	*3333*	*4444*	*5555*	*6666*	*7777*	*8888*	*9999*
2	*1111*	*2222*	*3333*	*4444*	*5555*	*6666*	*7777*	*8888*	*9999*
3	*1111*	*2222*	*3333*	*4444*	*5555*	*6666*	*7777*	*8888*	*9999*
4	*1111*	*2222*	*3333*	*4444*	*5555*	*6666*	*7777*	*8888*	*9999*

Row Index ("i_tot" or "i")

Column Index ("k_tot" or "k")

For Horizontal Scrolling:
Row Index remains fixed; only Column Index changes.

Figure 5.3 A Schematic of the Variable "Array_Contents"

5 Horizontal Scrolling: Method 1

In the "var" section of the declaration, the variable ("hll") stands for horizontal line length and is represented by the expression ("brc - tlc + 1") in the subprocedures. This expression causes both the first and last columns of the window to be counted as part of the length of the horizontal line. Likewise, ("vll") stands for vertical line length and is represented by the expression ("brr - tlr + 1") in the subprocedures. This expression also will include both the first and last rows of the scrolling window's vertical border.

The variables, adjusted top left column ("adj_tl_col") and adjusted bottom right column ("adj_br_col") are defined at lines 1000 and 1010 of the main body of H_SCROLL1 procedure. They are used in the parameter lists of the subprocedures MOVE_PARTSCR_LEFT and MOVE_PARTSCR_RIGHT to supply the needed information to correctly move sections of the display window to the right or to the left inside the overall display window. In the MOVE_PARTSCR... procedures, the adjusted top left column is abbreviated as "atlc," and the adjusted bottom right column is abbreviated as "abrc."

The variables row total ("i_tot") and column total ("k_tot") are essential to this routine. "I_tot" is initially given a value of 1 at line 1020 and is unchanged throughout the whole horizontal scrolling routine because in a horizontal scroll, the rows remain unchanged. "K_tot" is initially given a value of 1 at line 1025 and changes each time the Left or Right Arrow keys (keys 4 and 5 on the numeric keypad) are pressed. "K tot" is the column index of the data array variable "array_contents."

Horizontal Scrolling: Method 1 5

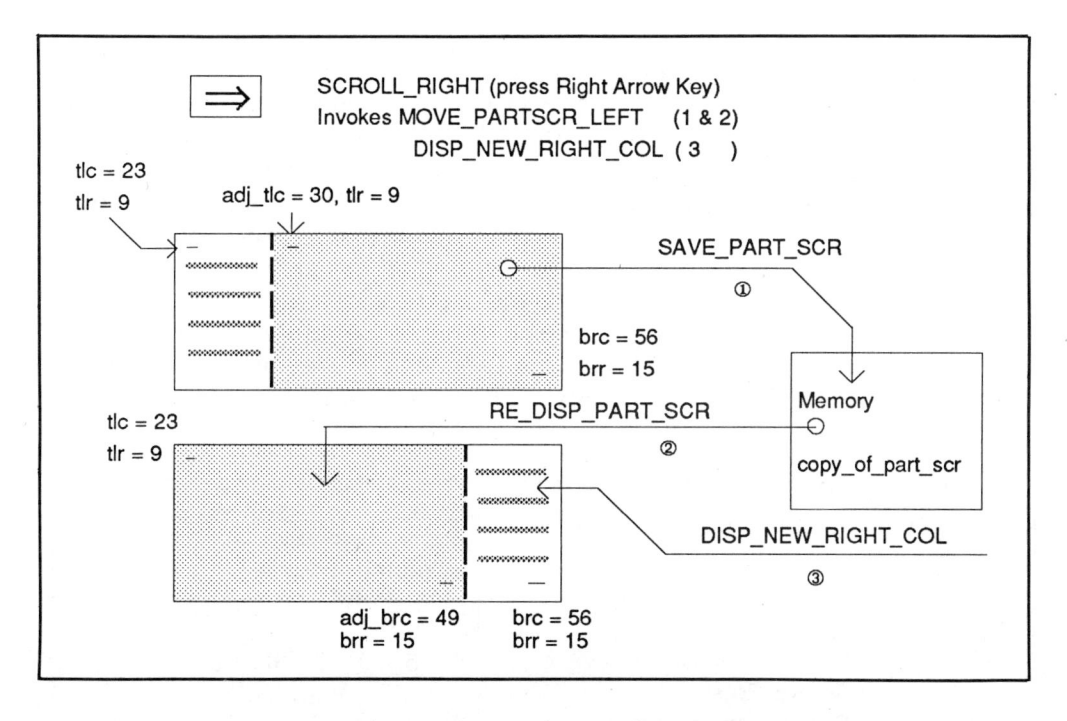

![Figure 5.4 diagram showing horizontal scroll mechanism with SCROLL_RIGHT invoking MOVE_PARTSCR_LEFT and DISP_NEW_RIGHT_COL, with tlc=23, tlr=9, adj_tlc=30, brc=56, brr=15, adj_brc=49, and memory copy_of_part_scr]

Figure 5.4 Horizontal Scroll — Press Right Arrow Key

If the Right Arrow key is pressed, as in a "scroll_right" at line 1130, then "k_tot" *increases* by 1. The procedure MOVE_PARTSCR_LEFT performs its task (see Figure 5.4), followed by writing of the new right-hand data column of "array_contents" using the parameter "k." See lines 0700 and 0740 in DISP_NEW_RIGHT_COL along with Figure 5.5 for an example.

Lines 1145-1160 were written to prevent the scrolling routine from scrolling beyond the last (ninth) column of the data variable "array_contents." The DISP_NEW_RIGHT_COL procedure adjusts the "k" index by adding 4 to it to get the next greater column of "array_contents" to be displayed on the right-hand side of the scroll window. If "k" is, say, 6, then the column to next be displayed when scrolling to the right would be (6 + 4 = 10), but the variable "array_contents" has only 9 columns. Line 1145 thus prevents overshooting the defined maximum number of columns.

5 Horizontal Scrolling: Method 1

If the Left Arrow key is pressed as in "scroll_left" at line 1060, then "k_tot" *decreases* by 1. If "k_tot" is already 1, then "k_tot" would become less than 1 (line 1075). If "k_tot" is less than 1, line 1085 resets "k_tot" to 1 and control is passed back to the label at line 1040 for a retry. Assuming "k_tot" is greater than 1, then "k_tot" is changed to k_tot - 1 (line 1070). The procedure MOVE_PARTSCR_RIGHT will make room for 1 six-character-wide display column at the left-hand side of the scrolling window, starting at column 23. The procedure DISP_NEW_LEFT_COL using the parameters "k_tot" and "i_tot" then writes out the appropriate column of "array_contents" to the computer screen. Note that "k" (line 0925) is used without adjustment in the subprocedure DISP_NEW_LEFT_COL (see Figure 5.7 for an example).

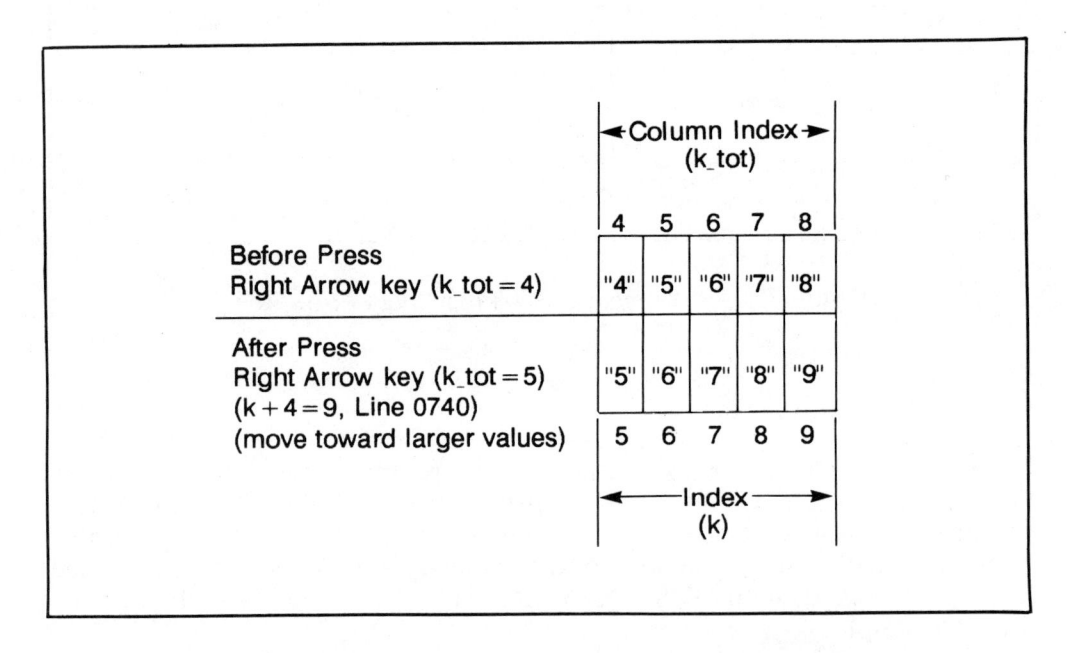

	Column Index (k_tot)
	4 5 6 7 8
Before Press Right Arrow key (k_tot = 4)	"4" "5" "6" "7" "8"
After Press Right Arrow key (k_tot = 5) (k + 4 = 9, Line 0740) (move toward larger values)	"5" "6" "7" "8" "9" 5 6 7 8 9 Index (k)

Figure 5.5 Schematic of Subprocedure Display_New_Right_Col

88

The variables "x_coord" and "y_coord" (read as "x_coordinate, y_coordinate") are used in more than just one of the subprocedures, so, like "hll" and "vll," they are included in the declaration section of the H SCROLL1 procedure. "X_coord" and "y_coord" are used for cursor positioning preceding the "Write" statements in the procedures DISP NEW_LEFT_COL and DISP_NEW_RIGHT_COL.

SAVE_PART_SCR/RE_DISP_PART_SCR

The detailed workings of these two subprocedures have been discussed at length in Chapter 4. A few points bear repeating at this time.

In SAVE_PART_SCR at line 0180, the procedure CHR_IN performs a read screen function; that is, it will read or assign the character contents of screen memory offset location "j" *from* "j" and into the character "ch." The variable "ch" is then passed out of the procedure and into the array variable "copy_of_part_scr[i,k]" in ordinary memory where it will be stored for later recall. The assignment statement

```
ch := CHR(MEM[bwseg : bwofs + j]);
```

in the external procedure CHR_IN supplies a single character-type variable, "ch," for the character array variable "copy_of_part_scr[i,k]" at line 0265.

In the procedure RE_DISP_PART_SCR at line 0315, a preliminary step must be accomplished (lines 0390-0430) before the screen character can be written directly from memory to the screen via the external procedure CHR_OUT at linie 0460. The preliminary step is to transform the two-dimensional array "copy_of_part_scr" into a one-dimensional array, "screen_copy_buffer." Why? Because the procedure CHR_OUT, which writes into a single-dimensioned array, MEM[bwseg : bwofs + j], can only take characters from a source array that is one-dimensional; otherwise, an array type incompatability error would occur. Characters from a two-dimensional array cannot be assigned into a one-dimensional array.

5 Horizontal Scrolling: Method 1

After the preliminary step, character data stored in ordinary memory in the array variable "screen_copy_buffer[count]" is written to the screen memory array at the proper offset value "j." The assignment statement

```
MEM[bwseg : bwofs + j] := ch;
```

in CHR_OUT accomplishes the task. Note that "ch" has already been converted into an integer-type variable by the ORD function in the procedure call. Remember that the video memory can only store integers — not characters.

MOVE_PARTSCR_LEFT

This subprocedure performs the first of two steps involved in scrolling the data in "array_contents" horizontally to the right. The first step is to save into ordinary memory the right-most four columns in the display window and then immediately redisplay them as a unit back onto the screen *but* at 1 six-character-wide display column to the *left* of their original position. This action will produce the scrolling effect mentioned earlier and will leave the right-most column of the display screen blank (see Figure 5.4).

The variables "atlc" and "tlr" define the upper left corner of the display screen to be saved by SAVE_PART_SCR. "Atlc" is the adjusted top left column and is defined as follows:

$$atlc = tlc + (col\_width + sp\_betw\_cols)....or$$
$$23 + (6 + 1) = 30$$

See Figure 5.4. The bottom right corner of the screen section to be saved is brc = 56 and brr = 15.

Immediately after this section of screen is saved into the two-dimensional variable "copy_of_part_scr," the screen area *into* which it will be redisplayed is cleared (lines 0610 & 0615). This screen area has its top left corner defined by "tlc" = 23 and its top left row defined as "tlr" = 9. The adjusted bottom right column ("abrc") is defined by the following expression:

$$abrc = brc - (col\_width + sp\_betw\_cols);$$
$$56 - (6 + 1) = 49;$$

"Brr" (the bottom right row) is 15. Note that "brc," "col_width," and "sp_betw_cols" are global to this subprocedure, as they are part of the parameter line of the H_SCROLL1 procedure.

Once the defined area is cleared (lines 0610 & 0615), the procedure RE DISP_PART_SCR will use the same parameters to redisplay the contents of "copy_of_part_scr" into the newly blanked screen area (23,9,49,15). This procedure completes the first step of horizontal data scrolling to the right.

DISP_NEW_RIGHT_COL

The second step of the horizontal scroll to the right is to write out the appropriate column into the space vacated at the right-hand side of the display window. The parameter "k_tot" in the procedures parameter list at line 0660 provides the proper starting column index of the data array "array_contents." "I_tot" provides the unchanging row index (note the assignment at line 0700). The screen location for writing of the next column is provided at lines 0705 and 0715. The variable "start_of_rightmost_col" is defined as

$$\text{start\_of\_rightmost\_col} = \text{brc} - (\text{col\_width} - 1)$$
$$56 - (6 - 1) = 51$$

Refer to Figure 5.4. Note that "brc" and "col_width" are global to this subprocedure, having been passed into the parameter list of the procedure H_SCROLL1. The new column to be displayed on the screen is written in a loop starting at line 0725. Note line 0740, where the starting column index "k" is increased by four.

On the display screen, "k" (the index of "array_contents") must always refer to the index of the contents of the left-most column. Since the scroll direction is toward larger indexes, "k" will change from, say, 4 to 5, but the index of the new column to be displayed at the right-hand side of the display window must be "k + 4" or, in this case, (5 + 4) or 9. Figure 5.5 clarifies this concept.

5 Horizontal Scrolling: Method 1

MOVE_PARTSCR_RIGHT

This procedure, like its counterpart, shifts a predefined section of the display screen one six-character display column to the *right* to make room at the left-hand side. In this case, the column contents of the display screen are moved *from* the screen area bounded by "tlc" = 23, "tlr" = 9 at the top left corner and "abrc" = 49, "brr" = 15 on the bottom right corner *to* the new screen location bounded by "atlc" = 30, "tlr" = 9 on the top left corner and "brc" = 56, "brr" = 15 on the bottom right. The shifting action that you see on the screen is a result of the screen save subprocedure at line 0820, followed immediately by the screen redisplay subprocedure at line 0860. The end result of the procedure MOVE_PARTSCR_RIGHT is a blank six-character-wide display column at the *left*-hand side of the screen. Activate the second part of line 0840 to see this effect (also see Figure 5.6).

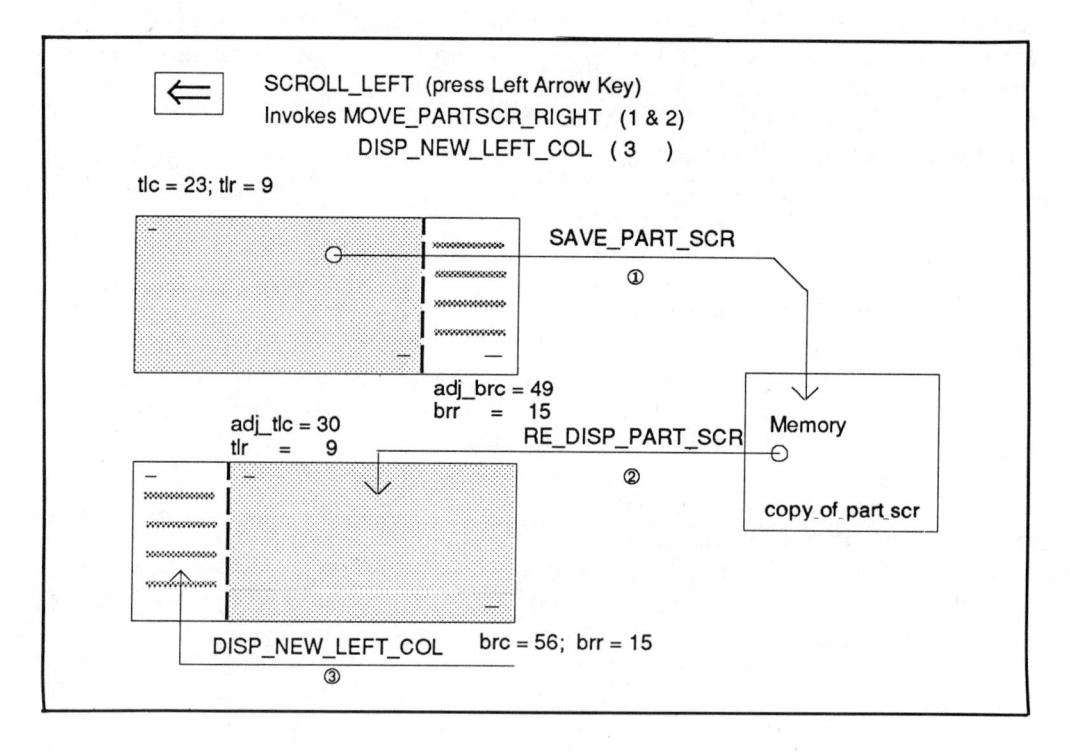

Figure 5.6 Horizontal Scroll — Press Left Arrow Key

DISPLAY_NEW_LEFT_COL

After the predefined screen area has been moved to the right by one column width, the second step can be performed. The task here is to display the appropriate column of string text from "array_contents" at the left-hand side of the screen display window. Exactly which column of "array_contents" is determined by the variable "k_tot" in the main routine at line 1115. Since the Left Arrow key was pressed, the "k_tot" index has been decreased by one. So, for example, if "k_tot" was 4 before the Left Arrow key was pressed, then "k_tot" will change to 3 after the key is pressed (note the assignment statement at line 0925). Now the column with "k" = 3 as an index will become the new left-hand column to be written from "array_contents" into the blanked screen area. To clarify the operation of this subprocedure, activate the second part of line 0950 and refer to Figure 5.7.

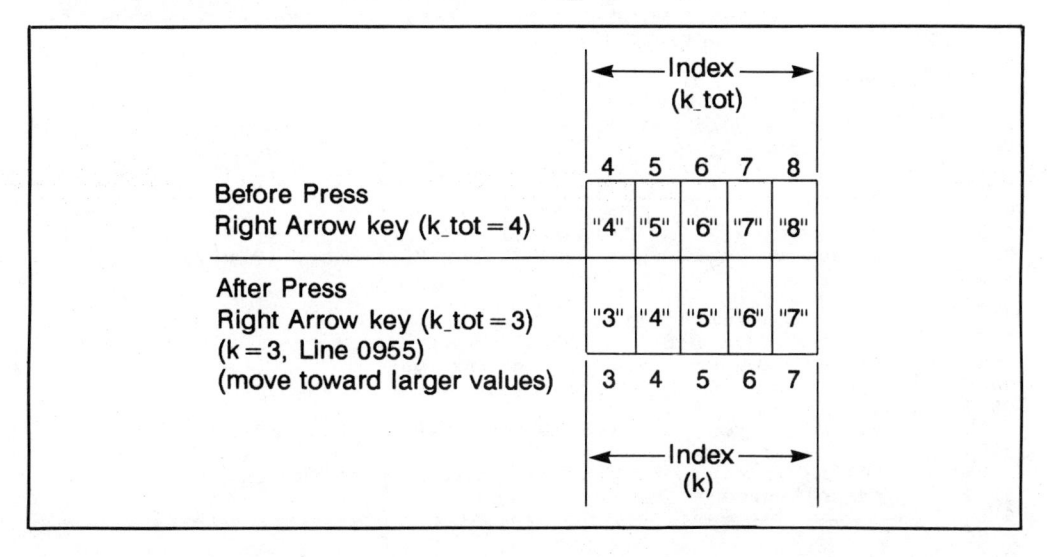

	Index (k_tot)
Before Press Right Arrow key (k_tot = 4)	4 5 6 7 8 "4" "5" "6" "7" "8"
After Press Right Arrow key (k_tot = 3) (k = 3, Line 0955) (move toward larger values)	"3" "4" "5" "6" "7" 3 4 5 6 7
	Index (k)

Figure 5.7 Schematic of Subprocedure Display_New_Left_Col

5 Horizontal Scrolling: Method 1

MODULE: H_S1.DRV

The driver program H_S1.DRV enables the horizontal scrolling module H_S1.INC to do its job. H_S1.DRV performs three main enabling tasks. First, it creates the data that will actually be scrolled on the display screen (procedure CREATE_SCROLL_DATA). Second, it sets up the starting position for the data in the scrolling window (procedure INITIALIZE_SCROLL_WINDOW). Third, it supplies the horizontal scrolling routine (H_SCROLL1) with the correct parameters to perform the horizontal scrolling. The procedure H_SCROLL1, in case you haven't been able to find it, is one of the procedures in the H_S1.INC module, an external procedure invoked at line 0135 in the driver routine. The code for this driver routine is presented below:

```
{======================================================================}
0005 program     h_s1(input,output);
0010 {
0015   horizontal scrolling driver program.
0020   On disk as "h_s1.drv"
0025 }
0030
0035 type
0040       str 6               = string[6];
0045       a                   = ARRAY[1..9,1..4] of str6;  {9 colx4 rows}
0050       screen_copy         = ARRAY[1..7,1..27] of char;
0055       screen_copy_buf     = ARRAY[1..189] of char; {7 x 27}
0060
0065 var
0070       array_contents      : a;
0075       copy_of_part_str    : screen_copy;
0080       screen_copy_buffer  : screen_copy_buf;
0085       i,k                 : integer;
0090
0095       t1_col,t1_row,
0100       br_col,br_row,      {scrolling window parameters}
0105       column_width,       {screen formatting parameters}
0110       space_between_columns : integer;
0115 {======================================================================}
0120
0125 {$i chrinout.inc}
0130 {$i windows.inc}
0135 {$i h_s1.inc}
0140
0145 {======================================================================}
0150
0155 procedure CREATE_COMMAND_LINE;
0160
0165 Begin
0170       window(1,1,80,25);
```

continued...

Horizontal Scrolling: Method 1 **5**

...from previous page

```
0175        TEXTCOLOR(0);TEXTBACKGROUND(15); {black char on white}
0180        gotoxy(27,2);write(' HORIZONTAL SCROLLING DEMO ');
0185        gotoxy(36,3);write(' CHAPTER 5 ');
0190        TEXTCOLOR(15);TEXTBACKGROUND(0); {white char on black}
0195        gotoxy(17,22);
0200        write('Use RIGHT and LEFT Arrow Keys on Numeric Keypad');
0205        gotoxy(27,23);
0210        write('(Be Sure NUM LOCK Key is OFF));
0215 End;        {procedure create_command_line}
0220 {------------------------------------------------------------------}
0225
0230 procedure      CREATE_SCROLL_DATA(var array_contents : a);
0235
0240 var
0245     i,k  : integer;    {indexes for use in this procedure}
0250
0255 Begin     {procedure create_scroll_data}
0260      window(1,1,80,25);
0265      FOR k := 1 to 9 DO       {col 1 to 9}
0270      Begin
0275          FOR i := 1 to 4 DO       {row 1 to 4}
0280          Begin
0285              CASE (k) OF
0290
0295              1   : array_contents[k,i] := '*1111*';
0300              2   : array_contents[k,i] := '*2222*';
0305              3   : array_contents[k,i] := '*3333*';
0310              4   : array_contents[k,i] := '*4444*';
0315              5   : array_contents[k,i] := '*5555*';
0320              6   : array_contents[k,i] := '*6666*';
0325              7   : array_contents[k,i] := '*7777*';
0330              8   : array_contents[k,i] := '*8888*';
0335              9   : array_contents[k,i] := '*9999*';
0340
0345              END; {case}
0350          End;
0355      End;
0360 End;      {procedure create_scroll_data}
0365 {------------------------------------------------------------------}
0370
0375 procedure      INITIALIZE_SCROLL_WINDOW(var array_contents : a);
0380
0385 var
0390     i,k       : integer;
0395     x_coord,            {x_coord is the column}
0400     y_coord   : integer {y_coord is the row       }
0405
0410 Begin    {procedure initialize_scroll_window}
0415      window(1,1,80,25);
0420      gotoxy(23,9);
0425      x_coord := WHEREX ; y_coord := WHEREY;
0430
0435      FOR i := 1 to 4 DO       {4 rows....}
0440      Begin
0445          gotoxy(x_coord,y_coord);
0450          FOR k := 1 to 5 DO       {5 columns....}
```

continued...

95

5   Horizontal Scrolling: Method 1

...from previous page

```
0455              Begin
0460                   write(array_contents[k,i]);
0465                   {* delay(500); *}
0470                   gotoxy(x_coord + (k * 7) , y_coord);
0475                   {across columns in a given row}
0480              End;
0485              x_coord := x_coord;       {col 23}
0490              y_coord := y_coord + 2; {next row : 9 + 2 = 11}
0495         End;
0500 End;     {procedure initialize_scroll_window}
0505 {------------------------------------------------------------------}
0510
0515 Begin    {driver}
0520      window(1,1,80,25);clrscr;
0525      CREATE_COMMAND_LINE;
0530      WINDOW_BORDER(21,8,58,16,2); {border style #2}
0535      CREATE_SCROLL_DATA(array_contents);
0540      INITIALIZE_SCROLL_WINDOW(array_contents);
0545
0550      tl_col := 23 ; tl_row := 9;        {overall window dimensions of}
0555      br_col := 56 ; br_row := 15;       {screen area to be scrolled}
0560      column_width := 6;
0565      space_between_columns := 1;
0570      H_SCROLL1(tl_col,tl_row,br_col,br_row,
0575                column_width,space_between_columns,
0580                array_contents);
0585 End.     {driver}
{==================================================================}
```

H_S1.DRV: NOTES

Before the details of the above procedures are described, a clear distinction should be made between the variable "array_contents" and the variable "copy_of_part_scr" found in the declaration section at lines 0070 and 0075.

First, "array_contents" is a 9-column by 4-row array containing the actual data or information that is to be scrolled on the screen. This information can be created by a separate computation in the driver program; it can be fed into the array from data held on a disk; or it can be created solely for demonstration purposes as has been done in this routine. Each data element of the 9-column by 4-row array is a string of six characters consisting of

   a "*"|1 digit|1 digit|1 digit|1 digit|a "*"

Each screen display column then is six characters wide.

Second, "copy_of_part_scr" (read as "copy of part screen") represents a two-dimensional, rectangular area on the computer screen. Refer now to Figure 5.6. Inside the computer's memory, this screen area is represented by "copy_of_part_scr" whose type is "screen_copy," an array whose depth is 7 rows deep by 27 columns wide. Note that the full display column width of the layout sheet is (col 56 - col 23 + 1) or 34 columns total. This computation *excludes* the cursor positioning columns, 22 and 57. Why only 27 columns? Because with each press of a Right or Left Arrow key, you are only saving and redisplaying the screen data in 4 columns along with the 3 spaces between them:

((4 col x 6 spaces/col) + 3 spaces) = 27 spaces

Why 7 rows instead of 4? Because in the Screen Layout, one space between each of the 4 rows has been specified so that you need

((1 space/row x 4 rows) + 3 spaces) = 7 spaces

Note that the variable "screen_copy_buffer" at line 0080 is the one-dimensional equivalent of "copy_of_part_scr." It has 27 x 7 = 189 single-character elements and is used in the subprocedure RE_DISP PART_SCR to map saved screen characters back from memory and into the one-dimensional screen memory array MEM[bwseg:bwof + j].

The first task of the driver routine is to create some data to scroll. The procedure CREATE_SCROLL_DATA performs this job. Since this is only a demonstration, the method of data creation (generation) will be simple. You will simply define the data as shown by the array in Figure 5.3. The loops at lines 0265 and 0275 along with the CASE..END structure will store all the six-character string elements into their proper locations in "array contents."

Having "created" and stored the data into the array, you then need to prepare for scrolling with the procedure INITIALIZE_SCROLL_WINDOW. The object is to put the first five columns of the data array onto the display screen. This task is performed by the loops at lines 0435 and 0450. The variable "i" is the row index, and "k" is the column index. Formatting on the screen itself is performed using the GOTOXY procedure, the WHEREX and WHEREY functions, and the variables "x coord" and "y_coord." The number "7" at line 0470 represents the number of spaces from the start of one column to the start of the next

5 Horizontal Scrolling: Method 1

adjacent column (6 spaces/col + 1 space between columns). Again, note that this procedure refers to the array "array_contents" in the parameter list at line 0230. After this procedure is finished, the screen will appear as shown in Figure 5.2.

The final task of this demonstration program is to define the parameters that will be required by the H_SCROLL1 procedure to "drive it" or make it work. Feeding the procedure its needed parameters begins at line 0550. Observe that the dimensions of the scrolling window are based on (and relative to) the whole display window. Observe also that the display column width of 6 is the same width as the data elements in the data array "array_contents." Then observe at line 0565 and in Figure 5.2 that a variable called "space_between_columns" has been defined. This variable, along with "column_width," enables the sub-procedures inside the H_SCROLL1 procedure to calculate "adj_tl_col" or "atlc" (adjusted top left column) and "adj_br_col" or "abrc" (adjusted bottom right column) values.

CHAPTER 6

HORIZONTAL SCROLLING: METHOD 2

6 Horizontal Scrolling: Method 2

In Chapter 5, you learned to perform a horizontal scroll using the "save/redisplay part screen" method. The advantages of this method are as follows:

- incorporates a screen saving technique, which was covered in Chapter 4
- concept for the scrolling is intuitively appealing; it is easy to visualize and comprehend

There are, however, a few disdvantages:

- it takes a fair amount of code to get the scrolling job done
- due to the limits of the "include" compiler directive, the procedures SAVE_PART_SCR and RE_DISP_PARTSCR cannot be split out of their scrolling procedures and used as separate modules

The "save/redisplay part screen" method, in spite of its disadvantages, is a good basic technique. Its speed is good, especially for scrolls where the row depth of the data on the screen is not too great. The horizontal scrolling technique introduced in this chapter is called the "index address" method. This method requires much less code to get the scrolling task done and is not redundant in its use of already written routines as was the first method. It is also fast. The compensating difficulty is the computation of the index of the array element to be written to the screen. This technique will take getting used to, but once mastered will prove to be powerful indeed.

The following statement sums up the "index address" method of scrolling:

You can display a subset of characters from the one-dimensional video memory array onto the screen by first systematically accessing and then assigning the correct subset of index values of a corresponding one-dimensional array of characters in regular memory into the video memory.

It may sound confusing, but as you read through this chapter, your understanding should crystallize.

Horizontal Scrolling: Method 2 6

MODULE: H_S2.INC

The overall objective of this module is to scroll a display screen of data either to the left or the right using the Left and Right Arrow keys on the Numeric Keypad. This module consists of two procedures. H_SCROLL2 is the main controlling procedure in which the arrow keys are pressed and the cumulative row and column indexes ("k_tot" and "i_tot") of the data array to be scrolled are calculated. It is, however, the responsibility of the subprocedure REWRITE_SCR_BYCOL (rewrite screen by column) to actually horizontally scroll the columns of data back and forth across the screen. This procedure is analogous to the subprocedure combinations MOVE_PARTSCR_RIGHT/DISP_NEW_LEFT_COL or MOVE_PARTSCR_LEFT/DISP_NEW_RIGHT_COL in the previous chapter, but, as you will see, the way of achieving the same result on the screen is radically different. The code is presented below.

```
{=======================================================================}
0005  {h_s2.inc}
0010  { This ".inc" file contains all the file saving and scrolling
0015      routines that are OVERHEAD REQUIREMENTS of the program
0020      "h_s2.drv".
0025      On disk as "h_s2.inc".
0030  }
0035
0040  {-----------------------------------------------------------------}
0045
0050  procedure     H_SCROLL2(tlc,tlr           : integer;
0055                  var screen_copy_buffer    : scr_copy_buf);
0060
0065  label
0070      rep_read;
0075
0080  const
0085      bell           = #$07;
0090      scroll_left    = #$4b;
0095      scroll_right   = #$4d;
0100      carrige_ret    = #$0d;
0105
0110  var
0115      scroll_choice  : char;
0120      exit_scroll    : boolean;
0125      i_tot,k_tot    : integer;
0130  {-----------------------------------------------------------------}
0135
0140      procedure REWRITE_SCR_BYCOL(k_tot , i_tot  : integer;
0145                      var screen_copy_buffer     : scr_copy_buf);
0150
```

continued...

6 Horizontal Scrolling: Method 2

...from previous page

```
0155   var
0160         bx,bp,
0165         count,
0170         j,
0175         row,col,
0180         k,i      : integer;
0185   {-----------------------------------------------------------------}
0190
0195         Begin      {sub procedure rewrite_scr_by_col}
0200              col := tlc ; row := tlr; {start loc. for screen write}
0205              j := ((row - 1) * 160) + ((col - 1) * 2);
0210              FOR k := (k_tot) to (k_tot + 4) DO {5 columns}
0215              Begin
0220                   FOR i := (i_tot) to (i_tot + 3) DO {1 to 1+3 rows}
0225                   Begin
0230                        bp := (k - 1) * 6;       {6 chars/col}
0235                        bx := (i - 1) * 54;      {54 chars/row}
0240                        FOR count := 1 to 6 DO {6 chars per display column}
0245                        Begin
0250                             CHR_OUT(j,ORD(screen_copy_buffer[bx+bp+count]));
0255
0260                             {* delay(1000) *}
0265                             j := j + 2;
0270                        End;
0275                        col := col ; row := row + 2;
0280                        {same column , down 2 rows}
0285                        j := ((row - 1) * 160) + ((col - 1) * 2);
0290                   End;
0295                   col := col + 7 ; row := tlr;
0300                   {next disp col (6 + 1);top row of display window}
0305                   j := ((row - 1) * 160) + ((col - 1) * 2);{recalc j}
0310              End;
0315         End;       {sub procedure rewrite_scr bycol}
0320   {-----------------------------------------------------------------}
0325
0330   Begin    {procedure h_scroll2}
0335         window(1,1,80,25);
0340         exit_scroll := false; {initialize exit condition}
0345         k_tot := 1;
0350         i_tot := 1;
0355
0360         REPEAT
0365              rep_read: {a label}
0370              read(KBD,scroll_choice);
0375              CASE (Scroll_Choice) OF
0380
0385              scroll_left   : Begin   {press Left Arrow key}
0390                                   i_tot := i_tot + 0;
0395                                   k_tot := k_tot - 1;
0400                                   IF (k_tot < 1) THEN
0405                                   Begin
0410                                        k_tot := 1;
0415                                        goto rep_read;
0420                                   End;
0425                                   REWRITE_SCR_BYCOL(k_tot,i_tot,
0430                                                    screen_copy buffer);
0435                              End; {scroll_left}
0440
```

continued...

102

...from previous page

```
0445                scroll_right  : Begin {press Right Arrow key}
0450                                    i_tot := i_tot + 0;
0455                                    k_tot := k_tot + 1;
0460                                    IF (k_tot > 5) THEN
0465                                    Begin
0470                                        k_tot := 5;
0475                                        goto rep_read;
0480                                    End;
0485                                    REWRITE_SCR_BYCOL(k_tot,i_tot,
0490                                                  screen_copy_buffer);
0495                                End; {scroll_right}
0500
0505                carriage_ret  : Begin
0510                                    exit_scroll := true;
0515                                    write(bell);
0520                                End;
0525
0530                ELSE
0535                         {if none of the above choices are selected...}
0540                         {no action. go back & press one of above keys}
0545                END   {case statement}
0550          UNTIL exit_scroll = true;
0555 End;          {procedure h_scroll2}
{================== END OF "h_s2.inc" overhead file ===================}
```

H_S2.INC: NOTES

H_SCROLL2

As mentioned above, this procedure sets up the horizontal scrolling of data on the screen. H_SCROLL2 has three parameters fed to it from the main driver routine. The first two, "tlc" and "tlr," are the starting top left column and starting top left row of the screen where the scrolled data will be displayed. These parameters are used in the subprocedure REWRITE_SCR_BYCOL (rewrite screen by column) later on. The third parameter, "screen_copy_buffer," is a one-dimensional array consisting of 216 characters (ARRAY[1..216] of char). This variable is the one-dimensional equivalent of the two-dimensional array "screen_copy," which is of the type "ARRAY[1..4,1..9] of string[6]" and is equivalent in that it too has 216 character elements (4 x 9 x 6 = 216). This one-dimensional array is necessary because mapping from a two-dimensional array directly onto the one-dimensional screen memory array MEM[bwseg:bwofs + j] is illegal in Turbo Pascal.

103

6 Horizontal Scrolling: Method 2

In the declaration section, not too much is different from the procedure H_SCROLL1 in Chapter 5. Note, however, that far fewer screen formatting variables are used here than were used in H_SCROLL1. Note also that the individual array elements that you are scrolling on the screen — whether in the previous chapter, this chapter, or in future chapters — are all six-character strings of the form "*####*". Maintaining consistency in the definition of *what* is scrolled should create a better understanding of *how* the scrolling process works.

The scrolling is controlled in the body of the procedure. As long as the Return key is not pressed, you can scroll the data for as long as you like. This feature is guaranteed by the REPEAT...UNTIL loop starting at line 0360. If you choose to scroll the data to the left, press the Left Arrow key (key #4 on the Numeric Keypad). The cumulative column total variable "k_tot" is then decreased by 1. Pressing the Left Arrow key means that you want to display the column of data immediately to the left (but out of sight) of the column of data currently located at the left-most position in the screen display window. If "k_tot" is already 1, then line 0395 will force it to be less than 1 (1 - 1 = 0). Then you are outside the minimum value of 1 in the allowed column range of 1 to 9 inclusive. This situation is corrected at lines 0400 to 0410 and tried again at line 0365. Assuming "k_tot" is a value greater than 2, pressing the Left Arrow key will decrease "k_tot" by 1, and since the revised "k_tot" value is inside the legal 1-9 range, you can call for a display screen rewrite at line 0425 via the procedure REWRITE_SCR BYCOL (rewrite screen by column).

If you want to scroll the screen data to the right, press the Right Arrow key (key #6 on the Numeric Keypad). The effect will be to increment the "k_tot" variable by 1, meaning that you want to display the column of data immediately to the right of the column of data currently at the right-most position in the display window.

Lines 0460-0470 were designed to prevent the column index variable "k tot" from exceeding 5. A "k_tot" value above 5 (in the demo program) will result in your trying to access a column whose index is greater than 9 (line 0210 in REWRITE_SCREEN_BYCOL). A column index value greater than 9 for the array variable "screen_copy" is out of range and is therefore illegal. As with "scroll_left" above, an illegal "k_tot" value will reset "k_tot" back to 5 and force a jump to the label "rep_read" for a retry.

Assuming that "k_tot" starts within the allowed range of 1-4 inclusive, pressing the Right Arrow key will increment "k_tot" by 1. Since the revised "k_tot" is still within the allowed range of 1-5 inclusive, you can bypass the error handling code and call the REWRITE_SCR_BYCOL procedure with "k_tot" and "i_tot" and the one-dimensional array "screen_copy_buffer." Note that "i_tot" (the row index of "screen copy") remains unchanged because during a horizontal scroll, the rows of the array remain unchanged while only the columns change.

REWRITE_SCR_BYCOL

This procedure actually performs the screen scroll you see after pressing either a Right or Left Arrow key. The technique used to achieve the horizontal scroll is radically different from the method discussed in Chapter 5 where predefined areas of the display screen were saved to memory then moved so new columns could be written into vacated screen areas. Here, the scrolling effect is achieved by arithmetic recalculation of the index values of the one-dimensional array variable "screen_copy_buffer." Each time a new "k_tot" value is selected in the H_SCROLL2 procedure, a different set (group) of 120 index values of the 216 possible is computed, and then the reindexed variables "screen copy_buffer[count]" are written directly to the screen display memory at line 0250.

Figure 6.1 shows a schematic of the array variable "screen_copy," which has been created for demonstration purposes. This memory array can be visualized and laid out as you see in the figure. There are 9 columns numbered 1-9 inclusive and 4 rows numbered 1-4 inclusive. Note that at each array location, there is a six-character string (or display column) and that each of these nine columns has the same string value. The strings were set up in this manner to best demonstrate horizontal scrolling. If you compute the number of characters in this array, you should find that there are

    9 x 4 positions x 6 characters/position = 216 characters

6 Horizontal Scrolling: Method 2

	Col 1	Col 2	Col 3	Col 4	Col 5	Col 6	Col 7	Col 8	Col 9
Row 1	*1111*	*2222*	*3333*	*4444*	*5555*	*6666*	*7777*	*8888*	*9999*
Row 2	*1111*	*2222*	*3333*	*4444*	*5555*	*6666*	*7777*	*8888*	*9999*
Row 3	*1111*	*2222*	*3333*	*4444*	*5555*	*6666*	*7777*	*8888*	*9999*
Row 4	*1111*	*2222*	*3333*	*4444*	*5555*	*6666*	*7777*	*8888*	*9999*

Figure 6.1 Schematic of Two-dimensional Array
Variable: Screen Copy = Array [1..4, 1..9] of String[6]

Figure 6.2 shows a schematic of the array variable "screen_copy_buffer," the one-dimensional equivalent of the two-dimensional array "screen copy" in Figure 6.1. It too has 216 indexed address locations with each location filled up by one character (after all, CHR_OUT can only work on a single character at a time). If you place "screen_copy" into successive memory locations one character at a time, starting with the first character of Col 1, Row 1 ("*") and ending with the last character of Col 9, Row 4 ("*"), you would create the one-dimensional equivalent of "screen_copy," namely "screen_copy_buffer." The manipulation of these 216 index values enables you to perform horizontal scrolling using the "index address" method.

Horizontal Scrolling: Method 2　6

1	*	55	*	109	*	163	*
2	1	56	1	110	1	164	1
3	1	57	1	111	1	165	1
4	1	58	1	112	1	166	1
5	1	59	1	113	1	167	1
6	*	60	*	114	*	168	*
7	*	61	*	115	*	169	*
8	2	62	2	116	2	170	2
9	2	63	2	117	2	171	2
10	2	64	2	118	2	172	2
11	2	65	2	119	2	173	2
12	*	66	*	120	*	174	*
13	*	67	*	121	*	175	*
14	3	68	3	122	3	176	3
15	3	69	3	123	3	177	3
16	3	70	3	124	3	178	3
17	3	71	3	125	3	179	3
18	*	72	*	126	*	180	*
19	*	73	*	127	*	181	*
20	4	74	4	128	4	182	4
21	4	75	4	129	4	183	4
22	4	76	4	130	4	184	4
23	4	77	4	131	4	185	4
24	*	78	*	132	*	186	*
25	*	79	*	133	*	187	*
26	5	80	5	134	5	188	5
27	5	81	5	135	5	189	5
28	5	82	5	136	5	190	5
29	5	83	5	137	5	191	5
30	*	84	*	138	*	192	*
31	*	85	*	139	*	193	*
32	6	86	6	140	6	194	6
33	6	87	6	141	6	195	6
34	6	88	6	142	6	196	6
35	6	89	6	143	6	197	6
36	*	90	*	144	*	198	*
37	*	91	*	145	*	199	*
38	7	92	7	146	7	200	7
39	7	93	7	147	7	201	7
40	7	94	7	148	7	202	7
41	7	95	7	149	7	203	7
42	*	96	*	150	*	204	*
43	*	97	*	151	*	205	*
44	8	98	8	152	8	206	8
45	8	99	8	153	8	207	8
46	8	100	8	154	8	208	8
47	8	101	8	155	8	209	8
48	*	102	*	156	*	210	*
49	*	103	*	157	*	211	*
50	9	104	9	158	9	212	9
51	9	105	9	159	9	213	9
52	9	106	9	160	9	214	9
53	9	107	9	161	9	215	9
54	*	108	*	162	*	216	*

Screen_Copy_Buffer [bx + bp + count]

Contents
Index Values

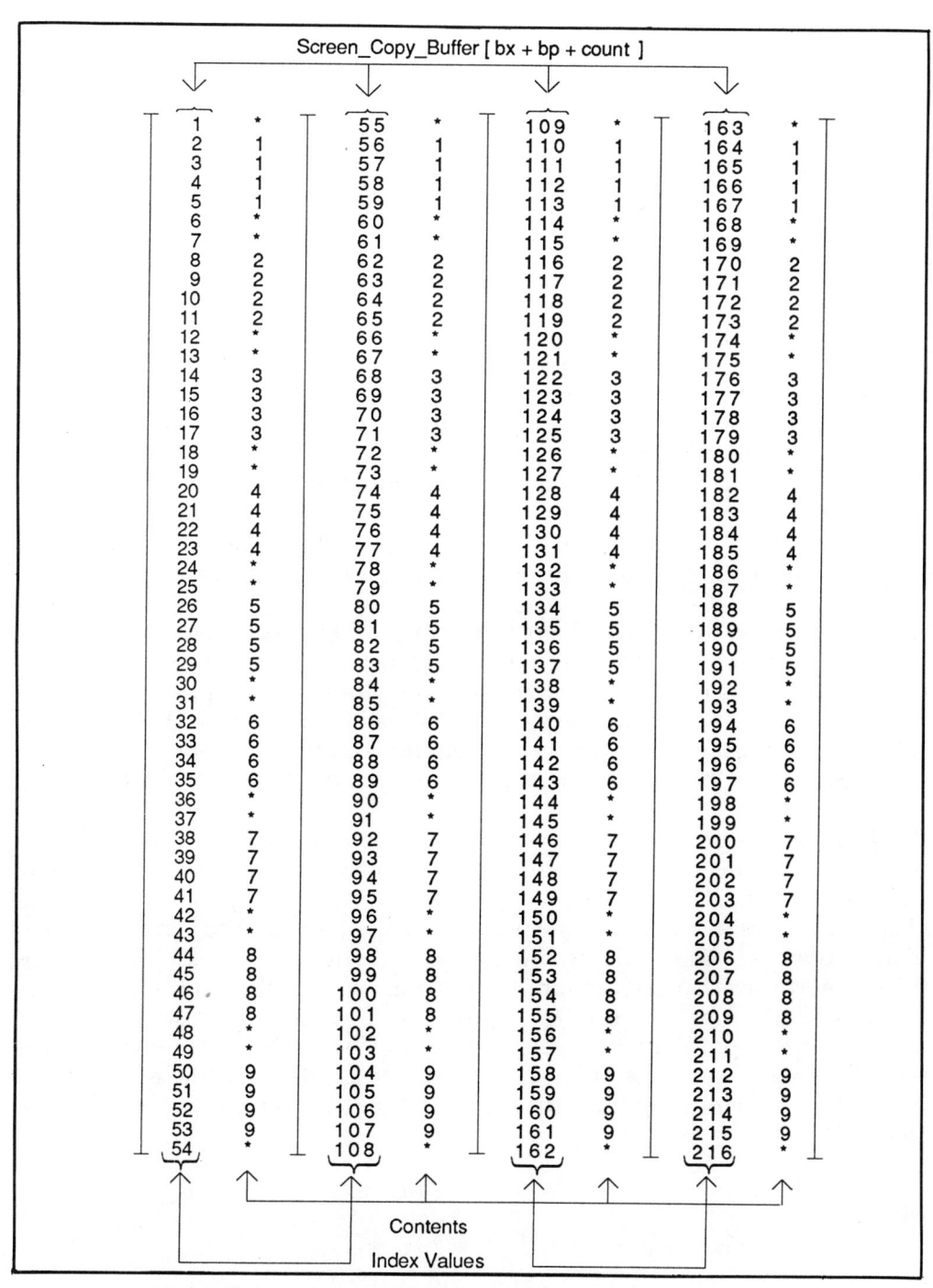

Figure 6.2　Schematic of One-dimensional Array Variable Screen Copy Buffer = ARRAY [1..216] of char.

6 Horizontal Scrolling: Method 2

The scrolling effect above was achieved by calculating and displaying to screen memory different sets of 120 indexed variables of the 216 possible. Refer to Figure 6.3. There you will see that the screen display width is 5 columns. It was decided beforehand that 5 columns would be the chosen width. So, for example, if you have columns 3-7 inclusive on your display screen, you have a set of

5 col x 6 chars/col * 4 rows = 120 indexed values

Each time you press a Left or Right Arrow key, you get a different set of 120 index values of "screen_copy_buffer" displayed in the display window of the screen, depending on the values of "k_tot" and "i_tot."

A specific example will illustrate the inner workings of REWRITE_SCR BYCOL. Assume from Figure 6.1 that the display screen is bounded by column 3 (rows 1 to 4) on the left and column 7 (rows 1 to 4) on the right. The current value of "k_tot" is 3 and "i_tot" is 1 and of no further interest. You now want to scroll towards the right so that columns 4-8 inclusive in Figure 6.1 will be displayed on the video screen.

When you press the Right Arrow key, "k_tot" changes from "k_tot" = 3 to "k_tot" = 4. "I_tot" stays unchanged at 1. These values are passed to the REWRITE_SCR_BYCOL subprocedure. Also included in the package of values are the "tlc" and "tlr" values by way of H_SCROLL2. These two formatting parameters enable you to calculate the starting screen memory location for screen rewrite at lines 0200 and 0295.

Now track this routine step by step. The loop starting at line 0210 will give "k" a range of values from 4-8 inclusive (5 columns total). The loop at line 0220 will give "i" a range of values from 1-4 rows deep. Together, these two indexes span the new part of the array "screen copy" that you want to display on the screen. The next lines (0225-0290) perform the conversion from what you can easily see in two-dimensional terms (Figure 6.1) into the not-so-easily visualized one-dimensional equivalent ("screen_copy_buffer[bx + bp + count]"). This variable is the pivot of this procedure. It is the variable upon which CHR_OUT operates at line 0250 to produce the results you see on the screen.

Horizontal Scrolling: Method 2 **6**

Figure 6.3 Schematic Example of Subprocedure REWRITE_SCREEN_BYCOL

6 Horizontal Scrolling: Method 2

Back up a moment and consider the following question: If you want to display the very first character of column 4, row 1, how do you calculate its equivalent one-dimensional index value in "screen_copy_buffer"? This is the job of lines 0230-0250. Note that the integer index value of "screen_copy_buffer" is built up from three component values: "bp," "bx," and "count."

In the example, starting at line 0230, calculate

    bp = (4 - 1) * 6   = 18   {using column 4}
    bx = (1 - 1) * 54 = 0   {using row 1}
    count   = 1   {first of 6 characters:col 4, row 1}

The first value of "screen_copy_buffer[bp + bx + count]" = 19. If you look at Figures 6.2 and 6.3, you will see that the index value of 19 is the correct one-dimensional equivalent of the first character of col 4, row 1. Take another example. You know that col 6, row 3 (4th character) will be on the display screen. What is its one-dimensional index equivalent then? Starting at line 0230, you see that

    bp = (6 - 1) * 6   = 30   {using column 6}
    bx = (3 - 1) * 54 = 108   {using row 3 }
    count   = 4   {4th of 6 characters: col 6, row 3}

The index value of "screen_copy_buffer" that is equivalent to col 6, row 3 of "screen_copy" is built up from the sum of "bp," "bx," and "count" and equals 30 + 108 + 4 or 142. Again, look at Figures 6.2 and 6.3. Continuing in the systematic manner prescribed by the three loops at lines 0230 (column), 0235 (row), and 0240 (each character of the six-character string located at each column/row location), you would build up a set of 120 index values as shown in Figure 6.3. The numbers written sideways are the calculated index values of "screen_copy_buffer," and the numbers written upright represent the order in which each of the indexes is calculated in the loops (1 is the first index to be calculated, and 120 is the last index calculated). You can trace the operation of this section of code if you unbracket line 0260. The actual contents of the indexed locations are seen in Figure 6.2.

Horizontal Scrolling: Method 2   6

Transferring the properly indexed character of "screen_copy_buffer" to screen memory is accomplished by the now familiar CHR_OUT procedure at line 0250. Exactly where the character is displayed on the screen is determined by the calculated offset value "j" intially at line 0205 for the starting location; later, it is incremented at line 0265 as you proceed with the display of each character in a given column of a given row; still later it is recalculated at line 0285 as you drop down two screen rows in any given column; and still later it is recalculated at line 0305 as you proceed to the next display column to the right on the screen. Each of these computed "j" values feeds the CHROUT procedure at line 0250 at different times as you systematically traverse the three FOR..DO loops of this subprocedure. All the above description of character screen location will make the most sense if you can see it. So unbracket line 0260 and see for yourself how it works. The number "7" (line 0295) represents 7 screen columns consisting of 6 characters and 1 space between the columns.

In the expressions "i - 1" and "k - 1" starting at line 0230 you may wonder why the subtraction of 1? The answer is that this adjustment must be made if access to the very first column and the very first row of "screen_copy_buffer" is to be achieved. If you assume that the variable bp := k * 6, that bx := i * 54, and that you want to access the first character (count := 1) of column 1, row 1 of "screen_copy," you would find that the calculated index of "screen_copy_buffer" would be [6 + 54 + 1] = 61. That calculation is wrong. How can the index of the very first value in the array have a value of 61? On the other hand, if you believe that bp := (k - 1) * 6, that bx := (i - 1) * 54, and that count := 1, then access to the first character at column 1, row 1 of "screen_copy" would provide you with an index whose value is [0 + 0 + 1] = 1, which is correct and corresponds to the index found in Figure 6.2.

In summary then, the procedure REWRITE_SCR_BYCOL when called will rewrite the whole display screen with 120 different indexed values of "screen_copy_buffer" each time either the Left or Right Arrow key is pressed. Using "k_tot" (via "k"), "i_tot" (via "i"), and count (1-6), a single unique index value is calculated, and the character stored in the array "screen_copy_buffer" at that indexed position is displayed at a specific location on the display screen using the CHR_OUT procedure at line 0250. Each time a Right or Left Arrow key is pressed, this process is repeated 120 times.

6 Horizontal Scrolling: Method 2

MODULE: H_S2.DRV

This driver routine (in the same spirit of any typical driver routine) creates the preconditions or environment in which the horizontal scrolling package "h_s2.inc" can function. The first task of the driver routine is performed in the Declaration Section, where you define the needed array and formatting variables. The second task of the driver is to call the prewritten "include" or ".inc" external routines. The third task is to create the data array whose contents are to be scrolled. This task is accomplished using the declared variable in the procedure CREATE SCROLL_DATA. The fourth task is to create a starting point from which to begin the scrolling. The procedure INITIALIZE_SCROLL DATA will display on the screen the first 4 rows and the first 5 columns of the array "screen_copy." The fifth and final task, once all the preparation is completed, is to call the procedure H_SCROLL2 — an external procedure from the "h_s2.inc" module. This module and its member procedures actually perform the horizontal scrolling function that you will see on the screen. The Pascal coding is presented below, followed by a more detailed discussion of the operation.

```
{=================================================================}
0005   program       h_s2(input,output);
0010      { Horizontal scroll using index address method.
0015        On disk as "h_s2.drv".
0020      }
0025
0030   type
0035        str6           = string[6];
0040        b              = ARRAY[1..4,1..9] of str6;
0045        scr_copy_buf   = ARRAY[1..216] of char;  {4 x 9 x 6}
0050
0055   var
0060        tl_col,tl_row       : integer;
0065        screen_copy         : b;
0070        screen_copy_buffer  : scr_copy_buf;
0075   {=================================================================}
0080
0085   {$i chrinout.inc}
0090   {$i windows.inc}
0095   {$i h_s2.inc}
0100
0105   {=================================================================}
0110
0115   procedure       CREATE_COMMAND_LINE;
0120
0125   Begin
0130        window(1,1,80,25);
0135        TEXTCOLOR(0);TEXTBACKGROUND(15);    {black char on white}
0140        gotoxy(27,2);write(' HORIZONTAL SCROLLING DEMO ');
0145        gotoxy(36,3);write(' CHAPTER 6 ');
0150        TEXTCOLOR(15);TEXTBACKGROUND(0);    {white char on black}
```

continued...

112

Horizontal Scrolling: Method 2   6

...from previous page

```
0155        gotoxy(17,22);
0160        write('Use RIGHT and LEFT Arrow Keys on Numeric Keypad');
0165        gotoxy(27,23);
0170        write('(Be Sure NUM LOCK Key is OFF)');
0175 End;        {procedure create_command_line}
0180 {----------------------------------------------------------------}
0185
0190 procedure      CREATE_SCROLL_DATA(var screen_copy_buffer :
0195                                      scr_copy_buf);
0200
0205 var
0210       count: integer;
0215
0220 Begin    {procedure create_scroll_data}
0225      FOR count := 1 to 216 DO
0230      Begin
0235           CASE (count MOD 54) OF
0240
0245             2..5 : screen_copy_buffer[count] := '1';
0250             8..11: screen_copy_buffer[count] := '2';
0255            14..17: screen_copy_buffer[count] := '3';
0260            20..23: screen_copy_buffer[count] := '4';
0265            26..29: screen_copy_buffer[count] := '5';
0270            32..35: screen_copy_buffer[count] := '6';
0275            38..41: screen_copy_buffer[count] := '7';
0280            44..47: screen_copy_buffer[count] := '8';
0285            50..53: screen_copy_buffer[count] := '9'
0290
0295           ELSE    screen_copy_buffer[count] := '*'
0300
0305           END; {case}
0310      End;
0315 End;      {procedure create_scroll_data}
0320 {--------------------------------------------------------}
0325
0330 procedure INITIALIZE_SCROLL_WINDOW(var screen_copy_buffer :
0335                                        scr_copy_buf);
0340
0345 var
0350      i,k,
0355      bx,bp,
0360      count,
0365      j,
0370      row,col  : integer;
0375
0380 Begin    {procedure initialize_scroll_window}
0385      col := 23 ; row := 9;
0390      j := ((row - 1) * 160) + ((col - 1) * 2);
0395      FOR i := 1 to 4 DO    { 4 rows }
0400      Begin
0405           FOR k := 1 to 5 DO { 5 cols }
0410           Begin
0415                bx := (i - 1) * 54;   {54 chars/row}
0420                bp := (k - 1) * 6;    {6 chars/col }
0425                FOR count := 1 to 6 DO
0430                Begin
0435                     CHR_OUT(j,ORD(screen_copy_buffer[bx + bp +
0440                                                      count]));
```

continued...

113

6 Horizontal Scrolling: Method 2

...from previous page

```
0445                         {* delay(1000); *}
0450                         j := j + 2;
0455                    End;
0460                    j := j + 2;      {skip a space between screen cols}
0465               End;
0470               col := col ; row := row + 2;
0475               j := ((row - 1) * 160) + ((col - 1) * 2);
0480          End;
0485 End;     {procedure initialize scroll_window}
0490 {----------------------------------------------------------------}
0495
0500 Begin    {driver}
0505     window(1,1,80,25);clrscr;
0510     CREATE_COMMAND_LINE;
0515     WINDOW_BORDER(21 , 8 , 58 , 16 , 4); {border style #4}
0520     CREATE_SCROLL_DATA(screen_copy_buffer);
0525     INITIALIZE_SCROLL_WINDOW(screen_copy_buffer);
0530
0535     tl_col := 23 ; tl_row := 9; {top_left col,top_left row}
0540     H_SCROLL2(tl_col,tl_row,screen_copy_buffer);
0545 End.     {driver}
{================================================================}
```

H_S2.DRV: NOTES

In the declaration section, the two-dimensional array variable "screen copy" has been created. It has 4 rows and 9 columns with each array element being a six-character string (lines 0065 & 0040). Note that "screen_copy" does not appear in any of the parameter lists in the main routine H_S2.DRV. "Screen_copy" is included for instructional purposes

- to assist you in visualizing the data structure you will eventually be manipulating. From the Type definition provided at line 0040, you can orient yourself by producing a diagram similar to that in Figure 6.1.

- to enable you to correctly define the Type of "screen_copy"'s one-dimensional equivalent, "screen_copy_buffer." Note that the Type of "screen_copy_buffer" could not have been defined without first looking at the Type of "screen_copy." Note also that this defined Type (line 0045) is used throughout all the procedure parameter lists in the external module "h_s2.inc."

Horizontal Scrolling: Method 2 6

The unused two-dimensional variable ("screen_copy") is the logical precursor of the one-dimensional array that you actually use and is only included to show how the type of "screen_copy_buffer" was derived.

Above, you saw that the first task of the driver routine is to supply the proper Type definitions for all the variables in the parameter lists of all the external (".inc" modules) procedures that will be used by it. The second task of the driver routine is to orchestrate the calling of all external modules that are dedicated to the performance of specialized tasks required by the driver. Line 0085 invokes the set of external procedures embodied within "chrinout.inc." You want to use the procedure CHR_OUT to write the characters from "screen_copy_buffer" directly to the screen via MEM[bwseg:bwofs + j]. Line 0090 invokes "windows.inc." You want to use all these procedures to create your window borders. Finally, line 0095 invokes the package of procedures "h s2.inc" including H_SCROLL2, which provides you with the necessary horizontal data scrolling capabilities.

The third task for the driver routine is to create a suitable array of data to use with the horizontal scrolling demonstration routines. The procedure CREATE_SCROLL_DATA provides the needed data. Figure 6.1 provides the form of data that you can best visualize. The one-dimensional equivalent of "screen_copy" is the variable "screen_copy_buffer" in Figure 6.2 and at line 0070 in the procedure. Note that with the "var" prefix, the scrolling data is created "from the inside out"; it is only after exit from this procedure that the screen data to be used in the scrolling operation is created. The word "suitable" is used above because the screen memory array MEM[bwseg:bwofs + j] is a one-dimensional array and can only be mapped onto by another one-dimensional array. So while you can better visualize with a two-dimensional array, the computer can better "visualize" with a one-dimensional array (see Figure 6.2). Therefore, you must convert from the more comfortable two-dimensional point of view into a less comfortable one-dimensional point of view.

Mapping the contents of "screen_copy" from its two-dimensional form (Figure 6.1) to its one-dimensional form "screen_copy_buffer" is accomplished by the FOR...DO loop starting at line 0225 and the CASE statement at line 0235. This process is pretty straight-forward. But why MOD 54 at line 0235? If you look at Figure 6.1, you will see that each of the 4 rows (moving from left to right) has exactly the same pattern of characters and that each row is 54 characters long (Figure 6.2). The

6 Horizontal Scrolling: Method 2

MOD function at line 0235 is a specially provided divisor function, but instead of calculating the quotient, it calculates the *remainder*. So, for example, if the count at line 0235 is 189, the value of "count MOD 54" would be 27 (the quotient would be 3). Looking at line 0265 in the CASE list, you can see that "screen_copy_buffer[189] := '5' ." You can also see this result if you consult Figure 6.2.

The fourth task of the driver routine is to initialize the scroll data, that is, to display on the screen the 4 rows and first 5 columns of the array as seen in Figure 6.4. This code should be familiar to you by now, as it was explained in detail above. Since this is an initialization, however, note that the "k" loop at line 0405 starts at 1. If you were to take the code between lines 0395 and 0480 and work out the index values based on their "bp," "bx," and "count" components in the same manner as prescribed in Figure 6.3, you would calculate the index values to be as follows:

    001-030 inclusive for row 1, columns 1-5, count 1-6
    055-084 inclusive for row 2, columns 1-5, count 1-6
    109-138 inclusive for row 3, columns 1-5, count 1-6
    163-192 inclusive for row 4, columns 1-5, count 1-6

You would also see these indexes and their corresponding character values if you consulted Figure 6.2.

The final task is to call the procedure H_SCROLL2 from the procedure module "h_s2.inc" to perform the scrolling function on the prepared data.

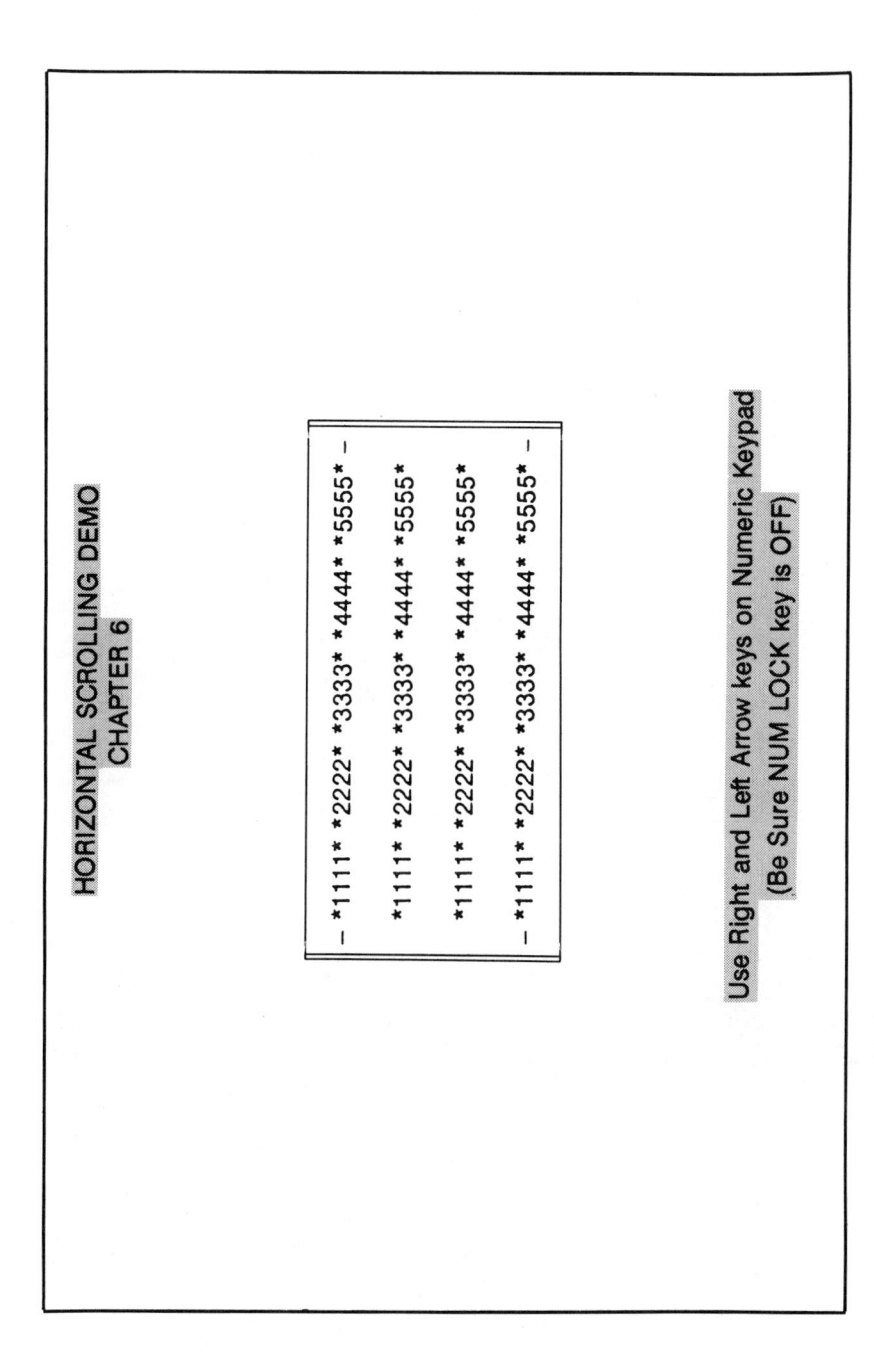

Figure 6.4 Initialized Screen for Horizontal Scroll – Index Address Method

CHAPTER 7

VERTICAL SCROLLING: METHOD 1

7 Vertical Scrolling: Method 1

So far, two different methods of horizontal scrolling have been covered in detail: the screen save/redisplay method (Chapter 5) and the indexed address method (Chapter 6). Both of these techniques have their vertical scrolling counterparts. This chapter will cover vertical scrolling in detail using the screen save/resdisplay method. Chapter 8 will explain vertical scrolling using the indexed address method. Further, Chapter 9 will take up yet a third method using Turbo Pascal's built-in functions INSLINE and DELLINE. Like the horizontal scrolling techniques covered earlier, each vertical technique has its advantages and disadvantages in terms of speed, smoothness, ease of learning, code size, and suitability within a chosen application. They all do the same job, and you must decide which tool is best for the application at hand.

MODULE: V_S1.INC

Below, the module V_S1.INC (read as "Vertical Scroll One Include") is presented. The overall layout of this module is illustrated in Figure 7.1. The main procedure here is V_SCROLL1, and it incorporates six additional subprocedures as shown in that figure.

```
Main Procedure:     V_Scroll1

Subprocedures:      Save_Part_Scr

                    Re_Disp_Part_Scr

                    Move_Partscr_Up
                       (a) Save_Part_Scr
                       (b) Re_Disp_Part_Scr

                    Disp_New_Bottom_Row

                    Move_Partscr_Down
                       (a) Save_Part_Scr
                       (b) Re_Disp_Part_Scr

                    Disp_New_Top_Row

       Note:  Move_Partscr_Down    (Read as Move Part Screen Downward)
              Move_Partscr_Up      (Read as Move Part Screen Upward)
```

Figure 7.1 Procedures and Subprocedures of Module "v_s1.inc"

To accomplish the vertical scrolling effect, assume that the screen already holds 5 six-character-wide display columns of scrollable data in 4 rows as shown in Figure 7.2.

To achieve a "scrolling down" effect (towards larger integers), the already displayed bottom three rows starting at row 2 are first saved into memory using the variable "copy_of_part_scr." This saved portion of the screen is then immediately redisplayed from memory back onto the screen, but starting at the first row (row 1). Once this three-row section of screen has been moved, the next larger row of the data array "array contents" is written to the screen with "write" statements in the loop starting at line 0710 of the subprocedure DISP_NEW_BOTTOM_ROW.

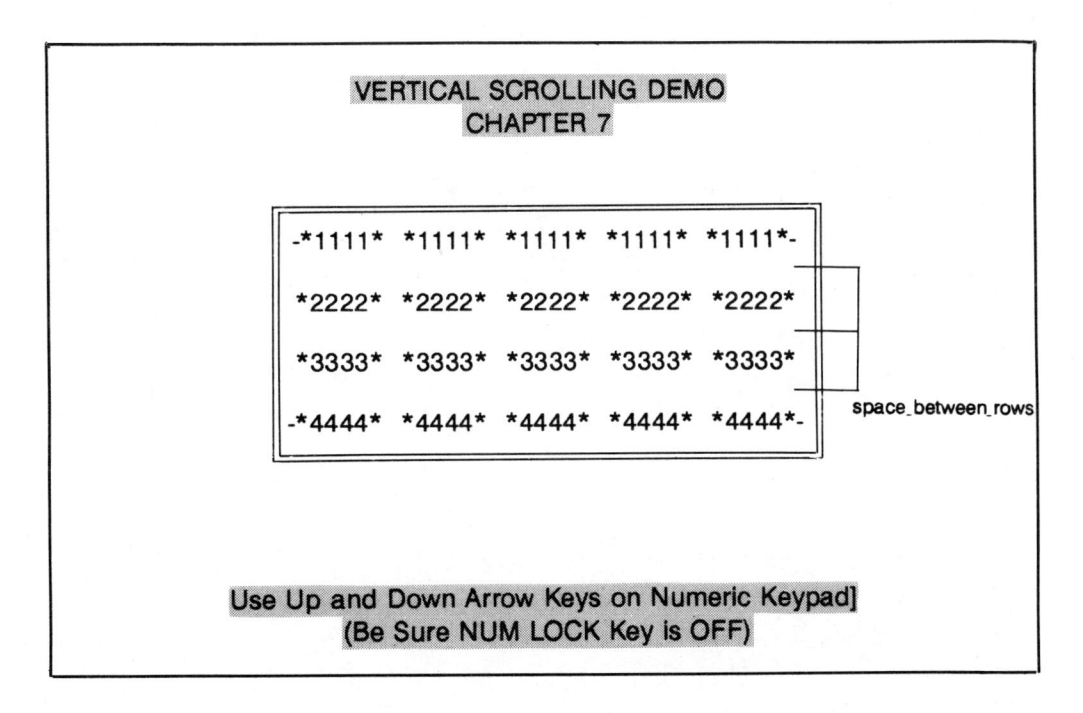

Figure 7.2 Initialized Screen Layout for Vertical Scrolling — Save/Redisplay Method

7 Vertical Scrolling: Method 1

To achieve a "scroll up" effect towards smaller index values, the already displayed three top rows (starting at row 1) are first saved into memory using the variable "copy_of_part_scr." This saved portion of the screen is then immediately redisplayed from the variable back to the screen but now starting at row 2. Once this task is done, the next smaller row of the data array "array_contents" is written to the screen with the write statement in the loop at line 0935 in the procedure DISP_NEW_TOP ROW.

Following is the code for the module V_S1.INC (vertical scroll using method 1 — the screen save/redisplay technique):

```
{=============================================================}
0005  {v_s1.inc}
0010  { This ".inc" file contains all the file saving and scrolling
0015    routines that are OVERHEAD REQUIREMENTS of the program
0020    "v_s1.drv".
0025    On disk as "v_s1.inc".
0030  }
0035
0040  {-----------------------------------------------------------}
0043
0045  procedure     V_SCROLL1(tlc,tlr,brc,brr,
0050                          sp_betw_rows      : integer;
0055                          var array_contents : a);
0060
0065  label
0070        rep_read;
0075
0080  const
0085        bell           = #$07;
0090        scroll_up      = #$48;
0095        scroll_down    = #$50;
0100        carriage_ret   = #$0d;
0105
0110  var
0115        h11,v11        : integer;  {derived from tlc,tlr etc....}
0120        adj_tl_row,
0125        adj_br_row     : integer;
0130        scroll_choice  : char;
0135        exit_scroll    : boolean;
0140        i,j            : integer;      {counter variables....}
0145
0150        i_tot , k_tot  : integer;
0155        x_coord,y_coord: integer;
0160  {-----------------------------------------------------------}
0163
0165        procedure SAVE_PART_SCR(tlc,tlr,brc,brr,
0170                          var copy_of_part_scr : screen_copy);
0175
0180        var
0185             i,k       : integer;
0190             h11,v11   : integer;
0195
0200        Begin    {sub procedure save_part_scr}
0205             window(1,1,80,25);
0210             h11 := brc - tlc + 1;
```

continued...

122

Vertical Scrolling: Method 1   7

...from previous page

```
0215                vll := brr - tlr + 1;
0220                gotoxy(tlc,tlr);
0225                FOR i := 1 to vll DO      {down thru rows}
0230                Begin
0235                    j := ((tlr - 1) * 160) + ((tlc - 1) * 2);
0240                    FOR k := 1 to hll DO   {across thru columns}
0245                    Begin
0250                        CHR_IN(j,copy_of_part_scr[i,k]);
0255                        { source(j) , destination(copy......) }
0260                        j := j + 2;
0265                    End;
0270                    tlc := tlc;            {same column.........}
0275                    tlr := tlr + 1;        {drop down to next row}
0280                End;
0285        End;       {sub procedure save_part_scr}
0290 {-----------------------------------------------------------------}
0295
0300        procedure    RE_DISP_PART_SCR(tlc,tlr,brc,brr  : integer;
0305                                     var copy_of_part_scr   :
0310                                                      screen_copy);
0315
0320        var
0325            i,j,k,
0330            hll,vll,
0335            count,
0340            count_of_chars_per_line : integer;
0345
0350        Begin    {sub procedure re_disp_part_scr}
0355            window(1,1,80,25);
0360            hll := brc - tlc + 1;
0365            vll := brc - tlc + 1;
0370            count_of_chars_per_line := 1;
0375            count := 0;
0380            FOR i := 1 to vll DO           {down thru rows.....}
0385            Begin
0390                FOR k := 1 to hll DO {across thru columns}
0395                Begin
0400                    count := count + 1;
0405                    screen_copy_buffer[count] :=
0410                    copy_of_part_scr[i,k];
0415                End;
0420            End;
0425            j := ((tlr - 1) * 160) + ((tlc - 1) * 2);
0430            {supply CHR_OUT with it's initial value....}
0435            FOR count := 1 to 170 DO     {5 * 35}
0440            Begin
0445                CHR_OUT(j,ORD(screen_copy_buffer[count]));
0450                {   destination(j) , source(ORD(.......) }
0455                count_of_chars_per_line := count_of_chars_per_line
0460                                           + 1;
0465                IF (count_of_chars_per_line > hll) THEN
0470                Begin
0475                    tlr := tlr + 1;
0480                    j := ((tlr - 1) * 160) + ((tlc - 1) * 2);
0485                    count_of_chars_per_line := 1;
0490                End
0495                ELSE
0500                    j := j + 2;     {every second, even numbered }
0505                                    {screen memory loc. is the   }
0510                                    {character part.             }
```

continued...

123

7 Vertical Scrolling: Method 1

...from previous page

```
0515            End;
0520        End;      {sub procedure re_disp_part_scr}
0525  {------------------------------------------------------------}
0527
0530        procedure MOVE_PARTSCR_UP(tlc,tlr,atlr,
0535                               brc,brr,abrr  : integer);
0540                     {make room on the bottom row         }
0545                     {assoc. with "disp_new_bottom_row"}
0550
0555        Begin     {sub-procedure move_partscr_up}
0560            {   tlc := 23 ; atlr:= 11;        }
0565            {   brc := 56 ; brr := 15;        }
0570            {   contains info to be moved up  }
0575            SAVE_PART_SCR(tlc,atlr,brc,brr,
0580                          copy_of_part_scr);
0585            {* delay(2000); *}
0590
0595            window(tlc,tlr,brc,abrr);  {(23,9,56,13);}
0600            clrscr;
0605            {* delay(2000); *}
0610            {   tlc := 23 ; tlr := 9;        }
0615            {   brc := 49 ; abrr := 13;      }
0620            RE_DISP_PART_SCR(tlc,tlr,brc,abrr,
0625                             copy_of_part_scr);
0630        End;      {sub-procedure move_partscr_up}
0635  {------------------------------------------------------------}
0637
0640        procedure DISP_NEW_BOTTOM_ROW(k_tot,i_tot : integer);
0645               {associated with "move_partscr_up"}
0650        var
0655            i,k : integer;
0660
0665        Begin     {sub-procedure disp_new_bottom_row}
0670            window(1,1,80,25);
0675            k := k_tot;
0680            i := i_tot;
0685            gotoxy(tlc,brr);   {(23,15)}
0690            x_coord := WHEREX ; y_coord := WHEREY;
0695            FOR k := 1 to 5 DO
0700            Begin
0705                gotoxy(x_coord,y_coord);
0710                write(array_contents[i + 3 , k]);
0715                {* delay(2000); *}
0720                x_coord := x_coord + 7 ; y_coord := y_coord;
0725            End;
0730        End;      {sub-procedure disp_new_bottom_row}
0735  {------------------------------------------------------------}
0737
0740        procedure    MOVE_PARTSCR_DOWN(tlc,tlr,atlr,
0745                                brc,brr,abrr : integer);
0750                     {make room on the top row           }
0755                     {associated with "disp_new_top_row"}
0760
0765        Begin     {sub-procedure move_partscr_down}
0770            {   tlc := 23 ; tlr := 9;        }
0775            {   brc := 56 ; abrr:= 13;       }
0780            {   contains info to be moved TO bottom}
0785            SAVE_PART_SCR(tlc,tlr,brc,brr,
0790                          copy_of_part_scr);
0795            {* delay(2000) *}
0800
```

continued...

...from previous page

```
0805              window(tlc,atlr,brc,brr);    {window(23,11,56,15);}
0810              clrscr;
0815              {* delay(2000) *}
0820              {   tlc := 23 ; atlr := 11;   }
0825              {   brc := 56 ; brr  := 15;   }
0830              {info saved FROM top is moved TO bottom}
0835              RE_DISP_PART_SCR(tlc,atlr,brc,brr,
0840                                        copy_of_part_scr);
0845        End;       {sub-procedure move_partscr_down}
0850   {--------------------------------------------------------------}
0855
0860        procedure DISP_NEW_TOP_ROW(k_tot,i_tot : integer);
0865                  {associated with "move_partscr_down"}
0870
0875        var
0880            i,k  : integer;
0885
0890        Begin      {sub-procedure disp_new_top_row}
0895            window(1,1,80,25);
0900            k := k_tot;
0905            i := i_tot;
0910            gotoxy(tlc,tlr);      {  (23,9);}
0915            x_coord := WHEREX ; y_coord := WHEREY;
0920            FOR k := 1 to 5 DO {same row,changing cols.}
0925            Begin
0930                gotoxy(x_coord,y_coord);
0935                write(array_contents[i,k]);
0940                x_coord := x_coord + 7 ; y_coord := y_coord;
0945            End;
0950        End;       {sub-procedure disp_new_top_row}
0955   {--------------------------------------------------------------}
0960
0965   Begin      {procedure v_scroll1}
0970        window(tlc,tlr,brc,brr);
0975        exit_scroll := false; {initialize exit condition}
0980        adj_tl_row := tlr  + (sp_betw_rows    + 1);
0985                     { 9   + (   1            + 1) = 11 }
0990        adj_br_row := brr  - (sp_betw_rows    + 1);
0995                     { 15  - (   1            + 1) = 13 }
1000        i_tot := 1;
1005        k_tot := 1;
1010
1015        REPEAT
1020            rep_read:  {a label with colon}
1025            read(KBD,scroll_choice);
1030            CASE(scroll_choice) OF
1035
1040            scroll_up      :    Begin     {Up Arrow key pressed}
1045                                    i_tot := i_tot - 1;
1050                                    k_tot := k_tot + 0;
1055                                    IF(i_tot < 1) THEN
1060                                    Begin
1065                                        i_tot := 1;
1070                                        goto rep_read;
1075                                    End;
1080                                    MOVE_PARTSCR_DOWN(tlc,tlr,adj_tl_row,
1085                                                brc,brr,adj_br_row);
1090                                    DISP_NEW_TOP_ROW(k_tot,i_tot);
```

continued...

7 Vertical Scrolling: Method 1

...from previous page

```
1095                                End; {scroll_up}
1100
1105           scroll_down : Begin      {Down Arrow key pressed}
1110                                i_tot := i_tot + 1;
1115                                k_tot := k_tot + 0;
1120                                IF(i_tot > 6) THEN {7 + 3 > 9}
1125                                Begin
1130                                    k_tot := 6;
1135                                    goto rep_read;
1140                                End;
1145                                MOVE_PARTSCR_UP(tlc,tlr,adj_tl_row,
1150                                                brc,brr,adj_br_row);
1155                                DISP_NEW_BOTTOM_ROW(k_tot,i_tot);
1160                           End;      {scroll_up}
1165
1170           carriage_ret : Begin
1175                                exit_scroll := true;
1180                                write(bell);
1185                           End;
1190
1195           ELSE
1200                       {if none of above choices is selected...}
1205                       {nothing--go back and press correct key.}
1210           END;        {case statement}
1215        UNTIL exit_scroll = true;
1220 End;     {procedure v_scroll1}
{================== END OF "v_s1.inc" overhead file ==================}
```

V_S1.INC: NOTES

V_SCROLL1

The procedure V_SCROLL1 orchestrates the activities of the five sub-procedures in this module. The parameters listed starting at line 0045 are

- the overall dimensions of the scrolling display window: top left column ("tlc"), top left row ("tlr"), bottom right column ("brr"), and bottom right row ("brr").

- the space between rows ("sp_betw_rows"), which is another required formatting variable used to separate the rows on the screen display. In this example, only one space has been placed between vertically adjacent rows.

- the array variable used to hold the actual data that is to be scrolled on the screen. This variable is called "array_contents." Refer to Figure 7.3.

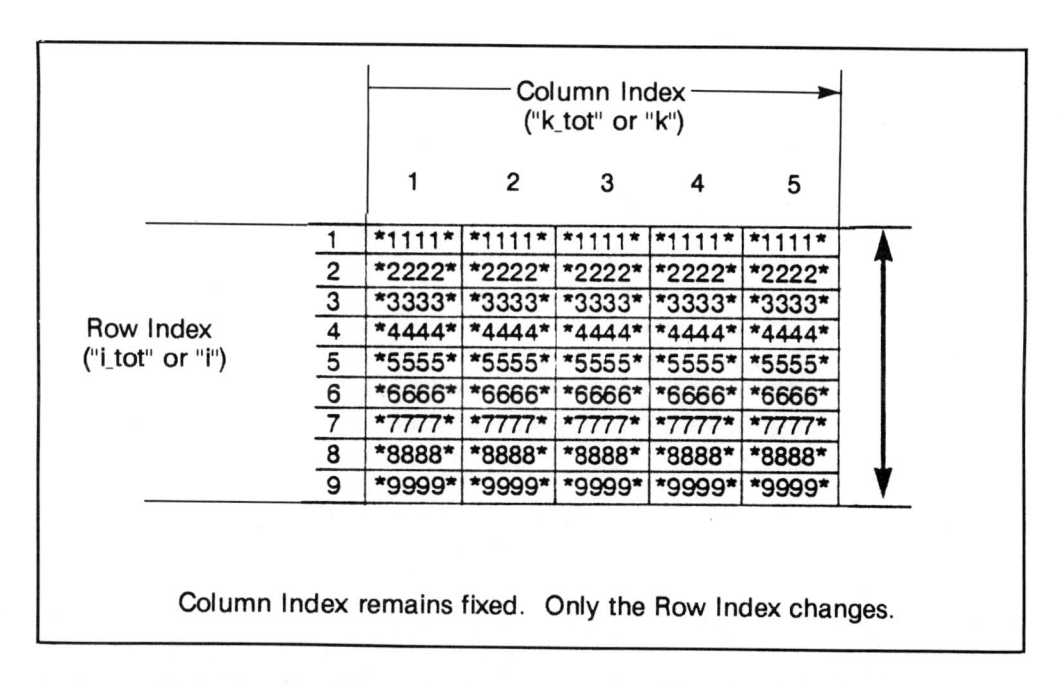

	Column Index 1	2	3	4	5
1	*1111*	*1111*	*1111*	*1111*	*1111*
2	*2222*	*2222*	*2222*	*2222*	*2222*
3	*3333*	*3333*	*3333*	*3333*	*3333*
4	*4444*	*4444*	*4444*	*4444*	*4444*
5	*5555*	*5555*	*5555*	*5555*	*5555*
6	*6666*	*6666*	*6666*	*6666*	*6666*
7	*7777*	*7777*	*7777*	*7777*	*7777*
8	*8888*	*8888*	*8888*	*8888*	*8888*
9	*9999*	*9999*	*9999*	*9999*	*9999*

Column Index ("k_tot" or "k")

Row Index ("i_tot" or "i")

Column Index remains fixed. Only the Row Index changes.

Figure 7.3 A Schematic of the Two-dimensional Array Variable "Array_Contents" for a Vertical Scroll

In the "const" section of the declaration, the scan code of the Up Arrow key is represented as a constant at line 0090. Likewise, the scan codes of the Down Arrow and Return keys are shown at lines 0095 and 0100.

In the "var" section of the declaration, the variable ("hll") stands for horizontal line length and is represented by the expression ("brc - tlc + 1"). This expression causes both the first and last columns of the defined scrolling window to be counted as part of the length of the horizontal line. Likewise, ("vll") stands for vertical line length and is represented by the expression ("brr - tlr + 1"). This expression also will include both the first and last rows of the vertical border of the scrolling window.

7 Vertical Scrolling: Method 1

The variables "adj_tl_row" (adjusted top left row) and "adj_br_row" (adjusted bottom right row) are defined at lines 0980 and 0990 of the main body of the V_SCROLL1 procedure and are used in the parameter lists of the subprocedures MOVE_ PARTSCR_ UP and MOVE_ PARTSCR DOWN to supply the needed information to correctly move parts of the display window vertically inside the overall display window. In the MOVE_PARTSCR... procedures, the adjusted top left row is abbreviated "atlr," and the adjusted bottom right row is abbreviated "abrr."

The variables "i_tot" (row total) and "k_tot" (column total) are essential to this routine. "K_tot" is initially given a value of 1 at line 1005 and is unchanged throughout the whole horizontal scrolling routine because in a vertical scroll, the columns remain unchanged. "I_ tot" is initially given a value of 1 at line 1000 and changes each time the Up or Down Arrow keys (keys 8 and 2 on the numeric keypad) are pressed. "I_tot" or "i in the subprocedures is the row index of the data array variable "array_contents."

If the Down Arrow key is pressed, as in a "scroll_down" at line 1105, then "i_tot" *increases* by 1. The procedure MOVE_PARTSCR_UP performs its task (see Figure 7.4), followed by writing of the new bottom row of "array_contents" using the parameters "k" and "i" as indexes.

Lines 1120-1130 were written to prevent the scrolling routine from scrolling down past the last (ninth) row of the array variable "array_contents." DISP_NEW_BOTTOM_ROW adjusts the "i" index by adding 3 to it to display the next larger display row of "array_contents." If "i" is, say, 7, then the row to next be displayed when scrolling down would be (7 + 3 = 10), but the variable "array_contents" has only 9 rows. Line 1120 prevents overshooting the defined maximum number of rows.

If the Up Arrow key is pressed, as in "scroll_up" at line 1025, then "i tot" is decreased by 1. But if "i_tot" is already 1, then "i_tot" would become less than 1 (line 1045). If "i_tot" is less than 1, line 1065 resets "i tot" to 1 and control is passed back to the label at line 1020 for a retry. Assuming "i_tot" is greater than 1, then "i_tot" is changed to i_tot - 1 (line 1045). The procedure MOVE_PARTSCR_DOWN will make room for one row at the top of the scrolling window at line 1. The procedure DISP_NEW_TOP_ROW, using the parameters "k" and "i," then writes out the appropriate row of "array_contents" to the computer screen. Note that "i" is used without adjustment in the subprocedure DISP NEW_TOP_ROW.

Vertical Scrolling: Method 1 7

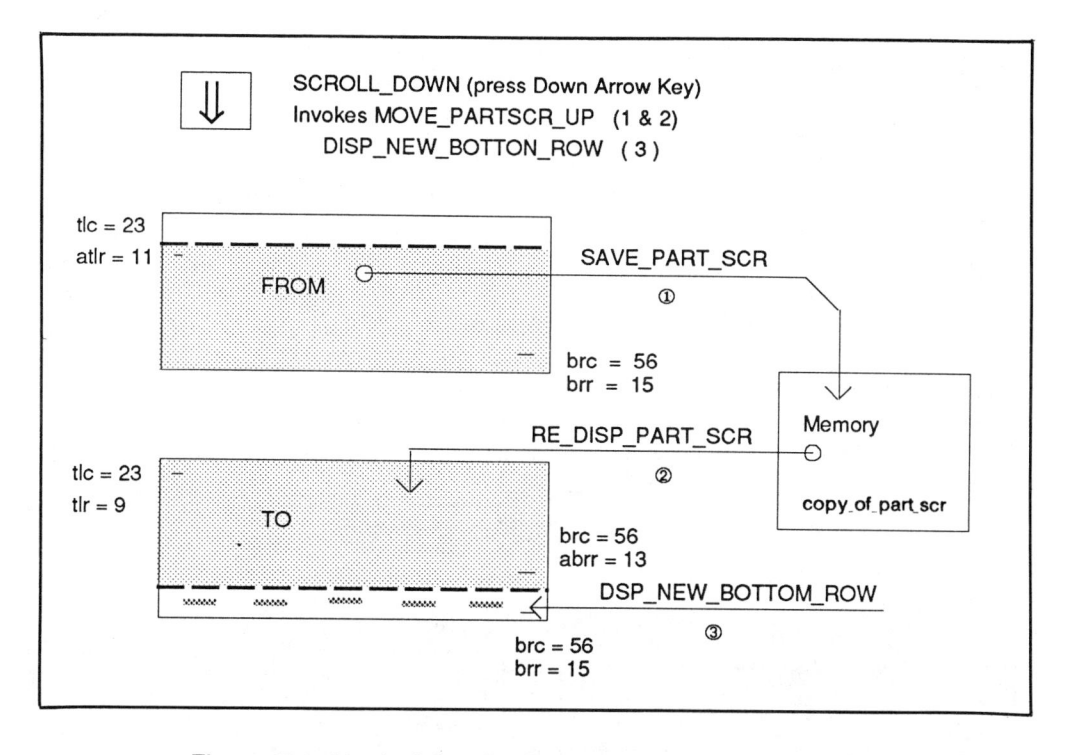

Figure 7.4 Vertical Scroll — Pressing the Down Arrow Key

The variables, "x_coord" and "y_coord" (read as "x_coordinate, y_coordinate") are used in more than just one of the subprocedures, and, like "hll" and "vll," they are included in the declaration section of the V SCROLL1 procedure. "X_coord" and "y_coord" are used for cursor positioning preceding the "Write" statements in the procedures DISP NEW_TOP_ROW and DISP_NEW_BOTTOM_ROW.

SAVE_PART_SCR/RE_DISP_PART_SCR

The mechanics of these two subprocedures were discussed in Chapter 4 and Chapter 5. Refer to the appropriate pages in these chapters if you do not understand how these procedures work.

129

7 Vertical Scrolling: Method 1

MOVE_PART_SCR_DOWN

This subprocedure performs the first of two steps involved in scrolling the data in "array_contents" upwards in the direction of the smaller numbers. The first step is to save to ordinary memory the top three rows (and the spaces between them) in the display window and then immediately redisplay them as a unit back onto the screen, *but* two rows *below* their original position (note the spacing between the screen rows of Figure 7.2). This action will produce the downward scrolling effect mentioned earlier and will leave the top row (row 9) of the display screen open (see Figure 7.5).

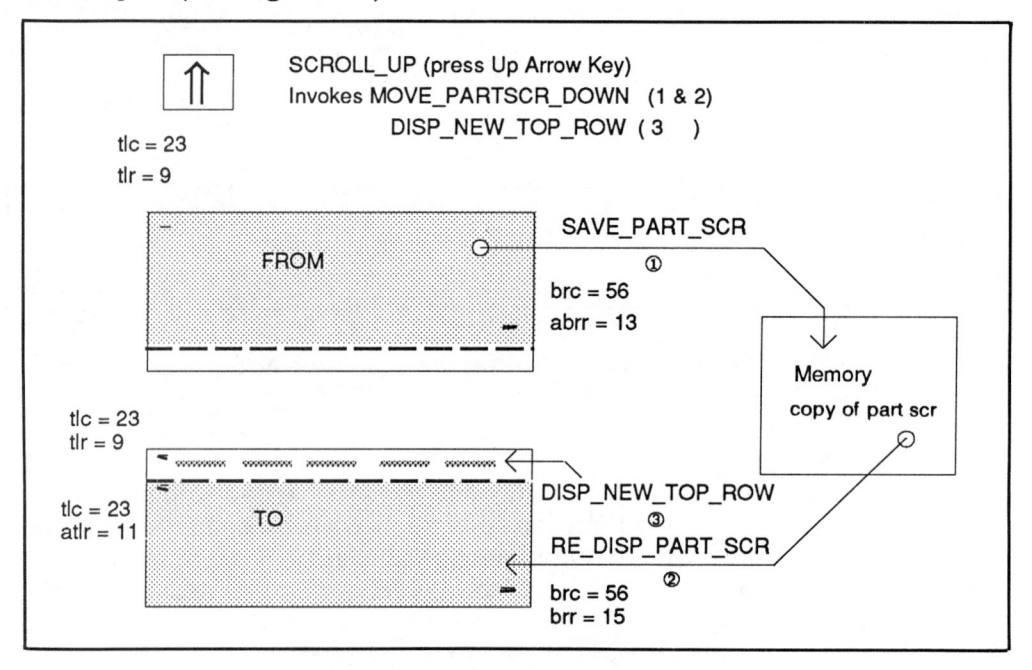

Figure 7.5 Vertical Scroll — Pressing the Up Arrow Key

Vertical Scrolling: Method 1 7

The variables "tlc" and "tlr" define the upper left corner of the display screen to be saved by SAVE_PART_SCR. "Abrr" is the adjusted bottom right row and is defined as follows (see Figure 7.5):

  abrr = brr - sp_betw_rows - 1 ....or
         15 -   1   - 1 = 13

The bottom right corner of the screen section to be saved is brc = 56.

Immediately after this section of screen is saved into the two-dimensional variable "copy_of_part_scr," the screen area *into* which it will be redisplayed is cleared (lines 0805 & 0810). This screen area has its top left corner defined by "tlc" = 23 and its adjusted top left row defined by the following expression:

  atlr = tlr + sp_betw_rows + 1 ....or
          9 +   1   + 1 = 11;

"Brc" (bottom right column) is 56 and "brr" (bottom right row) is 15. Note that "sp_betw_rows" is global to this subprocedure as it is part of the parameter line of the V_SCROLL1 procedure.

Once the defined area is cleared, the procedure RE_DISP_PART_SCR will use the same parameters to rewrite the contents of "copy_of_part scr" into the newly blanked screen area. This procedure completes the first step of scrolling data vertically in the upward direction.

DISP_NEW_TOP_ROW

The second step of the upward vertical scroll is to write out the appropriate row into the space vacated at the top of the display window. The variable "i_tot" in the subprocedure's parameter list at line 0860 provides the proper starting row index of "array_contents." "K_tot" provides the unchanging column index (note the assignment statements at lines 0900 and 0905). The screen location for writing the next smaller row is provided at lines 0915 and 0930. The new top row to be displayed to screen is written in a loop starting at line 0920.

On the display screen, "i" (the index of "array_contents") always refers to the index of the top-most row's contents. Since the scroll direction is toward smaller indexes, "i_tot" (line 1045) will change from, say, 4 to 3, and the index of the new row to be displayed from the subprocedure DISP_NEW_TOP_ROWwill be "i" = 3. Figure 7.5 shows how the "scroll_up" operation at line 0935 would look.

7 Vertical Scrolling: Method 1

MOVE_PARTSCR_UP

This subprocedure, like its counterpart, shifts a predefined section of the display screen two rows up to make room at the bottom of the display screen. In this case, the row contents of the display screen are moved *from* the screen area bounded by "tlc" = 23, "atlr" = 11 at the top left corner and "brc" = 56, "brr" = 15 at the bottom right corner *to* the new screen location bounded by "tlc" = 23, "tlr" = 9 at the top left corner and "brc" = 56, "abrr" = 13 at the bottom right corner. The vertical upward shifting action that you see on the screen is a result of the screen save subprocedure at line 0575, followed immediately by the screen redisplay subprocedure at line 0620. The end result of the procedure MOVE_PARTSCR_UP is a blank row at the bottom of the display window. Activate line 0605 to see this effect. Also see Figure 7.4.

DISP_NEW_BOTTOM_ROW

After the predefined screen area has been moved upward by two rows, the second step can be performed. This task is to display the appropriate row of character text from "array_contents" at the bottom of the screen display window. Exactly which row of "array_contents" is determined by the variable "i" (defined at line 0680) and some constant number whose value is 1 less than the number of rows shown in the display window. In this case, that constant value is (4 - 1 = 3). Since the Down Arrow key was pressed, the "i_tot" index has been increased by 1 (line 1110). So, for example, if "i_tot" is 4 before the Down Arrow key is pressed, then "i_tot" will change to 5 after the key is pressed. Note, however, that the display row with "i" = 8 (5 + 3) as the index will become the new bottom row to be written from "array_contents" into the cleared bottom row of the display screen window (see Figure 7.4 and line 0710).

MODULE: V_S1.DRV

The driver program V_S1.DRV enables the vertical scrolling module V_S1.INC to do its job. Besides invoking V_S1.INC, the driver program also performs three enabling tasks. The first is to create the data that will actually be scrolled on the display screen (procedure CREATE_SCROLL_DATA). The second is to set up the starting position for the data in the scrolling window (procedure INITIALIZE_SCROLL_WINDOW). And the third is to supply the vertical scrolling routine (V_SCROLL1) with the correct parameters to perform the vertical scroll-

Vertical Scrolling: Method 1 — 7

ing. The procedure V_SCROLL1 is one of the procedures in the V S1.INC module, an external procedure invoked at line 0125 in the driver routine. Following is the code for the driver routine:

```
{========================================================================}
0005  program   v_s1(input,output);
0010  { Vertical scrolling driver program.
0015    On disk as "v_s1.drv"
0020  }
0025
0030  type
0035        str 6           = string[6];
0040        a               = ARRAY[1..9,1..5] of str6;  {9 rows x 5 cols}
0045        screen_copy     = ARRAY[1..5,1..34] of char;
0050        screen_copy_buf = ARRAY[1..170] of char; {5 x 34}
0055
0060  var
0065        array_contents      : a;
0070        copy_of_part_str    : screen_copy;
0075        screen_copy_buffer  : screen_copy_buf;
0080        i,k                 : integer;
0085
0090        tl_col,tl_row,      {scrolling window parameters}
0095        br_col,br_row,
0100        space_between_rows  : integer;
0105  {========================================================================}
0110
0115  {$i chrinout.inc}
0120  {$i windows.inc}
0125  {$i v_s1.inc}
0130
0135  {========================================================================}
0140
0145  procedure       CREATE_COMMAND_LINE;
0150
0155  Begin    {procedure create_command_line}
0160        window(1,1,80,25);
0165        TEXTCOLOR(0);TEXTBACKGROUND(15); {black char on white}
0170        gotoxy(29,2);write(' VERTICAL SCROLLING DEMO ');
0175        gotoxy(36,3);write(' CHAPTER 7 ');
0180        TEXTCOLOR(15);TEXTBACKGROUND(0); {white char on black}
0185        gotoxy(19,22);
0190        write('Use UP and DOWN Arrow Keys on Numeric Keypad');
0195        gotoxy(27,23);
0200        write('(Be Sure NUM LOCK Key is OFF)');
0205  End;       {procedure create_command_line}
0210  {------------------------------------------------------------------------}
0213
0215  procedure       CREATE_SCROLL_DATA(var array_contents : a);
0220
0225  var
0230        i,k : integer;   {indexes for use in procedure}
0235
0240  Begin    {procedure create_scroll_data}
0245        window(1,1,80,25);
0250        FOR i := 1 to 9 DO   {ROW 1 to 9}
0255        Begin
0260             FOR k := 1 to 5 DO   {COL 1 to 5}
```

continued...

133

7 Vertical Scrolling: Method 1

...from previous page

```
0265                Begin
0270                    CASE (i) OF
0275
0280                       1   : array_contents[i,k] := '*1111*';
0285                       2   : array_contents[i,k] := '*2222*';
0290                       3   : array_contents[i,k] := '*3333*';
0295                       4   : array_contents[i,k] := '*4444*';
0300                       5   : array_contents[i,k] := '*5555*';
0305                       6   : array_contents[i,k] := '*6666*';
0310                       7   : array_contents[i,k] := '*7777*';
0315                       8   : array_contents[i,k] := '*8888*';
0320                       9   : array_contents[i,k] := '*9999*';
0325
0330                    END; {case}
0335                End;
0340        End;
0345 End;        {procedure create_scroll_data}
0350 {----------------------------------------------------------------}
0355
0360 procedure     INITIALIZE_SCROLL_WINDOW(var array_contents : a);
0365
0370 var
0375      i,k        : integer;
0380      x_coord,               {x_coord is the column }
0385      y_coord    : integer;{y_coord is the row         }
0390
0395 Begin    {procedure initialize_scroll_window}
0400       window(1,1,80,25);
0405       gotoxy(23,9);
0410       x_coord := WHEREX ; y_coord := WHEREY;
0415
0420       FOR i := 1 to 4 DO            {4 rows....}
0425       Begin
0430           gotoxy(x_coord,y_coord);
0435           FOR k := 1 to 5 DO       {5 columns....}
0440           Begin
0445               write(array_contents[i,k]);
0450               {* delay(500); *}
0455               gotoxy(x_coord + (k * 7) , y_coord);
0460               {across columns in a given row}
0465           End;
0470           x_coord := x_coord;          {col 23}
0475           y_coord := y_coord + 2;      {next row : 9 + 2 = 11}
0480       End;
0485 End;      {procedure initialize scroll_window}
0490 {----------------------------------------------------------------}
0495
0500 Begin    {driver}
0510       window(1,1,80,25);clrscr;
0515       CREATE_COMMAND_LINE;
0520       WINDOW_BORDER(21,8,58,16,1);   {border style #1}
0525       CREATE_SCROLL_DATA(array_contents);
0530       INITIALIZE_SCROLL_WINDOW(array_contents);
0535
0540       tl_col := 23 ; tl_row := 9;    {overall window dimensions of}
0545       br_col := 56 ; br_row := 15;   {screen area to be scrolled  }
0550       space_between_rows : = 1;
0555       V_SCROLL1(tl_col,tl_row,br_col,br_row,
0560                 space_between_rows,
0565                 array_contents);
0570 End.       {driver}
{================================================================}
```

134

V_S1.DRV: NOTES

Before some of the details of the above procedures are described, a clear distinction needs to be made between the variable "array_contents" and the variable "copy_of_part_scr" found in the declaration section at lines 0065 and 0070.

"Array_contents" is a 9-row by 5-column array containing the actual data or information that is scrolled up and down on the screen. This information can be created by a separate computation elsewhere in the driver program; it can be fed into the array from data held on a disk; or it can be created solely for demonstration purposes as was done in this routine. Each data element of the 9-row by 5-column data array is a string of 6 characters consisting of

a "*"|1 digit|1 digit|1 digit|1 digit|a "*"

Each row of "array_contents" has a total of five of these individual six-character elements.

"Copy_of_part_scr" (read as "copy of part screen") represents a two-dimensional, rectangular area of the computer screen. Remember that it is only a part of the full scrolling display window—that part first saved into memory and then later redisplayed back onto the screen at a different location (per the subprocedures SAVE_PART_SCR and RE DISP_PART_SCR that are invoked by MOVE_PARTSCR_UP and MOVE_PARTSCR_DOWN). See Figures 7.4 and 7.5. This screen area is represented inside the computer's memory by the variable "copy of_part_scr" whose Type is "screen_copy"—an array whose dimensions are only 5 rows deep (remember that you are saving or redisplaying only 5 of the 7 screen display rows at a time) and 34 columns wide. Note that the full display column width of the Layout is (col 56 - col 23 + 1) or 34 columns total. This computation *excludes* the cursor positioning columns, 22 and 57.

Note that the variable "screen_copy_buffer" at line 0075 is the one-dimensional equivalent of "copy_of_part_sc." It has $34 \times 5 = 170$ single character elements and is used in the subprocedure RE_DISP_PART SCR to map saved screen characters back from memory and onto the one-dimensional memory array MEM[bwseg:bwofs + j] for display on the screen.

7 Vertical Scrolling: Method 1

The first task of the driver routine is to create some data to scroll. The procedure CREATE_SCROLL_DATA performs this job. Since this is only a demonstration, the method of data creation (generation) will be simple. Data will be defined as shown in Figure 7.3. The loops at lines 0250 and 0260 together with the CASE..END structure will store all the six-character string elements into their proper locations in "array_contents."

Once data has been created and stored into the array, preparation for scrolling is needed. The procedure INITIALIZE_SCROLL_WINDOW handles this task. The object is to put the first 4 rows of the data array onto the display screen. This task is performed by the loops at lines 0420 and 0435. The variable "i" is the row index, and "k" is the column index. Formatting on the screen itself is performed using the GOTOXY procedure, the WHEREX and WHEREY functions, and the variables "x_coord" and "y_coord." The number "7" at line 0455 represents the number of spaces from the start of one column to the start of the next adjacent column (6 spaces/col + 1 space between columns). Again, note that this procedure refers to the array "array_contents" in the parameter list at line 0065. After this procedure is finished, the screen will appear as shown in Figure 7.2.

The final task of this demonstration program is to define the parameters that will be required by the V_SCROLL1 procedure to "drive" the program or make it work. Feeding the procedure its needed parameters begins at line 0540. Observe that the dimensions of the scrolling window are relative to the whole 80×25 screen display window. Also observe that the column width of 6 is the same width as the data elements in the data array "array_contents." Finally, observe at line 0550 and in Figure 7.2 that a variable called "space_between_rows" has been defined. This variable enables the subprocedures inside the V SCROLL1 procedure to calculate "adj_tl_row" or "atlr" (adjusted top left row) and "adj_br_row" or "abrr" (adjusted bottom right row) values.

CHAPTER 8

VERTICAL SCROLLING: METHOD 2

8 Vertical Scrolling: Method 2

Chapter 7 discussed how to vertically scroll screen data using the "save/redisplay screen" method. Along with learning the technique itself, you also became aware of its operational strengths and weaknesses in terms of speed, amount of coding, and flexibility. This chapter will show you how to perform the same vertical scrolling operation using the same data but implementing it with the faster "index address" method. If you have understood this technique as introduced in Chapter 6, this chapter should present no difficulties; however, if you did have trouble, this chapter will reinforce the index calculation concept by approaching it from the vertical scrolling perspective. The repetition plus change in point of view should enhance your understanding of this technique.

At this point you may be wondering why there are all these different methods for doing the same thing. Why not just learn one method and go on to something else? The answer is that success in learning the same task from different points of view or with different approaches will always provide you with a certain creative flexibility you would otherwise lack; that is, you will be able to produce better, more imaginative solutions to applications problems because you have a broader perspective from which to work. For example, in Chapter 12, you will create an applications program that scrolls a bar graph horizontally across the screen using the "index address" method. If you understand the operational mechanics of the program, you should find yourself asking "creative" questions: Was this approach the best one to use? Would it still be suitable if the graph data was represented as a set of points on a graphics screen? Will looking at the problem as an alternative approach ("save/redisplay screen" method) reveal important characteristics of the problem that would otherwise remain hidden because of a committment to the current approach?

These questions and others like them can only be asked (and answered) by the programmer who has experience in approaching problems from more than one point of view. Creative imagination is not a cheap commodity. It can only come after you have acquired a strong command of operational detail.

MODULE: V_S2.INC

The overall objective of this module is to show you how to scroll a display screen of data up or down using the Up and Down Arrow keys on the Numeric Keypad. This module consists of two procedures. V SCROLL2 is the main controlling procedure in which the arrow keys

Vertical Scrolling: Method 2   8

are pressed and the cumulative row and column indexes of the data array to be scrolled are calculated. The subprocedure REWRITE_SCR BYROW (rewrite screen by row) actually performs vertical scrolling of data up and down the screen and is analagous to the procedure combinations MOVE_PARTSCR_DOWN/DISP_NEW_TOP_ROW or MOVE PARTSCR_UP/DISP_NEW_BOTTOM_ROW from Chapter 7. Following is the code for this module:

```
{=========================================================================}
0005 {v_s2.inc}
0010 { This ".inc" file contains all the file saving and scrolling
0015   routines that are OVERHEAD REQUIREMENTS of the program
0020   "v_s2.drv".
0025   On disk as "v_s2.inc".
0030 }
0035
0040 {-----------------------------------------------------------------}
0045
0050 procedure V_SCROLL2(tlc,tlr : integer;
0055             var screen_copy_buffer : scr_copy_buf);
0060
0065 label
0070     rep_read;
0075
0080 const
0085     bell           = #$07;
0090     scroll_up      = #$48;
0095     scroll_down    = #$50;
0100     carrige_ret    = #$0d;
0105
0110 var
0115     scroll_choice  : char;
0120     exit_scroll    : boolean;
0125     i_tot,k_tot    : integer;
0130 {-----------------------------------------------------------------}
0135
0140     procedure   REWRITE_SCR_BYROW(k_tot , i_tot  : integer;
0145                     var screen_copy_buffer : scr_copy_buf);
0150
0155 var
0160     bx,bp,
0165     count,
0170     j,
0175     row,col,
0180     k,i            : integer;
0185
0190 {-----------------------------------------------------------------}
0195
0200     Begin    {sub procedure rewrite_scr_by_row}
0205         col := tlc ; row := tlr; {start loc. for screen write}
0210         j := ((row - 1) * 160) + ((col - 1) * 2);
0215         FOR i := (i_tot) to (i_tot + 3) DO {4 rows}
0220         Begin
0225             FOR k := (k_tot) to (k_tot + 4) DO {1 to 1+4}
0230             Begin
0235                 bx := (i - 1) * 30;  {30 chars/row}
```

...continued

8 Vertical Scrolling: Method 2

...from previous page

```
0240                          bp := (k - 1) * 6;   {6 chars/col }
0245                          FOR count := 1 to 6 DO {6 chars per display column}
0250                          Begin
0255                             CHR_OUT(j,ORD(screen_copy_buffer
0260                                                    [bx + bp + count]));
0265                             {* delay(1000) *}
0270                             j := j + 2;
0275                          End;
0280                          j := j + 2; {skip a space between scr. cols}
0285                       End;
0290                       col := col ; row := row + 2; {same col;next line}
0295                       j := ((row - 1) * 160) + ((col - 1) * 2);
0300                       {recalculate j}
0305                    End;
0310          End;      {sub procedure rewrite_scr_byrow}
0315   {----------------------------------------------------------------}
0320
0325   Begin     {procedure v_scroll2}
0330        window(1,1,80,25);
0335        exit_scroll := false; {initialize exit condition}
0340        k_tot := 1;
0345        i_tot := 1;
0350
0355        REPEAT
0360           rep_read: {a label followed by a colon}
0365           read(KBD,scroll_choice);      {hit a key}
0370           CASE (scoll_choice) OF
0375
0380              scroll_up      : Begin   {press Up Arrow key}
0385                                  i_tot := i_tot - 1;
0390                                  k_tot := k_tot + 0;
0395                                  IF (i_tot < 1) THEN
0400                                  Begin
0405                                     i_tot := 1;
0410                                     goto rep_read;
0415                                  End;
0420                                  REWRITE_SCR_BYROW(k_tot,i_tot,
0425                                              screen_copy_buffer);
0430                               End;   {scroll_up}
0435
0440              scroll_down    : Begin {press Down Arrow key}
0445                                  i_tot := i_tot + 1;
0450                                  k_tot := k_tot + 0;
0455                                  IF (i_tot > 6) THEN
0460                                  Begin
0465                                     i_tot := 6;
0470                                     goto rep_read;
0475                                  End;
0480                                  REWRITE_SCR_BYROW(k_tot,i_tot,
0485                                              screen_copy_buffer);
0490                               End; {scroll_down}
0495
0500              carriage_ret   : Begin
0505                                  exit_scroll := true;
0510                                  write(bell);
0515                               End;
0520
0525              ELSE
0530                 {if none of the above choices are selected...}
0535                 {no action. go back & press one of above keys}
0540           END; {case statement}
0545        UNTIL exit_scroll = true;
0550   End;      {procedure v_scroll2}
0555   {================ END OF "v_s2.inc" overhead file ================}
```

V_S2.INC: NOTES

V_SCROLL2

As mentioned above, this procedure sets up the vertical scrolling of data on the screen. V_SCROLL2 has three parameters fed to it from the main driver routine. The first two, "tlc" and "tlr," are the starting top left column and starting top left row of the screen where the scrolled data will be displayed. These parameters are used in the subprocedure later. The third parameter, "screen_copy_buffer," is a one-dimensional array consisting of 270 characters (ARRAY[1..270] of char). This variable is the one-dimensional equivalent of the two-dimensional array "screen_copy," which is of the type "ARRAY[1..9,1..5] of string[6]" and is equivalent in that it too has 270 character elements (9 x 5 x 6 = 270). This one-dimensional array is necessary because mapping from a two-dimensional array onto the one-dimensional screen memory array MEM[bwseg:bwofs + j] is illegal in Pascal.

In the declaration section, not too much is different from the procedure V_SCROLL1 in Chapter 7. Note, however, that far fewer screen formatting variables are used here than were used in V_SCROLL1.

The scrolling is controlled in the body of the procedure. As long as the Return key is not pressed, you can scroll data up and down for as long as you like. This feature is guaranteed by the REPEAT...UNTIL loop starting at line 0355. If you choose to scroll data upward, press the Up Arrow key (key #8 on the Numeric Keypad). The cumulative row total variable "i_tot" is then decreased by 1. Pressing the Up Arrow key means that you want to display the row of data immediately above (but out of sight) of the row of data currently located at the top-most row position in the screen display window. If "i_tot" is already 1, then line 0385 will force it to be less than 1 (1 - 1 = 0). Then you are outside the minimum value of 1 in the allowed row range of 1-9 inclusive. This situation is corrected at lines 0395-0405 and tried again at line 0365. Assuming "i_tot" is a value greater than 2, pressing the Up Arrow key will decrease "i_tot" by 1, and since the revised "i_tot" value is inside the legal 1-9 range, you can call for a display screen rewrite at line 0420 via the procedure REWRITE_SCR_BYROW (rewrite screen by row).

8 Vertical Scrolling: Method 2

If you want to scroll screen data downwards, press the Down Arrow key (key #2 on the Numeric Keypad). The "i_tot" variable will then be incremented by 1, meaning that you want to display the row of data immediately below the row of data currently at the bottom position in the display window.

Lines 0450-0465 were designed to prevent the row index variable "i_tot" from exceeding 6. An "i_tot" value above 6 (in the demo program) will result in trying to access a row whose index is greater than 9. A row index value greater than 9 for the array variable "screen_copy" is out of range and is therefore illegal. As with "scroll_up" above, an illegal "i_tot" value will reset "i_tot" back to 6 and force a jump to the label "rep read" for a retry.

Assuming that "i_tot" starts within the allowed range of 1-5 inclusive, pressing the Down Arrow key will increment "i_tot" by 1. Since the revised "i_tot" is still within the allowed range of 1 to 6 inclusive, you can bypass the error-handling code and call the REWRITE_SCR BYROW procedure with "i_tot" and "k_tot" and the one-dimensional array "screen_copy_buffer." Note that "k_tot" (the column index of "screen_copy") remains unchanged because during a vertical scroll, the columns of the array remain unchanged while only the rows change.

REWRITE_SCR_BYROW

This procedure actually performs the screen scroll you see after pressing either an Up or Down Arrow key. The technique used to achieve the vertical scroll is radically different from the method in Chapter 7 where predefined areas of the display screen were saved to memory, then moved, and new rows were written into vacated screen areas. Here, the scrolling effect is achieved by arithmetic recalculation of the index values of the array variable "screen_copy_buffer." Each time a new "i_tot" value is calculated in the V_SCROLL2 procedure, a different set of 120 index variables of the 270 possible is computed, and then the reindexed variables "screen_copy_buffer[bx + bp + count]" are written directly to the screen display memory at line 0255.

Vertical Scrolling: Method 2   8

Figure 8.1 shows a schematic of the array variable "screen_copy," which has been created for demonstration purposes. This array can be visualized and laid out as you see in the figure. There are 5 columns numbered 1-5 inclusive and 9 rows numbered 1-9 inclusive. Note that at each array location, there is a six-character string and that each row has the same string value. The strings are set up in this manner to best demonstrate vertical scrolling. If you compute the number of characters in this array, you should find that there are

$$9 \times 5 \text{ positions} \times 6 \text{ characters/position} = 270 \text{ characters}$$

Figure 8.2 shows a schematic of the array variable "screen_copy_buffer," the one-dimensional equivalent of the two-dimensional array "screen copy" in Figure 8.1. It too has 270 locations with each location filled up by one character. If you were to place "screen_copy" into successive memory locations one character at a time starting with the first character of Col 1, Row 1 ("*") and ending with the last character of Col 5, Row 9 ("*"), you would create the one-dimensional equivalent of "screen_copy," namely "screen_copy_buffer." The arithmetic manipulation of the 270 index values within three FOR..DO loops enables you to perform vertical scrolling.

As mentioned above, the scrolling effect was achieved by calculating and displaying to screen memory different sets of 120 indexed variables of the 270 possible. Refer to Figure 8.1. There you will see that the screen display width is 5 columns. Five columns was previously selected as the chosen width. So, for example, if you have rows 3-6 inclusive up on your display screen, you have a set of

$$5 \text{ col.} \times 6 \text{ chars./col.} \times 4 \text{ rows} = 120 \text{ indexed values}$$

Each time you press an Up or Down Arrow key, you see a different set of 120 values of "screen_copy_buffer" displayed in the screen window.

Here is a specific example of how REWRITE_SCR_BYCOL works. Assume from Figure 8.1 that the display screen is bounded by row 3, columns 1 to 5 on the top and row 6, columns 1 to 5 on the bottom. The current value of "i_tot" is 3, and "k_tot" is 1 and of no further interest. You now want to scroll down so that rows 4 through 7 of Figure 8.1 will be displayed on the screen.

143

8 Vertical Scrolling: Method 2

	Col 1	Col 2	Col 3	Col 4	Col 5
Row 1	*1111*	*1111*	*1111*	*1111*	*1111*
Row 2	*2222*	*2222*	*2222*	*2222*	*2222*
Row 3	*3333*	*3333*	*3333*	*3333*	*3333*
Row 4	*4444*	*4444*	*4444*	*4444*	*4444*
Row 5	*5555*	*5555*	*5555*	*5555*	*5555*
Row 6	*6666*	*6666*	*6666*	*6666*	*6666*
Row 7	*7777*	*7777*	*7777*	*7777*	*7777*
Row 8	*8888*	*8888*	*8888*	*8888*	*8888*
Row 9	*9999*	*9999*	*9999*	*9999*	*9999*

Figure 8.1 Schematic of Two-dimensional Array variable: screen_copy = ARRAY[1..9, 1..5] of str6

Vertical Scrolling: Method 2   8

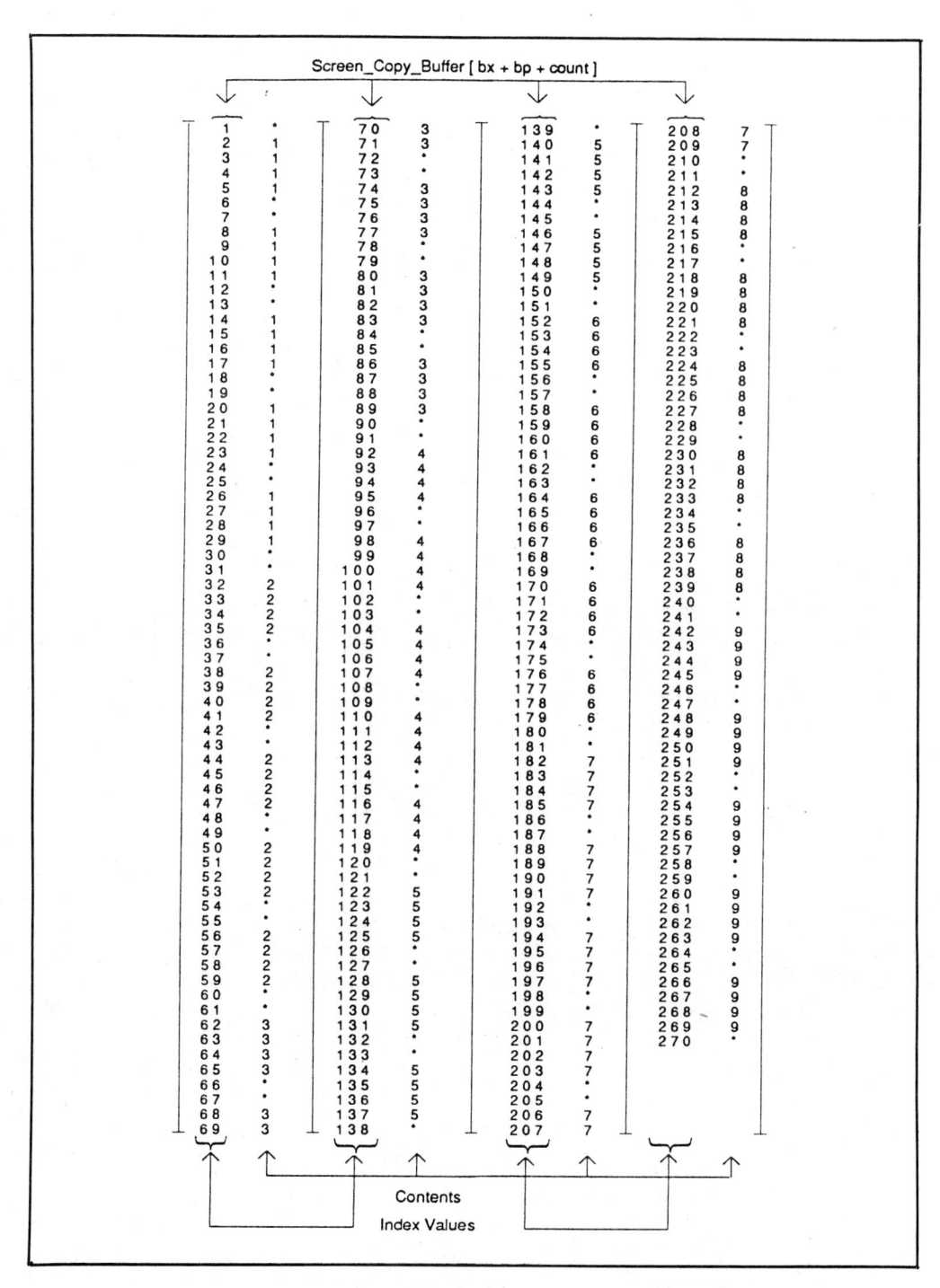

Figure 8.2 Schematic of One-dimensional Array Variable Screen Copy Buffer = ARRAY [1..270] of char.

8 Vertical Scrolling: Method 2

When you press the Down Arrow key, "i_tot" changes from "i_tot" = 3 to "i_tot" = 4. "K_tot" stays unchanged at 1. These values are passed to the REWRITE_SCR_BYROW subprocedure. Also included in the package of values are the "tlc" and "tlr" values by way of V_SCROLL2. These two formatting parameters enable you to calculate the starting screen memory location for screen rewrite at lines 0205 and 0210.

Now track this routine. The loop starting at line 0215 will give "i" a range of values from 4-7 inclusive (4 rows total). The loop at line 0225 will give "k" a range of values from 1-5 columns wide. These two indexes cover the new part of the array "screen_copy" that you want to display on the screen. The next lines convert what you can easily see in two-dimensional terms into the not-so-easily seen one-dimensional equivalent that the mapping procedure CHR_OUT needs to perform its task at line 0255.

If you want to display the very first character of row 4, display column 1 (an "*"), how do you figure out its equivalent one-dimensional index value in "screen_copy_buffer"? This is the job of lines 0235-0245. The integer index value of "screen_copy_buffer" is built up from three component values: "bx," "bp," and "count."

In the example starting at line 0235, you can calculate

```
bx = (4 - 1) * 30  = 90     {row 4    }
bp = (1 - 1) * 6   = 0      {column 1}
count              = 1
```

The first value of "screen_copy_buffer[bp + bx + count]" = 91. If you look at Figure 8.2, you will see that the index value of 91 is the correct one-dimensional equivalent of the first character of row 4, column 1. Take another example. You know that row 6, display column 3 (4th character, a "6") will be on the display screen. What is its one-dimensional index equivalent then? Starting at line 0235, you see that

```
bx = (6 - 1) * 30  = 150    {row 6    }
bp = (3 - 1) * 6   = 12     {column 3}
count              = 4
```

Vertical Scrolling: Method 2   8

The equivalent index value of "screen_copy_buffer" is built up from the sum of "bx," "bp," and "count" and equals 150 + 12 + 4 or 166 (see Figure 8.2). Continuing in the systematic manner as prescribed by the three loops at lines 0235 (row), 0240 (display column), and 0245 (each of the 6 characters in a given display column), you would build up a set of 120 index values as shown in Figure 8.3.

The numbers written sideways are the calculated index values of "screen copy_ buffer," and the numbers written upright represent the order in which each of the indexes is calculated in the loops (1 is the first index to be calculated, and 120 is the last index calculated).

Transferring the properly indexed character of "screen_copy_buffer" to screen memory is accomplished by the now familiar CHR_OUT procedure. Exactly where the character is displayed on the screen is determined by the calculated offset value "j" intitially at line 0210 for the starting location, later at line 0270 as you adjust the screen location after the display of each character in a given column of a given row, still later at line 0280 where you adjust in order to skip a space between display columns, and finally at line 0295 as you drop down two screen rows to start the next row of display columns. Remember, a display column is a string of characters of the form "*####*" (quotes not included).

At this point, the expressions "i - 1" and "k - 1" starting at line 0235 need to be explained. Why the subtraction of 1? The answer is that this adjustment must be made if access to the very first column and the very first row of "screen_copy_buffer" is to be achieved. If you assume that the variable bp := k * 6, that bx := i * 30, and that you want to access the first character (count := 1) of display column 1, row 1 of "screen_copy," you would find that the calculated index of "screen_copy buffer" would be [6 + 30 + 1] = 37. That calculation is wrong. How can the index of the very first value in the array have a value of 37? On the other hand, if you believe that bx := (i - 1) * 30, that bp := (k - 1) * 6, and that count := 1, then access to the first character at column 1, row 1 of "screen_ copy" would provide you with an index whose value is [0 + 0 + 1] = 1, which is correct and corresponds to the index found in Figure 8.2.

In summary, the procedure REWRITE_SCR_BYROW, when called, will rewrite the whole display screen with 120 different indexed values of "screen_copy_buffer" each time either the Up or Down Arrow key is pressed. Using "i_tot" (via "i"), "k_tot" (via "k"), and "count" (1 to 6),

8 Vertical Scrolling: Method 2

Figure 8.3 Subprocedure REWRITE_SCREEN_BYROW

a single unique index value is calculated, and the character stored in the one-dimensional array "screen_copy_buffer" at that indexed position is displayed at a specific location on the display screen using the CHR OUT procedure at line 0255. Each time an Up or Down Arrow key is pressed, this process is repeated 120 times within the three nested FOR..DO loops.

MODULE: V_S2.DRV

This driver routine creates the environment in which the vertical scrolling package "v_s2.inc" can function correctly. The driver routine's tasks are to

- define the required array and formatting variables (this task is performed in the Declaration section of the program)

- call the required external or ".inc" modules

- create a data structure with enough "dummy data" so that the vertical scrolling can be demonstrated (procedure CREATE_SCROLL_DATA)

- initialize the array created above (procedure INITIALIZE SCROLL_DATA)

- call the procedure V_SCROLL2 from the "include" module "v_s2.inc" to actually perform the vertical scrolling function

Note that this driver routine supplies three variables to the vertical scrolling procedure. The first two — top left column ("tl_col") and top right column ("tl_row") — are formatting variables. All data to be written to the screen starts at this column and row location. The third parameter is the one-dimensional data array that contains the actual data to be scrolled on the screen. The driver routine (and the programmer who writes it) defines exactly what data is transferred to the vertical scrolling routine. Thus, the statement

   V_SCROLL2 (tl_col,tl_row,screen_copy_buffer);

8 Vertical Scrolling: Method 2

provides two important types of information needed by the vertical scrolling procedure:

- WHERE — type information given by "tl_col" and "tl_row"

- WHAT — type information given by "screen_copy_buffer"

Following is the Pascal code for this module:

```
{=========================================================================}
0005 program    v_s2(input,output);       {"vertical scroll" }
0010 { "Vertical scroll" (index calculation method)
0015   On disk as "v_s2.drv"
0020 }
0025
0030 type
0035       str6           = string[6];
0040       c              = ARRAY[1..9,1..5] of str6;
0045       scr_copy_buf   = ARRAY[1..270] of char; {9 x 5 x 6}
0050
0055 var
0060       tl_col,tl_row       : integer;
0065       screen_copy         : c;
0070       screen_copy_buffer  : scr_copy_buf;
0075 {=========================================================================}
0080
0085 {$i chrinout.inc}
0090 {$i windows.inc}
0095 {$i v_s2.inc}
0100
0105 {=========================================================================}
0110
0115 procedure       CREATE_COMMAND_LINE;
0120
0125 Begin    {procedure create_command_line}
0130       window(1,1,80,25);
0135       TEXTCOLOR(0);TEXTBACKGROUND(15);   {black char on white}
0140       gotoxy(29,2);write(' VERTICAL SCROLLING DEMO ');
0145       gotoxy(36,3);write(' CHAPTER 8 ');
0150       TEXTCOLOR(15);TEXTBACKGROUND(0);   {white char on black}
0155       gotoxy(22,22);
0160       write('Use UP and DOWN Arrow Keys on Numeric Keypad');
0165       gotoxy(27,23);
0170       write('(Be Sure NUM LOCK Key is OFF)');
0175 End;     {procedure create_command_line}
0180 {-----------------------------------------------------------------}
0185
0190 procedure       CREATE_SCROLL_DATA(var screen_copy_buffer :
0195                                       scr_copy_buf);
0200
0205 var
0210       count    : integer;
```

...*continued*

Vertical Scrolling: Method 2   8

...from previous page

```
0215
0220 Begin      {procedure create_scroll_data}
0225     FOR count := 1 to 270 DO
0230     Begin
0235         CASE (count MOD 30) OF
0240         0..1,
0245         6..7,
0250         12..13,
0255         18..19,
0260         24..25    : screen_copy_buffer[count] := '*'
0265         ELSE
0270         Begin
0275             CASE (count) OF
0280             2..29      : screen_copy_buffer[count] := '1';
0285             32..59     : screen_copy_buffer[count] := '2';
0290             62..89     : screen_copy_buffer[count] := '3';
0295             92..119    : screen_copy_buffer[count] := '4';
0300             122..149   : screen_copy_buffer[count] := '5';
0305             152..179   : screen_copy_buffer[count] := '6';
0310             182..209   : screen_copy_buffer[count] := '7';
0315             212..239   : screen_copy_buffer[count] := '8';
0320             242..269   : screen_copy_buffer[count] := '9'
0325             END; {case}
0330         End;
0335         END; {case}
0340     End;
0345 End;      {procedure create_scroll_data}
0350 {-----------------------------------------------------------}
0355
0360 procedure   INITIALIZE_SCROLL_WINDOW(var screen_copy_buffer :
0365                                     scr_copy_buf);
0370
0375 var
0380     i,k,
0385     bx,bp,
0390     count,
0395     j,
0400     row,col:      integer;
0405 {-----------------------------------------------------------}
0410
0415 Begin     {procedure initialize_scroll_window}
0420     col := 23 ; row := 9;
0425     j := ((row - 1) * 160) + ((col - 1) * 2);
0430     FOR i := 1 to 4 DO     { 4 rows }
0435     Begin
0440         FOR k := 1 to 5 DO { 5 cols }
0445         Begin
0450             bx := (i - 1) * 30;   {30 chars/row}
0455             bp := (k - 1) * 6;    {6 chars/col }
0460             FOR count := 1 to 6 DO
0465             Begin
0470                 CHR_OUT(j,ORD(screen_copy_buffer
0475                              [bx + bp + count]));
0480                 {* delay(1000); *}
0485                 j := j + 2;
0490             End;
0495             j := j + 2;    {skip a space between scr. cols}
0500         End;
```

...continued

151

8 Vertical Scrolling: Method 2

...from previous page

```
0505                col := col ; row := row + 2;
0510                j := ((row - 1) * 160) + ((col - 1) * 2);
0515          End;
0520 End;           {procedure initialize_scroll_window}
0525 {----------------------------------------------------------------}
0530
0535 Begin          {driver}
0540          window(1,1,80,25);clrscr;
0545          CREATE_COMMAND_LINE;
0550          WINDOW_BORDER(21 , 8 , 58 , 16 , 3);   {border style #3}
0555          CREATE_SCROLL_DATA(screen_copy_buffer);
0560          INITIALIZE_SCROLL_WINDOW(screen_copy_buffer);
0565
0570          tl_col := 23 ; tl_row := 9; {top_left col,top_left row}
0575          V_SCROLL2(tl_col,tl_row,screen_copy_buffer);
0580 End.           {driver}
{================================================================}
```

V_S2.DRV: NOTES

In the Declaration Section, the two-dimensional array variable "screen copy" has been created, which has 9 rows and 5 display columns with each array element being a six-character string (lines 0065 & 0040). Note that "screen_copy" does not appear in any of the parameter lists of the main routine V S2.DRV. It has been included in the Declaration Section for instructional clarification and to

- assist you in visualizing the data structure you will eventually be manipulating from a different (one-dimensional) point of view. From the Type definition provided at line 0040, you can visually understand things by creating a diagram similar to that in Figure 8.1.

- enable you to correctly define the Type of "screen_copy's" one-dimensional equivalent, "screen_copy_buffer." Note that the Type of "screen_copy_buffer" could not have been properly defined without first looking at the Type of its two-dimensional counterpart, "screen_copy." Note also that this defined Type (line 0045) is used throughout all the procedure parameter lists in the external procedure module "v s2.inc."

Vertical Scrolling: Method 2   8

The unused two-dimensional variable ("screen_copy") is important because it is the logical precursor of the one-dimensional array that you actually use in the program; it is only included to show how the Type of "screen_copy_buffer" was derived.

Above, you saw that the first task of the driver routine was to supply the proper data Type definitions for all the variables in the parameter lists of all the external (".inc" suffixed modules) procedures that will be used by it. The second task of the driver routine is to orchestrate the calling of all external modules. Line 0085 invokes the set of external procedures embodied within "chrinout.inc." The procedure CHR_OUT is used to display the characters from within the memory variable "screen_copy_buffer" directly onto the screen via the screen memory array MEM[bwseg : bwofs + j]. Line 0090 invokes "windows.inc." Finally, line 0095 invokes the package of external procedures "v_s2.inc," including V_SCROLL2, which provides the program with the necessary vertical data scrolling capabilities.

The third task for the driver routine is to create a suitable array of data to use with the vertical scrolling demonstration routines. The procedure CREATE_SCROLL_DATA provides the necessary data. Figure 8.1 provides the form of data that you can best visualize. The one-dimensional equivalent of "screen_copy" is the variable "screen_copy buffer" in Figure 8.2 and at line 0190 in the procedure. The word "suitable" is used above because the screen memory array MEM[bwseg:bwofs + j] is a one-dimensional array and can only be mapped onto by another one-dimensional array. While you can better visulize with a two-dimensional array, the computer can better "visualize" with a one-dimensional array (see Figure 8.2); therefore, the comfortable two-dimensional point of view must be converted into a less comfortable one-dimensional point of view.

The mapping of the contents of "screen_copy" from its two-dimensional form (Figure 8.1) into its one-dimensional form, "screen_copy_buffer" (Figure 8.2), is accomplished by the FOR...DO loop starting at line 0225 and the pair of CASE statements at lines 0235 and 0275. Why MOD 30 at line 0235? If you look at Figure 8.1, you will see that each of the 9 rows has its own unique pattern of characters: row 1 has "*"

8 Vertical Scrolling: Method 2

characters and all "1's" while row 8 has "*" characters and all "8's," etc. These rows all have two characteristics in common:

- each row contains 30 characters.
- the "*" characters are all in the same relative positions within each of the rows.

These two observations should provide enough clues to show how the "*" characters are assigned their index values at line 0260. This section is a little tricky. If you don't understand exactly how it works, don't worry too much. What is most important is understanding how the scrolling of data on the screen is accomplished.

The assignment of the characters "1" through "9" is handled by the CASE statement at line 0275. Look at line 0265, which contains the ELSE statement. It says that if "count MOD 30" is not any of the numbers indicated at lines 0240-0260, then the character to be assigned to "screen_copy_buffer" must lie somewhere between "1" and "9" inclusive. Exactly which character will be assigned is a function of the range that the index variable "count" falls into (lines 0280-0320). Just how these ranges are determined is shown in Figure 8.2, which is a one-dimensional equivalent of the two-dimensional contents of Figure 8.1. Note that you count from left to right across the columns, with the index value of the first portion of any "next" row being 1 greater than the last index value of the row directly above it.

The fourth task of the driver routine is to initialize the data to start the vertical scrolling demonstration. Initialization consists of displaying to the screen the first 4 rows and all 5 display columns of "screen_copy buffer" (alias "screen_copy") as you can see in Figure 8.4. If you were to take the code between lines 0450 and 0460 and calculate by hand the index values at line 0475, based on their "bx," "bp," and "count" components as was prescribed in Figure 8.3, you would notice the pattern of index values is as shown below:

001-030 inclusive for row 1, columns 1-5, count 1-6
031-060 inclusive for row 2, columns 1-5, count 1-6
061-090 inclusive for row 3, columns 1-5, count 1-6
091-120 inclusive for row 4, columns 1-5, count 1-6

Vertical Scrolling: Method 2   8

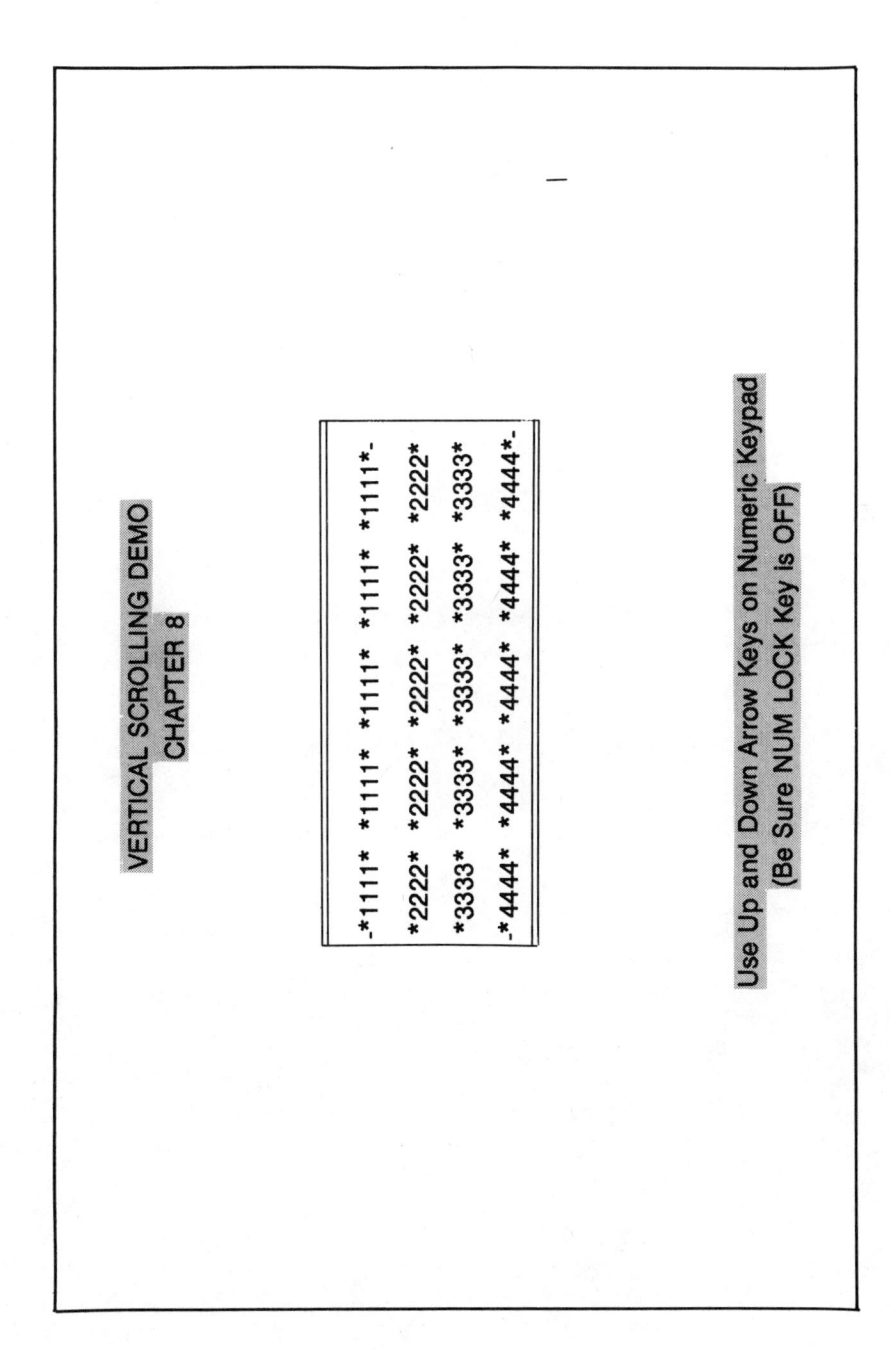

```
VERTICAL SCROLLING DEMO
     CHAPTER 8

-*1111*  *1111*  *1111*  *1111*  *1111*-
 *2222*  *2222*  *2222*  *2222*  *2222*
 *3333*  *3333*  *3333*  *3333*  *3333*
-*4444*  *4444*  *4444*  *4444*  *4444*-

Use Up and Down Arrow Keys on Numeric Keypad
       (Be Sure NUM LOCK Key is OFF)
```

Figure 8.4 Initialized Screen Layout for Vertical Scrolling — Index Address Method

8 Vertical Scrolling: Method 2

If you consulted Figure 8.2 directly, you would see the same index values there.

The final task of the driver routine is to call the procedure V SCROLL2 from the procedure module "v_s2.inc" to perform the vertical scrolling function on the hypothetical screen data.

CHAPTER 9

VERTICAL SCROLLING: METHOD 3

9 Vertical Scrolling: Method 3

This chapter presents the last of the three vertical scrolling methods discussed in this book. Of the three, it is the simplest and the shortest in terms of written code. It uses two functions that have been built into the Turbo Pascal compiler: INSLINE and DELLINE. For the sake of reference this vertical scrolling method is called the "insline/delline" method. Interestingly, there is no built-in Turbo procedure to perform horizontal scrolling.

MODULE: V_S3.INC

The overall objective of this module is to implement the vertical scroll of predefined screen data. The driver routine V_S3.DRV supplies the required parameters. There are three procedures in the "v_s3.inc" package: the main procedure V_SCROLL3 (vertical scroll method 3) and the two subprocedures, SCRL_UP (scroll up) and SCRL_DOWN (scroll down).

The main tasks of V_SCROLL3 are as follows:

- to control the up and down direction of the scroll by adjusting the index variable "k_tot," and then calling the appropriate subprocedure.

- to protect against any erroneous attempt by the user to scroll outside the index limits of the predefined data array.

The main task of the subprocedure SCRL_UP is to actually scroll upward the data on the display screen, that is, scroll the data *from* the upper window boundary *toward* the lower window boundary on the screen. So if you want to move toward the beginning of a table, you would press the Up Arrow key. The task of the other subprocedure, SCRL_DOWN, is to scroll down the screen data, that is, scroll the data *from* the lower window boundary *toward* the upper boundary. In other words, you would press the Down Arrow key if you want to reach the largest value at the end of a table. The code for the module "v_s3.inc" is as follows:

Vertical Scrolling: Method 3

```
{=========================================================================}
0005  {v_s3.inc}
0010  {  This ".inc" module contains all the vertical scrolling
0015     routines that are overhead requirements of the program
0020     "v_s3.drv".
0025     On disk as "v_s3.inc".
0030  }
0035
0040  {-----------------------------------------------------------------}
0045
0050  procedure      V_SCROLL3(tlc,tlr,brc,brr : integer;
0055                           var array_contents : a);
0060
0065  label
0070       rep_read;
0075
0080  const
0085       scroll_up     = #$48;
0090       scroll_down   = #$50;
0095       carriage_ret  = #$0d;
0100       bell          = #$07;
0105
0110  var
0115       scroll_choice  : char;
0120       exit_scroll    : boolean;
0125       i,k            : integer;
0130       i_tot,k_tot    : integer;
0135       x_coord,y_coord: integer;
0140
0145  {-----------------------------------------------------------------}
0150
0155       procedure  SCRL_UP(k_tot,i_tot : integer);
0160
0165       var
0170            k : integer;
0175
0180       Begin    {sub procedure scrl_up}
0185            window(tlc,tlr,brc,brr);      {23,9,56,15}
0190            gotoxy(1,1);
0195            DELLINE;DELLINE;
0200            window(1,1,80,25);
0205            gotoxy(tlc,brr);    {lower left corner (23,15)}
0210            x_coord := WHEREX ; y_coord := WHEREY;
0215            For k := 1 to 5 DO
0220            Begin
0225                 gotoxy(x_coord,y_coord);
0230                 write(array_contents[i_tot + 3,k]);
0235                 x_coord := tlc + (k * 7);    {tlc = 23}
0240                 y_coord := y_coord;
0245            End;
0250       End;     {sub procedure scrl_up}
0255  {-----------------------------------------------------------------}
0260
0265       procedure  SCRL_DOWN(k_tot,i_tot : integer);
0270
0275       var
0280            k : integer;
0285
0290       Begin    {sub procedure scrl_down}
0295            window(tlc,tlr,brc,brr); {(23,9,56,15)}
```

...*continued*

9 Vertical Scrolling: Method 3

...from previous page

```
0300                gotoxy(1,1);
0305                INSLINE;INSLINE;
0310                window(1,1,80,25);
0315                gotoxy(tlc,tlr);        {top left corner (23,9)}
0320                x_coord := WHEREX ; y_coord := WHEREY;
0325                FOR k := 1 to 5 DO
0330                Begin
0335                   gotoxy(x_coord,y_coord);
0340                   write(array_contents[i_tot,k]);
0345                   x_coord := tlc + (k * 7);  {tlc = 23}
0350                   y_coord := y_coord;
0355                End;
0360           End;       {sub procedure scrl_down}
0365 {------------------------------------------------------------------}
0370
0375 Begin      {procedure v_scroll3}
0380        window(tlc,tlr,brc,brr);
0385        exit_scroll := false;
0390        i_tot := 1;
0395        k_tot := 1;
0400
0405        REPEAT
0410            rep_read: {....a label with colon}
0415            read(KBD,scroll_choice);
0420            CASE (scroll_choice) OF
0425
0430                scroll_up      : Begin   {press Up Arrow Key}
0435                                    i_tot := i_tot - 1;
0440                                    k_tot := k_tot + 0;
0445                                    IF (i_tot < 1) THEN
0450                                    Begin
0455                                        i_tot := 1;
0460                                        goto rep_read;
0465                                    End
0470                                    ELSE
0475                                        SCRL_DOWN(k_tot,i_tot);
0480                                 End;   {scroll_up}
0485
0490                scroll_down    : Begin   {press Down Arrow Key}
0495                                    i_tot := i_tot + 1;
0500                                    k_tot := k_tot + 0;
0505                                    IF (i_tot > 6) THEN
0510                                    Begin
0515                                        i_tot := 6;
0520                                        goto rep_read;
0525                                    End
0530                                    ELSE
0535                                        SCRL_UP(k_tot,i_tot);
0540                                 End;   {scroll_down}
0545
0550                carriage_ret:  Begin
0555                                    exit_scroll := true;
0560                                    write(bell);
0565                                End;
0570
0575            ELSE
0580                {enters here if any other key is pressed}
0585
0590            END; {case}
0595        UNTIL (exit_scroll = true);
0600 End;       {procedure v_scroll3}
0605 {===================== END OF V_S3.INC MODULE =====================}
```

160

V_S3.INC: NOTES

In the declaration section of "v_s3.inc," note that V_SCROLL receives five parameters from the driver routine V_S3.DRV. The first four— "tlc," "tlr," "brc," and "brr"—define the upper-left and lower-right corners of the scrolling window. The fifth, "array_contents," is the 9-row by 5-column array that holds the data to be scrolled in the predefined screen display window. Note the prefix "var" in the parameter list. This prefix means that the procedure accesses the array that has already been created for global access by the driver routine (it doesn't neccessarily need to have the same name, but *must* be of the same type). When a variable is prefixed by "var" in a parameter list of a procedure, two things happen. First, available memory is saved because the procedure is spared the job of creating its own copy of the array for internal use. The procedure simply accesses the already created array through address reference (the effect of the prefix, "var"). Second, any changes that are made to the "var'd" variable inside the procedure parameter list will be transmitted directly from the procedure back into the original copy declared in the driver routine. So if you do *not* want changes made to the original, then *do not* prefix it with "var" in the parameter list of a procedure.

Within the main body of V_SCROLL3 nothing is new or unusual. The REPEAT..UNTIL loop starting at line 0405 enables you to continue scrolling the screen data up and down until you press the Return key at line 0550. The CASE statement at line 0420 enables you to select one of three keys to scroll up, scroll down, or exit from scrolling. Within the "scroll_up" and "scroll_down" options, "k_tot" index selection and error protection are provided as in the other demonstration routines.

SCRL_UP

This subprocedure is called from line 0535 after the Down Arrow key on the numeric keypad has been pressed. How is it that when you want to go "deeper" into an array, a "scroll_up" function is selected? It seems backwards, but it is not. The paradox is resolved if you can understand the DELLINE function at line 0195. The DELLINE function operates in the same fashion as the subprocedure MOVE_PARTSCR UP in Chapter 7. What happened there was that the lower 5 of 7 screen display rows were each moved 2 lines up, thus leaving a blank line at the *bottom* of the display window at line 15. This blank line is where the next larger row would be written to the screen. The index

9 Vertical Scrolling: Method 3

value used in the demonstration program at line 0230 is "i_tot + 3." The addition of the number "3" is an adjustment that must be made to translate the index value into a different index value, which, when displayed on the screen, will show a properly increasing row index of the variable "array_contents." Vary line 0230 to change the value "3" to some other value and see the difference it makes.

The procedure DELLINE has been called twice at line 0195 because in referring to Figure 9.1, you will see that a blank space has been included between the displayed rows. DELLINE is constructed to scroll only one line at a time in the upward direction.

To use the DELLINE function correctly, you must first set up the properly sized scrolling window. This is done at line 0185 where the WINDOW procedure uses the parameters supplied by the driver routine. DELLINE is then called to perform its task, and at line 0200 the window is changed back to full size. This is done prior to writing the new bottom line of data because the window parameters ("tlc," "tlr," "brc," "brr") were created in the context of a full-sized window, and any other window size would cause the new line of data to be written at the wrong place on the screen.

SCRL_DOWN

This subprocedure is called from line 0475 after the Up Arrow key has been pressed. Again, the same paradox arises. How is it that when you want to go "shallower" in the array, a "scroll down" function is called? The key to understanding this subprocedure lies with the built-in INSLINE function at line 0305. The INSLINE function operates similarly to the subprocedure MOVE_PARTSCR_DOWN in Chapter 7. There, the top 5 of 7 display screen rows were each moved down 2 lines, leaving a blank line at the top of the display window. This blank line at the top is the location where the next smaller row of the data array "array_contents" would be displayed. The index value used in the example at line 0340 is "i_tot." Unlike SCRL_UP, no adjustment is needed here because the calculated index value "i_tot" is already a properly decreasing row index of "array_contents" when it is displayed to the screen.

INSLINE is called twice at line 0305 for the same reasons that DELLINE was called twice in SCRL_UP. Experiment yourself by changing the number of INSLINE function calls and watching the different results.

VERTICAL SCROLLING DEMO
CHAPTER 9

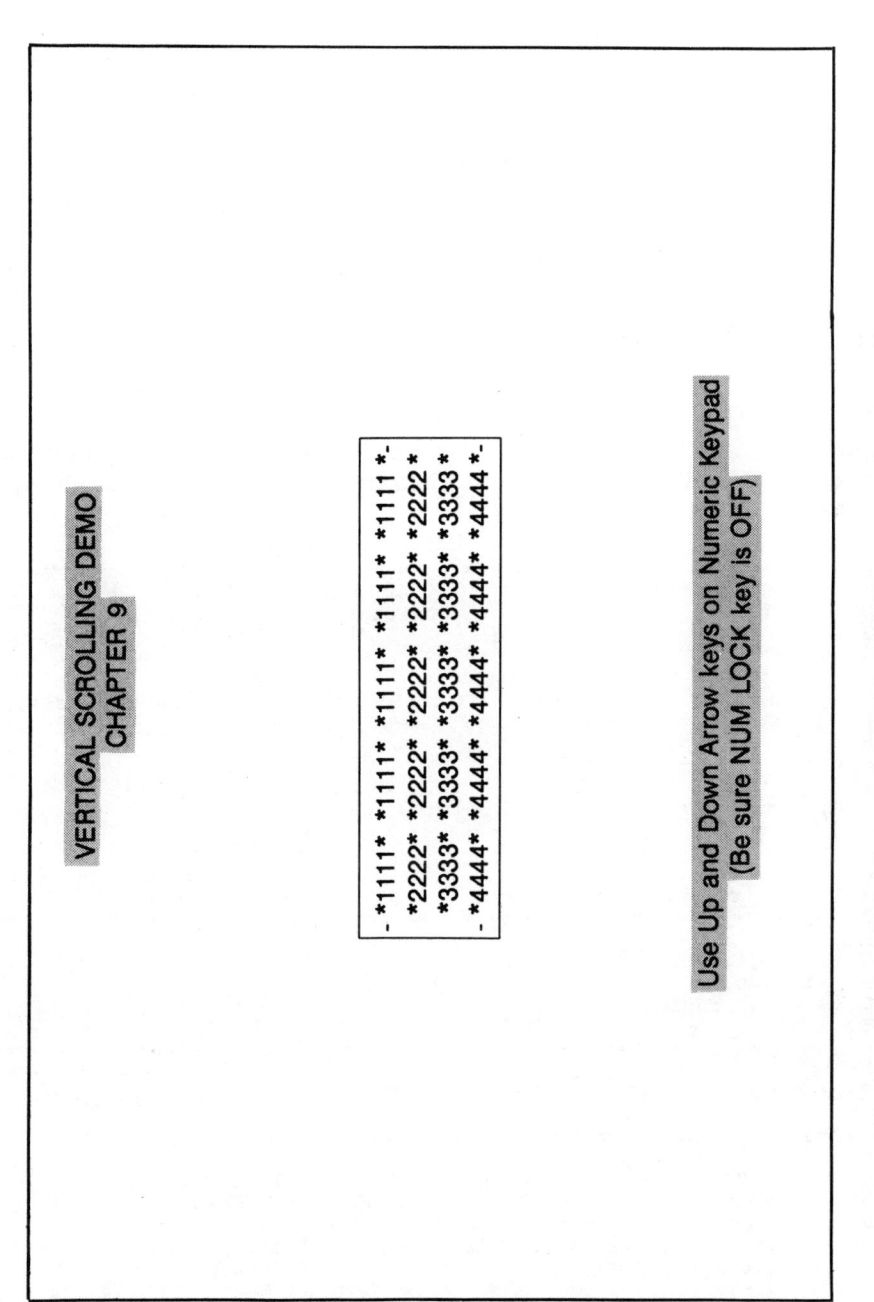

```
-*1111* *1111* *1111* *1111* *-
*2222* *2222* *2222* *2222*
*3333* *3333* *3333* *3333*
*4444* *4444* *4444* *4444*
-                              -
```

Use Up and Down Arrow keys on Numeric Keypad
(Be sure NUM LOCK key is OFF)

Figure 9.1 Initialized Screen for Vertical Scrolling — Insline/Delline Method

9 Vertical Scrolling: Method 3

To use the INSLINE function correctly, you must first set up the properly sized scrolling window. This is done at line 0295 where the WINDOW procedure uses the parameters supplied by the driver routine. INSLINE is then called to perform its task, and at line 0310 the window is changed back to full size. This change is done prior to writing the new top line of data because the window parameters ("tlc," "tlr," "brc," "brr") were created in the context of a full-sized window, and any other window size would cause the new line of data to be written at the wrong screen line.

MODULE: V_S3.DRV

This driver routine is similar to all of its predecessors in the earlier chapters. It performs the variable declarations, external function calls, data creation, and data initialization functions. Following is the code:

```
{===========================================================================}
0005  program    v_s3(input,output);   {"Vertical scroll 3"     }
0010                                    {On disk as "v_s3.drv"  }
0015
0020  type
0025        str6         = string[6];
0030        a            = ARRAY[1..9,1..5] of str6;  {9 row x 5 cols}
0035        screen_copy  = ARRAY[1..25,1..80] of char;
0040
0045  var
0050        array_contents : a;
0055        copy_of_screen : screen_copy;
0060        any_key        : char;
0065
0070        tl_col,tl_row,              {scrolling window parameters....}
0075        br_col,br_row  : integer;
0080  {===========================================================================}
0085
0090  {$i chrinout.inc}
0095  {$i windows.inc}
0100  {$i v_s3.inc}
0105
0110  {===========================================================================}
0115
0120  procedure     CREATE_COMMAND_LINE;
0125
0130  Begin      {procedure create_command_line}
0135        window(1,1,80,25);
0140        TEXTCOLOR(0);TEXTBACKGROUND(15);    {black char on white}
0145        gotoxy(29,2);write(' VERTICAL SCROLLING DEMO ');
0150        gotoxy(36,3);write(' CHAPTER 9 ');
0155        TEXTCOLOR(15);TEXTBACKGROUND(0);    {white char on black}
0160        gotoxy(19,22);
0165        write('Use UP and DOWN Arrow Keys on Numeric Keypad');
0170        gotoxy(27,23);
```

...continued

Vertical Scrolling: Method 3   9

...from previous page

```
0175            write('(Be Sure NUM LOCK Key is OFF)');
0180     End;        {procedure create_command_line}
0185 {-------------------------------------------------------------------}
0190
0195 procedure        CREATE_SCROLL_DATA(var array_contents : a);
0200
0205 var
0210        i,k : integer;       {indexes for use in procedure}
0215
0220 Begin      {procedure create_scroll_data}
0225        window(1,1,80,25);
0230        FOR i := 1 to 9 DO   {ROW 1 to 9}
0235        Begin
0240             FOR k := 1 to 5 DO    {COL 1 to 5}
0245             Begin
0250                  CASE (i) OF
0255
0260                  1 : array_contents[i,k] := '*1111*';
0265                  2 : array_contents[i,k] := '*2222*';
0270                  3 : array_contents[i,k] := '*3333*';
0275                  4 : array_contents[i,k] := '*4444*';
0280                  5 : array_contents[i,k] := '*5555*';
0285                  6 : array_contents[i,k] := '*6666*';
0290                  7 : array_contents[i,k] := '*7777*';
0295                  8 : array_contents[i,k] := '*8888*';
0300                  9 : array_contents[i,k] := '*9999*';
0305
0310                  END; {case}
0315                  {* writeln(i,' ',k,' ',array_contents[i,k]); *}
0320                  {* delay(1000); *}
0325             End;
0330        End;
0335 End;       {procedure create_scroll_data}
0340 {-------------------------------------------------------------------}
0345
0350 procedure        INITIALIZE_SCROLL_WINDOW(var array_contents : a);
0355
0360 var
0365        i,k       : integer;
0370        x_coord,              {x_coord is column }
0375        y_coord   : integer;  {y_coord is row    }
0380
0385 Begin      {procedure initialize_scroll_window}
0390        window(1,1,80,25);
0395        gotoxy(23,9);
0400        x_coord := WHEREX ; y_coord := WHEREY;
0405
0410        FOR i := 1 to 4 DO          {4 rows....}
0415        Begin
0420             gotoxy(x_coord,y_coord);
0425             FOR k := 1 to 5 DO     {5 cols....}
0430             Begin
0435                  write(array_contents[i,k]);
0440                  {* delay(500); *}
0445                  gotoxy(x_coord + (k * 7) , y_coord);
0450                  {across the columns in a given row....}
0455                  { column_width(6) + space_between_columns(1) = 7}
0460             End;
```

...continued

165

9 Vertical Scrolling: Method 3

...from previous page

```
0465              x_coord := x_coord;       {col 23}
0470              y_coord := y_coord + 2;   {next row = 9 + 2 = 11}
0475         End;
0480 End;         {procedure initialize scroll_window}
0485 {------------------------------------------------------------------}
0490
0495 Begin   {driver}
0500      window(1,1,80,25);clrscr;
0505      CREATE_COMMAND_LINE;
0510      WINDOW_BORDER(21,8,58,16,2); {border style #2}
0515
0520      CREATE_SCROLL_DATA(array_contents);
0525      INITIALIZE_SCROLL_WINDOW(array_contents);
0530
0535      tl_col := 23 ; tl_row := 9; {overall window dimensions of}
0540      br_col := 56 ; br_row := 15;{screen area to be scrolled  }
0545      V_SCROLL3(tl_col,tl_row,br_col,br_row,
0550                array_contents);
0555 End.     {driver}
{==================================================================}
```

V_S3.DRV: NOTES

Since the driver routine's operation has been described before, only one further comment is necessary before this chapter is concluded. Look at the procedure CREATE_SCROLL_DATA. There, at line 0315, you will see a few bracketed statements. If you remove the brackets and run the program, you will see that the row and column index as well as the contents of the array variable are written onto the screen. This type of bracketed statement embedded within the code is a good debugging tool to test if the array variables that you create inside the computer's memory are correct.

CONCLUSION

You have now completed the set of demonstration programs that illustrate the mechanics of screen saving/redisplay and horizontal/vertical scrolling. In Part 2, you will be working with several applications programs designed to achieve the following two goals:

- to demonstrate screen I/O techniques in a more practical context.

- to reinforce and expand the concepts you have learned by seeing them work in more realistic operating environments.

Up to this point, the focus has been the output side of screen I/O programming. In the next chapter, the focus will shift to the input side. In particular, the following topics will be covered:

- input data entry

- input data validation

- input data revision

PART II

APPLICATIONS

Note to programmers: The program listings in this book have been printed directly from the original program disks to ensure that no errors were introduced through rekeyboarding.

The letter "l" and the number "1" are represented in the program code by the same character (see examples on p.1 for clarification).

CHAPTER 10

DATA INPUT AND REVISION

10 Data Input and Revision

So far, the primary focus has been on screen output. Through the techniques of window bordering, screen saving and redisplay, and scrolling, you have seen how the computer can present screen output data in an easily readable and comprehensive form. Behind these techniques are two underlying assumptions. First, the input data has been correctly entered into the computer from the keyboard. Second, the calculations performed on the input data will produce correct results. Of course, there has been no input data or computing algorithms presented so far. Only invented, hypothetical output has been used to demonstrate the screen display techniques.

In this chapter, attention will shift to the topic of data input. The prime objective will be to learn how to write a computer input program that will format, validate, and revise some hypothetical data input for use by a computer program. The input medium will be the computer keyboard as opposed to modems, disk drives, etc.

Formatting means laying out the data input on the screen to make entering data into the computer and reading data off the screen easy tasks.

Validation of input data means testing the candidate data for correctness before it is accepted into the computer as valid input data. In this chapter, validation will be tested first from the point of view of the computer and then from the point of view of the user. These two points of view will comprise "stage 1 validation" and "stage 2 validation" respectively.

Revision means revising or changing an input data item that has already been entered and accepted by the computer as valid input.

Taken together, these three features will enable you to enter data into a computer program with three advantages:

1) You can see exactly what you have entered and in what units and ranges—that is the advantage of clarity.

2) You don't need to fear making a mistake—that is the advantage of security.

3) You have the luxury of being able to change your mind—that is the advantage of flexibility.

Data Input and Revision 10

Similar to the previous chapters in this book, demonstrations will be done by program example. This time, however, instead of output being created with no entered input, input will be created without any output.

The validation portion of the demonstration program will be set up as seen in the Screen Layout in Figure 10.1. Here, input data of several different types will be displayed at screen line 22, and the validated data input will be displayed at screen lines 6-10.

The revision portion of the demonstration program will be set up as seen in Figure 10.2. Here, by typing, say, <r5><Ret>, you can ask to revise entry #5, a previously entered date string.

To better understand the phrase "input data of several different types," refer to Figure 10.3. There, you will see that the data input is divided into two main types: numbers and non-numbers. Numbers are subdivided into **reals** and **integers**. Percentages, floating point scientific numbers, and dollar amounts are all examples of real numbers. Exact values used for counting, such as the number of days and number of people, are examples of integers.

The only catagory of non-numbers is **strings**. Strings are used for entering any data that are comprised of characters only or mixed characters and numbers, such as names, social security numbers, dates, zip codes, or, as you will see in Chapter 13, file names in the Disk Directory.

Of course, entering data into the computer in either numeric or non-numeric format isn't the end of it. What if you need to convert a date into a numeric value for computations, or what if you need to enter data in a numeric form and then need to scroll the data on the screen at a later time? These tasks would require using the following Turbo string procedures and functions:

Task	Description
COPY	parsing (splitting apart) a string
CONCAT	joining together of separate strings
STR	converting from numbers to strings for display
VAL	converting from strings to values for computations

Aside from formatting, validating, and revising input data, this demonstration program will also illustrate these operations in a meaningful context.

10 Data Input and Revision

```
┌─────────────────────────────────────────────┐
│                                             │
│      DATA INPUT/REVISION DEMO               │
│            CHAPTER 10                       │
│                                             │
│      01.   Enter an INTEGER      . . . :    │
│      02.   Enter a PERCENTAGE    . . . :    │
│      03.   Enter a DOLLAR AMOUNT . . . :    │
│      04.   Enter a REAL NUMBER   . . . :    │
│      05.   Enter a DATE          . . . :    │
│                                             │
│                                             │
│           Input Validation. . . . . Input:  │
│                       . . . . Units:  ▓▓▓   │
│                         Your Entry: ▓▓▓-▓▓-▓▓▓▓ │
│                                             │
└─────────────────────────────────────────────┘
```

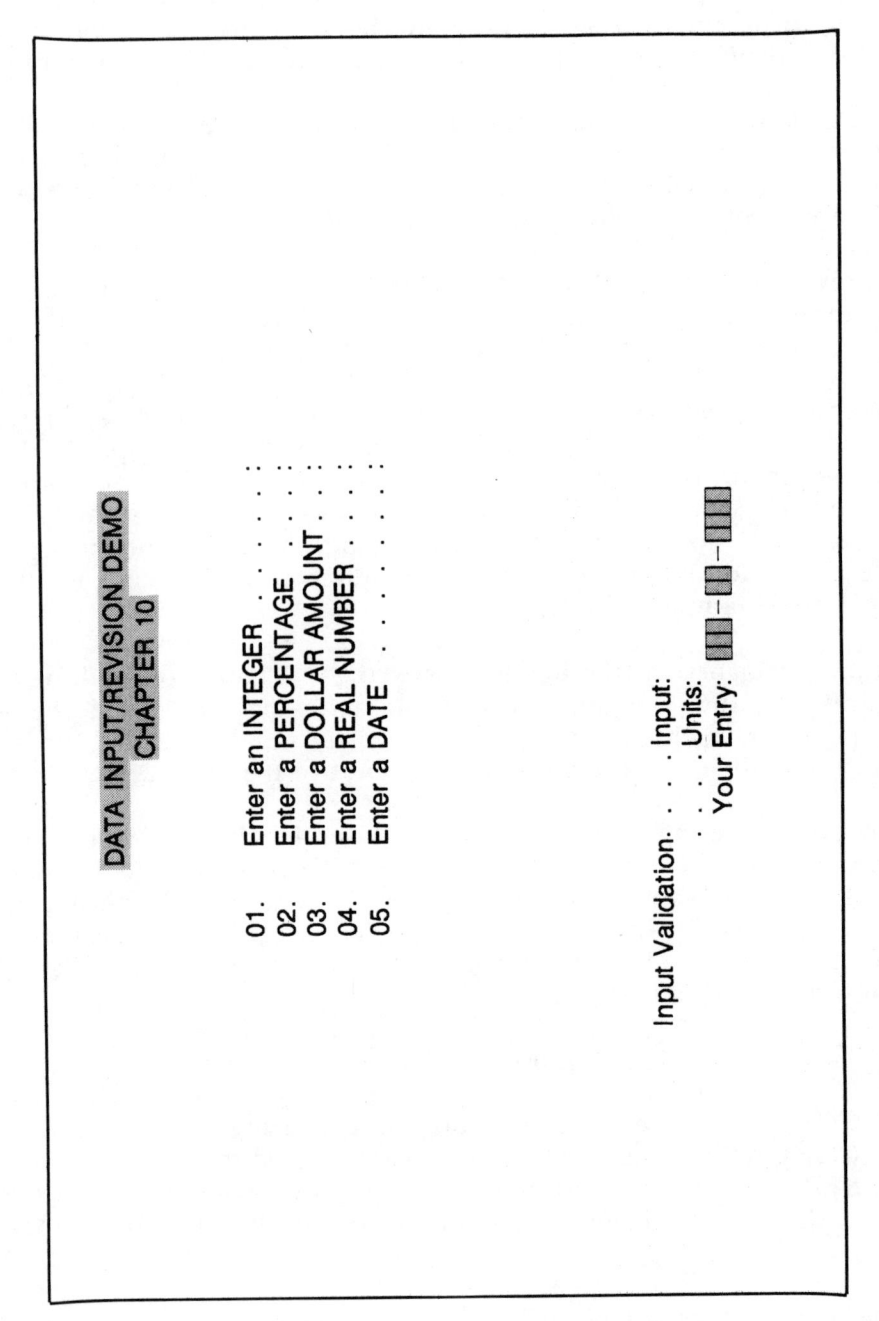

Figure 10.1 Initialized Screen for Data Input Portion of the Driver Program

Data Input and Revision 10

```
┌─────────────────────────────────────────────┐
│                                             │
│                                             │
│                                             │
│      DATA INPUT/REVISION DEMO               │
│            CHAPTER 10                       │
│                                             │
│      01.  Enter an INTEGER    . . . . :     │
│      02.  Enter a PERCENTAGE  . . . . :     │
│      03.  Enter a DOLLAR AMOUNT . . . :     │
│      04.  Enter a REAL NUMBER . . . . :     │
│      05.  Enter a DATE        . . . . :     │
│                                             │
│                                             │
│              REVISIONS??                    │
│                                             │
│        -YES-              -NO-              │
│                                             │
│     e.g., to revise           to exit, type │
│     entry #4, type            <q> <RET>     │
│     <r 4 RET>                               │
│                                             │
└─────────────────────────────────────────────┘
```

Figure 10.2 Initialized Screen for the Data Revision Portion of the Driver Program

175

10 Data Input and Revision

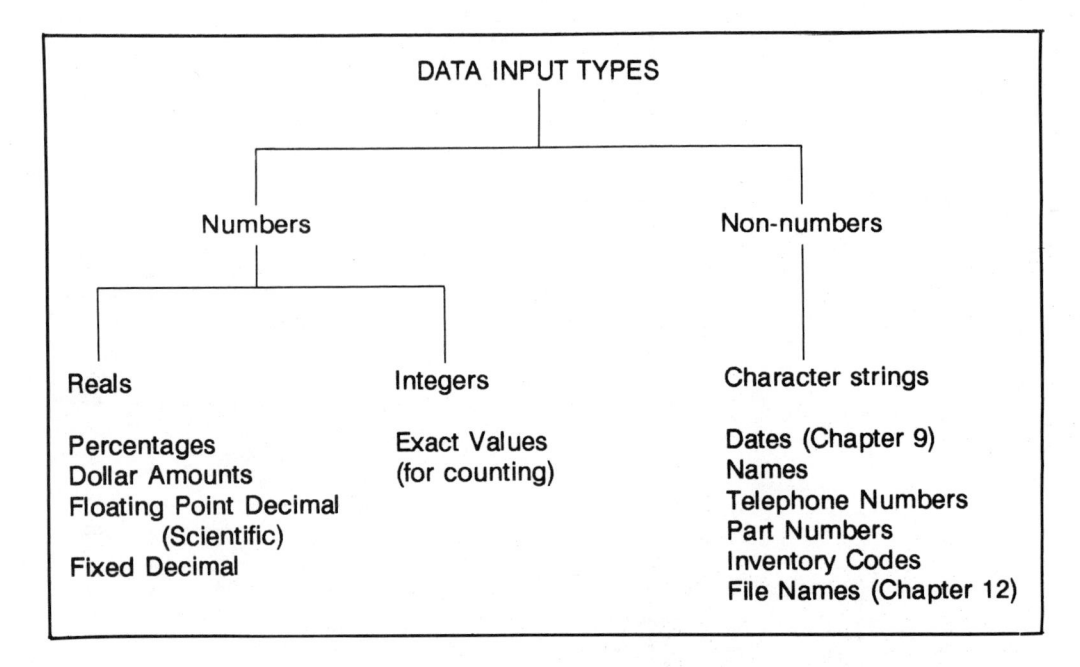

```
                        DATA INPUT TYPES
                               |
              +----------------+----------------+
              |                                 |
           Numbers                          Non-numbers
              |                                 |
        +-----+-----+                           |
        |           |                           |
      Reals      Integers                Character strings

   Percentages   Exact Values            Dates (Chapter 9)
   Dollar Amounts (for counting)         Names
   Floating Point Decimal                Telephone Numbers
        (Scientific)                     Part Numbers
   Fixed Decimal                         Inventory Codes
                                         File Names (Chapter 12)
```

Figure 10.3 Data Input Classification

MODULE: EI_ER.INC (ENTER INTEGER, ENTER REAL)

```
{=========================================================================}
0005 {ei_er.inc}      {"Enter integer , enter real"}
0010                  {On disk as "ei_er.inc"        }
0015 { This ".inc" module enables the user to enter any integer
0020   or any real value from the keyboard using the built-in
0025     function "IORESULT"
0030 }
0035
```

   ...continued

176

Data Input and Revision 10

...from previous page

```
0040  {======================================================================}
0045
0050  procedure ENTER_INTEGER(var int_val         : integer;
0055                          var valid_int_ent   : boolean);
0060
0065  Begin       {procedure enter_integer}
0070       {$i-}  read(int_val); {$i+}  {note punctuation!}
0075       IF (IORESULT = 0) THEN
0080            valid_int_ent := true;
0085  End;        {procedure enter_integer}
0090  {======================================================================}
0095
0100  procedure ENTER_REAL(var real_val         : real;
0105                       var valid_real_ent : boolean);
0110
0115  Begin       {procedure enter_real}
0120       {$i-}  read(real_val); {$i+}  {note punctuation!}
0125       IF (IORESULT = 0) THEN
0130            valid_real_ent := true;
0135  End;        {procedure enter_real}
{============== end of module "ei_er.inc ================================}
```

EI_ER.INC: NOTES

This module, as the name suggests, consists of two procedures, one for keyboard entry of integer data and the other for keyboard entry of real number data.

ENTER_INTEGER

This procedure allows you to enter integer input data. This procedure takes two values in its parameter list. The first is "int_val" (integer value). Note that this variable is preceded by the reserved word "var," which means that the integer value is either created or altered inside the procedure, and the result can be transferred back out to the driver routine. If the program has just begun, the original value of "int_val" going into the procedure would be undefined. And the value going back out to the driver routine would be the value typed in at the keyboard at line 0070. The second parameter in the parameter list is the Boolean variable, "valid_int_ent" (valid integer entry). The value passed out from this procedure determines the next action in the inner REPEAT..UNTIL loop in the driver routine at line 1195, that is, whether program execution drops through to line 1210 or whether it goes back up to line 1170 for a retry.

177

10 Data Input and Revision

Look at line 0070. There, you see the compiler directive {$i-} in front of the "read" (type in from the keyboard) statement, followed by another compiler directive {$i+}. When Turbo Pascal is first booted, the "i" compiler directive is automatically set to active ({$i+}). So if a programmer were to respond to a program's request for keyboard-entered integer input with, say, 55.74, then an I/O error (input/output error) would be triggered, and the program execution would halt with a message that looks like this:

    I/O error NN, PC = addr
    Program aborted

where "NN" is the Turbo system's I/O error number, and "addr" is the address in the program code where the error occurred.

While the compiler has caught the attempted entry of illegal data on the one hand, the price, on the other hand, is a disrupted program that has to be rerun again from the beginning. Imagine how inconvenient that could be if, for example, your program required 12 input entries and you made an entry error on the last entry.

The statement {$i-} at line 0070 will prevent this automatic termination of program execution in response to erroneously entered input data. The burden of responding to an I/O error, however, is shifted from the computer to the programmer. What the programmer responds to is an error code number generated by the standard, built-in error-checking function appropriately named IORESULT (line 0075). A value of *zero* returned by this function means that the compiler has looked at the input data and determined that it is *correct*. A non-zero result means that there was some kind of error committed by the programmer during the "read" operation.

As mentioned, the burden is on the programmer to respond to the error code number generated by the built-in system variable IORESULT. In this case, you are interested in responding to one of two values of IORESULT: "0" (no entry error) or any non-zero value (signifying some catagory of entry error). If the typed-in candidate integer is valid, then the Boolean variable "valid_int_ent" (valid integer entry) is set to "true" at line 0080, and that "true" value is passed back out to the driver routine via the parameter list. Otherwise, if IORESULT was non-zero, then line 0080 would never be reached, and the "false" value of "valid_int_ent" previously set in the driver routine would remain in effect.

Look more carefully at what the function IORESULT actually does. What must happen before IORESULT will respond to data input with a zero error code value?

- First, the integer must be entered in the proper format; that is, only a number or a minus sign is a legal character here. Letters, function keys, commas, blank spaces, and decimal points are all illegal, and their presence will cause IORESULT to generate a non-zero error code value. Note that prefixing with "+" signs is also illegal.

- Second, given that the integer is in the proper format, the integer must be in the Turbo system's predefined range of -32768 through 32767. If not, the error code number returned is non-zero, signifying an entry error at the system level.

Before leaving this procedure, note that the code at lines 0075 and 0080 is often written in articles and manuals as

valid_int_ent := (IORESULT = 0);

So if you see this form and understand it, then you can use it as it stands; otherwise, the equivalent version at lines 0075 and 0080 is just as good.

ENTER_REAL

This procedure allows the programmer to enter a valid real number into the program via the keyboard. Like ENTER_INTEGER, this procedure takes two "var" parameters, "real_val" (real value) and "valid_real ent" (valid real entry). Prior to a read operation, the default compiler I/O checking mechanism is turned off ({$i-}). The typed-in data is then held in the variable "real_val" (real value), and the compiler I/O checking mechanism is turned on again ({$i+}). IORESULT looks at the candidate input variable "real_val" and checks it for validity from the system's point of view. If the candidate value is valid, then it is passed from the procedure into the driver routine by way of the address reference or the "var" mechanism. At the same time, the Boolean variable is changed from "false" to "true" and also passed to the main

10 Data Input and Revision

routine. If the candidate value is not valid, then "real_val" is left undefined, and "valid_real_ent" is left as it was originally set in the main routine—"false." Here is what IORESULT looks for when validating a real number data entry:

- **correct format**: Legal characters for reals include minus signs, the letters "e" or "E" (as part of the floating point notation signifying the presence of exponents), decimal points, and any of the digits 0-9. Note that if you enter a real number in floating point format, watch out for two warnings concerning "+" signs. First, an entry such as +2.34e+14 is *illegal* because of the "+" preceding the number "2." It is not needed. Second, an entry such as +55.4572 in non-floating point format is illegal because of the same prefixed "+" sign. Note that either a "+" or "-" sign in front of the exponent part of a number in floating point format is legal.

- **illegal characters** such as any letter other than "e" or "E," as well as any function key, commas, tabs, blanks, and symbol characters such as dollar signs, etc.

- **correct range**: The predefined value limits for the computer are quite large, 1e - 38 at the lower end and 1e + 38 at the upper end. Any real value outside of these limits would force IORESULT to generate a non-zero error code value signifying an input entry error.

- If a **"0" error code** is generated by IORESULT, then, as far as the computer is concerned, the data entered is valid.

The predefined standard function IORESULT is powerful indeed. As you have seen, it is capable of performing all the required error checks on numeric data—integer or real. For programmers to code all those error conditions themselves would be tedious and time consuming.

Powerful as it is, however, there is one aspect of input data validation that IORESULT cannot anticipate — your own requirements for what constitutes a valid range for your computing purposes. For example, if you are entering an integer value to represent an amortization period in mortgage analysis, IORESULT can tell you that the candidate entry is correct if it lies between -32768 and 32767. But suppose your requirements are more demanding than that. First, you must have a positive value; second, assume its lower limit should be no less than 15 years and no greater than 30 years. As you can see, these requirements are specialized and peculiar to your application. For these reasons, in the input validation programs of this chapter, a second level of input validation has been provided.

MODULE: DOLLARS.INC

This module consists of two procedures: DISPLAY_DOLLARS and a subprocedure, INSERT_COMMAS. These procedures change an otherwise unreadable dollar amount such as 999999999.99 into a form more suitable for display: $999,999,999.99. Following is the code for these two procedures.

```
{==============================================================}
0005 {dollars.inc}      {"Dollars include.inc"          }
0010                    {On disk as "dollars.inc"       }
0015 { this module converts a dollar entry from its real format
0020   into a display version with 2 decimal places,dollar sign,
0025   commas and a negative sign if needed.
0030 }
0035 {==============================================================}
0040
0045 procedure      DISPLAY_DOLLARS(d_val       : real;
0050                                var d_str   : str16);
0055 type
0060      str13 = string[13];
0065
0070 var
0075      d_str_temp : str13; {max = -999999999.99    }
0080      blanks,
0085      characters : integer; { characters = 13 - blanks }
0090      i          : integer;
0095      exit_flag  : boolean;
0100 {--------------------------------------------------------------}
0105
0110      procedure      INSERT_COMMAS(d_str_temp : str13;
0115                                   characters: integer;
0120                                   var d_str : str16);
0125
0130      Begin    {sub procedure insert_commas}
0135
```

...continued

10 Data Input and Revision

...from previous page

```
0140              CASE (characters) OF
0145                3   : d_str := CONCAT('$',COPY(d_str_temp,1,3));
0150                4   : d_str := CONCAT('$',COPY(d_str_temp,1,4));
0155                5   : d_str := CONCAT('$',COPY(d_str_temp,1,5));
0160                6   : d_str := CONCAT('$',COPY(d_str_temp,1,6));
0165
0170
0175                7   : IF (d_val <= 0) THEN        {-999.99}
0180                        d_str := CONCAT('$',COPY(d_str_temp,1,7))
0185                      ELSE                        {9999.99}
0190                         d_str := CONCAT('$',COPY(d_str_temp,1,1),','
0195                                          ,COPY(d_str_temp,2,6));
0200
0205
0210                8   : d_str := CONCAT('$',COPY(d_str_temp,1,2),','
0215                                       ,COPY(d_str_temp,3,6));
0220
0225                9   : d_str := CONCAT('$',COPY(d_str_temp,1,3),','
0230                                       ,COPY(d_str_temp,4,6));
0235
0240
0245               10   : IF (d_val <= 0) THEN        {-999999.99}
0250                        d_str := CONCAT('$',COPY(d_str_temp,1,4),','
0255                                         ,COPY(d_str_temp,5,6))
0260                      ELSE                        {9999999.99}
0265                         d_str := CONCAT('$',COPY(d_str_temp,1,1),','
0270                                          ,COPY(d_str_temp,2,3),','
0275                                          ,COPY(d_str_temp,5,6));
0280
0285            { -9999999.99    = ($)-9(,)999(,)999.99 }
0290              11   : d_str := CONCAT('$',COPY(d_str_temp,1,2),','
0295                                       ,COPY(d_str_temp,3,3),','
0300                                       ,COPY(d_str_temp,6,6));
0305
0310            { -99999999.99   = ($)-99(,)999(,)999.99 }
0315              12   : d_str := CONCAT('$',COPY(d_str_temp,1,3),','
0320                                       ,COPY(d_str_temp,4,3),','
0325                                       ,COPY(d_str_temp,7,6));
0330
0335            { -999999999.99 = ($)-999(,)999(,)999.99 }
0340              13   : d_str := CONCAT('$',COPY(d_str_temp,1,4),','
0345                                       ,COPY(d_str_temp,5,3),','
0350                                       ,COPY(d_str_temp,8,6));
0355
0360              END; {case}
0365        End;       {sub procedure insert_commas}
0370 {------------------------------------------------------------------}
0375
0380 Begin     {procedure display_dollars}
0385       {* gotoxy(1,11);write(d_val:13:2); *}
0390       {13 chars including "-" and "."} {11 is max mantissa size}
0395       STR(d_val:13:2 , d_str_temp);
0400       {* gotoxy(1,12);write('*',d_str_temp,'*'); *}
0405       i := 1 ; blanks := 0; exit_flag := false;
0410       REPEAT
0415            IF (d_str_temp[i] = ' ') THEN   {1 blank}
0420            Begin
0425                {* write(bell);delay(1000); *}
0430                blanks := blanks + 1;
0435                i := i + 1;
```

...continued

Data Input and Revision 10

...from previous page

```
0440                    End
0445                ELSE
0450                    exit_flag := true;
0455            UNTIL (exit_flag = true);
0460            characters := 13 - blanks; { # of chars = 13 - blanks}
0465            {* gotoxy(1,13);write(characters,'     ',blanks); *}
0470            d_str_temp := COPY(d_str_temp,blanks + 1,characters);
0475            {strip out the blanks....}
0480            {* gotoxy(1,14);write('*',d_str_temp,'*'); *}
0485            INSERT_COMMAS(d_str_temp,    {...passed in}
0490                          characters,
0495                          d_str);        {...passed back out}
0500        End;      {procedure display_dollars}
{============ end of module "display_dollars.inc" =====================}
```

DOLLARS.INC.: NOTES

DISPLAY_DOLLARS

This procedure takes two parameters from the driver routine. The first is "d_val" (dollar value), a real number (the number form in which dollar amounts will be expressed). The second is the "var" variable "d_str (dollar string), which is created inside the procedure and then passed out to the driver routine where it is displayed. "D_str" is of type str16 (string[16]).

The main local variables created each time that DISPLAY_DOLLARS is called are "d_str_temp" (dollar string temporary), "blanks," and "characters." Note that "d_str_temp" is of type str13 (string[13]) because entry of a real number in non-exponential format allows for a maximum mantissa size of 11 significant digits as well as a decimal and a minus sign (plus signs are illegal); therefore, a maximum of 13 characters is allowed. Note that just because the maximum allowable number of characters is 13 does not mean that all dollar amounts entered must be of length 13.

Look now at the body of the procedure. The first step in changing the real value into a suitable display version is to convert it into its string equivalent using the built-in numeric value-to-string conversion function STR at line 0395. Here, the expression "d_val:13:2" (d_val : with 13 characters total : with 2 digits to the right of the decimal) is converted into a string equivalent called "d_str_temp" of type str13. As hinted above, if "d_str_temp" contains fewer than 13 characters, there will be

10 Data Input and Revision

leading blanks after the string variables are "right adjusted" or packed against the right-hand end of the allowable 13-character field defined for it. For example, if "d_val" was entered as 999999.99, then "d str temp" would appear in its 13-character field as |bbbb999999.99| with 4 leading blanks. Commas cannot be directly entered into "d_str_temp" until it is converted into a form that is first stripped of its leading blanks. This is the job of the REPEAT..UNTIL loop starting at line 0410. The number of blanks is computed and then subtracted from 13 at line 0460. Once the number of blanks is known, "d_str_temp" can be converted into its blankless form using the COPY procedure at line 0470. From the above example, you know there are 13 characters total in the field. You also know that there are 4 blanks; therefore, there are 9 characters to work with. The COPY function will extract (parse) the rightmost 9 characters of "d_str_temp," starting at position (4 + 1) = 5 in "d_str_temp." The expression would look like this:

    d_str_temp := COPY(d_str_temp,5,9)

or graphically like this:

				position #:								
1	2	3	4	5	6	7	8	9	10	11	12	13
b	b	b	b	9	9	9	9	9	9	9	9	9
				1	2	3	4	5	6	7	8	9
				character #:								

In words, the above expression would say "take 'd_str_temp,' begin at position #5, and take 9 characters starting from there (position 5). This resulting string of characters is the new 'd_str_temp' (line 0470)."

The result of the COPY procedure is a revised "d_str_temp," which now looks like this:

    |999999.99|

and is the form in which "d_str_temp" is passed into the subprocedure INSERT_COMMAS.

INSERT_COMMAS

This subprocedure takes three parameters. The first is "d_str_temp" (dollar string temporary) whose maximum number of characters allowed is 13. The second is the calculated number of characters actually present in "d_str_temp." The last is "d_str" (dollar_string). This variable is created inside this procedure and then passed out through DISPLAY_DOLLARS ("var'd") to the driver routine where it is displayed. "D_str" is of type str16 (string[16]) because 16 is the maximum number of characters that can result when you insert one dollar sign and two commas into a real value that already has 11 significant digits along with a decimal and a minus sign (see line 0335).

This procedure is a good example of a practical application of the string CONCAT (string combining) procedure and the string COPY (string partitioning or parsing) procedure. The way in which "d_str_temp" will be broken up and then recombined with the inserted dollar sign and commas will depend on the number of characters in the string. The variable "characters" supplies this information at line 0115. For example, say there are 13 characters in the string (line 0340). This concept can be illustrated as follows:

position #:

1	2	3	4	5	6	7	8	9	10	11	12	13
-	9	9	9	9	9	9	9	9	.	9	9	
1	2	3	4									
				1	2	3						
							1	2	3	4	5	6

character #:

The code COPY (d_str_temp,1,4) at line 0340 essentially says "subdivide (parse, extract, partition) that part of 'd_str_temp' starting at position #1 and continuing for 4 consecutive characters. The result is '-999." Line 0345 essentially says "partition that part of 'd_str_temp' starting at position #5 and continuing for 3 characters. The result is '999.'" Line 0350 essentially says "parse that portion of 'd_str_temp' starting at position #8 and continuing for 6 characters. The result is '999.99.'"

10   Data Input and Revision

Once the string -999999999.99 is parsed into "-999," "999," and "999.99," the CONCAT or string-combining procedure is invoked. The "$" sign is combined with "-999" to give "$-999"; a comma is added to give "$-999,"; the "999" is added to give "$-999,999, followed by another comma to give "$-999,999," followed by "999.99." The final result turns out to be "$-999,999,999.99."

Finally, note that the CASE selection variable "character" has a minimum value of 3. This value will handle the smallest dollar amount that can be entered: .01. The result, "$.01," would then be passed out of INSERT_COMMAS (with only a "$" added) via the string variable "d_str." Remember, "d_str" can be a string of any size up to a maximum of 16 typed characters.

MODULE: DATES.INC

This module is comprised of two procedures. ENTER_DATE allows you to input a date from the keyboard and to validate that date for correct month, day, and year. Once the date is validated, the second procedure, CONVERT_DATETOVALUE (convert date to value), will convert the string entry into an integer value for use in computations such as finding the number of days between two dates, which is useful in calculating interest owing on your mortgage. Following is the code:

```
{=================================================================}
0005  {dates.inc}       {"dates include"}
0010                    {On disk as "dates.inc"}
0015  { This module allows the user to input a date in string value
0020    from the keyboard. This module then validates that date and
0025    if valid, will calculate that day's number value. This is
0030    useful in applications where the number of days between 2
0035    different dates is needed.
0040  }
0045  {=================================================================}
0050
0055  procedure       ENTER_DATE(var dat_str   : str11;
0060                             var vde       : boolean;
0065                             var yr_val    : integer;
0070                             var dat_val   : integer);
0075
0080  const
0085       bell = #$07;
0090
0095  type
0100       str3 = string[3];
0105       str2 = string[2];
```

...*continued*

Data Input and Revision 10

...from previous page

```
0110        str4 = string[4];
0115        str36= string[36];
0120
0125 var
0130        all_months_str       : str36;
0135        month_str            : str3;
0140        month_val            : integer;
0145        day_str              : str2;
0150        day_val              : integer;
0155        year_str             : str4;
0160        year_val             : integer;
0165        code                 : integer; {used in VAL function}
0170        legal_month_found    : boolean;
0175        leap_year            : boolean;
0180        vde1,vde2,vde3,
0185        vde4,vde5            : boolean;
0190  {----------------------------------------------------------------}
0195
0200        procedure CONVERT_DATETOVAL;
0205
0210        var
0215            days : integer;
0220
0225        Begin {sub procedure convert_datetoval}
0230            {* gotoxy(1,24);write('month_val = ',month_val); *}
0235            {* gotoxy(16,24);write('day_val = ',day_val);   *}
0240            {* gotoxy(30,24);write('year_val = ',year_val); *}
0245            date_val := 0; {clear to 0}
0250            year_val := year_val - 1920;
0255            {* gotoxy(50,24);write('adj_year_val = ',year_val); *}
0260            CASE (month_val) OF
0265              1: days  :=      0;   2: days :=      31;   3: days :=  59
0270              4: days  :=     90;   5: days :=     120;   6: days := 151;
0275              7: days  :=    181;   8: days :=     212;   9: days := 243;
0280             10: days  :=    273;  11: days :=     304;  12: days := 334;
0285            END; {case}
0290            {* delay(8000);write(bell);gotoxy(1,24);clreol; *}
0295            {* gotoxy(1,24); *}
0300            {* write(days,'       '); *}
0305            {* write(year_val*365,'    '); *}
0310            {* write(year_val DIV 4,'   '); *}
0315            write(day_val);
0320               dat_val := days+(year_val*365)+(year_val DIV 4) + 1 +
0325                       day_val;
0330            IF (year_val MOD 4 = 0) AND (month_val <= 2) THEN
0335                  dat_val := dat_val - 1;
0340        End;      {sub-procedure convert_datetoval}
0345  {----------------------------------------------------------------}
0350
0355 Begin    {procedure enter_date}
0360        month_str := '   ' ; month_val:= 0;    {3 blanks}
0365        day_str   := '  ' ; day_val   := 0;    {2 blanks}
0370        year_str  := '    '; year_val := 0;    {4 blanks}
0375        code := 0;      {code of 0 means no error in VAL conversion}
0380
0385        vde1 := true ; vde2 := true ; vde3 := true ; vde4 := true;
0390        vde5 := true;
0395        read(dat_str);         {TYPE THE DATE STRING}
0400
```

...continued

10 Data Input and Revision

...from previous page

```
0405            {vde1 check:}
0410             IF (COPY(dat_str,4,1) <>' ') OR (COPY(dat_str,7,1)<>' ')
0415            THEN
0420                 vde1 := false;
0425
0430            {vde2 check:}
0435            all_months_str := 'janfebmaraprmayjunjulaugsepoctnovdec';
0440            month_str := COPY(dat_str, 1 , 3); {first three characters}
0445            month_val := 1;
0450            legal_month_found := false;
0455            REPEAT
0460                    IF (month_str = COPY(all_months_str,3 * month_val -
0465                                                         2,3)) THEN
0470                       legal_month_found := true
0475                    ELSE
0480                       month_val := month_val + 1;
0485            UNTIL ((month_val > 12) OR (legal_month_found = true));
0490            IF (legal_month_found = false) THEN
0495                 vde2 := false;
0500
0505            {vde3 check:}
0510            day_str := COPY(dat_str , 5 , 2); {2 positions: 5 & 6}
0515            VAL(day_str , day_val , code);
0520            IF (code > 0) THEN
0525                 vde3 := false;
0530
0535            IF (day_val < 1) OR (day_val > 31) THEN
0540                 vde3 := false;
0545
0550            {vde4 check:}
0555            IF (month_str = 'feb') AND (day_val = 30) THEN vde4 := false;
0560            IF (month_str = 'feb') AND (day_val = 31) THEN vde4 := false;
0565            IF (month_str = 'apr') AND (day_val = 31) THEN vde4 := false;
0570            IF (month_str = 'jun') AND (day_val = 31) THEN vde4 := false;
0575            IF (month_str = 'sep') AND (day_val = 31) THEN vde4 := false;
0580            IF (month_str = 'nov') AND (day_val = 31) THEN vde4 := false;
0583
0585            {vde5 check:}
0590            year_str := COPY(dat_str , 8 , 4); {4 positions: 8,9,10 & 11}
0595            VAL(year_str , year_val , code);
0600            IF (code > 0) THEN
0605                 vde5 := false;
0610
0615            yr_val := year_val; {"yr_val" to be passed to main routine}
0620                               {for test of limits 1920 to 1999      }
0625            IF (year_val MOD 4 = 0) AND ((year_val MOD 400 = 0) OR NOT
0630                (year_val MOD 100 = 0)) THEN       {notice DOUBLE BRACKETS
0635                                                    format}
0640
0645                 leap_year := true
0650            ELSE
0655                 leap_year := false;
0660
0665            IF (month_val = 2) AND (day_val = 29) AND (leap_year = false)
0670            THEN
0675                 vde5 := false;
0680
0685            {vde1..vde5 check for false:}
0690            IF ((vde1 = false) OR (vde2 = false) OR (vde3 = false) OR
```

...continued

...from previous page

```
0695                (vde4 = false) OR (vde5 = false)) THEN {double brackets}
0700
0705            vde := false   {result passed out to main routine}
0710        ELSE
0715        Begin
0720            vde := true;   {result passed to out main routine}
0725            CONVERT_DATETOVAL;
0730        End;
0735 End;        {procedure enter_date}
{============ end of the module "dates.inc" ===========================}
```

DATES.INC: NOTES

ENTER_DATE

The purpose of this procedure is two-fold. First, it will accept a date entered from the keyboard and will validate it for correct format. Second, it will return the integer equivalent values for the month, day, and year portions of the date for use in the subprocedure CONVERT DATETOVAL (convert date to value). This procedure has four parameters. The first, "dat_str" (date string), is of type str11 (string[11]) and is in the form MMMbDDbYYYY. "Yr_val" (year value) is an integer value used in the second stage of the date validation and will be fully explained later. "Vde" (valid date entry) is a Boolean variable that communicates to the driver routine whether or not the date string entered is valid or not. "Date_val" (date value) is of type integer and represents the integer value corresponding to the date entered in string form. The values of all these parameters are created from within the procedure and then passed on to the driver routine by the "var" prefix in the parameter list.

The local variables, while high in number, are quite straightforward. The variables, "vde1, vde2,..,vde5" are all Boolean and read as "valid date entry test 1," "valid date entry test 2," etc. The first five lines of the procedure clear the string and value variables for the month, day, and year. Lines 0385 and 0390 set all the flags to true. You then type in the candidate date entry at line 0395 using the variable "dat_str" (date string). The expected format is a three-letter month, a space, a two-digit month, a space, and, finally, a four-digit year.

10 Data Input and Revision

The validation section of the procedure follows with five checkpoints, each assigned the job of checking the date string for a particular type of entry error.

- **{vde1 check:}** at line 0405 checks for a blank character at positions 4 and 7 of "dat_str." If a non-blank character is detected instead, then "vde1" is set to the value "false."

- **{vde2 check:}** at line 0430 checks that a valid three-character month string has been entered. Line 0435 defines the variable "all_months_string" as shown. Line 0440 extracts from the entered date string the left-hand three characters starting at position 1. The code between lines 0455 and 0485 performs two tasks: first, it attempts to match what has been typed as a month with one of "jan," "feb," "mar," "apr," "may," "jun," "jul," "aug," "sep," "oct," "nov," or "dec" contained in "all_months_str." Second, if a valid three-character month string is matched to the candidate month string, the integer variable "month_val" (month value) is also returned. For example, if you were to type the candidate month string "may," the code in the REPEAT..UNTIL loop (lines 0455-0485) would answer two questions: Is "may" a legal month? And, if so, what is its integer month value, assuming that "jan" is month number 1? Look at Figure 10.4 to see how line 0460 works.

Line 0460 makes a comparison. On the left-hand side, there is the three-character month string that was typed, namely "may." On the right-hand side, there is a changing three-character partition of the 36-character variable "all_months_str." When "month_val" is 1 (from line 0445), then the 3 characters extracted by using COPY are "jan." You can make the comparison between "may" and "jan." They are not equal, so "month_val" is increased to 2 at line 0480. Since *neither* of the tests "(month_val > 12)" or "(legal month_found)" is true, you return to line 0460 with a "month_val" of 2. The right-hand side of the comparison then yields

COPY(all_months_str,4,3);

Data Input and Revision **10**

```
1  2  3  1  2  3  1  2  3  1  2  3  1  2  3  1  2  3  1  2  3  1  2  3  1  2  3  1  2  3  1  2  3  1  2  3
j  a  n  f  e  b  m  a  r  a  p  r  m  a  y  j  u  n  j  u  l  a  u  g  s  e  p  o  c  t  n  o  v  d  e  c
1  2  3  4  5  6  7  8  9  10 11 12 13 14 15 16 17 18 19 20 21 22 23 24 25 26 27 28 29 30 31 32 33 34 35 36
```

month_val	3 * month_val - 2	3 positions	characters
start: 1	1	position 1 2 3	j a n
2	4	4 5 6	f e b
3	7	7 8 9	m a r
4	10	10 11 12	a p r
5	13	13 14 15	m a y
6	16	16 17 18	j u n
7	19	19 20 21	j u l
8	22	22 23 24	a u g
9	25	25 26 27	s e p
10	28	28 29 30	o c t
11	31	31 32 33	n o v
12	34	34 35 36	d e c

Figure 10.4 {vde2.check:} Detail

10 Data Input and Revision

and the character string "may" is compared with "feb" located inside of "all_months_str." Again, the tests at line 0460 fail. Continuing in this manner inside the loop, you come to "month_val" = 5. The right-hand side of the comparison now yields

   COPY(all_months_str,13,3)

and the character string "may" on the left-hand side is compared with "may" on the right. Since these two strings are equal, "legal_month_found" is changed from "false" to "true" at line 0470, and the bottom of line 0485 drops out since *at least one* of the exit tests has been satisfied. Since "legal_month_found" was set to true, lines 0490 and 0495 would have been ignored and you would continue to line 0505.

What if you had typed an illegal month, say, "xyz"? In that case, "xyz" would have been compared to each of "jan"..."dec" and failed the comparison test each time. After "month_val" had failed the comparison test for "dec" (month 12), "month_val" would be changed to 13. At line 0485, the "(month_val 12)" exit condition would become true and you would fall through. Since a match for the candidate month, "xyz," had not been found, "legal_month_found" would still be false, so the Boolean flag variable "vde2" would be set to false (line 495).

- {vde3 check:} at line 0505 checks the day portion of "dat_str" for a legal entry. Unlike the month portion above, where strings were matched, it is necessary here to take the extracted day portion and match it against a range of legal integer values. To do this, you first need the services of another special conversion procedure called VAL. This built-in procedure will convert a given string into a numeric value—if it is possible to make the conversion. For example, if "day_str" had a string value of "15," then applying the VAL conversion procedure to it would result in "day val" (here defined as an integer type) having the numeric value 15 and the Turbo system integer variable "code" having the value 0 (meaning no errors detected during conversion); however, if "day_str" had a string value of, say, "5w," then the VAL procedure, when it attempted to convert

"5w" into an integer, would be unable to do so. The result of the failed conversion attempt would be a "code" value *greater than 0* and an undefined integer value. This in itself is enough to set the Boolean "vde3" to "false" at line 0525 and will cause the code to skip down to Line 0535 for the next test. But, assuming the string-to-integer conversion was successful, the next test comes up immediately at line 0535 where a test for the legal day range is made. If the "day val" candidate is less than 1 or greater than 31, then "vde3" is set to "false," as no month has 0 days or more than 31 days.

So "vde3" can be set to "false" for two reasons: either the conversion from "day_str" to a legal integer "day_val" is not possible ("code" > 0), or, given that the original conversion succeeds ("code" = 0), the resulting integer value representing the day value is not between 1 and 31 inclusive.

If you don't know why or where the integer variable "code" came from, read on. Remember that when using the built_in VAL conversion routine, you are responsible for supplying its three parameters in this order: the string to be converted, the variable that is to hold the forthcoming numeric value of the converted string, and a status variable that gives the resulting status of the conversion operation once it is done (either "0" or greater than "0," as you saw above). A value of "code" greater than 0 means that the attempt to convert from string to numeric value failed at the system level and that the failure occurred at position number "code" in the string. This string-to-value conversion status variable has been named "code" and is the same variable name used in the Turbo Pascal user's manual.

- {vde4 check:} at line 0550 is straightforward. Here, illegal february, april, june, and november days are tested for. If any of the six conditions is "true," then the Boolean flag variable "vde4" will be set to "false." There are more elegant ways to code this checkpoint, but this method is the most instructive.

10 Data Input and Revision

- **{vde5 check:}** at line 0585 first parses the right-hand four characters of "dat_str" (starting at position #8 in the string) and assigns them to the string variable "year_str." It then checks for illegal non-numeric characters in "year_str" by attempting to convert it into the integer variable "year_val" using the VAL procedure. If, at this point, "year_str" did contain a non-numeric character, VAL's attempt to convert it into the integer "year_val" would fail. "Code" would be set to an integer value greater than zero, and "year_val" would be left undefined. Since "year_val" was undefined, "vde5" would be set to "false" at line 0605. Assuming that "year_str" was successfully converted to an integer, lines 0625 and 0630 then test for a leap year. Line 0665 tests to see whether feb 29 of a non-leap year was entered. If it was entered, then "vde5" is set to "false."

The main idea behind this procedure is to type in a date input and then run it down through a filter of five check points. If the entered date fails at any one of the points, then the date is deemed illegal in some way. This is what lines 0690 and 0695 are saying: if the values of any one of "vde1" through "vde5" inclusive are "false," then the Boolean variable "vde" (valid data entry) for the whole date entry is set to "false." If none of "vde1" through "vde5" is "false," then all are "true" and so is "vde," the master validation flag.

Regardless of the outcome, the assigned value of "vde" (valid data entry) is passed out to the driver routine. One more point: if "vde" is "true," then the date entry string is qualified to enter the subprocedure CONVERT_DATETOVAL (convert date to value) at line 0725.

CONVERT_DATETOVAL

The inputs for this subprocedure are all found in the list of local variables of ENTER_DATE and have all been calculated there. They are "month_val," "day_val," and "year_val." The output from this subprocedure is "dat_val," an integer found in the parameter list of ENTER_DATE at line 0070. Note that the calculated value of "dat_val" (date value) will be passed to the driver routine via the "var" prefix. The variable "days" is the only one that is set up locally in this subprocedure. "Days" is the number of days from the beginning of the year and up to, but not including, the first day of each of the 12 months.

Because "dat_val" is defined as an integer, the range of "dat_val" must be kept under the allowed integer maximum of 32767. For this reason, the adjustment to "year_val" is made at line 0250. With this adjustment, jan 01 1920 becomes day number 1, and dec 31 1999 becomes day number 29,220.

The formula for "dat_val" is given at line 0320. For example, what is the day number corresponding to mar 17 1986? The value of "days" will be 59, the number of days from the start of the year up to, but not including, mar 1, that is, 31 days for january and 28 days for all of february (1986 is not a leap year). The value of "year_val" is 66 * 365 = 24090, based again on a non-leap year of 365 days. The third section of the formula then makes an adjustment for the number of leap years from 1920-1986 inclusive, so "(year_val DIV 4) + 1" = 17. 17 more days must be added to account for the number of leap years up to the start of 1986. The fourth section of the formula adds the number of days from march 01 1986 up to and including mar 17. This number is 17. "Dat_val" is then the sum of

$$59 + 24090 + (16 + 1) + 17 = 24183$$

One more adjustment must be made at line 0330 to avoid double counting. If the current year is a leap year and the current month value is either january or february, then the third part of the formula at line 0320 will have overstated the adjusted number of leap year days by 1 because you haven't yet gone beyond the end of february, yet an extra leap year day has been included (prematurely) in the third part of the formula at line 0320, "(year_val DIV 4) + 1." For example, if the date is jan 15 1988, then the value of "(1988 DIV 4) + 1" would be 18, but the value would be 18 only if you have a date *after* mar 01 1988. Note that because you are dealing exclusively with integer values here, the integer functions DIV and MOD are used.

MODULE: DATA_IR.DRV (DATA INPUT REVISE)

Unlike all the driver programs so far, this one is much longer and seems to be much more complex. It is longer because you are dealing with more than just one type of input. You are dealing with five types of input. It is apparently more complex because it is performing three

10 Data Input and Revision

main tasks. The first is the formatting, which takes up the first third of the program in the form of procedures. The second is the actual entry and validation of each of the five different input types:

- integer amount
- percentage amount
- dollar amount
- real number amount
- date

The third is the revision of these data inputs. This task takes up the last third of the program code. Following is the code:

```
{================================================================}
0005 program   data_ir(input,output);     {"Data input revise"}
0010                                      {On disk as "data_ir.drv"}
0015 {
0020   This program takes a selection of data input
0025   types and enters them via the keyboard, validates them and
0030   converts them from strings to numeric values and also
0035   asks if revisions are wanted.
0040 }
0045
0050 label     REVISE;                {for data input revisions}
0055
0060 const
0065       r1  = 163 ; r2 = 164 ; r3 = 165 ; r4 = 166 ; r5 = 167;
0070       q   = 113 ; bell = #$07;
0075
0080       {'r' = ascii 114 ; '1' = ascii 49 ; 'r1' = ascii 163 }
0085
0090 type
0095       str6  = string[6];       {for integer}
0100       str7  = string[7];       {for percentage str "+12.75%"}
0105       str11 = string[11];      {for date}
0110       str16 = string[16];
0115       str17 = string[17];
0120       str4  = string[4];       {input revisions}
0125
0130 var
0135       integer_val         : integer;   {for integer CANDIDATES}
0140       valid_integer_entry : boolean;   { entry #1 on screen    }
0145
0150       real_val            : real;      {for real CANDIDATES...}
0155       valid_real_entry    : boolean;   { #2,#3,#4 on screen    }
0160
           ...continued
```

196

Data Input and Revision 10

...from previous page

```
0165        date_str                : str11;     {for date CANDIDATES...(str. #11)}
0170        valid_date_entry        : boolean;   { entry #5 on screen        }
0175        year_val                : integer;
0180        date_val                : integer;
0185
0190        integer_val1            : integer;   {integer..(value #1)}
0195        valid_integer_entry1    : boolean;   {entry #1 }
0200        integer_str1            : str6;      {(string #1)}
0205
0210        percent_val1            : real;      {percentage..(value #1)}
0215        valid_percent_entry1    : boolean;   {entry #2 }
0220        percent_str1            : str7;      {(string #1)}
0225
0230        dollar_val1             : real;      {dollar..value #1}
0235        valid_dollar_entry1     : boolean;   {entry #3}
0240        dollar_str              : str16;
0245        dollar_str1             : str16;     {(string #1)}
0250
0255        real_val1               : real;      {real number..(value #1)}
0260        valid_real_entry1       : boolean;   {entry #4 }
0265        real_str1               : str17;
0270
0275        date_str1               : str11;     {date....}
0280        valid_date_entry1       : boolean;   {entry #5}
0285        year_val1               : integer;   (value #1)
0290        date_val1               : integer;   (value #1)
0295
0300        i                       : integer;   {for revisions....}
0305        ascii_sum               : integer;
0310        character               : char;
0315        revise_choice           : str4;
0320        exit_revise             : boolean;
0325        vf1,vf2,vf3,vf4,
0330        vf5                     : boolean;
0335  {================================================================}
0340  {$i ei_er.inc}         {"enter integer enter real"}
0345  {$i dollars.inc}
0350  {$i dates.inc}
0355  {================================================================}
0360
0365  procedure     CREATE_INPUT_VALIDATION_HEADER;
0370
0375  Begin
0380        gotoxy(14,18);         {col 14 : row 18}
0385        writeln('Input Validation.....Input:');
0390        gotoxy(30,20);
0395        writeln('.....Units:');
0400        gotoxy(30,22);
0405        writeln('Your Entry:');
0410  End;
0415  {================================================================}
0420
0425  procedure     ERASE_INPUT_VALIDATION_HEADER;{both Header and Data
0430                                                              parts}
0435
0440  Begin     {procedure erase_input_validation_header}
0445        window(3,16,78,22);    {row 16-22 ; col 3-78}
0450        clrscr;
0455        window(1,1,80,25)
0460  End;     {procedure erase_input_validation_header}
```

...continued

10 Data Input and Revision

...from previous page

```
0465   {======================================================================}
0470
0475   procedure          ERASE_INPUT_VALIDATION_DATA;
0480
0485   Begin      {procedure erase_input_validation_data}
0490        window(41,18,55,22);      {row 18-22 ; col 41-55}
0495        clrscr;
0500        window(1,1,80,25);
0505   End;        {procedure erase_input_validation_data}
0510   {======================================================================}
0515
0520   procedure          ERASE_DATA_ENTRY_LINE;
0525
0530   Begin      {procedure erase_data_entry_line}
0535        {* write(bell); *}
0540        gotoxy(42,22);for i := 1 to 20 do write(' ');
0545        {clears data entry line}
0550        gotoxy(42,22);
0555   End;        {procedure erase_data_entry_line}
0560   {======================================================================}
0565
0570   procedure          INTEGER_ENTRY_HEADER;
0575   Begin      {procedure integer_entry_header}
0580        gotoxy(42,18);
0585        writeln('INTEGER ENTRY');
0590        gotoxy(42,20);CLREOL;gotoxy(42,21);CLREOL;
0595        gotoxy(42,20);
0600        writeln('Legal Range: (-4783 to 12731)');
0605        gotoxy(42,22);
0610        FOR  i := 1 to 6 DO write(chr(176));
0615        gotoxy(42,22);
0620   End;        {procedure integer_entry_header}
0625   {======================================================================}
0630
0635   procedure          PERCENT_ENTRY_HEADER;
0640   Begin      {procedure percent_entry_header}
0645        gotoxy(42,18);
0650        writeln('PERCENTAGE');
0655        gotoxy(42,20);CLREOL;gotoxy(42,21);CLREOL;
0660        gotoxy(42,20);
0665        writeln('Legal Range: (0.00 to 99.999)');
0670        gotoxy(42,22);
0675        FOR i := 1 to 6 DO write(chr(176));
0680        gotoxy(42,22);
0685   End;        {procedure percent_entry_header}
0690   {======================================================================}
0695
0700   procedure          DOLLAR_AMOUNT_ENTRY_HEADER;
0705   Begin      {procedure dollar_amount_entry_header}
0710        gotoxy(42,18);
0715        writeln('DOLLAR AMOUNT');
0720        gotoxy(42,20);CLREOL;gotoxy(42,21);CLREOL;
0725        gotoxy(42,20);
0730        writeln('Legal Range: (-999999999.99');
0735        gotoxy(42,21);
0740        writeln('            to 999999999.99)');  {12 blanks}
0745        gotoxy(42,22);
0750        FOR i := 1 to 13 DO write(chr(176));
0755        gotoxy(42,22);
0760   End;       {procedure dollar_amount_entry_header}
```

...continued

Data Input and Revision 10

...from previous page

```
0765   {===================================================================}
0770
0775   procedure       REAL_ENTRY_HEADER;
0780   Begin      {procedure real_entry_header}
0785        gotoxy(42,18);
0790        writeln('REAL NUMBER');
0795        gotoxy(42,20);CLREOL;gotoxy(42,21);CLREOL;
0800        gotoxy(42,20);
0805        writeln('Legal Range: (-15000 to 15000)');
0810        gotoxy(42,22);
0815        FOR i := 1 to 11 DO write(chr(176));  {allows -14999.9999}
0820        gotoxy(42,22);
0825   End;      {procedure real_entry_header}
0830   {===================================================================}
0835
0840   procedure       DATE_ENTRY_HEADER;
0845   Begin      {procedure date_entry_header}
0850        gotoxy(42,18);
0855        writeln('DATE ENTRY');
0860        gotoxy(42,20);CLREOL;gotoxy(42,21);CLREOL;
0865        gotoxy(42,20);
0870        writeln('MMM DD YYYY   Range: (1920 to 1999)');
0875        gotoxy(42,22);
0880        FOR i := 1 to 3 DO write(chr(176));
0885        write(' ');  {1 blank}
0890        FOR i := 1 to 2 DO write(chr(176));
0895        write(' ');
0900        FOR i := 1 to 4 DO write(chr(176));
0905        gotoxy(42,22);
0910   End;      {procedure date_entry_header}
0915   {===================================================================}
0920
0925   procedure       REVISION_MENU;
0930   Begin      {procedure revision_menu}
0935        ERASE_INPUT_VALIDATION_HEADER;
0940        HIGHVIDEO;
0945        gotoxy(35,16);
0950        writeln('REVISIONS??');
0955        gotoxy(24,18);writeln('-YES-');
0960        gotoxy(20,20);writeln('Eg. to Revise');
0965        gotoxy(20,21);writeln('entry #4, type');
0970        gotoxy(20,22);writeln(' <r4RET> ');
0975
0980        gotoxy(53,18);writeln('-NO-');
0985        gotoxy(51,20);writeln('To Exit');
0990        gotoxy(51,21);writeln('type...');
0995        gotoxy(51,22);writeln('<qRET> ');
1000   End;      {procedure revision_menu}
1005   {============================================================}1010
1015   procedure       GENERAL_HEADER;
1020
1025   Begin      {procedure general_header}
1030        window(1,1,80,25);
1035        TEXTCOLOR(0);TEXTBACKGROUND(15);
1040        gotoxy(28,2);write(' DATA INPUT/REVISION DEMO ');
1045        gotoxy(35,3);write(' CHAPTER 10 ');
1050        TEXTCOLOR(15);TEXTBACKGROUND(0); {white on black bckgrd}
1055        gotoxy(21,6);write('01. Enter an INTEGER.......: ');
1060        gotoxy(21,7);write('02. Enter a PERCENTAGE.....: ');
1065        gotoxy(21,8);write('03. Enter a DOLLAR AMOUNT..: ');
```

...continued

10 Data Input and Revision

...from previous page

```
1070         gotoxy(21,9);write('04. Enter a REAL NUMBER....: ');
1075         gotoxy(21,10);write('05. Enter a DATE............: ');
1080   End;         {procedure general_header}
1085   {===================================================================}
1090
1095   Begin       {driver routine}
1100         window(1,1,80,25);clrscr;
1105         GENERAL_HEADER;
1110
1115         vf1 := true; vf2 := true;      {initialize validation flags}
1120         vf3 := true; vf4 := true;
1125         vf5 := true;                   {all flags unlocked}
1130         ERASE_INPUT_VALIDATION_HEADER; {both Header & Data parts}
1135         REVISE:     {A LABEL FOLLOWED BY A COLON}
1140         CREATE_INPUT_VALIDATION_HEADER;
1145
1150         WHILE (vf1 = true) DO          { INTEGER AMOUNT }
1155         Begin
1160              REPEAT
1165                   valid_integer_entry1 := false;
1170                   REPEAT
1175                        BUFLEN := 6;
1180                        valid_integer_entry := false;
1185                        ERASE_DATA_ENTRY_LINE;
1190                        INTEGER_ENTRY_HEADER;
1195                        ENTER_INTEGER(integer_val,
1200                                      valid_integer_entry);
1205                   UNTIL(valid_integer_entry = true);
1210                   IF ((integer_val >= -4783) AND
1215                       (integer_val <= 12731)) THEN
1220                        valid_integer_entry1 := true;
1225              UNTIL(valid_integer_entry1 = true);
1230              integer_val1 := integer_val;
1235              STR(integer_val,integer_str1);   {STR(from..,to..)}
1240              vf1 := false;          {lock out further changes}
1245              ERASE_INPUT_VALIDATION_DATA;
1250              gotoxy(50,6) ; for i := 1 to 20 do write(' ');
1255              gotoxy(50,6) ; write(integer_str1);
1260         End;       {while}
1265
1270         WHILE (vf2 = true) DO          {PERCENTAGE}
1275         Begin
1280              REPEAT
1285                   valid_percent_entry1 := false;
1290                   REPEAT
1295                        BUFLEN := 6;
1300                        valid_real_entry := false;
1305                        ERASE_DATA_ENTRY_LINE;
1310                        PERCENT_ENTRY_HEADER;
1315                        ENTER_REAL(real_val,
1320                                   valid_real_entry);
1325                   UNTIL(valid_real_entry = true);
1330
1335                   IF ((real_val > 0.01) AND
1340                       (real_val < 100)) THEN
1345                        valid_percent_entry1 := true
1350              UNTIL (valid_percent_entry1 = true);
1355              percent_val1 := real_val/100;   {convert to decimal for
1360                                               calculations}
```

...continued

200

Data Input and Revision 10

...from previous page

```
1365              STR(real_val:6:2,percent_str1);     {STR(from..,to..)}
1370              percent_str1 := CONCAT(percent_str1,'%');
1375              vf2 := false;          {lock out further revisions}
1380              ERASE_INPUT_VALIDATION_DATA;
1385              gotoxy(50,7) ; for i := 1 to 20 do write(' ');
1390              gotoxy(50,7) ; write(percent_str1);
1395          End;        {while}
1400
1405          WHILE (vf3 = true) DO          { DOLLAR AMOUNT }
1410          Begin
1415              REPEAT
1420                  valid_dollar_entry1 := false;
1425                  REPEAT
1430                      BUFLEN := 13; {includes "-" and "."}
1435                      valid_real_entry := false;
1440                      ERASE_DATA_ENTRY_LINE;
1445                      DOLLAR_AMOUNT_ENTRY_HEADER;
1450                      ENTER_REAL(real_val,
1455                                 valid_real_entry);
1460                  UNTIL(valid_real_entry = true);
1465                  IF((real_val >= -999999999.99) AND
1470                     (real_val <= 999999999.99)) THEN
1475                      valid_dollar_entry1 := true
1480              UNTIL (valid_dollar_entry1 = true);
1485              DISPLAY_DOLLARS(real_val,     {does string conversion}
1490                              dollar_str);
1495              dollar_val1 := real_val;
1500              dollar_str1 := dollar_str;
1505
1510              vf3 := false;      {lock out further revisions}
1515              ERASE_INPUT_VALIDATION_DATA;
1520              gotoxy(50,8) ; for i := 1 to 20 do write(' ');
1525              gotoxy(50,8) ; write(dollar_str1);
1530          End;        {while}
1535
1540          WHILE (vf4 = true) DO          { REAL NUMBER AMOUNT }
1545          Begin
1550              REPEAT
1555                  valid_real_entry1 := false;
1560                  REPEAT
1565                      BUFLEN := 11;
1570                      valid_real_entry := false;
1575                      ERASE_DATA_ENTRY_LINE;
1580                      REAL_ENTRY_HEADER;
1585                      ENTER_REAL(real_val,
1590                                 valid_real_entry);
1595                  UNTIL(valid_real_entry = true);
1600                  IF   ((real_val >= -15000) AND
1605                       (real_val <= 15000)) THEN
1610                       valid_real_entry1 := true
1615              UNTIL (valid_real_entry1 = true);
1620
1625              real_val1 := real_val;
1630              STR(real_val:11:4,real_str1);
1635              {":11:4" includes both "-" & "." | STR(from #,to string)}
1640              vf4 := false;          {lock out further revisions}
1645              ERASE_INPUT_VALIDATION_DATA;
1650              gotoxy(50,9) ; for i := 1 to 30 do write(' ');
1655              gotoxy(50,9) ; write(real_str1); {choose your format..}
1660              {* gotoxy(50,9) ; write(real_val1); *}
1665          End;        {while}
```

...continued

10 Data Input and Revision

...from previous page

```
1670
1675         WHILE (vf5 = true) DO         { DATE }
1680         Begin
1685             BUFLEN := 11;
1690             REPEAT
1695                 valid_date_entry1 := false;
1700                 REPEAT
1705                     BUFLEN := 11;
1710                     valid_date_entry := false;
1715                     ERASE_DATA_ENTRY_LINE;
1720                     DATE_ENTRY_HEADER;
1725                     ENTER_DATE(date_str,
1730                                valid_date_entry,
1735                                year_val,
1740                                date_val);
1745                 UNTIL(valid_date_entry = true);
1750                 IF (year_val >= 1920) AND (year_val <= 1999) THEN
1755                     valid_date_entry1 := true;
1760             UNTIL(valid_date_entry1 = true);
1765             date_str1 := date_str;   {for display.........}
1770             { year_val1 := year_val (optional) }
1775             date_val1 := date_val;   {for computations....}
1780             vf5 := false;            {lock out further changes}
1785             ERASE_INPUT_VALIDATION_DATA;
1790             gotoxy(50,10) ; for i := 1 to 20 do write(' ');
1795             gotoxy(50,10) ; write(date_str1);
1800             {* gotoxy(1,12);for i := 1 to 30 do write(' '); *}
1805             {* gotoxy(1,12); *}
1810             {* write('NUMBER ASSOCIATED WITH DATE = ',date_val1);*}
1815         End;        {while}
1820 {------------ revision section of driver ------------------------}
1825
1830         ERASE_INPUT_VALIDATION_HEADER;{erase whole lower area}
1835         REVISION_MENU;                {displays revision menu}
1840
1845         REPEAT
1850             BUFLEN := 4;
1855             exit_revise := false;
1860             ascii_sum := 0;
1865             gotoxy(39,24);write('    ');gotoxy(39,24); {4 blanks}
1870             read(revise_choice);       {Type in from the keyboard}
1875             FOR i := 1 to LENGTH(revise_choice) DO
1880             Begin
1885                 character := COPY(revise_choice , i , 1);
1890                 ascii_sum := ascii_sum + ORD(character);
1895             End;
1900             CASE (ascii_sum) OF
1905
1910             r1 : Begin                       {INTEGER}
1915                     TEXTCOLOR(0);TEXTBACKGROUND(15);
1920                     gotoxy(50,6);write(integer_str1);
1925                     TEXTCOLOR(15);TEXTBACKGROUND(0);
1930                     ERASE_INPUT_VALIDATION_HEADER;
1935                     vf1 := true;
1940                     goto REVISE;    {the label}
1945                  End;
1950
1955             r2 : Begin                       {PERCENTAGE}
1960                     TEXTCOLOR(0);TEXTBACKGROUND(15);
1965                     gotoxy(50,7);write(percent_str1);
```

...continued

...from previous page

```
1970                        TEXTCOLOR(15);TEXTBACKGROUND(0);
1975                        ERASE_INPUT_VALIDATION_HEADER;
1980                        vf2 := true;
1985                        goto REVISE;    {the label}
1990                End;
1995
2000           r3 : Begin                  {DOLLAR AMOUNT}
2005                        TEXTCOLOR(0);TEXTBACKGROUND(15);
2010                        gotoxy(50,8);write(dollar_str1);
2015                        TEXTCOLOR(15);TEXTBACKGROUND(0);
2020                        ERASE_INPUT_VALIDATION_HEADER;
2025                        vf3 := true;
2030                        goto REVISE;    {the label}
2035                End;
2037
2040           r4 : Begin                  {REAL AMOUNT}
2045                        TEXTCOLOR(0);TEXTBACKGROUND(15);
2050                        gotoxy(50,9);write(real_str1);
2055                        {* gotoxy(50,9);write(real_val);  *}
2060                        TEXTCOLOR(15);TEXTBACKGROUND(0);
2065                        ERASE_INPUT_VALIDATION_HEADER;
2070                        vf4 := true;
2075                        goto REVISE;    {the label}
2080                End;
2085
2090           r5 : Begin                  {DATE}
2095                        TEXTCOLOR(0);TEXTBACKGROUND(15);
2100                        gotoxy(50,10);write(date_str1);
2105                        TEXTCOLOR(15);TEXTBACKGROUND(0);
2110                        ERASE_INPUT_VALIDATION_HEADER;
2115                        vf5 := true;
2120                        goto REVISE; {the label}
2125                End;
2130
2135           q  : Begin
2140                        ERASE_INPUT_VALIDATION_HEADER;
2145                        gotoxy(32,20);
2150                        writeln('WILL EXIT AND QUIT');
2155                        exit_revise := true;
2160                End
2165
2170           ELSE       {make keyboard entry until correct}
2175
2180           END; {case}
2185        UNTIL (exit_revise = true);
2190 End.       {driver routine}
{====================================================================}
```

DATA_IR.DRV: NOTES

The declaration section of this driver routine is fairly extensive but not hard to understand. At line 0050 a label called REVISE has been declared. This label is an address or location in the program to which a jump is made from certain lines in the revision section of the driver routine. The REVISE label is located at the beginning of the routine's data entry section (line 1135).

10   Data Input and Revision

At line 0065, the declaration of constants begins, and they are assigned integer values of 163..167 and 113. What are these values and why are they so strange looking? First, "r1" means "revise entry number 1," and "q" means "quit revising and exit." The value of 163 is derived from "r1" as follows. If you look at a standard ASCII table, you will see that the ASCII value for "r" is 114 and that the ASCII value for the number "1" is 49. So pressing the keys <r> and then <1> translates as the constant value 114 + 49 = 163. The same idea follows with "r2".."r5." With "q," the ASCII value is 113 according to the table, so pressing the <q> key translates as the constant 113.

The "var" section is long but has been laid out in such a way to clarify its meaning. First, note that the variables of each of the input types have been grouped together in the order in which they would appear on the screen. Second, note lines 0135-0155. The variables "integer val" (integer value) and "valid_integer_entry" (valid integer entry) are the driver routine parameters into which the procedure ENTER_INTEGER (in "ei_er.inc") places its results. Likewise, the variables "real val" (real value) and "valid_real_entry" (valid real entry) hold the results of the procedure ENTER_REAL (also in "ei_er.inc").

For any *numeric* data entry to qualify as valid input, it must successfully pass two validating tests. The first test is format and machine-acceptable value range. This test was performed by ENTER_INTEGER and ENTER_REAL in the module "ei_er.inc," and the value and validity status were passed to the driver via the variables described above. The *inner* REPEAT..UNTIL loops at lines

     1170-1205 for Integers
     1290-1325 for Percentages
     1425-1460 for Dollar Amounts
     1560-1595 for Real Numbers

test for the validity of the numeric entry under the first validity test. If this test is passed ("valid_integer_entry" or "valid_real_entry" is "true"), then the numeric input candidate will enter the second of the two tests in the *outer* REPEAT..UNTIL loops at lines:

     1160-1225 for Integers
     1280-1350 for Percentages
     1415-1480 for Dollar Amounts
     1550-1615 for Real Numbers

Data Input and Revision **10**

The second validation test fine tunes or narrows the acceptable minimum and maximum limits of integers and reals. For integers, you know from ENTER_INTEGER that the candidate lies between -32768 and 32767. For reals, you know from ENTER_REAL that the candidate lies somewhere between 1e-38 and 1e+38.

What if, for a certain integer data input, *you* designated a legal entry as lying between, say, -4783 and 12731? And what if, for a certain real data input, *you* designated a legal entry as lying between a value greater than 0.00 and less than 100.00?

In the main routine, these and the other hypothetical program requirements are reflected for each of the numeric input types at lines

    1210 for Integers
    1335 for Percentages
    1465 for Dollar Amounts
    1600 for Real Numbers

If each of the numeric input types lies within its user-defined minimum and maximum limits, then its corresponding Boolean values

    "valid_integer_entry1"   for Integers
    "valid_percent_entry1"   for Percentages
    "valid_dollar_entry1"   for Dollar Amounts
    "valid_real_entry1"   for Real Numbers

will be set to "true." This setting permits exit from the outer REPEAT..UNTIL loop, and the candidate values will "graduate" and be assigned their program input values as follows:

    integer_val1   := integer_val   (line 1230)
    percent_val1   := real_val/100 (line 1355)
    dollar_val1   := real_val   (line 1495)
    real_val1   := real_val   (line 1625)

10 Data Input and Revision

These program input values have been suffixed with "1's" to distinguish them as fully validated input values that would be used in the program computations. In a real application program, these values could be named to represent any quantity that you want them to represent. Note the distinction made between the Boolean variables at the end of each of the REPEAT..UNTIL loops. Those in the inner REPEAT..UNTIL loops, such as "valid_real_entry," are not suffixed, while those in the outer REPEAT..UNTIL loops are suffixed with "1's," as you see in "valid_real_entry1" at line 1610.

Please note that suffixing of the Boolean validity flag variables with the number "1" is in no way connected with suffixing of the validated program input values.

What about non-numeric or mixed input types such as dates, which are entered into the computer as strings and not as numbers? The two-stage validation strategy still applies. The only difference lies in the first step of the process. With all integers or real numbers, the standard procedure, IORESULT, was used to handle all the formatting and machine-defined value limits. With a date (as with any string data), a customized string analogue to IORESULT must be created. The procedure ENTER_DATE was written to provide the first step in the validation of date string input. ENTER_DATE lies within the *inner* REPEAT..UNTIL loop between lines 1700 and 1745 and performs the first step in the validation of a date entry in a manner analogous to the other integer and real data inputs. Because ENTER_DATE is a customized string entry routine, the expected outputs would be a string value "date_str" (date string) and the Boolean "valid_date_entry." Unlike numeric input, each string entry routine is unique and may need other supplemental outputs as well. How can you use the sting variable "date_str" on its own to perform the second part of the two-stage validation process? You can't unless you get some help. For the date routine, two variables have therefore been added. The first is "year val" (year value) and the second is "date_val" (date value). Both were created inside ENTER_DATE and were passed out to the driver routine as integers for further use in the second stage of validation.

To test whether the "date_str" lies within the defined lower and upper limits of 1920 and 1999 respectively, its integerized year value component, "year_ val," is tested at line 1750 within the *outer* REPEAT..UNTIL loop (lines 1690-1760). If "year_val" is within the defined limits, the Boolean "valid_date_entry1" is set to "true"; therefore, "date_str" itself has successfully passed the second step of the two-step validation test for a date.

As was mentioned above, the procedure ENTER_DATE is a customized string entry routine. Strictly speaking, the variable "date_val" could be excluded from the coding, and there would be no effect on the validation process. It was included as a matter of efficiency. To calculate an integer value corresponding to a given date string, almost all the same variables would need to be used as were created inside ENTER_DATE. Instead of duplicating exactly the same code in a separate procedure, the job was finished here and the same code created from a small sub-procedure, CONVERT_DATETOVALUE, located inside ENTER DATE. "Date_value," although a by-product of the main objectives at this time, is quite useful in applications where the number of days between two dates needs to be calculated.

Dates have been used as a general model to illustrate how you can enter and validate string (non-numeric) data. There are all kinds of string input data types: names, inventory codes, zip codes, telephone numbers, part numbers, etc. Each of these, like the date, has its own unique characteristics, and each will require a customized routine written along the same lines as the date model created above. Following is a brief review of the method.

First, use the overall format as shown above between lines 1675 and 1815 of the driver routine. The double REPEAT..UNTIL loops are essential. The inner loop holds the outline for the first step of the validation, and the outer loop holds the outline for the second.

Second, write your specialized string entry and validation routine using ENTER_DATE as a general model. Pick out the unique characteristics of your string input variable, as was done with the Date, and test for correctness using the Boolean flag variables to hold the result as it was done in ENTER_DATE.

Third, if your string input variable needs to be in a predefined value range, integerize that section of the candidate data input string using the COPY and VAL string conversion routines. Earlier, these routines were used to convert the year portion of "date_str" into the integer "year_val" inside ENTER_DATE.

Finally, you can now perform the second part of the two-stage validation process by comparing your obtained integer value against some preset minimum and maximum limits. This step was done at line 1750 where "year_val" was compared against 1920 and 1999. Note that just as was done for numeric entries above, "date_val" has been designated

10 Data Input and Revision

as a candidate value, and "date_val1" has been designated for use in the program computations. Feel free to use your own variable naming conventions.

The description of the variables under the "var" section of the driver routine concludes here. The few remaining variables will be clarified shortly. The next section explains how the body of the driver routine operates.

DRIVER ROUTINE: DATA ENTRY SECTION (LINES 1100-1815)

This demonstration program features five different input types; however, the general structure of each type's code is identical, so only one will be discussed here. Use the percentage data entry as a typical example. First, notice the WHILE..DO loop starting at line 1270. This loop is the key to original entry when the program is first run and the key to revised data entry when you want to change the data inputs. Prior to original entry, the access flag "vf2" (valid flag2) is set to "true." This setting allows access to the section of code contained within the WHILE..DO loop, and you are allowed to enter input data for a percentage value. As you will recall from the discussion above, the set of double REPEAT..UNTIL loops is then entered. The inner loop starting at line 1290 provides the first step in the validation process. If you type in a syntactically illegal entry or a value that is out of the predefined maximum range, "valid_real_entry" (line 1300) stays "false," and you must remain inside the *inner* REPEAT..UNTIL loop and type in another percentage entry from within the ENTER_REAL procedure at line 1315. Once "valid_real_entry" (line 1325) is set to "true," the second stage of validation in the *outer* loop can begin, starting at line 1335. If the candidate entry "real_val" is out of the prespecified range (lines 1335 & 1340), then "valid_percent_entry1" is left as "false," and you must re-enter the double REPEAT..UNTIL loops again at line 1280 and type in another percentage entry using the external procedure ENTER_REAL (line 1315). This time, if the candidate entry is valid at step 1 and within the range required by step 2 (line 1335), you drop through at line 1350 and assign the candidate "real_val/100" to the variable "percent_val1" (line 1355). "Percent_val1" can then be used in the program as validated data input. "Real_val" is now free to become a candidate input value for "dollar_amount" in the following section of code. Line 1375 is important here. Once a valid percentage value has been entered, "vf2" is changed from "true" to "false." If you were to return to line 1270 at a later time, you would not be able to re-enter this section of code. A "false" value in "vf2" would deny you access. This will be important later when you want to revise the input data.

What does "BUFLEN := 6" mean at line 1295? BUFLEN stands for "buffer length" and is a Turbo predefined variable whose default value is 128. You could type in up to 128 characters from the keyboard to represent this little percentage entry. Since you want to limit the maximum number of digits in the entry to six, you can set BUFLEN to 6, and if you tried to type more than 6 digits, you would find that you could not — a nice piece of insurance against those messy 128-character data entries.

DRIVER ROUTINE: DATA REVISION SECTION (LINES 1820-2190)

The data revision section is composed of three main parts. The first is a large REPEAT..UNTIL loop starting at line 1845. As long as the Boolean variable "exit_revise" is true, you will stay inside the loop. You can then revise any one of the five data input values as many times as you like. Only by pressing the <q> key and setting "exit_revise" to true at line 2155 can you exit this loop and terminate the program.

The second main part is the CASE..END structure starting at line 1900. The case selector value "ascii_sum" can take only 1 of 5 legal values:

$r1 = 163$; $r2 = 164$; $r3 = 165$; $r4 = 166$; $r5 = 167$; $q = 113$

If any other key combination is pressed, nothing will happen. Continue with the example and assume that you want to revise the percentage input value just entered above. You respond to the message printed by the procedure REVISION_MENU by pressing the keys <r><2>; that is, you press the letter "r" (for revise) and then the number "2" (for entry number 2). Pressing the keys <r><2> will cause the case selector variable "ascii_sum" to take on the value 163 as defined above in the Constant Section (line 0060). You then enter the section of code starting at line 1955 that specializes in the revision of a percentage value. Lines 1960-1965 highlight the value that you want to change. Line 1980 changes "vf2" from "false" back to "true." Recall that on original entry, "vf2" was set to "false" at line 1375. Line 1980 then uses a "goto" statement to transfer program control to the label REVISE at line 1135 in the Data Entry Section above. Notice that REVISE is located at the beginning of the five data input WHILE..DO loops. What is it that allows you to enter *only* the percent loop and, at the same time, prevents you from entering any of the other four loops? Recall

10 Data Input and Revision

that each time a valid data input was entered, its flag "vf1".."vf5" was set to a value of "false." Setting the flags "vf1".."vf5" to "false" would prevent any further entry to that particular section of code. By pressing <r><2>, you have selectively unlocked the "vf2" flag and reset it back to a value of "true," thus allowing re-entry into that section of code. No other sections of the code can be accessed since their guard flags, "vf1" and "vf3".."vf5," are still "false."

The third main part of revision centers around lines 1870-1895 and answers the question, how can you type in a string of characters that will activate the section of code you want executed? Specifically, how is it that typing <r><2> (line 1955) will enable you to revise entry number 2 starting at line 1270 above? The key to the answer lies in constructing the integer, "ascii_ sum." The CASE selector statement is restricted by the Pascal language to working only with **scalar** (linearly or sequentially ordered) data types, most notably integers (but not reals). The CASE selector statement cannot take string values. You must somehow translate keystrokes (or series of keystrokes) into integer values. This translation is performed in the code between lines 1870 and 1895.

This method is simple: translate each keystroke into its corresponding integer ASCII value, and then add up the individual ASCII values to derive the integer value representing the series of keystrokes. "Ascii sum" is the result (line 1890). For example, if you typed the keys <r><2> (revise entry #2), the calculated value of "ascii_ sum" returned at line 1890 would be

114 (ascii value for <r>) + 50 (ascii value for <2>) = 164.

The CASE statement would take its "ascii_sum" value of 164 and check the Case List to see if 164 (<r><2>) is a legal value. Since the value 164 matches the predefined constant value of <r><2> (line 1955), the keystroke combination is legal, and you can revise the percentage entry. On the other hand, if you entered, say, the keystroke combination <r><8>, the calculated "ascii_sum" would be (114 + 56 = 170). Since 170 is not equal to any of <r><1> (163)...<r><5> (167) or <q> (113), the keystrokes <r><8> are illegal, and you would jump back up to the REPEAT statement at line 1845 for a retry.

BUFLEN is set to 4 to prevent you from physically typing any more than four keystrokes. "Exit_revise" (line 1855) is set to "false" so that as long as you do not press <q>, you can revise for as long as you want. You type in the keystroke combination from the keyboard at line 1870, and BUFLEN is set to 4 to allow a maximum possible range of keystrokes from <r><1> to <r><99> plus a carriage return. Each character in the keystroke combination is handled separately in the loop starting at line 1875. The character string is parsed one character at a time from left to right at line 1885. Each character is then converted into its ASCII value and added into "ascii_sum" at line 1890. Note that you must use the built-in ORD function to get the ASCII integer value that corresponds to the isolated character created by the built-in COPY function at line 1885. To help you visualize the overall operation of the driver routine, refer to Figure 10.5.

10 Data Input and Revision

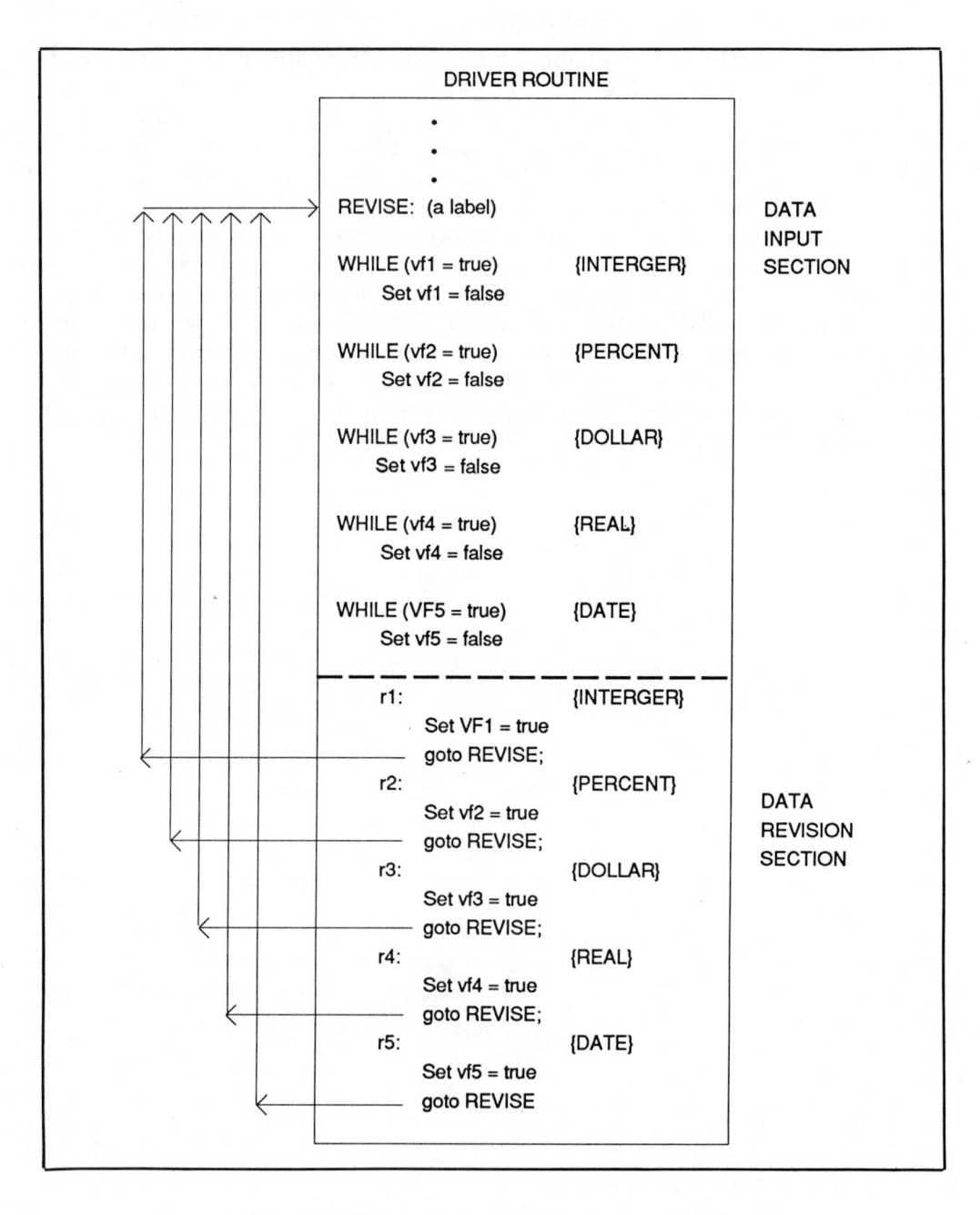

```
                        DRIVER ROUTINE
                             •
                             •
                             •
        REVISE: (a label)                          DATA
                                                   INPUT
        WHILE (vf1 = true)          {INTERGER}     SECTION
            Set vf1 = false

        WHILE (vf2 = true)          {PERCENT}
            Set vf2 = false

        WHILE (vf3 = true)          {DOLLAR}
            Set vf3 = false

        WHILE (vf4 = true)          {REAL}
            Set vf4 = false

        WHILE (VF5 = true)          {DATE}
            Set vf5 = false
        - - - - - - - - - - - - - - - - - -
            r1:                     {INTERGER}
                Set VF1 = true
                goto REVISE;
            r2:                     {PERCENT}
                Set vf2 = true                     DATA
                goto REVISE;                       REVISION
            r3:                     {DOLLAR}      SECTION
                Set vf3 = true
                goto REVISE;
            r4:                     {REAL}
                Set vf4 = true
                goto REVISE;
            r5:                     {DATE}
                Set vf5 = true
                goto REVISE
```

Figure 10.5   Driver Routine: Overall Layout

CHAPTER 11

VERTICAL AND HORIZONTAL SCROLLING WINDOWS

11 Vertical and Horizontal Scrolling Windows

The basics of the next applications program have already been established in Chapters 6 and 8. Chapter 6 explained the detailed mechanics of horizontal scrolling, and Chapter 8 did the same for vertical scrolling. In this chapter, the two techniques are brought together to create a bi-directional scrolling program, which, when customized to a particular user's needs, will prove an invaluable screen display tool.

VH_S2.INC

This ".inc" module supplies the driver program with the machinery to perform both vertical and horizontal scrolling of data contained within a 20×20 multiplication table. The above title refers to Part 1 of the book, where vertical and horizontal scrolling were introduced separately. Method "2" refers to the bi-directional scrolling technique using the "index address" method seen in Chapters 6 and 8. The overall structure of "vh_s2.inc" is as follows:

```
procedure VHSCROLL2
    subprocedure REWRITE_COL_LABEL
    subprocedure REWRITE_ROW_LABEL
    subprocedure REWRITE_SCR
```

- column labels are the numbers (ranging between 1-20) that lie along the top of the display screen.

- row labels are the numbers (also ranging between 1-20) that lie along the left-hand side of the display screen.

Both row and column labels act together to index the multiplication table. If you want to look up the product of, say, 4 and 5, first locate 4 along the top of the screen and then locate 5 along the left-hand side. Where they intersect in the body of the table, you will see their product, 20.

To illustrate the workings of "vh_s2.inc," three figures, 11.1, 11.2, and 11.3, are provided.

Vertical and Horizontal Scrolling Windows 11

		multiplicand				
	-*	1.00**	2.00**	3.00**	4.00**	5.00**	6.00*-
1.00*	-*	1.00**	2.00**	3.00**	4.00**	5.00**	6.00*-
2.00*	-*	2.00**	4.00**	6.00**	8.00**	10.00**	12.00*-
3.00*	-*	3.00**	6.00**	9.00**	12.00**	15.00**	18.00*-
4.00*	-*	4.00**	8.00**	12.00**	16.00**	20.00**	24.00*-
5.00*	-*	5.00**	10.00**	15.00**	20.00**	25.00**	30.00*-
6.00*	-*	6.00**	12.00**	18.00**	24.00**	30.00**	36.00*-

BI-DIRECTIONAL SCROLLING APPLICATION CHAPTER 11

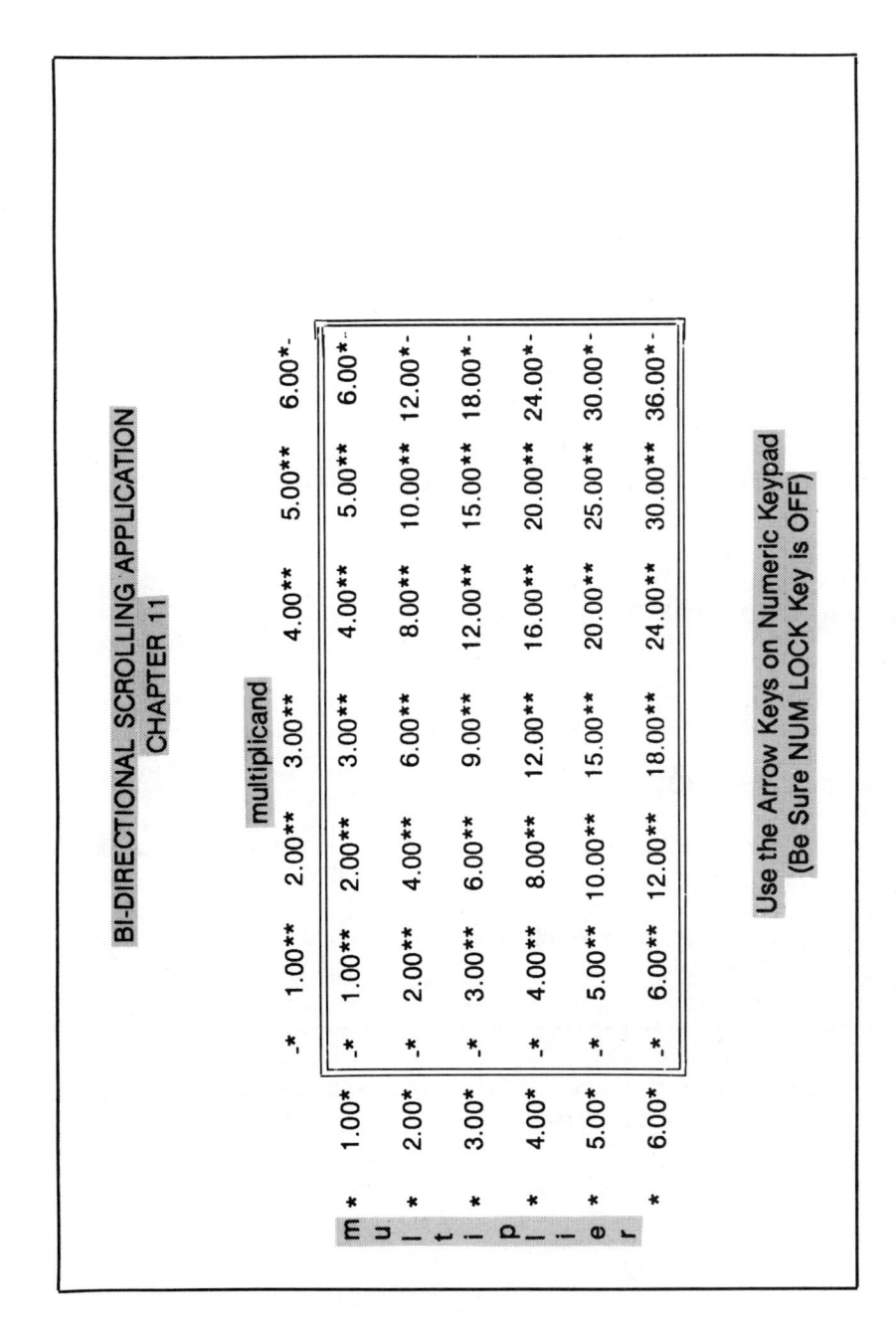

Use the Arrow Keys on Numeric Keypad (Be Sure NUM LOCK Key is OFF)

multiplier

Figure 11.1 Initialized Screen for Bi-directional Scroll Using the Computed Index Method

215

11 Vertical and Horizontal Scrolling Windows

```
                              subprocedure
                              REWRITE_COL_LABEL
                                      ↓
                        | 1 | 2 | 3 | 4 | 5 | 6 |

                  | 1 |  | 1 | 2 | 3 | 4 | 5 | 6 |
                  | 2 |  | 2 | 4 | 6 | 8 |10 |12 |
                  | 3 |  | 3 | 6 | 9 |12 |15 |18 |
                  | 4 |  | 4 | 8 |12 |16 |20 |24 |
                → | 5 |  | 5 |10 |15 |20 |25 |30 |
                  | 6 |  | 6 |12 |18 |24 |30 |36 |

  subprocedure                            subprocedure
  REWRITE_ROW_LABEL                       REWRITE_SCR
```

procedure "VHSCROLL2" — controls invocation of the subprocedures

procedure VHSCROLL2

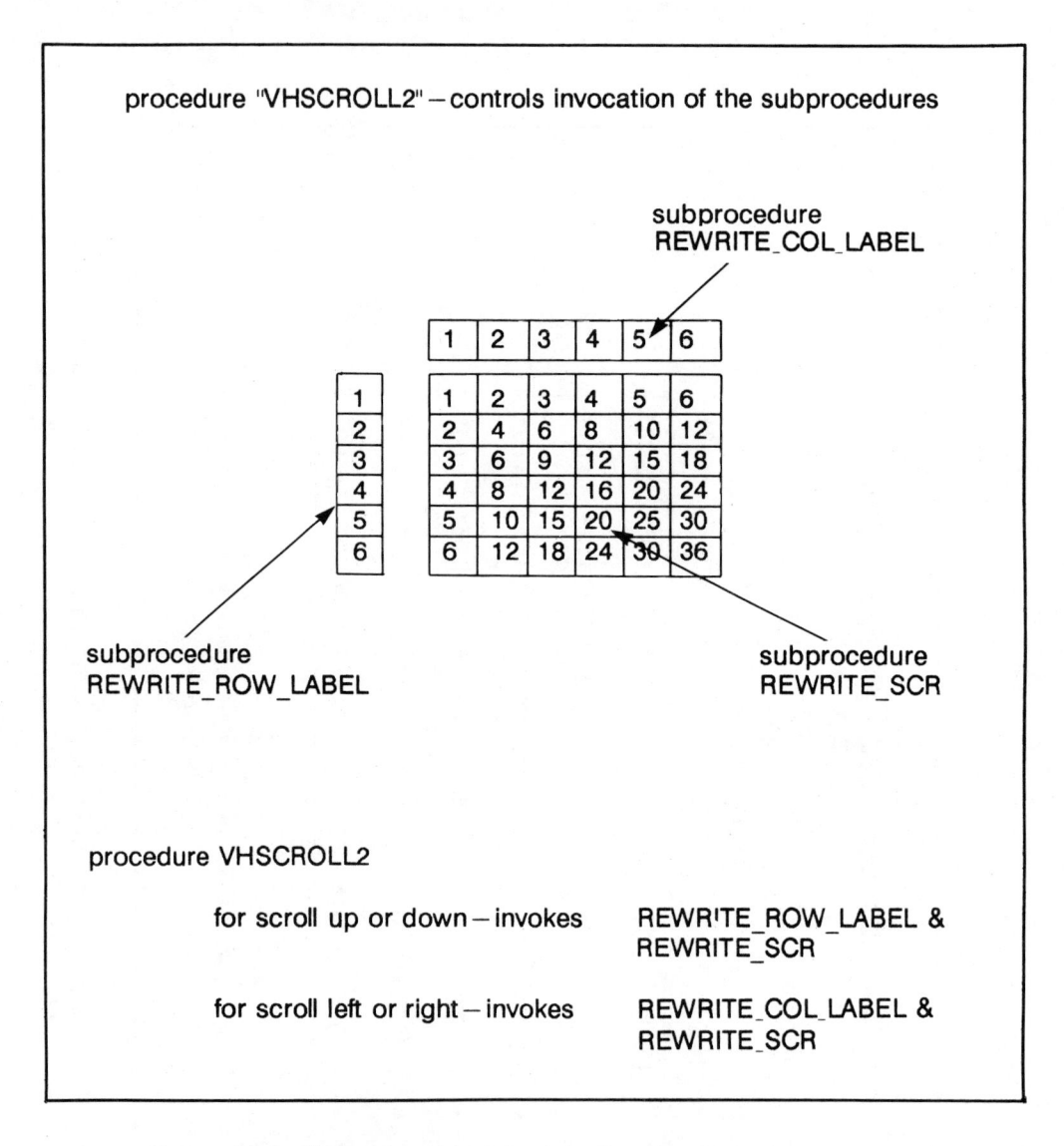

    for scroll up or down — invokes   REWRITE_ROW_LABEL & REWRITE_SCR

    for scroll left or right — invokes   REWRITE_COL_LABEL & REWRITE_SCR

Figure 11.2 Procedures in "vh_s2.inc" and where they operate on the screen

Vertical and Horizontal Scrolling Windows 11

From Start Position:

	1	2	3	4	5	6
1	1	2	3	4	5	6
2	2	4	6	8	10	12
3	3	6	9	12	15	18
4	4	8	12	16	20	24
5	5	10	15	20	25	30
6	6	12	18	24	30	36

i_tot := 1 (rows) k_tot := 1

Press Right Arrow key: k_tot = 2

	2	3	4	5	6	7
1	2	3	4	5	6	7
2	4	6	8	10	12	14
3	6	9	12	15	18	21
4	8	12	16	20	24	28
5	10	15	20	25	30	35
6	12	18	24	30	36	42

No change in i_tot

k_tot to k_tot + 5

Screen data appears from right and disappears at left

Then Press Down Arrow key: i_tot := 2

	2	3	4	5	6	7
2	4	6	8	10	12	14
3	6	9	12	15	18	21
4	8	12	16	20	24	28
5	10	15	20	25	30	35
6	12	18	24	30	36	42
7	14	21	28	35	42	49

i_tot: to i_tot + 5

No change in k_tot

Screen data appears from bottom and disappears at top

Figure 11.3 Operation of Procedures in "vh_s2inc"

11 Vertical and Horizontal Scrolling Windows

Fig. 11.1: Shows a detailed layout of the multiplication table just after it has been initialized and is ready to scroll. The "*" characters show the first and last characters respectively of the display strings and are included only to show where the strings begin and end. Observe here that the strings are located end-to-end and that there is, therefore, no variable to represent the blank space between the columns, as you saw in the earlier chapters. You will see the effect of the omission of this blank space when you come to look at the program coding at line 0520 in REWRITE_SCR, for example. Note also in Figure 11.1 that columns 21 and 76 (marked with the "-" character) are both deliberately left blank. This is crucial. If these column locations are not left blank, the vertical scroll will include the window borders.

Fig. 11.2: Shows the area on the screen where each subprocedure operates.

Fig. 11.3: Shows the relationship between the index variables "k_tot" and "i_tot" and the movement of the row and column labels relative to the body of the table.

The background provided in Part One, along with these introductory notes and figures, should make the code below easy to follow:

```
{========================================================================}
0005 {vh_s2.inc}
0010 { This ".inc" file contains all the file saving and scrolling
0015   routines that are OVERHEAD REQUIREMENTS of the program
0020   "vhscroll.drv".
0025   On disk as "vh_s2.inc".
0030 }
0035
0040 {------------------------------------------------------------------}
0045
0050 procedure        VHSCROLL2(tlc,tlr : integer;
0055                            var prod_buffer : pr_buf);
0060
0065 label
0070        rep_read;
0075
0080 const
0085       bell             = #$07;
0090       scroll_up        = #$48;
0095       scroll_down      = #$50;
0100       scroll_left      = #$4b;
0105       scroll_right     = #$4d;
0110       carriage_ret     = #$0d;
```
   ...*continued*

Vertical and Horizontal Scrolling Windows 11

...from previous page

```
0115
0120     var
0125         scroll_choice   : char;
0130         exit_scroll     : boolean;
0135         i_tot , k_tot   : integer;
0140  {-----------------------------------------------------------------}
0145
0150         procedure REWRITE_COL_LABEL(k_tot,i_tot : integer;
0155                                 var multand_buffer : multand_buf);
0160
0165         var
0170             bp,count,
0175             j,row,col,
0180             k               : integer;
0185
0190         Begin    {sub procedure rewrite_col_label}
0195             col := 22 ; row := 7;
0200             j := ((row - 1) * 160) + ((col - 1) * 2);
0205             FOR k := (k_tot) to (k_tot + 5) DO
0210             Begin
0215                 bp := (k - 1) * 9;
0220                 FOR count := 1 to 9 DO
0225                 Begin
0230                     CHR_OUT(j,ORD(multand_buffer[bp + count]));
0235                     j := j + 2;
0240                 End;
0245             End;
0250         End;     {sub procedure rewrite_col_label}
0255  {-----------------------------------------------------------------}
0260
0265         procedure REWRITE_ROW_LABEL(k_tot,i_tot       : integer;
0270                                 var multlr_buffer : multlr_buf);
0275
0280         var
0285             bp,count,
0290             j,row,col,
0295             i               : integer;
0300
0305         Begin    {sub procedure rewrite_row_label}
0310             col := 11 ; row := 9;
0315             j := ((row - 1) * 160) + ((col - 1) * 2);
0320             FOR i := (i_tot) to (i_tot + 5) DO
0325             Begin
0330                 bp := (i - 1) * 9;
0335                 FOR count := 1 to 9 DO
0340                 Begin
0345                     CHR_OUT(j,ORD(multlr_buffer[bp + count]));
0350                     j := j + 2;
0355                 End;
0360                 col := 11 ; row := row + 2;
0365                 j := ((row - 1) * 160) + ((col - 1) * 2);
0370             End;
0375         End;     {sub procedure rewrite_row_label}
0380  {-----------------------------------------------------------------}
0385
0390         procedure REWRITE_SCR(k_tot , i_tot    : integer;
0395                             var prod_buffer : pr_buf);
0400
```

...continued

11 Vertical and Horizontal Scrolling Windows

...from previous page

```
0405        var
0410            bx,bp,
0415            count,
0420            j,
0425            row,col,
0430            k,i         : integer;
0435
0440        Begin    {sub-procedure rewrite_scr}
0445            col := tlc ; row := tlr;
0450            {starting point for screen write}
0455            j := ((row - 1) * 160) + ((col - 1) * 2);
0460            FOR i := (i_tot) to (i_tot + 5) DO
0465            Begin
0470                FOR k := (k_tot) to (k_tot + 5) DO  { 1 to 1+5 }
0475                Begin
0480                    bx := (i - 1) * 180;    {180 chars/row}
0485                    bp := (k - 1) * 9;      {9 chars/col }
0490                    FOR count := 1 to 9 DO
0495                    Begin
0500                        CHR_OUT(j,ORD(prod_buffer[bx+bp+count]));
0505                        {* delay(500); *}
0510                        j := j + 2;
0515                    End;
0520                    { j := j + 2; }
0525                    {NB:NO space between screen display cols here}
0530                End;
0535                col := col ; row := row + 2;  {same col;next line}
0540                j := ((row - 1) * 160) + ((col - 1) * 2);
0545                { recalculate j with different row ; same column}
0550            End;
0555        End;       {sub-procedure rewrite_scr}
0560   {---------------------------------------------------------------}
0565
0570   Begin    {procedure vhscroll2}
0575        window(1,1,25,80);
0580        exit_scroll := false;    {initialize exit condition}
0585        k_tot := 1;              {initialize array row & col indexes}
0590        i_tot := 1;
0595
0600        REPEAT
0605            rep_read:       {a label with colon}
0610            read(KBD,scroll_choice);
0615            CASE(scroll_choice) OF
0620
0625            scroll_up       : Begin {press Up Arrow Key}
0630                                i_tot := i_tot - 1;
0635                                k_tot := k_tot + 0;
0640
0645                                IF(i_tot < 1) THEN
0650                                Begin
0655                                    i_tot := 1;
0660                                    goto rep_read;
0665                                End;
0670                                REWRITE_ROW_LABEL(k_tot,i_tot,
0675                                            multlr_buffer);
0680                                REWRITE_SCR(k_tot,i_tot,
0685                                            prod_buffer);
0690                              End; {scroll_up}
0695
```

...continued

Vertical and Horizontal Scrolling Windows 11

...from previous page

```
0700              scroll_down    : Begin {press Down Arrow Key}
0705                                    i_tot := i_tot + 1;
0710                                    k_tot := k_tot + 0;
0715
0720                                    IF(i_tot > 15) THEN
0725                                    Begin
0730                                        i_tot := 15;
0735                                        goto rep_read;
0740                                    End;
0745                                    REWRITE_ROW_LABEL(k_tot,i_tot,
0750                                                    multlr_buffer);
0755                                    REWRITE_SCR(k_tot,i_tot,
0760                                                    prod_buffer);
0765                              End;     {scroll_down}
0770
0775              scroll_left    : Begin {press Left Arrow Key}
0780                                    i_tot := i_tot + 0;
0785                                    k_tot := k_tot - 1;
0790
0795                                    IF(k_tot < 1) THEN
0800                                    Begin
0805                                        k_tot := 1;
0810                                        goto rep_read;
0815                                    End;
0820                                    REWRITE_COL_LABEL(k_tot,i_tot,
0825                                                    multand_buffer);
0830                                    REWRITE_SCR(k_tot,i_tot,
0835                                                    prod_buffer);
0840                              End;     {scroll_left}
0845
0850
0855              scroll_right   : Begin {press Right Arrow Key}
0860                                    i_tot := i_tot + 0;
0865                                    k_tot := k_tot + 1;
0870
0875                                    IF(k_tot > 15) THEN
0880                                    Begin
0885                                        k_tot := 15;
0890                                        goto rep_read;
0895                                    End;
0900                                    REWRITE_COL_LABEL(k_tot,i_tot,
0905                                                    multand_buffer);
0910                                    REWRITE_SCR(k_tot,i_tot,
0915                                                    prod_buffer);
0920                              End;     {scroll_right}
0925
0930
0935              carriage_ret   : Begin
0940                                    exit_scroll := true;
0945                                    write(bell);
0950                              End;
0955
0960              ELSE
0965                 {if none of above choices is selected...}
0970                 {nothing--go back and press correct key.}
0975         END; {case}
0980      UNTIL exit_scroll = true;
0985 End;       {procedure vhscroll2}
{=================== END OF "vh_s2.inc" overhead file ==================}
```

221

11 Vertical and Horizontal Scrolling Windows

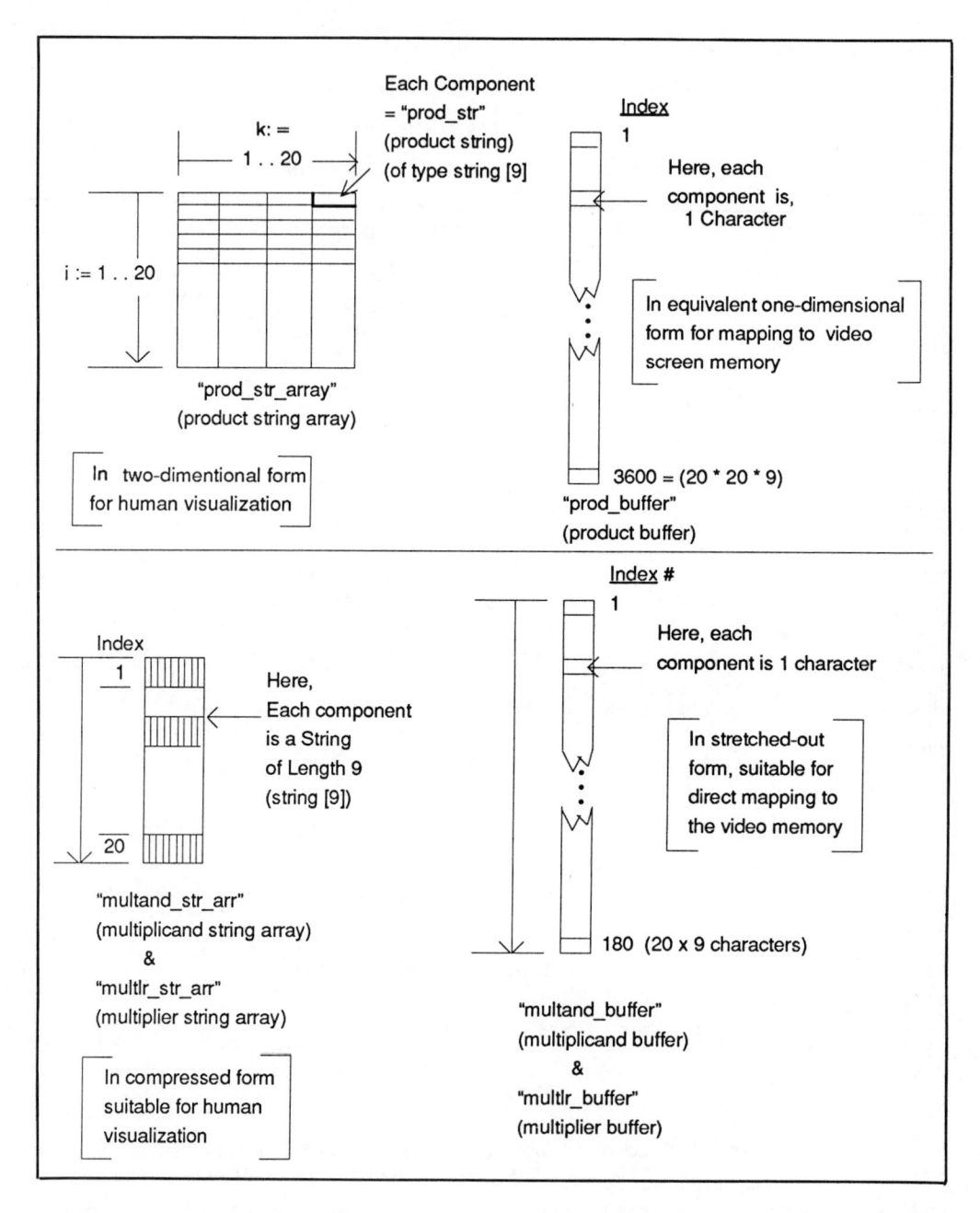

Figure 11.4 Visual Representation of One and Two-dimensional Array Variables

11 Vertical and Horizontal Scrolling Windows

MODULE: VHSCROLL.DRV

As stated above, the objective of this application program is to create a 20×20 multiplication table in the computer's memory and then scroll the whole table on the screen using only a 6×6 display array. Data on the screen is moved up, down, and side-to-side by pressing the vertical and horizontal Arrow keys on the numeric keypad. The initialized scrolling table is shown in Figure 11.1. To visualize the variables and their structural characteristics, refer to Figure 11.4

- remember that the "buffer" variables are needed because direct mapping to the video screen via the external CHR OUT procedure can only be done from a one-dimensional array whose components are single characters.

- remember also that the external CHR_OUT procedure takes the single characters of the "buffer" variables ("prod_buffer," "multand_buffer," and "multlr_buffer") and converts them to their equivalent ASCII number values by applying the ORD function. These number values are placed into the proper "j" screen memory locations and are then converted by the special video circuitry of the video memory to reproduce the characters that you see on the screen.

Keep this short refresher in mind. Following is the code for the bi-directional scrolling program:

```
{========================================================================}
0005 program vhscroll(input,output);
0010 {
0015   On disk as "vhscroll.drv"
0020   Application program for Chapter 11
0025 }
0030
0035 type
0040      str9           = string[9];
0045
0050      pr_array       = ARRAY[1..20,1..20] of str9;
0055      pr_buf         = ARRAY[1..3600] of char;   {20 * 20 * 9}
0060
0065      multand_str_arr   = ARRAY[1..20] of str9;
0070      multand_buf       = ARRAY[1..180] of char; {20 * 9}
0075
```

continued...

223

11 Vertical and Horizontal Scrolling Windows

...from previous page

```
0080         multlr_str_arr       = ARRAY[1..20] of str9;
0085         multlr_buf           = ARRAY[1..180] of char; {20 * 9}
0090
0095  var
0100         i,k,
0105         bx,bp,
0110         index,count,
0115         tl_col,tl_row        : integer;
0120
0125         prod_val             : real;
0130         prod_str             : str9;
0135         prod_str_array       : pr_array;
0140         prod_buffer          : pr_buf;
0145
0150         multand_val          : real;
0155         multand_str          : str9;
0160         multand_str_array    : multand_str_arr;
0165         multand_buffer       : multand_buf;
0170
0175         multlr_val           : real;
0180         multlr_str           : str9;
0185         multlr_str_array     : multlr_str_arr;
0190         multlr_buffer        : multlr_buf;
0195
0200  {================================================================}
0205  {$i chrinout.inc}
0210  {$i windows.inc}
0215  {$i vh_s2.inc}
0220  {================================================================}
0225
0230  procedure CREATE_COMMAND_LINE;
0235
0240  type
0245         str10 = string[10];
0250
0255  var
0260         i                    : integer;
0265         vertical_label       : str10;
0270         x_coord,
0275         y_coord              : integer;
0280         label_letter         : char;
0285
0290  {----------------------------------------------------------------}
0295
0300  Begin      {procedure create_command_line}
0305         window(1,1,80,25);
0310         TEXTCOLOR(0);TEXTBACKGROUND(15); {black on white}
0315         gotoxy(22,2);write(' BI-DIRECTIONAL SCROLLING APPLICATION ');
0320         gotoxy(35,3);write(' CHAPTER 11 ');
0325         TEXTCOLOR(15);TEXTBACKGROUND(0); {white on black}
0330         gotoxy(23,22);
0335         write('Use the ARROW KEYS on the Numeric Keypad');
0340         gotoxy(27,23);write('(Be Sure NUM LOCK Key is OFF)');
0345         TEXTCOLOR(0);TEXTBACKGROUND(15);
0350         {"black" letters on "white" background}
0355         gotoxy(41,5);write(' multiplicand ');
0360         vertical_label := 'multiplier';
0365         gotoxy(7,9) ; x_coord := WHEREX ; y_coord := WHEREY;
0370         FOR i := 1 to 10 DO
```

continued...

Vertical and Horizontal Scrolling Windows 11

...from previous page

```
0375        Begin
0380             gotoxy(x_coord,y_coord);
0385             label_letter := COPY(vertical_label,i,1);
0390             write(' ',label_letter,' ');
0395             {* delay(1000); *}
0400             x_coord := x_coord ; y_coord := y_coord + 1;
0405        End;
0410        TEXTCOLOR(15);TEXTBACKGROUND(0);
0415        {"white" letters on "black" background}
0420 End;     {procedure create_command_line}
0425 {------------------------------------------------------------------}
0430
0435 procedure CREATE_FIRST_STEP(var prod_str_array : pr_array);
0440
0445 Begin     {procedure create_first_step}
0450      FOR i := 1 to 20 DO
0455      Begin
0460           multand_val := i;
0465           FOR k := 1 to 20 DO
0470           Begin
0475                multlr_val := k;
0480                prod_val := multand_val * multlr_val;
0485                STR(prod_val:7:2,prod_str);
0490                prod_str := CONCAT('*',prod_str,'*');
0495                { change from 7 to defined width of 9....}
0500                prod_str_array[i,k] := prod_str;
0505           End;
0510      End;
0515 End;     {procedure create_first_step}
0520 {------------------------------------------------------------------}
0525
0530 procedure CREATE_SECOND_STEP(var prod_str_array  : pr_array;
0535                               var prod_buffer     : pr_buf);
0540
0545 Begin     {procedure create_second_step}
0550      index := 0;
0555      FOR i := 1 to 20 DO
0560      Begin
0565           FOR k := 1 to 20 DO
0570           Begin
0575                FOR count := 1 to 9 DO
0580                Begin
0585                     index := index + 1;
0590                     prod_buffer[index] :=
0595                          COPY(prod_str_array[i,k],count,1);
0600                End;
0605           End;
0610      End;
0615 End;     {procedure create_second_step}
0620 {------------------------------------------------------------------}
0625
0630 procedure CREATE_MULTAND_LABELS(var multand_str_array :
0635                                         multand_str_arr;
0640                                  var multand_buffer   :
0645                                         multand_buf);
0650
0655 var
0660      k,j       : integer;
0665      row,col   : integer;
0670
```

continued...

225

11 Vertical and Horizontal Scrolling Windows

...from previous page

```
0675 Begin       {procedure create_multand_labels}
0680      FOR k := 1 to 20 DO
0685      Begin
0690           multand_val := k;
0695           STR(multand_val:7:2,multand_str);
0700           multand_str := CONCAT('*',multand_str,'*');
0705           multand_str_array[k] := multand_str;
0710      End;
0715      index := 0;
0720      FOR k := 1 to 20 DO
0725      Begin
0730           FOR count := 1 to 9 DO
0735           Begin
0740                index := index + 1;
0745                multand_buffer[index] :=
0750                     COPY(multand_str_array[k],count,1);
0755           End;
0760      End;
0765
0770      {---- now initialize the multiplicand labels on screen ----}
0775      col := 22 ; row := 7;
0780      j := ((row - 1) * 160) + ((col - 1) * 2);
0785      FOR k := 1 to 6 DO
0790      Begin
0795           bp := (k - 1) * 9;
0800           FOR count := 1 to 9 DO
0805           Begin
0810                CHR_OUT(j,ORD(multand_buffer[bp + count]));
0815                {* delay(500); *}
0820                j := j + 2;
0825           End;
0830      End;
0835 End;      {procedure create_multand_labels}
0840 {------------------------------------------------------------------}
0845
0850 procedure CREATE_MULTLR_LABELS(var multlr_str_array   :
0855                                         multlr_str_arr;
0860                                var multlr_buffer      :
0865                                         multlr_buf);
0870
0875 var
0880      i,j       : integer;
0885      row,col   : integer;
0890
0895 Begin     {procedure create_multlr_labels}
0900      FOR i := 1 to 20 DO
0905      Begin
0910           multlr_val := i;
0915           STR(multlr_val:7:2,multlr_str);
0920           multlr_str := CONCAT('*',multlr_str,'*');
0925           multlr_str_array[i] := multlr_str;
0930      End;
0935      index := 0;
0940      FOR i := 1 to 20 DO
0945      Begin
0950           FOR count := 1 to 9 DO
0955           Begin
0960                index := index + 1;
0965                multlr_buffer[index] :=
0970                     COPY(multlr_str_array[i],count,1);
```

continued...

Vertical and Horizontal Scrolling Windows 11

...from previous page

```
0975              End;
0980          End;
0985
0990          {---- now initialize the multiplier labels on screen ----}
0995          col := 11 ; row := 9;
1000          j := ((row - 1) * 160) + ((col - 1) * 2);
1005          FOR i := 1 to 6 DO
1010          Begin
1015              bp := (i - 1) * 9;
1020              FOR count := 1 to 9 DO
1025              Begin
1030                  CHR_OUT(j,ORD(multlr_buffer[bp + count]));
1035                  {* delay(500); *}
1040                  j := j + 2;
1045              End;
1050              col := 11 ; row := row + 2;
1055              j := ((row - 1) * 160) + ((col - 1) * 2);
1060          End;
1065  End;       {procedure create_multlr_labels}
1070  {------------------------------------------------------------------}
1075
1080  procedure     INITIALIZE_SCROLL_WINDOW(var prod_buffer : pr_buf);
1085
1090  var
1095      j      : integer;
1100      col,
1105      row    : integer;
1110
1115  Begin     {procedure initialize_scroll_window}
1120      col := 22 ; row := 9;
1125      j := ((row - 1) * 160) + ((col - 1) * 2);
1130      FOR i := 1 to 6 DO    {6 rows}
1135      Begin
1140          FOR k := 1 to 6 DO    {6 columns}
1145          Begin
1150              bx := (i - 1) * 180; {180 chars/row}
1155              bp := (k - 1) * 9;   {9 chars/col}
1160              FOR count := 1 to 9 DO
1165              Begin
1170                  CHR_OUT(j,ORD(prod_buffer[bx + bp + count]));
1175                  {* delay 2000 *}
1180                  j := j + 2;
1185              End;
1190              { j := j + 2; }
1195              { NOTE: NO space between screen display cols here}
1200          End;
1205          col := col ; row := row + 2;
1210          j := ((row - 1) * 160) + ((col - 1) * 2);
1215      End;
1220  End;       {procedure initialize scroll window}
1225  {------------------------------------------------------------------}
1230
1235  Begin     {driver}
1240      window(1,1,80,25);clrscr;
1245      CREATE_COMMAND_LINE;
1250      WINDOW_BORDER(20 , 8 , 77 , 20 , 4); {border style #4}
1255      CREATE_FIRST_STEP(prod_str_array);
1260      CREATE_SECOND_STEP(prod_str_array,
```

continued...

227

11 Vertical and Horizontal Scrolling Windows

...from previous page

```
1265                              prod_buffer);
1270          CREATE_MULTAND_LABELS(multand_str_array,
1275                                multand_buffer);
1280          CREATE_MULTLR_LABELS(multlr_str_array,
1285                               multlr_buffer);
1290          INITIALIZE_SCROLL_WINDOW(prod_buffer);
1295          tl_col := 22 ; tl_row := 9;
1300          VHSCROLL2(tl_col,tl_row,
1305                    prod_buffer);
1310  End.         {driver}
{========================================================================}
```

VHSCROLL.DRV: NOTES

CREATE_FIRST_STEP and CREATE_SECOND_STEP

Together, these procedures create the contents of the 20×20 multiplication table. The overall process has been split into two separate procedures to better illustrate the steps involved. Figure 11.5 shows the detailed workings of CREATE_FIRST_STEP:

line 0485: the STR function acts as an assignment statement. It converts a numeric value into an equivalent string value. Note that here, it can only use at most seven of the nine possible string positions of "prod_str."

line 0490: the CONCAT function is used to add two "*" string delimiters and thus extend the string length from seven to its maximum defined length of nine characters.

line 0500: once "prod_str" is constructed, it is assigned to its properly indexed position in the variable "prod_str_array."

Vertical and Horizontal Scrolling Windows 11

... using the indexes i = 20 and k = 20 as an example.

Line 0480:   "prod_val"   400.00

| 4 | 0 | 0 | . | 0 | 0 | ␢ |

|← 7 →|

| ␢ | = blank

Line 0485:   str (prod_val : 7 : 2, prod_str)
(numbers are <u>left-adjusted</u> in their fields)

Line 0485:   str (prod_val : 7 : 2, prod_str)
(strings are <u>right-adjusted</u> in their fields)

| ␢ | 4 | 0 | 0 | . | 0 | 0 |

|← 7 →|

| * | ␢ | 4 | 0 | 0 | . | 0 | 0 | * |

|← 9 →|

Line 0490:   "prod_str"

Line 0450:

"prod_str_array [20, 20]"
[i, k]

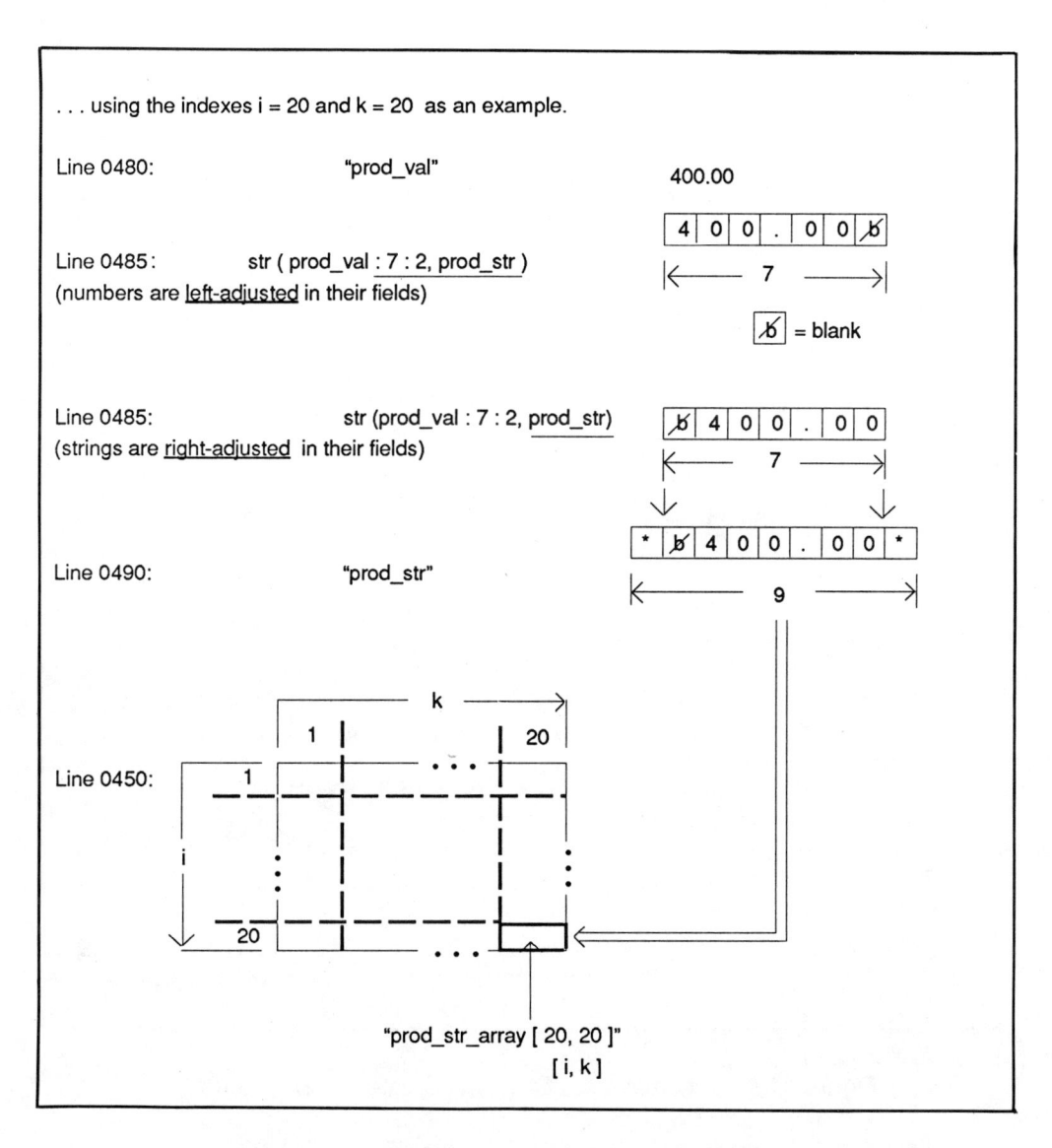

Figure 11.5   Schematic for Code of "Create_First_Step"

229

11 Vertical and Horizontal Scrolling Windows

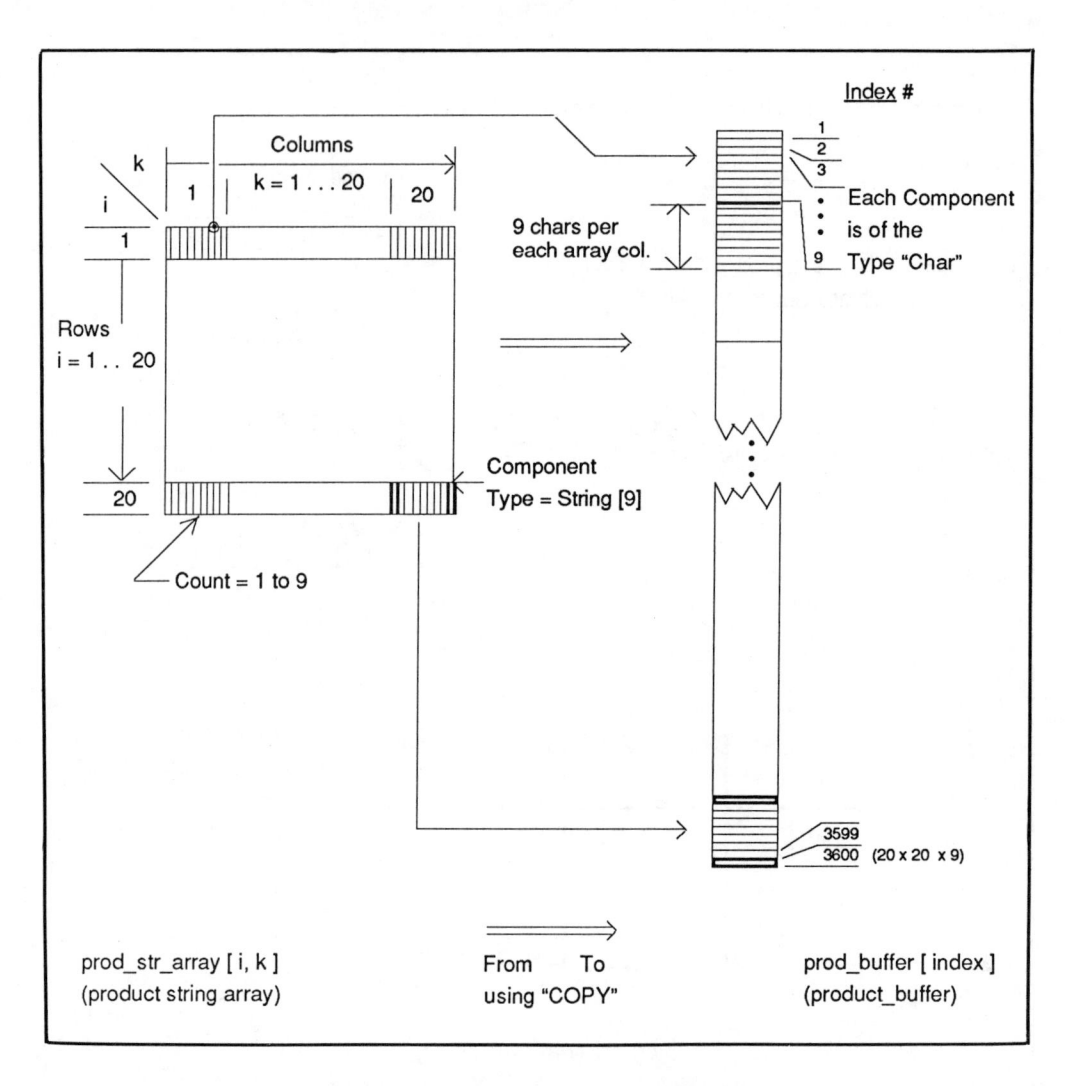

Figure 11.6 Schematic for Code of "Create_Second_Step"

Figure 11.6 shows the workings of CREATE_SECOND_STEP:

- the COPY function at line 0590 extracts each and every single character in the two-dimensional array, "prod_str array," and assigns it a unique index value in the one-dimensional array, "prod_buffer." The index values range from 1 to 3600 (20×20×9).

- note that the use of the reserved word "var" allows the changed contents of the array, "prod_buffer," to be used globally in the internal procedure INITIALIZE_SCROLL WINDOW and the external procedure VHSCROLL2 that follows.

CREATE_MULTAND_LABELS (Create Multiplicand Labels)
CREATE_MULTLR_LABELS (Create Multiplier Labels)

The procedure CREATE_MULTAND_LABELS creates the top border labels that move when the horizontal scroll keys are pressed. CREATE MULTLR_LABELS creates the left-hand border labels that move when the vertical scroll keys are pressed. For example, in the procedure CREATE_MULTAND_LABELS, lines 0685-0710 and lines 0720-0760 represent a two-step transition process to convert a number into a one-dimensional array of characters prior to initialization on the screen at lines 0770-0835.

Figure 11.7 illustrates the first step: the transition of the number value into its indexed string equivalent (lines 0685-0710). In step 2, the further conversion from the array of 20 (9 character) strings into an array of (20×9) 180 individual characters is accomplished at lines 0720-0760 (see Figure 11.8). Note that both of the above procedures closely resemble CREATE_FIRST_STEP. The only difference is that the "buffer" variables are created from one-dimensional arrays (lines 0705 and 0745) instead of a two-dimensional array variable (line 0500).

11 Vertical and Horizontal Scrolling Windows

– use "CREATE_MULTAND_LABELS" [lines 0680 - 0710] to illustrate both procedures

K = 20   Line 0690: "multand_val"   20.00
            (multiplicand value)

                                                                    ｢b｣ = blank

            Line 0695: str (multand_val: 7:2, multand_str) | 2 | 0 | . | 0 | 0 | b | b |
            (multiplicand value)
            (Numbers are left-adjusted in their fields) |←—— 7 ——→|

            Line 0695: str (multand_val: 7:2, multand_str) | b | b | 2 | 0 | . | 0 | 0 |
            (multiplicand string)
            (Strings are right-adjusted in their fields) |←—— 7 ——→|

            Line 0700: "multand_str" | * | b | b | 2 | 0 | . | 0 | 0 | * |
            (expanded to defined length of 9)
                                                                   |←———— 9 ————→|

                              9
                           characters
                             wide

Index
values
[k]

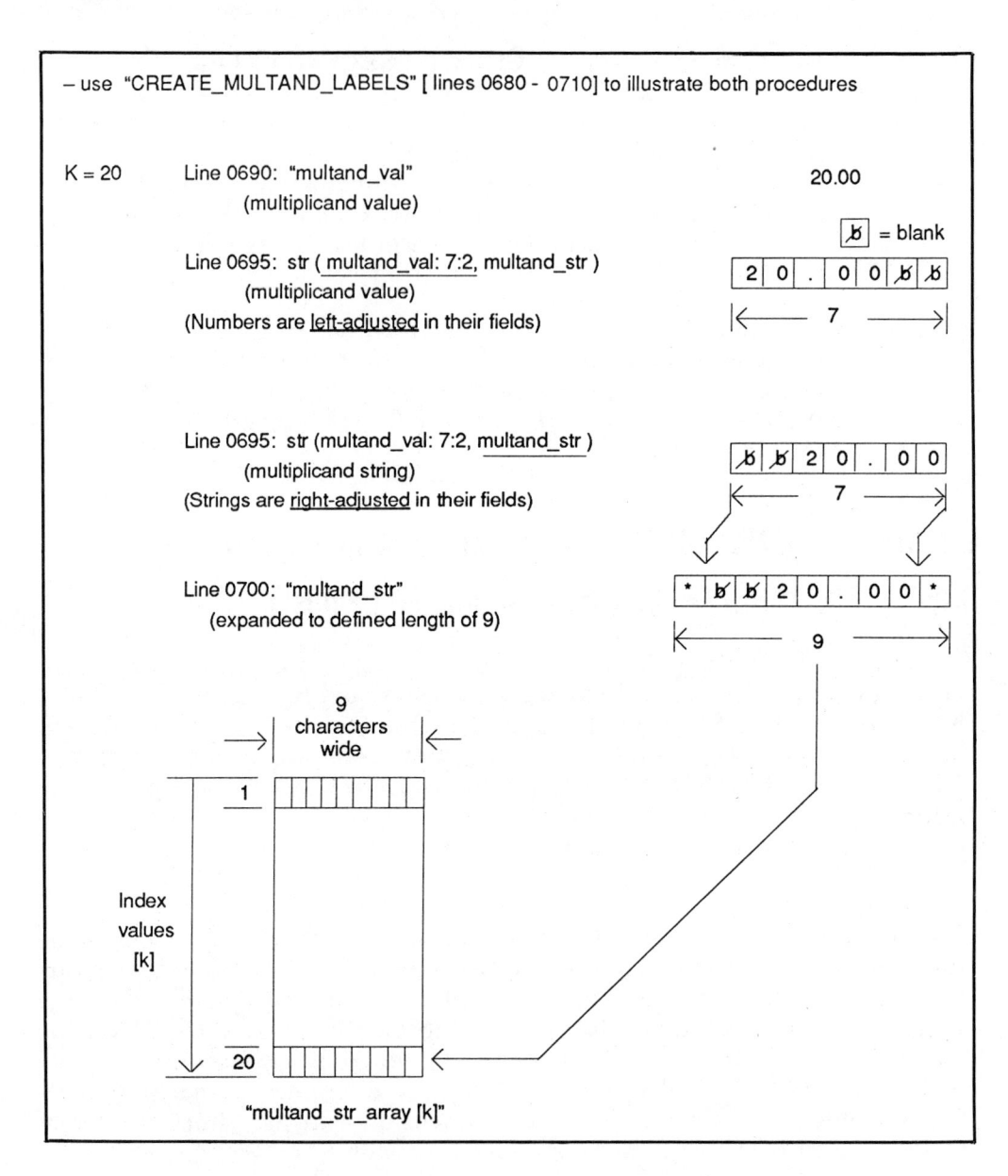

                             1
                            20

                      "multand_str_array [k]"

Figure 11.7 Schematic for Code of "Create_Multand_Labels"

Once all the multiplicand labels are assigned to "multand_buffer" (line 0745), the first 6 columns of the 20 are initialized; that is, 54 (6×9) characters are written into video memory and then displayed along the top of the table (see Figure 11.8). The "bp" and "count" index values used by CHR_OUT at line 0810 to produce the characters on the screen are calculated as follows (see lines 0785-0830):

label value	col k	bp offset value	bp + count range
1.00	1	(1 - 1) * 9 = 0	0-8 inclusive
2.00	2	(2 - 1) * 9 = 9	9-17 inclusive
3.00	3	(3 - 1) * 9 = 18	18-26 inclusive
4.00	4	(4 - 1) * 9 = 27	27-35 inclusive
5.00	5	(5 - 1) * 9 = 36	36-44 inclusive
6.00	6	(6 - 1) * 9 = 45	45-53 inclusive

What was said about the multiplicand labels also holds for the initialization of the multiplier labels in the procedure CREATE_MULTLR_LABELS. The only difference is that after each label is written, the row is increased by two in a vertical direction at line 1050, and a new screen memory location, "j," is calculated on the basis of the changed row (same column). To trace the action of these procedures, release the brackets around the "delay" procedure at lines 0815 and 1035.

INITIALIZE_SCROLL_WINDOW

This procedure writes the first 36 table string values onto the screen table prior to calling the external scrolling procedure VHSCROLL2. The screen memory write procedure CHR_OUT displays to the screen the selected characters that are created inside the one-dimensional array "prod_buffer" by CREATE_SECOND_STEP. If you have forgotten how the index values at line 1170 are arrived at, reread the detailed discussions in Chapter 6 or Chapter 8. To trace the operation of the procedure, remove the brackets at line 1175.

11 Vertical and Horizontal Scrolling Windows

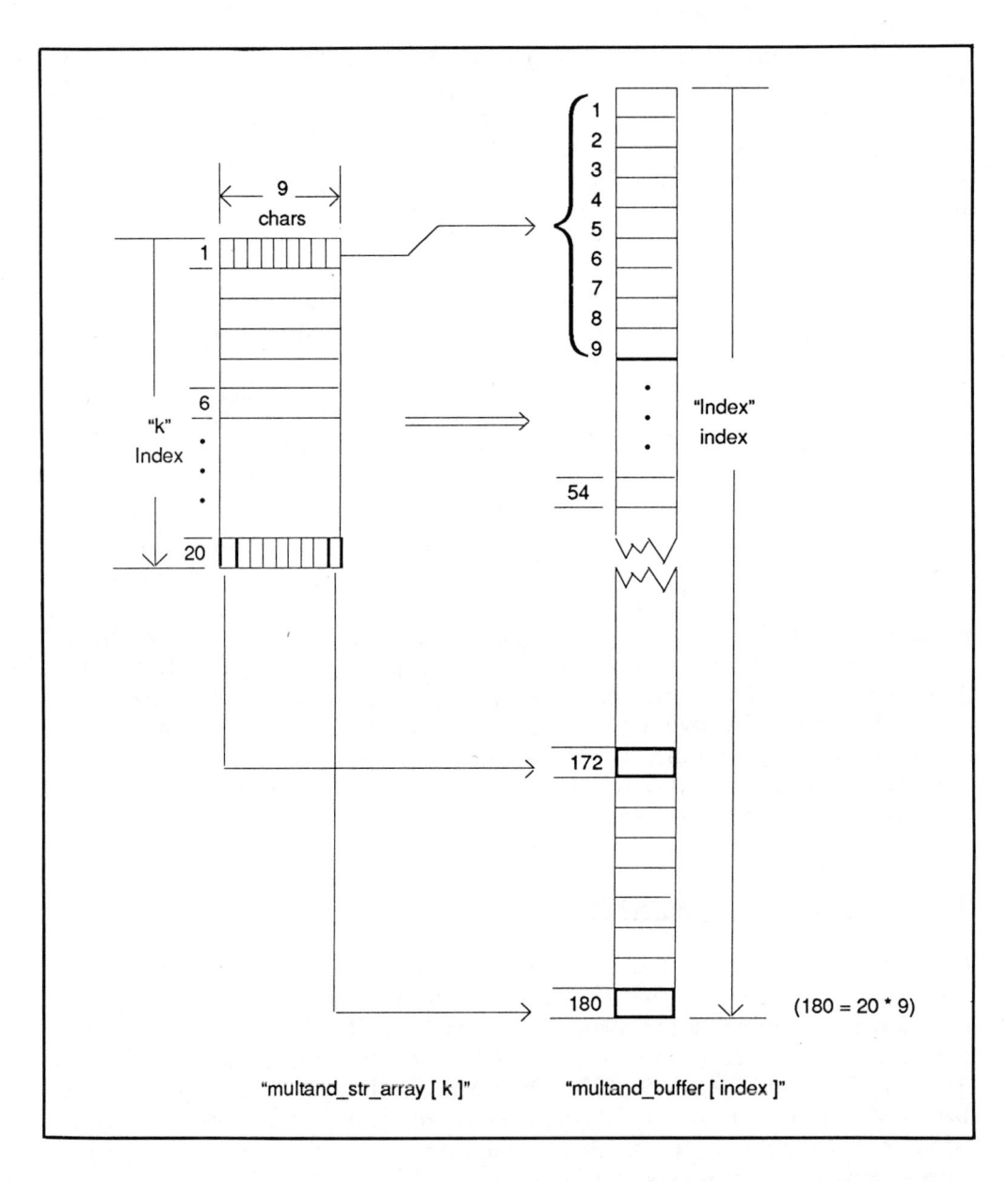

Figure 11.8 Schematic for Code of "Create_Multand_Labels" [lines 0720-0760]

234

Vertical and Horizontal Scrolling Windows 11

V_SCROLL2

This procedure actually controls the scrolling of the multiplication table and its associated labels. It is an external procedure located inside the external module, "vh_s2.inc," which in this program was invoked along with "chrinout.inc" and "windows.inc" at line 0215. Note again that these external procedures must use procedure parameters whose types are declared and sent in *from the driver routine*. These external modules *must not* declare scrolling table variable types internally and then try to send results back out to the driver routine. If they did, the basic concept of Pascal Scope rules would be violated; that is, called procedures cannot define new variables and expect to have their calling procedures recognize those new variables. So the driver routine would not know what it was getting because the type of the variable being sent out to it would not be recognized; the particular data Type it was being asked to handle was *not previously defined in the Type Declaration section of the driver routine*. Thus, in this case, it would be illegal to create (declare) the multiplication table array type "pr_buf" (line 0055) inside "vh_s2.inc" and then attempt to pass results out to the driver program. The rule is that any global Data Type that an ".inc" module uses internally *must* be declared in the Type Declaration section of the driver routine and made available to the module via the parameter list of a procedure (or function) and then passed back out using the reserved word prefix, "var."

LIMITATIONS

The bi-directional scrolling program just written provides a good format or template to use when you develop your own application programs. There are, however, a few deficiencies.

The first is its lack of generality. What if you wanted to develop a program that was capable of scrolling, say, 15 different tables instead of just one? What if each of these tables was a different size? Clearly, if you are to use static array variables, there would be no way that a single array could be many different sizes at once. Thus, if you use static (pre-declared) array variables, you must declare the type of each and every one inside the driver (calling) program and separately specify that variable's type in the parameter list of the ".inc" module. In addition, since each array variable may have different row and column dimensions, the increase in the complexity of code inside the body of

235

11 Vertical and Horizontal Scrolling Windows

the main scrolling routine (inside the REPEAT..UNTIL and CASE..END control structures of "vhscroll2.inc") would be significant.

A second deficiency with this program concerns the source of data for the scrolling table. In the above program, the source parameters that generated the table data turned out to be the index values themselves. The arithmetic product of these indexes created the body of the table. Thus, in the application, the source of table data turned out to be a procedure that was written in as part of the program (procedures CREATE FIRST_STEP and CREATE_SECOND_STEP). In commercial or research programs (or your own), the amount of computation would probably be great, relative to screen display overhead, and would probably be written as a separate program that would be called by the driver routine. Other sources of table data could be data already created by a program and stored to disk, data fed into the computer through modems over telephone wires, data created at one workstation and moved to another by way of local area networks, or data from data sensors connected to the external environment for scientific measurements.

Although the ultimate bi-directional scrolling program hasn't been developed here, understanding of how it works has come a long way. You now have a tool that is satisfactory in many practical applications and a vehicle that can supply a springboard to understanding and creating more complex applications.

CHAPTER 12

SCROLLING GRAPH AND NUMBER TABLE

12 Scrolling Graph and Number Table

Up to this point, the primary emphasis has been on horizontal and vertical scrolling. In this chapter, an application will be introduced where

- vertical scrolling will display a table of input data entered from the keyboard.

- horizontal scrolling will display a simple bar graph representation of the input table data.

- screen saving and redisplay techniques learned in Chapter 4 will be used to switch between scrolling the graph and scrolling the table of input data.

In a departure from the usual format, external routines have not been included here outside of the usual "chrinout.inc" and "windows.inc." As an exercise, you can choose which procedures you would externalize into ".inc" modules for your own future applications programs. Remember to ensure that all data Type definitions are included in the Declaration Section of the driver routine if you don't choose to use modules in your program design.

PROGRAM: H_GRAPH.DRV

In this program, you will enter into a table a series of 21 integer values, one value corresponding to each of the 21 years from 1950-1970 inclusive. After all the numbers are entered, you may then scroll these numbers vertically to inspect them. If you then press the Return key, a graphical representation of the input data just entered will appear on the screen. You can inspect this graphical data by pressing the horizontal scrolling keys on the Numeric Keypad. If you want to switch back to inspect the table of numbers, simply press the Home key, and the table of numbers will reappear over the top of the graph. After scrolling vertically, you can go back to the graph by pressing <Ret>. The table will disappear, and the graph will reappear, ready to scroll again. Following is the code for this program. Since this program is long, with many procedures, its structure is summarized in the following table (Figure 12.1).

Scrolling Graph and Number Table 12

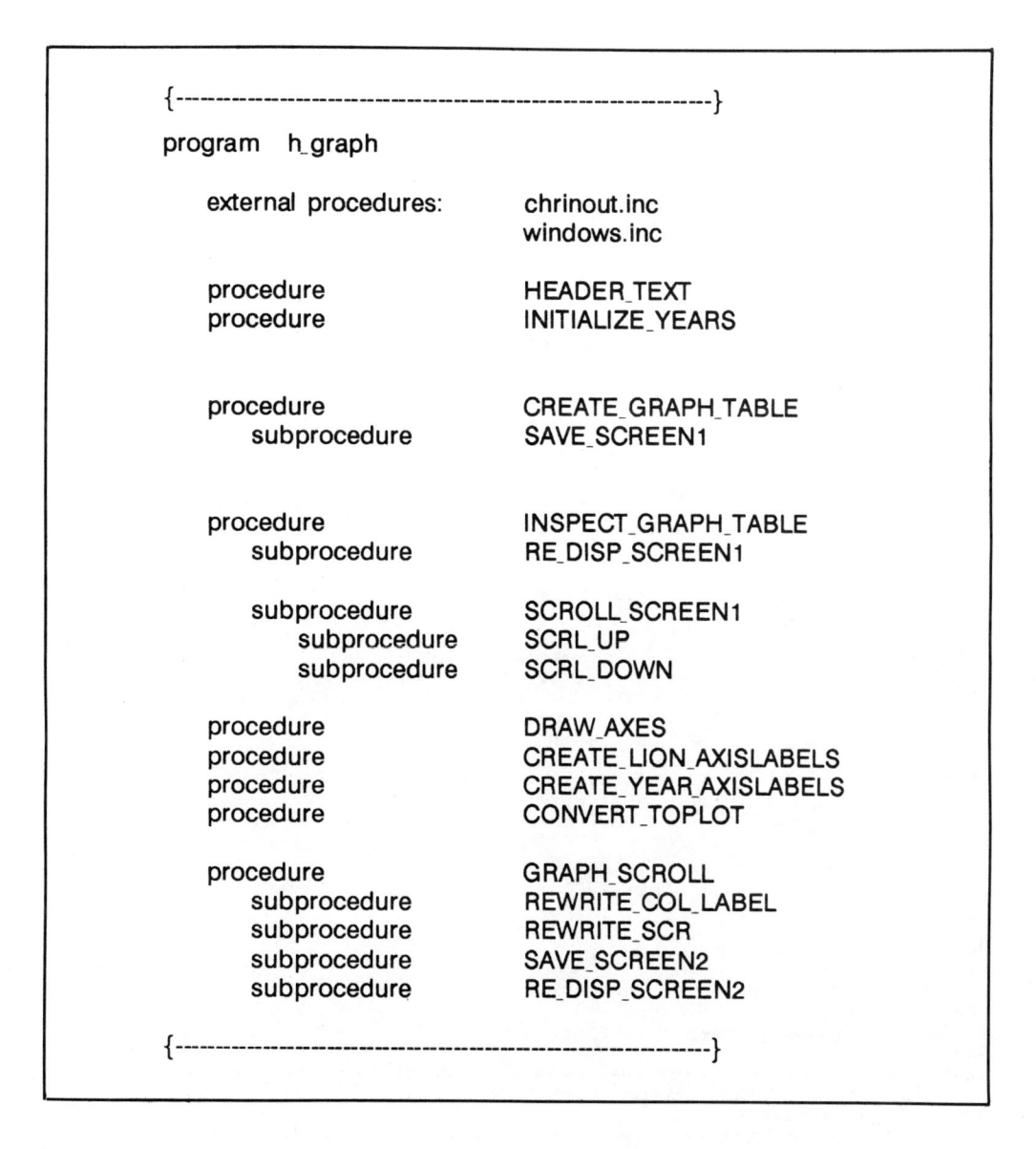

```
{--------------------------------------------------------------}
program   h_graph

        external procedures:        chrinout.inc
                                    windows.inc

        procedure                   HEADER_TEXT
        procedure                   INITIALIZE_YEARS


        procedure                   CREATE_GRAPH_TABLE
           subprocedure             SAVE_SCREEN1


        procedure                   INSPECT_GRAPH_TABLE
           subprocedure             RE_DISP_SCREEN1

           subprocedure             SCROLL_SCREEN1
              subprocedure          SCRL_UP
              subprocedure          SCRL_DOWN

        procedure                   DRAW_AXES
        procedure                   CREATE_LION_AXISLABELS
        procedure                   CREATE_YEAR_AXISLABELS
        procedure                   CONVERT_TOPLOT

        procedure                   GRAPH_SCROLL
           subprocedure             REWRITE_COL_LABEL
           subprocedure             REWRITE_SCR
           subprocedure             SAVE_SCREEN2
           subprocedure             RE_DISP_SCREEN2

{--------------------------------------------------------------}
```

Fig 12.1 Program H_GRAPH.DRV Procedure Layout

12 Scrolling Graph and Number Table

```
{========================================================================}
0005   program    h_graph(input,output);
0010 { On disk as "h_graph.drv"
0015   Application program Chapter 12.
0020 }
0025 const
0030       max_table_entries     = 21;
0035
0040 type
0045       str6              = string[6];
0050       year_array        = ARRAY[1..21] of integer;
0055       lion_array        = ARRAY[1..21] of integer;
0060
0065       scroll_txt_arr    = ARRAY[1..21,1..18] of char;
0070       init_scroll_txt   = ARRAY[1..180] of char; {10 * 18}
0075
0080       screen1           = ARRAY[1..13,1..20] of char;
0085
0090       year_str_arr      = ARRAY[1..21] of str6;   {'b1986b'}
0095       year_buf          = ARRAY[1..126] of char;  {21 * 6}
0100
0105       pl_arr            = ARRAY[1..13,1..21] of str6;
0110       pl_buf            = ARRAY[1..1638] of char; {13 * 21 * 6}
0115
0120 var
0125       start_year        : integer;
0130       year_val          : year_array;
0135       lion_val          : lion_array;
0140
0145       scroll_text       : scroll_txt_arr;
0150       init_scroll_text  : init_scroll_txt;
0155
0160       init_text,
0165       graph_text        : screen1;
0170
0175       year_str          : str6;
0180       year_str_array    : year_str_arr;
0185       year_buffer       : year_buf;
0190
0195       plot_array        : pl_arr;
0200       plot_buffer       : pl_buf;
0205
0210       screen1_tlc,
0215       screen1_tlr,
0220       screen1_brc,
0225       screen1_brr       : integer;
0230
0235       tl_col,tl_row     : integer;
0237
0240 {========================================================================}
0245 {$i chrinout.inc}   {always first!}
0250 {$i windows.inc}
0255 {========================================================================}
0260
0265 procedure      HEADER_TEXT;
0270
0275 Begin     {procedure header_text}
0280       window(1,1,80,25);
0285       TEXTCOLOR(0);TEXTBACKGROUND(15);
0290       gotoxy(21,2);
0295       write(' HORIZONTAL GRAPH SCROLLING APPLICATION ');
```

continued...

Scrolling Graph and Number Table 12

...from previous page

```
0300        gotoxy(34,3);write(' CHAPTER 12 ');
0305        TEXTCOLOR(15);TEXTBACKGROUND(0);
0310        WINDOW_BORDER(31,8,50,19,1); {border style #1}
0315        gotoxy(34,7);write('YEAR   LION POP.');
0320        gotoxy(8,7);write('Lion Population');
0325        gotoxy(5,9);write('Year Range: 1950-1970');
0330        gotoxy(5,10);write('Max Limit  :  7000 Lions');
0335        gotoxy(5,11);write('Min Limit  :  4000 Lions');
0340 End;        {procedure header_text}
0345 {-----------------------------------------------------------------}
0350
0355 procedure       INITIALIZE_YEARS(start_year   : integer;
0360                                  var year_val: year_array);
0365
0370 var
0375     i : integer;
0380
0385 Begin      {procedure initialize_years}
0390     FOR i := 1 to 21 DO     {1950 to 1970 INCLUSIVE is 21 years}
0395     Begin
0400         year_val[i]:= start_year;
0405         start_year := start_year + 1;
0410     End;
0415 End;       {procedure initialize_years}
0420 {-----------------------------------------------------------------}
0425
0430 procedure CREATE_GRAPH_TABLE(var scroll_text : scroll_txt_arr);
0435
0440 const
0445     chars_per_line = 18; {excludes left & right hand borders}
0450
0455 var
0460     i,k,j      : integer;
0465     entry_no   : integer;     {range 1..21}
0470     col,row    : integer;
0475 {-----------------------------------------------------------------}
0480
0485     procedure     SAVE_SCREEN1(tlc,tlr,brc,brr  : integer;
0490                                var init_text    : screen1);
0495
0500     var
0505         i,j,k     : integer;
0510         h11,v11   : integer;
0515
0520     Begin      {subprocedure save_screen1}
0525         window(1,1,80,25);
0530         h11 := brc - tlc + 1;
0535         v11 := brr - tlr + 1;
0540         gotoxy(tlc,tlr);
0545         FOR i := 1 to v11 DO        {down thru rows}
0550         Begin
0555             j := ((tlr - 1) * 160) + ((tlc - 1) * 2);
0560             FOR k := 1 to h11 DO  {across thru columns}
0565             Begin
0570                 CHR_IN(j,init_text[i,k]);
0575                 { source(j) , destination(init...) }
0580                 j := j + 2;
0585             End;
0590             tlc := tlc;        {same column.........}
0595             tlr := tlr + 1;    {drop down to next row}
0600         End;
```

continued...

12 Scrolling Graph and Number Table

...from previous page

```
0605        End;         {subprocedure save_screen1}
0610 {-------------------------------}
0615
0620 Begin       {procedure create_graph_table}
0625        window(1,1,80,25);
0630        gotoxy(32,9);
0635        col := WHEREX ; row := WHEREY;
0640        FOR entry_no := 1 to 10 DO    {10 is input screen depth}
0645        Begin
0650            gotoxy(col,row);    {32,9}
0655            write('  ',year_val[entry_no],'....'); {2 blanks}
0660            col := col ; row := row + 1;
0665        End;
0670        row := row - 10;   {get row back to starting place}
0675
0680        FOR entry_no := 1 to 10 DO
0685        Begin
0690            BUFLEN := 4;
0695            gotoxy(42,row);   {first one is 42,9}
0700            read(lion_val[entry_no]);    {type in a value from kbd}
0705            gotoxy(col,row); {first one is 32,9}
0710            j := ((row - 1) * 160) + ((col - 1) * 2);
0715            FOR k := 1 to chars_per_line DO
0720            Begin
0725                CHR_IN(j , scroll_text[entry_no,k]);
0730                j := j + 2;
0735            End;
0740            row := row + 1;
0745        End;
0750
0755        screen1_tlc := 31 ; screen1_tlr := 7;
0760        screen1_brc := 50 ; screen1_brr := 19;
0765        SAVE_SCREEN1(screen1_tlc , screen1_tlr,
0770                    screen1_brc , screen1_brr,
0775                    init_text);
0780
0785        col := 32 ; row := 18;  {now each row saved only from row 18}
0790        FOR entry_no := 11 to max_table_entries DO   {11 to 21}
0795        Begin
0800            window(32,9,49,18);
0805            gotoxy(1,1);    {locally, inside window}
0810            DELLINE;{* delay(2000); *}
0815            window(1,1,80,25);   {restore normal window}
0820            gotoxy(col,row);    {32,18}{bottom line of window}
0825            write('  ',year_val[entry_no],'....'); {2 blanks}
0830            BUFLEN := 4;        {max 4 character entry}
0835            gotoxy(42,18);      {bottom line of window}
0840            read(lion_val[entry_no]); {type in from kbd}
0845            gotoxy(col,row); {col 32,row 18 to save WHOLE LINE}
0850            j := ((row - 1) * 160) + ((col - 1) * 2);
0855            FOR k := 1 to chars_per_line DO
0860            Begin
0865                CHR_IN(j , scroll_text[entry_no,k]);
0870                j := j + 2;
0875            End;
0880        End;
0885 End;       {procedure create_graph_table}
0890 {---------------------------------------------------------------}
```

continued...

Scrolling Graph and Number Table 12

...from previous page

```
0895
0900    procedure       INSPECT_GRAPH_TABLE;
0905
0910    {------------------------------------------------------------------}
0915
0920        procedure       RE_DISP_SCREEN1(tlc,tlr,brc,brr : integer;
0925                                    var init_text         : screen1);
0930
0935        type
0940            screen1_buf = ARRAY[1..260] of char; {13 * 20}
0945
0950        var
0955            i,j,k,
0960            hll,vll                         : integer;
0965            count,
0970            count_of_chars_per_line         : integer;
0975
0980            init_text_buffer                : screen1_buf;
0985
0990        Begin       {subprocedure re_disp_screen1}
0995            window(1,1,80,25);
1000            hll := brc - tlc + 1;
1005            vll := brr - tlr + 1;
1010            count_of_chars_per_line := 1;
1015            count := 0;
1020            FOR i := 1 to vll DO            {down thru rows.....}
1025            Begin
1030                FOR k := 1 to hll DO {across thru columns}
1035                Begin
1040                    count := count + 1;
1045                    init_text_buffer[count] := init_text[i,k];
1050                End;
1055            End;
1060
1065            j := ((tlr - 1) * 160) + ((tlc - 1) * 2);
1070            {give CHR_OUT its first value of j....}
1075            FOR count:= 1 to 260 DO        {13 * 20}
1080            Begin
1085                CHR_OUT(j,ORD(init_text_buffer[count]));
1090                { destination(j) , source(ORD(.......) }
1095                count_of_chars_per_line :=
1100                                count_of_chars_per_line + 1;
1105                IF (count_of_chars_per_line > hll) THEN
1110                Begin
1115                    tlr := tlr + 1;
1120                    j := ((tlr - 1) * 160) + ((tlc - 1) * 2);
1125                    count_of_chars_per_line := 1;
1130                End
1135                ELSE
1140                    j := j + 2;
1145                    {every second, even numbered screen}
1150                    {memory loc. is the character part }
1155            End;
1160        End;        {subprocedure re_disp_screen1}
1165    {------------------------------------------------------------------}
1170
1175    procedure       SCROLL_SCREEN1(tlc,tlr,brc,brr : integer;
1180                                var scroll_text : scroll_txt_arr);
```

continued...

12 Scrolling Graph and Number Table

...from previous page

```
1185
1190   label
1195        rep_read;
1200
1205   const
1210        scroll_up       = #$48;
1215        scroll_down     = #$50;
1220        carriage_ret    = #$0d;
1225        bell            = #$07;
1230
1235   var
1240        scroll_choice   : char;
1245        exit_scroll     : boolean;
1250        i,k             : integer;
1255        i_tot,k_tot     : integer;
1260        x_coord,y_coord : integer;
1265
1270   {------------------------------------------------------------------}
1275
1280        procedure SCRL_UP(k_tot,i_tot : integer);
1285
1290        var
1295             k : integer;
1300
1305        Begin     {sub procedure scrl_up}
1310             window(tlc,tlr,brc,brr);      {32,9,49,18}
1315             gotoxy(1,1);   {window includes col 32,row 9 etc}
1320             DELLINE;
1325             window(1,1,80,25);
1330             gotoxy(tlc,brr);      {lower left corner 32,18}
1335             For k := 1 to 18 DO {18 chars/line in window}
1340             Begin
1345                  write(scroll_text[i_tot + 9,k]);
1350             End;
1355        End;      {sub procedure scrl_up}
1360   {------------------------------------------------------------------}
1365
1370        procedure SCRL_DOWN(k_tot,i_tot : integer);
1375
1380        var
1385             k : integer;
1390
1395        Begin     {sub procedure scrl_down}
1400             window(tlc,tlr,brc,brr);      {32,9,49,18}
1405             gotoxy(1,1);
1410             INSLINE;
1415             window(1,1,80,25);
1420             gotoxy(tlc,tlr);     {top left corner 32,9}
1425             FOR k := 1 to 18 DO {18 chars/line in window}
1430             Begin
1435                  write(scroll_text[i_tot,k]);
1440             End;
1445        End;      {sub procedure scrl_down}
1450   {------------------------------------------------------------------}
1455
1460   Begin     {subprocedure scroll_screen1}
1465        window(tlc,tlr,brc,brr); {32,9,49,18}
1470        exit_scroll := false;
1475        i_tot := 1;
```

continued...

Scrolling Graph and Number Table   12

...from previous page

```
1480        k_tot := 1;
1485
1490        REPEAT
1495            rep_read: {....a label with colon}
1500            read(KBD,scroll_choice);
1505            CASE (scroll_choice) OF
1510
1515                scroll_up      : Begin   {press Up Arrow Key}
1520                                    i_tot := i_tot - 1;
1525                                    k_tot := k_tot + 0;
1530                                    IF (i_tot < 1) THEN
1535                                    Begin
1540                                        i_tot := 1;
1545                                        goto rep_read;
1550                                    End
1555                                    ELSE
1560                                        SCRL_DOWN(k_tot,i_tot);
1565                                End;   {scroll_up}
1570
1575                scroll_down    : Begin   {press Down Arrow Key}
1580                                    i_tot := i_tot + 1;
1585                                    k_tot := k_tot + 0;
1590                                    IF (i_tot > 12) THEN {13 + 9 > 21}
1595                                    Begin
1600                                        i_tot := 12;
1605                                        goto rep_read;
1610                                    End
1615                                    ELSE
1620                                        SCRL_UP(k_tot,i_tot);
1625                                End;   {scroll_down}
1630
1635                carriage_ret   : Begin
1640                                    exit_scroll := true;
1645                                End;
1650
1655            ELSE
1660                {enters here if any other key is pressed}
1665
1670            END; {case}
1675        UNTIL (exit_scroll = true);
1680   End;    {subprocedure scroll_screen1}
1685   {----------------------------------------------------------------}
1690
1695   Begin   {procedure inspect_graph_table}
1700        screen1_tlc := 31 ; screen1_tlr := 7;
1705        screen1_brc := 50 ; screen1_brr := 19;
1710        RE_DISP_SCREEN1(screen1_tlc , screen1_tlr,
1715                        screen1_brc , screen1_brr,
1720                        init_text);
1725
1730        screen1_tlc := 32 ; screen1_tlr := 9;
1735        screen1_brc := 49 ; screen1_brr := 18;
1740        SCROLL_SCREEN1(screen1_tlc , screen1_tlr,
1745                        screen1_brc , screen1_brr,
1750                        scroll_text);
1755   End;    {procedure inspect_graph_table}
1760   {----------------------------------------------------------------}
1765
1770   procedure    DRAW_AXES;
```

continued...

12 Scrolling Graph and Number Table

...from previous page

```
1775
1780 var
1785        i    : integer;
1790        row,
1795        col  : integer;
1800
1805 Begin     {procedure draw_axes}
1810       gotoxy(13,7);              {vertical....}
1815       col := WHEREX ; row := WHEREY;
1820       FOR i := 1 to 14 DO
1825       Begin
1830            gotoxy(col,row);
1835            IF (i MOD 4 = 1) THEN
1840                 write(chr(197))
1845            ELSE
1850                 write(chr(179));
1855
1860            col := col ; row := row + 1;
1865       End;
1870       gotoxy(13,21);write(chr(192));   {elbow at origin}
1875
1880       gotoxy(14,21);             {horizontal....}
1885       col := WHEREX ; row := WHEREY;
1890       FOR i := 1 to 57 DO
1895       Begin
1900            gotoxy(col,row);
1905            IF (i MOD 7 = 1) THEN
1910                 write(chr(197))
1915            ELSE
1920                 write(chr(196));
1925
1930            col := col + 1 ; row := row;
1935       End;
1940 End;      {procedure draw_axes}
1945 {---------------------------------------------------------------}
1950
1955 procedure    CREATE_LION_AXISLABELS;
1960
1965 var
1970       i         : integer;
1975       row,
1980       col       : integer;
1985       max_lions : integer;
1990
1995 Begin     {procedure create_lion_axislabels}
2000       max_lions := 7000;
2005       gotoxy(9,7);
2010       col := WHEREX ; row := WHEREY;
2015       FOR i := 1 to 4 DO
2020       Begin
2025            gotoxy(col,row);
2030            write(max_lions);
2035            max_lions := max_lions - 1000;
2040            col := col ; row := row + 4;
2045       End;
2050 End;      {procedure create_lion_axislables}
2055 {---------------------------------------------------------------}
2060
```

continued...

Scrolling Graph and Number Table 12

...from previous page

```
2065   procedure CREATE_YEAR_AXISLABELS(var year_str_array  :
2070                                                     year_str_arr;
2075                                    var year_buffer   :
2080                                                     year_buf);
2085
2090   var
2095        i,j        : integer;
2100        row,col    : integer;
2105        index      : integer;
2110        bp,count   : integer;
2115
2120   Begin    {procedure create_year_axislabels}
2125        FOR i := 1 to 21 DO     {1950 - 1970 incl}
2130        Begin
2135             STR(year_val[i],year_str);
2140             year_str_array[i]:= CONCAT('*',year_str,'*');
2145        End;
2150        index := 0;
2155        FOR i := 1 to 21 DO
2160        Begin
2165             FOR count := 1 to 6 DO
2170             Begin
2175                  index := index + 1;   {max is 21 * 6 = 126}
2180                  year_buffer[index] :=
2185                                 COPY(year_str_array[i],count,1);
2190             End;
2195        End;
2200        {---- now initialize the year_axislabels on screen ----}
2205        col := 15 ; row := 22;
2210        j := ((row - 1) * 160) + ((col - 1) * 2);
2215        FOR i := 1 to 8 DO    {8 years on x axis}
2220        Begin
2225             bp := (i - 1) * 6;
2230             FOR count := 1 to 6 DO    {6 chars/entry}
2235             Begin
2240                  CHR_OUT(j,ORD(year_buffer[bp + count]));
2245                  j := j + 2;
2250             End;
2255             j := j + 2; {skip a space - cols 21,28,35,42,49,56 etc}
2260        End;
2265   End;     {procedure create_year_axislabels}
2270   {-------------------------------------------------------------}
2275
2280   procedure CONVERT_TOPLOT(var lion_val    : lion_array;
2285                            var plot_array  : pl_arr;
2290                            var plot_buffer : pl_buf);
2295
2300   const
2305        eight_blanks     = '        ';   {8 blanks}
2310
2315   type
2320        str6 = string[6];
2325        str4 = string[4];
2330        lion_plot_array = ARRAY[1..21] of integer;
2335
2340   var
2345        i,k,j             : integer;
2350        lion_plot_val     : lion_plot_array;
2355        temp_val          : integer;
```

continued...

247

12 Scrolling Graph and Number Table

...from previous page

```
2360        temp_str          : str4;
2365        code              : integer;
2370        best_candidate,
2375        base,quarter,
2380        half,
2385        three_quarter,
2390        full              : integer;
2395
2400        bx,bp,
2405        count,index       : integer;
2410        col,row           : integer;
2415        st,fin            : integer;
2420        color_bar         : str6;
2425
2430  Begin    {procedure convert_toplot}
2435      For i := 1 to 13 DO
2440      Begin                       {initialize array with blanks..}
2445          FOR k := 1 to 21 DO
2450          Begin
2455              plot_array[i,k] := eight_blanks;
2460          End;
2465      End;
2470
2475      color_bar := CONCAT(chr(176),chr(176),chr(176),
2480                          chr(176),chr(176),chr(176));
2485      FOR k := 1 to 21 DO    {for each of 21 yrs 1950 - 1970 incl}
2490      Begin
2495          temp_val := lion_val[k];
2500
2505          STR(temp_val,temp_str);
2510          temp_str := CONCAT(COPY(temp_str,1,1),'000');
2515          VAL(temp_str , base , code);
2520          quarter := base + 250;
2525          half := base + 500;
2530          three_quarter := base + 750;
2535          full := base + 1000;
2540
2545          best_candidate := base;
2550          IF (ABS(quarter - temp_val) <=
2555                              ABS(base - temp_val)) THEN
2560              best_candidate := quarter;
2565          IF (ABS(half - temp_val) <=
2570                              ABS(quarter - temp_val)) THEN
2575              best_candidate := half;
2580          IF (ABS(three_quarter - temp_val) <=
2585                              ABS(half - temp_val)) THEN
2590              best_candidate := three_quarter;
2595          IF (ABS(full - temp_val) <=
2600                              ABS(three_quarter - temp_val)) THEN
2605              best_candidate := full;
2610
2615          lion_plot_val[k] := best_candidate;
2620
2625          CASE (lion_plot_val[k]) OF
2630          {insertions into blank graph locations}
2635
2640          7000 : plot_array[1,k]   := color_bar;
2645          6750 : plot_array[2,k]   := color_bar;    {6 chars}
2650          6500 : plot_array[3,k]   := color_bar;
```

continued...

Scrolling Graph and Number Table 12

...from previous page

```
2655              6250 : plot_array[4,k]   := color_bar;
2660              6000 : plot_array[5,k]   := color_bar;
2665              5750 : plot_array[6,k]   := color_bar;
2670              5500 : plot_array[7,k]   := color_bar;
2675              5250 : plot_array[8,k]   := color_bar;
2680              5000 : plot_array[9,k]   := color_bar;
2685              4750 : plot_array[10,k]  := color_bar;
2690              4500 : plot_array[11,k]  := color_bar;
2695              4250 : plot_array[12,k]  := color_bar;
2700              4000 : plot_array[13,k]  := color_bar;
2705
2710           END; {case}
2715
2720      End;
2725 {
2730  RESULT: "CASE" statement will select only 1 of the 13 possible
2735  plot values.
2740  "Plot_array" is  now populated according to values entered
2745  from the keyboard
2750 }
2755
2760      FOR k := 1 to 21 DO
2765      Begin
2770           st    := ((7000 - lion_plot_val[k]) DIV 250) + 2;
2775           fin   := 13;
2780           FOR i := st to fin DO  {"st" = start   "fin" = finish}
2785           Begin
2790                plot_array[i,k] := color_bar;
2795           End;
2800      End;
2805 {Now, convert "plot_array" into "plot_buffer" ....}
2810      index := 0;
2815      FOR i := 1 to 13 DO
2820      {each of 13 possible plot values in each year....}
2825      Begin
2830           FOR k := 1 to 21 DO
2835           {21 year values in this graph}
2840           Begin
2845                FOR count := 1 to 6 DO
2850                Begin
2855                     index := index + 1;
2860                     plot_buffer[index] :=
2865                               COPY(plot_array[i,k],count,1);
2870                End;
2875           End;
2880      End;
2885      {Now, initialize the first 8 entered lion plot}
2890      {values on graph}
2895      col := 15 ; row := 7;    {start at top left corner}
2900      j := ((row - 1) * 160) + ((col - 1) * 2);
2905      FOR i := 1 to 13 DO
2910      Begin
2915           FOR k := 1 to 8 DO          {8 years on graph....}
2920           Begin
2925                bx := (i - 1) * 126; {each change in row}
2930                bp := (k - 1) * 6;   {each change in col}
2935                FOR count := 1 to 6 DO
```

continued...

249

12 Scrolling Graph and Number Table

...from previous page

```
2940                    Begin
2945                         CHR_OUT(j,ORD(plot_buffer[bx + bp + count]));
2950                         j := j + 2;
2955                    End;
2960                    j := j + 2;   {skip a space on screen}
2965               End;
2970               col := col ; row := row + 1; {drop down a row}
2975               j := ((row - 1) * 160) + ((col - 1) * 2);
2980               {recalculate j for new row}
2985          End;
2990 End;        {procedure convert_toplot}
2995 {---------------------------------------------------------------}
3000
3005 procedure    GRAPH_SCROLL(tlc,tlr : integer;
3010                           var plot_buffer : pl_buf);
3015
3020 label
3025      rep_read;
3030
3035 const
3040      bell            = #$07;
3045      scroll_left     = #$4b;
3050      scroll_right    = #$4d;
3055      home            = #$47;
3060      carriage_ret    = #$0d;
3065
3070   var
3075      scroll_choice   : char;
3080      exit_scroll     : boolean;
3085      i_tot , k_tot   : integer;
3090
3095 {---------------------------------------------------------------}
3100
3105      procedure REWRITE_COL_LABEL(k_tot,i_tot : integer;
3110                                  var year_buffer : year_buf);
3115
3120      var
3125          bp,count,
3130          j,row,col,
3135          k                   : integer;
3140
3145      Begin    {sub procedure rewrite_col_label}
3150          col := 15 ; row := 22;
3155          j := ((row - 1) * 160) + ((col - 1) * 2);
3160          FOR k := (k_tot) to (k_tot + 7) DO
3165          Begin
3170              bp := (k - 1) * 6;
3175              FOR count := 1 to 6 DO
3180              Begin
3185                  CHR_OUT(j,ORD(year_buffer[bp + count]));
3190                  j := j + 2;    {move over to next col.}
3195              End;
3200              j := j + 2;  {skip a column....}
3205          End;
3210      End;     {sub procedure rewrite_col_label}
3215 {---------------------------------------------------------------}
3220
3225      procedure REWRITE_SCR(k_tot , i_tot  : integer;
3230                            var plot_buffer: pl_buf);
```

continued...

250

Scrolling Graph and Number Table 12

...from previous page

```
3235
3240        var
3245            bx,bp,
3250            count,
3255            j,
3260            row,col,
3265            k,i         : integer;
3270
3275        Begin     {sub-procedure rewrite_scr}
3280            col := tlc ; row := tlr;
3285            {starting point for screen write}
3290            j := ((row - 1) * 160) + ((col - 1) * 2);
3295            FOR i := 1 to 13 DO {13 rows/each year column}
3300            Begin
3305                FOR k := (k_tot) to (k_tot + 7) DO
3310                {k to k+7 = 8 columns inclusive}
3315                Begin
3320                    bx := (i - 1) * 126;  {126 chars/full row}
3325                    bp := (k - 1) * 6;    {6 chars/col }
3330                    FOR count := 1 to 6 DO
3335                    Begin
3340                        CHR_OUT(j,ORD(plot_buffer[bx + bp +
3345                                                 count]));
3350                        {* delay(1000); *}
3355                        j := j + 2;
3360                    End;
3365                    j := j + 2; {skip space betw. scr. cols}
3370                End;
3375                col := col ; row := row + 1;   {same col;next line}
3380                j := ((row - 1) * 160) + ((col - 1) * 2);
3385                {recalculate j}
3390            End;
3395        End;      {sub-procedure rewrite_scr}
3400    {-----------------------------------------------------------------}
3405
3410        procedure    SAVE_SCREEN2(tlc,tlr,brc,brr : integer;
3415                                  var graph_text     : screen1);
3420
3425        var
3430            i,j,k      : integer;
3435            hll,vll    : integer;
3440
3445        Begin     {sub procedure save_screen2}
3450            window(1,1,80,25);
3455            hll := brc - tlc + 1;
3460            vll := brr - tlr + 1;
3465            gotoxy(tlc,tlr);
3470            FOR i := 1 to vll DO         {down thru rows}
3475            Begin
3480                j := ((tlr - 1) * 160) + ((tlc - 1) * 2);
3485                FOR k := 1 to hll DO  {across thru columns}
3490                Begin
3495                    CHR_IN(j,graph_text[i,k]);
3500                    { source(j) , destination(graph...) }
3505                    j := j + 2;
3510                End;
3515                tlc := tlc;           {same column.........}
3520                tlr := tlr + 1;       {drop down to next row}
3525            End;
```

continued...

251

12 Scrolling Graph and Number Table

...from previous page

```
3530          End;        {sub procedure save_screen2}
3535    {------------------------------------------------------------------}
3540
3545          procedure       RE_DISP_SCREEN2(tlc,tlr,brc,brr : integer;
3550                                      var graph_text : screen1);
3555
3560          type
3565              screen2_buf = ARRAY[1..260] of char;  {13 * 20}
3570
3575          var
3580              i,j,k,
3585              hll,vll                       : integer;
3590              count,
3595              count_of_chars_per_line       : integer;
3600
3605              graph_text_buffer             : screen2_buf;
3610
3615          Begin     {sub procedure re_disp_screen2}
3620              window(1,1,80,25);
3625              hll := brc - tlc + 1;
3630              vll := brr - tlr + 1;
3635              count_of_chars_per_line := 1;
3640              count := 0;
3645              FOR i := 1 to vll DO           {down thru rows.....}
3650              Begin
3655                  FOR k := 1 to hll DO       {across thru columns}
3660                  Begin
3665                      count := count + 1;
3670                      graph_text_buffer[count] := graph_text[i,k];
3675                  End;
3680              End;
3685
3690              j := ((tlr - 1) * 160) + ((tlc - 1) * 2);
3695              {give CHR_OUT its first value of j....}
3700              FOR count := 1 to 260 DO      {13 * 20}
3705              Begin
3710                  CHR_OUT(j,ORD(graph_text_buffer[count]));
3715                  { destination(j) , source(ORD(.......) }
3720                  count_of_chars_per_line :=
3725                                  count_of_chars_per_line + 1;
3730                  IF (count_of_chars_per_line > hll) THEN
3735                  Begin
3740                      tlr := tlr + 1;
3745                      j := ((tlr - 1) * 160) + ((tlc - 1) * 2);
3750                      count_of_chars_per_line := 1;
3755                  End
3760                  ELSE
3765                      j := j + 2;
3770                      {every second, even numbered screen  }
3775                      {memory location is the character part}
3780              End;
3785          End;      {sub procedure re_disp_screen2}
3790    {------------------------------------------------------------------}
3795
3800    Begin     {procedure graph_scroll}
3805        window(1,1,80,25);
3810        exit_scroll := false;    {initialize exit condition}
3815        k_tot := 1;
3820        i_tot := 1;
```

continued...

Scrolling Graph and Number Table 12

...from previous page

```
3825
3830        REPEAT
3835            rep_read:              {a label with colon}
3840            read(KBD,scroll_choice);
3845            CASE(scroll_choice) OF
3850
3855            scroll_left  : Begin {press Left Arrow Key}
3860                                 i_tot := i_tot + 0;
3865                                 k_tot := k_tot - 1;
3870
3875                                 IF(k_tot < 1) THEN
3880                                 Begin
3885                                    k_tot := 1;
3890                                    goto rep_read;
3895                                 End;
3900                                 REWRITE_COL_LABEL(k_tot,i_tot,
3905                                                 year_buffer);
3910                                 REWRITE_SCR(k_tot,i_tot,
3915                                             plot_buffer);
3920                           End;  {scroll_left}
3925
3930            scroll_right : Begin {press Right Arrow Key}
3935                                 i_tot := i_tot + 0;
3940                                 k_tot := k_tot + 1;
3945
3950                                 IF(k_tot > 14) THEN {15 + 7 = 22!}
3955                                 Begin               {max. is 21  }
3960                                    k_tot := 14;
3965                                    goto rep_read;
3970                                 End;
3975                                 REWRITE_COL_LABEL(k_tot,i_tot,
3980                                                 year_buffer);
3985                                 REWRITE_SCR(k_tot,i_tot,
3990                                             plot_buffer);
3995                           End;    {scroll_right}
4000
4005            home         : Begin {press upper left keypad key "7"}
4010                                 SAVE_SCREEN2(31,7,50,19,
4015                                              graph_text);
4020                                 INSPECT_GRAPH_TABLE;
4025                                 RE_DISP_SCREEN2(31,7,50,19,
4030                                                 graph_text);
4035                           End;   {display exact graph data}
4040
4045            carriage_ret : Begin
4050                                 exit_scroll := true;
4055                           End;
4060
4065            ELSE
4070                {if none of above choices is selected...}
4075                {nothing--go back and press correct key.}
4080            END;   {case}
4085        UNTIL exit_scroll = true;
4090 End;       {procedure graph_scroll}
4095 {-------------------------------------------------------------------}
4100
4105 Begin     {driver}
4110      window(1,1,80,25);clrscr;
4115      HEADER_TEXT;
```

continued...

253

12 Scrolling Graph and Number Table

...from previous page

```
4120        start_year := 1950;
4125        INITIALIZE_YEARS(start_year,year_val);
4130        CREATE_GRAPH_TABLE(scroll_text);
4135        INSPECT_GRAPH_TABLE;              {does vertical scroll}
4140        window(1,4,80,25);clrscr;window(1,1,80,25);
4145        DRAW_AXES;
4150        CREATE_LION_AXISLABELS;
4155        CREATE_YEAR_AXISLABELS(year_str_array,
4160                          year_buffer);
4165        CONVERT_TOPLOT(lion_val,
4170                    plot_array,
4175                    plot_buffer);
4180        tl_col := 15 ; tl_row := 7;
4185        GRAPH_SCROLL(tl_col,tl_row,        {does horizontal scroll}
4190                    plot_buffer);
4195 End.      {driver}
{================================================================}
```

H_GRAPH.DRV: NOTES

Below, some brief notes are presented, supplemented by diagrams to avoid tedious explanation of program details. Only those procedures that require explanation will be treated here. It is assumed that any procedure not covered here has either been covered elsewhere or does not require explanation.

INITIALIZE_YEARS

The task of this procedure is to create a one-dimensional array of the independent variable "years," which will be shown in the table in Figure 12.2 and in the graph in Figure 12.3. Note that the year range 1950-1970 inclusive contains 21 entries, not 20.

Scrolling Graph and Number Table **12**

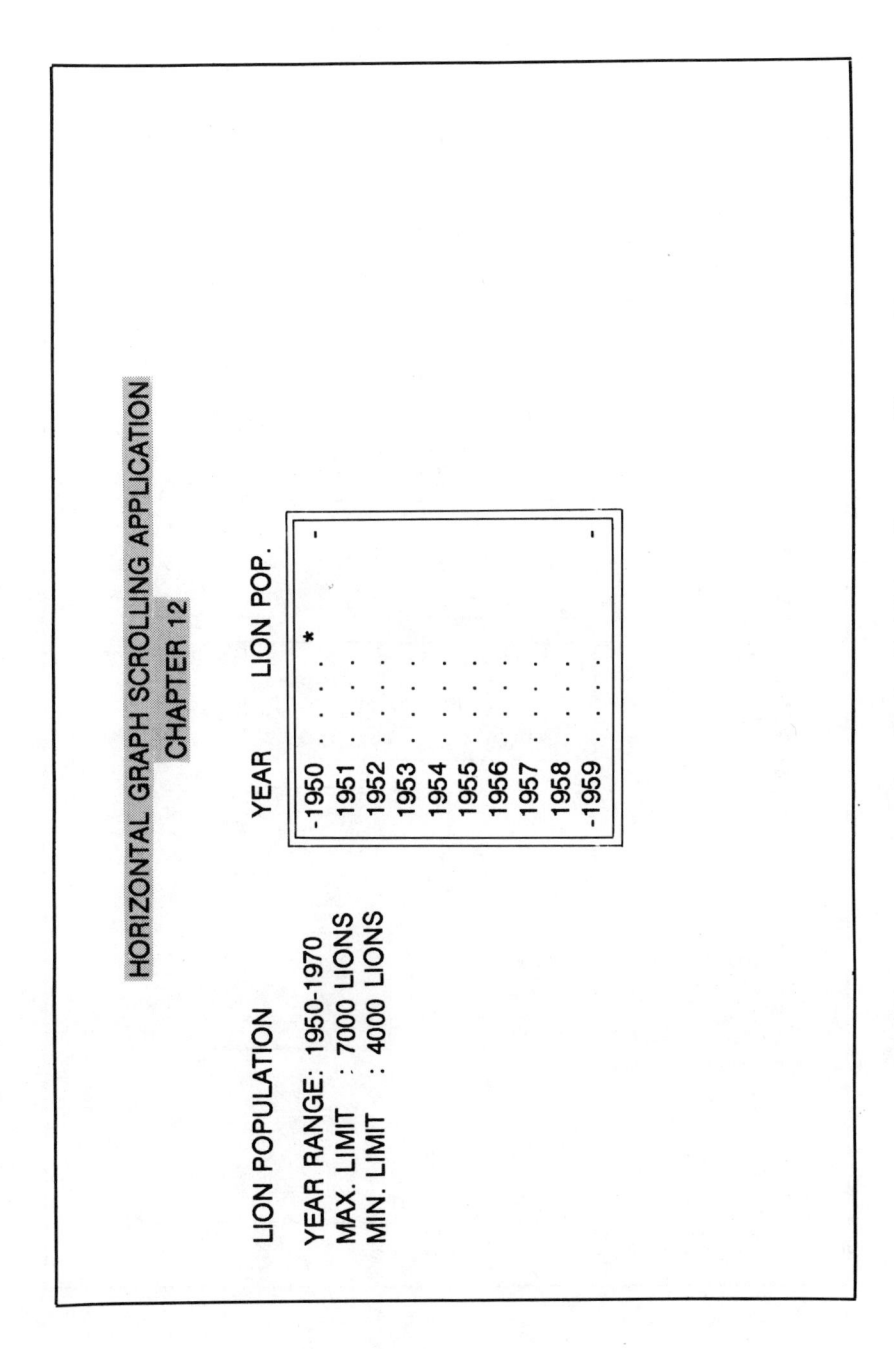

```
HORIZONTAL GRAPH SCROLLING APPLICATION
              CHAPTER 12

       YEAR    LION POP.
      ┌─────────────────────────┐
      │ -1950  . . . *  . . . - │
      │  1951  . . . .  . . . . │
      │  1952  . . . .  . . . . │
      │  1953  . . . .  . . . . │
      │  1954  . . . .  . . . . │
      │  1955  . . . .  . . . . │
      │  1956  . . . .  . . . . │
      │  1957  . . . .  . . . . │
      │  1958  . . . .  . . . . │
      │ -1959  . . . .  . . . - │
      └─────────────────────────┘


LION POPULATION

YEAR RANGE: 1950-1970
MAX. LIMIT : 7000 LIONS
MIN. LIMIT : 4000 LIONS
```

Figure 12.2 Initialized Screen for the Driver Program Chapter 12

12 Scrolling Graph and Number Table

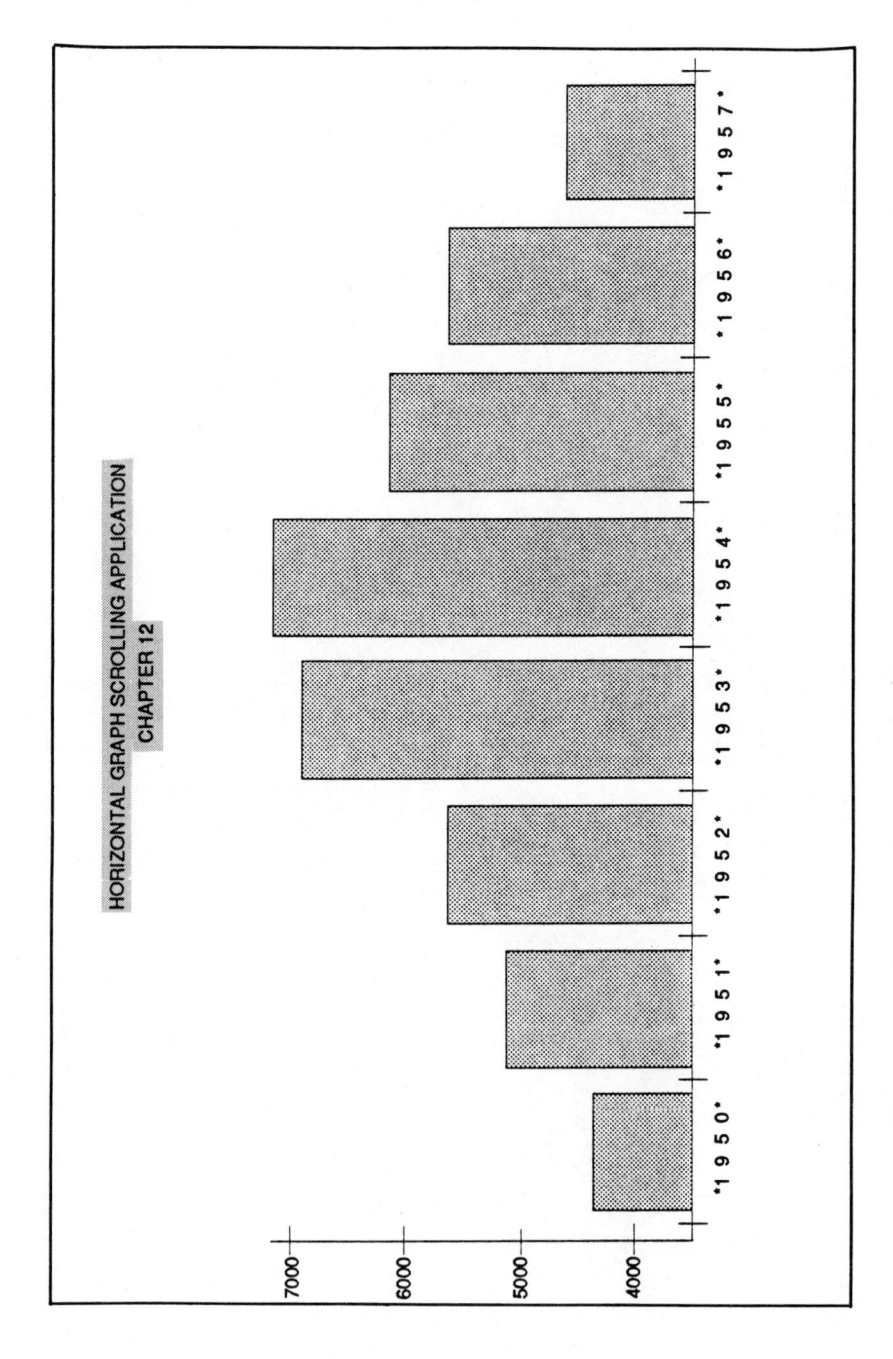

Figure 12.3 Screen Display of Hypothetical Data Entered in Figure12.2

CREATE_GRAPH_TABLE

The overall objective of this procedure is to create the set of 21 values of the dependent variable "lion pop" (derived from an ecology model — lion population) that correspond to each of the years between 1950 and 1970. You are responsible for typing in this information a year at a time (lines 0700 & 0840). For an understanding of the mechanical details, turn to Figures 12.4, 12.5, and 12.6. The FOR..DO loop (lines 0680-0745) is responsible for saving the first 10 lines of entered input data directly from the screen and into the two-dimensional array of characters, "scroll_text." This task is accomplished a single line at a time. The first 10 of the 21-year values (1950-1959) are displayed on the screen (lines 0640-0665). You first type on the screen the input data for 1950, and then that line is immediately saved one character at a time into a row of the array "scroll_text" by the external procedure CHR_IN (line 0725). This cycle of typing an input value, saving the full screen data line, and then moving down to the next line is repeated for each of the years 1950-1959. Once the screen is filled in with the data for 1959, the whole area of the screen as defined by lines 0755 and 0760 is saved into memory in the array variable "init_text" (initialized text). When initialization of the scrolling screen is needed later in INSPECT GRAPH_TABLE, this variable will be pulled out of memory and placed on the screen using the subprocedure RE_DISP_SCREEN1 (redisplay screen1).

Figure 12.5 shows the effect of the built-in DELLINE procedure at line 0810. The contents inside the window are moved up one line. The top line disappears, and a blank space appears at the bottom of the scrolling window at screen row 18.

Figure 12.6 illustrates how each successive data line starting at entry #11 and continuing down to entry #21 is written to the screen at row 18 and then saved directly from the screen at row 18 (cols 32-49 inclusive) into the scrolling array variable, "scroll_text."

12 Scrolling Graph and Number Table

```
                          SCREEN
                          COLUMN #
        31 32 33 34 35 36 37 38 39 40 41 42 43 44 45 46 47 48 49 50
 7
 8                     Y  E  A  R     L  I  O  N     P  O  P  .
 9              —      1  9  5  0  .  .  .  .  .  .  .  —
10                     1  9  5  1  .  .  .  .  .  5  0  0  1               A , B[1], C[1]
11                     1  9  5  2  .  .  .  .  .  5  6  7  7
12                     1  9  5  3  .  .  .  .  .  .  .  .  .  .  .  .  .
13                     1  9  5  4  .  .  .  .  .  .  .  .  .  .  .  .
14                     1  9  5  5  .  .  .  .  .  .  .  .  .  .
15                     1  9  5  6  .  .  .  .  .  .  .  .
16                     1  9  5  7  .  .  .  .  .  .
17                     1  9  5  8  .  .  .  .
18                     1  9  5  9  .  .  .  .  .  6  8  4  5               A , B[10], C[10]
19              —
```

Screen   A   Line 0680
Line   B [Entry_No]   Line 0700
Entry   C [Entry_N0]   Lines 0715 – 0735   A single line saved to "scroll_text" Line 0725
and Saving
Cycle:

Line 0765 : After the data for the year 1959 is saved to "scroll_text," then
the whole screen area is saved to memory and will be re-displayed as the initialized
scrolling screen in procedure "INSPECT_GRAPH_TABLE"

SCREEN ROW#

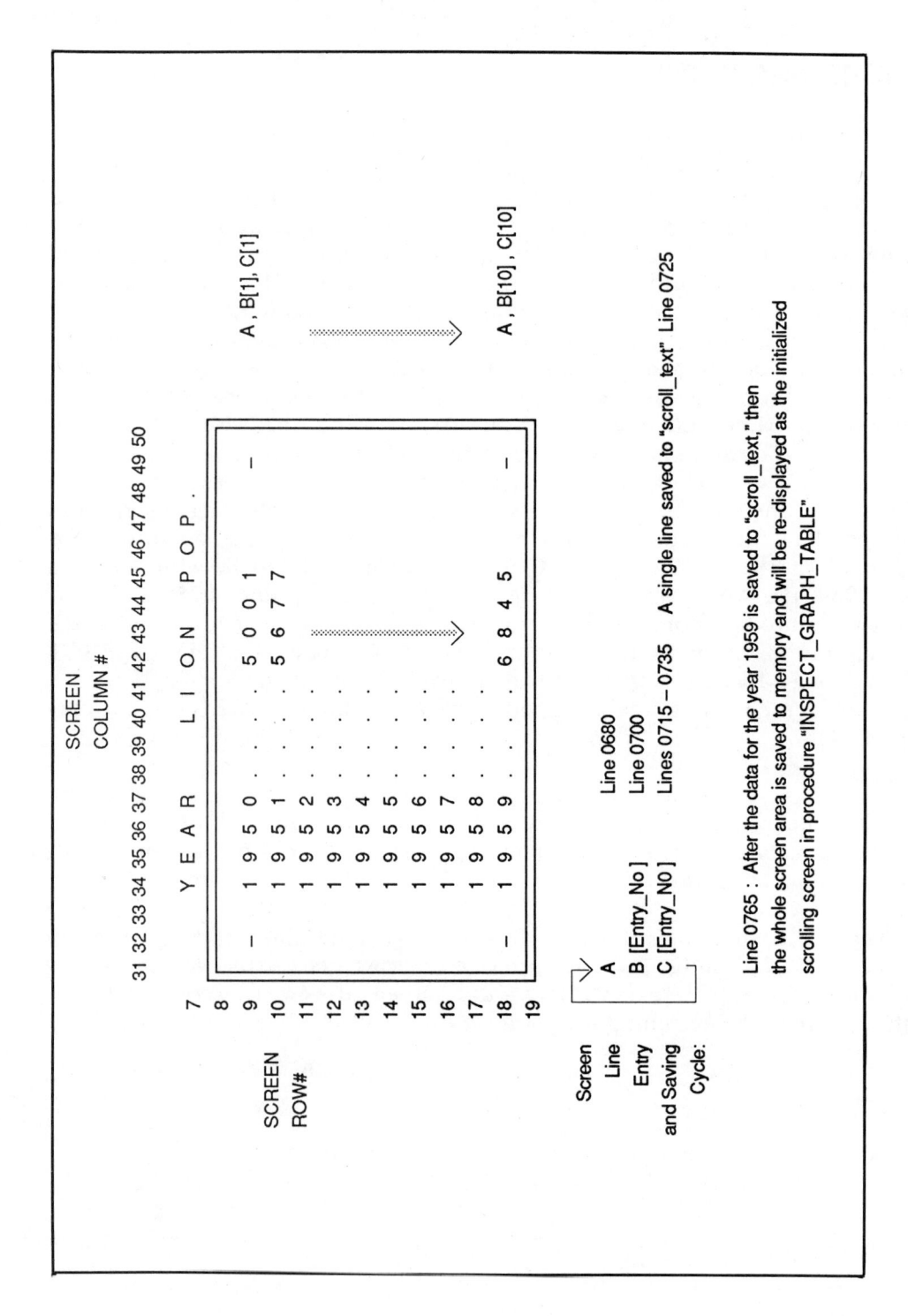

Figure 12.4 How Data for 1950-1959 is Entered and Saved in the Procedure "Create_Graph_Table"

258

12 Scrolling Graph and Number Table

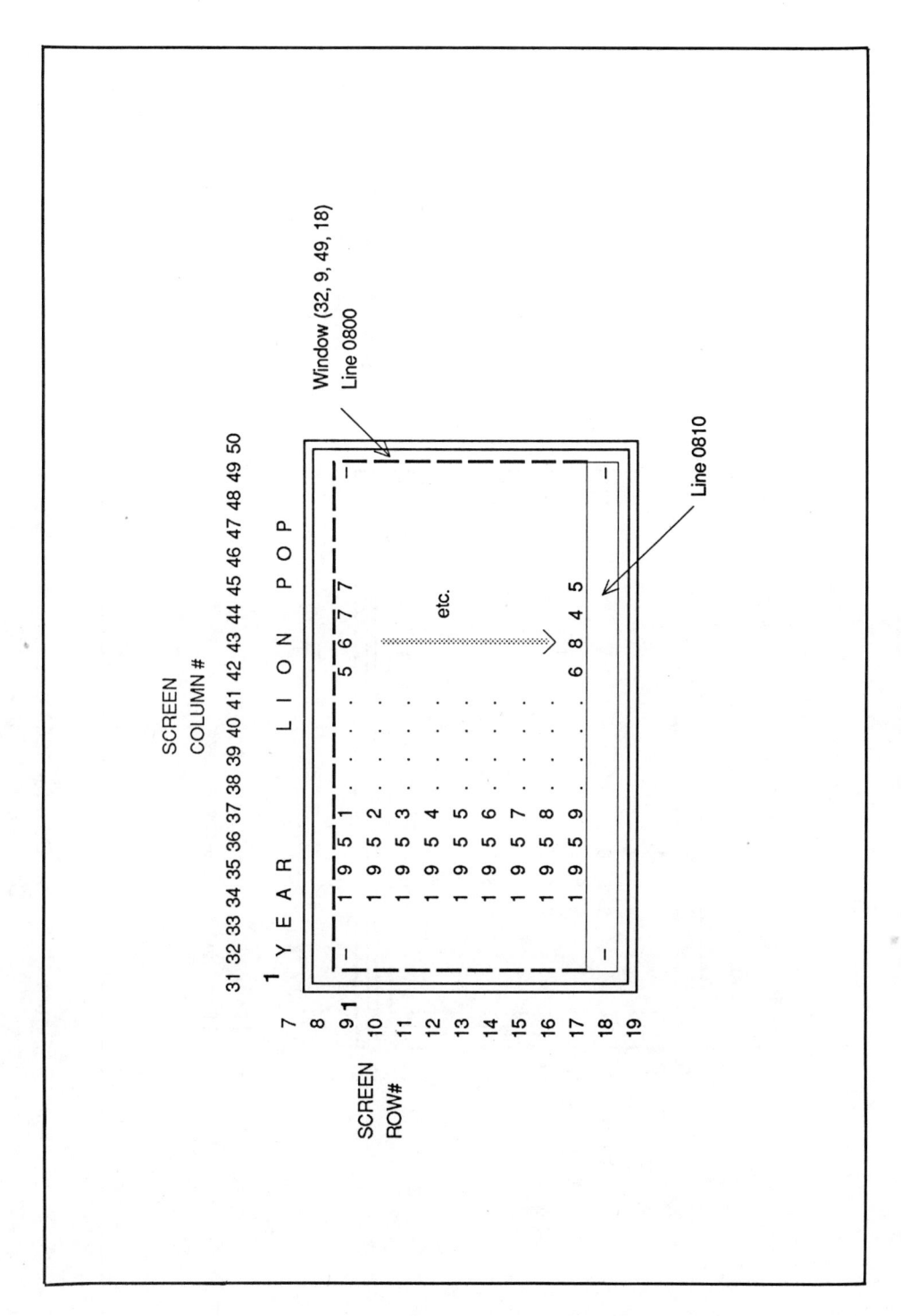

Figure 12.5 How Data for 1960 and Later is Entered in the Procedure "Create_Graph_Table" (Screen Scroll Up One Line)

12 Scrolling Graph and Number Table

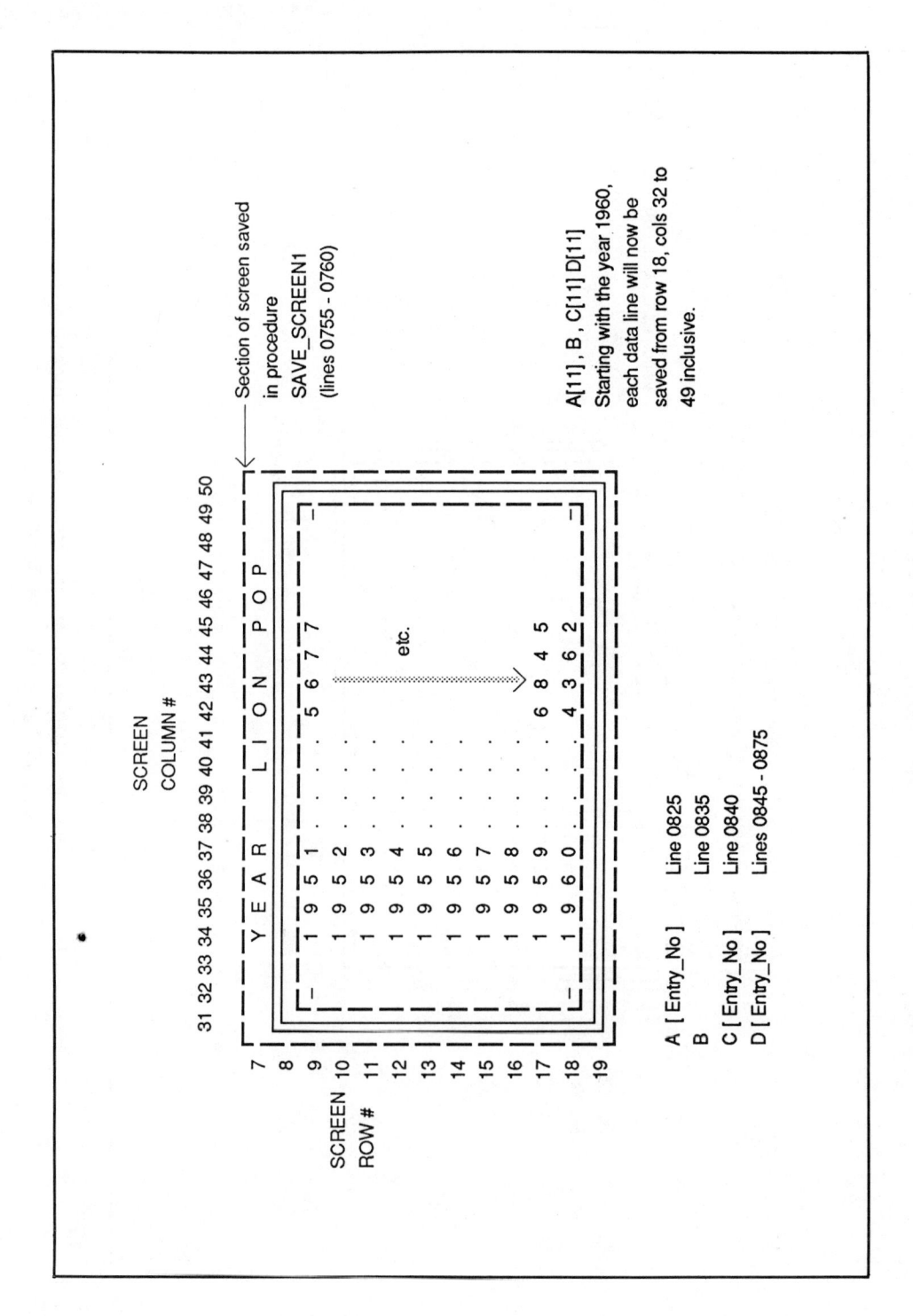

```
                                    SCREEN
                                    COLUMN #
      31 32 33 34 35 36 37 38 39 40 41 42 43 44 45 46 47 48 49 50
   7                                                                    ← Section of screen saved
   8                  Y  E  A  R        L  I  O  N     P  O  P              in procedure
   9                 ┌─                                              ─┐     SAVE_SCREEN1
  10                 │  1  9  5  1              .  .  .  5  6  7  7  │     (lines 0755 - 0760)
  11                 │  1  9  5  2              .  .  .              │
  12                 │  1  9  5  3              .  .  .              │
  13                 │  1  9  5  4              .  .  .       etc.   │
  14                 │  1  9  5  5              .  .  .              │
  15                 │  1  9  5  6              .  .  .              │
  16                 │  1  9  5  7              .  .  .              │
  17                 │  1  9  5  8              .  .  .  6  8  4  5  │  ← A[11], B, C[11] D[11]
  18                 │  1  9  5  9              .  .  .  4  3  6  2  │     Starting with the year 1960,
  19                 └─  1  9  6  0                                  ─┘     each data line will now be
SCREEN                                                                     saved from row 18, cols 32 to
ROW #                                                                      49 inclusive.

  A [ Entry_No ]        Line 0825
  B                     Line 0835
  C [ Entry_No ]        Line 0840
  D [ Entry_No ]        Lines 0845 - 0875
```

Figure 12.6 How Data for 1960 and Later is Entered in the Procedure "Create_Graph_Table" (Entry and Saving of Typed-in Data)

INSPECT_GRAPH_TABLE

Once the numeric data for the lion population is typed into the graph table, the procedure INSPECT_GRAPH_TABLE is invoked. This procedure allows you to inspect the data you have just entered. This procedure calls two subprocedures. The first is RE_DISP_SCREEN1, which was just mentioned. The border parameters that are set prior to requesting the screen display are exactly the same as those that were previously used to save the same screen. SCROLL_SCREEN1 is called next at line 1740 to vertically scroll the data saved in the array, "scroll_text." Note the dimensions of the scrolling window at line 1735 and in Figure 12.6. When laying out your display screens, always be sure to leave the corners of the scrolling windows blank. SCROLL_SCREEN1 invokes its own subprocedures, SCRL_UP (scroll up) and SCRL_DOWN (scroll down), to perform the mechanics of the vertical scroll on the numeric data table. Note that method 3 (INSLINE/DELLINE) is used here.

CONVERT_TO_PLOT

This procedure is a conversion procedure that adjusts the data entered from the keyboard so that it can be displayed on a bar graph (see Figure 12.3). But how do you convert, say, 5677 to a vertical location on the graph for Figure 12.3? For a start, each horizontal row will represent a block of 250 units (lion units). Thus, as you can see from Figure 12.3, each group of 1000 units is broken down into four subunits of 250 each. For example, between 5000 and 6000 units you have

```
5000 - 5249 inclusive for screen row 15
5250 - 5499 inclusive for screen row 14
5500 - 5749 inclusive for screen row 13
5750 - 5999 inclusive for screen row 12
```

The mechanics of converting a typical input value, say, 5677, to a plot-table value that is placed onto the screen graph is illustrated in Figure 12.7 and Figure 12.8. Study these figures carefully as they embody much explanation. Note that the ABSOLUTE function has been used because only magnitudes are dealt with and, therefore, the positive or negative signs of the values are of no concern.

12 Scrolling Graph and Number Table

Note also that the top of each bar is defined inside the CASE..END statement starting at line 2625 and that the rest of the bar from the top down to the base at the x-axis is filled in using the code of the FOR..DO loop starting at line 2760. The procedure concludes with two operations that are by now familiar: the first (line 2805) converts "plot array" into its one-dimensional screen memory mappable form called "plot_buffer"; the second (line 2885) initializes on screen the graphical representation of the first eight data table numbers that were entered from the keyboard inside CREATE_GRAPH_TABLE.

```
Line 2495     temp_val := lion_val = (5677)

Line 2510     5677→5000

Line 2515     Base             5000
Line 2520     Quarter          5250
Line 2525     Half             5500
Line 2530     Three-quarter    5750
Line 2535     Full             6000

Line 2545     Best Candidate   :=    5000 (Base)
Line 2550     |5250-5677|      ≤     |5000-5677|    ?
              427              ≤     677            Yes
Line 2560     Best Candidate   =     5250 (Quarter)
Line 2565     |5500-5677|      ≤     |5250-5677|    ?
              177              ≤     427            Yes
Line 2575     Best Candidate   =     5500 (Half)
Line 2580     |5750-5677|      ≤     |5500-5677|    ?
              73               ≤     177            Yes
Line 2590     Best Candidate   =     5750 (Three-quarter)
Line 2595     |6000-5677|      ≤     |5750-5677|    ?
              323              ≤     73             No
Line 2605     Not Applicable

Line 2615     Lion_Plot_val[k] :=    5750 (Best Candidate)


Continue by Feeding Lion_Plot_val[k], say, 5750, into CASE Statement Starting
at line 2625 . . . .
```

Figure 12.7 CONVERT_TOPLOT – Desk-Checked Example

Scrolling Graph and Number Table 12

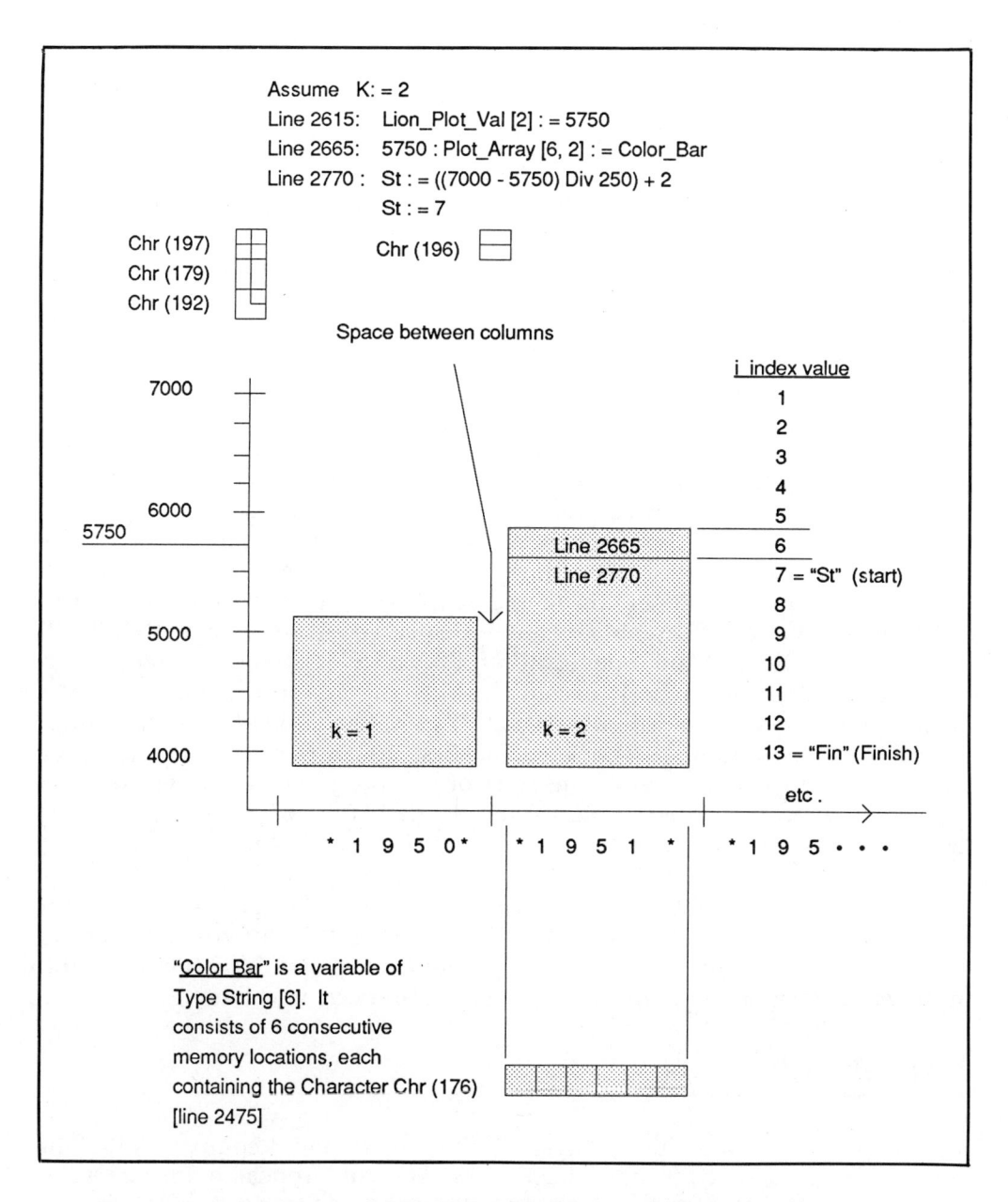

Assume K: = 2
Line 2615: Lion_Plot_Val [2] : = 5750
Line 2665: 5750 : Plot_Array [6, 2] : = Color_Bar
Line 2770 : St : = ((7000 - 5750) Div 250) + 2
St : = 7

Chr (197)
Chr (179)
Chr (192)

Chr (196)

Space between columns

i index value	
1	
2	
3	
4	
5	
6	Line 2665
7	= "St" (start) — Line 2770
8	
9	
10	
11	
12	
13	= "Fin" (Finish)
etc.	

7000
6000
5750
5000
4000

k = 1   k = 2

* 1 9 5 0 *   * 1 9 5 1 *   * 1 9 5 · · ·

"Color Bar" is a variable of
Type String [6]. It
consists of 6 consecutive
memory locations, each
containing the Character Chr (176)
[line 2475]

Figure 12.8 Procedure CONVERT_TOPLOT (cont.) (Detail of Figure 12.3)

263

12 Scrolling Graph and Number Table

GRAPH_SCROLL

The chief task of GRAPH_SCROLL is to control both the horizontal and the vertical scrolling action of the graph and data table—all within the scope of the REPEAT..UNTIL control structure starting at line 3830. The left and right scrolling of the graph table is accomplished starting at lines 3855 and 3930. Both of these operations utilize the subprocedures REWRITE_COL_LABEL (rewrite column label) and REWRITE_SCR (rewrite screen) in horizontally scrolling the graph table. The former rewrites the appropriate group of year values from "year_buffer" along the bottom of the graph, and the latter dynamically redisplays the bars of the graph into their new screen positions from "plot_buffer." Pressing the Home key enables vertical scrolling by activating the procedure INSPECT_GRAPH_TABLE so that you can check an exact value corresponding to the approximated value on the graph. There is a preliminary step, however. Before the numeric data table is redisplayed, the procedure SAVE_SCREEN2 is activated. It saves into memory that section of the graph screen that will be overwritten by the table of numbers to be displayed from within INSPECT_GRAPH_TABLE. The operation of SAVE_SCREEN2 is exactly the same as SAVE_SCREEN1 except for the name of the variable into which the screen data will be saved. INSPECT_GRAPH_TABLE then overlays the computer screen with the first 10 entries from the table of numbers originally created at the start of the program. Pressing the Vertical Arrow keys enables you to scroll this table of numbers up and down. The rest you already know. If you press <Ret>, you will exit INSPECT_GRAPH_TABLE; the procedure RE_DISP_SCREEN2 will overlay the number table with its saved section of the graph table. You may continue to inspect the graph by pressing the horizontal scrolling keys. This procedure allows you to switch back and forth between the number table and the graph table as many times as you like.

LIMITATIONS

As written, this application program is not in its most compact, efficient form. Sections of code have been expanded and repeated for the sake of exposition. If you have a text editor with the standard "cut and paste" (move text from one location to another) function, the extended length of this program won't pose a typing problem since many parts are repeated elswhere in the program text. In this section, possible

Scrolling Graph and Number Table 12

ways of building generality into your screen saving and scrolling routines will be discussed.

The first limitation and opportunity for improvement is in the area of data input and revision. Notice that the code does not validate for either type (integer vs. real vs. character) or for legal range. Notice also that there is no provision for revision of input data. These topics were covered in depth in Chapter 10; to include these features in this program would make it unnecessarily long.

The next opportunity for improvement lies with the screen saving and redisplay routines. The program, as written, contains the screen-saving subprocedures SAVE_ SCREEN1 and SAVE_ SCREEN2 (see Figure 12.1). Both save to memory the same size screen (of type "screen1"), but each holds different contents. The screen redisplay subprocedures RE_ DISP_ SCREEN1 and RE_ DISP_ SCREEN2 operate similarly. The following code fragments and accompanying notes show one method of building greater generality and efficiency into the program. To begin, SAVE_SCREEN1 (number table) and SAVE_SCREEN2 (graph) will be consolidated into the following, more efficient screen-saving routine. Only those parts of the code that need to be changed will be shown:

```
{------------------------------------------------------------------------}
     procedure       SAVE_SCREEN(tlc,tlr,brc,brr  : integer;
                                 var init_text    : screen1;
                                 init_text_active : boolean;
                                 var graph_text   : screen1;
                                 graph_text_active: boolean);

     var
           .
           .
           .
     Begin      {procedure save_screen}
           .
           .
           .
         Begin
             j := ((tlr - 1) + ((tlc - 1) * 2);
             FOR k := 1 to hll DO
             Begin
                 IF (init_text_active = true) THEN
                     CHR_IN(j,init_text[i,k]);
                 IF (graph_text_active = true) THEN
                     CHR_IN(j,graph_text[i,k]);
                     .
                     .
                     .
```

continued...

265

12 Scrolling Graph and Number Table

...from previous page

```
            End;
              .
              .
    End;      .   {procedure save_screen}
{----------------------------------------------------------------------}
```

In the driver routine, you need to declare two Boolean variables, "init text_active" and "graph_text_active." And each time you want to invoke SAVE_SCREEN for a certain variable, say, "graph_text," you must also include in the parameter list the variable "init_text" and its Boolean "init_text_active," even though they are not used on every procedure call. The advantage of avoiding code duplication, as in the original code, would be offset some by the need to include sometimes unneeded variables in the parameter list as seen in the above code fragment.

So if you want to save the character contents of the graph screen into the two-dimensional array "graph_text," your invocation of the new sub-procedure SCREEN_SAVE (via either CREATE_GRAPH_TABLE or GRAPH_SCROLL) in the driver routine would look like this:

```
        graph_text_active := true;    {turn it on for use}
        SAVE_SCREEN(31,7,50,19,
                    init_text,
                    init_text_active,
                    graph_text,
                    graph_text_active);
        graph_text_active := false;   {turn off after use}
```

Now consider consolidating the screen redisplay routines RE_DISP_SCREEN1 (number table) and RE_DISP_SCREEN2 (graph) into the hybrid, RE_DISP_SCREEN. The following code fragment shows only those parts of the code that would be different:

```
{-----------------------------------------------------------}
    procedure      RE_DISP_SCREEN(tlc,tlr,brc,brr,
                                  var init_text       : screen1;
                                  init_text_active    : boolean;
                                  var graph_text      : screen1;
                                  graph_text_active   : boolean);

    type
         screen1_buf   = array[1..260] of char;
         screen2_buf   = array[1..260] of char;

    continued...
```

266

Scrolling Graph and Number Table 12

...from previous page

```
    var
        .
        .
        .
        init_text_buffer  : screen1_buf;
        graph_text_buffer : screen2_buf;
Begin        {procedure re_disp_screen}
        .
        .
        .
        Begin
            FOR k := 1 to h11 DO
            Begin
                count := count + 1;
                IF (init_text_active = true) THEN
                    init_text_buffer[count] := init_text[i,k];
                IF (graph_text_active = true) THEN
                    graph_text_buffer[count] := graph_text[i,k];
            End;
        .
        .
        .
        FOR count := 1 to 260 DO
        Begin
            IF (init_text_active = true) THEN
                CHR_OUT(j,ORD(init_text_buffer[count]));
            IF (graph_text_active = true) THEN
                CHR_OUT(j,ORD(graph_text_buffer[count]));
            .
            .
            .

{------------------------------------------------------------}
```

In the main routine of the program, the Boolean variables "init_text_active" and "graph_text active" are needed for the procedure to act on the proper array variable. Each time you want to invoke RE_DISP SCREEN for a certain variable, say, "init_text" (initialized text), you would also have to include in your parameter list the other variable "graph_text" and its Boolean "graph_text_active," even though they are not needed in the present instance. This is the price paid for greater generality. So if you want to redisplay the initial screen of the scrolling data table, your invocation of RE_DISP_SCREEN as a subprocedure from within INSPECT_GRAPH_TABLE or GRAPH_SCROLL would look like this:

12 Scrolling Graph and Number Table

```
          init_text_active := true;      {turn on the boolean}
          RE_DISP_SCREEN(31,7,50,19,
                         init_text,
                         init_text_active,
                         graph_text,
                         graph_text_active);   {displays scroll text only}
          init_text_active := false;     {turn off boolean after use}
```

In theory, if the subprocedures SAVE_SCREEN1 and SAVE_SCREEN2 were consolidated into SAVE_SCREEN, and RE_DISP_SCREEN1 and RE_DISP_SCREEN2 were likewise consolidated into the more efficient RE_DISP_SCREEN, you could employ these two separate procedures inside an general screen saving and screen redisplay ".inc" module that could be named, say, "sc_sd.inc" (screen save display include module). In theory, this module would be capable of saving and redisplaying a large number of screen images of many different sizes. You will learn in detail the general principles behind saving, redisplaying, and scrolling multiple windows in chapters 14, 15, and 16.

Finally, note that there is code redundancy at lines 0690-0745 and lines 0830-0875 in the body of the procedure CREATE_GRAPH_TABLE. Judicious use of the IF..THEN structure could eliminate this duplication if desired (inside the IF..THEN structure you would need to perform a test to see whether "entry_no" (entry number) was between 1 and 10 or greater than 10). The code has been left in this less efficient form to better demonstrate saving data input text to an array in memory.

CHAPTER 13

SCREEN I/O AND THE DISK

13 Screen I/O and the Disk

Up to this point, all data entry into the computer has been by way of the keyboard. From the keyboard, data is then stored into memory variables (usually arrays) and used for scrolling and screen saving/redisplay. When you finish a session and turn off the computer, you lose all your data. In this chapter, a program has been developed that is capable of the following:

- accepting new data typed in from the keyboard, displaying it on screen, and then optionally storing it to disk for later use.

- retrieving an existing (previously created) data file from disk and storing it into computer memory variables for current use.

To implement the above capabilities in a smooth manner, the following screen I/O features have been added:

- scrolling of data typed into the computer or received from disk.

- on-screen revision capability of disk or keyboard-sourced data.

- validation of file name candidate entries prior to acceptance by the Disk Directory. This is another example of specialized non-numeric input data mentioned in Chapter 10.

- capability of displaying a different, scrollable text file over the top of existing screen data.

All of these features can be developed using the existing screen I/O tools. Figure 13.1 shows the overall relationship between the keyboard, screen, and disk in terms of the options "c" (create file), "s" (save file), "f" (fetch file), and "t" (display text file). Figures 13.2 and 13.3 provide a structural outline of all the procedures used in the program FILMAN.DRV (file manager drive). Refer to these figures as you continue reading.

Screen I/O and the Disk 13

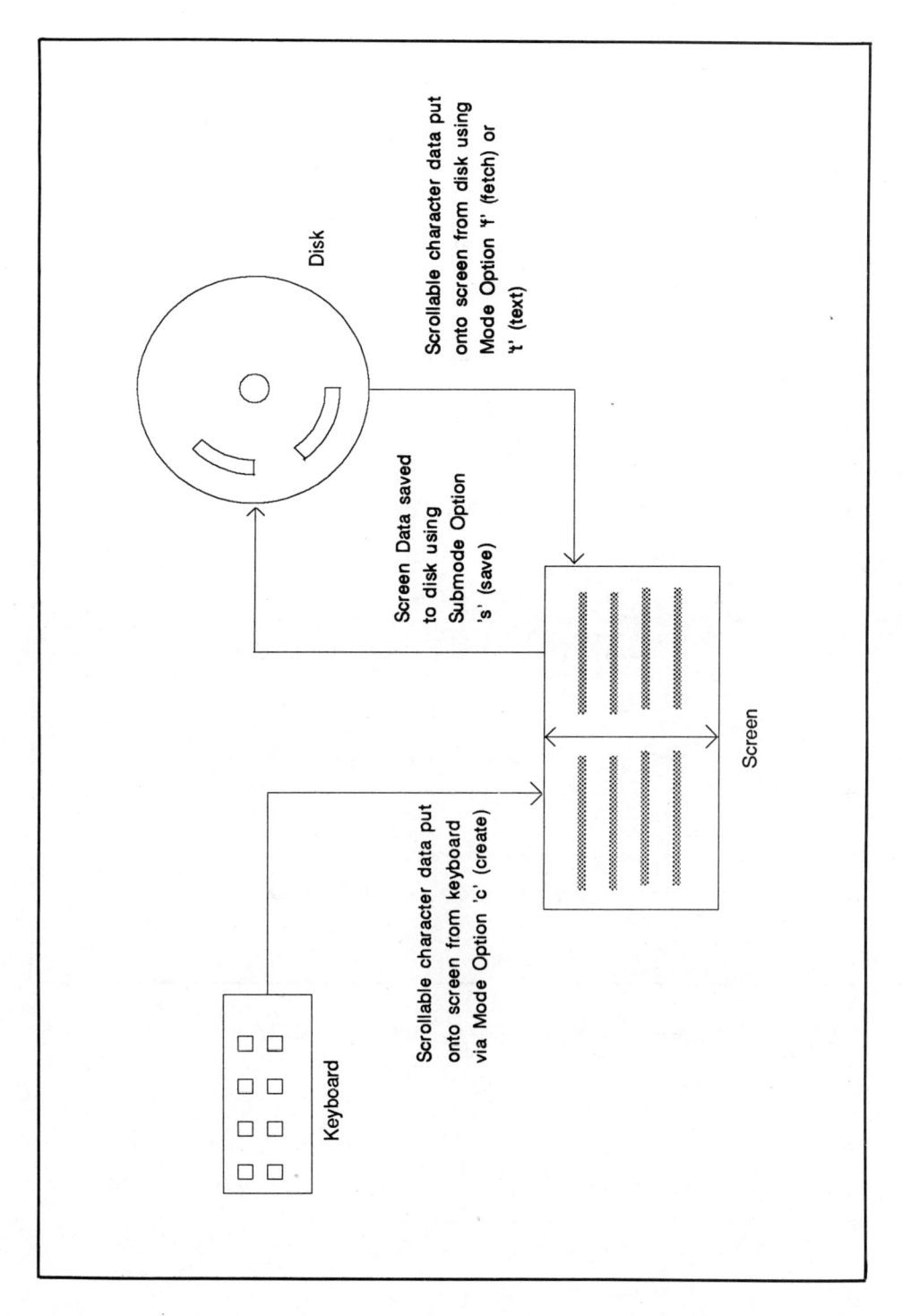

Figure 13.1 Schematic of General Structure

13 Screen I/O and the Disk

```
Line      Skeleton Code

0005 program   filman(input,output);

     EXTERNAL PROCEDURES:
0340 chrinout.inc
0345 windows.inc
0350 textwrit.inc
0355 filename.inc

     INTERNAL PROCEDURES:
0375 procedure INITIALIZE_SCROLL
0520 procedure SCROLL_IT
0625      sub-procedure  SCRL_DOWN
0705      sub-procedure  SCRL_UP
0795      sub-procedure  DISPLAY_PAGE

1405 procedure CREATE_A_FILE
1445      sub-procedure  CHANGING_INPUT_TEXT

1795 procedure SUB_MODE_HEADER
1880 procedure REVISE_DATA_INPUT
2215 procedure A_CALCULATION
2510 procedure SAVE_FILE
2720 procedure FETCH_A_FILE
2930 procedure CREATE_SHADOW_DATA_FILE_NAME
3005 procedure MODE_HEADER
{-----------------------------------------}


3160 Begin     {main program - FILMAN.DRV }

               (CONT'D)

See Figure 13.3 for layout of the procedures
inside the body of the main program

4260 End.      {main program - FILMAN.DRV }
```

Figure 13.2 Procedure Layout – FILMAN.DRV

Screen I/O and the Disk 13

```
Line        Skeleton Code

3160  Begin      {main program - FILMAN.DRV }
3165       REPEAT
3185         CASE (mode_choice) OF
3195           'c' : Begin {create new file mode}
3225                 REPEAT
3235                   REPEAT
3265                     ENTER_NEW_FILE_NAME
3275                   UNTIL
3345                 UNTIL
3370                 CREATE_SHADOW_DATA_FILE_NAME
3380                 CREATE_A_FILE
3405                 REPEAT
3430                   CASE(submode_choice) OF
3435                     'r' :     {revise}
3450                               REVISE_DATA_INPUT
3465                     'c' :     {calculate}
3480                               A_CALCULATION
3495                     's' :     {save file to disk}
3510                               SAVE_FILE
3535                     'q' :     {exit submodes}
3600                   END {case}
3605                 UNTIL {exit_submode_flag = true}
3610               End; {create new file mode}

3625           'f' : Begin {fetch existing file mode}
3650                 REPEAT
3660                   REPEAT
3690                     ENTER_OLD_FILE_NAME
3700                   UNTIL
3770                 UNTIL
3775                 CREATE_SHADOW_DATA_FILE_NAME
3805                 FETCH_A_FILE
3820                 REPEAT
3845                   CASE(submode_choice) OF
3850                     'r' :     {revise}
3865                               REVISE_DATA_INPUT
3880                     'c' :     {calculate}
3895                               A_CALCULATION
3910                     's' :     {save file to disk}
3925                               SAVE_FILE
3950                     'q' :     {exit submodes}  .
4015                   END {case}
4020                 UNTIL {exit_submode_flag = true}
4025               End; {fetch existing file mode}
4030
4035           't' : Begin {display supplemental text file}
4065                 REPEAT
4075                   REPEAT
4105                     ENTER_OLD_FILE_NAME
4115                   UNTIL
4140                 UNTIL
4150                 TXTWRIT
4155               End;  {display supplemental text file}


4165           'q' : Begin {display supplemental text file}
4185                       {enter one of Turbo System commands:}
4200                       press "d" for Disk Directory
4210                       press "r" to run program
4220                       press "q" to EXIT to DOS
4245               End
4250         END  {CASE (mode_choice) OF - ref line 3185}
4255       UNTIL    {ref. to REPEAT statement, line 3165}
4260  End. {ref. to Begin statement,line 3160}
```

Figure 13.3 Skeleton Layout of Main Routine Filman.drv

273

13 Screen I/O and the Disk

MODULE: FILENAME.INC

This ".inc" module performs a validation check on a candidate file name typed in at the keyboard. This module can be used in those situations where you want to create valid disk file names under program control; that is, prior to entering file data, you will assign a file name by typing in that name from the keyboard. "Filename.inc" is analogous to the input validation routines developed in Chapter 10. If you look at line 3265 and lines 3690 and 4105 of the driver routine, you will see that the member procedures ENTER_NEW_FILE_NAME and ENTER_OLD_FILE_NAME are called from within the familiar double REPEAT..UNTIL structures that you have become accustomed to in Chapter 10. Unlike with Integers and Reals, the Turbo system does not appear to check for the correct syntax of the file names at the time the candidate file name is typed in. While ASSIGN connects the typed-in file name with the data file, it does not then check for a syntactically correct file name string. If the entered file name string is syntactically wrong, the error will be caught by the system at the built-in file procedure REWRITE (for a new file) or RESET (for an existing file). The program will stop at this point, and the system will respond with an error message. It is therefore your job to construct some Pascal code that will prevent the system from stopping the program if an invalid file name is typed in from the keyboard. The code for the external procedure "filename.inc" is as follows:

```
{==================================================================}
0005  {filename.inc}
0010  {
0015    Used to perform system validation upon a filename entered
0020    from the keyboard.
0025    On disk as "filename.inc"
0030  }
0035
0040  {----------------------------------------------------------}
0045
0050  procedure   SYNTAX_CHECK(fil_nam        : str12;
0055                           var syntax_err : boolean);
0060  {
0065    Unlike Integers and Reals, the system does not appear
0070    to check for the correct syntax of file names. While
0075    "ASSIGN" connects the entered file name with the file
0080    data, it does NOT check for a syntactically valid
0085    filename string. If the entered filename is syntactically
0090    wrong the error is caught by the system at "REWRITE"
0095    (for a newly created file) or "RESET" for an existing file.
0100  }
0105
```

continued...

Screen I/O and the Disk 13

...from previous page

```
0110 var
0115        i                : integer;
0120        string_length    : integer;
0125        dot_count        : integer;
0130        valid_character,
0135        dot              : SET OF char;
0140
0145 Begin      {procedure syntax_check}
0150        dot_count := 0;
0155        string_length := LENGTH(fil_nam);
0160        valid_character := ['A'..'Z' , 'a'..'z' , '.' , '0'..'9'];
0165        dot             := ['.'];
0170        IF(string_length < 5) OR (string_length > 12) THEN syntax_err:=true;
0175        FOR i := 1 to string_length DO
0180        Begin
0185             IF NOT(fil_nam[i] IN valid_character) THEN
0190                  syntax_err := true;
0195             IF (fil_nam[i] IN dot) THEN
0200                  dot_count := dot_count + 1;
0205             IF (dot_count > 1) THEN
0210                  syntax_err := true;
0215             IF NOT(fil_nam[string_length - 3] IN dot) THEN
0220                  syntax_err := true;
0225        End;
0230 End;       {procedure syntax_check}
0235 {------------------------------------------------------------------}
0240
0245 procedure ENTER_NEW_FILE_NAME(var fil_nam        : str12;
0250                               var valid_file_nam : boolean);
0255
0260 var
0265        syntax_error    : boolean;
0270
0275 Begin      {procedure enter_new_file_name}
0280        syntax_error := false;
0285        read(fil_nam); {type in filename of a NEW disk file}
0290        SYNTAX_CHECK(fil_nam,syntax_error);
0295        IF (syntax_error = false) THEN
0300        Begin
0305             ASSIGN(filevar,fil_nam);        {"filevar" is global}
0310             {$i-} RESET(filevar); {$i+}
0315             IF (IORESULT = 0) THEN          {...a successful RESET...}
0320             Begin                           {can only RESET an EXISTING file}
0325                  gotoxy(23,12);clreol;
0330                  write('DUPLICATE FILE NAME EXISTS....');
0335                  valid_file_nam := false;
0340             End
0345             ELSE    {if IORESULT <> 0. ie a failed RESET}
0350             Begin
0355                  gotoxy(23,12);clreol;
0360                  write('NEW FILE....');
0365                  {$i-} REWRITE(filevar); {$i+}
0370                  {only use REWRITE when creating a new file}
0375                  valid_file_nam := true;
0380             End;
0385        End;
0390        IF (syntax_error = true) THEN {syntax error was made....}
0395        Begin
0400             gotoxy(23,12);clreol;
```

continued...

13 Screen I/O and the Disk

...from previous page

```
0405                write('SYNTAX ERROR IN FILE NAME....');
0410                valid_file_nam := false;
0415         End;
0420         delay(2000);gotoxy(23,12);clreol;
0425 End;          {procedure enter_new_file_name}
0430 {------------------------------------------------------------------}
0435
0440 procedure ENTER_OLD_FILE_NAME(var fil_nam        : str12;
0445                               var valid_file_nam : boolean);
0450
0455 var
0460         syntax_error : boolean;
0465
0470 Begin     {procedure enter_old_file_name}
0475      syntax_error := false;
0480      read(fil_nam); {type in file name of EXISTING disk file}
0485      SYNTAX_CHECK(fil_nam,syntax_error);
0490      IF (syntax_error = false) THEN
0495      Begin
0500           ASSIGN(filevar,fil_nam);       {"filevar" is global}
0505           {$i-} RESET(filevar); {$i+}
0510           IF (IORESULT = 0) THEN       {...a successful RESET...}
0515           Begin                        {can only RESET an EXISTING file}
0520                gotoxy(23,12);clreol;
0525                write('OLD FILE REQUEST GRANTED....');
0530                valid_file_nam := true;
0535           End
0540           ELSE  {if IORESULT <> 0. ie a failed RESET}
0545           Begin
0550                gotoxy(23,12);clreol;
0555                write(fil_nam,' IS NOT IN THE DIRECTORY....');
0560                valid_file_nam := false;
0565           End;
0570      End;
0575      IF (syntax_error = true) THEN {if a syntax error was made}
0580      Begin
0585           gotoxy(23,12);clreol;
0590           write('SYNTAX ERROR IN FILE NAME....');
0595           valid_file_nam := false;
0600      End;
0605      delay(2000);gotoxy(23,12);clreol;
0610 End;          {procedure enter_old_file_name}
{==========================================================================}
```

FILENAME.INC: NOTES

This module consists of the three following procedures:

procedure SYNTAX_CHECK
procedure ENTER_NEW_FILE_NAME (uses SYNTAX_CHECK}
procedure ENTER_OLD_FILE_NAME (uses SYNTAX_CHECK}

Screen I/O and the Disk **13**

SYNTAX_CHECK

As the name implies, SYNTAX_CHECK is the procedure that checks the syntactic correctness of the file name typed in from the keyboard. This procedure is called by both ENTER_NEW_FILE_NAME and ENTER_OLD_FILE_NAME and is therefore placed ahead of them both in "filename.inc." The parameter list at line 0050 accepts a file name in the variable "fil_nam" (file name). After the syntax validation has taken place, the Boolean variable "syntax_err" (syntax_error) returns either "true" or "false" to the calling routine (either ENTER_NEW_FILE_NAME or ENTER_OLD_FILE_NAME). For this program's purposes, it has been coded so that a valid file name has the following characteristics:

- line 0170   ensures that the length of a legal file name string is $>=5$ and $<=12$

- line 0185   members of the character set considered as valid characters are specified here (note: numbers and special characters have deliberately been excluded for this example)

- line 0205   only one dot is allowed to separate the file name prefix from the file name suffix

- line 0215   position of the dot separator must be exactly four positions from the end of the character string

Any violation of these programmer-predefined conditions will result in the Boolean variable "syntax_error" being set to "true," indicating that a syntactically invalid file name has been typed.

ENTER_NEW_FILE_NAME

This procedure is called from the main program at line 3265. Note that it is used only under the "create new data file option" (see Figure 13.4). Line 0285 allows you to actually type in the desired file name. Note that the variable "fil_nam" (file name) is prefixed by "var," which allows the typed-in file name to later be passed out to the main driver routine from the procedure. The procedure SYNTAX_CHECK is then called

13 Screen I/O and the Disk

immediately at line 0290. If a syntax error is detected, then "syntax error" is assigned the Boolean value "true." If a syntax error is *not* detected, then "syntax_ error" remains "false." Now trace the action after a candidate file name is typed in. If the file name is syntactically legal, you then enter the section of code starting at line 0300. At lines 0310-0315, check to see if the file name is a duplicate of a file name already existing in the disk directory. If you can successfully perform a RESET, then you know that the candidate file name is a duplicate, and you set "valid file_ nam" (valid file name) to the value "false" at line 0335. As this variable is also prefixed with "var" in the parameter list, the Boolean result is also passed out to the driver routine. If, however, you cannot successfully RESET the candidate file name, then IORESULT is non-zero, and you know that that file is *not* in the disk directory, and you proceed to write the message at line 0360, create the new file name (line 0365), create the new file name (line 0365), and exit at line 0415.

If the typed in file name is not syntactically legal, you then enter the section of code at line 0390, write the error message at line 0405, set the Boolean "valid_ file_ nam" to "false" at line 0410, and send the "false" value out to the main routine by way of the parameter list (line 0250).

ENTER_OLD_FILE_NAME

This procedure is called from the main program at lines 3690 and 4105. It is used only under the "fetch old file option" (line 3625 and Figure 13.4) when you want to pull an already created file from the disk and load it into the computer. Look at line 0495. If the entered file name is syntactically legal, you can enter the section of code starting at line 0500. At lines 0505-0510, a RESET is attempted on the entered file name.

If the RESET file function is successful (IORESULT = 0), the typed-in file name matches a file name that already exists in the file directory, and you are given the message at line 0525. If, however, you have requested a file name that does not exist in the directory, the result of RESET will be a non-zero IORESULT. In that case, you have not successfully matched the file name with any of those presently existing in the disk directory, and control will be transferred to line 0540 (ELSE statement) where you receive the message at line 0555. "Valid_file_ name" (line 0445) is set to "false" and returns you to the main routine (line 3660) for a retry inside the REPEAT..UNTIL loop there.

DISK FILE APPLICATIONS CHAPTER 13

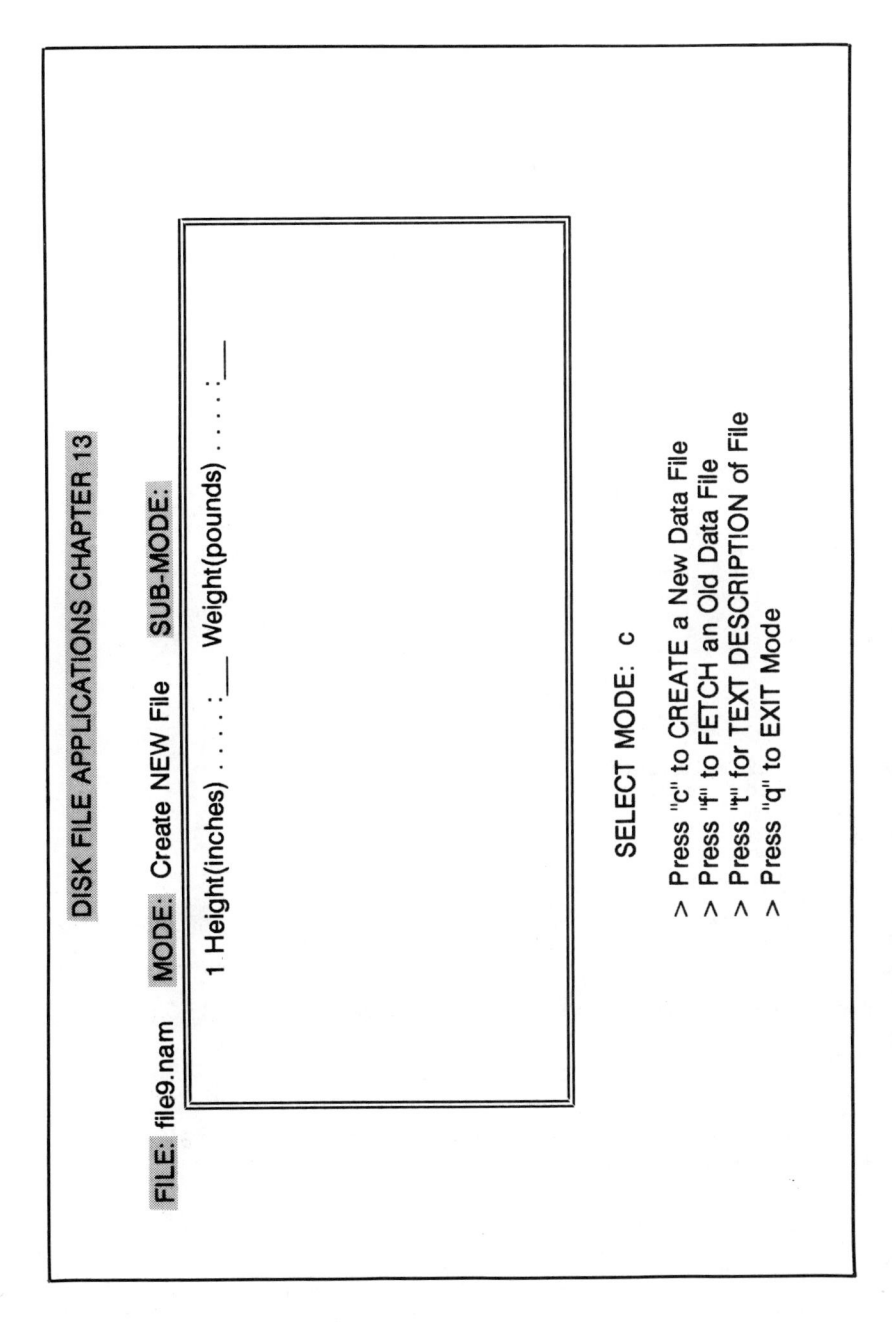

FILE: file9.nam **MODE:** Create NEW File **SUB-MODE:**

1 Height(inches) . . . . . :____ Weight(pounds) . . . . . :____

SELECT MODE: c

> Press "c" to CREATE a New Data File
> Press "f" to FETCH an Old Data File
> Press "t" for TEXT DESCRIPTION of File
> Press "q" to EXIT Mode

Figure 13.4 Initialized Screen Showing Mode Option Choices

13   Screen I/O and the Disk

MODULE: TEXTWRIT.INC

Oftentimes, when you are scrolling through a table of numbers or a graph, you can forget some of the background facts concerning the data in front of you. TEXTWRIT.INC (text write) was developed to address this problem. This module enables you—from within a program—to call to the screen and scroll a disk-based text file. This disk text file must be an existing text file, one created and saved to the disk at some earlier time. The code for "textwrit.inc" follows:

```
{=========================================================================}
0005 {textwrit.inc}
0010 {On disk as "textwrit.inc"}
0015
0020 {-----------------------------------------------------------------------}
0025
0030 procedure      TXTWRIT(var file_name : str12);
0035 { Assumes that the text file it displays has already been
0040   created. This procedure will accept any pre-created text file
0045   of up to 500, 80 character lines . It will pull this file from
0050   the disk storage and place it into a scrollable display array
0055   inside the computer's memory.
0060 }
0065
0070 const
0075       escape     = #$1b;
0080       bell       = #$07;
0085
0090 type
0095       str12 = string[12];
0100       str80 = string[80];
0105
0110 var
0115       line            : str80;
0120       line_count      : integer;
0125       k               : integer;
0130       mode_choice     : char;
0135       entry_error     : boolean;
0140 {-----------------------------------------------------------------------}
0145
0150 procedure      TEXT_FILE_TO_ARRAY(lin_ct : integer);
0155
0160 const
0165       max_file_lines : integer = 500;
0170
0175 type
0180       array_of_screen_text = array[1..500,1..80] of char;
0185       line_length_array    = array[1..500] of integer;
0190
0195 var
0200       screen_text : array_of_screen_text;
0205       i,k         : integer;
0210       line_length : line_length_array;
0215
0220 {-----------------------------------------------------------------------}
```

continued...

Screen I/O and the Disk 13

...from previous page

```
0225
0230         procedure       SCROLL_IT;
0235
0240         label
0245         REP_READ;       {a label}
0250
0255         const
0260             scroll_up       = #$48;
0265             scroll_down     = #$50;
0270             carriage_ret    = #$0d;
0275
0280         var
0285             scroll_choice   : char;
0290             exit_scroll     : boolean;
0295
0300         Begin    {sub procedure scroll_it}
0305             exit_scroll := false;
0310             i := 1;
0315             REPEAT
0320                 REP_READ:       {a label with colon}
0325                 read(KBD,scroll_choice);
0330                 CASE(scroll_choice) OF
0335
0340                     scroll_up   : Begin
0345                                       i := i - 1;
0350                                       IF (i < 1) THEN
0355                                       Begin
0360                                           i := 1;
0365                                           goto rep_read;
0370                                       End;
0375                                       gotoxy(1,1); {local to window}
0380                                       INSLINE;
0385                                       FOR k := 1 to line_length[i] DO
0390                                       Begin
0395                                           write(screen_text[i,k]);
0400                                       End;
0405                                   End;    {scroll_up}
0410
0415                     scroll_down : Begin
0420                                       i := i + 1;
0425                                       IF (i > lin_ct - 9) THEN
0430                                       Begin
0435                                           i := i - 1;
0440                                           goto rep_read;
0445                                       End;
0450                                       gotoxy(1,1); {local to window}
0455                                       DELLINE;
0460                                       gotoxy(1,10); {local to window}
0465                                       FOR k := 1 to line_length[i +
0470                                                                   9] DO
0475                                       Begin
0480                                           write(screen_text[i +
0485                                                              9,k]);
0490                                       End;
0495                                   End;    {scroll_down}
0500
0505                     carriage_ret: Begin
0510                                       exit_scroll := true;
0515                                   End
```

continued...

281

13 Screen I/O and the Disk

...from previous page

```
0520
0525                    ELSE
0530
0535                END;        {CASE}
0540        UNTIL(exit_scroll = true);
0545    End;        {sub procedure scroll_it}
0550 {----------------------------------------------------------------}
0555
0560 Begin    {procedure text_file_to_array}
0565        FOR i := 1 to max_file_lines DO   {500 in "const" section}
0570        Begin
0575            FOR k := 1 to 80 DO
0580            Begin
0585                screen_text[i,k] := ' ';    {1 blank}
0590            End;
0595        End;
0600
0605        RESET(filevar); {assumes EXISTING text file}
0610        FOR i := 1 to lin_ct DO    {line_count supplied by "TXTWRIT"}
0615        Begin
0620            readln(filevar,line);
0625            {FROM "filevar" TO file transfer variable, "line" }
0630            line_length[i] := LENGTH(line);
0635            FOR k := 1 to line_length[i] DO
0640            Begin
0645                screen_text[i,k] := line[k];
0650            End;
0655        End;
0660        CLOSE(filevar);
0665        {file now transferred from disk file via file transfer
0670        variable, "line" into an array in computer's memory}
0675
0680        clrscr;   {whole screen}
0685        TEXTCOLOR(0);TEXTBACKGROUND(15);
0690        gotoxy(31,2);write(' TEXT FILE SCROLLER ');
0695        gotoxy(1,4);for k := 1 to 80 do write('=');
0700        gotoxy(1,15);for k := 1 to 80 do write('=');
0705        {top and bottom scrolling borders}
0710        gotoxy(31,20);write(' Hit <RET> to Exit ');
0715        TEXTCOLOR(15);TEXTBACKGROUND(0);
0720        {initialize first 10 lines - to prepare for scrolling}
0725        window(1,5,80,14);
0730        gotoxy(1,1);    {local - inside the scrolling window}
0735        {scrolling window is 10 lines deep (5 to 14 inclusive = 10)
0740        and is 80 columns wide}
0745        FOR i := 1 to 10 DO
0750        Begin
0755            CASE i OF
0760
0765            1..9     : Begin
0770                        FOR k := 1 to line_length[i] DO
0775                        Begin
0780                            write(screen_text[i,k]);
0785                        End;
0790                        writeln;
0795                       End;
0800
```

continued...

282

...from previous page

```
0805                10          : Begin
0810                                   FOR k := 1 to line_length[i] DO
0815                                   Begin
0820                                         WRITE(screen_text[i,k]);
0825                                   End;
0830                             End;
0835                 END; {case}
0840         End;
0845         SCROLL_IT;          {sub-procedure using array - screen_text[i,k]}
0850 End;        {procedure text_file_to_array}
0855 {-----------------------------------------------------------------}
0860
0865 Begin     {procedure txtwrit}
0870      ASSIGN(filevar,file_name);
0875      RESET(filevar);
0880
0885      line_count := 0;
0890      WHILE not EOF(filevar) DO {line_count NOT known in advance}
0895      Begin
0900            readln(filevar,line);
0905            {transfer FROM "filevar" TO transfer variable, "line"}
0910            line_count := line_count + 1;
0915      End;
0920      CLOSE(filevar);
0925
0930      TEXT_FILE_TO_ARRAY(line_count);
0935      window(1,1,80,25);
0940 End;       {procedure txtwrit}
{===============================================================}
```

TEXTWRIT.INC: NOTES

This module contains the following procedures and subprocedures:

procedure   TXTWRIT(text write)
subprocedure TEXT_FILE_TO_ARRAY (within TXTWRIT)
subprocedure SCROLL_IT (within TEXT_FILE_TO_ARRAY)

This text file displaying module is activated at line 4150 in the driver routine by pressing the letter "t" from the list of mode choices (see Figure 13.4).

13   Screen I/O and the Disk

TEXTWRIT (Text Write)

This procedure performs two tasks. The first is performed between lines 0870 and 0920. Here, the name of an *existing* text file is assigned to "filevar" (a file of Type "text") and then opened with RESET. Having connected the typed-in file name with the Disk Operating System (DOS), the number of lines that the chosen text file contains is then determined. The variable "line_count" will hold this information. The number of lines in the chosen text file is determined by using the WHILE..DO loop structure starting at line 0890. Note that to obtain the value of "line_count," you must first read (copy) one at a time each component (an 80-character string) of the file into the data transfer variable "line." In this case, each component is a line of text plus an EOLN (end of line) marker. Only after the end of the file (EOF) has been reached can the size of the file be determined by the value contained in "line_count."

The second task performed inside of TXTWRIT is to call its subprocedure TEXT_FILE_TO_ARRAY with the value of the variable "line count" as its single parameter (line 0930). Line 0935 will change the window size back to normal size prior to exiting.

TEXT_FILE_TO_ARRAY

As the name suggests, this subprocedure takes a chosen text file (file of text characters) from the disk and places it into an array variable inside the computer. Once the file of text data is inside an array variable, it can be scrolled up and down on the screen using the array variable as the vehicle. Line 0605 opens the existing file for the transfer operation. You then enter a FOR..DO loop (line 0610) to transfer the file data into the array variable. "Lin_ ct" (line count) from the procedure TEXTWRIT tells you how many rows or lines the array will have.

Because data cannot be transferred directly from a file into an array, an intermediate or **file transfer variable** is required. This special file transfer variable must be compatible with the type of data held in the file. In this case, the file transfer variable is "line." It is of the Type STRING[80] and is compatible with TEXT, which is also defined as a file of characters. So each time you perform a READLN (filevar,line) at line 0620, you are actually copying (reading) a group of text file characters *from* the text file *into* the file transfer variable, "line." The "readln" procedure causes the text to be left-adjusted inside the variable "line"; that is, the characters are stored starting at the left end. If the file text line is less than 80 characters long, then the remaining characters are stored as blanks to fill up the reserved string space with a full complement of 80 characters.

To move the data from the file transfer variable "line" into the scrolling array variable "screen_text," you must first determine the actual number of characters in "line" and store that value (LENGTH(line)) into a variable "line_length[i]" where "i" is the row number of the array. Then use "line_length[i]" as the upper limit of the "k" index in the storage loop at line 0635. "Line[k]" at line 0645 is the k'th character in the file transfer variable "line," and "screen_text[i,k]" is the character located in the i'th row of the array and the k'th column position in that row. Figure 13.5 should help you visualize this file transfer process.

Once "screen_array" is populated with the text file data, you set up scrolling borders (lines 0695-0700), initialize the first 10 lines of the file (lines 0725-0840), and then call the procedure SCROLL_IT to perform the actual screen scrolling operation. To exit from scrolling the text file, simply press <Ret>, and you will return to the main routine in the program (see Figure 13.6).

This section will conclude with a brief outline of how to create a text file using Turbo. These text files are handy places to hold your program development notes or data file comments and can be structured in any way you please. You can even use this facility to "draw" your tables and templates directly onto the screen and then save them to disk for later use.

13 Screen I/O and the Disk

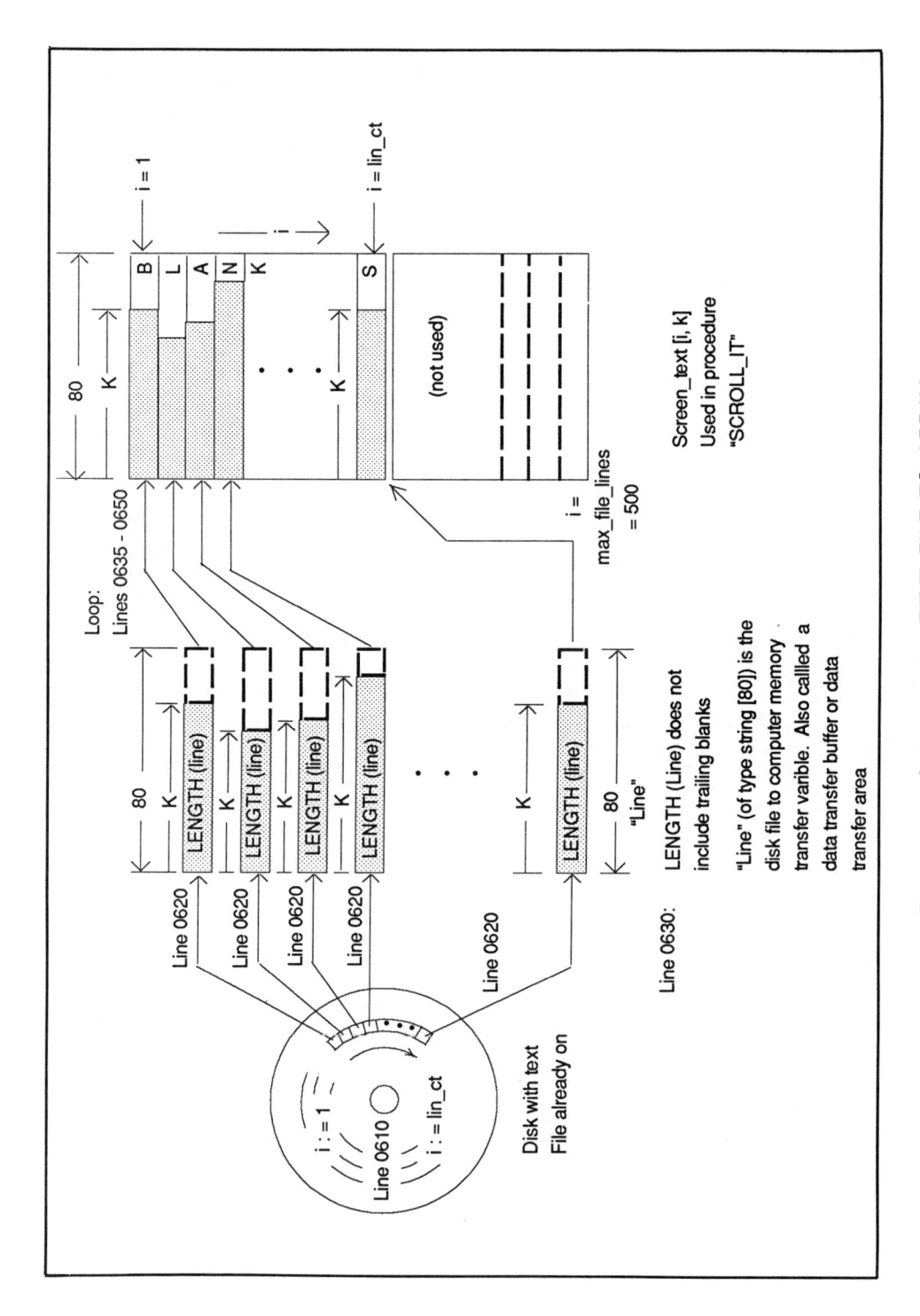

Figure 13.5 Subprocedure TEXT_FILE_TO_ARRAY

286

Screen I/O and the Disk 13

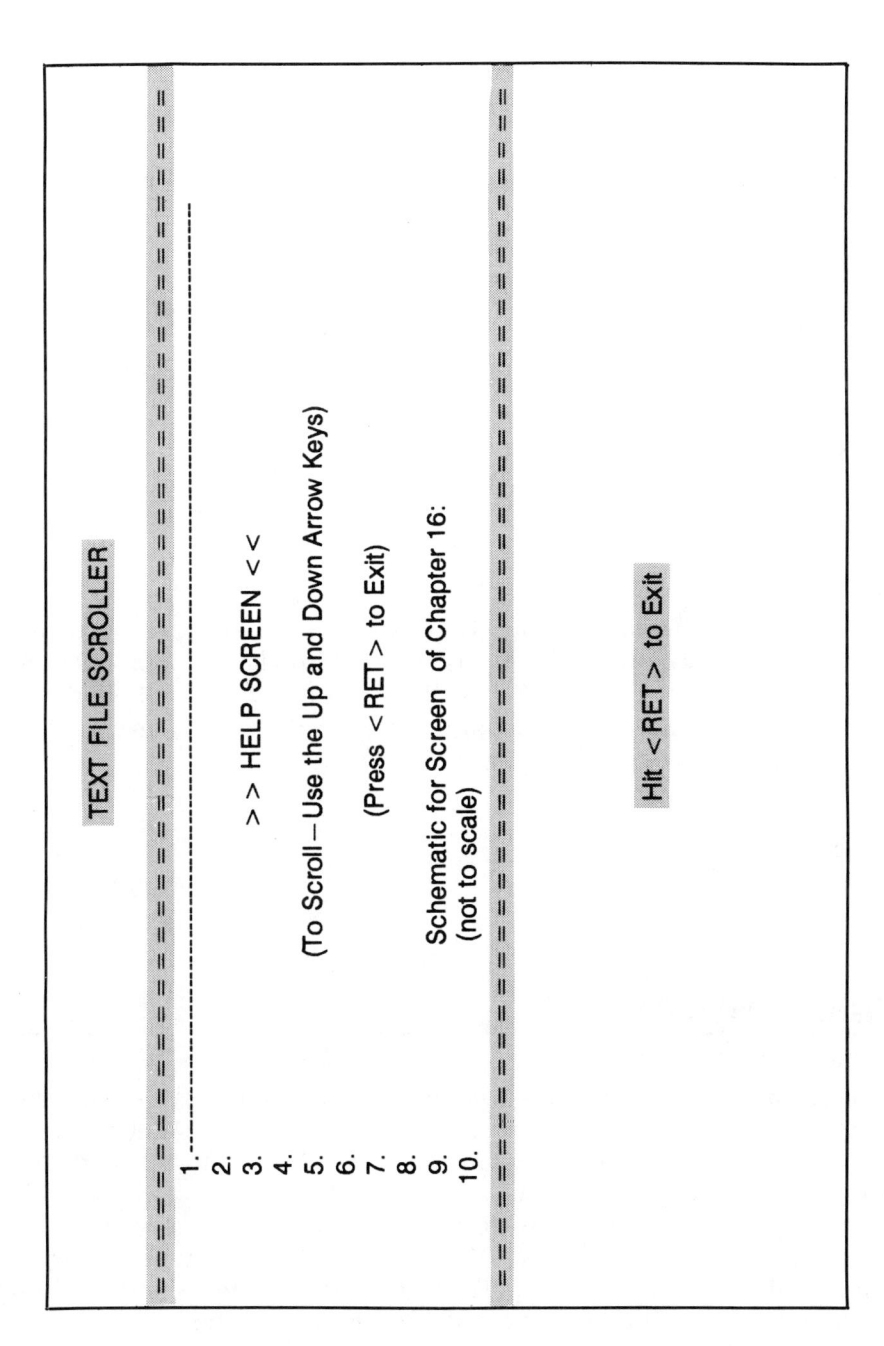

```
┌─────────────────────────────────────────────────┐
│  ║     ║                                        │
│  ║     ║        TEXT FILE SCROLLER              │
│  ║     ║                                        │
│  ║     ║                                        │
│  ║     ║          >> HELP SCREEN <<             │
│  ║     ║                                        │
│  ║     ║     (To Scroll—Use the Up and Down Arrow Keys)│
│  ║     ║                                        │
│  ║     ║              (Press <RET> to Exit)     │
│  ║  1. ║                                        │
│  ║  2. ║         Schematic for Screen of Chapter 16:│
│  ║  3. ║         (not to scale)                 │
│  ║  4. ║                                        │
│  ║  5. ║                                        │
│  ║  6. ║                                        │
│  ║  7. ║                                        │
│  ║  8. ║                                        │
│  ║  9. ║                Hit <RET> to Exit       │
│  ║ 10. ║                                        │
│  ║     ║                                        │
└─────────────────────────────────────────────────┘
```

Figure 13.6 Initialized Screen after Selection of "t" Mode Option

287

13 Screen I/O and the Disk

The text file production process is outlined as follows:

From the TURBO PROMPT (>)   press "w" (work file)

Response: Work file name: _   type, say, <aaa.txt>

Response: Loading B: AAA.TXT
               New File
               >__   press "e" (edit)

Response: (you will see the file editing line across top of
                  of the screen)

               Line 1 Col 1 Insert   Indent B:AAA.TXT

               (type your text here)

After you have finished typing your text file, chart, or other information, type these keystrokes: <Ctrl/K> <Ctrl/D>. These commands will write an EOF (end of file) marker onto the end of your text file and return you to the Turbo prompt (> _). Press "s" (save file).

Response: Saving AAA.TXT
               >__   if you press "d" you will
                                            see your file name in the
                                            directory

MODULE: FILMAN.DRV

This section of code provides a suitable environment in which you can combine basic Disk and Screen I/O operations. Within the large REPEAT..UNTIL loop (line 3165 and line 4255) you are able to either create a new file or fetch an existing file. Then, having created the new file or having fetched the existing one, you can (within the overall structure of smaller REPEAT..UNTIL loops) manipulate that file by scrolling it, revising its contents, performing calculations using its numeric data, or saving the file back to disk for use at a later time. Before the overall code is presented, refer back to Figures 13.2 and 13.3. These

Screen I/O and the Disk 13

figures summarize how the control structure is laid out and places the various procedures in a meaningful context. This section, although rather long, is quite simple in its overall structure and offers a good example of how procedures can be organized within nested REPEAT..UNTIL control structures. Following is the code:

```
{==========================================================================}
0005 program   filman(input,output);
0010 {
0015    On disk as "FILMAN.DRV"
0020    Application program for chapter 13
0025 }
0030
0035 const
0040      bell        = #$07;
0045      ret         = #$0d;
0050
0055      chars_per_line = 50;
0060      max_lines      = 20;
0065      {20 lines of data displayed on 10 line screen}
0070      max_buff_chars = 1000;
0075      {20 rows x 50 characters/line}
0080
0085 {--------------------------------------------------------------------}
0090
0095 type
0100      array_of_screen_text= array[1..max_lines ,
0105                                  1..chars_per_line] of char;
0110
0115      fast_display_buffer = array[1..max_buff_chars] of char;
0120
0125      input_integer_pair  = array[1..2] of integer;
0130      input_line          = string[50];
0135      file_transfer_area  = string[50];
0140
0145      str4                = string[4];
0150      str12               = string[12];
0155
0160 {--------------------------------------------------------------------}
0165 var
0170      screen_text        : array_of_screen_text;
0175      input_data_array   : array[1..max_lines,1..2] of integer;
0180           i,k           : integer;
0185
0190      x_coord            : integer; {result of function wherex COLUMN}
0195      y_coord            : integer; {result of function wherey ROW}
0200           j             : integer; {figured using x_coord & y_coord}
0205
0210      fd_buffer          : fast_display_buffer;
0215      count              : integer;
0220
0225      revise_choice      : char;   {ONLY "y" or "n" are valid}
0230
0235      filevar            : TEXT;                {a text file}
0240      input_file         : FILE OF input_line;  {string[50]}
0245      input_line_buffer  : file_transfer_area;
0250
```

continued...

13 Screen I/O and the Disk

...from previous page

```
0255        input_file_data       : FILE OF integer;
0260        integer_line_buffer   : input_integer_pair;
0265
0270        file_name             : str12;  {for scrolling display only}
0275        data_file_name        : str12;  {for numerical data only}
0280        choice                : char;
0285        entry_mode            : boolean;
0290
0295        valid_file_name,
0300        valid_file_name1      : boolean;
0305        suffix                : str4;
0310        mode_choice           : char;
0315        submode_choice        : char;
0320        exit_mode_flag        : boolean;
0325        exit_submode_flag     : boolean;
0330 {================================================================}
0335
0340 {$i chrinout.inc}
0345 {$i windows.inc}
0350 {$i textwrit.inc}
0355 {$i filename.inc}
0360
0365 {================================================================}
0370
0375 procedure    INITIALIZE_SCROLL(var screen_text :
0380                                   array_of_screen_text);
0385
0390 var
0395     i,k : integer;
0400
0405 Begin   {procedure initialize_scroll}
0410      FOR i := 1 to 10 DO       {window rows are 1..10}
0415      Begin
0420          IF i <= 9 THEN        {10 window rows - 1 = 9}
0425          Begin
0430              FOR k := 1 to chars_per_line DO
0435              Begin
0440                  write(screen_text[i,k]);
0445              End;
0450              writeln;   {drop cursor down one line....}
0455          End;
0460          IF i = 10 THEN
0465          Begin
0470              FOR k := 1 to chars_per_line DO
0475              Begin
0480                  write(screen_text[i,k]);
0485                  {hold cursor on bottom (20th) line}
0490              End;
0495          End;
0500      End;
0505 End;    {procedure initialize_scroll}
0510 {----------------------------------------------------------------}
0515
0520 procedure    SCROLL_IT(var screen_text : array_of_screen_text);
0525
0530   label
0535       rep_read;
0540
```

continued...

Screen I/O and the Disk 13

...from previous page

```
0545 const
0550      scroll_up          = #$48;
0555      scroll_down        = #$50;
0560      page_up            = #$49;
0565      page_down          = #$51;
0570      carriage_ret       = #$0d;
0575
0580 var
0585      sroll_choice       : char;
0590      exit_scroll        : boolean;
0595
0600      i_tot              : integer;
0605      k_tot              : integer;
0610
0615 {------------------------------------------------------------------}
0620
0625      procedure   SCRL_DOWN(kl,il : integer);
0630
0635      var
0640          k    : integer;
0645
0650      Begin    {sub procedure scrl_down}
0655          gotoxy(1,1);    {local to scrolling window}
0660          INSLINE;
0665          {Blanks row at cursor pos. Bottom line scrolls off}
0670          FOR k := 1 to chars_per_line DO
0675          Begin
0680              write(screen_text[il,k]);
0685          End;
0690      End;     {sub procedure scrl_down}
0695 {------------------------------------------------------------------}
0700
0705      procedure   SCRL_UP(kl,il : integer);
0710
0715      var
0720          k    : integer;
0725
0730      Begin    {sub procedure scrl_up}
0735          gotoxy(1,1);    {local to scrolling window}
0740          DELLINE;
0745          {text pushed up and blank line at bottom of screen}
0750          gotoxy(1,10); {bottom line of screen window}
0755          FOR k := 1 to chars_per_line DO
0760          Begin
0765              write(screen_text[il + 9,k]);
0770              {1 less than "depth" of scr. disp}
0775          End;
0780      End;     {sub procedure scrl_up}
0785 {------------------------------------------------------------------}
0790
0795      procedure   DISPLAY_PAGE(kl,il : integer);
0800
0805      var
0810          i,k          : integer;
0815          j            : integer;
0820          count        : integer;
0825
0830          tl_row,
```

continued...

13 Screen I/O and the Disk

...from previous page

```
0835                tl_col,
0840                h_line_len: integer;
0845                count_of_chars_per_line   : integer;
0850
0855        Begin      {sub procedure display_page}
0860            clrscr;
0865            tl_row := 5;    {global}
0870            tl_col := 15;   {global}
0875            h_line_len := chars_per_line;
0880            count_of_chars_per_line := 1;
0885            j := ((tl_row - 1) * 160) + ((tl_col - 1) * 2);
0890
0895            count := 0;
0900
0905            FOR i := i1 to i1 + 9 DO
0910            Begin
0915                FOR k := 1 to chars_per_line DO   {1..50}
0920                Begin
0925                    count := count + 1;
0930                    fd_buffer[count] := screen_text[i,k];
0935                End;
0940            End;
0945
0950            FOR count := 1 to 500 DO    {10 rows x 50 chars/row}
0955            Begin
0960                CHR_OUT(j,ORD(fd_buffer[count]));
0965                count_of_chars_per_line :=
0970                                 count_of_chars_per_line + 1;
0975                IF (count_of_chars_per_line > h_line_len) THEN
0980                Begin
0985                    tl_row := tl_row + 1;
0990                    {drop down 1 row, stay at same column}
0995                    j := ((tl_row - 1)*160) + ((tl_col - 1)*2);
1000                    {recalculate j}
1005                    count_of_chars_per_line := 1;   {reset to 1}
1010                End
1015                ELSE
1020                    j := j + 2;
1025            End;
1030        End;      {sub procedure display_page}
1035   {------------------------------------------------------------------}
1040
1045  Begin     {procedure scroll_it}
1050      exit_scroll := false;
1055      i_tot := 1;
1060      k_tot := 1;
1065
1070      REPEAT
1075          REP_READ:      {a label with colon}
1080          read(KBD,scroll_choice);
1085          CASE (scroll_choice) OF
1090
1095          scroll_up : Begin
1100                        i_tot := i_tot - 1;
1105                        k_tot := k_tot - 0;
1110                        IF (i_tot < 1) THEN
1115                        Begin
1120                            i_tot := 1;
1125                            goto rep_read;
```

continued...

...from previous page

```
1130                            End;
1135                            SCRL_DOWN(k_tot,i_tot);
1140                            {scrolls @ displays new top line}
1145                        End;
1150
1155            scroll_down:Begin
1160                            i_tot := i_tot + 1;
1165                            k_tot := k_tot + 0;
1170                            IF (i_tot > 11) THEN
1175                            Begin
1180                                    i_tot := 11;   {11 + 9 = 20}
1185                                    goto rep_read;
1190                            End;
1195                            SCRL_UP(k_tot,i_tot);
1200                            {scrolls @ displays new bottom line}
1205                        End;
1210
1215            page_up    :Begin
1220                            i_tot := i_tot - 10; {toward top}
1225                            k_tot := k_tot + 0;
1230                            IF (i_tot < 1) THEN
1235                            Begin
1240                                    i_tot := i_tot + 10;
1245                                    {back to what it was prior to
1250                                     hitting "page_up" key}
1255                                    goto rep_read;
1260                            End;
1265                            DISPLAY_PAGE(k_tot,i_tot);
1270                        End;
1275
1280            page_down  :Begin
1285                            i_tot := i_tot + 10; {toward bottom}
1290                            k_tot := k_tot + 0;
1295                            IF (i_tot > 11) THEN
1300                            Begin
1305                                    i_tot := i_tot - 10;
1310                                    {back to what it was prior to
1315                                     hitting "page_down" key}
1320                                    goto rep_read;
1325                            End;
1330                            DISPLAY_PAGE(k_tot,i_tot);
1335                        End;
1340
1345            carriage_ret:Begin
1350                            exit_scroll := true;
1355                        End
1360
1365            ELSE
1370                {if none of the above....}
1375
1380            END;                            {....case statement....}
1385        UNTIL exit_scroll = true;      {....repeat....}
1390 End;       {procedure scroll_it}
1395 {-----------------------------------------------------------------}
```

continued...

13 Screen I/O and the Disk

...from previous page

```
1400
1405    procedure       CREATE_A_FILE;
1410
1415    var
1420         height,weight : integer;
1425         i,j,k         : integer;
1430
1435    {------------------------------------------}
1440
1445         procedure CHANGING_INPUT_TEXT(i_print : integer;
1450                                       x_cd    : integer;
1455                                       y_cd    : integer);
1460
1465         Begin    {sub procedure changing_input_text}
1470              CASE (i_print) OF
1475
1480              1..max_lines : Begin
1485                                 gotoxy(x_cd,y_cd);
1490                                 {same column but different row}
1495              {2 blanks          }  write('  ',i_print:2,
1500              {1 blank , 3 spaces}         ' Height(inches)....:___',
1505              {1 blank , 3 spaces}         ' Weight(pounds)....:___');
1510                              End;
1515              END; {case}
1520         End;    {sub procedure changing_input_text}
1525    {--------------------------------------------------------------}
1530
1535    Begin    {procedure create_a_file}
1540         WINDOW_BORDER(14,4,66,15,1); {border style #1}
1545         {create scrolling input window....}
1550         window(15,5,65,14);clrscr;
1555         {clear out area for creation of file pending}
1560         window(1,1,80,25);gotoxy(15,5);
1565         {inside the window - x_coord & y_coord MUST BE GLOBAL}
1570         {window display is local. x_coord/y_coord & j GLOBAL}
1575         x_coord := WHEREX;   {COLUMN is 15}
1580         y_coord := WHEREY;   {ROW is 5    }
1585
1590         FOR i := 1 to max_lines DO      {1..20}
1595         Begin
1600              IF y_coord > 14 THEN
1605              Begin
1610                   window(15,5,65,14);gotoxy(1,1);
1615                   {inside the reduced window}
1620                   DELLINE;
1625                   {scroll window text 1 line up from bottom}
1630                   window(1,1,80,25);  {restore full global window}
1635                   y_coord := 14;      {in full global window}
1640              End;
1645              { makes small window,scroll up in it,
1650                then return window to full size }
1655
1660              CHANGING_INPUT_TEXT(i,x_coord,y_coord);
1665              {clear out old, unwanted entries....}
1670              input_data_array[i,1] := 0 ; input_data_array[i,2] := 0;
1675              BUFLEN := 3;
1680              gotoxy(39,y_coord);read(height); {inside_window coords.}
1685              BUFLEN := 3;
```

continued...

Screen I/O and the Disk 13

...from previous page

```
1690              gotoxy(62,y_coord);read(weight);{DROP cursor to next row}
1695              input_data_array[i,1] := height;
1700              input_data_array[i,2] := weight;
1705
1710              {save the just-written line from screen into the array}
1715              j := ((y_coord - 1) * 160) + ((x_coord - 1) * 2);
1720              {j is a GLOBAL screen address}
1725              FOR k := 1 to chars_per_line DO
1730              Begin
1735                  CHR_IN(j,screen_text[i,k]);
1740                  j := j + 2;
1745              End;
1750              {just-written screen line now saved into array....}
1755
1760              x_coord := x_coord; {same col. for next iteration}
1765              y_coord := y_coord + 1;
1770              {Increment row by 1 for next iteration}
1775          End;
1780 End;     {procedure create_a_file}
1785 {------------------------------------------------------------------}
1790
1795 procedure    SUB_MODE_HEADER;
1800
1805 Begin     {procedure sub_mode_header}
1810      window(1,1,80,25);{change window back to full screen}
1815      gotoxy(21,17);clreol;
1820      writeln('SELECT SUB-MODE: ');
1825      gotoxy(21,19);clreol;
1830      writeln('> Press "r" to REVISE File Data');
1835      gotoxy(21,20);clreol;
1840      writeln('> Press "c" to CALCULATE');
1845      gotoxy(21,21);clreol;
1850      writeln('> Press "s" to SAVE File to Disk');
1855      gotoxy(21,22);clreol;
1860      writeln('> Press "q" to EXIT Sub-Mode');
1865 End;     {procedure sub_mode_header}
1870 {------------------------------------------------------------------}
1875
1880 procedure    REVISE_DATA_INPUT;
1885
1890 label
1895      escape;
1900
1905 var
1910      i,j,k            : integer;
1915      height,weight    : integer;
1920      exit_revise      : boolean;
1925
1930 Begin     {procedure revise_data_input}
1935      REPEAT
1940          exit_revise := false;
1945          window(2,17,78,24);clrscr;window(1,1,80,25);
1950          gotoxy(23,18);clreol;
1955          write('Type # of Data Entry to Revise....: ');
1960          gotoxy(30,20);clreol;
1965          write('Press <99> to Exit');
1970
1975          window(15,5,65,14);clrscr;
1980          INITIALIZE_SCROLL(screen_text);
1985          SCROLL_IT(screen_text);      {ret key ends scrolling}
```

continued...

295

13 Screen I/O and the Disk

...from previous page

```
1990
1995              window(1,1,80,25);   {re_enable full screen}
2000              REPEAT
2005                  BUFLEN := 2;
2010                  gotoxy(59,18);clreol;
2015                  readln(i);              {TYPE in from KBD}
2020              UNTIL ((i >= 1) AND (i <= 20)) OR (i = 99);
2025              IF (i = 99) THEN
2030              Begin
2035                  exit_revise := true;
2040                  GOTO ESCAPE;     {a label}
2045              End
2050              ELSE     { i is within legal range 1..20}
2055                  gotoxy(34,20);clreol;
2060
2065              gotoxy(23,18);clreol;
2070              write('* ',i:2,' Height(inches)....:___',  {3 spaces}
2075                            ' Weight(pounds)....:___');
2080              {clear out old, unwanted entries....}
2085              input_data_array[i,1] := 0 ; input_data_array[i,2] := 0;
2090              BUFLEN := 3;gotoxy(47,18);read(height);
2095              BUFLEN := 3;gotoxy(70,18);readln(weight);
2100              input_data_array[i,1] := height;
2105              input_data_array[i,2] := weight;
2110
2115              gotoxy(23,18);      {save contents of this line to array}
2120              x_coord := WHEREX;  {col 23}
2125              y_coord := WHEREY;  {row 18}
2130              j := ((y_coord - 1) * 160) + ((x_coord - 1) * 2);
2135              FOR k := 1 to chars_per_line DO
2140              Begin
2145                  CHR_IN(j,screen_text[i,k]);
2150                  j := j + 2;
2155              End;
2160
2165              ESCAPE:   {a label with colon}
2170          UNTIL (exit_revise = true);
2175
2180          window(1,1,80,25);      {re_enable full screen}
2185          gotoxy(23,18);clreol;
2190          {erase text: "Data Item Number...<R>.."}
2195          SUB_MODE_HEADER;
2200 End; {procedure revise_data_input}
2205 {-----------------------------------------------------------------}
2210
2215 procedure     A_CALCULATION;
2220
2225 var
2230     cumulated_height,
2235     cumulated_weight   : integer;
2240     average_height,
2245     average_weight     : real;
2250
2255     i                  : integer;
2260     code               : integer;
2265     key_choice         : char;
2270     return_flag        : boolean;
2275
```

continued...

...from previous page

```
2280 Begin       {procedure a_calculation}
2285     window(1,1,80,25);       {re_enable full screen}
2290     cumulated_height := 0;
2295     cumulated_weight := 0;
2300     FOR i := 1 to max_lines DO
2305     Begin
2310         cumulated_height := cumulated_height +
2315                             input_data_array[i,1];
2320         cumulated_weight := cumulated_weight +
2325                             input_data_array[i,2];
2330     End;
2335     average_height := cumulated_height / max_lines;
2340     average_weight := cumulated_weight / max_lines;
2345
2350     window(2,17,78,24);clrscr;
2355     {clear an output display area of "window" size}
2360     window(1,1,80,25);       {back to regular sized window}
2365     gotoxy(14,20);
2370     write('Average Height :_____    Average Weight :_____');
2375     gotoxy(30,20);write(average_height:6:2);
2380     gotoxy(55,20);write(average_weight:6:2);
2385
2390     gotoxy(30,23);
2395     write('Press RETURN to Return to Submode....:');
2400     return_flag := false;
2405     REPEAT
2410         read(KBD,key_choice);
2415         IF (key_choice = ret) THEN
2420         Begin
2425             return_flag := true;
2430             window(2,17,78,24);clrscr;
2435             SUB_MODE_HEADER;
2440         End
2445         ELSE
2450         Begin
2455             write(bell);
2460         End;
2465     UNTIL (return_flag = true);
2470
2475     window(15,5,65,14);clrscr;
2480     INITIALIZE_SCROLL(screen_text); {scroll to check result }
2485     SCROLL_IT(screen_text);
2490     window(1,1,80,25);              {re_enable full screen}
2495 End;       {procedure a_calculation}
2500 {----------------------------------------------------------------}
2505
2510 procedure     SAVE_FILE(file_name,
2515                        data_file_name : str12;
2520                        mode_choice : char);
2525
2530 var
2535     i,k : integer;
2540
2545 Begin      {procedure save_file}
2550     ASSIGN(input_file,file_name);
2555     IF (mode_choice = 'c') THEN
2560         REWRITE(input_file);
2565     IF (mode_choice = 'f') THEN
2570         RESET(input_file);
```

continued...

13   Screen I/O and the Disk

...from previous page

```
2575
2580          FOR i := 1 to max_lines DO            {20 lines}
2585          Begin
2590              FOR k := 1 to chars_per_line DO {50 chars/line}
2595              Begin
2600                  input_line_buffer[k] := screen_text[i,k];
2605              End;
2610              write(input_file,input_line_buffer);
2615          End;
2620          CLOSE(input_file);
2625
2630          ASSIGN(input_file_data,data_file_name);
2635          IF (mode_choice = 'c') THEN
2640              REWRITE(input_file_data);
2645          IF (mode_choice = 'f') THEN
2650              RESET(input_file_data);
2655
2660          FOR i := 1 to max_lines DO
2665          Begin
2670              FOR k := 1 to 2 DO
2675              Begin
2680                  integer_line_buffer[k] := input_data_array[i,k];
2685                  write(input_file_data,integer_line_buffer[k]);
2690              End;
2695          End;
2700          CLOSE(input_file_data);
2705 End;       {procedure save_file}
2710 {--------------------------------------------------------------}
2715
2720 procedure     FETCH_A_FILE(file_name,
2725                            data_file_name : str12);
2730
2735 var
2740    i,k : integer;
2745
2750 Begin    {procedure fetch_a_file}
2755          WINDOW_BORDER(14,4,66,15,1); {border style #1}
2760          window(15,5,65,14);clrscr; {clear inside of window}
2765          gotoxy(1,1);
2770
2775          ASSIGN(input_file,file_name);
2780          RESET(input_file); {can only fetch an existing file}
2785          FOR i := 1 to max_lines DO              {20 lines}
2790          Begin
2795              read(input_file,input_line_buffer);
2800              FOR k := 1 to chars_per_line DO    {50 chars/line}
2805              Begin
2810                  screen_text[i,k] := input_line_buffer[k];
2815              End;
2820          End;
2825          CLOSE(input_file);
2830
2835          ASSIGN(input_file_data,data_file_name);
2840          RESET(input_file_data);
2845          FOR i := 1 to max_lines DO
2850          Begin
2855              FOR k := 1 to 2 DO
2860              Begin
2865                  read(input_file_data,integer_line_buffer[k]);
2870                  input_data_array[i,k] := integer_line_buffer[k];
```

continued...

Screen I/O and the Disk 13

...from previous page

```
2875            End;
2880        End;
2885        CLOSE(input_file_data);
2890
2895        window(15,5,65,14);clrscr;
2900        INITIALIZE_SCROLL(screen_text);
2905        SCROLL_IT(screen_text);
2910        window(1,1,80,25);
2915 End;    {procedure fetch_a_file}
2920 {----------------------------------------------------------------}
2925
2930 procedure CREATE_SHADOW_DATA_FILE_NAME(fil_nam : str12;
2935                                        VAR fil_nam_dat : str12);
2940
2945 type
2950     str8 = string[8];
2955
2960 var
2965     fil_nam_prefix : str8;   {max length of file name prefix}
2970
2975 Begin    {procedure create_shadow_data_file_name}
2980     fil_nam_prefix := COPY(fil_nam,1,LENGTH(fil_nam) - 4);
2985     fil_nam_dat    := CONCAT(fil_nam_prefix,'.dat');
2990 End;    {procedure create_shadow_data_file_name}
2995 {----------------------------------------------------------------}
3000
3005 procedure     MODE_HEADER;
3010
3015 Begin    {procedure mode_header}
3020     window(1,1,80,25);clrscr;
3025     TEXTCOLOR(0);TEXTBACKGROUND(15);
3030     gotoxy(24,1);
3035     writeln(' DISK FILE APPLICATIONS CHAPTER 13 ');
3040     gotoxy(4,3);clreol;
3045     write(' FILE:');
3050     gotoxy(24,3);
3055     write(' MODE:');
3060     gotoxy(50,3);
3065     writeln(' SUB-MODE:');
3070     TEXTCOLOR(15);TEXTBACKGROUND(0);
3075     window(9,18,70,23);clrscr;{clear text area for writing}
3080     window(1,1,80,25);        {window to regular size}
3085
3090     gotoxy(25,17);
3095     write('SELECT MODE: ');
3100     gotoxy(21,19);
3105     writeln('> Press "c" to CREATE a New Data File');
3110     gotoxy(21,20);
3115     writeln('> Press "f" to FETCH an Old Data File');
3120     gotoxy(21,21);
3125     writeln('> Press "t" for TEXT DESCRIPTION of File');
3130     gotoxy(21,22);
3135     writeln('> Press "q" to EXIT Mode');
3140     exit_mode_flag := false;
3145 End;    {procedure mode_header}
3150 {----------------------------------------------------------------}
3155
```

continued...

13 Screen I/O and the Disk

...from previous page

```
3160  Begin       {main program - FILMAN.DRV }
3165        REPEAT
3170        MODE_HEADER;
3175        gotoxy(38,17);
3180        readln(mode_choice);
3185        CASE (mode_choice) OF
3190
3195        'c' : Begin
3200                  gotoxy(31,3);
3205                  writeln('Create NEW File');
3210
3215                  gotoxy(23,10);
3220                  write('Enter a Valid File Name: ');
3225                  REPEAT
3230                      valid_file_name1 := false;
3235                      REPEAT
3240                          FOR i := 1 to 12 DO
3245                              file_name[i] := ' ';   {1 blank}
3250                          gotoxy(48,10);clreol;
3255                          BUFLEN := 12;
3260                          valid_file_name := false;
3265                          ENTER_NEW_FILE_NAME(file_name,
3270                                              valid_file_name);
3275                      UNTIL(valid_file_name = true);
3280                      suffix := COPY(file_name,LENGTH(file_name) -
3285                                              3,4);
3290                      IF ((suffix = '.txt') OR
3295                          (suffix = '.dat')) THEN
3300                      Begin
3305                          gotoxy(23,12);
3310                          write('".txt" and ".dat" Suffixes
3315                                              {1 bl}Illegal.');
3320                          delay(2000);
3325                          gotoxy(23,12);clreol;
3330                      End
3335                      ELSE
3340                          valid_file_name1 := true;
3345                  UNTIL(valid_file_name1 = true);
3350                  gotoxy(23,10);clreol;
3355                  gotoxy(11,3);
3360                  writeln(file_name);
3365
3370                  CREATE_SHADOW_DATA_FILE_NAME(file_name,
3375                                              data_file_name);
3380                  CREATE_A_FILE;
3385                  {file name doesn't matter until you come
3390                   to save the file}
3395                  SUB_MODE_HEADER;
3400
3405                  REPEAT
3410                      exit_submode_flag := false;
3415                      gotoxy(38,17);clreol;
3420                      readln(submode_choice);
3425
3430                      CASE (submode_choice) OF
3435                      'r' : Begin
3440                              gotoxy(61,3);clreol;
3445                              writeln('Revise Data Input');
3450                              REVISE_DATA_INPUT;
3455                            End;
```

continued...

...from previous page

```
3460
3465                    'c' : Begin
3470                              gotoxy(61,3);clreol;
3475                              writeln('Calculate Avg');
3480                              A_CALCULATION;
3485                          End;
3490
3495                    's' : Begin
3500                              gotoxy(61,3);clreol;
3505                              writeln('Save File');
3510                              SAVE_FILE(file_name,
3515                                        data_file_name,
3520                                        mode_choice);
3525                          End;
3530
3535                    'q' : Begin
3540                              gotoxy(61,3);clreol;
3545                              writeln('Exit Submode');
3550                              exit_submode_flag := true;
3555                              window(10,4,71,15);clrscr;
3560                              window(1,1,80,25);
3565                          End
3570
3575                    ELSE  {any other character is not valid}
3580                          Begin
3585                              gotoxy(38,17);writeln('       ');
3590                              gotoxy(38,17);
3595                          End;
3600                    END;  {case submode_choice}
3605                    UNTIL (exit_submode_flag = true);
3610                End;
3615
3620
3625        'f' : Begin
3630                  gotoxy(31,3);
3635                  writeln('Fetch an OLD File');
3640                  gotoxy(23,10);
3645                  write('Enter a Valid File Name: ');
3650                  REPEAT
3655                      valid_file_name1 := false;
3660                      REPEAT
3665                          FOR i := 1 to 12 DO
3670                              file_name[i] := ' ';   {1 blank}
3675                          gotoxy(48,10);clreol;
3680                          BUFLEN := 12;
3685                          valid_file_name := false;
3690                          ENTER_OLD_FILE_NAME(file_name,
3695                                              valid_file_name);
3700                      UNTIL(valid_file_name = true);
3705                      suffix := COPY(file_name,LENGTH(file_name) -
3710                                     3,4);
3715                      IF ((suffix = '.txt') OR
3720                          (suffix = '.dat')) THEN
3725                      Begin
3730                          gotoxy(23,12);
3735                          write('".txt" and ".dat" Suffixes
3740                                       {1 bl}Illegal.');
3745                          delay(2000);
3750                          gotoxy(23,12);clreol;
```

continued...

13 Screen I/O and the Disk

...from previous page

```
3755                        End
3760                        ELSE
3765                            valid_file_name1 := true;
3770                    UNTIL(valid_file_name1 = true);
3775                    CREATE_SHADOW_DATA_FILE_NAME(file_name,
3780                                                 data_file_name);
3785                    gotoxy(23,10);clreol;
3790                    gotoxy(11,3);
3795                    writeln(file_name);
3800
3805                    FETCH_A_FILE(file_name,
3810                                 data_file_name);
3815                    SUB_MODE_HEADER;
3820                    REPEAT
3825                        exit_submode_flag := false;
3830                        gotoxy(38,17);clreol;
3835                        readln(submode_choice);
3840
3845                        CASE (submode_choice) OF
3850                        'r' : Begin
3855                                  gotoxy(61,3);clreol;
3860                                  writeln('Revise Data Input');
3865                                  REVISE_DATA_INPUT;
3870                              End;
3875
3880                        'c' : Begin
3885                                  gotoxy(61,3);clreol;
3890                                  writeln('Calculate Avg');
3895                                  A_CALCULATION;
3900                              End;
3905
3910                        's' : Begin
3915                                  gotoxy(61,3);clreol;
3920                                  writeln('Save File');
3925                                  SAVE_FILE(file_name,
3930                                            data_file_name,
3935                                            mode_choice);
3940                              End;
3945
3950                        'q' : Begin
3955                                  gotoxy(61,3);clreol;
3960                                  writeln('Exit Submode');
3965                                  exit_submode_flag := true;
3970                                  window(14,4,66,15);clrscr;
3975                                  window(1,1,80,25);
3980                              End
3985
3990                        ELSE  {handles any invalid character}
3995                            Begin
4000                                gotoxy(38,17);writeln('      ');  {2bl}
4005                                gotoxy(38,17);
4010                            End;
4015                        END;  {case submode_choice}
4020                    UNTIL (exit_submode_flag = true);
4025                End;
```

continued...

Screen I/O and the Disk 13

...from previous page

```
4030
4035        't' : Begin
4040              gotoxy(31,3);
4045              writeln('Text Description');
4050              gotoxy(11,10);
4055              write('Enter a Valid Text File
4060                                   Name(".txt" suffix): ');
4065              REPEAT
4070                  valid_file_name1 := false;
4075                  REPEAT
4080                      FOR i := 1 to 12 DO
4085                          file_name[i] := ' ';   {1 blank}
4090                      gotoxy(56,10);clreol;
4095                      BUFLEN := 12;
4100                      valid_file_name := false;
4105                      ENTER_OLD_FILE_NAME(file_name,
4110                                         valid_file_name);
4115                  UNTIL(valid_file_name = true);
4120                  suffix := COPY(file_name,LENGTH(file_name) -
4125                                         3,4);
4130                  IF (suffix = '.txt') THEN
4135                      valid_file_name1 := true;
4140              UNTIL(valid_file_name1 = true);
4145              clrscr;
4150              TXTWRIT(file_name);
4155          End;
4160
4165        'q' : Begin
4170              exit_mode_flag := true;
4175              window(1,4,80,25);clrscr;window(1,1,80,25);
4180              gotoxy(21,20);TEXTCOLOR(0);TEXTBACKGROUND(15);
4185              write(' From TURBO System Prompt (" > "): ');
4190              TEXTCOLOR(15);TEXTBACKGROUND(0);
4195              gotoxy(21,22);
4200              write('- Press "d" for Disk DIRECTORY');
4205              gotoxy(21,23);
4210              write('- Press "r" to RUN Program');
4215              gotoxy(21,24);
4220              write('- Press "q" to EXIT to DOS');
4225              {NOTE: other SYSTEM commands "e" for edit "s" save
4230               program etc are not included here}
4235              gotoxy(1,5);    {position cursor properly}
4240              write(bell);
4245          End;
4250      END;          {case mode_choice}
4255    UNTIL(exit_mode_flag = true);
4260 End.     {main program - FILMAN.DRV}
{======================================================================}
```

303

13 Screen I/O and the Disk

FILMAN.DRV: NOTES

CREATE_A_FILE

This procedure is found under the "c" (Create) mode option at line 3380 and is invoked immediately after the procedure ENTER_NEW FILE_NAME and its complement procedure CREATE_SHADOW DATA_FILE_NAME. The first procedure names the newly created scrollable display file. The second procedure names the collection of numeric data in that file that will be used in calculations. This procedure "creates" a file only in that it populates two array data variables which are then capable of being saved to disk. Inside the procedure itself, the first variable is the global variable "screen_text" (line 1735). This variable is a 50-column × 20-line (row) array of characters. Its contents consist of text characters (created from the subprocedure CHANGING_INPUT_TEXT) and numbers (typed onto the screen by the user in the vacant spots and later converted into text). The variable "screen_text" is created solely to enable you to scroll the file information. The second variable is "input_data_array." This variable is a 2-column × 20-line (row) array of integers that is entered into the line of prepared text (created by the small subprocedure CHANGING_INPUT TEXT) at lines 1445-1520. The physical process of picking text directly off the computer screen and transferring it into the array "screen_text" is accomplished at lines 1725-1750. The process of transferring the numeric data to its array variable "input_data_array" is performed by assignment statements at lines 1695 and 1700 and is done *prior* to saving the whole screen line to the scrolling array "screen_text."

The detailed mechanics of transferring screen text one line at a time into the two arrays is pictured in Figure 13.7 and at lines 1725-1750, where the contents of screen memory offset location "j" are transferred directly *from* the screen (actually screen memory) and *into* the scrolling display variable by the external procedure CHR_IN at line 1735. Note that the entry numbers 1-9 inclusive are entered and saved to disk from different screen lines, and the entry numbers 10-20 inclusive are entered and saved only from the bottom line of the display window, that is, screen row 14 of Figure 13.7 (see lines 1600-1640 also).

Screen I/O and the Disk **13**

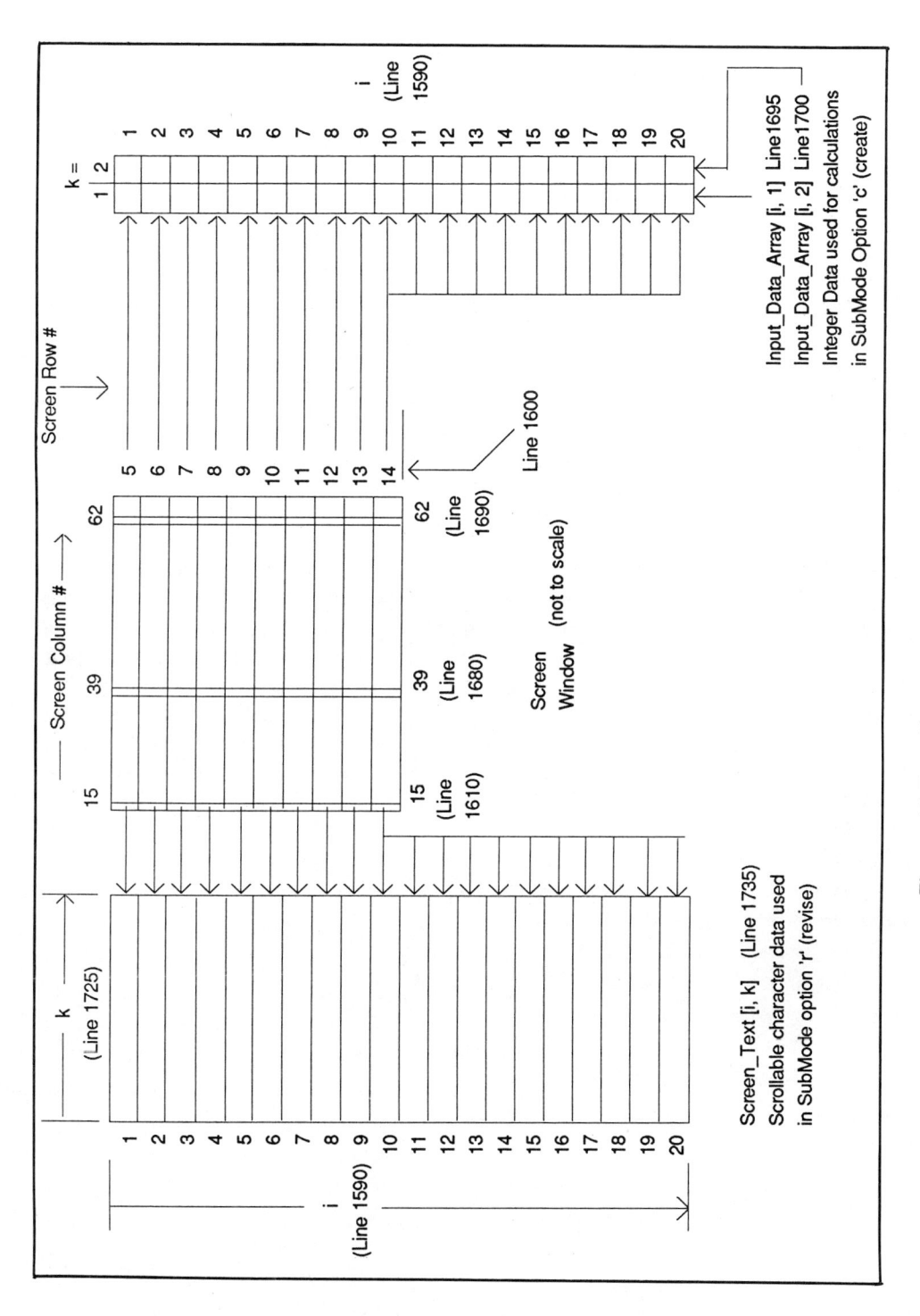

Figure 13.7 Procedure CREATE_A_FILE

13 Screen I/O and the Disk

REVISE_DATA_INPUT

This procedure is found at two different locations in the main routine: under "c" (Create) mode at line 3450 and under "f" (Fetch) mode at line 3865. In both cases, REVISE_DATA_INPUT is a submode option; that is, it can only be called after a mode option ("create," "fetch," "text," or "quit") but can be called on an equal footing with any of the other submode options ("calculate," "save," or "quit"; see Figure 13.8). This procedure enables you to revise the file information one line at a time. On entry, line 1955 asks for the number of the line you want to revise. The two procedures at lines 1980 and 1985 then enable you to scroll-inspect the file. Once you press <Ret>, the cursor leaves the scrolling window and moves to the first data entry location on the entry line to be revised. The template of the line to be revised is written onto the screen at line 2070. Note that this template, with the exception of the "*" prefix, is an exact replica of the text produced by the procedure CHANGING_INPUT_TEXT. How else could the revised line of text fit into the scrolling display array "screen_text"? To perform a revision, you then type in two (revised) numbers which are immediately saved to "input_data_array" in the properly indexed location, lines 2100 and 2105. Next, the whole line of scrollable text starting at screen location (23,18) is saved directly from the screen and inserted into "screen text" at the proper row location. Since this procedure is enclosed within a REPEAT..UNTIL loop, the revision process will continue until you type the number "99" and set the Boolean variable "exit revise" to "true," thus allowing exit from the revision procedure. Note the use of limited error checking at line 2020 and the use of the "goto" statement to provide a quick exit from the revision loop (line 2040). So much for having to create yet another REPEAT..UNTIL loop and Boolean exit variable.

Screen I/O and the Disk 13

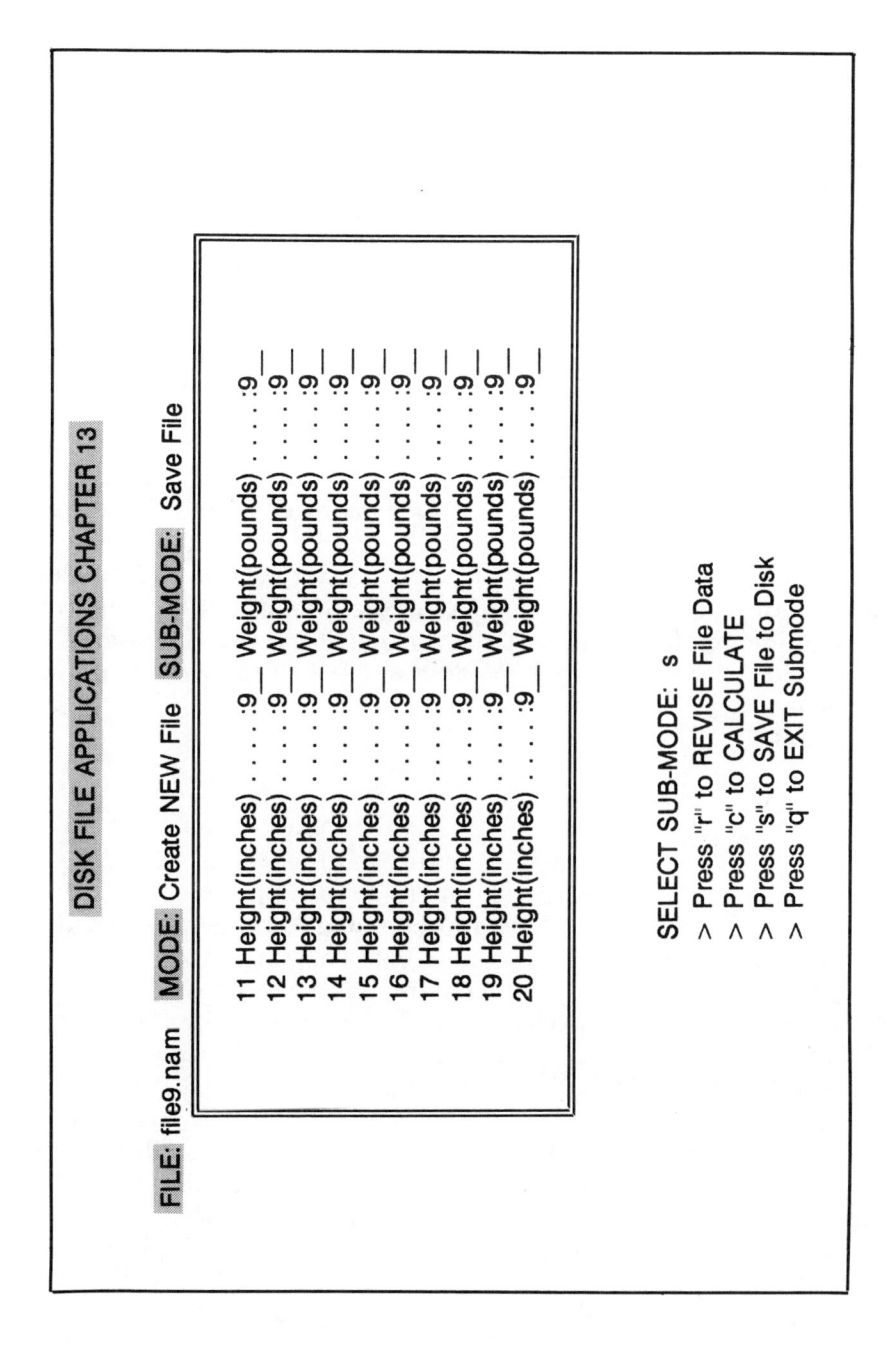

```
┌─────────────────────────────────────────────────────┐
│ ╔═══════════════════════════════════════════════╗  │
│ ║      DISK FILE APPLICATIONS CHAPTER 13        ║  │
│ ╚═══════════════════════════════════════════════╝  │
│  FILE: file9.nam   MODE: Create NEW File   SUB-MODE: Save File │
│                                                     │
│   11 Height(inches) ....:9_   Weight(pounds) ....:9_ │
│   12 Height(inches) ....:9_   Weight(pounds) ....:9_ │
│   13 Height(inches) ....:9_   Weight(pounds) ....:9_ │
│   14 Height(inches) ....:9_   Weight(pounds) ....:9_ │
│   15 Height(inches) ....:9_   Weight(pounds) ....:9_ │
│   16 Height(inches) ....:9_   Weight(pounds) ....:9_ │
│   17 Height(inches) ....:9_   Weight(pounds) ....:9_ │
│   18 Height(inches) ....:9_   Weight(pounds) ....:9_ │
│   19 Height(inches) ....:9_   Weight(pounds) ....:9_ │
│   20 Height(inches) ....:9_   Weight(pounds) ....:9_ │
│                                                     │
│   SELECT SUB-MODE:  s                               │
│   > Press "r" to REVISE File Data                   │
│   > Press "c" to CALCULATE                          │
│   > Press "s" to SAVE File to Disk                  │
│   > Press "q" to EXIT Submode                       │
└─────────────────────────────────────────────────────┘
```

Figure 13.8 Initialized Screen Showing the SUBMODE Option Choices

13 Screen I/O and the Disk

SAVE_FILE

In the main routine, this procedure is found under the Create Mode option ("c") at line 3510 and under the Fetch Mode option ("f") at line 3925. Note that this procedure is under the "s" (Save) submode option (Figure 13.8) and is also on equal footing with the other submode options; that is, you do not have to first revise or perform calculations before saving the file to disk. Saving prior to calculating or revising is equally permissible. SAVE_FILE is broken into two parts. Inside the procedure, lines 2580-2615 save the contents of the scrollable "screen text" array to disk. Note that the procedure must be told which mode option is in effect so that it can correctly open (ASSIGN) the file (lines 2555-2570). As described in TEXTWRIT.INC, computer memory variables cannot be transferred directly into a disk file. Both "input line_buffer" and "integer_line_buffer" are intermediate or data transfer variables that enable the transfer of data from computer memory to the external storage medium (disk) a single component at a time. Figure 13.9 illustrates the mechanics of the transfer. Lines 2660-2695 are similar in form except that they save the numeric file data from the computer memory to a separate file so that it can be referenced directly when needed for computations, as you will see in the procedure A_CALCULATION.

FETCH_A_FILE

This procedure is found in the main routine under the "f" (Fetch) mode option at line 3805 and, similar to its peer procedure CREATE_A_FILE, is only invoked after the proper name has been requested (lines 2775-2780). FETCH_A_FILE is the converse of SAVE_FILE. When called with the correct file name parameters (one of which you type in from the keyboard), this procedure will pull the contents of the desired file off the disk and place those contents into the memory variables "screen_text" (line 2810) and "input_data_array" (line 2870). Note again the crucial roles that the file transfer variables "input_line_buffer" and "integer_line_buffer" play. The "read" statements at lines 2795 and 2865 read (copy) one component at a time *from* the file on disk *to* the corresponding file transfer variables. Lines 2785-2820 transfer the scroll data, and lines 2845-2880 transfer the numeric data. The mechanics of this operation are illustrated in Figure 13.10. Within this procedure (at lines 2900-2905), the scrolling of the just fetched file is performed prior to exiting the procedure.

Screen I/O and the Disk 13

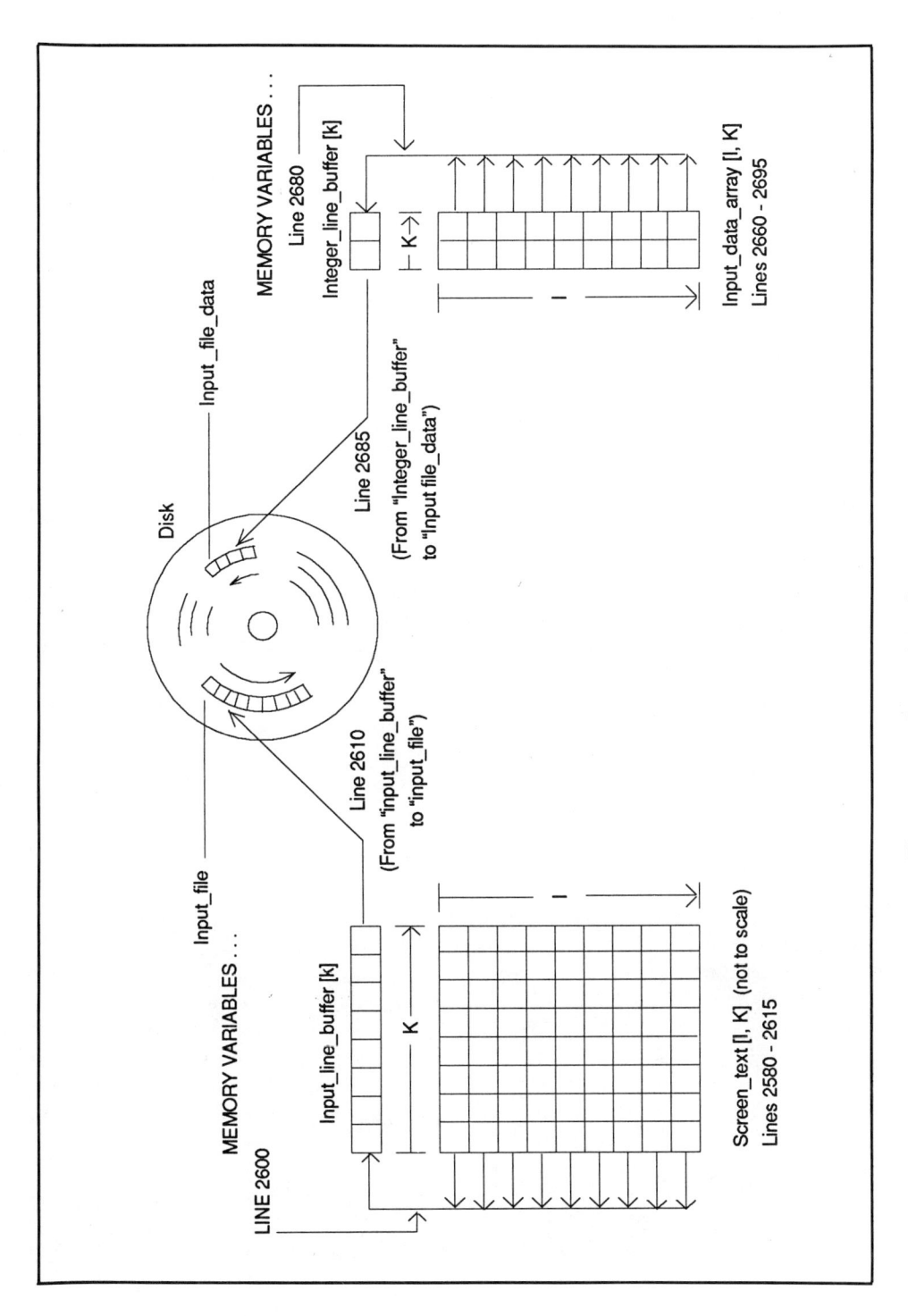

Figure 13.9 Procedure SAVE_FILE

13 Screen I/O and the Disk

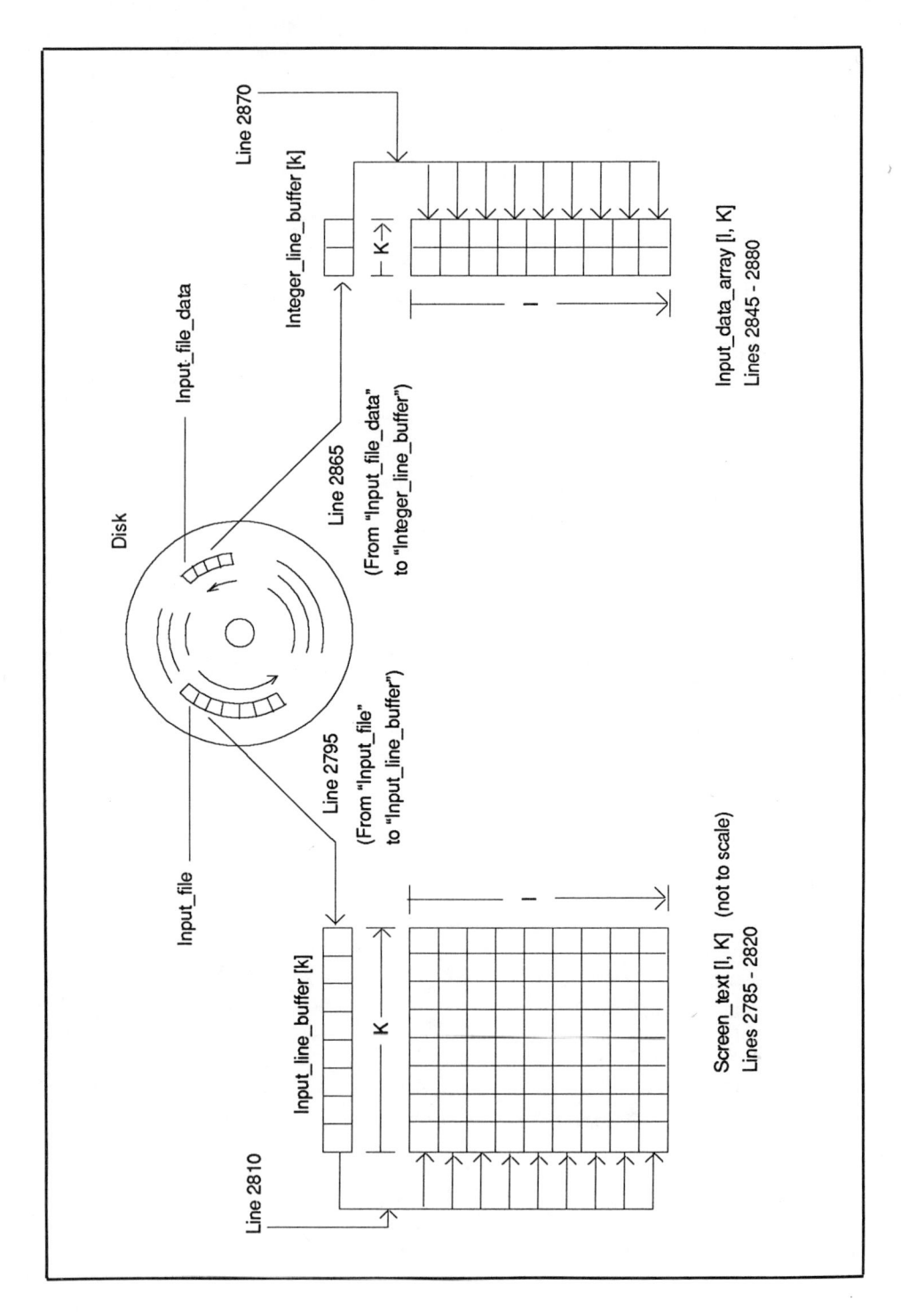

Figure 13.10 Procedure FETCH_A_FILE

CREATE_SHADOW_FILE_NAME

This procedure is found under the "c" option at line 3370 and under the "f" option at line 3775 in the main routine. As the words "shadow" and "name" imply, the procedure provides an automatic naming mechanism. After a valid file name (for the scrolling data file) is created, this procedure automatically names its numeric file counterpart. For example, if you type in the legal file name, say, "file.fil," this procedure will automatically create the file name "file.dat" for the numeric data file. The main routine supplies the procedure with a valid file name through the global variable "file_name" (file name). Inside the procedure, the corresponding parameter "fil_nam" is taken and adjusted at lines 2980 and 2985. Line 2980 chops off the suffix. Using the example above, the result would be "file". Line 2985 then takes the prefix and tacks on the pre-defined suffix, ".dat." The result, "file.dat," is then passed back to the main routine and into "data_file_name" through the "var'd" variable "data_file_name" in the parameter list at line 2935.

A_CALCULATION

This procedure is also found at two different locations in the main routine: under the "c" mode option at line 3480 and under the "f" mode option at line 3895. A_CALCULATION is a submode option procedure and on equal footing with the other submode options of either "r" or "s" (Figure 13.8). When invoked, this procedure will calculate the average value of both height and weight data of the numeric ".dat" file currently in the memory variables. This procedure is itself simple to understand. A few points are worth mentioning, however. First, note the interpretation of lines 2375-2380. The suffix part (" :6:2 ") says that the real number—including the decimal—lies in a field of length 6 with 2 decimal places reserved to the right of the decimal. This suffix allows a real number whose maximum value can be 999.99 (the decimal point takes up 1 of the 6 available field positions). Also, if the number is less than 3 digits to the left of the decimal point, that number will be right-adjusted in the 6-place number field. Thus, the real number 99.5 will have its first digit placed in the second location of the 6-place field. Remember, two places are reserved for the fractional portion to the right of the decimal. Also, this simple calculation procedure is included in this program only to show how a file's numeric data, which has been pulled from the disk and into memory, can be used in arithmetic calculations.

13 Screen I/O and the Disk

To conclude this section, attention will focus on the body of the main routine starting at line 3160. The overall structure of this section of code is summarized in Figure 13.3. You can see how most of the procedures described fit into the overall plan of the program.

Look first at the external procedure ENTER_NEW_FILE_NAME at line 3265 in the "c" (Create) mode section. Recall that ENTER_NEW_FILE NAME" is found inside "filename.inc." Note that it is embedded within two nested REPEAT..UNTIL loops (lines 3225 and 3235). Within the inner REPEAT..UNTIL loop (line 3235), the external procedure ENTER_NEW_FILE_NAME checks for syntactic correctness of the user-typed file name and checks to see that the file name is not a duplicate of a file name already in the Disk Directory. Once the candidate file name passes these two tests, it is then tested a third time in the outer REPEAT..UNTIL loop (lines 3225-3345) to ensure that the user-reserved suffixes ".txt" and ".dat" are not in the candidate file name. Recall that this double REPEAT..UNTIL loop method of validating input data was used extensively in Chapter 10.

Now look at the procedure ENTER_OLD_FILE NAME at line 3690 in the "f" (Fetch) mode section of the main routine. What has just been said above applies to the section of code between lines 3650 and 3770 *except* that it checks that the file name entered from the keyboard matches a file name that *already exists* in the directory.

Now, look at line 4105 in the "t" (Text) mode section of the main routine. Here again, you see the procedure ENTER_ OLD_ FILE_ NAME. This time, however, you see that you can fetch a text file only if, at the time of its creation, you had suffixed it with the file name extention ".txt." This suffix test is done at lines 4130-4135 where the entered file name is parsed and checked for a ".txt" suffix. You may exit the outer REPEAT..UNTIL loop (line 4140) only if the Boolean variable "valid_file_name1" is set to "true," that is, only if the suffix of the typed-in file name is ".txt." Line 4150 calls the TXTWRIT (text write) procedure from the "textwrit.inc" external procedures module only after a proper text file name has been typed. If you never enter a valid text file name, you will never be able to leave the outer loop.

Finally, look at the "q" (Quit) mode option. When "q" is selected in response to the keyboard input request at line 3180, the text between lines 4185 and 4220 is written to the screen (Figure 13.11) prior to the program ending and positioning the Turbo prompt ">" at column 1, row 5 (line 4235). You can use the "q" mode option if you need to check the directory of file names without having to interrupt the program. Note that besides the normal "d"(directory), "r"(run), and "q"(quit) options listed, you can also use the other "e"(edit), "w"(workfile), and "s"(save program) options as well. Note also that pressing the "r" option will cause the Turbo system to reactivate the program FILMAN.DRV, and the screen shown in Figure 13.4 will appear on the video monitor.

LIMITATIONS

One measurement of a truly robust program is its ability to recover gracefully from the user's I/O errors. The procedure REVISE_DATA_INPUT is designed to recover from some, but not all, such errors. The use of the predefined BUFLEN variable will limit the number of keystrokes that you can enter and thereby prevent a "run-on entry syndrome" (neutralize the BUFLEN function by bracketing it and then entering a long number). As you can see, it makes a real mess out of your screen. Line 2020 inside REVISE_DATA INPUT will prevent you from inadvertently typing an entry number whose value is outside of the legal integer range of 1-20 inclusive. Merely checking for a legal range is not enough. This section of code will not prevent a system error should you type in a candidate entry that is a fractional real number or contains an alphabetic character.

The procedure CREATE_A_FILE, where you type numeric input data into the input data array, is not too robust either. Again, there is no method to prevent entry of illegal input data (real numbers with decimal points and alphabetic characters). To prevent these potential dangers, you can use the tools of Chapter 10: the "ei_er.inc" (integer/real number checking module) in conjunction with the double REPEAT..UNTIL loop structure or the less comprehensive but faster technique illustrated inside the procedure REVISE_DATA_INPUT.

13 Screen I/O and the Disk

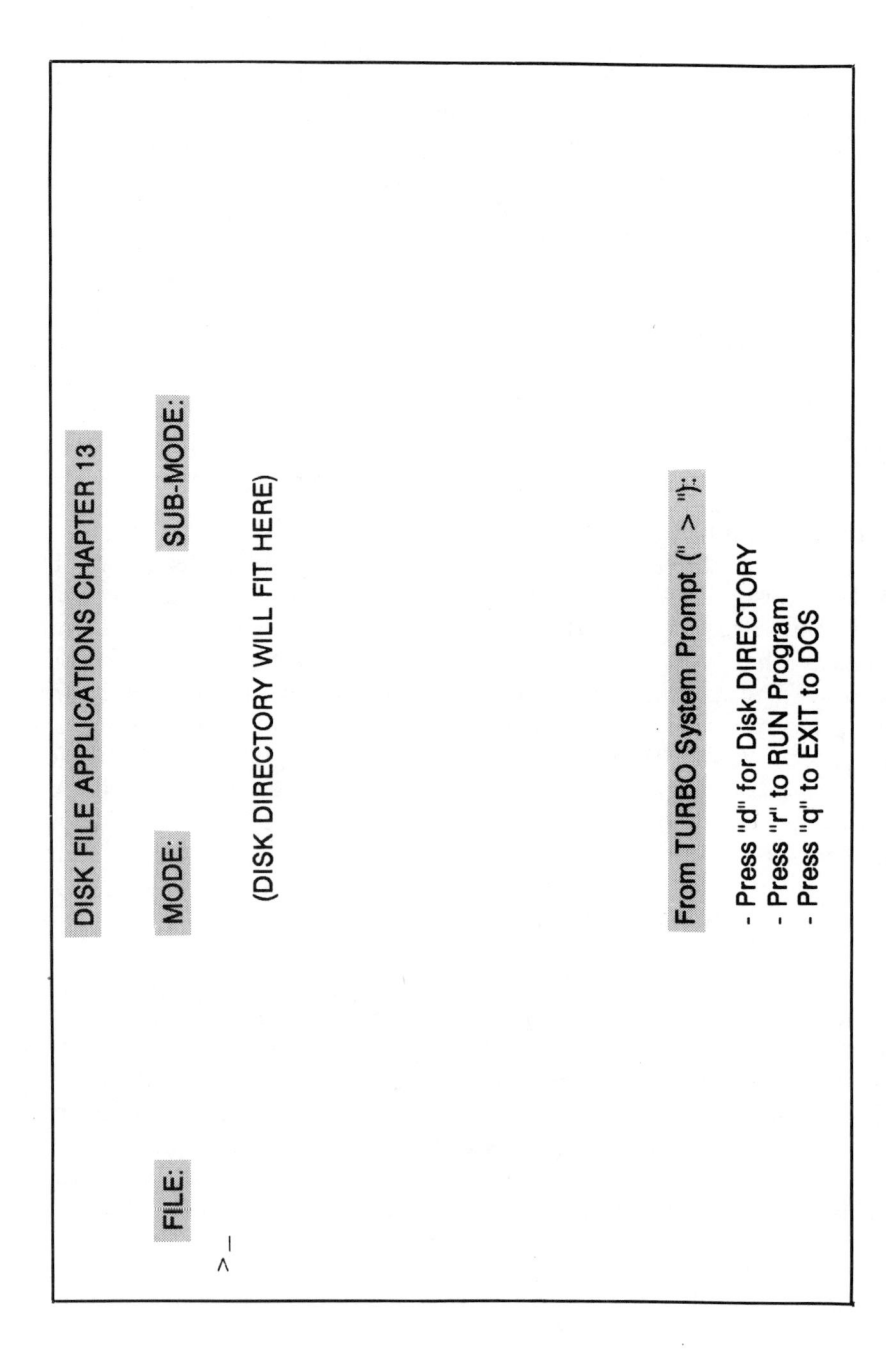

```
┌─────────────────────────────────────────────────┐
│                                                 │
│   DISK FILE APPLICATIONS CHAPTER 13             │
│                                                 │
│   MODE:              SUB-MODE:                  │
│                                                 │
│   (DISK DIRECTORY WILL FIT HERE)                │
│                                                 │
│                                                 │
│                          From TURBO System Prompt (" > "):  │
│                                                 │
│                          - Press "d" for Disk DIRECTORY     │
│                          - Press "r" to RUN Program         │
│                          - Press "q" to EXIT to DOS         │
│                                                 │
│   FILE:                                         │
│   ^                                             │
└─────────────────────────────────────────────────┘
```

Figure 13.11 Initialized Screen after Selection of the "q" Submode Option

Screen I/O and the Disk 13

Another limitation of this program is related to the selection of mode and submode options in the menu screens. The mode and submode options are geared to accept only lowercase letter choices. Also, if the NUM LOCK key is enabled, the scrolling keys on the numeric keypad will be disabled.

A fourth limitation that invites correction concerns operational flexibility. Once you have selected the "c," the "f," or the "t" modes, access is lost to the directory. So if you enter one of these modes and then forget which files are in the directory, you could theoretically attempt to create already existing files, fetch non-existent files, or fetch non-existent ".txt" files forever.

The program developed in this chapter is an overhead program; that is, it is designed to facilitate creation and display of file data as well as movement of file data back and forth between disk storage and the computer's memory. Properly speaking, the actual calculations on the numeric data are out of place in this overhead program. Input/Output operations are best separated from computing operations. To improve these modularity characteristics, you can do one of the following:

- rewrite A_CALCULATION as an external procedure (".inc" file).

- write A_CALCULATION as a separate stand-alone program and then use the built-in CHAIN procedure to activate it from the overhead program.

- if your computations are varied and complex, you could use the built-in procedure overlay facility provided as part of the Turbo Pascal compiler package.

Each of these methods has advantages and compensating disadvantages. You must use the tool that best suits your needs.

13 Screen I/O and the Disk

Before concluding this chapter, one more limitation must be discussed. Assume that you create a new file called "ugga.bug" using the "c" (Create File) mode option. Recall that under this option, the file name is placed into the directory, and the file has a length of 0 bytes. At this point, the scrollable file text is held in the memory variable "screen text[i,k]," and the associated numeric data is in "input_ data_ array[i,1&2]." Now, if you forget to save the newly created file to disk and then later try to fetch this unsaved file, Turbo will halt the program and display an I/O error message on the screen. You receive this message because the program (under the "f" mode) first looks for the directory name (which it finds) and then transfers the disk file information back into the memory variables inside the procedure FETCH_A_FILE.

At this point, the program will fail because the file was never saved from the memory variables onto the disk. FETCH_ A_ FILE cannot transfer an empty disk file that is 0 bytes in length. The program crashes and the Turbo system program generates an I/O error.

If you ever want to use the file name "ugga.bug" again or want to remove it from your diskette, you must return to DOS and use the ERASE command to erase it from the disk directory. Probably the simplest method of doing this would be to write some code that would make saving a newly created file a precondition to exiting from the "c" mode. There are other solutions, depending on your desired degree of "bulletproofing."

At this point, you may be asking, "Why present a program with so many deficiencies?" Remember, the prime purpose of this program is to demonstrate the transfer of text and numeric information between the disk and screen memory, as in Figure 13.1. These limitations are important, but are incidental to your main purpose. Remedying these deficiencies will provide good practice in building improvements to an existing "core" program. Feel free to experiment, change, and customize the programs to suit your needs.

CHAPTER 14

GENERAL PRINCIPLES

14 General Principles

So far, screen save/redisplay and scrolling routines have been used, which are not sufficiently general in nature to qualify as true stand-alone modules. If you refer back to the applications programs in Chapters 11 and 12, you see that their screen I/O procedures are riddled throughout with unnamed, undefined constant values. Up to this point, only fixed numbers have been used to establish a solid mechanical understanding of these screen I/O procedures. Introducing more general features at that time would only have been confusing and counterproductive. Now is the time to develop a naming system for these constant values and thereby provide the screen I/O modules with powerful facilities to handle multiple screens. The key to this next step lies with the creation of a separate ".inc" module whose sole purpose is to declare all of the constants, types, and variables associated with the screens you want to manipulate.

MODULE: TYPEDEF.INC (TYPE DEFINITIONS)

Saving, redisplaying, and scrolling multiple data windows on the same video screen calls for separate definitions of many constant and array variables. To do a proper job, you will need 20 constant values and 4 array values—24 in all—for a full definition of each screen window. Even two fully defined windows would take up a lot of space in the Declaration Section of any driver program and would confuse the overall intent of the program itself. There are so many variables floating around that it becomes difficult and frustrating to unravel how and what each one is doing to contribute to the overall programming effort. And what if you want to add or delete a screen from the driver routine? The best method of clearing up this potential confusion is to consolidate and split all of the screen definition parameters into a separate ".inc" module as has been done in the Declaration module called "typedef.inc." The module consists of three main sections. The "const" section fully defines each screen window used in the program. The "type" section builds on the "const" section and defines the array types these screens represent in terms of the defined constants. Finally, once the types are set, the screen array variables used in the driver are defined in the "var" section.

So far, all the demonstration and applications programs have defined all screen variables inside the Declaration Section of the driver routines. As stated, the reason for this was to maximize the scope of these variables so they could be referenced from any other ".inc" module you would choose to install. By creating and defining the screen variables

General Principles 14

inside a separate ".inc" module, you are breaking no scope rules. To ensure that this module is compiled before any other in the program, you must be sure that it is the very first module in the program and that it is placed immediately after the "program" statement in any program you write. Observe also that as long as there is no duplication of variables, you are allowed to have more than one "const," "type," and "var" header (one group in the ".inc" file and one at the head of the driver routine). It would even be permissible to split "typedef.inc" into three separate headings if you wanted to; however, the order of the reserved words "const," "type," and "var" must be strictly observed as each builds on its predecessor. After the code for "typedef.inc" is presented, its organization will be explained.

```
{=========================================================================}
0005 {typedef.inc}
0010
0015 const
0020
0025      {SCREEN1: screen save/redisplay constants}
0030      tlc1 = 5 ; tlr1 = 4 ; brc1 = 53 ; brr1 = 16;
0035      maxscrrows1 = 13;
0040      maxscrcols1 = 49;
0045      maxscrdisplaychars1 = 637;       {13 x 49}
0050
0055      {SCREEN1: array data scrolling constants}
0060      datacharsperrow1 = 45;       {cols 7 to 51 inclusive}
0065      datacharspercol1 = 3;        {first data col is cols. 7,8,9}
0070      maxcountofdatacharspercol1 = 3;{each data unit handled a  }
0075                                      {character at a time       }
0080      max_allowed_i_tot1 = 11; {to arrive at...count backwards }
0085      datarowdepth1       = 6; {marks at rows 5,7,9,11,13,15    }
0090      datarowdepthminusone1 = 5;
0095      datacolwidth1 = 15;          {15, 3 column data locations}
0100      datacolwidthminusone1 = 14;
0105      maxdatarows1 = 16;
0110      maxdatacols1 = 15;
0115      maxdatachars1 = 720;     {16 x 15 x 3 = 720}
0120
0125      scr1_init   : boolean = false;
0130      scr1_active : boolean = false;
0135      {-------------------------------------------------------------
0140
0145      {SCREEN2: screen save/redisplay constants}
0150      tlc2 = 32; tlr2 = 8 ; brc2 = 65 ; brr2 = 14;
0155      maxscrrows2 = 7;
0160      maxscrcols2 = 34;
0165      maxscrdisplaychars2 = 238;   {7 x 34}
0170
0175      {SCREEN2: array data scrolling constants}
0180      datacharsperrow2 = 30;   {cols 34 to 63 inclusive}
0185      datacharspercol2 = 3;    {first data col is cols. 34,35,36}
0190      maxcountofdatacharspercol2 = 3; {each data unit handled a }
0195                                       {character at a time      }
```

continued...

319

14 General Principles

...from previous page

```
0200        max_allowed_i_tot2 = 28; {to arrive at...count backwards  }
0205        datarowdepth2         = 3; {marks at rows 9,11,13 }
0210        datarowdepthminusone2 = 2;
0215        datacolwidth2 = 10;      {10, 3 column data locations}
0220        datacolwidthminusone2 = 9;
0225        maxdatarows2 = 30;
0230        maxdatacols2 = 10;
0235        maxdatachars2 = 900;     {30 x 10 x 3 = 900}
0240
0245        scr2_init   : boolean = false;
0250        scr2_active : boolean = false;
0255 {-------------------------------------------------------------------}
0260
0265        {SCREEN3 : screen save/redisplay constants}
0270        tlc3 = 57; tlr3 = 4 ; brc3 = 78 ; brr3 = 12;
0275        maxscrrows3 = 9;
0280        maxscrcols3 = 22;
0285        maxscrdisplaychars3 = 198;    {9 x 22}
0290
0295        {SCREEN3: array data scrolling constants}
0300        datacharsperrow3 = 18;    {cols 59 to 76 inclusive}
0305        datacharspercol3 = 3;     {first data col is cols. 59,60,61}
0310        maxcountofdatacharspercol3 = 3; {each data unit handled a }
0315                                        {character at a time      }
0320        max_allowed_i_tot3 = 21; {to arrive at...count backwards  }
0325        datarowdepth3         = 4; {marks at rows 5,7,9,11}
0330        datarowdepthminusone3 = 3;
0335        datacolwidth3 = 6;        {6, 3 column data locations}
0340        datacolwidthminusone3 = 5;
0345        maxdatarows3 = 24;
0350        maxdatacols3 = 6;
0355        maxdatachars3 = 432;      {24 x 6 x 3 = 432}
0360
0365        scr3_init   : boolean = false;
0370        scr3_active : boolean = false;
0375
0380
0385 type
0390        str3       = string[3];
0395
0400                                    {13}              {49}
0405        s1_arr     = ARRAY[1..maxscrrows1 , 1..maxscrcols1] of char;
0410                                    {637}
0415        s1_buf     = ARRAY[1..maxscrdisplaychars1] of char;
0420                                    {16}              {15}
0425        s1arr      = ARRAY[1..maxdatarows1 , 1..maxdatacols1] of str3;
0430                                    {720}
0435        s1buf      = ARRAY[1..maxdatachars1] of char;
0440
0445        s2_arr     = ARRAY[1..7,1..34] of char;
0450        s2_buf     = ARRAY[1..238] of char;   {7 rows x 34 cols}
0455        s2arr      = ARRAY[1..30,1..10] of str3;
0460        s2buf      = ARRAY[1..900] of char;    {30 x 10 x 3}
0465
0470                                    {9}              {22}
0475        s3_arr     = ARRAY[1..maxscrrows3,1..maxscrcols3] of char;
0480                                    {198}
0485        s3_buf     = ARRAY[1..maxdisplaychars3] of char; {9 x 22}
0490                                    {24}              {6}
```

continued...

...from previous page

```
0495        s3arr      = ARRAY[1..maxdatarows3,1..maxdatacols3] of str3;
0500                              {432}
0505        s3buf      = ARRAY[1..maxdatachars3] of char;   {24 x 6 x 3}
0510
0515   var
0520        scr1_array        : s1_arr;
0525        scr1_buffer       : s1_buf;
0530        scr1array         : s1arr;
0535        scr1buffer        : s1buf;
0540
0545        scr2_array        : s2_arr;
0550        scr2_buffer       : s2_buf;
0555        scr2array         : s2arr;
0560        scr2buffer        : s2buf;
0565
0570        scr3_array        : s3_arr;
0575        scr3_buffer       : s3_buf;
0580        scr3array         : s3arr;
0585        scr3buffer        : s3buf;
{=======================================================================}
```

TYPEDEF.INC: NOTES

This module creates and defines program and parameter variables that can be used by the procedures inside the driver routine. In one sense, these variables are the "output" of this module. Screen 3 (line 0265) will be used to trace this evolution from input (constants) to output (variables). To organize this approach, observe that each created screen window has two different sets of constants. One set pertains to the screen saving and redisplay parameters; the other defines those parameters needed to scroll the screen data.

Now, consider the screen saving and redisplay constants (lines 0270-0285). Here, seven of them need to be defined. The first four define the rectangular outline of the whole screen window by setting out its top left corner ("tlc3" & "tlr3") and its bottom right corner ("brc3" & "brr3"). The number of screen rows ("maxscrrows") is then defined as the number of rows from "tlr3" to "brr3" inclusive (line 0275). The number of screen columns ("maxscrcols3") is defined as the number of columns from "tlc3" to "brc3" inclusive (line 0280). Remember, you are saving to memory an image of the whole screen window and must therefore include both starting and ending row and columns. From "maxscrrows3" and "maxscrcols3," you can define the constant value "maxscrdisplaychars3" (maximum screen display characters for screen 3), which is their product (line 0285; see Figure 14.1).

14 General Principles

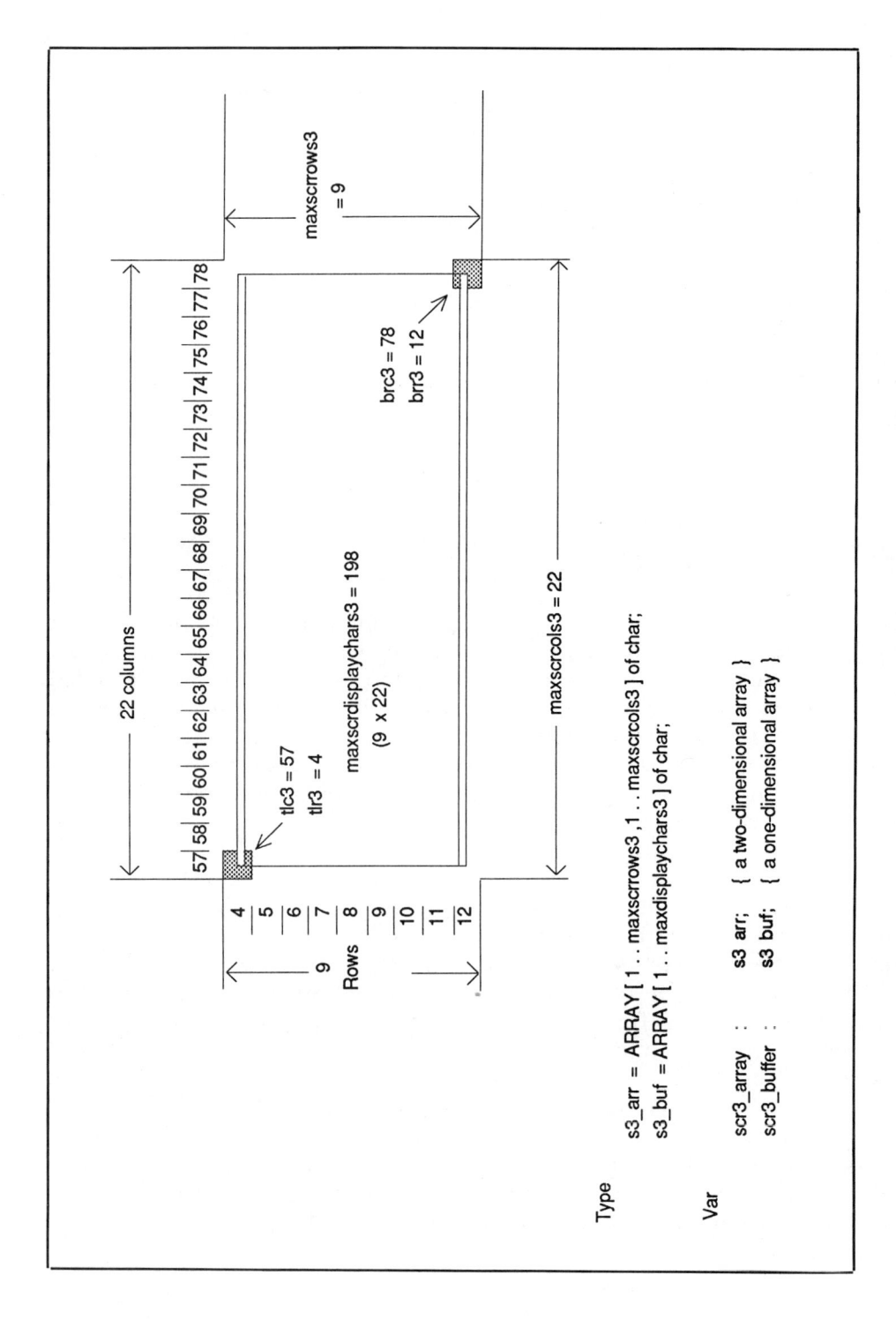

Figure 14.1 Screen3: Save/Redisplay Screen Parameters

General Principles 14

Once these screen save/redisplay constants have been defined, type definitions can be formulated from them. Line 0475 sets type definitions for the two-dimensional memory array representing the area of the video screen to be saved/redisplayed. Line 0485 then sets the type definition for the corresponding one-dimensional array of the same video screen. Remember, you need this one-dimensional array to map directly to the one-dimensional video memory array MEM[bwseg : bwofs + j]. With the type definitions in place, the two-dimensional and one-dimensional array variables to be used by the program for screen save/redisplay purposes are named.

Now, the array variables to scroll the screen data will be derived. Before looking at the parameters used for scrolling the screen data, however, consider line 0505. To scroll array data on the computer screen, you must first decide how large (in terms of the number of characters) each array element in the scrollable data array will be. This step is crucial when deciding how much screen width you will need to display one row of scrollable screen data. With Screen 3, it was arbitrarily decided to display six 3-character-long data elements per screen display row, that is, six array elements, each of size "str3" (line 0495). In most cases, the data creation algorithm will dictate the maximum width of the typical array data display element. This simple data creation algorithm (CREATE_SCREEN_ARRAYS) dictates a range of row values from 1 to 24; therefore, an array display element has been provided with a maximum width of 3 characters, which provides the appearance of at least 1 blank space between data fields. In reality, the data display fields are displayed end to end along any given row on the screen. See Figure 14.2 for an outline of CREATE_SCREEN_ARRAYS' output.

Now return to the constants used to define the screen scrolling data parameters for Screen 3 (line 0295). "Maxdatarows3" defines the maximum number of rows in the scrollable data array. "Maxdatacols3" defines the array's maximum number of columns. Here, the scrolling data array will have 24 rows of data, with each row having 6 data elements. Since each data element has 3 characters, the total number of characters in "maxdatachars3" is 432 (24 x 6 x 3).

323

14 General Principles

	Columns 1	2	3	4	5	6
1	1	1	1	1	1	1
2	2	2	2	2	2	2
3	3	3	3	3	3	3
4	4	4	4	4	4	4
5	5	5	5	5	5	5
6	6	6	6	6	6	6
7	7	7	7	7	7	7
8	8	8	8	8	8	8
9	9	9	9	9	9	9
10	10	10	10	10	10	10
11	11	11	11	11	11	11
12	12	12	12	12	12	12
13	13	13	13	13	13	13
14	14	14	14	14	14	14
15	15	15	15	15	15	15
16	16	16	16	16	16	16
17	17	17	17	17	17	17
18	18	18	18	18	18	18
19	19	19	19	19	19	19
20	20	20	20	20	20	20
21	21	21	21	21	21	21
22	22	22	22	22	22	22
23	23	23	23	23	23	23
24	24	24	24	24	24	24

Rows

```
Type
    Str3   =   String [3]
    S3arr  =   Array [1 . . maxdatarrows3, 1 . . maxdatacols3] of Str3;
                          {24}                       {6}
Var
    S3 array:  S3arr
```

Figure 14.2 Results of Procedure "CREATE_SCREEN_ARRAYS" "scr3array"

General Principles 14

From the previous discussion, you know why "datacharspercol3" (data characters per column for Screen 3) is 3. Because six data columns have been defined, you can now see why "datacharsperrow3" (data characters per row for Screen 3) is equal to 18. The variable "maxcountofdatacharspercol3" (maximum number of data characters per column for Screen 3) may not be obvious, but it should be familiar. This constant is used as an accounting device.

Once you have located a three-character data row element within the array (row range 1..24; column range 1..6), use this variable as the upper value of a FOR..DO loop to access each and every individual character within the data array element. Recall that this variable was embodied as a number in the earlier demonstration programs where horizontal and vertical scrolling were performed using the "index addressing method." This variable was embodied in the upper value of the variable "count" in the innermost FOR..DO loop of these programs (Chapters 6 and 8).

For this screen display, at any one time, four data rows from the data array will be displayed; therefore, "datarowdepth3" (data row depth for Screen 3) is assigned the constant value of 4. The variable "datarowdepthminusone3" is used in the vertical scrolling routine to help calculate the index of the highest-valued row to be displayed on the screen after pressing the Down Arrow key. Note the blank spaces between the data rows in Figure 14.3. From the point of view of the display of the data array, the blank lines are immaterial as they are created separately and are for screen formatting purposes only (see lines 0345-0350 of the subprocedure REWRITE_SCR and line 0585 of the procedure INIT SCREEN). In this program, only the vertical scroll of array data is performed, which is why the number of data columns in the display array ("maxdatacols3") exactly matches the number of physical data columns available on the screen ("datacolwidth3"). If you were to perform horizontal scrolling as well, you would need to use the variable "datacolwidthminusone3" to help calculate the index of the highest-valued display column to be displayed on the right-hand side of the screen after each press of the Right Arrow key. In this example, creating horizontal scrolling capability is left to you (don't forget to define "maxdatacols3" as some number greater than 6). If you can't figure out horizontal scrolling, don't despair. It will be developed in Chapter 15.

14 General Principles

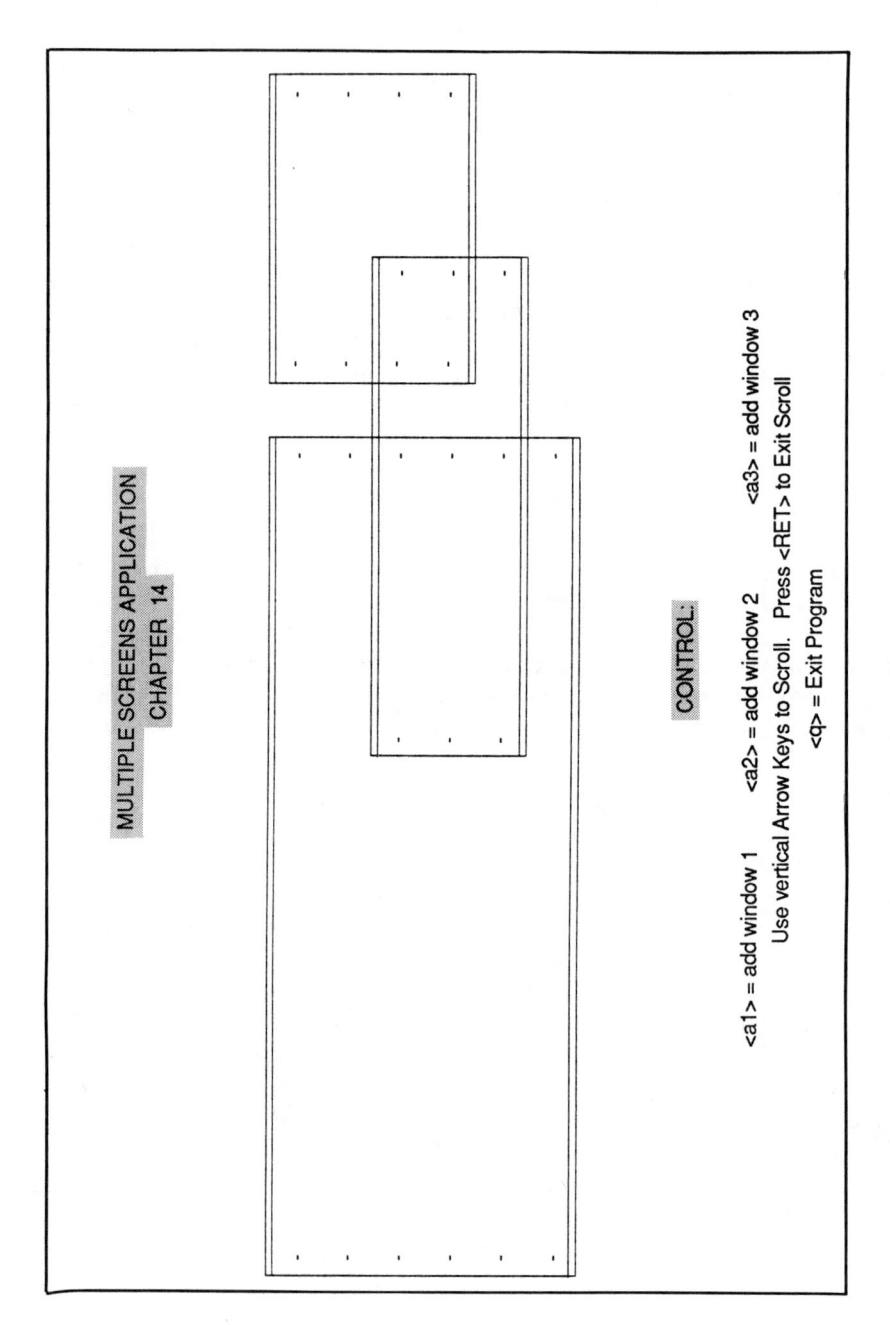

Figure 14.3 Layout Showing Location of Overlapping Screen Windows

"I_tot," as you will see later in VSCROLL_SCREEN, is the variable that keeps track of the current data row index value as you press the Up and Down Arrow keys during a vertical scroll of the data array. If you press the Down Arrow key to look at larger values in the data array, you know that the next value to apprear at the bottom of the screen window will not be those indexed by "i_tot." Instead, they will be the values indexed by "i_tot" plus a screen depth adjustment factor of 3 (datarowdepthminusone3 for Screen 3). Since the data array has a maximum depth of 24 rows, you should now be able to understand why the variable "max_allowed_i_tot3" should be assigned the value of 21. A simple method to derive the value of 21 is to imagine that you are at the last row of the scrolling array at row 24 (see Figure 14.4). To derive the value of 21, simply count backwards by 1 up the displayed screen rows until you reach the top display row. This method could also apply if you were coding a horizontal scroll of the screen data (with more than 6 data columns) and needed a value for the variable "max_allowed_k_tot3." Since you are not performing a horizontal scroll here, this variable has not been included in the list of data array scrolling constants.

Now that all of the data array screen scrolling constants have been defined, you can formulate the type definitions. Line 0495 sets out the type definition for the two-dimensional array that represents the whole scrollable data array. Note that each element of the data array is a 3-character string (of the type "str3" defined earlier). The type definition of the corresponding one-dimensional array is defined at line 0505. This one-dimensional equivalent is needed to map the contents directly into the one-dimensional video memory array MEM[bwseg : bwofs + j] during the actual scrolling operation. Remember that mapping to the video memory can only be done from a one-dimensional memory array.

With the type definitions in place, you then proceed to name the two array variables used by the driver routine to vertically scroll the data array.

14 General Principles

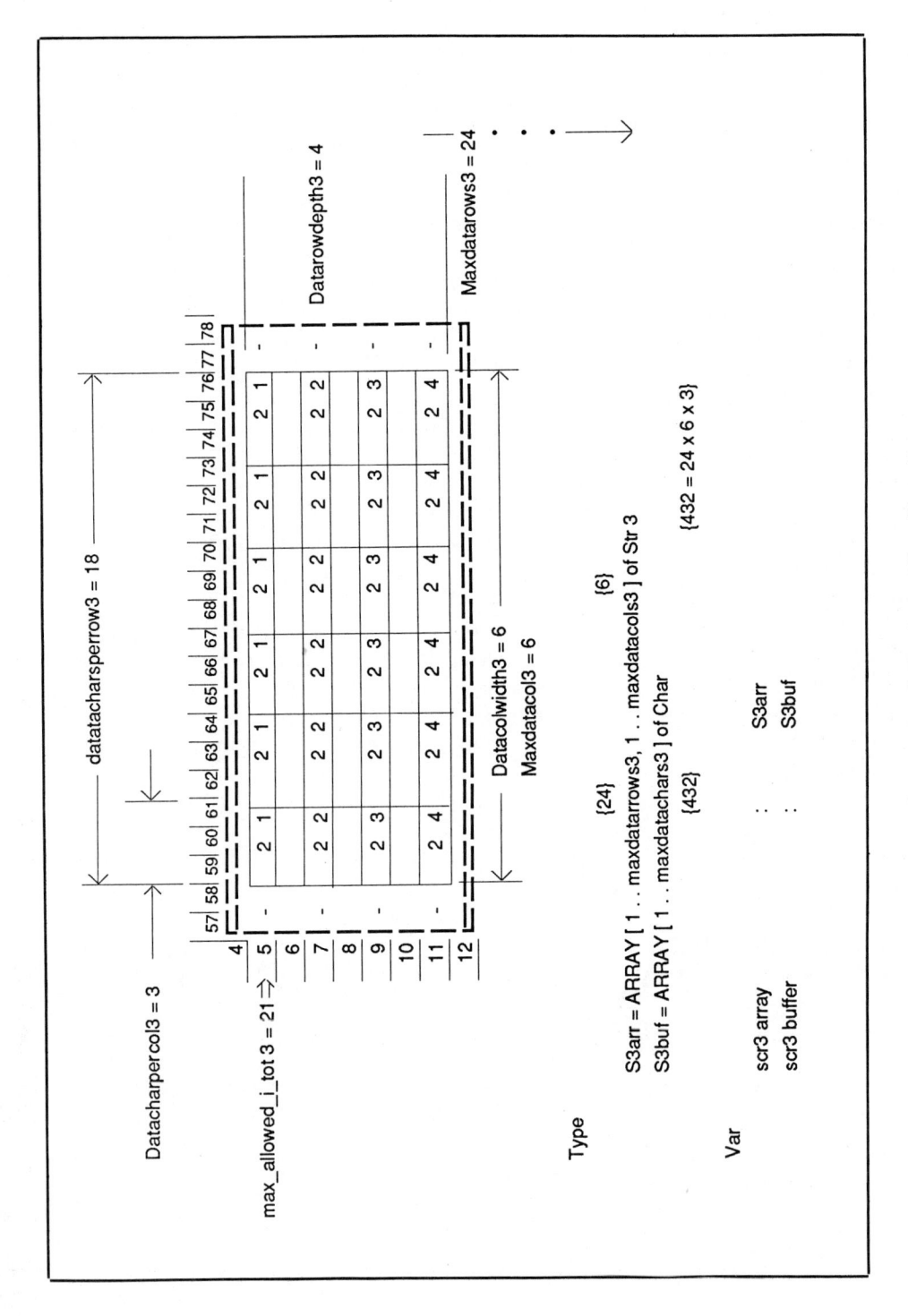

Figure 14.4 Screen3: Data Array Scrolling Parameters

General Principles 14

Before this section is concluded, consider a few short observations. First, the Boolean screen control variables "scr3_init" (screen 3 initialized) and "scr3_active" (screen 3 active) are both assigned the value "false" to start with. Once Screen 3 has been initialized, "scr3_init" will be set to "true" and stay that way. Now, depending on the order in which you bring up the data windows to the video screen, the variable "scr3_active" may flip back and forth many times between "true" and "false." You will come to appreciate this point later.

Second, the coding of lines 0365 and 0370 is equivalent to the following code fragment:

```
{typedef.inc}                        {SCREEN DECLARATION MODULE}
     .
     .
     .
     scr3_init    : boolean;
     scr3_active  : boolean;
     .
     .
     .
program   mult_scr(input,output);    {DRIVER PROGRAM}
     .
     .
Begin
     scr3_init    := false;
     scr3_active  := false;
     .
     .
```

You may choose whichever method is most comfortable for you.

14 General Principles

Third, if you look at Figures 14.3 and 14.4, you will see that a series of horizontal marks has been placed at certain rows inside columns 58 and 77. These columns have been included as a buffer to separate the screen border from the scrollable screen data, and these marks have been included to help you visualize which screen rows will hold the scrollable data array. Strictly speaking, the one-column buffer areas are not needed when you are scolling array data using the "index address method." They have been included here only for consistency as the other two scrolling methods definitely need them for correct scrolling operation.

Fourth, note the Type and Variable naming convention. Somewhere within the Type or Variable name, the number of the screen you are dealing with here has been embedded. Data types and variables pertaining to screen save/redisplay operations have been named using the "_" character. Data types and variables involved in the scrolling operations have been named *without* using the "_" symbol inside the name identifier. These conventions have been incorporated only to simplify handling a large number of Type and Variable names that are closely related in the type of descriptive work they do.

Finally, when you create your own multiple screen application programs, first lay out all your screen windows on a Screen Layout form similar to the one in Figure 14.3, and then define all your required screen parameters in a manner similar to the example in Figures 14.1 and 14.4. Taking this kind of trouble at the beginning will go a long way toward correctly organizing the mass of parameters required for complex multiple screen save/redisplay and scrolling operations and will make it a much simpler task to add or delete data screens at a future time.

MODULE: REWRITSC.INC (REWRITE SCREEN)

As the name implies, this module vertically scrolls the data arrays produced by the procedure CREATE_ SCREEN_ ARRAYS. This module will perform its scrolling job using the "index address method" introduced in Chapter 8. Like the routine in Chapter 8, it too has a main procedure and a subprocedure. VSCROLL_SCREEN provides the module with all the required parameters and the proper control parameters to perform the vertical scrolling. The subprocedure REWRITE_SCR (rewrite screen) actually performs the calculations that make the vertical scrolling possible. Unlike the scrolling procedure in Chapter 8, the present stand-alone module has been designed for more general use and is capable of scrolling any number of data windows, hence, the reason for the larger number of parameters. Following is the code and subsequent explanation:

```
{========================================================}
0005  {rewritsc.inc}
0010  {
0015    Read as: "rewrite screen include file"
0020    On disk as "rewritsc.inc"
0025  }
0030  procedure      VSCROLL_SCREEN(tlc,tlr                   : integer;
0035                             var saved_i_tot              : integer;
0040                             var saved_k_tot              : integer;
0045                                 datarowdepthminusone     : integer;
0050                                 datacolwidthminusone     : integer;
0055                                 datacharsperrow          : integer;
0060                                 datacharspercol          : integer;
0065                                 maxcountofdatacharspercol: integer;
0070                                 max_allowed_i_tot        : integer;
0075                             var scr1buffer               : s1buf;
0080                             var scr2buffer               : s2buf;
0085                             var scr3buffer               : s3buf);
0090
0095  label
0100       rep_read;
0105
0110  const
0115       scroll_up       = #$48;
0120       scroll_down     = #$50;
0125       carriage_ret    = #$0d;
0130
0135  var
0140       scroll_choice   : char;
0145       exit_scroll     : boolean;
0150       i_tot,k_tot     : integer;
0155                       {takes saved_i_tot , saved_k_tot}
```

continued...

14 General Principles

...from previous page

```
0160    {-------------------------------------------------------------}
0165
0170         procedure REWRITE_SCR;
0175
0180         var
0185              bx,bp,
0190              count,
0195              j,
0200              row,col,
0205              k,i        : integer;
0210
0215         Begin     {sub-procedure rewrite_scr}
0220              col := tlc + 2 ; row := tlr + 1;
0225              {adjust column and row for data display}
0230              j := ((row - 1) * 160) + ((col - 1) * 2);
0235              FOR i := (i_tot) to (i_tot + datarowdepthminusone) DO
0240              Begin
0245                   FOR k := (k_tot) TO
0250                             (k_tot + datacolwidthminusone) DO
0255                   Begin
0260                        bx := (i - 1) * datacharsperrow;
0265                        bp := (k - 1) * datacharspercol;
0270                        FOR count := 1 to maxcountofdatacharspercol DO
0275                        Begin
0280                             IF (scr1_active = true) THEN
0285                                CHR_OUT(j,ORD(scr1buffer[bx+bp+count]));
0290
0295                             IF (scr2_active = true) THEN
0300                                CHR_OUT(j,ORD(scr2buffer[bx+bp+count]));
0305
0310                             IF (scr3_active = true) THEN
0315                                CHR_OUT(j,ORD(scr3buffer[bx+bp+count]));
0320
0325                             {* delay(100); *}
0330                             j := j + 2;
0335                        End;
0340                   End;
0345                   col := col ; row := row + 2;
0350                   j := ((row - 1) * 160) + ((col - 1) * 2)
0355              End;
0360         End;      {sub-procedure rewrite_scr}
0365    {-------------------------------------------------------------}
0370
0375    Begin     {procedure vscroll_screen}
0380         window(1,1,80,25);
0375    Begin     {procedure vscroll_screen}
0380         window(1,1,80,25);
0385         exit_scroll := false;
0390         i_tot := saved_i_tot ; k_tot := saved_k_tot;
0395
0400         REPEAT
0405              rep_read:           {label with colon}
0410              gotoxy(40,21);
0415              read(KBD,scroll_choice);     {type in at keyboard}
0420              CASE (scroll_choice) of
0425
0430              scroll_up:    Begin           {press Up Arrow Key....}
0435                                i_tot := i_tot - 1;
0440                                k_tot := k_tot + 0;
0445                                IF (i_tot < 1) THEN
```

continued...

332

...from previous page

```
0450                            Begin
0455                                i_tot    := 1;
0460                                goto rep_read;
0465                            End;
0470                            REWRITE_SCR;
0475                       End;       {scroll_up}
0480
0485           scroll_down : Begin          {press Down Arrow Key....}
0490                            i_tot := i_tot + 1;
0495                            k_tot := k_tot + 0;
0500                            IF (i_tot > max_allowed_i_tot) THEN
0505                            Begin
0510                                i_tot := max_allowed_i_tot;
0515                                goto rep_read;
0520                            End;
0525                            REWRITE_SCR;
0530                       End;          {scroll_down}
0535
0540           carriage_ret : Begin
0545                            exit_scroll  := true;
0550                            saved_i_tot  := i_tot;
0555                            saved_k_tot  := k_tot;
0560                       End
0565
0570           ELSE
0575                            {any other entry is illegal}
0580
0585           END;          {case}
0590       UNTIL (exit_scroll = true);
0595       gotoxy(40,21);
0600  End;      {procedure vscroll_screen}
{=====================================================}
```

REWRITSC.INC: NOTES

VSCROLL_SCREEN

As mentioned, this module is adapted for general use as a separately installable vertical screen data scrolling module. The key to its utility and flexibility lies within its parameter list. If you look at this list (lines 0030-0085), you will see that the parameters can be classified into three main groups.

The first group contains the non-array parameters used to supply the module with information about the data array currently being scrolled. These values can all be found in the "const" section of "typedef.inc" and in Figure 14.4. Notice that these parameters are all unsuffixed and

14 General Principles

can take on whatever value is fed to them from the procedure calls in the driver routine. For example, if Screen 3 were currently being scrolled, then the value of "tlc" would be given the value of "tlc3," which is 57, etc. The parameters in this group include "tlc," "tlr," "datarowdepthminusone," "datacolwidthminusone," "datacharsperrow," "datacharspercol," "maxcountofdatacharspercol," and "max_allowed_i_tot." These values are all fixed at the time a particular screen is selected for scrolling in the driver routine. These values, with the exception of "max_allowed_i_tot," are all used inside the subprocedure REWRITE_SCR.

The second group of parameters consists of the control parameters "saved_i_tot" and "saved_k_tot." Unlike those in the first group, these two have their original values (of 1) set from within the driver routine at lines 0840 and 0845 of "mult_scr_drv" and not from within "typedef.inc." These two control parameters are prefixed with a "var" reserved word, which means that after the scrolling of a certain screen is completed (you press <Ret>), the current values of those variables are stored back into the corresponding variables of the calling procedure in the driver routine. For example, if you were scrolling Screen 3, you would, after pressing <Ret>, be saving the current values of "saved_i_tot" and "saved_k_tot" back into "saved_i_tot3" and "saved_k_tot3" in the driver routine. This would enable you to then scroll some other screen data and return to scrolling Screen 3 from the point where you left off. Notice at line 0390 that "saved_i_tot" and "saved_k_tot" have been saved into the local variables "i_tot" and "k_tot." This has been done to separate in your mind the dynamic operation of scrolling data up and down from the end process of saving the final values for future use. After the scrolling is finished, the final "i_tot" and "k_tot" values are reassigned into "saved_i_tot" and "saved_k_tot" (line 0550) for storage into "saved_i_tot#" and "saved_k_tot#" (with "#" depending on whether Screen 1, Screen 2, or Screen 3 is currently active). One final point: "Saved_k_tot" is the control variable used only if a horizontal scroll is in effect. As this procedure does not perform a horizontal scroll, this parameter never changes from its initialized value of 1. It has been included in case you want to adapt this procedure for horizontal scrolling and/or bi-directional scrolling of the array data.

The third group of parameters contains the scrollable data arrays themselves. Each of these arrays can be found under the "var" section of "typedef.inc," and if you trace them back through their type and into the "Const" section, you can determine their dimensions as well. There are several points to note about these variables. First, there are three of them, one to represent each of the three different data screens. If you had 10 screens, then you would need 10 of them; therefore, each time you add or delete a screen, you must change the parameter list of VSCROLL_SCREEN and add/delete the IF..THEN statements and associated CHR_OUT procedure calls you see at lines 0275-0320. Second, each of these data array variables is represented in its one-dimensional form so that it can be mapped immediately into the one-dimensional video memory array using the external CHR_OUT procedure inside REWRITE_SCR. Third, each of the array variables is prefixed with the reserved word "var," which allows the subprocedure REWRITE_SCR to map the appropriate group of data array characters to the screen from an array variable that can be defined one time and ahead of time in the "typedef.inc" module.

Turning now to the body of the procedure, VSCROLL_SCREEN, note that the control structures represented by REPEAT..UNTIL and CASE..END are both familiar. Be aware that the subprocedure REWRITE_SCR has no parameter list. All the variables that it uses are supplied from the parameter list of its calling procedure, VSCROLL SCREEN. Also, this procedure does not horizontally scroll array data within the display windows; however, expanding this procedure to provide for horizontal scrolling is easily accomplished; all the necessary clues have been provided throughout the book, and you can use this task to test your understanding.

REWRITE_SCR

This subprocedure actually vertically scrolls the window data using the "indexed address method." If you refer back to Chapter 8, you will see that the subprocedure REWRITE_SCR_BY_ROW (rewrite screen by row) is a close analogue; however, there are a few characteristics that make REWRITE_SCR much more flexible. First, the code (lines 0280-0310) allows you to scroll array data of more than just 1 screen window. Which window you scroll depends on which screen you activate. Aside from the group of IF..THEN screen selector statements, the overall structure of REWRITE_SCR is different from its Chapter 8 predecessor only in that it uses no numbers as stand-ins for parameters. Recall the

14 General Principles

earlier version of Chapter 8 where certain numbers were used in the FOR..DO loops and in the formulation of the local variables "bx" and "bp" of the procedure REWRITE_SCR_BYROW. The present procedure is more generally applicable in that parameters (whose values can now be changed) take the place of those fixed numbers. Referring to REWRITE_SCR_BYROW in Chapter 8, you can see that the number "3" is now replaced by the parameter "datarowdepthminusone," that the number "4" is now replaced with "datacolwidthminusone," that "30" is replaced by "datacharsperrow," that "6" is replaced by "datacharspercol," and, finally, that the number "6" is replaced by the parameter "maxcountofdatacharspercol."

The module as a whole has sufficient generality to qualify as a full stand-alone module. Note, however, that if you need to add or delete scrollable data screens, you must change the parameter list of VSCROLL_SCREEN and also make a change in the group of IF..THEN screen selector statements inside the subprocedure REWRITE_SCR.

MODULE: S_D_SC.INC (SAVE AND REDISPLAY SCREEN)

This module is charged with two separate yet related responsibilities. The first is to save a screen image (the whole screen or part of the screen) into a memory array variable. The second is to take a given memory array variable and map it back onto the video screen. The screen saving procedure SAVE_SCREEN is, therefore, the complement of the screen redsiplay procedure RE_DISPLAY_SCREEN. It is only natural that they are included together within the same module. In the context of the overall program, this module is invoked immediately after you have finished scrolling a data window (SAVE_SCREEN) and immediately after you select a screen by pressing <a1><Ret>, <a2><Ret>, or <a3><Ret> (RE_DISPLAY_SCREEN). These procedures together will allow you to call up a window of data, scroll it, exit the scroll, call up some other window and scroll it, and then return to the original window and continue scrolling it from the exact spot where you previously left it. This operation can only be accomplished if you know how to save and redisplay screen images. Recall that a similar though less robust module was developed in Chapter 4. That Chapter 4 module will be referred to throughout this section. Following is the code for the current save/redisplay module:

```
{=============================================================}
0005 {s_d_sc.inc}
0010 {
0015    Read as: "save and redisplay screen include module"
0020    General screen save and redisplay module
0025    On disk as "s_d_sc.inc"
0030 }
0035 {-------------------------------------------------------------}
0040
0045 procedure       SAVE_SCREEN(tlc,tlr,brc,brr      : integer;
0050                             var scr1_array      : s1_arr;
0055                             var scr2_array      : s2_arr;
0060                             var scr3_array      : s3_arr);
0065
0070 var
0075    i,j,k      : integer;
0080    hll,vll    : integer;
0085
0090 Begin     {procedure save_screen}
0095     window(1,1,80,25);
0100     hll := brc - tlc + 1;
0105     vll := brr - tlr + 1;
0110     gotoxy(tlc,tlr);
0115     For i := 1 to vll DO
0120     Begin
0125         j := ((tlr - 1) * 160) + ((tlc - 1) * 2);
0130         For k := 1 to hll DO
0135         Begin
0140             IF (scr1_active = true) THEN
0145                 CHR_IN(j,scr1_array[i,k]);
0150
0155             IF (scr2_active = true) THEN
0160                 CHR_IN(j,scr2_array[i,k]);
0165
0170             IF (scr3_active = true) THEN
0175                 CHR_IN(j,scr3_array[i,k]);
0180             {     FROM,  TO   }
0185             j := j + 2;
0190         End;
0195         tlc := tlc;
0200         tlr := tlr + 1;
0205     End;
0210 End;      {procedure save_screen}
0215 {-------------------------------------------------------------}
0220
0225 procedure       RE_DISPLAY_SCREEN(tlc,tlr,brc,brr      : integer;
0230                                   maxscrdisplaychars   : integer;
0235                                   var scr1_array       : s1_arr;
0240                                   var scr1_buffer      : s1_buf;
0245                                   var scr2_array       : s2_arr;
0250                                   var scr2_buffer      : s2_buf;
0255                                   var scr3_array       : s3_arr;
0260                                   var scr3_buffer      : s3_buf);
0265
0270 var
0275     i,j,k,
0280     hll,vll,
0285     count,
0290     count_of_chars_per_line    : integer;
0295
```

continued...

14 General Principles

...from previous page

```
0300 Begin       {procedure re_display_screen}
0305      window(1,1,80,25);
0310      hll := brc - tlc + 1;
0315      vll := brr - tlr + 1;
0320      count_of_chars_per_line := 1;
0325      count := 0;
0330      For i := 1 to vll DO
0335      Begin
0340              FOR k := 1 to hll DO
0345              Begin
0350                     count := count + 1;
0355                     IF (scr1_active = true) THEN
0360                          scr1_buffer[count] := scr1_array[i,k];
0365
0370                     IF (scr2_active = true) THEN
0375                          scr2_buffer[count] := scr2_array[i,k];
0380
0385                     IF (scr3_active = true) THEN
0390                          scr3_buffer[count] := scr3_array[i,k];
0395              End;
0400      End;
0405      j := ((tlr - 1) * 160) + ((tlc - 1) * 2);
0410      FOR count := 1 to maxscrdisplaychars DO
0415      Begin
0420              IF (scr1_active = true) THEN
0425                   CHR_OUT(j,ORD(scr1_buffer[count]));
0430
0435              IF (scr2_active = true) THEN
0440                   CHR_OUT(j,ORD(scr2_buffer[count]));
0445
0450              IF (scr3_active = true) THEN
0455                   CHR_OUT(j,ORD(scr3_buffer[count]));
0460              { destination(j) , source(ORD(.....) }
0465              count_of_chars_per_line := count_of_chars_per_line + 1;
0470              IF (count_of_chars_per_line > hll) THEN
0475              Begin
0480                   tlr := tlr + 1;
0485                   j := ((tlr - 1) * 160) + ((tlc - 1) * 2);
0490                   count_of_chars_per_line := 1;
0495              End
0500              ELSE
0505                   j := j + 2;
0510      End;
0515 End;       {procedure re_display_screen}
{=======================================================================}
```

S_D_SC.INC: NOTES

SAVE_SCREEN

A close look at the parameter list will show that it consists of two groups of parameters. The first group contains the non-array constants, which are defined for each screen in the "const" section of "typedef.inc." These parameters must always be present as they define the top left and bottom right corners of the rectangular screen area to be saved into memory. As with the previous module, note that these parameters are unsuffixed, signifying their capacity to take on many different values. The second group of parameters contains the memory array variables into which the character contents of the video screen will be saved. These array variables are also defined within "typedef.inc" and are global to all procedures as well.

The number of "var" prefixed array variables will vary depending on the number of screen images you want to save to memory. In this case, you need to save three of them. They are prefixed with the reserved word "var" so that the results of the screen image saving CHR_IN procedure may be passed out to these global variables. To communicate the result to a variable that is more broadly scoped, the procedure must signal its desire to access those variables by attaching the prefix "var." With the proper "var" signal given, the Pascal compiler can then perform the transfer of information from within the procedure and out to the proper globally defined array variable.

Remember, "hll" stands for "horizontal line length" (line 0080), and "vll" stands for "vertical line length." The values of these local variables are derived from the corner parameters and tell how many screen locations down from the starting point (line 0110) and how many locations across you must travel to save the section of video screen that concerns you.

14 General Principles

Look now at lines 0140-0180. Here, you see three IF..THEN statements, each followed by a CHR_IN procedure call using one of the three array parameters from the parameter list. At any given invocation of SAVE_SCREEN, only one of the three screens will be set to the "active" state so that only one will have its contents saved into a memory array variable. The global variable "scr#_active" (# = 1, 2, or 3) enables you to access only one array variable at a time even though more than one (three in this case) is included in the parameter list. This same principle was used in REWRITSC.INC above.

RE_DISPLAY_SCREEN

The parameter list for this external procedure is identical to that for SAVE_SCREEN except for two differences. The first is the existence of the parameter "maxscrdisplaychars" (maximum number of screen display characters). This parameter is equal to the product of the number of video screen rows and the number of video screen columns of a previously saved two-dimensional array variable. It is used in this procedure as the upper limit of the FOR..DO loop (line 0410), which displays the previously saved screen array from memory back onto the screen. If you refer back to Chapter 4, you will see that the main routine defines a two-dimensional array variable "copy_of_part_scr," which is of the type ARRAY[1..12,1..32] of char. If you then look inside the module "scr_s_d.inc," you see in the Declaration Section of the procedure RE_DISPLAY_PART_SCREEN a one-dimensional array of the type "part_scr_disp_buf," which is a one-dimensional array with 12 x 32 or 384 characters. The variable "maxscrdisplaychars" and the number 384 both represent the number of characters that would result from the conversion of a two-dimensional array into a one-dimensional array. The only difference between "maxdisplaychars" and "384" is flexibility. "Maxdisplaychars" is the product of "maxscrrows" and "maxscrcols" and can take on any number of different values up to 2000 (80 cols x 25 rows). The number "384," on the other hand, is obviously fixed by its defined rows (12) and columns (32).

The second difference is that each two-dimensional array variable has its one-dimensional equivalent included as well. If you refer again to Chapter 4, you will see that the one-dimensional equivalent is separately and locally defined under the "type" and "var" headers there. This was done at the time (thereby sacrificing true stand-alone modularity) because the idea of a separate Declaration Module to hold global "const," "type," and "var" declarations (i.e., a "typedef.inc" module) had not yet been developed.

General Principles 14

The body of the current procedure is very similar to that developed back in Chapter 4. The FOR..DO loop between lines 0330 and 0400 converts the already saved two-dimensional array (e.g., "scr3_ array") into its screen mappable one-dimensional equivalent (e.g., "scr3_ buffer"). The only difference is that only one of the three possible screens will be converted, depending on which Boolean variable (lines 0420, 0435, 0450) is activated or set to the value of "true."

The FOR..DO loop between lines 0410 and 0510 performs the crucial task of mapping the one-dimensional array variable onto the appropriate place on the video screen using the external procedure CHR OUT. This mapping is an almost instantaneous reappearace of the previously saved screen image. Note again that only one of the three possible screens will be redisplayed and that this will depend on which one of the three has been activated from the driver routine (lines 0420-0450).

As with the previous module, this one is quite capable of general use in many different program applications. To add or delete screen images, you must change the parameter lists and the IF..THEN statements in the procedure bodies as discussed above. Before leaving this section, note again that all the array variable definitions used have been set up and fully defined ahead of time in a separate module called "typedef.inc." In your own applications programs, you must first create a general Declaration Module similar to the one developed in this chapter. This module will organize the large number of parameters needed to give your programs multiple window save/redisplay and scrolling capabilities.

MODULE: MULT_SCR.DRV

To appreciate what this driver module does, read over the HEADER procedure in the code that follows (line 0615). There you will see that you can bring up onto the screen (in any order) any 1 of 3 different screen windows and that once the window is displayed on the screen you can scroll its data vertically using the Up and Down Arrow keys on the Numeric Keypad. To end the scrolling of data in the active window, just press the <Ret> key. You are free to "add" another window by again pressing one of <a1><Ret>, <a2><Ret>, or <a3><Ret> and then using the Up and Down Arrow keys to scroll its data. You can quit the program by pressing <q>. Following is the code for this driver module:

14 General Principles

```
{================================================================}
0005  program mult_scr(input,output);
0010  {
0015    Applications program Chapter 14
0020    On disk as "mult_scr.drv"
0025  }
0030  {================================================================
0035  {$i typedef.inc}
0040  {================================================================}
0045  const
0050        a1 = 146;         {ascii "a" = 97 ; ascii "1" = 49}
0055        a2 = 147;
0060        a3 = 148;
0065        q  = 113;         {ascii "q" = 113}
0070
0075        bell = #$07;
0080
0085  var
0090        i                 : integer;
0095        screen_choice     : str3;
0100        ascii_sum         : integer;
0105        character         : char;
0110        exit              : boolean;
0115        saved_i_tot1,saved_i_tot2,saved_i_tot3,
0120        saved_k_tot1,saved_k_tot2,saved_k_tot3   : integer;
0125
0130  {================================================================}
0135  {$i chrinout.inc}
0140  {$i windows.inc}
0145  {$i rewritsc.inc}   {for scrolling data in screen windows}
0150  {$i s_d_sc.inc}     {for save/redisplay sections of video screen}
0155  {================================================================}
0160
0165  procedure        CREATE_SCREEN_ARRAYS(maxdatarows     : integer;
0170                                        maxdatacols     : integer;
0175                              maxcountofdatacharspercol : integer;
0180                                    var scr1array       : s1arr;
0185                                    var scr1buffer      : s1buf;
0190                                    var scr2array       : s2arr;
0195                                    var scr2buffer      : s2buf;
0200                                    var scr3array       : s3arr;
0205                                    var scr3buffer      : s3buf);
0210
0215  var
0220        i,k,c : integer;
0225        count : integer;
0230
0235  Begin     {procedure create_screen_arrays}
0240       For i := 1 to maxdatarows DO
0245       Begin
0250            For k := 1 to maxdatacols DO
0255            Begin
0260                 IF (scr1_active = true) THEN
0265                      STR(i:3 , scr1array[i,k]);
0270
0275                 IF (scr2_active = true) THEN
0280                      STR(i:3 , scr2array[i,k]);
0285
0290                 IF (scr3_active = true) THEN
0295                      STR(i:3 , scr3array[i,k]);
0300            End;
0305       End;
```

continued...

...from previous page

```
0310
0315          count := 0;
0320          For i := 1 to maxdatarows DO
0325          Begin
0330               For k := 1 to maxdatacols DO
0335               Begin
0340                    For c := 1 to maxcountofdatacharspercol DO
0345                    Begin
0350                         count := count + 1;
0355                         IF (scr1_active = true) THEN
0360                              scr1buffer[count] :=
0365                              COPY(scr1array[i,k],c,1);
0370
0375                         IF (scr2_active = true) THEN
0380                              scr2buffer[count] :=
0385                              COPY(scr2array[i,k],c,1);
0390
0395                         IF (scr3_active = true) THEN
0400                              scr3buffer[count] :=
0405                              COPY(scr3array[i,k],c,1);
0410                    End;
0415               End;
0420          End;
0425 End;     {procedure create_screen_arrays}
0430 {------------------------------------------------------------------}
0435
0440 procedure     INIT_SCREEN(tlc,tlr,brc,brr : integer;
0445                          datarowdepth    : integer;
0450                          datacolwidth    : integer;
0455                          var scr1array   : s1arr;
0460                          var scr2array   : s2arr;
0465                          var scr3array   : s3arr);
0470
0475 var
0480     i,k,
0485     col,row   : integer;
0490
0495 Begin    {procedure init_screen}
0500     window(tlc,tlr,brc,brr);clrscr;window(1,1,80,25);
0505     WINDOW_BORDER(tlc,tlr,brc,brr,3);
0510     gotoxy(tlc + 2 ,tlr + 1) ; col := WHEREX ; row := WHEREY;
0515     FOR i := 1 to datarowdepth DO
0520     Begin
0525          FOR k := 1 to datacolwidth DO
0530          Begin
0535               IF (scr1_active = true) THEN
0540                    write(scr1array[i,k]);
0545
0550               IF (scr2_active = true) THEN
0555                    write(scr2array[i,k]);
0560
0565               IF (scr3_active = true) THEN
0570                    write(scr3array[i,k]);
0575                    {* delay(100); *}
0580          End;
0585          col := col ; row := row + 2;
0590          gotoxy(col,row);
0595     End;
0600 End;     {procedure init_screen}
0605 {------------------------------------------------------------------}
```

continued...

14 General Principles

...from previous page

```
0610
0615   procedure       HEADER;
0620
0625   Begin      {procedure header}
0630        TEXTCOLOR(0) ; TEXTBACKGROUND(15);
0635        gotoxy(26,1);write(' MULTIPLE SCREENS APPLICATION ');
0640        gotoxy(35,2);write(' CHAPTER 14 ');
0645        gotoxy(36,20);write(' CONTROL: ');
0650        TEXTCOLOR(15) ; TEXTBACKGROUND(0);
0655        gotoxy(5,22);write('<a1>  = add window1');
0660        gotoxy(30,22);write('<a2>  = add window2');
0665        gotoxy(55,22);write('<a3>  = add window3');
0670        gotoxy(9,23);write('Use Vertical Arrow Keys to Scroll.');
0675        gotoxy(45,23);write('Press <Ret> to Exit Scroll');
0680        gotoxy(32,24);write('<q> = Exit Program');
0685   End;      {procedure header}
0690   {-------------------------------------------------------------------}
0695
0700   Begin     {driver}
0705        window(1,1,80,25);clrscr;
0710        HEADER;
0715        scr1_active := true;     {activate screen1}
0720        CREATE_SCREEN_ARRAYS(maxdatarows1 , maxdatacols1,
0725                             maxcountofdatacharspercol1,
0730                             scr1array , scr1buffer,
0735                             scr2array , scr2buffer,
0740                             scr3array , scr3buffer);
0745        scr1_active := false;    {deactivate screen1}
0750
0755        scr2_active := true;     {activate screen2}
0760        CREATE_SCREEN_ARRAYS(maxdatarows2 , maxdatacols2,
0765                             maxcountofdatacharspercol2,
0770                             scr1array , scr1buffer,
0775                             scr2array , scr2buffer,
0780                             scr3array , scr3buffer);
0785        scr2_active := false;    {deactivate screen2}
0790
0795        scr3_active := true;     {activate screen3}
0800        CREATE_SCREEN_ARRAYS(maxdatarows3 , maxdatacols3,
0805                             maxcountofdatacharspercol3,
0810                             scr1array , scr1buffer,
0815                             scr2array , scr2buffer,
0820                             scr3array , scr3buffer);
0825        scr3_active := false;    {deactivate screen3}
0830
0835        write(bell);
0840        saved_i_tot1 := 1 ; saved_i_tot2 := 1 ; saved_i_tot3 := 1;
0845        saved_k_tot1 := 1 ; saved_k_tot2 := 1 ; saved_k_tot3 := 1;
0850        REPEAT
0855            BUFLEN := 3;
0860            exit := false;
0865            ascii_sum := 0;
0870            gotoxy(40,21) ; write('   ') ; gotoxy(40,21);{3 blanks}
0875            readln(screen_choice);       {type it in from keyboard}
0880            FOR i := 1 to LENGTH(screen_choice) DO
0885            Begin
0890                character := COPY(screen_choice, i , 1);
0895                ascii_sum := ascii_sum + ORD(character);
0900            End;
```

continued...

...from previous page

```
0905            CASE (ascii_sum) OF
0910
0915            a1  : Begin
0920                    scr1_active := true;
0925                    IF scr1_init = false THEN
0930                    Begin
0935                            INIT_SCREEN(tlc1,tlr1,brc1,brr1,
0940                                        datarowdepth1,
0945                                        datacolwidth1,
0950                                        scr1array,
0955                                        scr2array,
0960                                        scr3array);
0965
0970                            VSCROLL_SCREEN(tlc1,tlr1,
0975                                           saved_i_tot1,
0980                                           saved_k_tot1,
0985                                           datarowdepthminusone1,
0990                                           datacolwidthminusone1,
0995                                           datacharsperrow1,
1000                                           datacharspercol1,
1005                                           maxcountofdatacharspercol1,
1010                                           max_allowed_i_tot1,
1015                                           scr1buffer,
1020                                           scr2buffer,
1025                                           scr3buffer);
1030                            scr1_init := true;
1035                    End
1040                    ELSE
1045                    Begin
1050                            RE_DISPLAY_SCREEN(tlc1,tlr1,brc1,brr1,
1055                                              maxscrdisplaychars1,
1060                                              scr1_array,
1065                                              scr1_buffer,
1070                                              scr2_array,
1075                                              scr2_buffer,
1080                                              scr3_array,
1085                                              scr3_buffer);
1090
1095                            VSCROLL_SCREEN(tlc1,tlr1,
1100                                           saved_i_tot1,
1105                                           saved_k_tot1,
1110                                           datarowdepthminusone1,
1115                                           datacolwidthminusone1,
1120                                           datacharsperrow1,
1125                                           datacharspercol1,
1130                                           maxcountofdatacharspercol1,
1135                                           max_allowed_i_tot1,
1140                                           scr1buffer,
1145                                           scr2buffer,
1150                                           scr3buffer);
1155                    End;
1160                    SAVE_SCREEN(tlc1,tlr1,brc1,brr1,
1165                                scr1_array,
1170                                scr2_array,
1175                                scr3_array);
1180                    gotoxy(40,21);
1185                    scr1_active := false;
1190                End;
```

continued...

14   General Principles

...from previous page

```
1195
1200            a2    : Begin
1205                      scr2_active := true;
1210                      IF scr2_init = false THEN
1215                      Begin
1220                          INIT_SCREEN(tlc2,tlr2,brc2,brr2,
1225                                      datarowdepth2,
1230                                      datacolwidth2,
1235                                      scr1array,
1240                                      scr2array,
1245                                      scr3array);
1250
1255                          VSCROLL_SCREEN(tlc2,tlr2,
1260                                         saved_i_tot2,
1265                                         saved_k_tot2,
1270                                         datarowdepthminusone2,
1275                                         datacolwidthminusone2,
1280                                         datacharsperrow2,
1285                                         datacharspercol2,
1290                                         maxcountofdatacharspercol2,
1295                                         max_allowed_i_tot2,
1300                                         scr1buffer,
1305                                         scr2buffer,
1310                                         scr3buffer);
1315                         scr2_init := true;
1320                      End
1325                      ELSE
1330                      Begin
1335                          RE_DISPLAY_SCREEN(tlc2,tlr2,brc2,brr2,
1340                                            maxscrdisplaychars2,
1345                                            scr1_array,
1350                                            scr1_buffer,
1355                                            scr2_array,
1360                                            scr2_buffer,
1365                                            scr3_array,
1370                                            scr3_buffer);
1375
1380                          VSCROLL_SCREEN(tlc2,tlr2,
1385                                         saved_i_tot2,
1390                                         saved_k_tot2,
1395                                         datarowdepthminusone2,
1400                                         datacolwidthminusone2,
1405                                         datacharsperrow2,
1410                                         datacharspercol2,
1415                                         maxcountofdatacharspercol2,
1420                                         max_allowed_i_tot2,
1425                                         scr1buffer,
1430                                         scr2buffer,
1435                                         scr3buffer);
1440                      End;
1445                      SAVE_SCREEN(tlc2,tlr2,brc2,brr2,
1450                                  scr1_array,
1455                                  scr2_array,
1460                                  scr3_array);
1465                      gotoxy(40,21);
1470                      scr2_active := false;
1475                    End;
1480
```

continued...

...from previous page

```
1485            a3   : Begin
1490                     scr3_active := true;
1495                     IF scr3_init = false THEN
1500                     Begin
1505                         INIT_SCREEN(tlc3,tlr3,brc3,brr3,
1510                                     datarowdepth3,
1515                                     datacolwidth3,
1520                                     scr1array,
1525                                     scr2array,
1530                                     scr3array);
1535
1540                         VSCROLL_SCREEN(tlc3,tlr3,
1545                                        saved_i_tot3,
1550                                        saved_k_tot3,
1555                                        datarowdepthminusone3,
1560                                        datacolwidthminusone3,
1565                                        datacharsperrow3,
1570                                        datacharspercol3,
1575                                        maxcountofdatacharspercol3,
1580                                        max_allowed_i_tot3,
1585                                        scr1buffer,
1590                                        scr2buffer,
1595                                        scr3buffer);
1600                         scr3_init := true;
1605                     End
1610                     ELSE
1615                     Begin
1620                         RE_DISPLAY_SCREEN(tlc3,tlr3,brc3,brr3,
1625                                           maxscrdisplaychars3,
1630                                           scr1_array,
1635                                           scr1_buffer,
1640                                           scr2_array,
1645                                           scr2_buffer,
1650                                           scr3_array,
1655                                           scr3_buffer);
1660
1665                         VSCROLL_SCREEN(tlc3,tlr3,
1670                                        saved_i_tot3,
1675                                        saved_k_tot3,
1680                                        datarowdepthminusone3,
1685                                        datacolwidthminusone3,
1690                                        datacharsperrow3,
1695                                        datacharspercol3,
1700                                        maxcountofdatacharspercol3,
1705                                        max_allowed_i_tot3,
1710                                        scr1buffer,
1715                                        scr2buffer,
1720                                        scr3buffer);
1725                     End;
1730                     SAVE_SCREEN(tlc3,tlr3,brc3,brr3,
1725                     End;
1730                     SAVE_SCREEN(tlc3,tlr3,brc3,brr3,
1735                                 scr1_array,
1740                                 scr2_array,
1745                                 scr3_array);
1750                     gotoxy(40,21);
1755                     scr3_active := false;
1760                   End;
1765
```

continued...

14   General Principles

...from previous page

```
1770                    q    : exit := true
1775
1780               ELSE
1785                         {TRY ANOTHER KEYBOARD ENTRY}
1790
1795               END;     {case statement}
1800
1805        UNTIL (exit = true);
1810 End.        {driver}
{=======================================================================}
```

MULT_SCR.DRV: NOTES

Look at the Declaration Section first. "Typedef.inc" has been inserted prior to listing any of the driver's own constants or variables. Remember that "typedef.inc" has its own "const, "type," and "var" declaration headers and that it is legal to have more than one set of these headers as long as there is no duplication of definitions within the different headers. Next (by way of the ".inc" files at lines 0135-0150) all of the external modules and their procedures have been declared. In keeping with the adopted convention, they have been located just ahead of the coding for the driver's three internal procedures. Before considering the overall operation of the driver, look at two of these internal procedures.

CREATE_SCREEN_ARRAYS

This procedure creates the scrollable data arrays that will be used by the program's vertical scrolling routine. The procedure itself is broken into three main parts: the parameter list, the creation of the two-dimensional array, and then the creation of the equivalent one-dimensional array.

The parameter list itself is comprised of two parts (lines 0165-0205). The first is the group of parameters that take on the constant values passed in from the procedure calls located in the driver routine. Under the naming convention, note that their screen number reference suffixes have been omitted to show that they can take on the values from any one of the three different sets of screen defining constants. The second part of the parameter list is the "var'd" one- and two-dimensional array variables for each of the different screens. Unlike the first three parameters, these variables must refer *specifically* to the arrays they represent because this procedure creates the array data, which is then passed out to the globally defined array variables. Address reference and the "var" prefix in a procedure variable in one sense suspend the ordinary operation of the Pascal scope rules and allow information to be passed from a local procedure into global variables with greater scope or accessability.

In this case, there are three screens and, therefore, six global array variables that must be capable of being changed from within this procedure. The word "changed" is used here to mean being filled up with data from within the procedure.

The first FOR..DO loop of the procedure creates the two-dimensional data array. So, for example, if Screen 3 were set to active, then "maxdatarows3" would be set to 24; "maxdatacols3" would be set to 6; and "maxcountofdatacharspercol3" would be set to 3. Thus, a two-dimensional array is created with 24 rows, 6 columns per row, each row/column element having 3 characters. With Screen 3 active, you would be referencing only "scr3array" and "scr3buffer" in the parameter list. The other four array variables would not be used at this time. Note, however, that all "var" prefixed output array parameters must be included in the procedure parameter list even if they are not all used during a given procedure call. The potentially long length of these parameter lists is part of the price that must be paid to acquire generality in the procedures. This procedure will create an array of data whose rows are filled with the row number currently being processed in the FOR..DO loop (line 0295 in the example). See Figure

The second FOR..DO loop starting at line 0320 creates the one-dimensional equivalent of the two-dimensional array just created. As you can see from the Screen 3 example at line 0395, each character within each "i"/"k" array location is split out one character at a time by the built-in COPY procedure and assigned its proper place (indexed by "count") in the one-dimensional data array variable "scr3buffer."

14 General Principles

INIT_SCREEN (Initialize Screen)

Once all the array data has been created and safely stored into the array memory variables, this procedure (depending on which screen is activated) writes onto the video screen the first few lines of the scrolling data array in preparation for the forthcoming vertical data scrolling operation. The non-array parameters refer to physical aspects of the screen that you need to know to perform the initialization. So if Screen 3 were activated, then the area of the screen to be written to would use

```
tlc          = tlc3          = 57
tlr          = tlr3          = 4
brc          = brc3          = 78
brr          = brr3          = 12
datarowdepth = datarowdepth3 = 4
datacolwidth = datacolwidth3 = 6
```

That screen area would also use the contents of the first four rows and six columns of the array variable "scr3array," which would be written onto the screen by lines 0565-0570. Note that line 0510 represents a small adjustment to the top left column and top left row coordinates of the screen window to allow the initialized array to start at the predefined screen location as seen in Figure 14.1. Line 0585 is a formatting line that controls where on the screen the next row and column of the array will be written to. Note also that if "row" is not adjusted as "row + 2" but adjusted as "row + 1" instead, you would need a "datarowdepth" of 8 instead of 4 for Screen 3.

Finally, note the use of the "var" prefixed parameter variables in this procedure. In CREATE_SCREEN_ARRAYS, the "var" prefix allowed that procedure to alter the global array variables from the "inside-out," that is, from the local procedure out to the global variable. In the present procedure, the "var" prefix still allows access by the procedure to global variables, but this time only in the sense of looking at (or referring to) an array element from the "outside-in" for the purpose of writing that element to the screen and not altering it.

General Principles 14

Now look at how the body of the driver routine controls the operation of all the external and internal procedures previously described. The body of the driver routine is divided into two main parts. The first part (lines 0715-0835) is responsible for creating the data that will be scrolling within the screen windows. As you have seen, each invocation of CREATE_SCREEN_ARRAYS will create a different scrollable data array depending on which screen has been activated.

The second section enclosed within the large REPEAT..UNTIL loop controls the program as described at the beginning of this section. After you select the screen number that you want to call up (line 0875), control is passed to the CASE..END statement located between lines 0905 and 1795. Assume that you have pressed <a3><Ret> to activate Screen 3. Selecting Screen 3 automatically transfers program control to line 1485 where you continue with the execution of the code. Line 1490 sets the Boolean variable "scr3 active" to "true." All of the Screen 3 parameters as defined in "typedef.inc" are now ready for use in the procedures that follow. At this point, there are two different paths that can be taken.

If Screen 3 has *not* been selected previously, then the Boolean variable "scr3_init" is "false," and the code between lines 1500 and 1605 is executed. Here, the procedure INIT_SCREEN is called, using all the parameters that were previously defined in "typedef.inc." You can see the action of INIT_SCREEN in the first four rows of data in the small window at the right-hand side of the video screen. Once the screen is initialized, the procedure VSCROLL_SCREEN (line 1540), with its required complement of parameters, is called. Pressing the Up and Down Arrow keys enables you to scroll the 24 data rows of Screen 3. When you exit the scroll by pressing the <Ret> key, three things happen. First, the Boolean variable "scr3_init" (screen 3 now initialized) is set to "true." Second, the external procedure SAVE_SCREEN (line 1730) is activated and will save to memory the exact image of Screen 3 as it was immediately prior to pressing the <Ret> key. Third, execution skips over the ELSE statement section (lines 1610-1725) and sets the Boolean variable "scr3_active" back to "false" (line 1755). Since you did not press the <q> key, the Boolean variable "exit" is still "false," and an encounter with the UNTIL statement at line 1805 sends execution back up to its REPEAT statement at line 0850. At this point, you could select any one of the three screens by pressing <a1><Ret>, <a2><Ret>, or <a3><Ret> at line 0875. Again, select <a3><Ret>. When <a3><Ret> is selected, code execution inside the CASE..END will again jump to line 1485 and reactivate Screen 3.

351

14 General Principles

This time, "scr3_init" has the value of "true," lines 1500-1605 are skipped, and lines 1615-1725 of the ELSE section are executed instead. At line 1620, the external procedure REDISPLAY_SCREEN, with all the predefined Screen 3 parameters, is called. The screen image previously saved by SAVE_SCREEN is immediately redisplayed to the video screen. It will appear as if nothing has happened, since the image that was left on the screen from the time before is simply overwritten. You will appreciate how the memory images are redisplayed once you save and redisplay the screens that overlap each other.

Once the screen image is redisplayed from memory onto the screen, the procedure VSCROLL_SCREEN (line 1665) is called, and you can continue to scroll from where you previously left off. Pressing <Ret> causes two things to happen ("scr3 init" will be "false" until you exit the program). First, SAVE_SCREEN is activated, and the screen image as it was prior to pressing <Ret> will be saved to memory. Second, "scr3_active" will again be deactivated (set to "false") prior to exiting from this section.

What was said with respect to Screen 3 applies as well to Screen 1 and Screen 2 or to as many screens as you might care to define. Remember, though, that each screen you define will require its own set of parameters inside "typedef.inc" and its own driver routine control section similar to the one seen for Screen 3 (lines 1485-1760). To see how the procedures all connect and flow together, look at Figure 14.5. Screen 2, which overlaps the others, has been omitted to more clearly show how the procedures work together.

General Principles **14**

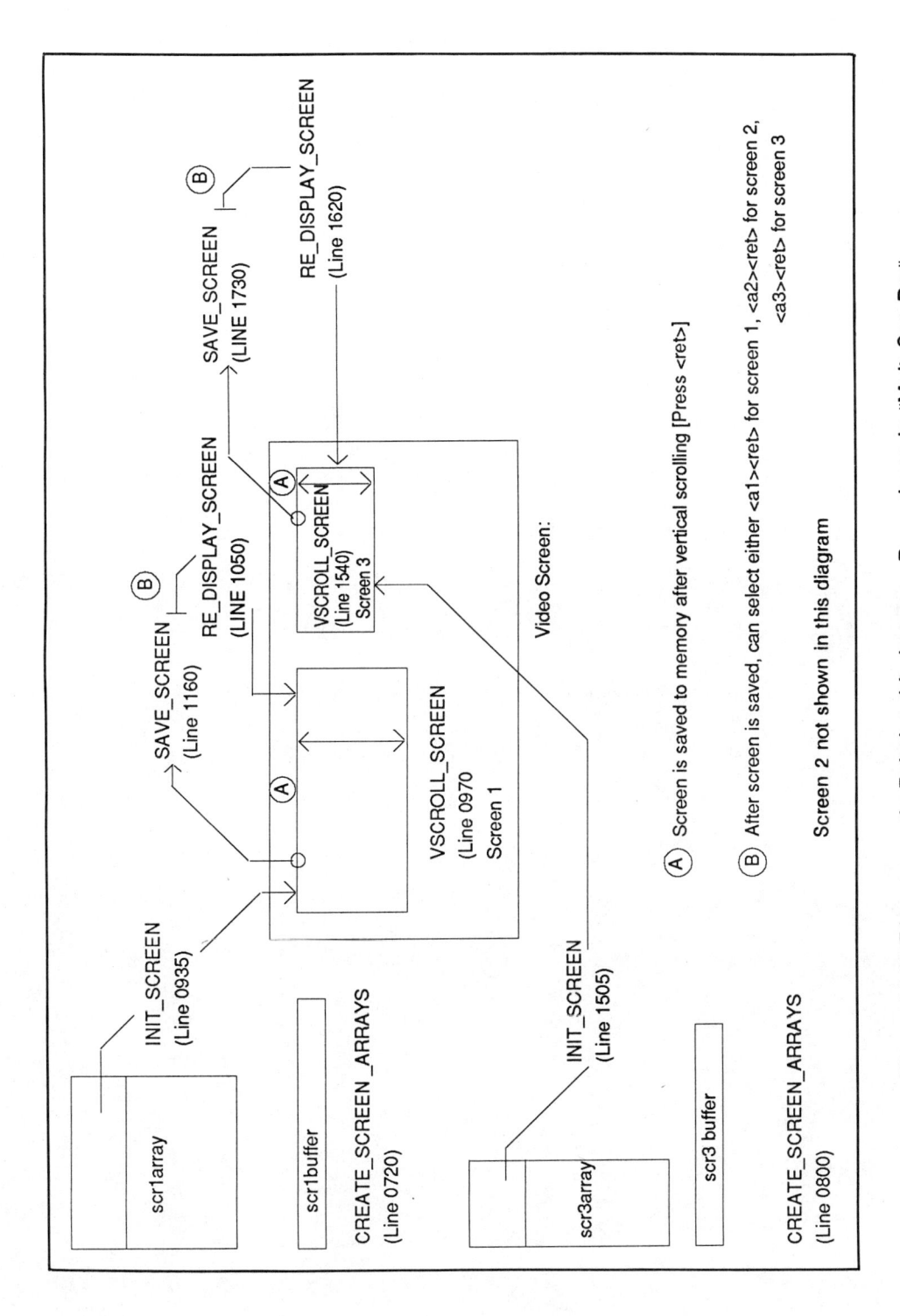

Figure 14.5 Diagrammatic Relationship between Procedures in "Mult_Scr_Drv"

353

CHAPTER 15

MORE GENERAL PRINCIPLES

15 More General Principles

In the previous chapter, with the screen save/redisplay and screen scrolling modules you learned about in Parts One and Two, a method was developed to make them more flexible and adaptable through the inclusion of an External Definition Module called "typedef.inc." Converting the previously number-specific screen I/O routines into a more robust stand-alone form was a large and important step. Still, one deficiency needs attention. The new scrolling module hasn't been provided with any horizontal scrolling capability, which is quite a limitation. In this chapter, one of the objectives is to show you how to build in that capability, using as a base the same driver routine and modules developed in Chapter 14.

In the second half of this chapter, what you've learned from this book will be put into perspective. In particular, a general model for the driver routine is discussed that you can use (and/or adapt) when you write your own applications programs using the screen I/O techniques developed in this book. This model is intended only as a guide, and through time and experience, your own models will evolve in response to your requirements and programming style.

INSTALLATION OF HORIZONTAL SCROLLING

Here, horizontal scrolling will be installed for Screen 3 from the previous chapter. Screens 1 and 2 will be left as is. You may convert them later if you want, using the method outlined next.

The installation process requires that you look at three modules: "typedef.inc," "rewritsc.inc," and "mult_scr.drv." After each of these three modules has been altered, it will be given a slightly different name. Once named, a different set of modules will be created from those originals in the previous chapter. This set performs the same tasks as those in Chapter 14 but with the added feature of horizontal scrolling for Screen 3 plus the potential of adding the same to Screens 1 and 2. Once you become skilled at the installation process, you can create and install data scrolling screens, some of which can only be scrolled horizontally, some only vertically, and some with capability in both horizontal and vertical directions.

More General Principles 15

TYPDEF15.INC (TYPEDEF.INC FROM CHAPTER 14)

Assume for now that you want to expand Screen 3 from six data columns to 16 data columns; that is, you want to increase the number of three-character (str3) data columns from 6 to 16. To do this, the following changes are made under the subheader {SCREEN 3...}:

- *Change* "datacharsperrow3 *from* 18 *to* 48
  {16 cols. × 3 chars/data column}

- *Change* "maxdatacols3" *from* 6 *to* 16

- *Change* "maxdatachars3 *from* 432 *to* 1152
  {24 rows × 16 cols. × 3}

The next change is to alter the bracketed "{typedef.inc}" to read "{typdef15.inc}." This external module will be compiled when the external procedure call "{$i typdef15.inc}" is made from the driver routine.

The last change to make to "typedef.inc" from Chapter 14 is to add three new constants: "max_allowed_k_tot1," max_allowed_k_tot2," and "max_allowed_k_tot3." Add these constants immediately after their "max_allowed_i_tot#" counterparts in the "const" section. These constants do for horizontal scrolling what the "max_allowed_i_tot#" values did for vertical scrolling. They prevent the horizontal scroll from exceeding its maximum column index value of 16 inside the procedure VHSCROLL_SCR. (After you read the section about VHSCROLL SCREEN, reread this section again.) In Screen 3, for example, this is achieved by assigning "max_allowed_k_tot3" the value 11. Why 11? Imagine that you are at the largest right-hand column in the horizontal scrolling window (column 16). Add to this the fact that the display screen is defined to hold only 6 data columns. So what is the index number of the data column at the left-hand side of the screen window? The answer is 11:

Data Column Index:

| 11 | 12 | 13 | 14 | 15 | 16 |

15 More General Principles

One simple way to derive this number is to count backwards from right to left inside the data display window. A second way to derive this number is to perform the following subtraction:

    maxdatacols3 - datacolwidthminusone3 : that is,
       16   -   5   = 11

Notice that you must assign the value of 0 to both "max_allowed_k_tot1" and "max_allowed_k_tot2" because screens 1 and 2 do *not* have horizontal scrolling.

Once the above changes have been made, use your Text Editor or DOS to change the name of the module *from* "typedef.inc" *to* "typdef15.inc," and then save this new file to disk under the new name.

REWRSC15.INC (REWRITSC.INC FROM CHAPTER 14)

Now load the module "rewritsc.inc" into your Editor and make the following changes and additions:

- *Change* the bracketed include file symbol "{rewrite.inc}" to read: "{rewrsc15.inc}" (do *not* include the quotation marks).

- *Change* the name of the procedure from VSCROLL_SCREEN to VHSCROLL_SCREEN to show that it can perform both vertical and horizontal scrolling.

- In the parameter list of the newly named VHSCROLL_SCREEN procedure, *add* the parameter "max_allowed_k_tot" immediately after "max_allowed_i_tot." Note: *no* number suffix.

- In the "const" section of VHSCROLL_SCREEN *add* the statements "scroll_left = #$4b;" and "scroll_right = #$4d;" immediately after the "scroll_down...." statement.

- Inside the body of VHSCROLL_SCREEN, install the following scrolling control code immediately following the code for "scroll_down":

358

More General Principles 15

```
scroll_left :  Begin     {Press Left Arrow Key}
                  i_tot := i_tot + 0;
                  k_tot := k_tot - 1;
                  IF (k_tot < 1) THEN
                  Begin
                        k_tot := 1;
                        goto rep_read;
                  End;
                  REWRITE_SCR;
               End;    {scroll_left}

scroll_right : Begin     {Press Right Arrow Key}
                  i_tot := i_tot + 0;
                  k_tot := k_tot + 1;
                  IF (k_tot > max_allowed_k_tot) THEN
                  Begin
                        k_tot := max_allowed_k_tot;
                        goto rep_read;
                  End;
                  REWRITE_SCR;
               End;    {scroll_right}
```

Once you've made the above changes and additions, use your Text Editor or DOS to change the module name *from* "rewritsc.inc" *to* "rewrsc15.inc," and then save this module to disk.

MULTSC15.DRV (MULT_SCR.DRV FROM CHAPTER 14)

Finally, load the module MULT_SCR.DRV into your Editor and perform the following changes and additions:

- *Change* "{$i typedef.inc}" to read as "{$i typdef15.inc}"

- *Change* "{$i rewritsc.inc}" to read as "{$i rewrsc15.inc}"

- *Change* the internal procedure name CREATE_SCREEN ARRAYS to read CREATE_SCREEN_ARRAYS15 and then be sure to make the same change at the three places at the start of the body of the driver routine as well.

- *Change* the code inside the renamed CREATE_SCREEN ARRAYS15 *from* this:

359

15 More General Principles

```
IF (scr3_active = true) THEN
    STR(i:3 , scr3array[i,k]);
```

to this:

```
IF (scr3_active = true) THEN
    scr3array[i,k] := CONCAT('  ' + chr(224 + RANDOM(29)));
```

What does this new code do exactly? It quickly and simply creates some screen data that will show you whether it has been scrolled horizontally or vertically (ask yourself: how could a horizontal row of 1's show a horizontal scroll?). What the assignment statement does each time it is encountered is to create a three-character data array element. The first two characters are blanks, and the third is an ASCII character symbol whose value lies between chr(224) and chr(252) inclusive. Recall that RANDOM(29) selects at random any integer between 0 and 28 inclusive.

- *Change* the "write" statements in the procedure HEADER as follows:

  ```
  gotoxy(35,2);write(' CHAPTER 15 ');
  and
  gotoxy(13,23);write(' Use Arrow Keys to Scroll.');
  ```

- In the body of the driver routine, *change* VSCROLL SCREEN to read VHSCROLL_SCREEN. You must make six changes, two for each of the CASE selectors: "a1," "a2," and "a3" inside the CASE..END statement.

- Under CASE selector "a1," *add* the constant "max_allowed_k tot1" to the parameter list of the newly named VHSCROLL SCREEN. Put it immediately after "max_allowed_i_tot1." You must do this for both VHSCROLL_SCREEN procedure calls under "a1."

- Under CASE selector "a2," *add* the constant "max_allowed_k tot2" to the parameter list of the newly named VHSCROLL SCREEN. Put it immediately after "max_allowed_i_tot2." You must do this for both VHSCROLL_SCREEN procedure calls under "a2."

More General Principles 15

- Under CASE selector "a3," *add* the constant "max_allowed_k_tot3" to the parameter list of the newly named VHSCROLL_SCREEN. Put it immediately after "max_allowed_i_tot3." You must do this for both VHSCROLL_SCREEN procedure calls under "a3."

Notice that the constants "max_allowed_k_tot1" and "max_allowed_k_tot2" have been included and assigned values (of 0) even though they are not going to be used at this time. You *must* do this to ensure that the number of parameters within each of the six calls to the procedure VHSCROLL_SCREEN inside the driver exactly matches the number of parameters in the procedure VHSCROLL_SCREEN located inside the external procedure module "rewrsc15.inc."

Once the above changes have been made, rename MULT_SCR.DRV as MULTSC15.DRV and save it to disk as well. Now, if you've made all of the above changes and additions correctly, you will find on running the module that Screen 1 and Screen 2 work exactly as before. Screen 3, however, will be filled with a random group of Greek letters that you may scroll both vertically and horizontally.

From now on, whenever you want to add or delete display windows, change their scrolling directions, or alter data array row/column dimensions, all you need to do is make the appropriate changes to the values inside the external Declaration module, "typdef15.inc." Feel free to choose your own module names.

OVERALL ORGANIZATION

Before concluding, a few ideas on program organization that could act as a starting framework to guide you in the development of your own applications programs will be discussed. It would be unfair to leave you with a set of screen I/O tools without at least suggesting an overall organizational scheme to connect them up with your own applications algorithms. Please note that this is only a suggested framework to start with and that once you begin to write your own applications programs, your own method of organization will naturally evolve. This scheme is only a suggested starting point.

15 More General Principles

A diagram of the overall framework for the driver programs of Chapters 14 and 15 appears in Figure 15.1. Look at the diagram's main features. Observe that the driver routine itself is broken down into three main parts: Declarations, Procedures, and Body. Each of these parts will be discussed in turn.

Declarations

The Declaration Section has been subdivided into two sections: External Declarations and Internal Declarations. The convention is to place the External Declarations before the Internal Declarations. The External Declarations contain all of the external Constant, Type, and Variable declarations needed to perform save/redisplay and scrolling operations on data entered onto the video screen. It is important to modularize and separate the declaration (as embodied in the "typdef15.inc" module) to facilitate any future adjustments that you might want to make. As hinted above, these changes could include the addition/deletion of whole screens, changes in screen location of the display windows, changes in the row and/or column dimensions of the scrollable array data itself, changes in the horizontal/vertical scrolling characteristics of the array data, and the like. Any of these alterations can be made easily as long as you have all the required information centrally located in one place.

Immediately following are the Internal Declarations specific to the driver module. These constants and variables are predominantly control-type variables whose job is to organize and control the execution of the many procedures located throughout the body of the driver routine.

Procedures

The Procedure Section is also divided into two different parts. The first contains the declarations of all of the External procedures used by the driver but located in separate files. The second consists of the Internal procedures located inside the driver routine. By convention, the External procedure calls have been set up ahead of the Internal ones so that the latter may reference the former if required.

More General Principles 15

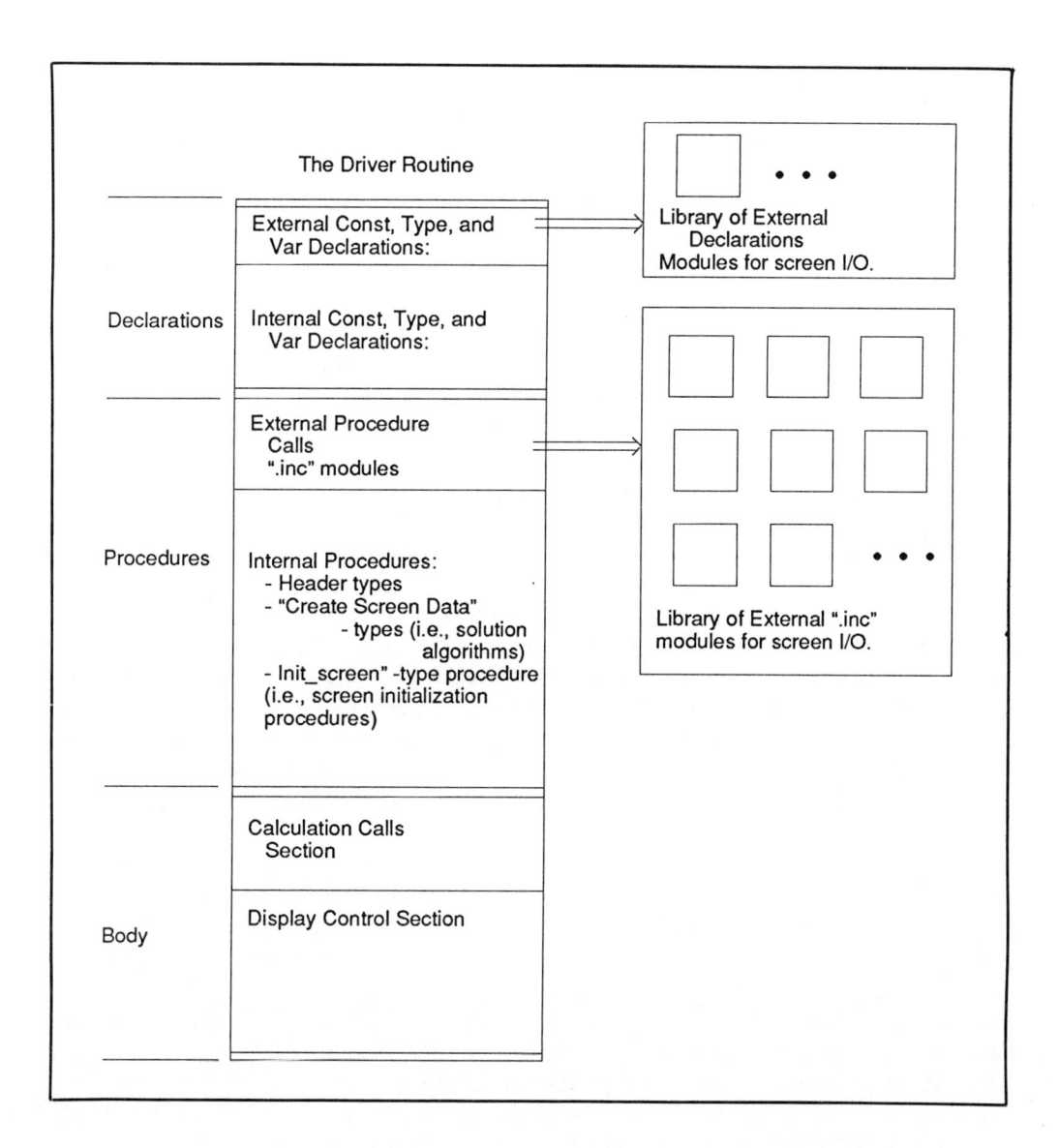

Figure 15.1 Overal Organization of Screen-oriented Applications Driver Program

15 More General Principles

The External procedures are all those stand-alone screen I/O routines that have been developed throughout this book. They handle all the screen I/O activities considered the common denominators of any good applications program, such as screen scrolling, data input/validation, and screen save/redisplay modules. By convention, the External screen I/O modules are distinguished by suffixing them with ".inc." Since these modules actually represent a library of generally useable screen I/O routines, they could just as easily be distinguished as ".lib" or ".scr" modules. The concept of external modules is not confined to screen I/O alone. Other specialty libraries can also be created using the Turbo Pascal "include file" concept, such as disk file handling (".fil"), printer handling (".prt"), sorting (".srt"), and graphics (".gph").

In contrast, the Internal procedures are narrowly specialized and are usually written when developing the applications program itself. In the general model (Figure 15.1), the Internal procedures fall into three catagories. The first contains the HEADER-type procedure(s), which design an introductory screen that states the program title and provides some general on-screen operating instructions for the user. The second catagory (one designated here as the CREATE_SCREEN_ARRAYS-type procedures) contains the most important procedures. They directly address the problem you want to solve. Because this book has focused on the mechanics of screen I/O techniques, this most important area (to you) has been relegated the task of producing "output" that is simple and suitable for demonstration purposes only.

In reality, the CREATE_SCREEN_DATA-type procedure(s) will represent the area where most of your programming energy will focus. In this section, you "solve" your problems; it will probably be the largest section of your whole programming effort. The third catagory of Internal procedures contains the Initialization or INIT_SCREEN-type procedures. Once the problem is solved, you need to display the results on the video screen. Two questions naturally arise: where and how do you start? The answers (at least for screen-oriented applications) are provided within the code for these procedures, which says where and what part of the overall "output" will be first displayed to the screen.

More General Principles **15**

Body

The Body section is divided into two main parts. The first part is called the "Calculation Call Section." It invokes those Internal procedures that are exclusively dedicated to solving the problem you want to solve. In the programs in Chapters 14 and 15, the "problem" was to create three different two-dimensional arrays of character data suitable for demonstrating the screen I/O modules. The invocation of the Internal procedures that you will design to solve your problems will be placed in this section of the Body (with the actual problem-solving procedure(s) being placed up above in the Internal Procedures Section). The second part of the Body is called the "Display Control Section." This is where the connection between your algorithmic output and the screen I/O tools to display that output becomes evident. This section is framed within two large, nested control structures: an outer REPEAT..UNTIL loop to control selection of screen choices and exiting and, within it, an inner CASE..END structure to control the pattern of procedure invocations, depending on the value of the Boolean variables at the time. Notice the mixture of Internal and External procedures here. The Internal INIT_SCREEN-type procedures will initialize the already created data onto the screen only if that particular screen has not been previously requested. Notice also that all of the other procedures used are External procedures dedicated solely to screen I/O operations *but* whose parameter lists also include all of the "output" (scrollable data array variables) created by the Internal "problem solving" procedures resident inside the driver routine. These procedures are at the heart of the connection between the output and the screen I/O modules used to display that output onto the video screen.

CHAPTER 16

REVIEW AND EXTENSIONS

16 Review and Extensions

The key words in this chapter are **extension** and **review**. In the previous two chapters, some fairly general screen I/O routines were developed, which were capable of vertical/horizontal scrolling of table data inside a screen display window. In this chapter, a generalized routine will be created, which will enable you to attach row and column index labels to the scrolling windows. This extension will be a great help when you start scrolling around in large, two-dimensional data tables. Recall that an earlier prototype of this routine was developed in Chapter 12, where you scrolled a bar chart back and forth along a horizontal axis. In this chapter, you will also review what you have learned in this book by seeing an applications program that brings together all the generalized screen saving, redisplay, and scrolling techniques covered.

As an application, a scrolling table of "j" (screen pointer) values has been created. This table of 25 rows by 80 columns has been created by using each value in the 1..25 range (for screen rows) and each value in the 1..80 range (for screen columns) in the familiar formula

$$j := ((row - 1) * 160) + ((col - 1) * 2)$$

to produce the "j" value corresponding to each possible row/column pair on the video screen. Recall that this "j" value is the offset value in the one-dimensional video memory array MEM[bwseg : bwofs + j] and that by placing an ASCII integer value into one of these video memory locations indexed by "j," you can produce the corresponding ASCII character at the equivalent row/column location on the video screen. A table like this would come in handy should you want to create sophisticated screen redisplay routines where the redisplay from memory back to the screen would originate from the the bottom of the screen, from the left of the screen toward the right, from right to left, or even from both left and right (bookend style). This table would save much calculation time when figuring out the "j" values corresponding to the different screen row/column combinations.

In this program, three different data tables are actually created. Each data table uses the formula above as its source of information; however, each table has different row and column dimensions:

    Screen 1:   25 rows by 80 columns

    Screen 2:   25 rows by 5 columns

    Screen 3:   5 rows by 80 columns

The data on each of these screens is independently scrollable and features scrollable row and column index labels as well (see Figure 16.1). Since the display windows have not been overlapped, the screen save/redisplay techniques are illustrated by installing a scrollable "help" screen (see Figure 16.2). If at any time, you want to leave the scrolling applications to read the "help" text file, you can do so without losing the information in the original screen display windows.

MODULE: TYPDEF16.INC

This module, like those of its predecessors in Chapters 14 and 15, contains all of the screen constant, type, and variable definitions that will be used by the other ".inc" modules and the driver routine. Each screen definition under the "const" section is now broken down into three parts, and not two as before. The first and second parts are familiar from Chapters 14 and 15. The third section is new. As mentioned, one of the goals in this chapter is to create scrollable data screens with attached row and column labels along the window axis on the screen. The constant values under the generic subheading "SCREEN #: row and column label constants" will allow you to do just that.

Before proceeding, note some of the naming conventions for the constants, types, and variables. Begin with the constants. First, the names are long, but if you pay close attention to the words and what they say, you can determine what their jobs are. Second, if the word has the word "data" embedded within it, you know that you are dealing with a constant used to define the actual table information inside a two-dimensional array. Third, if the word contains "label" along with either "row" or "col" (column), you know that you are dealing with either row label or column label constants. Fourth, if the word contains the number "1" at the end of it, you know that you are dealing with Screen number 1, and so on.

16 Review and Extensions

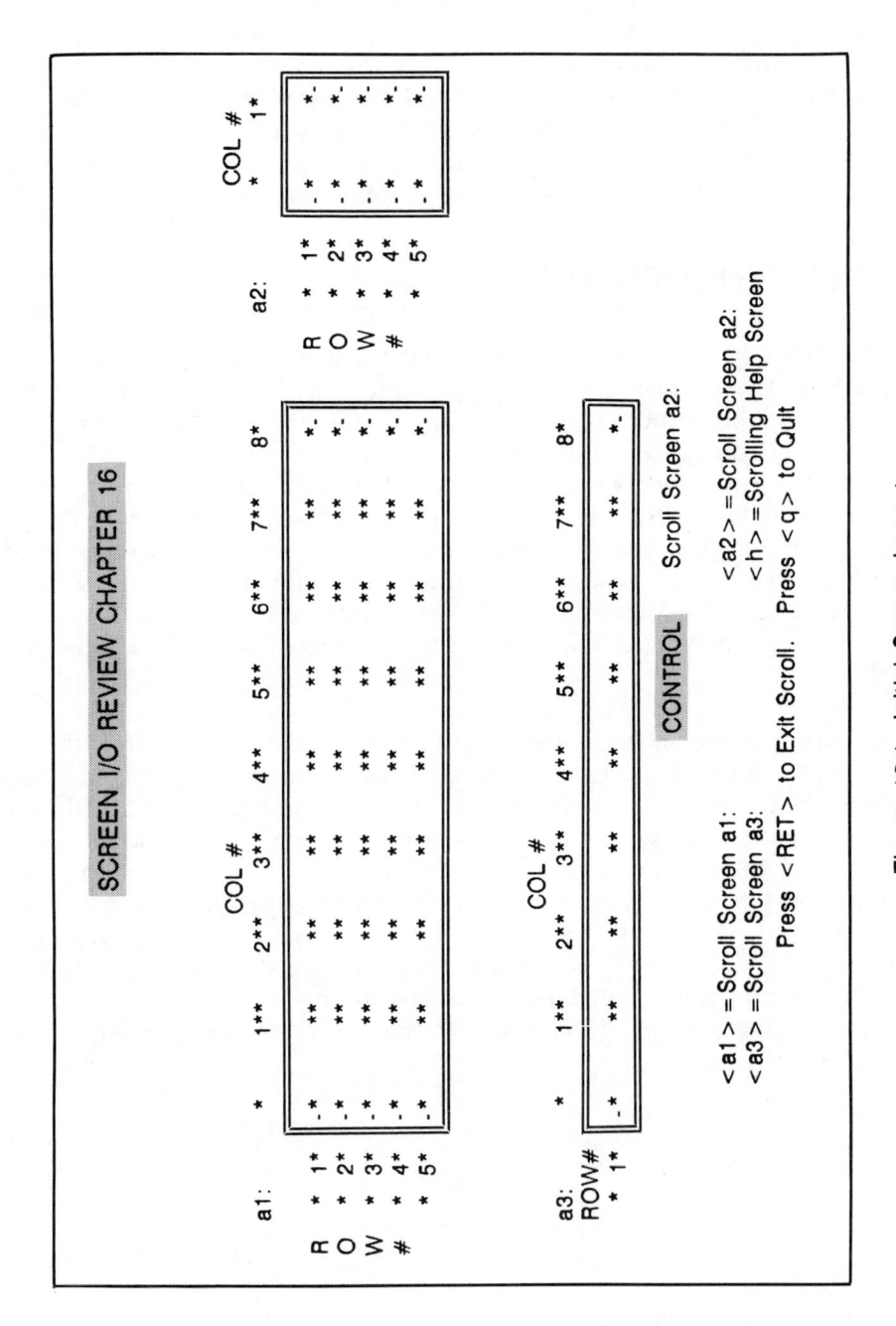

Figure 16.1 Initial Screen Layout

370

Review and Extensions 16

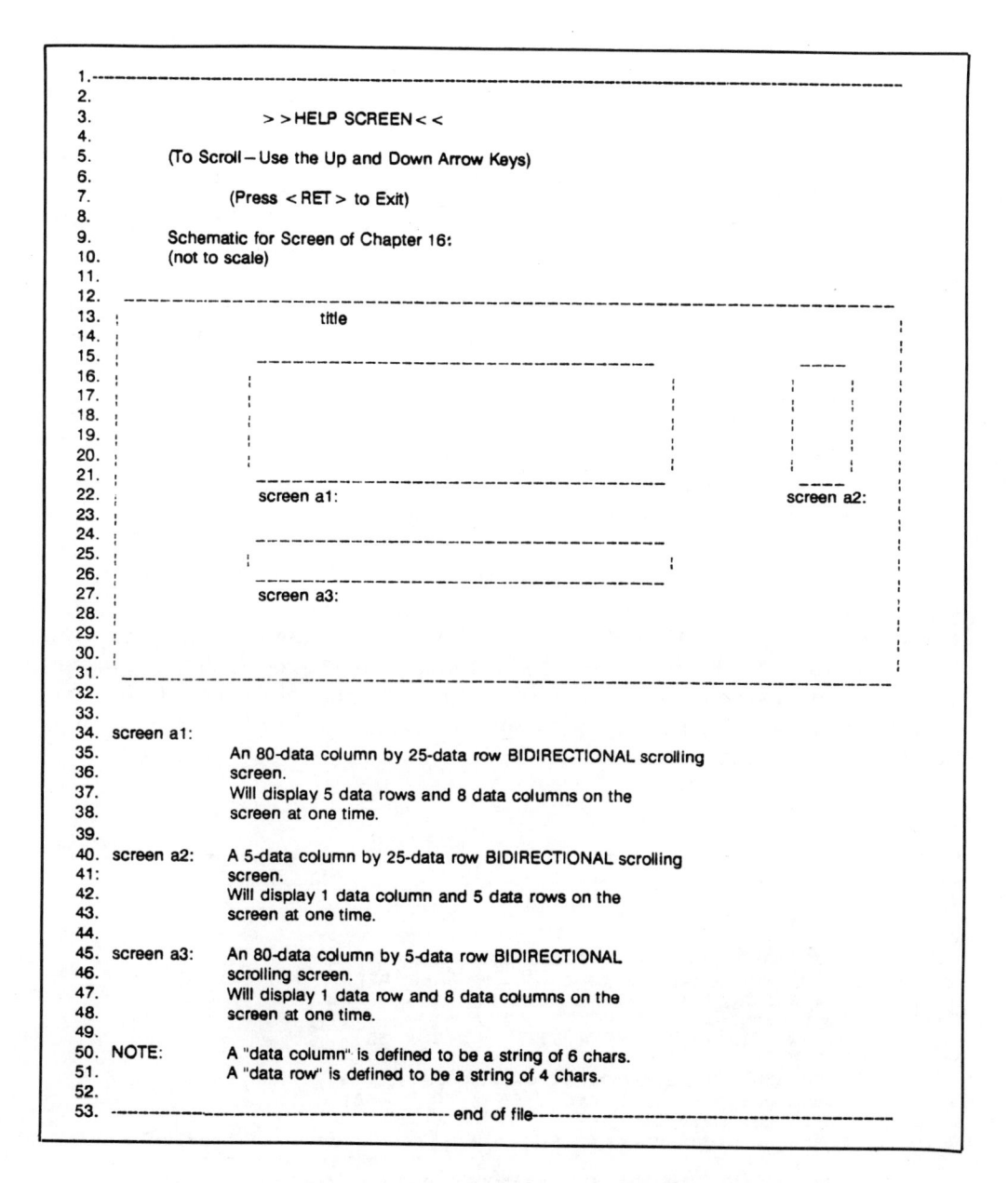

```
1.-----------------------------------------------------------------------------
2.
3.                    > >HELP SCREEN< <
4.
5.            (To Scroll—Use the Up and Down Arrow Keys)
6.
7.                    (Press <RET> to Exit)
8.
9.            Schematic for Screen of Chapter 16:
10.           (not to scale)
11.
12.        ------------------------------------------------------------------
13.       :                       title                                     :
14.       :                                                                 :
15.       :        --------------------------------            ----         :
16.       :        :                              :            :  :         :
17.       :        :                              :            :  :         :
18.       :        :                              :            :  :         :
19.       :        :                              :            :  :         :
20.       :        :                              :            :  :         :
21.       :        --------------------------------            ----         :
22.       :        screen a1:                                  screen a2:   :
23.       :                                                                 :
24.       :        --------------------------------                         :
25.       :        :                              :                         :
26.       :        --------------------------------                         :
27.       :        screen a3:                                               :
28.       :                                                                 :
29.       :                                                                 :
30.       :                                                                 :
31.        ------------------------------------------------------------------
32.
33.
34.   screen a1:
35.            An 80-data column by 25-data row BIDIRECTIONAL scrolling
36.            screen.
37.            Will display 5 data rows and 8 data columns on the
38.            screen at one time.
39.
40.   screen a2:   A 5-data column by 25-data row BIDIRECTIONAL scrolling
41.  :            screen.
42.            Will display 1 data column and 5 data rows on the
43.            screen at one time.
44.
45.   screen a3:   An 80-data column by 5-data row BIDIRECTIONAL
46.            scrolling screen.
47.            Will display 1 data row and 8 data columns on the
48.            screen at one time.
49.
50.   NOTE:    A "data column" is defined to be a string of 6 chars.
51.            A "data row" is defined to be a string of 4 chars.
52.
53.   -------------------------------- end of file--------------------------------
```

Figure 16.2 Scrollable Help Screen

371

16 Review and Extensions

Turning to the types, note first that any of the video screen Saving/Redisplay Types are named using an underscore ("_") with abbreviations. For example, for Screen 1, the Type "s1_arr" stands for "screen 1 array," and "s1_buf" stands for "screen 1 buffer." Second, any Data array Types (as opposed to physical screen types just discussed) are named using abbreviations *without* the underscore inserted. For example, "s1arr" reads as "screen 1 array" but refers to the data structure and *not* the physical dimensions of the video screen. Third, the prefix "r" stands for "row," and "c" stands for "column" so that "rlabel1arr" reads as "row label 1 array" and is a Type definition involving data in Screen 1. Similarly, "clabel1buf" would read "column label 1 buffer" and is also a Type definition involving data in Screen 1.

These points about Type definitions also apply to naming variables under the "var" heading. The only distinction is that in the variables, the names "array" and "buffer" are fully expanded.

The way the definitions have been set up, Screens 1, 2, and 3 are all capable of being saved/redisplayed, of having their internal data array contents scrolled, and of having their corresponding row and column labels scrolled as well. Note that Screen 4 has been defined only to have screen save/redisplay capability. Before the meaning of the row and column label scrolling constants is explained, the code for "typdef16.inc" is presented as follows:

```
{============================================================================}
0005   {typdef16.inc}
0010
0015   const
0020
0025         {SCREEN1: screen save/redisplay constants}
0030         tlc1 = 3 ; tlr1 = 3 ; brc1 = 60 ; brr1 = 11;
0035         maxscrrows1 = 9;
0040         maxscrcols1 = 58;
0045         maxscrdisplaychars1 = 522;      {9 x 58}
0050
0055         {SCREEN1: array data scrolling constants}
0060         datacharsperrow1 = 480;    {6 x 80 = 480}
0065         datacharspercol1 = 6;
0070         maxcountofdatacharspercol1 = 6; {each data unit handled a }
0075                                         {character at a time      }
0080         max_allowed_i_tot1 = 21; {count backwards from 25...}
0085         max_allowed_k_tot1 = 73; {count backwards from 80...}
0090         datarowdepth1       = 5;  {count, there are 5...    }
0095         datarowdepthminusone1 = 4;
0100         datacolwidth1 = 8;         {8, 6 column data locations}
0105         datacolwidthminusone1 = 7;
```

continued...

Review and Extensions 16

...from previous page

```
0110        maxdatarows1 = 25;          {25 rows on the video screen}
0115        maxdatacols1 = 80;          {80 columns on the video screen}
0120        maxdatachars1 = 12000;      {25 x 80 x 6 = 12000}
0125
0130        {SCREEN1: row and column label scrolling constants}
0135        labelcharsperrow1      = 4;
0140        maxcountoflabelcharsperrow1    = 4;
0145        labelcharspercol1      = 6;
0150        maxcountoflabelcharspercol1    = 6;
0155        labelrowdepth1 = 5;
0160        labelrowdepthminusone1         = 4;
0165        labelcolwidth1 = 8;
0170        labelcolwidthminusone1         = 7;
0175        maxlabelrows1  = 25;
0180        maxlabelcols1  = 80;
0185        maxlabelrowchars1      = 100;   {25 x 4}
0190        maxlabelcolchars1      = 480;   {80 x 6}
0195
0200        scr1_init    : boolean = false;
0205        scr1_active  : boolean = false;
0210
0215   {====================================================================}
0220
0225        {SCREEN2: screen save/redisplay constants}
0230        tlc2 = 64; tlr2 = 3 ; brc2 = 79 ; brr2 = 11;
0235        maxscrrows2 = 9;
0240        maxscrcols2 = 16;
0245        maxscrdisplaychars2 = 144;      {9 x 16}
0250
0255        {SCREEN2: array data scrolling constants}
0260        datacharsperrow2 = 30;   {5 per row x 6 chars/row unit}
0265        datacharspercol2 = 6;
0270        maxcountofdatacharspercol2 = 6; {each data unit handled a }
0275                                        {character at a time      }
0280        max_allowed_i_tot2 = 21; {count backwards from 25}
0285        max_allowed_k_tot2 = 5;  {count backwards from 5}
0290        datarowdepth2          = 5;   {5, 4 column row locations}
0295        datarowdepthminusone2 = 4;
0300        datacolwidth2 = 1;       {1, 6 column data locations}
0305        datacolwidthminusone2 = 0;
0310        maxdatarows2 = 25;
0315        maxdatacols2 = 5;
0320        maxdatachars2 = 750;     {25 x 5 x 6 = 750}
0325
0330        {SCREEN2: row and column label scrolling constants}
0335        labelcharsperrow2      = 4;
0340        maxcountoflabelcharsperrow2    = 4;
0345        labelcharspercol2      = 6;
0350        maxcountoflabelcharspercol2    = 6;
0355        labelrowdepth2 = 5;
0360        labelrowdepthminusone2         = 4;
0365        labelcolwidth2 = 1;
0370        labelcolwidthminusone2         = 0;
0375        maxlabelrows2  = 25;
0380        maxlabelcols2  = 5;             {only 5 defined here}
0385        maxlabelrowchars2      = 100;   {25 x 4}
0390        maxlabelcolchars2      = 30;    {5 x 6 = 30}
0395
0400        scr2_init    : boolean = false;
0405        scr2_active  : boolean = false;
```

continued...

16 Review and Extensions

...from previous page

```
0410
0415          {================================================================}
0420
0425          {SCREEN3 : screen save/redisplay constants}
0430          tlc3 = 3 ; tlr3 = 14 ; brc3 = 60 ; brr3 = 18;
0435          maxscrrows3 = 5;
0440          maxscrcols3 = 57;
0445          maxscrdisplaychars3 = 285;      {5 x 57}
0450
0455          {SCREEN3: array data scrolling constants}
0460          datacharsperrow3 = 480;   {80 columns of 6 chars/col = 480}
0465          datacharspercol3 = 6;
0470          maxcountofdatacharspercol3 = 6; {each data unit handled a }
0475                                          {character at a time     }
0480          max_allowed_i_tot3 = 5;    {count backwards from 5}
0485          max_allowed_k_tot3 = 73;   {backwards from 80: 80,79,...,73}
0490          datarowdepth3          = 1;
0495          datarowdepthminusone3 = 0;
0500          datacolwidth3 = 8;          {8, 6 column data locations}
0505          datacolwidthminusone3 = 7;
0510          maxdatarows3 = 5;
0515          maxdatacols3 = 80;
0520          maxdatachars3 = 2400;     {5 x 80 x 6 = 2400}
0525
0530          {SCREEN3: row and column label scrolling constants}
0535          labelcharsperrow3      = 4;
0540          maxcountoflabelcharsperrow3    = 4;
0545          labelcharspercol3      = 6;
0550          maxcountoflabelcharspercol3    = 6;
0555          labelrowdepth3 = 1;          {only 1 displayed row}
0560          labelrowdepthminusone3    = 0;
0565          labelcolwidth3 = 8;
0570          labelcolwidthminusone3         = 7;
0575          maxlabelrows3    = 5;        {only 5 defined here}
0580          maxlabelcols3    = 80;
0585          maxlabelrowchars3      = 20;    {5 x 4 = 20}
0590          maxlabelcolchars3      = 480;   {80 x 6}
0595
0600          scr3_init   : boolean = false;
0605          scr3_active : boolean = false;
0610
0615          {SCREEN4 : screen save/redisplay constants}
0620          tlc4 = 1 ; tlr4 = 1 ; brc4 = 80 ; brr4 = 25;
0625          maxscrrows4 = 25; {brr4 - tlr4 + 1 = 25 : rows 1 to 25 incl}
0630          maxscrcols4 = 80;
0635          maxscrdisplaychars4 = 2000;    {25 x 80}
0640
0645          scr4_init   : boolean = false;
0650          scr4_active : boolean = false;
0655
0660
0665 type
0670          str4     = string[4];
0675          str6     = string[6];
0680
```

continued...

Review and Extensions 16

...from previous page

```
0685            {SCREEN1:}
0690            s1_arr      = ARRAY[1..maxscrrows1,1..maxscrcols1] of char;
0695            s1_buf      = ARRAY[1..maxscrdisplaychars1] of char;
0700            s1arr       = ARRAY[1..maxdatarows1,1..maxdatacols1] of str6;
0705            s1buf       = ARRAY[1..maxdatachars1] of char;
0710
0715            rlabel1arr  = ARRAY[1..maxlabelrows1] of str4;
0720            rlabel1buf  = ARRAY[1..maxlabelrowchars1] of char;
0725            clabel1arr  = ARRAY[1..maxlabelcols1] of str6;
0730            clabel1buf  = ARRAY[1..maxlabelcolchars1] of char;
0735
0740
0745            {SCREEN2:}
0750            s2_arr      = ARRAY[1..maxscrrows2,1..maxscrcols2] of char;
0755            s2_buf      = ARRAY[1..maxscrdisplaychars2] of char;
0760            s2arr       = ARRAY[1..maxdatarows2,1..maxdatacols2] of str6;
0765            s2buf       = ARRAY[1..maxdatachars2] of char;
0770
0775            rlabel2arr  = ARRAY[1..maxlabelrows2] of str4;
0780            rlabel2buf  = ARRAY[1..maxlabelrowchars2] of char;
0785            clabel2arr  = ARRAY[1..maxlabelcols2] of str6;
0790            clabel2buf  = ARRAY[1..maxlabelcolchars2] of char;
0795
0800
0805            {SCREEN3:}
0810            s3_arr      = ARRAY[1..maxscrrows3,1..maxscrcols3] of char;
0815            s3_buf      = ARRAY[1..maxscrdisplaychars3] of char;    {9 x 22}
0820            s3arr       = ARRAY[1..maxdatarows3,1..maxdatacols3] of str6;
0825            s3buf       = ARRAY[1..maxdatachars3] of char;
0830
0835            rlabel3arr  = ARRAY[1..maxlabelrows3] of str4;
0840            rlabel3buf  = ARRAY[1..maxlabelrowchars3] of char;
0845            clabel3arr  = ARRAY[1..maxlabelcols3] of str6;
0850            clabel3buf  = ARRAY[1..maxlabelcolchars3] of char;
0855
0860
0865            {SCREEN4: for save and redisplay only}
0870            s4_arr      = ARRAY[1..maxscrrows4,1..maxscrcols4] of char;
0875            s4_buf      = ARRAY[1..maxscrdisplaychars4] of char;
0880
0885
0890  var
0895
0900            {SCREEN1:}
0905            scr1_array      : s1_arr;
0910            scr1_buffer     : s1_buf;
0915            scr1array       : s1arr;
0920            scr1buffer      : s1buf;
0925            rlabel1array    : rlabel1arr;
0930            rlabel1buffer   : rlabel1buf;
0935            clabel1array    : clabel1arr;
0940            clabel1buffer   : clabel1buf;
0945
0950
0955            {SCREEN2:}
0960            scr2_array      : s2_arr;
0965            scr2_buffer     : s2_buf;
0970            scr2array       : s2arr;
0975            scr2buffer      : s2buf;
```

continued...

375

16 Review and Extensions

...from previous page

```
0980        rlabel2array   : rlabel2arr;
0985        rlabel2buffer  : rlabel2buf;
0990        clabel2array   : clabel2arr;
0995        clabel2buffer  : clabel2buf;
1000
1005
1010        {SCREEN3:}
1015        scr3_array     : s3_arr;
1020        scr3_buffer    : s3_buf;
1025        scr3array      : s3arr;
1030        scr3buffer     : s3buf;
1035        rlabel3array   : rlabel3arr;
1040        rlabel3buffer  : rlabel3buf;
1045        clabel3array   : clabel3arr;
1050        clabel3buffer  : clabel3buf;
1055
1060
1065        {SCREEN4:}
1070        scr4_array     : s4_arr;
1075        scr4_buffer    : s4_buf;
{===============================================================}
```

TYPDEF16.INC: NOTES

Consider the row and column label constants for Screen 1. Refer to Figure 16.3 (for row and column labels) and Figure 16.4 (for actual table data) as you read along.

"Maxlabelrows1" is assigned a value of 25, indicating that each row of the data array has a corresponding number index between 1 and 25. Note that "maxdatarows1" is equal to "maxlabelrows1." "Labelcharsperrow1" focuses on each of the 25 row labels and tells you that each one is made up of four characters.

Review and Extensions 16

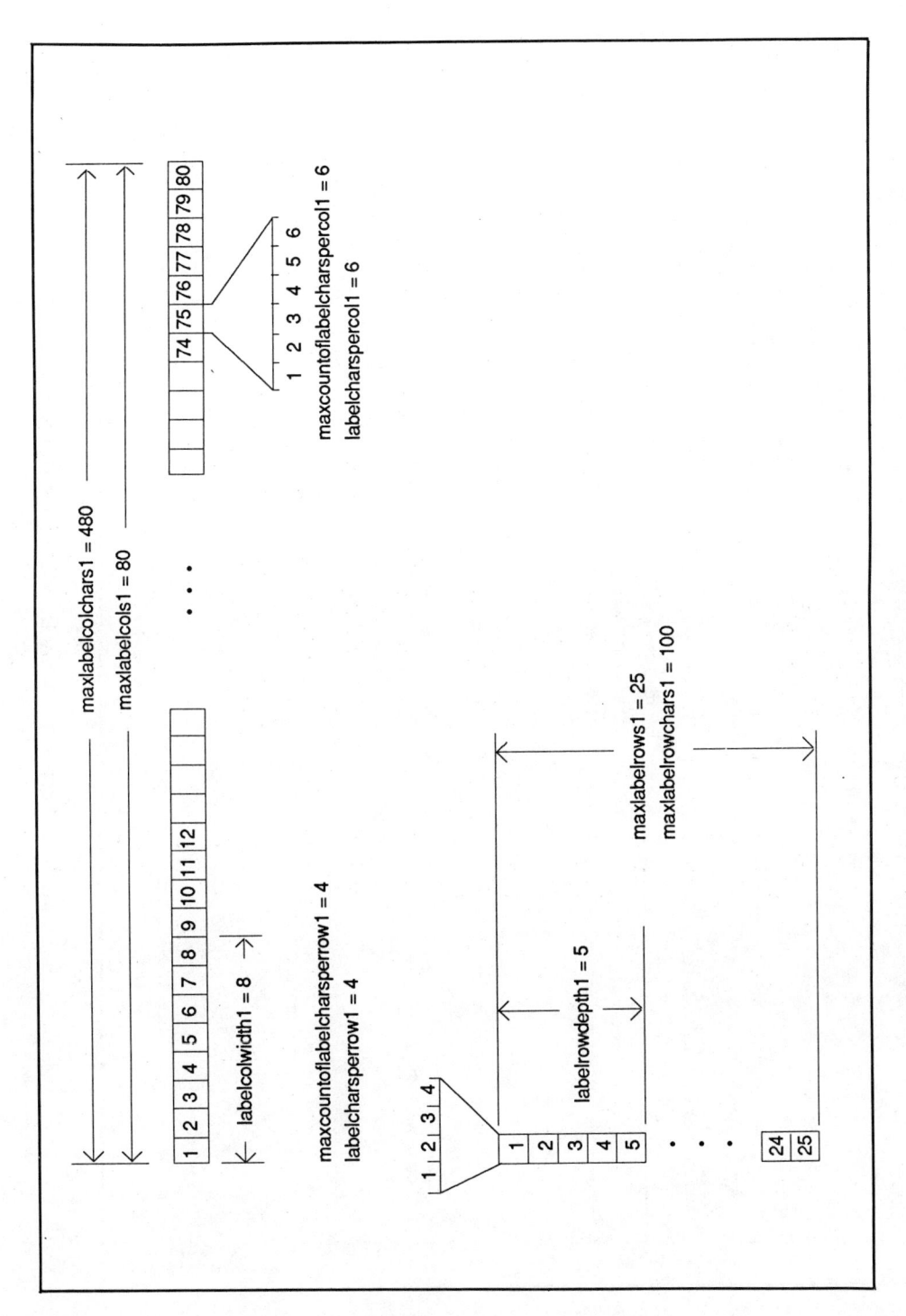

Figure 16.3 Screen 1: Row and Column Label Scrolling Constants

377

16   Review and Extensions

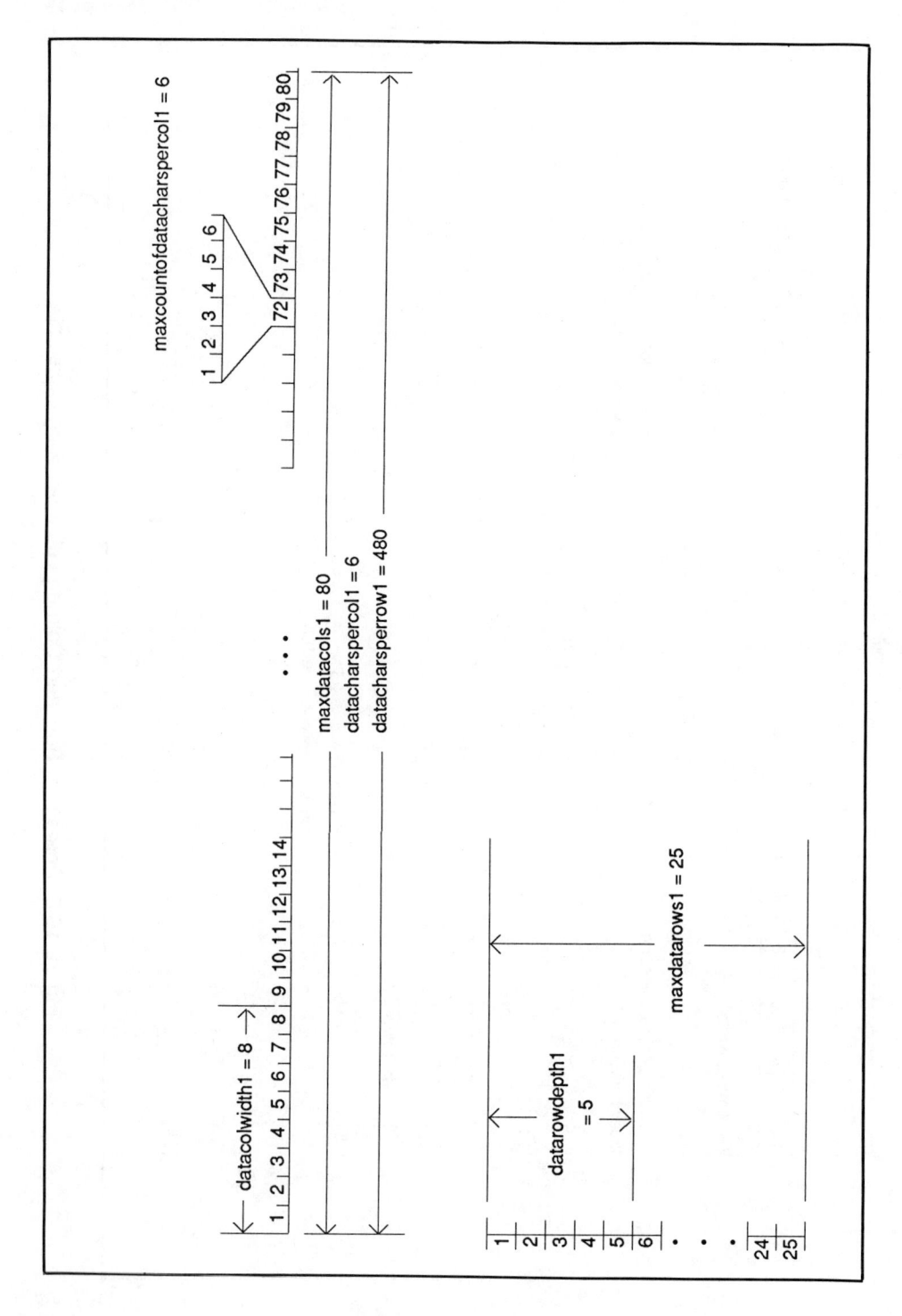

Figure 16.4   Screen 1: Array Data Scrolling Constants

"Maxcountoflabelcharsperrow1" has the same value of 4. Although these constants have the same number value, they refer to different things, which will be explained shortly. "Maxlabelcols1" for Screen 1 is assigned a value of 80. This tells you that each column of data in the data array has a corresponding index number between 1 and 80. Again, "maxlabelcols1" is equal to "maxdatacols1." "Labelcharspercol1" has a value of 6 and says that each column label is composed of a group of 6 characters. The difference between "labelcharspercol1" and "maxcountoflabelcharspercol1" will also be discussed later. "Labelrowdepth1" is given the value 5 and tells you that the display screen will display 5 label values down the left-hand side of the screen data window. "Labelrowdepthminusone1" is equal to 4 and is used to calculate the next larger label value (row index value) to be displayed during a Scroll Down operation (toward larger values in a vertical direction). Note that the data array has "datarowdepth1" equal to 5 and "datarowdepthminusone1" equal to 4 as analogues to the row label array. "Labelcolwidth1" is given the value 8, which tells you that the display screen will show 8 column labels along the top of the screen display window. "Labelcolwidthminusone1" equals 7 and is used to calculate the next larger column label value to be shown at the right-hand side of the display screen during a Scroll Right operation (toward larger values in a horizontal direction). Again, note the data array analogues "datacolwidth1" equals 8 and "datcolwidthminusone1" equals 7. "Maxlabelrowchars1" is assigned the value 100 and is the product of "maxlabelrows1" (25) and "labelcharsperrow1" (4). You need to understand the distinction between "maxlabelrows1" and "maxlabelrowchars1." The former says that Screen 1 has 25 four-character strings, and the latter says that Screen 1 also has 100 one-character strings. You need to perform this conversion from an array of strings (of length 4) into an array of characters (of length 1) to display the row labels on the video screen, using the single-character screen display procedure CHR_OUT inside the external procedure REWRITE_ROW_LABEL (in module "rewrsc16.inc").

"Maxlabelcolchars1" is assigned the value of 480 and is the product of "maxlabelcols1" (80) and "labelcharspercol1" (6). Again, note the difference between "maxlabelcols1" and "maxlabelcolchars1." The former says that Screen 1 has 80 six-character strings, and the latter says that Screen 1 also has 480 one-character strings. You need to make this conversion from an array of strings (length 6) into an array of characters (length 1) to display the column labels onto the screen using the single-character video display procedure CHR_OUT inside the external procedure REWRITE_COL_LABEL (inside "rewrsc16.inc").

16 Review and Extensions

Now consider the "type" section of "typedef16.inc." Each screen has two defined types for the row label (lines 0715 and 0720 for Screen 1) and two defined types for the column label (lines 0725 and 0730 for Screen 1). "Rlabel1arr" (row label 1 array) is an array of 25 four-character strings. "Rlabel1buf" (row label 1 buffer) is an equivalent array of 100 one-character strings. Similarly, "clabel1arr" (column label 1 array) is an array of 80 six-character strings, and "clabel1buf" (column label 1 buffer) is an equivalent array of 480 one-character strings.

As you move down to the "var" section (lines 0790-0940 for Screen 1), you see the variable names (and their corresponding types) that you will use when you display the row and column labels on the screen. These variables will be found in the procedures of the external screen data and row/label scrolling module "rewrsc16.inc" (rewrite screen chapter 16 inc. file).

Before leaving this section, note the following points:

- The constant names, although long-winded, are descriptive enough. Feel free to invent your own screen-naming conventions.

- Each row/column label constant value has an analogue among the data array constant values, which performs a similar task. So even though the number of constant values is large, a large amount of parallel function exists among them, which reduces the complexity considerably.

- Use the layout of the "const" section along with Figures 16.3 and Fig 16.4 as a reference when you come to define your own scrolling data screens. Feel free to mix and match. If you do not need row/col labels, then omit the appropriate part of the screen definition constants.

- What has been said about Screen 1 above applies to all of the other screens as well.

Review and Extensions **16**

MODULE: REWRSC16.INC

This module was developed directly from the module "rewritsc.inc" in Chapter 14. Unlike its predecessor, this stand-alone module is capable of vertically and horizontally scrolling both array table data as well as accompanying row and column labels used to index the table data.

The structure of "rewrsc16.inc" is as follows:

>procedure VHRLCLSCROLL_SCREEN (with a big parameter list....)
>{"vertical/horizontal row label/column label scroll screen" }
>
>>subprocedure REWRITE_SCR (with no parameter list)
>>{"rewrite screen"}
>>
>>subprocedure REWRITE_ROWLABEL (with no parameter list)
>>{"rewrite row label"}
>>
>>subprocedure REWRITE_COLLABEL (with no parameter list)
>>{"rewrite column label"}

This scrolling module is the most general and powerful scrolling module presented in this book. Following is the code, which will be explained afterwards:

```
{========================================================================}
0005 {rewrsc16.inc}
0010 { This ".inc" file is a general data array scrolling
0015   module. Used in "multsc16.drv".
0020   It contains all the routines to allow for bidirectional,
0025   vertical, or horizontal only scrolling of data windows
0030   and row or column labels. On disk as "rewrsc16.inc"
0035 }
0040
0045 {------------------------------------------------------------------}
0050
0055 procedure VHRLCLSCROLL_SCREEN(tlc,tlr               : integer;
0060                      var saved_i_tot               : integer;
0065                      var saved_k_tot               : integer;
0070                      datarowdepthminusone          : integer;
0075                      datacolwidthminusone          : integer;
0080                      labelrowdepthminusone         : integer;
```

continued...

16 Review and Extensions

...from previous page

```
0085                         labelcolwidthminusone          : integer;
0090                         datacharsperrow                : integer;
0095                         datacharspercol                : integer;
0100                         labelcharsperrow               : integer;
0105                         labelcharspercol               : integer;
0110                         maxcountofdatacharspercol      : integer;
0115                         maxcountoflabelcharsperrow     : integer;
0120                         maxcountoflabelcharspercol     : integer;
0125                         max_allowed_i_tot              : integer;
0130                         max_allowed_k_tot              : integer;
0135                     var scr1buffer                     : s1buf;
0140                     var scr2buffer                     : s2buf;
0145                     var scr3buffer                     : s3buf;
0150                     var rlabel1buffer                  : rlabel1buf;
0155                     var clabel1buffer                  : clabel1buf;
0160                     var rlabel2buffer                  : rlabel2buf;
0165                     var clabel2buffer                  : clabel2buf;
0170                     var rlabel3buffer                  : rlabel3buf;
0175                     var clabel3buffer                  : clabel3buf);
0180
0185
0190   label
0195        rep_read;
0200
0205   const
0210        scroll_up     = #$48;
0215        scroll_down   = #$50;
0220        scroll_left   = #$4b;
0225        scroll_right  = #$4d;
0230        carriage_ret  = #$0d;
0235
0240   var
0245        scroll_choice : char;
0250        exit_scroll   : boolean;
0255        i_tot,k_tot   : integer;   {takes saved_i_tot , saved_k_tot}
0260   {----------------------------------------------------------------}
0265
0270        procedure REWRITE_SCR;
0275
0280        var
0285            bx,bp,
0290            count,
0295            j,
0300            row,col,
0305            k,i       : integer;
0310
0315        Begin     {sub-procedure rewrite_scr}
0320            col := tlc + 8 ; row := tlr + 3;
0325            {adjust for data display}
0330            j := ((row - 1) * 160) + ((col - 1) * 2);
0335            FOR i := (i_tot) to (i_tot + datarowdepthminusone) DO
0340            Begin
0345                FOR k := (k_tot) to
0350                        (k_tot + datacolwidthminusone) DO
```

continued...

...from previous page

```
0355                    Begin
0360                        bx := (i - 1) * datacharsperrow;    {480}
0365                        bp := (k - 1) * datacharspercol;
0370                        FOR count := 1 to maxcountofdatacharspercol DO
0375                        Begin
0380                            IF (scr1_active = true) THEN
0385                                CHR_OUT(j,ORD(scr1buffer[bx+bp+count]));
0390
0395                            IF (scr2_active = true) THEN
0400                                CHR_OUT(j,ORD(scr2buffer[bx+bp+count]));
0405
0410                            IF (scr3_active = true) THEN
0415                                CHR_OUT(j,ORD(scr3buffer[bx+bp+count]));
0420
0425                            {* delay(100); *}
0430                            j := j + 2;
0435                        End;
0440                    End;
0445                    col := col ; row := row + 1;
0450                    j := ((row - 1) * 160) + ((col - 1) * 2)
0455                End;
0460        End;       {sub-procedure rewrite_scr}
0465    {----------------------------------------------------------------}
0470
0475        procedure REWRITE_ROWLABEL;
0480
0485        var
0490            bx,bp,
0495            count,
0500            j,
0505            row,col,
0510            k,i         : integer;
0515
0520        Begin     {sub-procedure rewrite_rowlabel}
0525            col := tlc + 2 ; row := tlr + 3;
0530            {adjust for data display}
0535            j := ((row - 1) * 160) + ((col - 1) * 2);
0540            FOR i := (i_tot) to (i_tot + labelrowdepthminusone) DO
0545            Begin
0550                bx := (i - 1) * labelcharsperrow;
0555                FOR count := 1 to maxcountoflabelcharsperrow DO
0560                Begin
0565                    IF (scr1_active = true) THEN
0570                        CHR_OUT(j,ORD(rlabel1buffer[bx+count]));
0575
0580                    IF (scr2_active = true) THEN
0585                        CHR_OUT(j,ORD(rlabel2buffer[bx+count]));
0590
0595                    IF (scr3_active = true) THEN
0600                        CHR_OUT(j,ORD(rlabel3buffer[bx+count]));
0605
0610                    {* delay(100); *}
0615                    j := j + 2;
0620                End;
0625                col := col ; row := row + 1;
0630                j := ((row - 1) * 160) + ((col - 1) * 2)
0635            End;
0640        End;       {sub-procedure rewrite_rowlabel}
0645    {----------------------------------------------------------------}
```

continued...

16 Review and Extensions

...from previous page

```
0650
0655          procedure REWRITE_COLLABEL;
0660
0665          var
0670              bx,bp,
0675              count,
0680              j,
0685              row,col,
0690              k,i         : integer;
0695
0700          Begin      {sub-procedure rewrite_collabel}
0705              col := tlc + 8 ; row := tlr + 1;
0710              {adjust for data display}
0715              j := ((row - 1) * 160) + ((col - 1) * 2);
0720              FOR k := (k_tot) to (k_tot + labelcolwidthminusone) DO
0725              Begin
0730                  bp := (k - 1) * labelcharspercol;
0735                  FOR count := 1 to maxcountoflabelcharspercol DO
0740                  Begin
0745                      IF (scr1_active = true) THEN
0750                          CHR_OUT(j,ORD(clabel1buffer[bp+count]));
0755
0760                      IF (scr2_active = true) THEN
0765                          CHR_OUT(j,ORD(clabel2buffer[bp+count]));
0770
0775                      IF (scr3_active = true) THEN
0780                          CHR_OUT(j,ORD(clabel3buffer[bp+count]));
0785
0790                      {* delay(100); *}
0795                      j := j + 2;
0800                  End;
0805                  col := col + 6 ; row := row;
0810                  j := ((row - 1) * 160) + ((col - 1) * 2)
0815              End;
0820          End;       {sub-procedure rewrite_collabel}
0825  {----------------------------------------------------------------}
0830
0835  Begin     {procedure vhrlclscroll_screen}
0840      window(1,1,80,25);
0845      exit_scroll := false;
0850      i_tot := saved_i_tot ; k_tot := saved_k_tot;
0855
0860      REPEAT
0865          rep_read:       {label with colon}
0870          gotoxy(40,21);
0875          read(KBD,scroll_choice);   {type in at keyboard}
0880          CASE (scroll_choice) of
0885
0890          scroll_up : Begin              {press Up Arrow Key....}
0895                          i_tot := i_tot - 1;
0900                          k_tot := k_tot + 0;
0905                          IF (i_tot < 1) THEN
0910                          Begin
0915                              i_tot := 1;
0920                              goto rep_read;
0925                          End;
0930                          REWRITE_SCR;
0935                          REWRITE_ROWLABEL;
0940                      End;    {scroll_up}
```

continued...

Review and Extensions 16

...from previous page

```
0945
0950            scroll_down : Begin              {press Down Arrow Key....}
0955                              i_tot := i_tot + 1;
0960                              k_tot := k_tot + 0;
0965                              IF (i_tot > max_allowed_i_tot) THEN
0970                              Begin
0975                                  i_tot := max_allowed_i_tot;
0980                                  goto rep_read;
0985                              End;
0990                              REWRITE_SCR;
0995                              REWRITE_ROWLABEL;
1000                          End;    {scroll_down}
1005
1010            scroll_left : Begin              {press Left Arrow Key....}
1015                              i_tot := i_tot + 0;
1020                              k_tot := k_tot - 1;
1025                              IF (k_tot < 1) THEN
1030                              Begin
1035                                  k_tot := 1;
1040                                  goto rep_read;
1045                              End;
1050                              REWRITE_SCR;
1055                              REWRITE_COLLABEL;
1060                          End;    {scroll_left}
1065
1070            scroll_right : Begin             {press Right Arrow Key....}
1075                              i_tot := i_tot + 0;
1080                              k_tot := k_tot + 1;
1085                              IF (k_tot > max_allowed_k_tot) THEN
1090                              Begin
1095                                  k_tot := max_allowed_k_tot;
1100                                  goto rep_read;
1105                              End;
1110                              REWRITE_SCR;
1115                              REWRITE_COLLABEL;
1120                          End;    {scroll_right}
1125
1130            carriage_ret : Begin
1135                              Exit_scroll := true;
1140                              saved_i_tot := i_tot;
1145                              saved_k_tot := k_tot;
1150                          End
1155
1160        ELSE
1165                  {any other entry is illegal}
1170
1175            END;        {case}
1180        UNTIL (exit_scroll = true);
1185        gotoxy(40,21);
1190 End;     {procedure vhrlclscroll_screen}
{======================================================================}
```

16 Review and Extensions

REWRSC16.INC: NOTES

VHRLCLSCROLL_SCREEN (Vertical/Horizontal Row Label/Column Label)

This procedure is the control procedure for this module and has two jobs. First, it supplies the subprocedures (the workhorses) with all the external parameters they will need to perform their respective scrolling tasks (i.e., scrolling of array data, row labels, or column labels). Second, it provides a control mechanism to ensure that the proper procedures are called in accordance with pressing the Arrow Keys on the Numeric Keypad. The REPEAT..UNTIL structure (lines 0860-1180) along with the CASE..END structure (lines 0880-1175) provide such a control mechanism.

Now look at the parameter list in more detail. As noted, the procedure VHRLCLSCROLL_SCREEN features horizontal scrolling and the scrolling of row index labels and column index labels in addition to vertical scrolling. The following new parameters were added to provide these additional capabilities:

1) saved_i_tot
2) labelrowdepthminusone
3) labelcolwidthminusone
4) labelcharsperrow
5) labelcharspercol
6) maxcountoflabelcharsperrow
7) maxcountoflabelcharspercol
8) max_allowed_k_tot
9) rlabel1buffer
10) clabel1buffer
11) rlabel2buffer
12) clabel2buffer
13) rlabel3buffer
14) clabel3buffer

Review and Extensions 16

From the list, you can see that the parameters numbered 2 through 7 are the non-array parameters found in the "const" section of "typdef16.inc." They supply information about the row and column labels that will be used as moving indexes into the scrollable table data inside the display screen. Parameters numbered 2, 4, and 6 are found inside the subprocedure REWRITE_ROWLABEL, while parameters numbered 3, 5, and 7 are found inside REWRITE_COLLABEL. Parameter number 8, "max_allowed_k_tot," like the others, has its value fixed depending on which Screen number has been called for scrolling. Recall that this parameter represents the upper limit of the horizontal scrolling index k_tot for both the scrollable screen data as well as the column labels (line 1085). (Table data and column indexes move together in lockstep during a horizontal scrolling operation; see lines 1110-1115.) Take Screen 1 as an example. Notice that the value of "max_allowed_k_tot1" is only 73 (not 80 as you might expect) to prevent a rightward horizontal scroll from trying to display more than its 80-column limit. Look at line 1085 inside the procedure VHRLCLSCROLL_SCREEN. In the Screen 1 example, "k_tot" is not allowed to exceed the value of 73. Look now at line 0720 inside REWRITE_COLLABEL. Here, you see that if you were at the rightmost portion of the scrolling screen, the label index value "k" would have the range "k_tot" (73) to "k_tot" + "labelcolwidthminusone" (7) or 73 to 80 inclusive. "Max_allowed_k_tot" has been used to represent the upper limit of both the column label index and the screen data since they are scrolled together as a unit (lines 1050-1055 and 1110-1115 inside VHRLCLSCROLL_SCREEN). See Figure 16.5 for Screen 1 and Figures 16.6 and 16.7 for Screens 2 and 3.

16 Review and Extensions

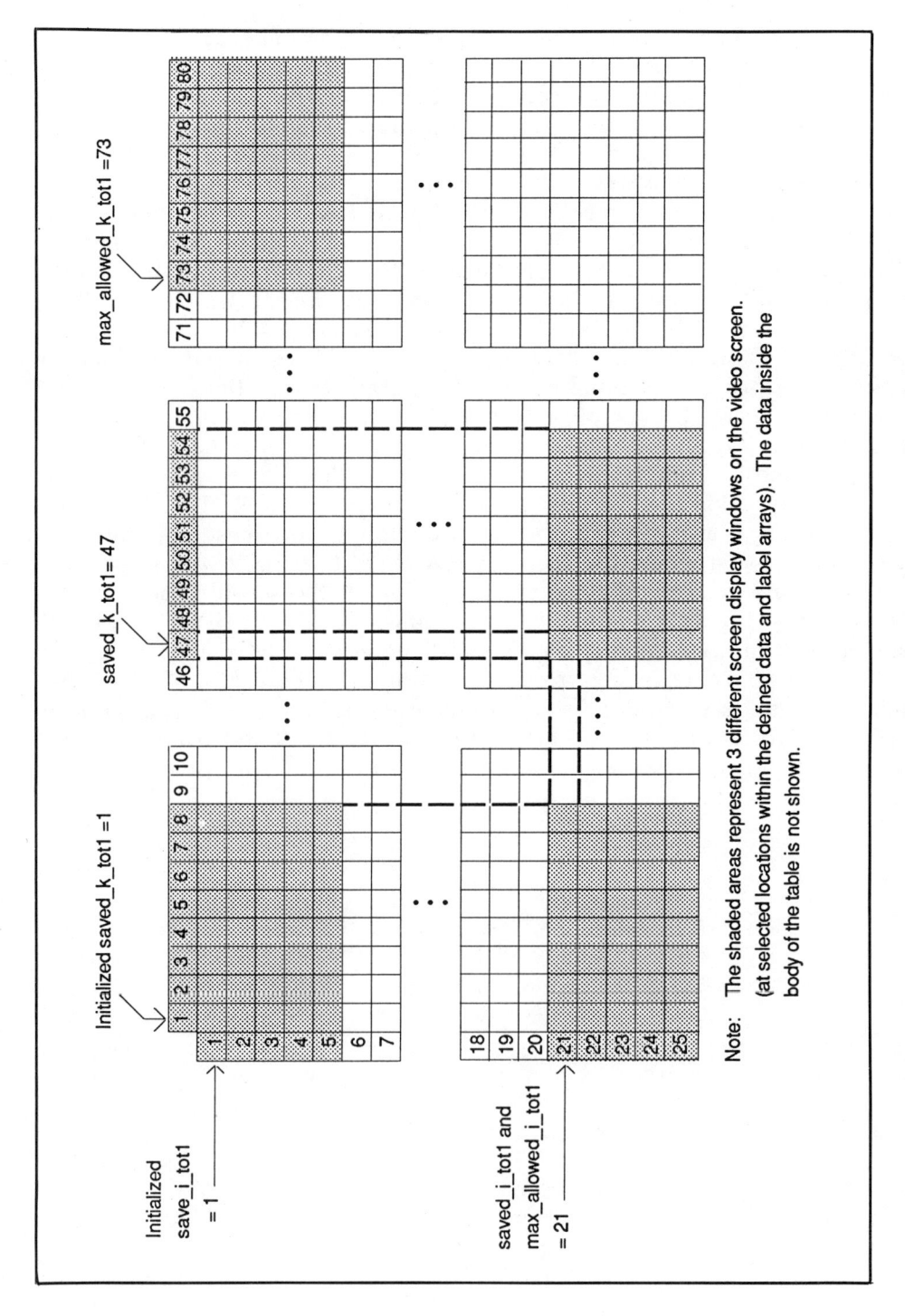

Figure 16.5 Screen 1: Relationship Between Data Array and the Video Display Window

388

Review and Extensions 16

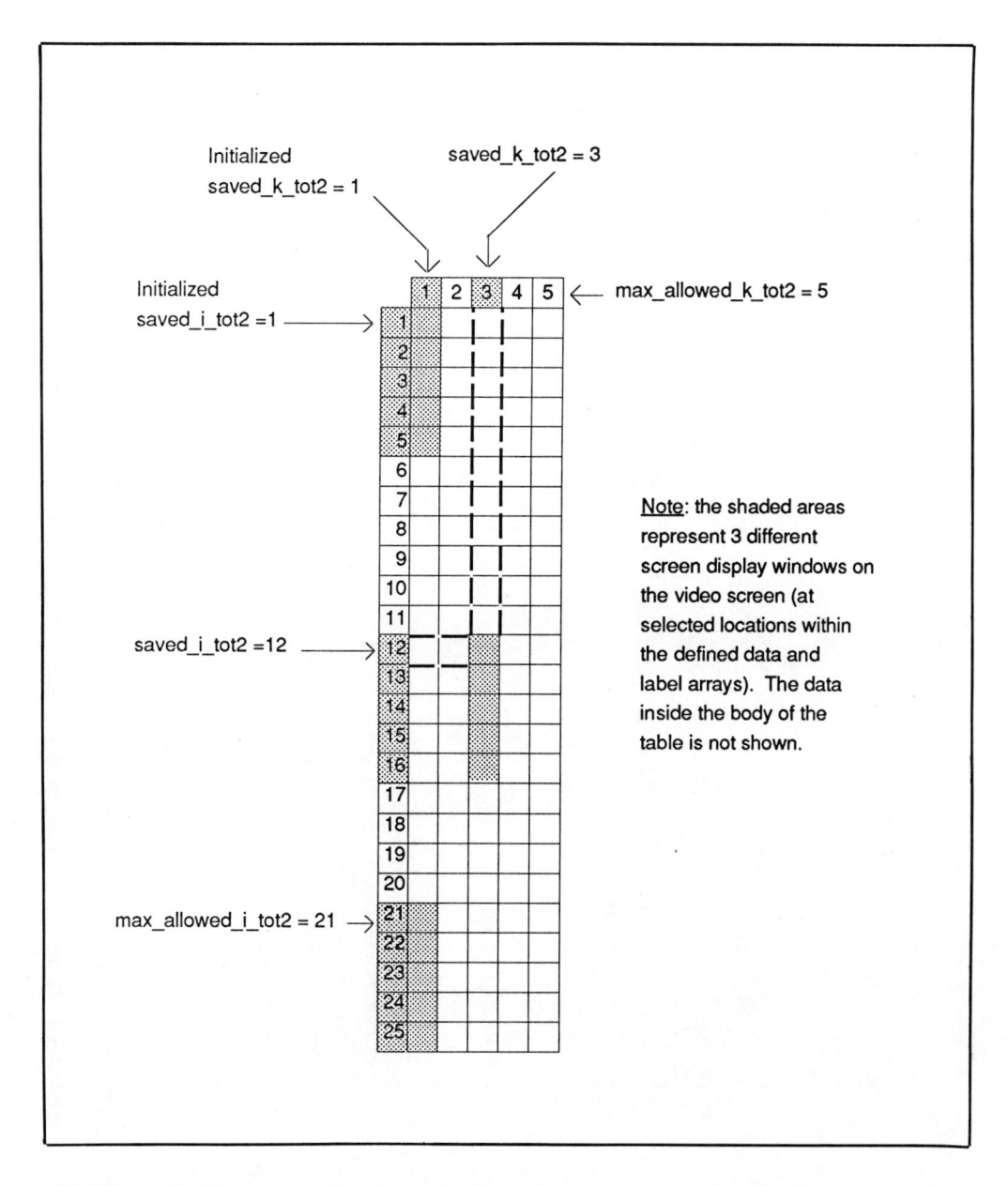

Figure 16.6 Screen 2: Relationship Between Data Array and the Video Display Window

Note: the shaded areas represent 3 different screen display windows on the video screen (at selected locations within the defined data and label arrays). The data inside the body of the table is not shown.

16 Review and Extensions

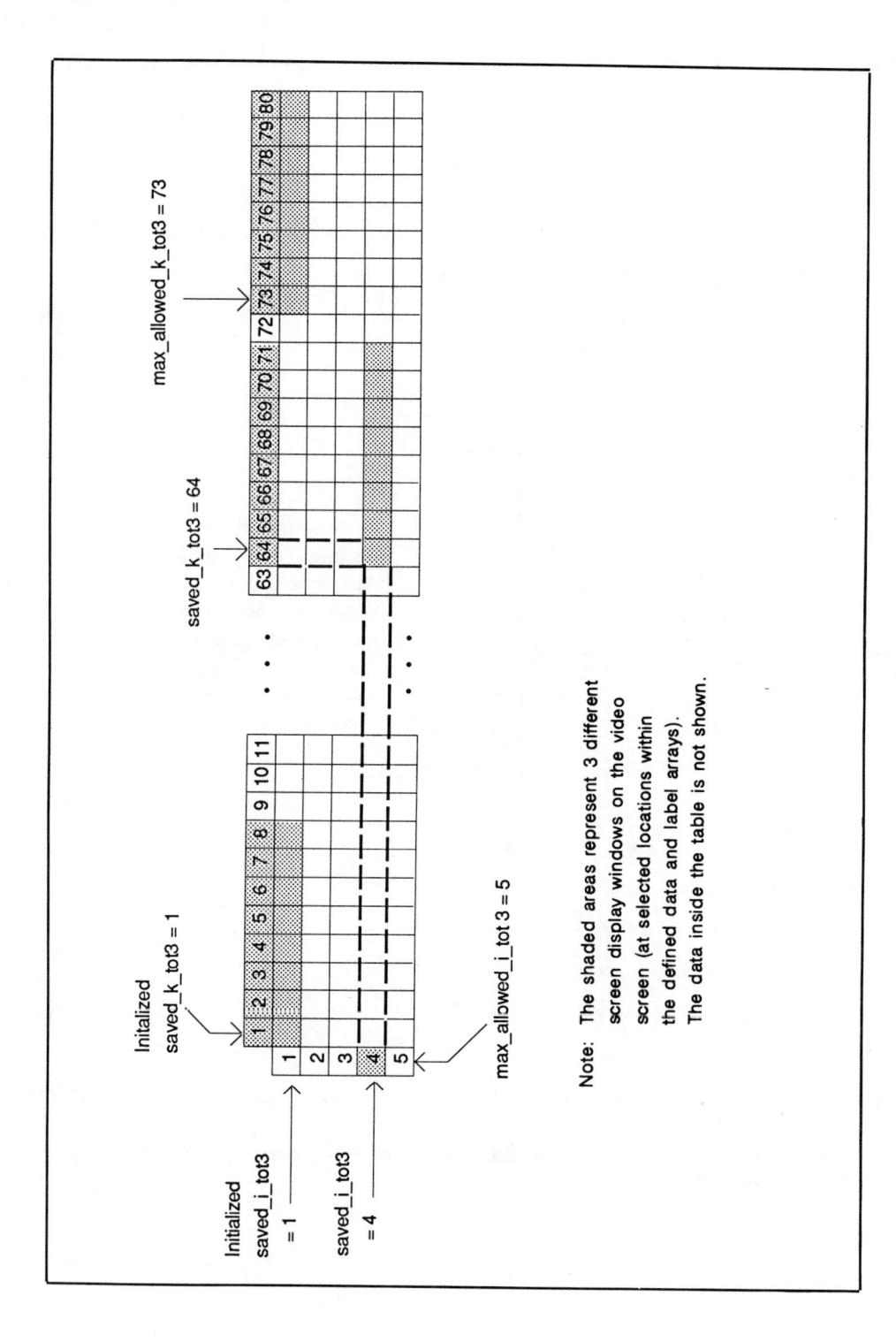

Figure 16.7 Screen 3: Relationship Between Data Array and the Video Display Window

Parameter #1, "saved_k_tot," was detailed in Chapter 14. When horizontal scrolling of column labels and data is in effect, the local variable "k_tot" is active, and its value will increase by 1 or decrease by 1, depending on which horizontal scrolling key you press (lines 1010 and 1070 via line 0875); however, once you press <Ret>, the current value of "k_tot" is assigned to "saved_k_tot" (line 1145) and that value is passed out of the procedure by way of the "var"'d parameter list variable and into the main routine's global variable (either "saved_k_tot1," "saved_k_tot2," or "saved_k_tot3," depending on which Screen was active at the time). This control variable enables you to scroll a given screen, leave it, scroll a different screen, and then return to the first screen and continue the scroll from where you left off.

Parameter numbers 9 through 14 are scrollable row and column label arrays. Representing the row and column label arrays are parameters 9 and 10 for Screen 1, 11 and 12 for Screen 2, and 13 and 14 for Screen 3. Notice that each of these one-dimensional arrays has a "var" prefix that enables the subprocedures of VHRLCLSCROLL_SCREEN to reference the contents of these global array variables prior to displaying the relevant portion on the screen using CHR_OUT. Remember, placing a "var" prefix in front of a variable in its parameter list allows a procedure to extend its scope or sphere of influence over that variable while the procedure is active.

As mentioned, the second main job of VHRLCLSCROLL_SCREEN is to provide a control environment. Control of scrolling the two-dimensional table data and the one-dimensional index labels (row or column) is really at two levels. One level might be called the **macro** level. Here, the REPEAT..UNTIL and CASE..END structures control what happens when a certain key is pressed. The phrase "what happens" refers to exactly which procedure teams will be called. For example, when you press the Right Arrow key (line 0875), the subprocedures REWRITE_SCREEN and REWRITE_COLLABEL are called together as a unit. The second level of control might be called the **micro** level. Here, all row or column label indexes and data table indexes are checked to ensure that they are within their preset legal bounds as per the constant values set out in "typdef16.inc." For example, if you perform a horizontal scroll, you would first check that both the column label index and the data table index values (both represented by "k_tot") are "in bounds" before you call the subprocedure team REWRITE_SCR and REWRITE_COLLABEL. Now look at the subprocedures.

16 Review and Extensions

REWRITE.SCR

Whenever you press an Up, Down, Left, or Right Arrow key, this subprocedure scrolls the table data inside the screen display window. All of the parameters used by this subprocedure are supplied from the parameter list of VHRLCLSCROLL_SCREEN. Since the size of the data array greatly exceeds the size of the screen display area (see Figure 16.5), you need a method of translating the press of an Arrow Key into the display of the appropriate section of the data table onto the limited screen display window.

In this procedure, the above scrolling task is accomplished in three stages. In the first stage, the two-dimensional area of the data array to be displayed is delimited. Line 0335 of the procedure sets the row range using the variable "i." Note that the "i_tot" values are supplied from the control section inside the body of VHRLCLSCROLL_ SCREEN (lines 0895, 0955, 1015, and 1075) and that the upper limit is the sum of "i_tot" and "datarowdepthminusone" (line 0335). Line 0345 sets the column range using the variable "k." Again, "k_tot" is supplied from VHRLCLSCROLL_ SCREEN (lines 0900, 0960, 1020, and 1080), and the upper limit of "k" is the sum of "k_ tot" and "datacolwidthminusone" (line 0345).

Once the row and column ranges of the data table have been defined, you then need to use these derived "i" (row) and "k" (column) ranges to display the appropriate subsections of the one-dimensional displaying arrays "scr1buffer," "scr2buffer," or "scr3buffer" (depending on which screen is active). See Figure 16.8.

To display the appropriate section of "scr#buffer" ("#" can represent either the number 1, 2, or 3) on the screen to produce the screen scrolling effect, you must first calculate the appropriate set of index values of the display array (one-dimensional "buffer" array) and then apply CHR OUT to the buffer array variable, using those calculated index values (lines 0385, 0400, and 0415).

Review and Extensions **16**

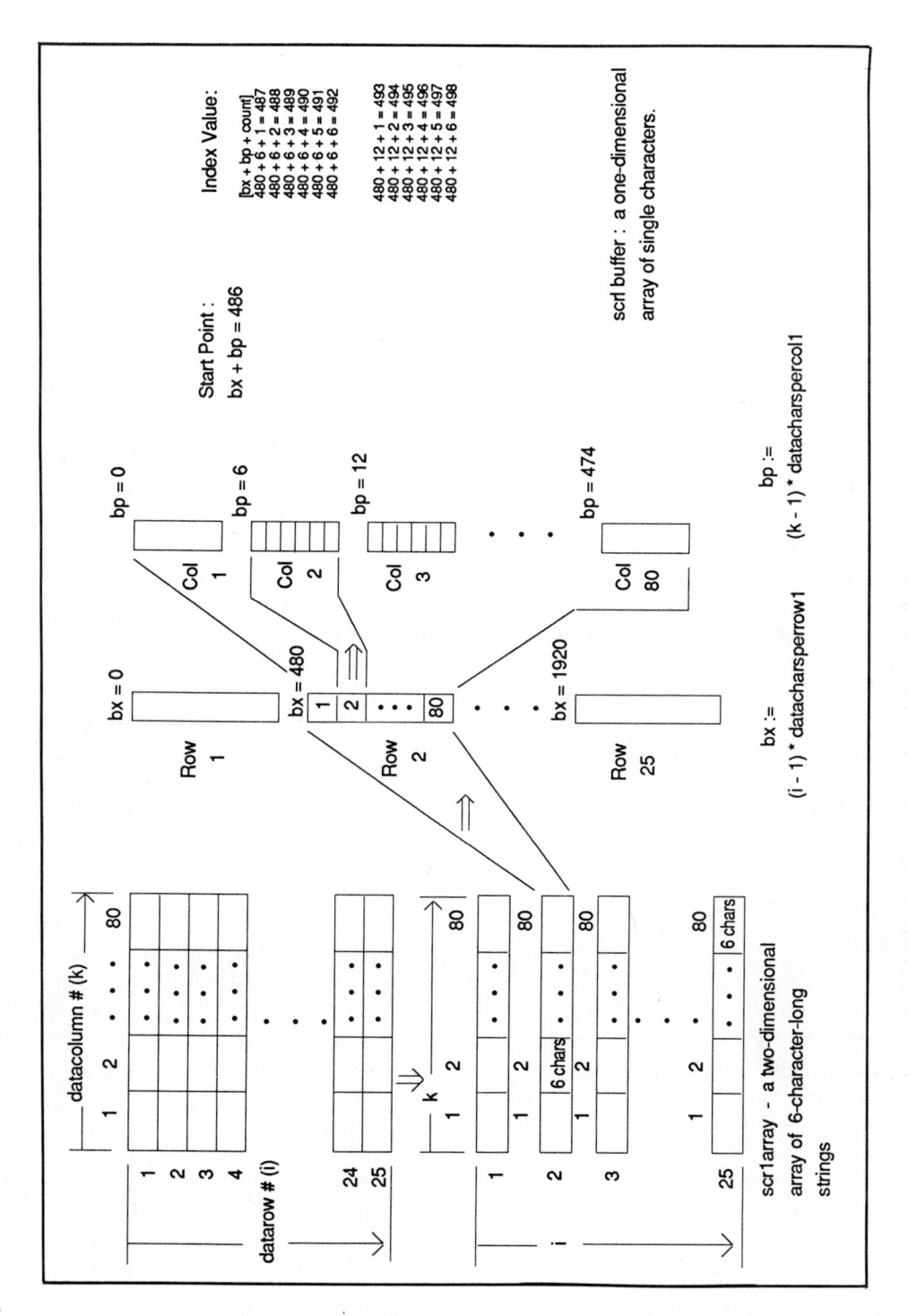

Figure 16.8 Table Data: Screen 1 Schematic of Conversion from Two-dimensional to One-dimensional Array

16 Review and Extensions

Since the scrolling data array was originally a two-dimensional array ("scr#array"), you need two index values to access any given element of the corresponding one-dimensional display array ("scr#buffer"). Look at lines 0360 and 0365 together with Figure 16.8. Line 0360 calculates the value of "bx," the defined row starting point of the two-dimensional array. Line 0365 calculates "bp," the defined column starting point of the same two-dimensional array. The sum of "bx" and "bp," then, is the calculated starting point inside the one-dimensional array "scr#buffer," expressed in terms of the equivalent two-dimensional array "scr#array." In Figure 16.8, you can see how each row of the two-dimensional array separates from its neighbours, rotates 90 degrees, and stretches out into its equivalent one-dimensional form.

Now, having reached the "bx + "bp" starting point of the one-dimensional array "scr#buffer," how do you display the contents located at that calculated starting point, and how far do you travel from that starting point for the display of each data element? Remember that the one-dimensional display array is an array of characters and that each display element is six characters long. The FOR..DO loop at line 0370 should make more sense now. Each six-character data element is built up on the screen one character at a time by traversing this FOR..DO loop — one loop traversal for each of the six characters that make up the six-character-wide display element. With each traversal of this inner loop, "bx + bp" (lines 0385, 0400, and 0415) stays the same, but "count" is increased by 1 so that CHR_OUT can place the character into the appropriate "j"-valued screen location (line 0430 for a different column on a given row and lines 0445-0450 for a change of rows). To slow down the action of this procedure, remove the curly brackets at line 0425 and watch how each character is displayed one by one to the screen by CHR_OUT. Assuming you are scrolling the data table for Screen 1, can you see why pressing once any of the Arrow Keys will result in the calculation of 40 "bx + bp" starting points and 240 calls to CHR_OUT (line 0385)? With five different rows and eight different columns, you have 40 different starting points. Since each data element residing at a given starting point has six characters, you have 240 separate calls to CHR_OUT — one for the display of each character on the screen.

Before you leave this subprocedure, look again at lines 0360-0365. Why (using Screen 1 as an example) do you use "datacharsperrow1" = 480 when the number of data characters on the screen is only 6 x 8 or 48? Remember that in calculating the row starting point, you must use the parameters of the data structure you are displaying and not those of the display screen. Look at Figure 16.8 again. A final question: why do the parameters "datacharspercol" and "maxcountofdatacharspercol" have exactly the same value all the time? The answer: only because of the way the screen parameters were defined above in "typdef16.inc." It only makes sense that if you define "datacharspercol" to be equal to 6 and if you were to go back and count how many characters you had ("maxcountofdatacharspercol"), you would have 6.

REWRITE_ROWLABEL

Whenever you press an Up or Down Arrow key, this subprocedure will scroll the row label data on the outside left of the screen display window. All of the parameters used by this subprocedure are supplied from the parameter list of VHRLCLSCROLL_SCREEN. Since the size of the row label array greatly exceeds the size of the screen display area reserved for its display (see Figure 16.5), you need a method of translating the press of an Arrow Key into the display of the appropriate section of the data table onto the limited screen display window.

In this procedure, the above task is accomplished in three stages. In the first stage, the two-dimensional area of the data array to be displayed is delimited. Line 0540 sets the row range using the variable "i." Note that the "i_tot" value is supplied from the control section inside the body of VHRLCLSCROLL_SCREEN (lines 0895 and 0955) and that the upper limit is the sum of "i_tot" and the parameter "labelrowdepthminusone" (line 0540).

Once you have defined the row range of the data table, you need to use the derived "i" (row) range to display the appropriate subsection of the one-dimensional arrays "rlabel1buffer," "rlabel2buffer," or "rlabel3buffer" (depending on which Screen is active). See Figure 16.9.

16 Review and Extensions

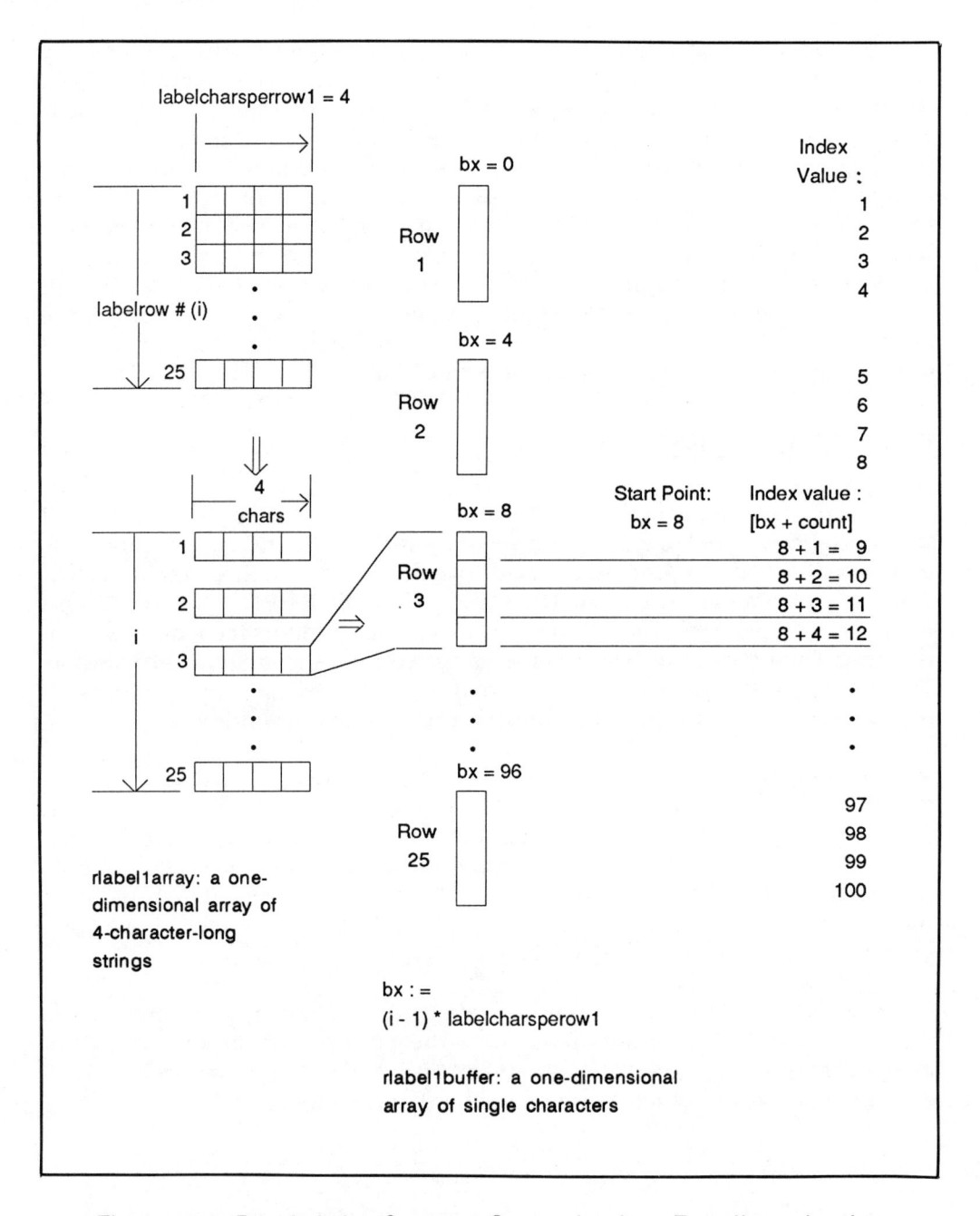

Figure 16.9 Row Labels: Screen 1 Conversion from Two-dimensional to One-dimensional Array

396

Review and Extensions 16

To display the appropriate section of "rlabel#buffer" to the screen, first calculate the appropriate set of index values of the display array (one-dimensional "buffer" array) and then apply CHR_OUT to the buffer variable, using those calculated index values (lines 0570, 0585, and 0600).

Since the scrolling label index array was originally a one-dimensional array ("rlabel#array"), you only need one index value to access any given element of the corresponding one-dimensional display array ("rlabel#buffer"). Look at line 0540 together with Figure 16.9. Line 0550 calculates the value of "bx," the defined row starting point. "Bx," then, is the calculated starting point inside the one-dimensional array, "rlabel#buffer," expressed in terms of the equivalent two-dimensional array "rlabel#array." In Figure 16.9, you can see how this one-dimensional array "unglues" between its rows, and how each row rotates 90 degrees to change into its equivalent one-dimensional form.

Now, having reached the "bx" starting point of the one-dimensional array "rlabel#buffer," how do you display the contents located at that calculated starting point, and how far do you travel from that starting point for the display of each data element? Remember that the one-dimensional display array is an array of characters and that each display element is four characters long. The FOR..DO loop at line 0555 should make more sense now. Each data element is created on the screen one character at a time by traversing this FOR..DO loop four times — one loop traversal for each of the four characters that make up the four-character-wide display element. With each traversal of this inner loop, "bx" (lines 0570, 0585, and 0600) stays the same, but "count" is increased by 1 so that CHR_OUT can put the character to the appropriate "j"-valued screen location (line 0615 for a different column on a given row and lines 0625-0630 for a change of rows). To slow down this procedure, remove the curly brackets at line 0610, and then watch how each character is displayed one by one to the screen by CHR_OUT.

Before leaving this subprocedure, consider a final question: why (using Screen 1) do the parameters "labelcharsperrow1" and "maxcountoflabelcharsperrow1" have exactly the same value all the time? The answer: only because of the way the screen parameters were defined above in "typdef16.inc." It only makes sense that if you define "labelcharsperrow1" to be equal to 4 and if you were to go back and count how many characters you had in "maxcountoflabelcharsperrow1," you would have 4.

16 Review and Extensions

REWRITE_COLLABEL

Whenever you press an Up or Down Arrow key, this subprocedure will scroll the row label data on the outside left of the screen display window. All of the parameters used by this subprocedure are supplied from the parameter list of VHRLCLSCROLL_SCREEN. Since the size of the row label array greatly exceeds the size of the screen display area reserved for its display (see Figure 16.5), you need a method of translating the press of an Arrow Key into the display of the appropriate section of the data table onto the limited screen display window.

In this procedure, the above task is accomplished in three stages. In the first stage, the one-dimensional area of the label array to be displayed is delimited. Line 0720 sets the column range using the variable "k." Note that the "k_tot" value is supplied from the control section inside the body of VHRLCLSCROLL_SCREEN (lines 1020 and 1080) and that the upper limit is the sum of "k_tot" and the parameter "labelcolwidthminusone."

Once you have defined the column range of the data table, you then need to use the derived "k" (column) range to display the appropriate subsection of one-dimensional arrays "clabel1buffer," "clabel2buffer," or "clabel3buffer" (depending on which screen is active). See Figure 16.10 for Screen 1 as an example.

To display the appropriate section of "clabel#buffer" to the screen, first calculate the appropriate set of index values of the display array (one-dimensional "buffer" array) and then apply CHR_OUT to the buffer variable, using the calculated index values (lines 0750, 0765, and 0780).

Since the scrolling label index array was originally a one-dimensional array ("clabel#array"), you only need one index value to access any given element of the corresponding one-dimensional display array ("clabel#buffer"). The character "#" represents either the number 1, 2, or 3. Look at line 0720 together with Figure 16.10. Line 0730 calculates the value of "bp," the defined column starting point. "Bp," then, is the calculated starting point inside the one-dimensional array "clabel#buffer," expressed in terms of the equivalent two-dimensional array "clabel#array." In Figure 16.10, you can see how the one-dimensional array "unglues" between its rows, and how each row rotates 90 degrees to change into its equivalent one-dimensional form. Note that the column labels are represented here as a one-dimensional array of rows in Figure 16.10.

Review and Extensions 16

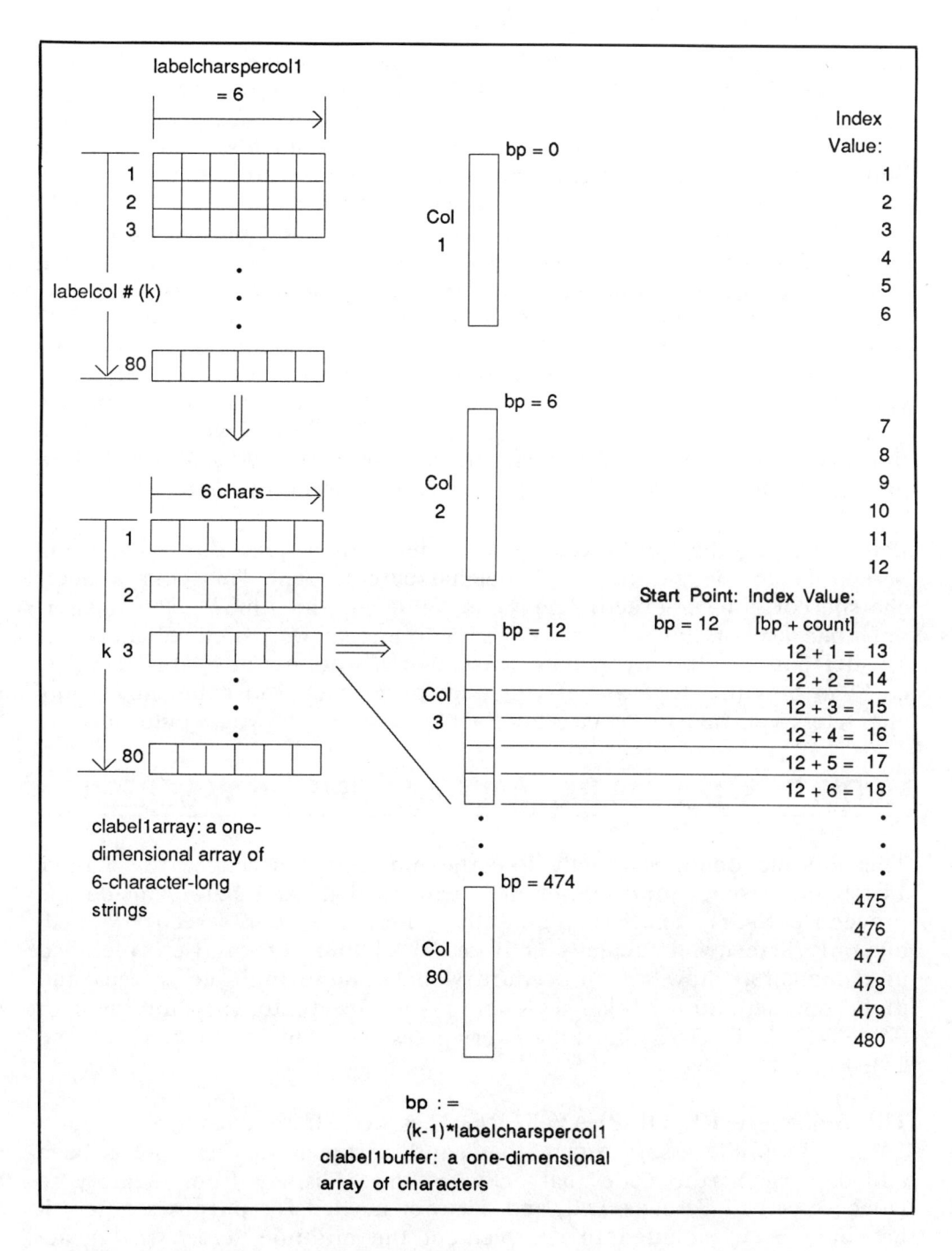

Figure 16.10 Column Labels: Screen 1 Conversion from Two-dimensional to One-dimensional Array

399

16 Review and Extensions

Now, having reached the "bp" starting point of the one-dimensional array "clabel#buffer," how do you display the contents located at that calculated starting point, and how far do you travel from that starting point for the display of each data element? Remember that the one-dimensional display array is an array of characters and that each display element is six characters long. The FOR..DO loop at line 0735 should make more sense now. Each data element is created on the screen one character at a time by traversing this FOR..DO loop six times, one loop traversal for each of the six characters that make up the six-character-wide display element. With each traversal of this inner loop, "bp" (lines 0750, 0765, and 0780) stays the same, but "count" is increased by 1 so that CHR_OUT can place the character at the appropriate "j"-valued screen location (line 0795 for a different column on a given row and lines 0805-0810 for a change of rows). To slow down the action of this procedure, remove the curly brackets at line 0790 and watch how each character is displayed one by one to the screen by CHR_OUT.

Before leaving this subprocedure, consider a final question: why (using Screen 1) do the parameters "labelcharspercol1" and "maxcountoflabelcharspercol1" have exactly the same value all the time? The answer: only because of the way the screen parameters were defined above in "typdef16.inc." It only makes sense that if you define "labelcharspercol1" to be equal to 6 and if you were to go back and count how many characters you had in "maxcountoflabelcharspercol1," you would have 6.

MODULE: S_D_SC16.INC (SAVE AND REDISPLAY SCREEN)

This module operates exactly like the module "s_d_sc.inc" in Chapter 14, so only some minor differences will be discussed here. Inside the procedure SAVE_SCREEN, note that there are four screens defined, but only Screen 4 is actually activated. All four screens were included to demonstrate how this procedure would handle multiple screens and to accomodate future changes should you decide to vary the sizes of Screens 1, 2, or 3 so that they overlap (as they did in Chapters 14 and 15).

The procedure RE_DISPLAY_SCREEN is no different from its Chapter 14 and 15 predecessors except that another screen (Screen 4) has been added. Again, the code that activates the redisplay from memory to video screen of Screens 1, 2, and 3 is not needed for purposes here. It has only been included to complement the multiple screen saving activity of SAVE_SCREEN. Following is the code for this module:

```
{========================================================================}
0005  {s_d_sc16.inc}
0010  {
0015     General screen save and redisplay module
0020     On disk as "s_d_sc16.inc"
0025  }
0030  {------------------------------------------------------------------}
0035
0040  procedure       SAVE_SCREEN(tlc,tlr,brc,brr :  integer;
0045                              var scr1_array :  s1_arr;
0050                              var scr2_array :  s2_arr;
0055                              var scr3_array :  s3_arr;
0060                              var scr4_array :  s4_arr);
0065
0070  var
0075      i,j,k      : integer;
0080      hll,vll    : integer;
0085
0090  Begin     {procedure save_screen}
0095      window(1,1,80,25);
0100      hll := brc - tlc + 1;
0105      vll := brr - tlr + 1;
0110      gotoxy(tlc,tlr);
0115      For i := 1 to vll DO
0120      Begin
0125          j := ((tlr - 1) * 160) + ((tlc - 1) * 2);
0130          For k := 1 to hll DO
0135          Begin
0140              IF (scr1_active = true) THEN
0145                  CHR_IN(j,scr1_array[i,k]);
0150
0155              IF (scr2_active = true) THEN
0160                  CHR_IN(j,scr2_array[i,k]);
0165
0170              IF (scr3_active = true) THEN
0175                  CHR_IN(j,scr3_array[i,k]);
0180                  {    FROM, TO  }
0185
0190              IF (scr4_active = true) THEN
0195                  CHR_IN(j,scr4_array[i,k]);
0200                  {    FROM, TO  }
0205
0210              j := j + 2;
0215          End;
0220          tlc := tlc;
0225          tlr := tlr + 1;
0230      End;
0235  End;      {procedure save_screen}
0240  {------------------------------------------------------------------}
0245
0250  procedure       RE_DISPLAY_SCREEN(tlc,tlr,brc,brr   : integer;
0255                                    maxscrdisplaychars : integer;
0260                                    var scr1_array   :  s1_arr;
0265                                    var scr1_buffer  :  s1_buf;
0270                                    var scr2_array   :  s2_arr;
0275                                    var scr2_buffer  :  s2_buf;
0280                                    var scr3_array   :  s3_arr;
0285                                    var scr3_buffer  :  s3_buf;
0290                                    var scr4_array   :  s4_arr;
0295                                    var scr4_buffer  :  s4_buf);
0300
```

continued...

16 Review and Extensions

...from previous page

```
0305
0310  var
0315        i,j,k,
0320        hll,vll,
0325        count,
0330        count_of_chars_per_line   : integer;
0333
0335  Begin       {procedure re_display_screen}
0340       window(1,1,80,25);
0345       hll := brc - tlc + 1;
0350       vll := brr - tlr + 1;
0355       count_of_chars_per_line := 1;
0360       count := 0;
0365       For i := 1 to vll DO
0370       Begin
0375            FOR k := 1 to hll DO
0380            Begin
0385                 count := count + 1;
0390                 IF (scr1_active = true) THEN
0395                      scr1_buffer[count] := scr1_array[i,k];
0400
0405                 IF (scr2_active = true) THEN
0410                      scr2_buffer[count] := scr2_array[i,k];
0415
0420                 IF (scr3_active = true) THEN
0425                      scr3_buffer[count] := scr3_array[i,k];
0430
0435                 IF (scr4_active = true) THEN
0440                      scr4_buffer[count] := scr4_array[i,k];
0445            End;
0450       End;
0455       j := ((tlr - 1) * 160) + ((tlc - 1) * 2);
0460       FOR count := 1 to maxscrdisplaychars DO
0465       Begin
0470            IF (scr1_active = true) THEN
0475                 CHR_OUT(j,ORD(scr1_buffer[count]));
0480
0485            IF (scr2_active = true) THEN
0490                 CHR_OUT(j,ORD(scr2_buffer[count]));
0495
0500            IF (scr3_active = true) THEN
0505                 CHR_OUT(j,ORD(scr3_buffer[count]));
0510            { destination(j) , source(ORD(.....) }
0515
0520            IF (scr4_active = true) THEN
0525                 CHR_OUT(j,ORD(scr4_buffer[count]));
0530            { destination(j) , source(ORD(.....) }
0535
0540            count_of_chars_per_line := count_of_chars_per_line + 1;
0545
0550            IF (count_of_chars_per_line > hll) THEN
0555            Begin
0560                 tlr := tlr + 1;
0565                 j := ((tlr - 1) * 160) + ((tlc - 1) * 2);
0570                 count_of_chars_per_line := 1;
0575            End
0580            ELSE
0585                 j := j + 2;
0590       End;
0595  End;       {procedure re_display_screen}
{=========================================================================}
```

Review and Extensions 16

MODULE: TXTWR16.INC (TEXT WRITE)

This module is very similar in structure and function to a module developed earlier in Chapter 13 called "textwrit.inc" (textwrite include). In this chapter, changes have been made to the original to increase the size of the text display area and to increase the scrolling speed. You do not need to retype all that follows. Just fetch "textwrit.inc" from the disk and resave it under the new name; then make the changes you see in the following code:

```
{========================================================================}
0005 {txtwr16.inc}
0010
0015 {On disk as "txtwr16.inc"}
0020
0025 {------------------------------------------------------------------}
0030
0035 procedure      TXTWRIT(var file_name : str12);
0040 {
0045   Assumes that the text file it displays has already been
0050   created. This procedure will accept any pre-created text
0055   file of indefinite length (60 lines or less).
0060   It will pull this file from the disk storage and place
0065   it into a display array inside the computer's memory.
0070   This array will also be scrollable.
0075 }
0080
0085 const
0090       escape     = #$1b;
0095       bell       = #$07;
0100
0105 type
0110       str12      = string[12];
0115       str80      = string[80];
0120
0125 var
0130       line             : str80;
0135       line_count       : integer;
0140       k                : integer;
0145       mode_choice      : char;
0150       entry_error      : boolean;
0155 {------------------------------------------------------------------}
0160
0165 procedure      TEXT_FILE_TO_ARRAY(lin_ct : integer);
0170
0175 const
0180       max_file_lines = 60;
0185
0190 type
0195       array_of_screen_text  = ARRAY[1..max_file_lines,1..80]of char;
0200       line_length_array     = ARRAY[1..max_file_lines] of integer;
0205
0210 var
```

continued...

403

16 Review and Extensions

...from previous page

```
0215        screen_text      : array_of_screen_text;
0220        i,k              : integer;
0225        line_length      : line_length_array;
0230
0235     {------------------------------------------------------------}
0240
0245        procedure      SCROLL_IT;
0250
0255        label
0260           REP_READ;         {a label}
0265
0270        const
0275           scroll_up      = #$48;
0280           scroll_down    = #$50;
0285           page_up        = #$49;
0290           page_down      = #$51;
0295           carriage_ret   = #$0d;
0300
0305        var
0310           i_tot,i          : integer;
0315           col,row          : integer;   {for "page_up" & "page_down"}
0320           scroll_choice    : char;
0325           exit_scroll      : boolean;
0330
0335        Begin     {sub procedure scroll_it}
0340           exit_scroll := false;
0345           i := 1;
0350           REPEAT
0355              REP_READ:       {a label with colon}
0360              read(KBD,scroll_choice);
0365              CASE(scroll_choice) OF
0370
0375                 scroll_up  :  Begin   {towards top of screen}
0380                                  window(1,5,80,19);
0385                                  {for INSLINE}
0390                                  i_tot := i_tot - 1;
0395                                  IF (i_tot < 1) THEN
0400                                  Begin
0405                                     i_tot := 1;
0410                                     goto rep_read;
0415                                  End;
0420                                  gotoxy(1,1); {local to window}
0425                                  INSLINE;
0430                                  FOR k := 1 to
0435                                          line_length[i_tot] DO
0440                                  Begin
0445                                     write(screen_text[i_tot,k]);
0450                                  End;
0455                               End;    {scroll_up}
0460
0465                 scroll_down :  Begin
0470                                  window(1,5,80,19);
0475                                  {for DELLINE}
0480                                  i_tot := i_tot + 1;
0485                                  IF (i_tot > lin_ct - 14) THEN
0490                                  Begin
0495                                     i_tot := i_tot - 1;
0500                                     goto rep_read;
0505                                  End;
```

continued...

404

...from previous page

```
0510                         gotoxy(1,1); {local to window}
0515                         DELLINE;
0520                         gotoxy(1,10);
0525                         FOR k := 1 to
0530                                 line_length[i_tot + 14] DO
0535                         Begin
0540                             write(screen_text[i+14,k]);
0545                         End;
0550                     End;      {scroll_down}
0555
0560             page_up    : Begin
0565                         window(1,1,80,25);
0570                         {for WHEREX & WHEREY}
0575                         i_tot := i_tot - 15;
0580                         IF (i_tot < 1) THEN
0585                         Begin
0590                             i_tot := i_tot + 15;
0595                             {back to original i_tot}
0600                             goto rep_read;
0605                         End;
0610                         gotoxy(1,5); {global coords}}
0615                         col := WHEREX ; row := WHEREY;
0620                         FOR i := i_tot to i_tot + 14 DO
0625                         Begin
0630                             gotoxy(col,row);clreol;
0635                             FOR k := 1 to line_length[i]
0640                             DO Begin
0645                                 write(screen_text[i,k]);
0650                             End;
0655                             col := col ; row := row + 1;
0660                         End;
0665                     End;      {page_up}
0670
0675             page_down  : Begin
0680                         window(1,1,80,25);
0685                         {for WHEREX & WHEREY}
0690                         i_tot := i_tot + 15;
0695                         IF (i_tot > lin_ct - 14) THEN
0700                         Begin
0705                             i_tot := i_tot - 15;
0710                             {back to original i_tot}
0715                             goto rep_read;
0720                         End;
0725                         gotoxy(1,5); {global coords}
0730                         col := WHEREX ; row := WHEREY;
0735                         FOR i := i_tot to i_tot + 14 DO
0740                         Begin
0745                             gotoxy(col,row);clreol;
0750                             FOR k := 1 to line_length[i]
0755                             DO Begin
0760                                 write(screen_text[i,k]);
0765                             End;
0770                             col := col ; row := row + 1;
0775                         End;
0780                     End;      {page_down}
```

continued...

16 Review and Extensions

...from previous page

```
0785
0790                    carriage_ret:  Begin
0795                                        exit_scroll := true;
0800                                   End
0805
0810                ELSE
0815
0820                END;       {CASE}
0825           UNTIL(exit_scroll = true);
0830     End;      {sub procedure scroll_it}
0835  {------------------------------------------------------------------}
0840
0845  Begin    {procedure text_file_to_array}
0850       FOR i := 1 to max_file_lines DO
0855       Begin
0860            FOR k := 1 to 80 DO
0865            Begin
0870                 screen_text[i,k] := ' ';    {1 blank}
0875            End;
0880       End;
0885
0890       RESET(filevar);
0895       FOR i := 1 to lin_ct DO   {line_count NOT known in advance}
0900       Begin
0905            readln(filevar,line);
0910            {FROM filevar TO file transfer variable, "line" }
0915            line_length[i] := LENGTH(line);
0920            FOR k := 1 to line_length[i] DO
0925            Begin
0930                 screen_text[i,k] := line[k];
0935            End;
0940       End;
0945       CLOSE(filevar);
0950       {file now transferred from disk file via file transfer
0955        variable, "line" into an array in computer's memory}
0960
0965       clrscr;   {whole screen}
0970       TEXTCOLOR(0);TEXTBACKGROUND(15);
0975       gotoxy(31,2);write(' TEXT FILE SCROLLER ');
0980       gotoxy(1,4);for k := 1 to 80 do write('=');
0985       gotoxy(1,20);for k := 1 to 80 do write('=');
0990       { scrolling borders }
0995       gotoxy(31,21);write(' Hit <RET> to Exit ');
1000       TEXTCOLOR(15);TEXTBACKGROUND(0);
1005
1010       {initialize first 15 lines - to prepare for scrolling}
1015       window(1,5,80,19);
1020       gotoxy(1,1);    {inside the scrolling window}
1025       {scrolling window is 15 lines deep (5 to 19 inclusive = 15)
1030        on screen and is 80 columns wide}
1035       FOR i := 1 to 15 DO
1040       Begin
1045            CASE i OF
1050
1055            1..14  : Begin
1060                          FOR k := 1 to line_length[i] DO
1065                          Begin
1070                               write(screen_text[i,k]);
1075                          End;
```

continued...

...from previous page

```
1080                              writeln;
1085                          End;
1090
1095            15      : Begin
1100                          FOR k := 1 to line_length[i] DO
1105                          Begin
1110                              WRITE(screen_text[i,k]);
1115                          End;
1120                      End;
1125            END;       {case}
1130      End;
1135      SCROLL_IT;       {procedure using  array - screen_text[i,k]}
1140 End;                  {procedure text_file_to_array}
1145 {---------------------------------------------------------------}
1150
1155 Begin     {procedure txtwrit}
1160     ASSIGN(filevar,file_name);
1165     RESET(filevar);
1170
1175     line_count := 0;
1180     WHILE not EOF(filevar) DO
1185     Begin
1190         readln(filevar,line);
1195         line_count := line_count + 1;
1200     End;
1205     CLOSE(filevar);
1210
1215     TEXT_FILE_TO_ARRAY(line_count);
1220     window(1,1,80,25);clrscr;
1225 End;      {procedure txtwrit}
{=================================================================}
```

TXTWR16.INC: NOTES

To deepen the scrolling text display area from 10 to 15 lines, several small changes have been made to the code in the body of the procedure TEXT_FILE_TO_ARRAY. Here, you set up the scrolling borders, adjust the local scrolling window size, and then initialize the first 15 lines of text onto the scrolling screen (lines 1035-1130). The other change to note is at line 0180 where the value of the constant "max_file_lines" has been changed to 60. There is no need to take any more array space than you think you will need.

The second major adjustment made here is to increase the speed of the scrolling. This increase was achieved by adding the "page_up" and "page_down" operations inside the subprocedure SCROLL_IT. With these operations, you can scroll whole 15-line chunks of text data up and down with the touch of a key.

407

16 Review and Extensions

Notice at line 0575 of "page_up" and line 0690 of "page_down" that the "i" index will be decreased by 15 as you move toward the top of the scrolling array "screen_text" and that it will increase by 15 as you move toward the bottom. In "page_down" you might be wondering why the number "lin_ct - 14" (line count minus 14) is used as the upper limit of the scrolling index, "i." Assume for the moment that the value "lin_ct" is 53. If you had the last 15 lines of text on the screen, what would be the index value of the top line on the screen? Counting 15 backwards from "lin_ct" or 53 (using 53 as 1 in your counting), you would come to the number 39 ("lin_ct - 14"). Can you now see why the number 14 is used in these "scroll_down," "page_up," and "page_down" operations? (If you include end points in the lower and upper limits of the FOR..DO loops, the number of displayed lines will be 15, even though you only add 14 to the lower limit value.)

Before continuing, there are three more points to consider. First, the window sizes for the "scroll_up" and "scroll_down" operations are local windows designed for use with the INLSINE and DELLINE functions, while the window sizes for the "page_up" and "page_down" operations are global because they use the WHEREX and WHEREY functions. Second, in the "page_up" and "page_down" operations, you need to blank the display line prior to writing the text there in case the line coming into the location is shorter than the one that previously occupied it. Finally, unlike its predecessor routine in Chapter 13, this routine displays the text characters one line at a time on the screen by writing them from an array of characters ("screen text"). To trace the difference in the way the "scroll" operations and the "page" operations work, insert "delay(100);" statements immediately after the four "write" statements in each of these operations.

As mentioned above, 60 lines were reserved for the scrolling text file. In case you can't think of anything to type, try HELP16.TXT as shown in Figure 16.2. This file is slightly under 60 lines and can be used to demonstrate how TXTWR16.INC works. Note line 0180.

To create this file, do the following: get to the Turbo ">" prompt and type "w" for "workfile"; next, type in the file name HELP16.TXT (upper- or lowercase letters can be used). A new file will be created by the system, and the Turbo Editor will appear on the top line of the blank screen. At this point, just type in what you see in Figure 16.2. After typing, press <Ctrl/k> <Ctr/D> and then type "s" (save) in response to the Turbo prompt. The text file will be saved to disk and can be used with TXTWR16.INC, the text file scrolling module.

MODULE: MULTSC16.DRV (MULTIPLE SCREEN)

To understand what this module does, look at the internal procedure SET_UP_SCREEN. At the start of this program, three blank windows appear on the screen, labelled "a1," "a2," and "a3," denoting Screen a1, Screen a2, and Screen a3. Along the top of each window, the text "COL #" (column number) appears. Down the side the text "ROW #" (row number) appears. These are the row and column number indexes for the table data to be displayed inside the windows on the screen. Following this, the text displayed at the bottom of the screen (see Figure 16.1) invites you to press any one of the four key combinations. Pressing one of the first three <a1><RET>, <a2><RET>, or <a3><RET> will bring up onto the screen a table of information along with its corresponding row and column index (labels). At this point, you can press any of the four Arrow Keys on the Numeric Keypad to scroll the data inside the window. To end scrolling of a given window, you would press <RET>. You can select another window to scroll or press <h><RET> for help. If you press <h><RET>, the displayed screen will disappear and a new screen will appear in its place, which contains a scrollable (previously created) text file that explains the information inside the screen windows. After you scroll this information, you can press <RET> again, and the original screen will reappear in place of the text screen. You can then elect to continue scrolling the screens, reenter the "help" or text screen, or press <q><RET> to "quit" or exit the program.

MULTSCR16.DRV is quite long, so to keep things straight in your mind, refer to Figures 16.11 and 16.12. The first presents an outline of the Declaration Section, showing all the procedures used; the second presents an outline of the Body of the program, which details how these procedures are coordinated into a working unit. Following Figures 16.11 and 16.12 is the code.

16 Review and Extensions

```
Program  multsc16.drv

{$i typdef16.inc}
                           External Procedures:

{$i chrinout.inc}          CHR_IN, CHR_OUT
{$i windows.inc}           WINDOW_BORDER
{$i rewrsc16.inc}          VHRLCLSCROLL_SCREEN (REWRITE_SCR,
                                REWRITE_ROWLABEL, REWRITE_COLLABEL)
{$i s_d_sc16.inc}          SAVE_SCREEN, RE_DISPLAY_SCREEN
{$i txtwr16.inc}           TXTWRIT

                           Internal Procedures:

procedure                  REVERSE_SCREEN
procedure                  NORMAL_SCREEN
procedure                  SET_UP_SCREEN
procedure                  CREATE_VIDEO_JTABLES
procedure                  CREATE_ROW_LABELS
procedure                  CREATE_COL_LABELS
procedure                  INIT_VIDEO_JTABLES
procedure                  INIT_ROW_LABELS
procedure                  INIT_COL_LABELS

{----------------------------------------------------------------}

                      BODY of multsc16.drv
                      see Figure 16.12
```

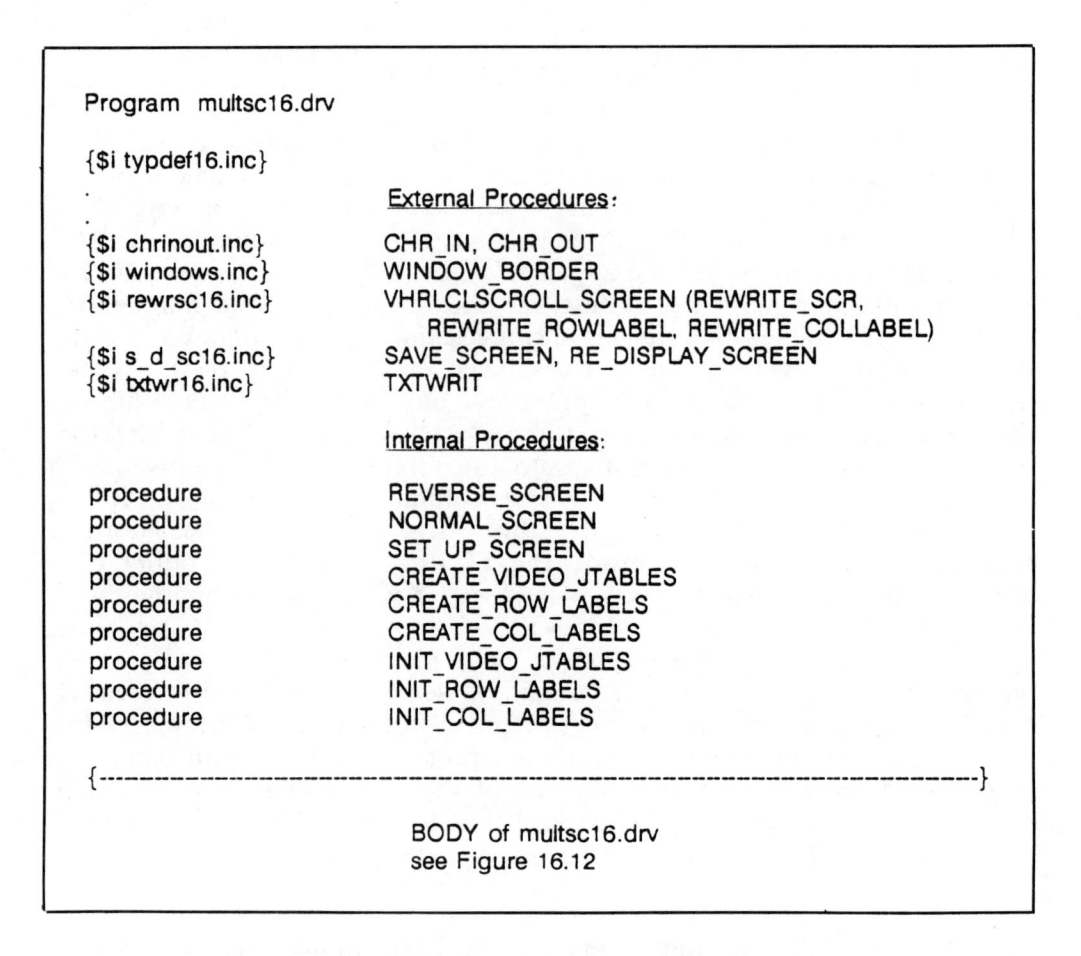

Figure 16.11 MULTSC16.DRV — Declaration Section

410

Review and Extensions 16

```
                        Declarations
                        See Figure 16.11
{------------------------------------------------------}
Begin
SET_UP_SCREEN
                                    CREATE_VIDEO_JTABLES
      for each of Screen 1,        CREATE_ROW_LABELS
      Screen 2, and Screen 3       CREATE_COL_LABELS

      REPEAT
          CASE (Choice of Screen 1, Screen 2, or Screen 3)

          a1:   Begin
                    IF (Screen 1 is not initialized) THEN
                       INIT_VIDEO_JTABLES
                       INIT_ROW_LABELS      (for Screen 1)
                       INIT_COL_LABELS
                       VHRLCLSCROLL_SCREEN
                       {Screen 1 now initialized}
                    End
                    ELSE {if Screen 1 has been initialized}
                    Begin
                       VHRLCLSCROLL_SCREEN
                    End

          a2:   Begin
                    IF (Screen 2 not initialized) THEN
                       INIT_VIDEO_JTABLES
                       INIT_ROW_LABELS
                       INIT_COL_LABELS
                       VHRLCLSCROLL_SCREEN
                       {Screen 2 now initialized}
                    End
                    ELSE {if Screen 2 has been initialized}
                    Begin
                       VHRLCLSCROLL_SCREEN
                    End

          a3:   Begin
                    IF (Screen 3 not initialized) THEN
                       INIT_VIDEO_JTABLES
                       INIT_ROW_LABELS      (for Screen 3)
                       INIT_COL_LABELS
                       VHRLCLSCROLL_SCREEN
                       {Screen 3 now initialized}
                    End
                    ELSE {if Screen 3 has been initialized}
                    Begin
                       VHRLCLSCROLL_SCREEN
                    End

          h:    Begin
                    SAVE_SCREEN (25 x 80 holding all 3 windows)
                    TXTWRIT
                    RE_DISPLAY_SCREEN
                End

          q:    exit:=true

          ELSE

          END  {case}
      UNTIL  (exit=true)
```

Figure 16.12 MULTSC16.DRV – Body

16 Review and Extensions

```
{==============================================================}
0005 program   multscl6(input,output);
0010
0015 {
0020   On disk as "multscl6.drv"
0025 }
0030
0035 {==============================================================}
0040 {$i typdef16.inc}
0045 {==============================================================}
0050
0055 const
0060       a1   = 146;      {ascii "a" = 97 ; ascii "1" = 49}
0065       a2   = 147;
0070       a3   = 148;
0075       h    = 104;      {ascii "h" = 104}
0080       q    = 113;      {ascii "q" = 113}
0085
0090       bell = #$07;
0095
0100
0105 type
0110       str3  =  string[3];
0115       str12 =  string[12];
0120
0125 var
0130       i                : integer;
0135       screen_choice    : str3;    {includes the carriage return}
0140       ascii_sum        : integer;
0145       character        : char;
0150       exit             : boolean;
0155       saved_i_tot1,saved_i_tot2,saved_i_tot3,
0160       saved_k_tot1,saved_k_tot2,saved_k_tot3  : integer;
0165
0170       filename         : str12;
0175       filevar          : TEXT;
0180
0185 {==============================================================}
0190 {$i chrinout.inc}
0195 {$i windows.inc}
0200 {$i rewrscl6.inc}
0205 {$i s_d_scl6.inc}
0210 {$i txtwr16.inc}
0215 {==============================================================}
0220
0225 procedure      REVERSE_SCREEN;
0230
0235 Begin      {procedure reverse_screen}
0240       TEXTCOLOR(0);        {"0"  = black, or no color}
0245       TEXTBACKGROUND(15);  {"15" = white, or all colors}
0250 End;       {procedure reverse_screen}
0255 {--------------------------------------------------------------}
0260
0265 procedure      NORMAL_SCREEN;
0270
0275 Begin      {procedure normal_screen}
0280       TEXTCOLOR(15);       {"15" = white, or all colors}
0285       TEXTBACKGROUND(0);   {"0"  = black, no color}
0290 End;       {procedure normal_screen}
0295 {--------------------------------------------------------------}
0300
```

continued...

Review and Extensions 16

...from previous page

```
0305  procedure        SET_UP_SCREEN;
0310
0315  type
0320      str4 = string[4];
0325
0330  var
0335        i                   : integer;
0340        vertical_label      : str4;
0345        x_coord,
0350        y_coord             : integer;
0355        label_letter        : char;
0360
0365  Begin      {procedure set_up_screen}
0370       window(1,1,80,25);
0375       REVERSE_SCREEN;gotoxy(26,1);
0380       write(' SCREEN I/O REVIEW CHAPTER 16 ');
0385       gotoxy(37,20);
0390       write(' CONTROL ');
0395       NORMAL_SCREEN;
0400       gotoxy(8,22);write('<a1> = Scroll Screen a1:');
0405       gotoxy(48,22);write('<a2> = Scroll Screen a2:');
0410       gotoxy(8,23);write('<a3> = Scroll Screen a3:');
0415       gotoxy(48,23);write('<h> = Scrolling Help Screen');
0420       gotoxy(19,24);write('Press <RET> to Exit Scroll. '); {1 bl}
0425                  write('Press <q> to Quit');
0430
0435       vertical_label := 'ROW#';
0440       WINDOW_BORDER(9,5,60,11,1);    {border style #1}
0445       gotoxy(4,4);write('a1:');
0450       gotoxy(3,6) ; x_coord := WHEREX ; y_coord := WHEREY;
0455       FOR i := 1 to 4 DO
0460       Begin
0465            gotoxy(x_coord,y_coord);
0470            label_letter := COPY(vertical_label,i,1);
0475            write(label_letter);
0480            {* delay(500); *}
0485            x_coord := x_coord ; y_coord := y_coord + 1;
0490       End;
0495       gotoxy(24,3);write('COL #');
0500
0505       WINDOW_BORDER(70,5,79,11,4);   {border style #4}
0510       gotoxy(66,4);write('a2:');
0515       gotoxy(64,6) ; x_coord := WHEREX ; y_coord := WHEREY;
0520       FOR i := 1 to 4 DO
0525       Begin
0530            gotoxy(x_coord,y_coord);
0535            label_letter := COPY(vertical_label,i,1);
0540            write(label_letter);
0545            {* delay(500); *}
0550            x_coord := x_coord ; y_coord := y_coord + 1;
0555       End;
0560       gotoxy(72,3);write('COL #');
0565
0570       WINDOW_BORDER(9,16,60,18,3);   {border style #3}
0575       gotoxy(4,15);write('a3:');
0580       gotoxy(4,16);write('ROW# ');
0585       gotoxy(24,14);write('COL #');
0590       gotoxy(8,22);write('<a1> = Scroll Screen a1:');
0595       gotoxy(48,22);write('<a2> = Scroll Screen a2:');
0600       gotoxy(8,23);write('<a3> = Scroll Screen a3:');
```

continued...

16 Review and Extensions

...from previous page

```
0605            gotoxy(48,23);write('<h> = Scrolling Help Screen');
0610            gotoxy(19,24);write('Press <RET>  to Exit Scroll. '); {1 bl}
0615                         write('Press <q> to Quit');
0620            gotoxy(40,21);
0625    End;        {procedure set_up_screen}
0630    {-----------------------------------------------------------------}
0635
0640    procedure CREATE_VIDEO_JTABLES(var scrlarray   : slarr;
0645                                   var scrlbuffer  : slbuf;
0650                                   var scr2array   : s2arr;
0655                                   var scr2buffer  : s2buf;
0660                                   var scr3array   : s3arr;
0665                                   var scr3buffer  : s3buf);
0670
0675    type
0680        str6      = string[6];
0685
0690    var
0695        row,col    : integer;
0700        j          : integer;
0705        index      : integer;
0710        jstr1      : str6;
0715        jstr2      : str6;
0720        jstr3      : str6;
0725        count      : integer;
0730
0735    Begin     {procedure create_video_jtables}
0740        IF (scrl_active = true) THEN
0745        Begin
0750            FOR row := 1 to maxdatarows1 DO
0755            Begin
0760                FOR col := 1 to maxdatacols1 DO
0765                Begin
0770                    j := ((row - 1) * 160) + ((col - 1) * 2);
0775                    STR(j:4 , jstr1);
0780                    jstr1 := CONCAT('*',jstr1,'*');
0785                    scrlarray[row,col] := jstr1;
0790                End;
0795            End;
0800
0805            {assign 2 dimensional array into 1 dimensional buffer}
0810            index := 0;
0815            FOR row := 1 to maxdatarows1 DO
0820            Begin
0825                FOR col := 1 to maxdatacols1 DO
0830                Begin
0835                    FOR count := 1 to
0840                                maxcountofdatacharspercol1 DO
0845                    Begin
0850                        index := index + 1;
0855                        scrlbuffer[index] :=
0860                                COPY(scrlarray[row,col],
0865                                                       count,
0870                                                       1);
0875                    End;
```

continued...

Review and Extensions 16

...from previous page

```
0880                          End;
0885                    End;
0890              End;        {screen1 active}
0895
0900
0905        IF (scr2_active = true) THEN
0910        Begin
0915              FOR row := 1 to maxdatarows2 DO
0920              Begin
0925                    FOR col := 1 to maxdatacols2 DO
0930                    Begin
0935                          j := ((row - 1) * 160) + ((col - 1) * 2);
0940                          STR(j:4 , jstr2);
0945                          jstr2 := CONCAT('*',jstr2,'*');
0950                          scr2array[row,col] := jstr2;
0955                    End;
0960              End;
0965
0970              {assign 2 dimensional array into 1 dimensional buffer}
0975              index := 0;
0980              FOR row := 1 to maxdatarows2 DO
0985              Begin
0990                    FOR col := 1 to maxdatacols2 DO
0995                    Begin
1000                          FOR count := 1 to
1005                                      maxcountofdatacharspercol2 DO
1010                          Begin
1015                                index := index + 1;
1020                                scr2buffer[index] :=
1025                                            COPY(scr2array[row,col],
1030                                                          count,
1035                                                          1);
1040                          End;
1045                    End;
1050              End;
1055        End;          {screen2 active}
1060
1065        IF (scr3_active = true) THEN
1070        Begin
1075              FOR row := 1 to maxdatarows3 DO
1080              Begin
1085                    FOR col := 1 to maxdatacols3 DO
1090                    Begin
1095                          j := ((row - 1) * 160) + ((col - 1) * 2);
1100                          STR(j:4 , jstr3);
1105                          jstr3 := CONCAT('*',jstr3,'*');
1110                          scr3array[row,col] := jstr3;
1115                    End;
1120              End;
1125
1130              {assign 2 dimensional array into 1 dimensional buffer}
1135              index := 0;
1140              FOR row := 1 to maxdatarows3 DO
1145              Begin
1150                    FOR col := 1 to maxdatacols3 DO
1155                    Begin
1160                          FOR count := 1 to
1165                                      maxcountofdatacharspercol3 DO
```

continued...

415

16 Review and Extensions

...from previous page

```
1170                          Begin
1175                              index := index + 1;
1180                              scr3buffer[index] :=
1185                                  COPY(scr3array[row,col],
1190                                                    count,
1195                                                    1);
1200                          End;
1205                      End;
1210              End;
1215      End;         {screen3 active}
1220 End;         {procedure create_video_jtables}
1225 {----------------------------------------------------------------}
1230
1235 procedure CREATE_ROW_LABELS(var rlabel1array      : rlabel1arr;
1240                             var rlabel1buffer     : rlabel1buf;
1245                             var rlabel2array      : rlabel2arr;
1250                             var rlabel2buffer     : rlabel2buf;
1255                             var rlabel3array      : rlabel3arr;
1260                             var rlabel3buffer     : rlabel3buf);
1265
1270 type
1275     str4       = string[4];
1280
1285 var
1290     rowval1    : integer;
1295     rowval2    : integer;
1300     rowval3    : integer;
1305
1310     rowstr1    : str4;
1315     rowstr2    : str4;
1320     rowstr3    : str4;
1325
1330     i,j,
1335     row,col,
1340     index,
1345     count   : integer;
1350
1355 Begin      {procedure create_row_labels}
1360     IF (scr1_active = true) THEN
1365     Begin
1370         FOR i := 1 to maxlabelrows1 DO
1375             Begin
1380                 rowval1 := i;       {value of row is value of index}
1385                 STR(rowval1:2 , rowstr1);    {max size 2}
1390                 rlabel1array[i] := CONCAT('*',rowstr1,'*');
1395                                              {now size 4}
1400             End;
1405         {convert from 2 dim array to 1 dim buffer}
1410         index := 0;
1415         FOR i := 1 to maxlabelrows1 DO
1420         Begin
1425             FOR count := 1 to maxcountoflabelcharsperrow1 DO
1430             Begin
1435                 index := index + 1;
1440                 rlabel1buffer[index] :=
1445                          COPY(rlabel1array[i],count,1);
1450             End;
1455         End;
1460     End;       {screen1 active}
```

continued...

...from previous page

```
1465
1470
1475        IF (scr2_active = true) THEN
1480        Begin
1485        FOR i := 1 to maxlabelrows2 DO
1490            Begin
1495                rowval2 := i;       {value of row is value of index}
1500                STR(rowval2:2 , rowstr2);    {max size 2}
1505                rlabel2array[i] := CONCAT('*',rowstr2,'*');
1510                                             {now size 4}
1515            End;
1520
1525        {convert from 2 dim array to 1 dim buffer}
1530        index := 0;
1535        FOR i := 1 to maxlabelrows2 DO
1540        Begin
1545            FOR count := 1 to maxcountoflabelcharsperrow2 DO
1550            Begin
1555                index := index + 1;
1560                rlabel2buffer[index] :=
1565                            COPY(rlabel2array[i],count,1);
1570            End;
1575        End;
1580    End;        {screen2 active}
1585
1590
1595        IF (scr3_active = true) THEN
1600        Begin
1605        FOR i := 1 to maxlabelrows3 DO
1610            Begin
1615                rowval3 := i;       {value of row is value of index}
1620                STR(rowval3:2 , rowstr3);    {max size 2}
1625                rlabel3array[i] := CONCAT('*',rowstr3,'*');
1630                                             {now size 4}
1635            End;
1640
1645        {convert from 2 dim array to 1 dim buffer}
1650        index := 0;
1655        FOR i := 1 to maxlabelrows3 DO
1660        Begin
1665            FOR count := 1 to maxcountoflabelcharsperrow3 DO
1670            Begin
1675                index := index + 1;
1680                rlabel3buffer[index] :=
1685                            COPY(rlabel3array[i],count,1);
1690            End;
1695        End;
1700    End;        {screen3 active}
1705 End;       {procedure create_row_labels}
1710 {-----------------------------------------------------------------}
1715
1720 procedure CREATE_COL_LABELS(var clabel1array  : clabel1arr;
1725                             var clabel1buffer : clabel1buf;
1730                             var clabel2array  : clabel2arr;
1735                             var clabel2buffer : clabel2buf;
1740                             var clabel3array  : clabel3arr;
1745                             var clabel3buffer : clabel3buf);
1750
```

continued...

16 Review and Extensions

...from previous page

```
1755  type
1760        str6       = string[6];
1765
1770  var
1775        colval1    : integer;
1780        colval2    : integer;
1785        colval3    : integer;
1790
1795        colstr1    : str6;
1800        colstr2    : str6;
1805        colstr3    : str6;
1810
1815        k,j,
1820        row,col,
1825        index,
1830        count    : integer;
1835
1840  Begin      {procedure create_col_labels}
1845        IF (scr1_active = true) THEN
1850        Begin
1855        FOR k := 1 to maxlabelcols1 DO
1860             Begin
1865                  colval1 := k;         {value of row is value of index}
1870                  STR(colval1:4 , colstr1);   {max size 4}
1875                  clabel1array[k] := CONCAT('*',colstr1,'*');
1880                                               {now size 6}
1885             End;
1890
1895             {convert from 2 dim array to 1 dim buffer}
1900             index := 0;
1905             FOR k := 1 to maxlabelcols1 DO
1910             Begin
1915                  FOR count := 1 to maxcountoflabelcharspercol1 DO
1920                  Begin
1925                       index := index + 1;
1930                       clabel1buffer[index] :=
1935                                COPY(clabel1array[k],count,1);
1940                  End;
1945             End;
1950        End;      {screen1 active}
1955
1960
1965        IF (scr2_active = true) THEN
1970        Begin
1975        FOR k := 1 to maxlabelcols2 DO
1980             Begin
1985                  colval2 := k;         {value of row is value of index}
1990                  STR(colval2:4 , colstr2);   {max size 4}
1995                  clabel2array[k] := CONCAT('*',colstr2,'*');
2000                                               {now size 6}
2005             End;
2010
2015             {convert from 2 dim array to 1 dim buffer}
2020             index := 0;
2025             FOR k := 1 to maxlabelcols2 DO
2030             Begin
2035                  FOR count := 1 to maxcountoflabelcharspercol2 DO
2040                  Begin
2045                       index := index + 1;
```

continued...

Review and Extensions 16

...from previous page

```
2050                          clabel2buffer[index] :=
2055                                   COPY(clabel2array[k],count,1);
2060                End;
2065            End;
2070      End;       {screen2 active}
2075
2080
2085      IF (scr3_active = true) THEN
2090      Begin
2095          FOR k := 1 to maxlabelcols3 DO
2100          Begin
2105              colval3 := k;       {value of row is value of index}
2110              STR(colval3:4 , colstr3);    {max size 2}
2115              clabel3array[k] := CONCAT('*',colstr3,'*');
2120                                           {now size 6}
2125          End;
2130
2135          {convert from 2 dim array to 1 dim buffer}
2140          index := 0;
2145          FOR k := 1 to maxlabelcols3 DO
2150          Begin
2155              FOR count := 1 to maxcountoflabelcharspercol3 DO
2160              Begin
2165                  index := index + 1;
2170                  clabel3buffer[index] :=
2175                          COPY(clabel3array[k],count,1);
2180              End;
2185          End;
2190      End;       {screen3 active}
2195 End;       {procedure create_col_labels}
2200 {----------------------------------------------------------------}
2205
2210 procedure  INIT_VIDEO_JTABLES(var scr1buffer  : s1buf;
2215                               var scr2buffer  : s2buf;
2220                               var scr3buffer  : s3buf);
2225 var
2230      bx,bp,
2235      i,k,j,
2240      col,row,
2245      count     : integer;
2250
2255 Begin      {procedure init_video_jtables}
2260      IF (scr1_active = true) THEN
2265      Begin
2270          col := tlc1 + 8 ; row := tlr1 + 3;
2275          j := ((row - 1) * 160) + ((col - 1) * 2);
2280          FOR i := 1 to datarowdepth1 DO
2285          Begin
2290              FOR k := 1 to datacolwidth1 DO
2295              Begin
2300                  bx := (i - 1) * datacharsperrow1;
2305                  bp := (k - 1) * datacharspercol1;
2310                  FOR count := 1 to
2315                          maxcountofdatacharspercol1 DO
2320                  Begin
2325                      CHR_OUT(j,ORD(scr1buffer[bx+bp+count]));
2330                      j := j + 2;
2335                  End;
2340              End;
```

continued...

16 Review and Extensions

...from previous page

```
2345                         row := row + 1 ; col := col;
2350                         j := ((row - 1) * 160) + ((col - 1) * 2);
2355                 End;
2360         End;
2365
2370         IF (scr2_active = true) THEN
2375         Begin
2380             col := tlc2 + 8 ; row := tlr2 + 3;
2385             j := ((row - 1) * 160) + ((col - 1) * 2);
2390             FOR i := 1 to datarowdepth2 DO
2395             Begin
2400                 FOR k := 1 to datacolwidth2 DO
2405                 Begin
2410                     bx := (i - 1) * datacharsperrow2;
2415                     bp := (k - 1) * datacharspercol2;
2420                     FOR count := 1 to
2425                                     maxcountofdatacharspercol2 DO
2430                     Begin
2435                         CHR_OUT(j,ORD(scr2buffer[bx+bp+count]));
2440                         j := j + 2;
2445                     End;
2450                 End;
2455                 row := row + 1 ; col := col;
2460                 j := ((row - 1) * 160) + ((col - 1) * 2);
2465             End;
2470         End;
2475
2480         IF (scr3_active = true) THEN
2485         Begin
2490             col := tlc3 + 8 ; row := tlr3 + 3;
2495             j := ((row - 1) * 160) + ((col - 1) * 2);
2500             FOR i := 1 to datarowdepth3 DO
2505             Begin
2510                 FOR k := 1 to datacolwidth3 DO
2515                 Begin
2520                     bx := (i - 1) * datacharsperrow3;
2525                     bp := (k - 1) * datacharspercol3;
2530                     FOR count := 1 to
2535                                     maxcountofdatacharspercol3 DO
2540                     Begin
2545                         CHR_OUT(j,ORD(scr3buffer[bx+bp+count]));
2550                         j := j + 2;
2555                     End;
2560                 End;
2565                 row := row + 1 ; col := col;
2570                 j := ((row - 1) * 160) + ((col - 1) * 2);
2575             End;
2580         End;
2585 End;       {procedure init_video_jtables}
2590 {------------------------------------------------------------------}
2595
2600 procedure    INIT_ROW_LABELS(var rlabellbuffer : rlabellbuf;
2605                              var rlabel2buffer : rlabel2buf;
2610                              var rlabel3buffer : rlabel3buf);
2615
2620 var
2625      i,k,
2630      j,
2635      col,row,
2640      bx,count   : integer;
```

continued...

420

...from previous page

```
2645
2650  Begin        {procedure init_row_labels}
2655       IF (scr1_active = true) THEN
2660       Begin
2665            col := 5 ; row := 6;
2670            j := ((row - 1) * 160) + ((col - 1) * 2);
2675            FOR i := 1 to labelrowdepth1 DO
2680                 Begin
2685                      bx := (i - 1) * labelcharsperrow1; {4}
2690                      FOR count := 1 to maxcountoflabelcharsperrow1 DO
2695                      Begin
2700                           CHR_OUT(j,ORD(rlabellbuffer[bx + count]));
2705                           j := j + 2;
2710                      End;
2715                      row := row + 1; col := col;
2720                      j := ((row - 1) * 160) + ((col - 1) * 2);
2725                 End;
2730       End;
2735
2740       IF (scr2_active = true) THEN
2745       Begin
2750            col := 66 ; row := 6;
2755            j := ((row - 1) * 160) + ((col - 1) * 2);
2760            FOR i := 1 to labelrowdepth2 DO
2765                 Begin
2770                      bx := (i - 1) * labelcharsperrow2; {4}
2775                      FOR count := 1 to maxcountoflabelcharsperrow2 DO
2780                      Begin
2785                           CHR_OUT(j,ORD(rlabel2buffer[bx + count]));
2790                           j := j + 2;
2795                      End;
2800                      row := row + 1; col := col;
2805                      j := ((row - 1) * 160) + ((col - 1) * 2);
2810                 End;
2815       End;
2820
2825       IF (scr3_active = true) THEN
2830       Begin
2835            col := 5 ; row := 17;
2840            j := ((row - 1) * 160) + ((col - 1) * 2);
2845
2850            FOR i := 1 to labelrowdepth3 DO
2855                 Begin
2860                      bx := (i - 1) * labelcharsperrow3; {4}
2865                      FOR count := 1 to maxcountoflabelcharsperrow3 DO
2870                      Begin
2875                           CHR_OUT(j,ORD(rlabel3buffer[bx + count]));
2880                           j := j + 2;
2885                      End;
2890                      row := row + 1; col := col;
2895                      j := ((row - 1) * 160) + ((col - 1) * 2);
2900                 End;
2905       End;
2910  End;         {init_row_labels}
2915  {-----------------------------------------------------------------}
2920
2925  procedure   INIT_COL_LABELS(var clabellbuffer : clabellbuf;
2930                              var clabel2buffer : clabel2buf;
2935                              var clabel3buffer : clabel3buf);
```

continued...

16 Review and Extensions

...from previous page

```
2940
2945    var
2950           i,k,
2955           j,
2960           col,row,
2965           bp,count  : integer;
2970
2975    Begin         {procedure init_col_labels}
2980          IF (scr1_active = true) THEN
2985          Begin
2990              col := 11 ; row := 4;
2995              j := ((row - 1) * 160) + ((col - 1) * 2);
3000              FOR k := 1 to labelcolwidth1 DO
3005              {8, 6 character data units}
3010              Begin
3015                  bp := (k - 1) * labelcharspercol1; {6}
3020                  FOR count := 1 to maxcountoflabelcharspercol1 DO
3025                  Begin
3030                      CHR_OUT(j,ORD(clabel1buffer[bp + count]));
3035                      j := j + 2;
3040                  End;
3045              End;
3050          End;
3055
3060
3065          IF (scr2_active = true) THEN
3070          Begin
3075              col := 72 ; row := 4;
3080              j := ((row - 1) * 160) + ((col - 1) * 2);
3085              FOR k := 1 to labelcolwidth2 DO
3090              {1, 6 character data unit}
3095              Begin
3100                  bp := (k - 1) * labelcharspercol2; {6}
3105                  FOR count := 1 to maxcountoflabelcharspercol2 DO
3110                  Begin
3115                      CHR_OUT(j,ORD(clabel2buffer[bp + count]));
3120                      j := j + 2;
3125                  End;
3130              End;
3135          End;
3140
3145          IF (scr3_active = true) THEN
3150          Begin
3155              col := 11 ; row := 15;
3160              j := ((row - 1) * 160) + ((col - 1) * 2);
3165              FOR k := 1 to labelcolwidth3 DO
3170              {8, 6 character data units}
3175              Begin
3180                  bp := (k - 1) * labelcharspercol3; {6}
3185                  FOR count := 1 to maxcountoflabelcharspercol3 DO
3190                  Begin
3195                      CHR_OUT(j,ORD(clabel3buffer[bp + count]));
3200                      j := j + 2;
3205                  End;
3210              End;
3215          End;
3220    End;       {init_col_labels}
3225    {------------------------------------------------------------------}
3230
```

continued...

Review and Extensions **16**

...from previous page

```
3235  Begin        {main}
3240       window(1,1,80,25);clrscr;
3245       SET_UP_SCREEN;
3250
3255       scr1_active := true;     {activate screen 1}
3260       CREATE_VIDEO_JTABLES(scr1array , scr1buffer,
3265                            scr2array , scr2buffer,
3270                            scr3array , scr3buffer);
3275
3280       CREATE_ROW_LABELS(rlabel1array , rlabel1buffer,
3285                         rlabel2array , rlabel2buffer,
3290                         rlabel3array , rlabel3buffer);
3295
3300       CREATE_COL_LABELS(clabel1array , clabel1buffer,
3305                         clabel2array , clabel2buffer,
3310                         clabel3array , clabel3buffer);
3315       scr1_active := false;    {deactivate screen 1}
3320
3325       scr2_active := true;     {activate screen 2}
3330       CREATE_VIDEO_JTABLES(scr1array , scr1buffer,
3335                            scr2array , scr2buffer,
3340                            scr3array , scr3buffer);
3345
3350       CREATE_ROW_LABELS(rlabel1array , rlabel1buffer,
3355                         rlabel2array , rlabel2buffer,
3360                         rlabel3array , rlabel3buffer);
3365
3370
3375       CREATE_COL_LABELS(clabel1array , clabel1buffer,
3380                         clabel2array , clabel2buffer,
3385                         clabel3array , clabel3buffer);
3390       scr2_active := false;    {deactivate screen 2}
3395
3400       scr3_active := true;     {activate screen 3}
3405       CREATE_VIDEO_JTABLES(scr1array , scr1buffer,
3410                            scr2array , scr2buffer,
3415                            scr3array , scr3buffer);
3420
3425       CREATE_ROW_LABELS(rlabel1array , rlabel1buffer,
3430                         rlabel2array , rlabel2buffer,
3435                         rlabel3array , rlabel3buffer);
3440
3445       CREATE_COL_LABELS(clabel1array , clabel1buffer,
3450                         clabel2array , clabel2buffer,
3455                         clabel3array , clabel3buffer);
3460       scr3_active := false;    {deactivate screen 3}
3465
3470       write(bell);   {all tables and labels created}
3475       saved_i_tot1 := 1 ; saved_i_tot2 := 1 ; saved_i_tot3 := 1;
3480       saved_k_tot1 := 1 ; saved_k_tot2 := 1 ; saved_k_tot3 := 1;
3485       REPEAT
3490          BUFLEN := 3;
3495          exit := false;
3500          ascii_sum := 0;
3505          gotoxy(40,21) ; write('   ') ; gotoxy(40,21); {3 blanks}
3510          readln(screen_choice);
3515          FOR i := 1 to LENGTH(screen_choice) DO
3520          Begin
3525             character := COPY(screen_choice , i , 1);
3530             ascii_sum := ascii_sum + ORD(character);
```

continued...

16 Review and Extensions

...from previous page

```
3535              End;
3540              CASE (ascii_sum) OF
3545
3550              a1   : Begin                          {SCREEN 1}
3555                       scrl_active := true;
3560                       IF (scrl_init = false) THEN
3565                       Begin
3570                              INIT_VIDEO_JTABLES(scrlbuffer,
3575                                                 scr2buffer,
3580                                                 scr3buffer);
3585
3590                              INIT_ROW_LABELS(rlabellbuffer,
3595                                              rlabel2buffer,
3600                                              rlabel3buffer);
3605
3610                              INIT_COL_LABELS(clabellbuffer,
3615                                              clabel2buffer,
3620                                              clabel3buffer);
3625
3630                              gotoxy(50,20);clreol;
3635                              write('Scroll Screen a1:');
3640
3645                              VHRLCLSCROLL_SCREEN(tlcl,tlrl,
3650                                                  saved_i_totl,
3655                                                  saved_k_totl,
3660                                             datarowdepthminusonel,
3665                                             datacolwidthminusonel,
3670                                             labelrowdepthminusonel,
3675                                             labelcolwidthminusonel,
3680                                                  datacharsperrowl,
3685                                                  datacharspercoll,
3690
3695                                                  labelcharsperrowl,
3700                                                  labelcharspercoll,
3705                                          maxcountofdatacharspercoll,
3710                                          maxcountoflabelcharsperrowl,
3715                                          maxcountoflabelcharspercoll,
3720                                                  max_allowed_i_totl,
3725                                                  max_allowed_k_totl,
3730                                                  scrlbuffer,
3735                                                  scr2buffer,
3740                                                  scr3buffer,
3745                                                  rlabellbuffer,
3750                                                  clabellbuffer,
3755                                                  rlabel2buffer,
3760                                                  clabel2buffer,
3765                                                  rlabel3buffer,
3770                                                  clabel3buffer);
3775
3780                              scrl_init := true;
3785                       End
3790                       ELSE
3795                       Begin
3800                              gotoxy(50,20);clreol;
3805                              write('Scroll Screen a1:');
3810                              VHRLCLSCROLL_SCREEN(tlcl,tlrl,
3815                                                  saved_i_totl,
3820                                                  saved_k_totl,
```

continued...

...from previous page

```
3825                                  datarowdepthminusone1,
3830                                  datacolwidthminusone1,
3835                                  labelrowdepthminusone1,
3840                                  labelcolwidthminusone1,
3845                                     datacharsperrow1,
3850                                     datacharspercol1,
3855                                     labelcharsperrow1,
3860                                     labelcharspercol1,
3865                               maxcountofdatacharspercol1,
3870                               maxcountoflabelcharsperrow1,
3875                               maxcountoflabelcharspercol1,
3880                                      max_allowed_i_tot1,
3885                                      max_allowed_k_tot1,
3890                                         scr1buffer,
3895                                         scr2buffer,
3900                                         scr3buffer,
3905                                         rlabel1buffer,
3910                                         clabel1buffer,
3915                                         rlabel2buffer,
3920                                         clabel2buffer,
3925                                         rlabel3buffer,
3930                                         clabel3buffer);
3935
3940              End;
3945              gotoxy(40,21);
3950              scr1_active := false;
3955           End;    {a1}
3960
3965
3970        a2 : Begin                            {SCREEN 2}
3975              scr2_active := true;
3980              IF (scr2_init = false) THEN
3985              Begin
3990                 INIT_VIDEO_JTABLES(scr1buffer,
3995                                    scr2buffer,
4000                                    scr3buffer);
4005
4010                 INIT_ROW_LABELS(rlabel1buffer,
4015                                 rlabel2buffer,
4020                                 rlabel3buffer);
4025
4030                 INIT_COL_LABELS(clabel1buffer,
4035                                 clabel2buffer,
4040                                 clabel3buffer);
4045
4050                 gotoxy(50,20);clreol;
4055                 write('Scroll Screen a2:');
4060
4065                 VHRLCLSCROLL_SCREEN(tlc2,tlr2,
4070                                     saved_i_tot2,
4075                                     saved_k_tot2,
4080                                  datarowdepthminusone2,
4085                                  datacolwidthminusone2,
4090                                  labelrowdepthminusone2,
4095                                  labelcolwidthminusone2,
4100                                     datacharsperrow2,
4105                                     datacharspercol2,
4110                                     labelcharsperrow2,
4115                                     labelcharspercol2,
```

continued...

16 Review and Extensions

...from previous page

```
4120                              maxcountofdatacharspercol2,
4125                              maxcountoflabelcharsperrow2,
4130                              maxcountoflabelcharspercol2,
4135                                    max_allowed_i_tot2,
4140                                    max_allowed_k_tot2,
4145                                            scr1buffer,
4150                                            scr2buffer,
4155                                            scr3buffer,
4160                                          rlabel1buffer,
4165                                          clabel1buffer,
4170                                          rlabel2buffer,
4175                                          clabel2buffer,
4180                                          rlabel3buffer,
4185                                          clabel3buffer);
4190
4195                  scr2_init := true;
4200              End
4205              ELSE
4210              Begin
4215                  gotoxy(50,20);clreol;
4220                  write('Scroll Screen a2:');
4225                  VHRLCLSCROLL_SCREEN(tlc2,tlr2,
4230                                            saved_i_tot2,
4235                                            saved_k_tot2,
4240                              datarowdepthminusone2,
4245                              datacolwidthminusone2,
4250                              labelrowdepthminusone2,
4255                              labelcolwidthminusone2,
4260                                    datacharsperrow2,
4265                                    datacharspercol2,
4270                                    labelcharsperrow2,
4275                                    labelcharspercol2,
4280                              maxcountofdatacharspercol2,
4285                              maxcountoflabelcharsperrow2,
4290                              maxcountoflabelcharspercol2,
4295                                    max_allowed_i_tot2,
4300                                    max_allowed_k_tot2,
4305                                            scr1buffer,
4310                                            scr2buffer,
4315                                            scr3buffer,
4320                                          rlabel1buffer,
4325                                          clabel1buffer,
4330                                          rlabel2buffer,
4335                                          clabel2buffer,
4340                                          rlabel3buffer,
4345                                          clabel3buffer);
4350              End;
4355
4360          gotoxy(40,21);
4365          scr2_active := false;
4370      End;     {a2}
4375
4380
4385      a3 : Begin                              {SCREEN 3}
4390          scr3_active := true;
4395          IF (scr3_init = false) THEN
4400          Begin
4405              INIT_VIDEO_JTABLES(scr1buffer,
4410                                            scr2buffer,
4415                                            scr3buffer);
```

continued...

426

...from previous page

```
4420
4425                        INIT_ROW_LABELS(rlabel1buffer,
4430                                        rlabel2buffer,
4435                                        rlabel3buffer);
4440
4445                        INIT_COL_LABELS(clabel1buffer,
4450                                        clabel2buffer,
4455                                        clabel3buffer);
4460
4465                        gotoxy(50,20);clreol;
4470                        write('Scroll Screen a3:');
4475
4480                        VHRLCLSCROLL_SCREEN(tlc3,tlr3,
4485                                            saved_i_tot3,
4490                                            saved_k_tot3,
4495                                    datarowdepthminusone3,
4500                                    datacolwidthminusone3,
4505                                    labelrowdepthminusone3,
4510                                    labelcolwidthminusone3,
4515                                        datacharsperrow3,
4520                                        datacharspercol3,
4525                                       labelcharsperrow3,
4530                                       labelcharspercol3,
4535                            maxcountofdatacharspercol3,
4540                            maxcountoflabelcharsperrow3,
4545                            maxcountoflabelcharspercol3,
4550                                      max_allowed_i_tot3,
4555                                      max_allowed_k_tot3,
4560                                           scr1buffer,
4565                                           scr2buffer,
4570                                           scr3buffer,
4575                                         rlabel1buffer,
4580                                         clabel1buffer,
4585                                         rlabel2buffer,
4590                                         clabel2buffer,
4595                                         rlabel3buffer,
4600                                         clabel3buffer);
4605
4610                        scr3_init := true;
4615                    End
4620                    ELSE
4625                    Begin
4630                        gotoxy(50,20);clreol;
4635                        write('Scroll Screen a3:');
4640                        VHRLCLSCROLL_SCREEN(tlc3,tlr3,
4645                                            saved_i_tot3,
4650                                            saved_k_tot3,
4655                                    datarowdepthminusone3,
4660                                    datacolwidthminusone3,
4665                                    labelrowdepthminusone3,
4670                                    labelcolwidthminusone3,
4675                                        datacharsperrow3,
4680                                        datacharspercol3,
4685                                       labelcharsperrow3,
```

continued...

16 Review and Extensions

...from previous page

```
4690                                      labelcharspercol3,
4695                            maxcountofdatacharspercol3,
4700                            maxcountoflabelcharsperrow3,
4705                            maxcountoflabelcharspercol3,
4710                                       max_allowed_i_tot3,
4715                                       max_allowed_k_tot3,
4720                                              scr1buffer,
4725                                              scr2buffer,
4730                                              scr3buffer,
4735                                            rlabel1buffer,
4740                                            clabel1buffer,
4745                                            rlabel2buffer,
4750                                            clabel2buffer,
4755                                            rlabel3buffer,
4760                                            clabel3buffer);
4765
4770              End;
4775
4780              gotoxy(40,21);
4785              scr3_active := false;
4790          End;    {a3}
4795
4800     h   : Begin
4805              scr4_active := true;
4810              gotoxy(50,20);clreol;
4815              write('Scroll Help Screen');
4820              SAVE_SCREEN(tlc4,tlr4,brc4,brr4,
4825                          scr1_array,
4830                          scr2_array,
4835                          scr3_array,
4840                          scr4_array);
4845              filename := 'help16.txt';
4850              TXTWRIT(filename);
4855              write(bell);
4860              RE_DISPLAY_SCREEN(tlc4,tlr4,brc4,brr4,
4865                                maxscrdisplaychars4,
4870                                scr1_array,scr1_buffer,
4875                                scr2_array,scr2_buffer,
4880                                scr3_array,scr3_buffer,
4885                                scr4_array,scr4_buffer);
4890              scr4_active := false;
4895          End;
4900
4905
4910     q    : exit := true;
4915
4920     ELSE
4925         {TRY ANOTHER KEYBOARD ENTRY}
4930
4935     END;    {case statement}
4940
4945  UNTIL (exit = true);
4950 End.    {driver}
{========================================================================}
```

428

Review and Extensions 16

MULTSC16.DRV: NOTES

CREATE_VIDEO_JTABLES

In accordance with the general program organization chart (Figure 16.11), this procedure is used to create the scrollable table data.

The "jtables" referred to in the procedure name are the table of "j" values (screen pointers) that result from the repeated application of the formula

j := ((row - 1) * 160) + ((col - 1) * 2)

which calculates a video memory location index in terms of the screen's row and column coordinates. Since the video screen has 25 rows and 80 columns, this table can be represented in the computer's memory as a 25-row by 80-column two-dimensional array (e.g., "scr1array" at line 0640).

Before the creation of the scrollable tables is explained, look at the parameter list. In contrast to the analogue procedure CREATE_SCREEN_ARRAYS in Chapter 14, note that CREATE_VIDEO_JTABLES contains only array variables and does not include any other parameters. This difference in the way that the parameter lists are set up leads to two different ways of creating the required array and buffer variables used for scrolling.

In the main routine in Chapter 14, the number-suffixed parameters from "typedef.inc" were included directly inside the procedure calls of the main routine. In the parameter list of CREATE_SCREEN_ARRAYS, they were represented as non-number-suffixed value parameters. For example, for Screen 1, "maxdatarows1" in the parameter list of the call CREATE_SCREEN_ARRAYS in the main routine was represented by the corresponding value parameter "maxdatarows" (no suffix number) inside that procedure's parameter list. This parameter access strategy made for longer parameter lists on the one hand, but for much shorter procedure code on the other. Once the relevant parameters were accessed, the only task that remained was to assign the arrays "scr#array[...]" and "scr#buffer[...]" their values from within the procedure, depending on which screen number was currently active.

429

16 Review and Extensions

In this chapter, a different strategy has been used for the set of internal procedures to demonstrate the difference. Here, the relevant non-array parameters as defined under the "const" heading in "typdef16.inc" are not included inside the procedure calls of the main routine. Instead, they are referenced directly from within the procedure CREATE_JTABLES in accordance with which screen is active at the time. For example, if Screen 1 is set to "active" in the main routine, then only the code between lines 0750 and 0795 of CREATE_VIDEO_JTABLES is actually executed. Also, only the non-array parameters with a number suffix of "1" are used to create the required arrays, and only those arrays, "scr1array" and "scr1buffer," are created and exported from the procedure for future use. What was said about Screen 1 applies equally to Screens 2 and 3 or any number of screens you want to create (subject to memory limits).

Now examine the mechanics of creating the scrollable data table arrays that you see in the parameter list of CREATE_VIDEO_JTABLES (lines 0640-0665). Only the creation of "scr1array" and "scr1buffer" is explained. The others are created in the same way.

Lines 0745-0795 create "scr1array," the two-dimensional data array of six character strings, and make it globally accessible by way of the "var" prefix. It is created inside a pair of FOR..DO loops. The outer row loop (line 0750) has a range of 1 to "maxdatarows1" (25), while the inner column loop (line 0760) has a range of 1 to "maxdatacols1" (80). For each row/column pair, a unique value of "j" is calculated at line 0770. At this point, "j" is an integer and must be converted into an equivalent string value if it is to be part of a scrollable array. This integer-to-string conversion takes place at lines 0775-0780. At line 0775, the value of "j" is converted into a four-character string, "jstr1." To build "jstr1" up from a string of four characters to the required six, the CONCAT function is used to add a "*" character at each end of "jstr1." The "*" character is included only to show the limits of the string field. Once the six-character string has been created, it is assigned to its proper location inside "scr1array," using the current values of "row" and "col" as the location index. Since there are 25 rows and 80 columns for Screen 1, this process will be repeated 2000 (25 x 80) times to populate "scr1array."

Lines 0815-0890 then create "scr1buffer," the corresponding one-dimensional array of characters actually used in the scrolling operations of VHRLCLSCROLL_ SCREEN. "Scr1buffer" is created inside three FOR..DO loops. The outer "row" loop (line 0815) has a range of 1 to "maxdatarows1" (25); the second "col" loop (line 0825) has a range of 1 to "maxdatacols1" (80); and the innermost "count" loop has a range of 1 to "maxcountofdatacharspercol1" (6). This innermost loop is needed because a one-dimensional array of characters is being created as opposed to a two-dimensional array of (6 character) strings. For each "row," "column," "count" triple, a unique "index" value is assigned (line 0850). This "index" value takes on the range 1 to 12,000 (25 x 80 x 6) and is the index of the one-dimensional array "scr1buffer." The conversion of the two-dimensional array "scr1array" into "scr1buffer" is accomplished at line 0855. The COPY function parses each six-character string element into a single character and assigns it over to "scr1buffer[index]". Since there are 2000 elements and each element is a string of six characters in length, line 0855 is executed 12,000 times for Screen 1. Now is a good time to look again at Figure 16.8.

What was said about Screen 1 applies equally to the other two screens. The form of the code is exactly the same. Only the values used by the code are different, depending on which screen is currently active.

CREATE_ROW_LABELS

This procedure creates the scrollable row index labels for each of the three tables of data produced by CREATE_VIDEO_JTABLES. Since Screen 1 has 25 rows of data, it must also have a corresponding row index array, "rlabel1array," consisting of 25 four-character strings. It must also have an equivalent array, "rlabel1buffer," consisting of 100 one-character strings that will be used by VHRLCLSCROLL_SCREEN to actually scroll the row labels in tandem with scrolling the table data. Notice that both "rlabel1array" and "rlabel1buffer" are only one-dimensional arrays. Since Screen 2 will have 25 rows, it must also have 2 one-dimensional arrays the same size as those for Screen 1. Notice, however, that Screen 3 is different. Since it only has 5 rows of data, it will only need a row index array, "rlabel3array," consisting of 5 four-character strings and, along with it, an equivalent one-dimensional array, "rlabel3buffer," comprised of 20 one-character strings.

16 Review and Extensions

Operationally, CREATE_ROW_LABELS is very similar to CREATE VIDEO_JTABLES. The parameter list holds only global array variables, which are populated from within the procedure and then exported for use outside. A second similarity is that each time the procedure is activated, only part of the code is executed. For example, if Screen 1 were set to "active" in the main routine, only lines 1360-1460 of CREATE_ROW_LABELS would be activated, and only the reference variables (the "var"'d variables) "rlabel1array" and "rlabel1buffer" would be populated. The same holds for Screens 2 and 3. A third similarity is that each section of the procedure body has its own special parameters (as defined by "typdef16.inc") to work with and no others. If Screen 1 is active, only the parameters pertaining to Screen 1 are activated (i.e., "maxlabelrows1" and "maxcountoflabelcharsperrow1"). A fourth similarity concerns the creation and conversion of the row label index values into a scrollable form. As with CREATE_ VIDEO JLABELS, the process involves three steps. Since you are dealing only with one-dimensional data, however, the scrollable labels are created using only one FOR..DO loop (line 1370). Line 1380 takes the "i" index value found at line 1370 and assigns it into the local integer variable "rowval1." Line 1385 uses the STR function to convert "rowval1" into a four-character string. Notice that the size of the integer has been restricted to a maximum field width of two (row values of 1-25 only need a field width of 2). Line 1390 then uses the CONCAT function to expand "rowstr1" to fill up all four-character locations in its four-character field. The expanded value of "rowstr1" is then assigned into "rlabel1array" at the current index value, "i." After 25 iterations, "rlabel1array" will be fully populated with 25 four-character string values:

|* 1*|* 2*|* 3*|...|*11*|*12*|...|*25*|

The process of converting "rlabel1array" into its equivalent one-dimensional array of characters (not strings) is accomplished between lines 1415 and 1460. There is an "index" variable whose range will go between 1 and 100 (25 x 4). Since you are dealing only with the conversion of a one-dimensional array of strings into a one-dimensional array of characters, only two FOR..DO loops are needed. The outer "i" loop (line 1415) runs from 1 to "maxlabelrows1" (25). The inner "count" loop runs from 1 to "maxcountoflabelcharsperrow1" (4). Each time line 1435 is reached, the "index" value is incremented by 1. Each time line 1440 is reached, the COPY function will split out (parse) a single character of the four-character array element of "rlabel1array" and assign it into "rlabel1buffer" at position number "index." In all, line 1440 is executed 100 times (25 data rows x 4 characters/data row). Now look again at Figure 16.9 for a visual representation of the conversion process from a one-dimensional array of strings into an equivalent one-dimensional array of characters.

Screen 1 is used as an example here. The coding used to handle Screens 2 and 3 is exactly the same. The only difference lies with the parameters used in the different sections of the procedure.

CREATE_COL_LABELS

This procedure creates the scrollable column index labels for each of the three tables of data produced by CREATE_VIDEO_JTABLES. Since Screen 1 has 80 columns of data, it must also have a corresponding column index array "clabel1array" consisting of 80 six-character strings. It must also have an equivalent array, "clabel1buffer," consisting of 480 one-character strings that will be used by VHRLCLSCROLL SCREEN to actually scroll the column labels in tandem with scrolling the table data. Notice that both "clabel1array" and "clabel1buffer" are only one-dimensional arrays. Since Screen 3 will also have only 80 columns, it must also have 2 one-dimensional arrays the same size as those for Screen 1. Notice, however, that Screen 2 is different. Since it only has 5 columns of data, it will only need a column index array, "clabel3array," consisting of 5 six-character strings and, along with it, an equivalent one-dimensional array, "clabel3buffer," comprised of 30 one-character strings.

Operationally, CREATE_COL_LABELS is also very similar to CREATE VIDEO_JTABLES. The parameter list holds only global array variables, which are populated from within the procedure and then exported for use outside. A second similarity is that each time the procedure is activated, only part of the code is executed. For example, if Screen 1 were set to "active" in the main routine, only lines 1845-1950 of CREATE_COL_LABELS would be activated, and only the reference variables (the "var"'d variables) "clabel1array" and "clabel1buffer" would be populated. The same holds for Screens 2 and 3. A third similarity is that each section of the procedure body has its own special parameters (as defined by "typdef16.inc") to work with and no others. If Screen 1 is active, only the parameters pertaining to Screen 1 are activated (i.e., "maxlabelcols1" and "maxcountoflabelcharspercol1"). A

16 Review and Extensions

fourth similarity concerns the creation and conversion of the column label index values into a scrollable form. As with CREATE_VIDEO JLABELS, the process involves three steps. Since you are dealing only with one-dimensional data, however, the scrollable labels are created using only one main FOR..DO loop indexed by "k" only (line 1905).

Line 1865 takes the "k" index value found at line 1855 and assigns it into the local integer variable "colval1." Line 1870 uses the STR function to convert "colval1" into a four-character string. Notice that the size of the integer has been restricted to a maximum field width of 4 (column values of 1-80 only need a field width of 2, but the integer was made 4 wide to match the width of the data inside the display window). Line 1875 then uses the CONCAT function to expand "colstr1" to fill up all six character locations in its preset six-character field. The expanded value of "colstr1" is then assigned into "clabel1array" at the current index value, "k." After 80 iterations, "clabel1array" will be fully populated with 80 six-character string values:

|*   1*|*   2*|*   3*|...|*   67*|*   68*|...|*   80*|

The process of converting "clabel1array" into its equivalent one-dimensional array of characters (not strings) is accomplished between lines 1895 and 1950. There is an "index" variable whose range will go between 1 and 480 (80 x 6). Since you are dealing only with the conversion of a one-dimensional array of strings into a one-dimensional array of characters, only two FOR..DO loops are needed. The outer "k" loop (line 1905) runs from 1 to "maxlabelcols1" (80). The inner "count" loop runs from 1 to "maxcountoflabelcharspercol1" (6). Each time line 1925 is reached, the "index" value is incremented by 1. Each time line 1930 is reached, the COPY function will split out (parse) a single character of the six-character array element of "clabel1array" and assign it into "clabel1buffer" at position number "index." In all, line 1930 is executed 480 times (80 data columns x 6 characters/data column). Now look at Figure 16.10 again to see a visual representation of the conversion process from a one-dimensional array of strings into an equivalent one-dimensional array of characters.

Screen 1 is used as an example here. The coding used to handle Screens 2 and 3 is exactly the same. The only difference lies with the parameters used in the different sections of the procedure.

Review and Extensions 16

INIT_VIDEO_JTABLES

This procedure is invoked three times during the course of a program run. Its purpose is to set up or initialize the screen table data prior to calling the external scrolling procedure. As you can see from the main routine, it is called one time only for each of Screen 1 (line 3570), Screen 2 (line 3990), and Screen 3 (line 4405).

This procedure is similar in structure to the other internal procedures that created the j tables, the row labels, and the column labels; that is, it is comprised of four main parts:

- a parameter list containing only array data structures.

- a section of code customized to handle only Screen 1 table data (lines 2260-2360). Notice that for initialization purposes, the range of the row index "i" is 1 to "datarowdepth1" (5), and the range of the column index "k" is 1 to "datacolwidth1" (8).

- a section of code customized to handle only Screen 2 table data (lines 2370-2470). Notice that for initialization, the range of the row index "i" is 1 to "datarowdepth2" (5), and the range of the column index "k" is 1 to "datacolwidth2" (1). An upper limit of 1 in a FOR..DO loop is legal as long as it is greater than or equal to the lower limit.

- a section of code customized to handle only Screen 3 table data (lines 2480-2580). Notice that for initialization purposes, the range of the row index "i" is 1 to "datarowdepth3" (1), and the range of the column index "k" is 1 to "datacolwidth1" (8).

With the exception of the fixed "i" and "k" FOR..DO loops that are used to delimit the upper left corners of each of these two-dimensional data tables, notice that the code responsible for displaying the initialized table into the respective screen windows is remarkably similar to the code in the external procedure REWRITE_SCR discussed earlier.

16 Review and Extensions

INIT_ROW_LABELS/INIT_COL_LABELS

These two procedures are exact analogues of INIT_VIDEO_JTABLES. Each sets up the screen row/column labels prior to calling the external scrolling procedure VHRLCLSCROLL_SCREEN. Each procedure is called only once to perform its initialization function for the rows/columns of Screens 1, 2, and 3. Also, observe that the four-part structure of the coding is no different from that of INIT_VIDEO_JTABLES.

Since the row and column label arrays are one-dimensional, the procedures only use one FOR..DO loop to define the number of row/column array elements to be displayed on the screen. Notice too that the code used to display the row/column labels on the screen is very close to the external procedures REWRITE_ROWLABEL and REWRITE_COLLABEL, whose operation was described earlier.

MULTSC16.DRV (Body)

There is a close similarity between the operation of this driver routine and that of Chapters 14 and 15. Their differences will be addressed here. Since you are adding row and column index labels to the scrolling windows, the number of procedure calls prior to the REPEAT statement at line 3485 jumps from 3 to 9—an additional 2 for each screen. Once inside the REPEAT..UNTIL control loop, the number of initialization procedure calls jumps from one to three for each screen, thus raising the total number of initialization procedures from three to nine again.

Another conspicuous difference between this driver routine and that of the previous two chapters is the general absence of the external procedures SAVE_SCREEN and RE_DISPLAY_SCREEN. Since none of the screens was physically overlapping, there was no need to use these procedures. Notice lines 0155 & 0160 where this eventuality has been provided for in the parameter list of these procedures, just in case you want to experiment with the screen sizes on your own.

Review and Extensions 16

One of this particular program's features is a facility to bring up a scrollable text file that completely overlays the display screen and its three windows. Here (line 4800), the screen saving and redisplay procedures have been utilized. Assume that you have been scrolling the screens and would now like to refer to some notes that you had previously typed and saved into a separate text file on disk. To look at these notes, you would simply press the Help key (the "h" option). As you can see (line 4800), the entire contents of Screen 4 (defined as the whole 25-row by 80-column video screen) would be saved into the memory variable "scr4_ array" using the external procedure SAVE SCREEN. Since at this point "filename" has been assigned the disk file name "help16.txt" (line 4845), the external procedure TXTWRIT (from "textwr16.inc") is called with it as the parameter. The scrolling window screen suddenly disappears, and a full-screen scrolling window containing the contents of "help16.txt" appears (see Figure 16.2). You can now scroll this file to look up whatever it is you want to know. To exit, press <Ret>, at which time the external procedure RE_ DISPLAY SCREEN brings back the original screen full of scrolling display windows exactly as they had been left. Pressing any one of <a1><Ret>, <a2><Ret>, or <a3><Ret> will again allow you to scroll from the points where you had previously left off.

APPENDIX A

SCREEN LAYOUT FORM

SCREEN LAYOUT

SYSTEM: _____ PROGRAM: _____ INITIALS: _____

SCREEN DESCRIPTION: _____ DATE: _____ PAGE: _____ OF _____

REMARKS: _____

INDEX

A

array
    video screen as one dimensional   10-13
    one-dimensional, two-dimensional   (see "conversions")

ASCII
    and menu choices   204
    attribute   13, 44
    character   13, 44
    and printer   71

ASSIGN   274

B

bar graph   238

BUFLEN   209

C

CASE..END
    use in revision of data input   208, 210
    use in creation of data   262
    use in selection of scrolling keys   161
    use in activating screens   351

CH2DEM1.DRV
    code   29
    notes   29

CH2DEM2.DRV
    code   31
    notes   32

CH2DEM3.DRV
    code   33
    notes   35

CHRINOUT.INC
    code 24
    notes 26

circuitry
    and video memory 10, 62, 223

CODE
    as status variable in VAL function 193

CONCAT 173, 185-186, 228, 430, 432, 434

COPY 173, 184-185, 207, 211, 231, 349, 431, 432, 434

constants
    screen redisplay (see TYPDEF16.INC or TYPEDEF.INC)
    screen saving (see TYPDEF16.INC or TYPEDEF.INC)
    use in menu selection 209

conversions
    screen row and column to "j" offsets 13
    KBD data to graphic plot (see CONVERT_TO_PLOT)
    ASCII characters to printable characters 72
    real to string 183
    two-dimensional arrays into one-dimensional arrays 59, 89, 103, 143, 54, 349
    one-dimensional array into video memory 327, 379, 394, 397, 398

compiler directive 47, 178, 179

D

.dat
    as reserved suffix 311

data entry and validation 172
    integer 177
    real numbers 179
    dollar amounts 183
    dates 189
    mixed strings 207
    example using percentages 208

DATA_IR.DRV
    code 196
    notes 203

data revision
    program layout 212
    revision choice 209
    example using percentages 209
    and labels 203

data validation — numeric
    stage 1 204
    stage 2 204

data validation — strings
    stage 1 206
    stage 2 206

DATES.INC
    code 186
    notes 189

DELLINE
    and scrollable data input 257
    and vertical scrolling 161, 162

DIRECTORY
    and creation of new file 278
    and fetching of existing file 278, 316

display column
    defined for horizontal scroll 96, 104, 325
    defined for vertical scroll 135, 147

DOLLARS.INC
    code 181
    notes 183

Down Arrow key   127, 142, 325, 392

driver routine   46

.drv   46

E

EI_ER.INC
   code   176
   notes   177

external procedures   (see procedures in ".inc" modules, 363)

external definition module   356

F

FILENAME.INC
   code   274
   notes   276

file names
   validation of   277-278

file transfer variables   284, 308

files
   revision of data input   306
   creation of numeric data for   304
   creation of scrollable text for   288
   on-screen save to disk   308-309
   calculation on data in   311
   transfer from disk to memory   285-286, 308, 310

FILMAN.DRV   313
   code   289
   notes   304

FILLCHAR 66

filters
   and SCRTOPR.DRV 74
   use in input validation 190-194

G

goto statement 209, 306
   in input revison (see "label")

GOTOXY 16, 97

H

H_GRAPH.DRV
   code 238
   notes 254

H_S1.DRV
   code 94
   notes 96

H_S2.DRV
   code 112
   notes 114

H_S1.INC
   code 79
   notes 84

H_S2.INC
   code 101
   notes 103

HOME key 264

horizontal scrolling (see scrolling)

I

.INC (include) files
    defined 9
    location in programs 9, 318-319

index address method
    as horizontal scrolling method 100
    as vertical scrolling method 138, 331

initialization
    of display screens 364

input entry (see data entry and validation)

input revision (see data revision)

input validation (see data entry and validation)

INSLINE
    and vertical scrolling 158, 164

INSLINE/DELLINE method
    for vertical scrolling 158, 408

installation 17

IORESULT
    and integer input 178
    and real number input 179, 180
    and creation of new disk file 278
    and fetching of existing disk file 278

J

"j" (the variable) defined 13
"j" values 58, 304
jtables 368, 429

L

label
    statement in data revision 203, 212
    statement in vertical scrolling 88, 142

labels —scrollable
    in H_GRAPH.DRV 238
    on multiplication tables 214
    on video "j" value offset tables 387, 395, 398
    in TYPDEF16.INC 369
    in REWRSC16.INC 386

Left Arrow Key 83, 223, 264, 392

library 9, 363

Life (game of) 35

limitations
    of FILMAN.DRV 313
    of H_GRAPH.DRV 264
    of VHSCROLL.DRV 235

M

mapping
    horizontal scroll method 2 223
    vertical scroll method 2 223

MEM (memory array) 9, 11

MOD 115, 153

MODE (DOS command)
    monochrome screens 18
    black and white graphics 18
    color graphics 18

mode options — FILMAN.DRV
    'c' (create new file) 304
    'f' (fetch existing file) 308
    't' (fetch existing text file) 312
    'q' (as exit mode options) 303

modular programming
    concept 8
    wrt multiple windows 362

monitors
    monochrome 18
    black and white graphics 20
    color graphics 20

multiple screens
    general redisplay of 266
    general saving of 265
    general organization of (see TYPEDEF.INC and TYPDEF16.INC)
    and IF..THEN statements 335, 331, 337, 338, 342-344
    naming conventions (see "naming conventions")

multiplication tables 223, 228

MULT_SCR.DRV
    code 342
    notes 348

MULTSC15.DRV
    notes 359, 361

MULTSC16.DRV
    code 412
    notes 429

N

naming conventions — multiple screens
    constants 319-320, 369
    types 320-321, 330, 372
    variables 321, 330, 372
    parameter lists 348-349

NUM LOCK   315

O

offset   9

options   (see "mode options" or "submode options")

ORD   29, 62, 72, 211, 223

P

PAGE UP/PAGE DOWN   407, 408

parameter   14

pop-up screens
    how to save and redisplay   55, 59
    overlaying one over the other   238
    and graphs   264

printer
    and screen image   71
    ASCII conversion   71, 72

procedures
    external   112, 115, 312, 362-364
    internal   362-364

procedures — Chapter 2
    CHR_IN   26
    CHR_OUT   26
    INITIALIZE   35
    DISPLAY_NEW_SCREEN   36
    VISIT_NEIGHBOUR   36

procedures — Chapter 3
    BORDER_STYLE_TABLE   43
    WINDOW_LINE   43

procedures — Chapter 4
    SAVE_PART_SCR 55
    RE_DISPLAY_PART_SCREEN 59
    FILTER 69, 72
    SET_UP 72

procedures — Chapter 5
    H_SCROLL1 84
    SAVE_PART_SCR 89
    RE_DISP_PART_SCR 89
    MOVE_PARTSCR_LEFT 90
    DISP_NEW_RIGHT_COL 91
    MOVE_PARTSCR_RIGHT 92
    DISP_NEW_LEFT_COL 93

procedures — Chapter 6
    H_SCROLL2 103
    REWRITE_SCR_BYCOL 105

procedures — Chapter 7
    V_SCROLL1 126
    SAVE_PART_SCR 129
    RE_DISP_PART_SCR 129
    MOVE_PARTSCR_UP 132
    DISP_NEW_BOTTOM_ROW 132
    MOVE_PARTSCR_DOWN 130
    DISP_NEW_TOP_ROW 131

procedures — Chapter 8
    V_SCROLL2 141
    REWRITE_SCR_BYROW 142

procedures — Chapter 9
    V_SCROLL3 160
    SCRL_UP 161
    SCRL_DOWN 162

procedures — Chapter 10
    ENTER_INTEGER 177
    ENTER_REAL 179
    DISPLAY_DOLLARS 183
    INSERT_COMMAS 185
    ENTER_DATE 189
    CONVERT_DATE_TOVALUE 194

procedures — Chapter 11
    CREATE_FIRST_STEP 228
    CREATE_SECOND_STEP 228
    CREATE_MULTAND_LABELS 231
    CREATE_MULTLR_LABELS 231
    INITIALIZE_SCROLL_WINDOW 233
    VHSCROLL2 235

procedures — Chapter 12
    INITIALIZE_YEARS 254
    CREATE_GRAPH_TABLE 257
    INSPECT_GRAPH_TABLE 261
    CONVERT_TOPLOT 261
    GRAPH_SCROLL 264
    REWRITE_COL_LABEL 264
    SAVE_SCREEN1 264
    SAVE_SCREEN2 264
    RE_DISP_SCREEN1 264
    RE_DISP_SCREEN2 264

procedures — Chapter 13
    SYNTAX_CHECK 277
    ENTER_NEW_FILE_NAME 277
    ENTER_OLD_FILE_NAME 278
    TEXTWRIT 284
    TEXT_FILE_TO_ARRAY 284
    CREATE_A_FILE 304
    REVISE_DATA_INPUT 306
    SAVE_FILE 308
    FETCH_A_FILE 308
    CREATE_SHADOW_FILE_NAME 311
    A_CALCULATION 311

procedures — Chapter 14
   VSCROLL_SCREEN   333
   REWRITE_SCR   335
   SAVE_SCREEN   339
   RE_DISPLAY_SCREEN   340
   CREATE_SCREEN_ARRAYS   348
   INIT_SCREEN   350

procedures — Chapter 15
   VHSCROLL_SCREEN   358
   CREATE_SCREEN_ARRAYS15   359

procedures — Chapter 16
   VHRLCLSCROLL_SCREEN   386
   REWRITE_SCR   392
   REWRITE_ROWLABEL   395
   REWRITE_COLLABEL   398
   CREATE_VIDEO_JTABLES   429
   CREATE_ROW_LABELS   431
   CREATE_COL_LABELS   433
   INIT_VIDEO_JTABLES   435
   INIT_ROW_LABELS   436
   INIT_COL_LABELS   436

program organization   361

R

RANDOM   29, 360

readln
   to transfer disk data into memory   284

REPEAT..UNTIL
   used in data input   177, 204-208, 312
   used in multiple screen display   410
   to validate file names   278, 312
   to control file mode functions   288
   to control file submode functions   288
   to control horizontal scrolling   104
   to control vertical scrolling   141
   to control scrolling graph table   264

RESET   274, 278

revision
    of data input   172

REWRITE   274

REWRITSC.INC
    code   330
    notes   332

REWRSC15.INC
    notes   358

REWRITSC16.INC
    code   381
    notes   386

Right Arrow key   84, 223, 264, 325, 392

S

save/redisplay part screen
    as horizontal scrolling method   76
    as vertical scrolling method   120

screen
    save to memory   55
    redisplay from memory   59
    relation to variable, "j"   13

screen memory   (see video memory)

screen pointer
    "j" values as   10, 50, 368, 429

scrolling
    and index address method 100, 138, 214
    and insline/delline method 158
    and screen save/redisplay method 76, 120
    bidirectional 214
    with labels 214
    horizontal—method 1 76
    horizontal—method 2 100
    vertical—method 1 120
    vertical—method 2 138
    vertical—method 3 158
    installation of horizontal 356-361

scrolling tables
    multiplication table 214
    table of "j" (screen pointer) values 368
    of lion population 257

scrolling windows
    adding or deleting 400

SCRTOPR.DRV
    code 69
    notes 71

segment 9-12

SSD.DRV
    code 62
    notes 65

strings 173

STR 173, 183, 228, 432, 434

syntax error
    and file names 277

submode options—FILMAN.DRV
    "r" (revise file data) 306
    "c" (perform a calculation) 311
    "s" (save file to disk) 308
    "q" (exit submode) 301, 302

S_D_SC.INC
    code 337
    notes 339

S_D_SC16.INC
    code 400

SCR_S_D.INC
    code 53
    notes 55

T

text files
    scrollable 285, 403
    creation using Turbo 288, 408
    and saving to arrays 284

TEXTWRIT.INC
    code 280
    notes 283

TINST 21

TXTWR16.INC
    code 403
    notes 407

TYPDEF15.INC
    notes 357

TYPDEF16.INC
    code 372
    notes 376

.txt
    as reserved suffix 312

TYPEDEF.INC
    code 319
    notes 321

typing conventions 4-7

U

Up Arrow key 127, 141, 392

V

variables
    naming conventions
    distinction between #1 and letter "l" 1, 169

vertical scrolling (see scrolling)

VAL 173, 192, 207

validation (see data entry and validation)

var
    in parameter lists 55, 277-278, 335, 391
    and scope rules 161, 231, 349, 350

VHSCROLL.DRV
    code 223
    notes 228

VH_S2.INC
    code 218
    notes 214

V_S1.DRV
    code 133
    notes 135

V_S2.DRV
    code 150
    notes 152

V_S3.DRV
    code 164
    notes 166

V_S1.INC
    code 122
    notes 126

V_S2.INC
    code 139
    notes 141

V_S3.INC
    code 159
    notes 161

video memory
    vs ordinary memory 55
    as holder of ASCII integers 13, 368

W

WHILE..DO
    to text files to disk for scrolling 284
    in data input and revision 208-211

WINDOW.DRV
    code 45
    notes 46

WINDOWS.INC
    code 40
    notes 42

WINDOW 15

WHEREX 16, 97, 408

WHEREY 16, 97, 408

window borders
    creation of 40
    variations on 49

windows 14

ORDER FORM FOR
PROGRAM LISTINGS ON DISKETTE

*T*his diskette contains the complete program listings for all programs and applications contained in this book. By using this diskette, you will eliminate time spent typing in pages of program code.

*I*f you did not buy this book with diskette, use this form to order now:

*O*nly:
$20.00

MANAGEMENT INFORMATION SOURCE, INC.
1107 N.W. 14th • Portland, Oregon 97209

NAME (Please print or type)

ADDRESS

CITY   STATE   ZIP

*C*all free
1-800-MANUALS

☐ Screen I/O Diskette only $20.00

Please add $2.00 for shipping and handling.
Please check
☐ VISA   ☐ MasterCharge   ☐ American Express
☐ Check enclosed $_____

ACCT.

EXP. DATE

SIGNATURE

MIS: PRESS

M A N A G E M E N T   I N F O R M A T I O N   S O U R C E ,   I N C .

Related Titles in the MIS: Press Programmer Series

Memory Resident Utilities, Interrupts, and Disk Management with MS and PC DOS
An indispensable resource for serious DOS programmers. Includes chapters on disk data storage, BIOS and DOS interrupts, utility programming, and memory resident utilities.

Michael Hyman   0-943518-73-3 $22.95   Book/Disk: $44.95

Assembly Language Interfacing in Turbo Pascal
Allows Turbo Pascal programmers to bring the power and speed of assembly language code to their programs. Includes an assembly language primer and reference section, communications and graphics routines, Turbo Pascal inline machine code, and several ready-to-use routines

Sanjiva Nath   0-943518-25-3 $20.95   Book/Disk: $40.95

Linear and Dynamic Programming with Lotus 1-2-3 Release 2
Explains and illustrates the basic concepts of Linear and Dynamic Programming within the Lotus 1-2-3 spreadsheet environment, with numerous examples from business and industry.

James Ho   0-943518-72-5 $19.95   Book/Disk: $39.95

Turbo Prolog Features for Programmers
Explores the limits of Turbo Prolog's possibilities and provides programmers with numerous ready-to-use routines.

Sanjiva Nath   0-943518-68-7 $22.95

dBASE III Plus Networking and Multi-user Systems
Includes a discussion of the benefits and limitations of networking, accessing mainframe data through a network, and step-by-step programming instructions for developing applications and installing the dBASE III Plus network.

Joseph Carrabis   0-943518-26-1 $20.95   Book/Disk: $40.95

dBASE III Plus Power Tools
Outlines integrating data into spreadsheets and documents, accessing mainframe data, installing memory resident utilities, debugging and compiling the program, and expanding dBASE III Plus into a comprehensive computing system.

Rob Krumm   0-943518-66-0 $21.95

Screen I/O Programming Techniques using Turbo Pascal
Explains how students and professionals alike can write customized applications programs, saving hours of programming time and lending visual appeal and professionalism to programming efforts.

Andy Stuart   0-943518-28-8 $24.95   Book/Disk: $44.95

Turbo C: Memory Resident Utilities, Screen I/O and Programming Techniques
Covers topics and techniques including memory management, ROM BIOS functions, programming screen input/output, and writing memory resident utility programs in Turbo C. .

Al Stevens   0-943518-35-0 $24.95

C Database Development
All the tools programmers need for writing C database programs—with complete, detailed instructions on how to use them.

Al Stevens   0-943518-33-4 $23.95   Book/Disk: $43.95

Available where fine books are sold.

MIS: Press   1107 N.W. 14th Ave., Portland OR 97209   (503) 222-2399   1-800-MANUALS